Copyright © 2020 by Houghton Mifflin Harcourt Publishing Company

All rights reserved. No part of this work may be reproduced or transmitted in any form or by any means, electronic or mechanical, including photocopying or recording, or by any information storage or retrieval system, without the prior written permission of the copyright owner unless such copying is expressly permitted by federal copyright law. Requests for permission to make copies of any part of the work should be submitted through our Permissions website at https://customercare.hmhco.com/contactus/Permissions.html or mailed to Houghton Mifflin Harcourt Publishing Company, Attn: Intellectual Property Licensing, 9400 Southpark Center Loop, Orlando, Florida 32819-8647.

Front Cover Photo Credits: (t overlay): © Carlos Caetano/Shutterstock, (outer ring): ©Willyam Bradberry/Shutterstock, (inner ring): ©jeep5d/Shutterstock, (c): ©Carrie Garcia/Houghton Mifflin Harcourt, (tc overlay): ©Eyewire/Getty Images, (bc overlay): ©elenamiv/Shutterstock

Back Cover Photo Credits: (Units 1-6): ©Michal Bednarek/Photocreo/Shutterstock; ©Digital Vision/Getty Images; ©Everett Historical/Shutterstock; ©Yulia Grigoryeva/Shutterstock; ©nazmoo/Fotolia; ©Photoraidz/Shutterstock

Printed in the U.S.A.

ISBN 978-1-328-55673-8

5 6 7 8 9 10   0868   27 26 25 24 23 22 21 20

4500799609   B C D E F G

If you have received these materials as examination copies free of charge, Houghton Mifflin Harcourt Publishing Company retains title to the materials and they may not be resold. Resale of examination copies is strictly prohibited.

Possession of this publication in print format does not entitle users to convert this publication, or any portion of it, into electronic format.

GRADE 6

Program Consultants:
Kylene Beers
Martha Hougen
Elena Izquierdo
Carol Jago
Erik Palmer
Robert E. Probst

HMH *Into Literature*
PROGRAM CONSULTANTS

Kylene Beers

Nationally known lecturer and author on reading and literacy; coauthor with Robert Probst of *Disrupting Thinking, Notice & Note: Strategies for Close Reading,* and *Reading Nonfiction;* former president of the National Council of Teachers of English. Dr. Beers is the author of *When Kids Can't Read: What Teachers Can Do* and coeditor of *Adolescent Literacy: Turning Promise into Practice,* as well as articles in the *Journal of Adolescent and Adult Literacy.* Former editor of *Voices from the Middle,* she is the 2001 recipient of NCTE's Richard W. Halle Award, given for outstanding contributions to middle school literacy. She recently served as Senior Reading Researcher at the Comer School Development Program at Yale University as well as Senior Reading Advisor to Secondary Schools for the Reading and Writing Project at Teachers College.

Martha Hougen

National consultant, presenter, researcher, and author. Areas of expertise include differentiating instruction for students with learning difficulties, including those with learning disabilities and dyslexia; and teacher and leader preparation improvement. Dr. Hougen has taught at the middle school through graduate levels. In addition to peer-reviewed articles, curricular documents, and presentations, Dr. Hougen has published two college textbooks: *The Fundamentals of Literacy Assessment and Instruction Pre-K–6* (2012) and *The Fundamentals of Literacy Assessment and Instruction 6–12* (2014). Dr. Hougen has supported Educator Preparation Program reforms while working at the Meadows Center for Preventing Educational Risk at The University of Texas at Austin and at the CEEDAR Center, University of Florida.

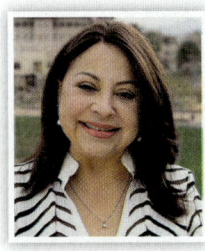

Elena Izquierdo

Nationally recognized teacher educator and advocate for English language learners. Dr. Izquierdo is a linguist by training, with a Ph.D. in Applied Linguistics and Bilingual Education from Georgetown University. She has served on various state and national boards working to close the achievement gaps for bilingual students and English language learners. Dr. Izquierdo is a member of the Hispanic Leadership Council, which supports Hispanic students and educators at both the state and federal levels. She served as Vice President on the Executive Board of the National Association of Bilingual Education and as Publications and Professional Development Chair.

Carol Jago

Teacher of English with 32 years of experience at Santa Monica High School in California; author and nationally known lecturer; former president of the National Council of Teachers of English. Ms. Jago currently serves as Associate Director of the California Reading and Literature Project at UCLA. With expertise in standards assessment and secondary education, Ms. Jago is the author of numerous books on education, including *With Rigor for All* and *Papers, Papers, Papers,* and is active with the California Association of Teachers of English, editing its scholarly journal *California English* since 1996. Ms. Jago also served on the planning committee for the 2009 NAEP Reading Framework and the 2011 NAEP Writing Framework.

Erik Palmer

Veteran teacher and education consultant based in Denver, Colorado. Author of *Well Spoken: Teaching Speaking to All Students* and *Digitally Speaking: How to Improve Student Presentations.* His areas of focus include improving oral communication, promoting technology in classroom presentations, and updating instruction through the use of digital tools. He holds a bachelor's degree from Oberlin College and a master's degree in curriculum and instruction from the University of Colorado.

Robert E. Probst

Nationally respected authority on the teaching of literature; Professor Emeritus of English Education at Georgia State University. Dr. Probst's publications include numerous articles in *English Journal* and *Voices from the Middle,* as well as professional texts including (as coeditor) *Adolescent Literacy: Turning Promise into Practice* and (as coauthor with Kylene Beers) *Disrupting Thinking, Notice & Note: Strategies for Close Reading,* and *Reading Nonfiction.* He regularly speaks at national and international conventions including those of the International Literacy Association, the National Council of Teachers of English, the Association of Supervisors and Curriculum Developers, and the National Association of Secondary School Principals. He has served NCTE in various leadership roles, including the Conference on English Leadership Board of Directors, the Commission on Reading, and column editor of the NCTE journal *Voices from the Middle.* He is also the 2004 recipient of the CEL Exemplary Leader Award.

UNIT 1
FINDING COURAGE
PAGE 1

? ESSENTIAL QUESTION

How do you find courage in the face of fear?

ANALYZE & APPLY

NOTICE & NOTE READING MODEL

NOVEL
from **The Breadwinner** 4
by Deborah Ellis

POEM
Life Doesn't Frighten Me 20
by Maya Angelou

INFORMATIONAL TEXT   **MENTOR TEXT**

Fears and Phobias 28
by kidshealth.org

VIDEO
Wired for Fear 42
by the California Science Center

COLLABORATE & COMPARE

COMPARE THEMES AND MAIN IDEAS

INFORMATIONAL TEXT

Embarrassed? Blame Your Brain 46
by Jennifer Connor-Smith

SHORT STORY

The Ravine 58
by Graham Salisbury

FM6 Grade 6

UNIT 1

 INDEPENDENT READING 78
These selections can be accessed through the digital edition.

POEM
Horrors
by Lewis Carroll

SHORT STORY
Vanquishing the Hungry Chinese Zombie
by Claudine Gueh

NARRATIVE NONFICTION
Running into Danger on an Alaskan Trail
by Cinthia Ritchie

INFORMATIONAL TEXT
Face Your Fears: Choking Under Pressure Is Every Athlete's Worst Nightmare
by Dana Hudepohl

Suggested Novel Connection

NOVEL
Behind Rebel Lines
by Seymour Reit

Unit 1 Tasks
- Write an Informational Essay 80
- Give a Presentation 87

Reflect on the Unit 89

Key Learning Objectives
- Analyze character and plot
- Analyze setting
- Analyze speaker
- Analyze refrain
- Cite evidence
- Analyze structure
- Analyze digital texts
- Make predictions
- Make inferences

 Visit the Interactive Student Edition for:
- Unit and Selection Videos
- Media Selections
- Selection Audio Recordings
- Enhanced Digital Instruction

UNIT 2
THROUGH AN ANIMAL'S EYES
PAGE 90

? ESSENTIAL QUESTION

What can you learn by seeing the world through an animal's eyes?

ANALYZE & APPLY

NOTICE & NOTE READING MODEL

NOVEL
from **Pax** 94
by Sara Pennypacker

SCIENCE FICTION
Zoo 106
by Edward Hoch

INFORMATIONAL TEXT
from **Animal Snoops: The Wondrous World of Wildlife Spies** 116
by Peter Christie

COLLABORATE & COMPARE

COMPARE THEMES

POEM
Animal Wisdom 130
by Nancy Wood

POEM
The Last Wolf 136
by Mary TallMountain

COMPARE ARGUMENTS

ARGUMENT   **MENTOR TEXT**
Wild Animals Aren't Pets 142
by USA Today

ARGUMENT   **MENTOR TEXT**
Let People Own Exotic Animals 148
by Zuzana Kukol

FM8   Grade 6

UNIT 2

INDEPENDENT READING 158
These selections can be accessed through the digital edition.

POEM
The Caterpillar
by Robert Graves

POEM
The Flying Cat
by Naomi Shihab Nye

SHORT STORY
The Pod
by Maureen Crane Wartski

SPEECH
Tribute to the Dog
by George Graham Vest

ARGUMENTS
Views on Zoos

Suggested Novel Connection

NOVEL
Black Beauty
by Anna Sewell

Unit Tasks
- Write an Argument 160
- Present an Argument 167

Reflect on the Unit 169

Key Learning Objectives
- Analyze point of view
- Analyze voice
- Infer theme
- Analyze text structure
- Determine key ideas
- Analyze imagery
- Analyze arguments

 Visit the Interactive Student Edition for:
- Unit and Selection Videos
- Media Selections
- Selection Audio Recordings
- Enhanced Digital Instruction

UNIT 3
SURVIVING THE UNTHINKABLE
PAGE 170

? ESSENTIAL QUESTION

What does it take to be a survivor?

ANALYZE & APPLY

NOTICE & NOTE READING MODEL

NOVEL
from *A Long Walk to Water* 174
by Linda Sue Park

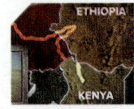
DOCUMENTARY
Salva's Story 188
by POVRoseMedia

MEMOIR   **MENTOR TEXT**
Into the Lifeboat
from *Titanic Survivor* 192
by Violet Jessop

COLLABORATE & COMPARE

COMPARE ACROSS GENRES

POEM
from *After the Hurricane* 206
by Rita Williams-Garcia

NOVEL
from *Ninth Ward* 220
by Jewell Parker Rhodes

UNIT 3

 INDEPENDENT READING 234
These selections can be accessed through the digital edition.

POEM
Watcher: After Katrina, 2005
by Natasha D. Trethewey

SHORT STORY
The Day I Didn't Go to the Pool
by Leslie J. Wyatt

SHORT STORY
Tuesday of the Other June
by Norma Fox Mazer

SPEECH
In Event of Moon Disaster
by Bill Safire

INFORMATIONAL TEXT
Ready: Preparing Your Pets for Emergencies Makes Sense
by Ready.gov

Suggested Novel Connection

NOVEL
Hatchet
by Gary Paulsen

Unit **Task**
- Write a Nonfiction Narrative 236

Reflect on the Unit 243

Key Learning Objectives

- Analyze setting
- Analyze character
- Analyze digital texts
- Explain author's purpose
- Analyze structure and meter
- Describe use of figurative language
- Analyze language

 Visit the Interactive Student Edition for:
- Unit and Selection Videos
- Media Selections
- Selection Audio Recordings
- Enhanced Digital Instruction

Contents FM11

UNIT 4
DISCOVERING YOUR VOICE
PAGE 244

? ESSENTIAL QUESTION

What are the ways you can make yourself heard?

ANALYZE & APPLY

NOTICE & NOTE READING MODEL

MULTIMODAL TEXT
from Selfie: The Changing Face of Self-Portraits 248
by Susie Brooks

MEMOIR IN VERSE
from Brown Girl Dreaming 264
by Jacqueline Woodson

HUMOR
What's So Funny, Mr. Scieszka? 276
by Jon Scieszka

COLLABORATE & COMPARE

COMPARE POEMS

POEM
A Voice 288
by Pat Mora

POEM
Words Like Freedom 294
by Langston Hughes

COMPARE ARGUMENTS

ARGUMENT
Better Than Words: Say It with a Selfie 300
by Gloria Chang

ARGUMENT   **MENTOR TEXT**
OMG, Not *Another* Selfie! 308
by Shermakaye Bass

UNIT 4

 INDEPENDENT READING 320
These selections can be accessed through the digital edition.

POEM
I Was a Skinny Tomboy Kid
by Alma Luz Villanueva

POEM
Words are birds
by Francisco X. Alarcón

SHORT STORY
Eleven
by Sandra Cisneros

SHORT STORY
On Dragonwings
by Lucy D. Ford

INFORMATIONAL TEXT
Carved on the Walls
by Judy Yung

Suggested Novel Connection

NOVEL
The Giver
by Lois Lowry

Unit 4 Task
- Create a Multimodal Argument 322

Reflect on the Unit 329

Key Learning Objectives
- Analyze multimodal texts
- Analyze text structure
- Analyze purpose
- Make inferences
- Analyze figurative language
- Make connections
- Analyze rhetorical devices
- Identify audience

 Visit the Interactive Student Edition for:
- Unit and Selection Videos
- Media Selections
- Selection Audio Recordings
- Enhanced Digital Instruction

Contents FM13

UNIT 5
NEVER GIVE UP
PAGE 330

? ESSENTIAL QUESTION

What keeps people from giving up?

ANALYZE & APPLY

NOTICE & NOTE READING MODEL

MEMOIR
A Schoolgirl's Diary
from I Am Malala 334
by Malala Yousafzai
with Patricia McCormick

SHORT STORY
The First Day of School 352
by R. V. Cassill

POEM
Speech to the Young: Speech to the Progress-Toward 366
by Gwendolyn Brooks

COLLABORATE & COMPARE

COMPARE PRESENTATIONS

GRAPHIC BIOGRAPHY
from **Into the Air** 374
by Robert Burleigh
illustrated by Bill Wylie

BIOGRAPHY   **MENTOR TEXT**
from **The Wright Brothers: How They Invented the Airplane** 390
by Russell Freedman

UNIT 5

INDEPENDENT READING 406
These selections can be accessed through the digital edition.

POEM
Paul Revere's Ride
by Henry Wadsworth Longfellow

POEM
The Road Not Taken
by Robert Frost

DRAMA
Damon and Pythias
dramatized by Fan Kissen

SPEECH
Education First *from* **Malala's Speech to the United Nations**
by Malala Yousafzai

Suggested Novel Connection

NOVEL
The Outsiders
by S. E. Hinton

Unit 5 Tasks
- Write a Biographical Report 408
- Produce and Present a Podcast 415

Reflect on the Unit 417

Key Learning Objectives
- Analyze text features
- Generate questions
- Analyze plot
- Analyze setting
- Analyze structure
- Make inferences about theme
- Analyze multimodal texts
- Determine key ideas

 Visit the Interactive Student Edition for:
- Unit and Selection Videos
- Media Selections
- Selection Audio Recordings
- Enhanced Digital Instruction

UNIT 6
HIDDEN TRUTHS
PAGE 418

? ESSENTIAL QUESTION

What hidden truths about people and the world are revealed in stories?

ANALYZE & APPLY

NOTICE & NOTE READING MODEL

BOOK INTRODUCTION
from **Storytelling** 422
by Josepha Sherman

The Prince and the Pauper 434
by Mark Twain
dramatized by Joellen Bland

COLLABORATE & COMPARE

COMPARE POEMS

POEM
Archetype 458
by Margarita Engle

POEM
Fairy-tale Logic 464
by A. E. Stallings

COMPARE THEMES

FOLKTALE
The Boatman's Flute 470
retold by Sherry Garland

FOLKTALE   **MENTOR TEXT**
The Mouse Bride 484
retold by Heather Forest

FM16   Grade 6

UNIT 6

INDEPENDENT READING 502

These selections can be accessed through the digital edition.

FABLE
The Golden Serpent
retold by Walter Dean Myers

MYTH
Echo and Narcissus
retold by Lancelyn Green

FOLKTALE
The Fisherman and the Chamberlain
retold by Jane Yolen

INFORMATIONAL TEXT
Urban Legends, Suburban Myths
by Robert T. Carroll

Suggested Novel Connection

NOVEL
The Jungle Book
by Rudyard Kipling

Unit 6   Task
- Write a Short Story 504

Reflect on the Unit 511

Key Learning Objectives

- Analyze informational text structures
- Make inferences about ideas
- Analyze character development in drama
- Analyze structure in poetry
- Make connections
- Analyze plot
- Identify point of view
- Infer theme
- Analyze purpose

Visit the Interactive Student Edition for:
- Unit and Selection Videos
- Media Selections
- Selection Audio Recordings
- Enhanced Digital Instruction

Contents   FM17

SELECTIONS BY GENRE

FICTION

NOVEL

from **The Breadwinner** Deborah Ellis . . 4

from **A Long Walk to Water** Linda Sue Park 174

from **Ninth Ward** Jewell Parker Rhodes . . 220

from **Pax** Sara Pennypacker 94

SHORT STORY

The Day I Didn't Go to the Pool Leslie J. Wyatt . . . . Online

Eleven Sandra Cisneros . . . . Online

The First Day of School R. V. Cassill . . 352

On Dragonwings Lucy D. Ford . . . . . . Online

The Pod Maureen Crane Wartski . . . . . Online

The Ravine Graham Salisbury 58

Tuesday of the Other June Norma Fox Mazer . . . . Online

Vanquishing the Hungry Chinese Zombie Claudine Gueh . . . . . Online

Zoo Edward Hoch SCIENCE FICTION 106

ORAL TRADITION

The Boatman's Flute *retold by* Sherry Garland FOLKTALE 470

Echo and Narcissus *retold by* Lancelyn Green MYTH . . . . . . Online

The Fisherman and the Chamberlain *retold by* Jane Yolen FOLKTALE . . . . Online

The Golden Serpent *retold by* Walter Dean Myers FABLE . . . . . . Online

The Mouse Bride *retold by* Heather Forest FOLKTALE 484

NONFICTION

INFORMATIONAL TEXT

from **Animal Snoops: The Wondrous World of Wildlife Spies** Peter Christie 116

Carved on the Walls Judy Yung . . . . . Online

Embarrassed? Blame Your Brain Jennifer Connor-Smith 46

Face Your Fears: Choking Under Pressure Is Every Athlete's Worst Nightmare Dana Hudepohl . . . . Online

Fears and Phobias kidshealth.org 28

Ready: Preparing Your Pets for Emergencies Makes Sense Ready.gov . . . . Online

from **Storytelling** Josepha Sherman BOOK INTRODUCTION 422

Urban Legends, Suburban Myths Robert T. Carroll . . . . Online

NARRATIVE NONFICTION

Running into Danger on an Alaskan Trail Cinthia Ritchie . . . . Online

ARGUMENT

Better Than Words: Say It with a Selfie Gloria Chang 300

Let People Own Exotic Animals Zuzana Kukol 148

OMG, Not *Another* Selfie! Shermakaye Bass 308

Views on Zoos	Online
Wild Animals Aren't Pets USA Today	142

SPEECH

In Event of Moon Disaster Bill Safire	Online
Education First from Malala's Speech to the United Nations Malala Yousafzai	Online
Tribute to the Dog George Graham Vest	Online

AUTOBIOGRAPHY/MEMOIR

from **Brown Girl Dreaming** Jacqueline Woodson MEMOIR IN VERSE . . .	264
Into the Lifeboat *from* **Titanic Survivor** Violet Jessup	192
A Schoolgirl's Diary *from* **I Am Malala** Malala Yousafzai with Patricia McCormick	334
What's So Funny, Mr. Scieszka? Jon Scieszka HUMOR	276

BIOGRAPHY

from **Into the Air** Robert Burleigh, *illustrated* by Bill Wylie GRAPHIC BIOGRAPHY	374
from **The Wright Brothers: How They Invented the Airplane** Russell Freedman	390

POETRY

from **After the Hurricane** Rita Williams-Garcia	206
Animal Wisdom Nancy Wood	130
Archetype Margarita Engle	458
The Caterpillar Robert Graves	Online
Fairy-tale Logic A. E. Stallings	464
The Flying Cat Naomi Shihab Nye	Online
Horrors Lewis Carroll	Online

I Was a Skinny Tomboy Kid Alma Luz Villanueva	Online
The Last Wolf Mary TallMountain	136
Life Doesn't Frighten Me Maya Angelou	20
Paul Revere's Ride Henry Wadsworth Longfellow	Online
The Road Not Taken Robert Frost . . .	Online
Speech to the Young: Speech to the Progress-Toward Gwendolyn Brooks	366
A Voice Pat Mora	288
Watcher: After Katrina, 2005 Natasha D. Trethewey	Online
Words are birds Francisco X. Alarcón . .	Online
Words Like Freedom Langston Hughes	294

DRAMA

Damon and Pythias *dramatized by* Fan Kissen	Online
The Prince and the Pauper Mark Twain *dramatized by* Joellen Bland	434

MEDIA STUDY

Salva's Story POVRoseMedia DOCUMENTARY	188
from **Selfie: The Changing Face of Self-Portraits** Susie Brooks MULTIMODAL TEXT	248
Wired for Fear the California Science Center VIDEO	42

HMH
Into Literature Dashboard

Easy to use and personalized for your learning.

 Explore Online to Experience the Power of HMH Into Literature

All in One Place
Readings and assignments are supported by a variety of resources to bring literature to life and give you the tools you need to succeed.

Supporting 21st Century Skills
Whether you're working alone or collaborating with others, it takes effort to analyze the complex texts and competing ideas that bombard us in this fast-paced world. What will help you succeed? Staying engaged and organized. The digital tools in this program will help you take charge of your learning.

Ignite Your Investigation
You learn best when you're engaged. The **Stream to Start** videos at the beginning of every unit are designed to spark your interest before you read. Get curious and start reading!

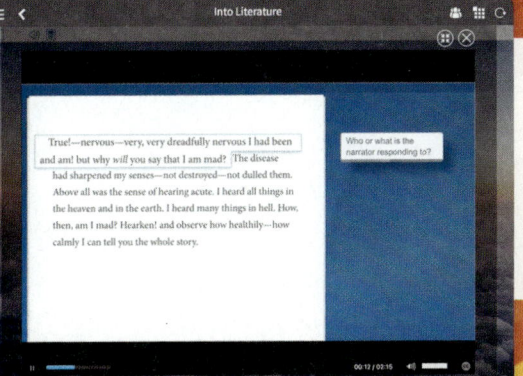

Learn How to Close Read
Close reading effectively is all about examining the details. See how it's done by watching the **Close Read Screencasts** in your eBook. Hear modeled conversations on targeted passages.

Bring the Meaning into Focus
Text in Focus videos dig deeper into complex texts by offering visual explanations for potential stumbling blocks.

Personalized Annotations
My Notes encourages you to take notes as you read and allows you to mark the text in your own customized way. You can easily access annotations to review later as you prepare for exams.

Interactive Graphic Organizers
Graphic organizers help you process, summarize, and keep track of your learning and prepare for end-of-unit writing tasks. **Word Networks** help you learn academic vocabulary, and **Response Logs** help you explore and deepen your understanding of the **Essential Question** in each unit.

No Wi-Fi? No problem!
With HMH *Into Literature,* you always have access: download when you're online and access what you need when you're offline. Work offline and then upload when you're back online.

Communicate "Raise a Hand" to ask or answer questions without having to be in the same room as your teacher.

Collaborate Collaborate with your teacher via chat and work with a classmate to improve your writing.

HMH
Into Literature
STUDIOS

All the help you need to be successful in your literature class is one click away with the Studios. These digital-only lessons are here to tap into the skills that you already use and help you sharpen those skills for the future.

Easy-to-find resources, organized in five separate STUDIOS. On demand and on ED!

Look for links in each lesson to take you to the appropriate Studio.

READING STUDIO
Go beyond the book with the Reading Studio. With over 100 full-length downloadable titles to choose from, find the right story to continue your journey.

WRITING STUDIO
Being able to write clearly and effectively is a skill that will help you throughout life. The Writing Studio will help you become an expert communicator—in print or online.

SPEAKING & LISTENING STUDIO
Communication is more than just writing. The Speaking & Listening Studio will help you become an effective speaker and a focused listener.

GRAMMAR STUDIO
Go beyond traditional worksheets with the Grammar Studio. These engaging, interactive lessons will sharpen your grammar skills.

VOCABULARY STUDIO
Learn the skills you need to expand your vocabulary. The interactive lessons in the Vocabulary Studio will grow your vocabulary to improve your reading.

An ABSOLUTELY, POSITIVELY, MUST READ ESSAY in the FRONT of your Literature Book

BY TWO PEOPLE YOU HAVE NEVER HEARD OF
Dr. Kylene Beers and Dr. Robert E. Probst

If you are reading this essay when we think you are, it's early in the school year. You have this big book in front of you and, for some reason, your teacher has asked you to read these pages by two people you've never met.

Let's begin by telling you something about us.

From Dr. Beers:

> I've been a teacher all my adult life. I've worked with students at all grades and now I spend most of my time working with teachers, maybe even your teacher! I live in Texas and when I'm not on an airplane flying off to work in a school, I'm on my ranch, plowing a field. I like to read, cook, read, garden, read, spend time with my family and friends, and (did I mention?) read!

From Dr. Probst:

> I've also been a teacher all my adult life. When I first started teaching, I taught kids in middle school and high school, and then I spent most of my career teaching people how to be teachers. For many years now, Dr. Beers and I have written books together, books that are about teaching kids how to be better readers. I live in Florida and when I'm not in schools working with teachers and kids, I enjoy watching my grandkids play soccer and baseball and I love going out on my boat. And, like Dr. Beers, I love reading a great book, too.

So, we're teachers. And we're writers. Specifically, we write books for teachers, books teachers read so that they can help their students become better readers...

. . . and we're going to try to help you become a better reader this year.

We will because we both believe TWO things.

First, we've never met a kid who didn't want to get better at reading. <u>Reading is important for almost everything you do, so doing it well is important.</u>

Second, we believe that reading can change you. Reading something can open up your mind, your thinking, your ideas, your understanding of the world and all the people in it, so that you might choose to change yourself. <u>Reading can help you change yourself.</u>

We think too often it's easy to forget why reading is important. You can come to believe that you need to read better just so your grades will go up, or you need to read better so that you do well on a big state test. Those things are important—you bet—but they aren't as important as reading better so that you can become better. Yes, reading can help you change.

How would that happen—how can reading help you change yourself? Sometimes it is obvious. You read something about the importance of exercise and you <u>start walking a little more.</u>

How can reading help me change myself?

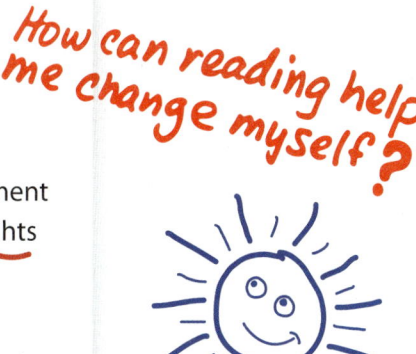

Or, you read something about energy and the environment and you <u>decide to make sure you always turn off the lights</u> when you leave any room.

Other times, it might be less obvious. You might read *Wonder* and begin to <u>think about what it really means to be a good friend.</u> Maybe you walk over to that person sitting alone in the cafeteria and sit with him or her. Perhaps you'll read *Stella by Starlight* and that book helps you become someone who stands against racism. Or maybe it happens as you read *Mexican Whiteboy* and discover that <u>who you are is more about what you are on the inside than what anyone ever sees on the outside.</u> And when you realize that,

FM25

"Hello! I wanted to discuss the Important Message with you!"

perhaps it will give you the courage you need to be truer to yourself, to be the person you really want to be.

Reading gives us moments to think, and as we think we just might discover something about ourselves that we want to change. And that's why we say reading can help us change ourselves.

Finding Important Messages

It sure would be easy to find important messages in the things we read if the authors would just label them and then maybe give us a call.

The reality is, though, that would make the reading less interesting. And it would mean that every reader is supposed to find the same message. Not true! While the author has a message he or she wants to share, the reader—that's you!—has at least three jobs to do:

My Job

1 → **First,** enjoy what you are reading.

2 → **Second,** figure out the message the author wanted to share. Authors write for a reason (no, not to make a lot of money!), and part of that reason is to share something important. That's the author's message, and this year we'll be showing you some ways to really focus in on that.

3 → **Third,** you need to figure out the message that matters most to **YOU.** (YES, WE SAVED THE BEST FOR LAST!!!) Sometimes the author's message and what matters most to you will be the same; sometimes not. For instance, it's obvious that J.K. Rowling wrote the Harry Potter series to show us all the sustaining power of love.

From Dr. Beers:
❝ But when I read these books, what really touched my heart was the importance of standing up to our fears. ❞

From Dr. Probst:
❝ And what mattered most to me was the idea that one person, one small person, can make a huge difference in the world. I think that's a critically important point. ❞

Understanding the author's message requires you to do some work while you read, work that requires you to read the text closely. No. You don't need a magnifying glass. But you do need to learn how to notice some things in the text we call SIGNPOSTS.

A signpost is simply something the author says in the text that helps you understand how characters are changing, how conflicts are being resolved, and, ultimately, what theme—or lesson—the author is trying to convey.

You can also use signposts to help you figure out the author's purpose when you are reading nonfiction. If you can identify the author's purpose—why she or he wrote that particular piece of nonfiction—then you'll be better able to decide whether or not you agree, and whether you need more information.

We do want you thinking about signposts, but first, as you read, we want you to remember three letters: BHH.

B	Book	As you read, we want you to remember that you have to pay attention to what's in the book (or article).
H	Head	And, you need to think about what you are reading as you read—so you have to think about *what's in your head.*
H	Heart	And sometimes, maybe as you finish what you're reading, you'll ask yourself *what you have taken to heart.*

To think carefully about what's in the book and what's in your head, you need to become an alert reader, one who notices things. If you're reading fiction, for instance, you ought to pay attention to how characters act. When a character starts acting in a way you don't expect, something is up! That's as if the author has put up a blinking sign that says "Pay attention here!" Or, if you are reading nonfiction, and the author starts using a lot of numbers, that's the same as the author waving a huge flag that says "Slow down! Pay attention! I'm trying to show you something!"

How do I find the author's message?

So, as I read, I have to think about something called signposts?

Pay attention HERE!

Don't worry about memorizing all the signposts. You'll learn them this year. Your teacher will probably have you make some notes—perhaps as the student above did.

Some of the things you'll read this year, you might not like. (OK—just being honest!) But most of the things we bet you will. What we hope you'll do, throughout this year, is keep reading.

- » Read every day.
- » Read something hard.
- » Read something easy.
- » Read something you choose.
- » Read what your teachers ask you to read.
- » Read something that makes you laugh.
- » And it's OK if sometimes what you read makes you cry.

One of us LOVES to read scary books while the other much prefers survival books, so don't worry if you like something your best friend doesn't. Read joke books and how-to books and love stories and mysteries and absolutely be sure you read about people who aren't like you. That's the best way to learn about the world around you, about other people, about other ways of thinking. The best way to become a more open person is to live for a while, in the pages of a book, the life of someone you are not.

We hope you have a great year. Stay alert for signposts that you'll be learning throughout this book.

And remember . . .

. . . reading is something that can help you become the person you most want to be.

NOTICE & NOTE SIGNPOSTS

Signpost	Definition	Anchor Question(s)
FICTION		
Contrasts and Contradictions	A sharp contrast between what we would expect and what we observe the character doing; behavior that contradicts previous behavior or well-established patterns	Why would the character act (feel) this way?
Aha Moment	A character's realization of something that shifts his actions or understanding of himself, others, or the world around him	How might this change things?
Tough Questions	Questions a character raises that reveal his or her inner struggles	What does this question make me wonder about?
Words of the Wiser	The advice or insight about life that a wiser character, who is usually older, offers to the main character	What is the life lesson, and how might this affect the character?
Again and Again	Events, images, or particular words that recur over a portion of the story	Why might the author bring this up again and again?
Memory Moment	A recollection by a character that interrupts the forward progress of the story	Why might this memory be important?
NONFICTION		
Contrasts and Contradictions	A sharp contrast between what we would expect and what we observe happening. A difference between two or more elements in the text.	What is the difference, and why does it matter?
Extreme or Absolute Language	Language that leaves no doubt about a situation or an event, allows no compromise, or seems to exaggerate or overstate a case.	Why did the author use this language?
Numbers and Stats	Specific quantities or comparisons to depict the amount, size, or scale. Or, the writer is vague and imprecise about numbers when we would expect more precision.	Why did the author use these numbers or amounts?
Quoted Words	Opinions or conclusions of someone who is an expert on the subject, or someone who might be a participant in or a witness to an event. Or, the author might cite other people to provide support for a point.	Why was this person quoted or cited, and what did this add?
Word Gaps	Vocabulary that is unfamiliar to the reader—for example, a word with multiple meanings, a rare or technical word, a discipline-specific word, or one with a far-removed antecedent.	Do I know this word from someplace else? Does it seem like technical talk for this topic? Can I find clues in the sentence to help me understand the word?

READING AND WRITING ACROSS GENRES

by Carol Jago

Reading is a first-class ticket around the world. Not only can you explore other lands and cultures, but you can also travel to the past and future. That journey is sometimes a wild ride. Other books can feel like comfort food, enveloping you in an imaginative landscape full of friends and good times. Making time for reading is making time for life.

Genre

One of the first things readers do when we pick up something to read is notice its genre. You might not think of it exactly in those terms, but consider how you approach a word problem in math class compared to how you read a science fiction story. Readers go to different kinds of text for different purposes. When you need to know how to do or make something, you want a reliable, trusted source of information. When you're in the mood to spend some time in a world of fantasy, you happily suspend your normal disbelief in dragons.

In every unit of *Into Literature,* you'll find a diverse mix of genres all connected by a common theme, allowing you to explore a topic from many different angles.

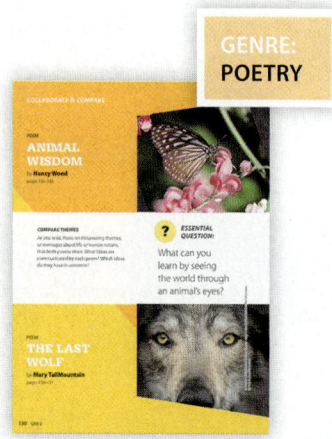

Writer's Craft

Learning how writers use genre to inform, to explain, to entertain, or to surprise readers will help you better understand—as well as enjoy—your reading. Imitating how professional writers employ the tools of their craft—descriptive language, repetition, sensory images, sentence structure, and a variety of other features—will give you many ideas for making your own writing more lively.

GENRE ELEMENTS: SHORT STORY
- is a work of short fiction that centers on a single idea and can be read in one sitting
- usually includes one main conflict that involves the characters and keeps moving
- includes the basic elements of fiction—plot, character, setting, and theme
- may be based on real and historical events

GENRE ELEMENTS: INFORMATIONAL TEXT
- provides factual information
- includes evidence to support ideas
- contains text features
- includes many forms, such as news articles and essays

GENRE ELEMENTS: HISTORICAL FICTION
- includes the basic elements of fiction: setting, character, plot, conflict, and theme
- is set in the past and includes real places and real events of historical importance
- is a type of realistic in which fictional characters behave like real people, use human abilities with life's challenges

GENRE ELEMENTS: POETRY
- may use figurative language, including personification
- often includes imagery that appeals to the five senses
- expresses a theme, or a "big idea" message about life

Into Literature provides you with the tools you need to understand the elements of all the critical genres and advice on how to learn from professional texts to improve your own writing in those genres.

Reading with Independence

Finding a good book can sometimes be a challenge. Like every other reader, you have probably experienced "book desert" when nothing you pick up seems to have what you are looking for (not that it's easy to explain exactly what you are looking for, but whatever it is, "this" isn't it). If you find yourself in this kind of reading funk, bored by everything you pick up, give yourself permission to range more widely, exploring graphic novels, contemporary biographies, books of poetry, historical fiction. And remember that long doesn't necessarily mean boring. My favorite kind of book is one that I never want to end.

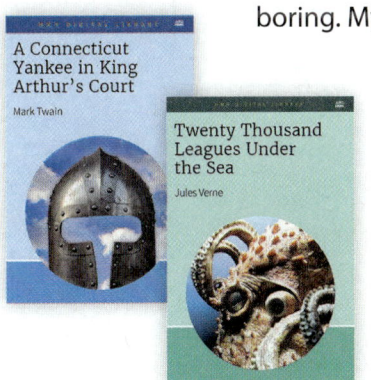

Take control over your own reading with *Into Literature's* Reader's Choice selections and the HMH Digital Library. And don't forget: your teacher, librarian, and friends can offer you many more suggestions.

SHORT STORY
Vanquishing the Hungry Chinese Zombie
Claudine Gueh

A girl faces terror to protect her parents and the family store.

POEM
Horrors
Lewis Carroll

What are those terrible things that go bump in the night?

NARRATIVE NONFICTION
Running into Danger on an Alaskan Trail
Cinthia Ritchie

A long-distance runner has a terrifying encounter with a bear.

UNIT 1

FINDING COURAGE

? ESSENTIAL QUESTION:

How do you find courage in the face of fear?

> " I learned that courage was not the absence of fear, but the triumph over it. "
>
> Nelson Mandela

UNIT 1

ACADEMIC VOCABULARY

Academic Vocabulary words are words you use to discuss and write about texts. In this unit, you will learn and practice using five words.

☑ evident   ☐ factor   ☐ indicate   ☐ similar   ☐ specific

Study the Word Network to learn more about the word **evident**.

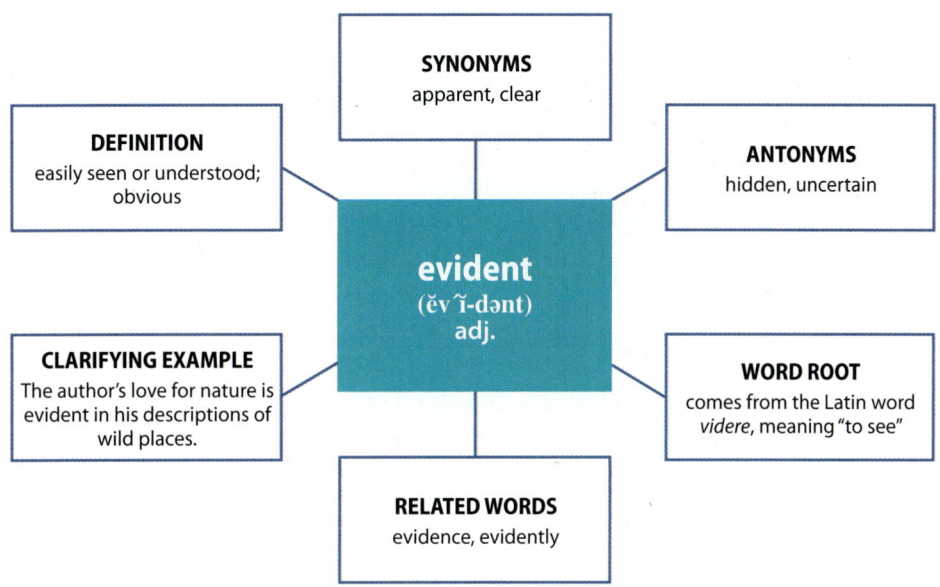

Write and Discuss Discuss the completed Word Network with a partner, making sure to talk through all of the boxes until you both understand the word, its synonyms, antonyms, and related forms. Then, fill out Word Networks for the remaining four words. Use a dictionary or online resource to help you complete the activity.

 Go online to access the Word Networks.

RESPOND TO THE ESSENTIAL QUESTION

In this unit, you will explore how different people find courage in the face of many kinds of fear. As you read, you will revisit the **Essential Question** and gather your ideas about it in the **Response Log** that appears on page R1. At the end of the unit, you will write an **informational essay** about how people find the courage to face their fears. You will also give a presentation. Filling out the Response Log will help you prepare for these tasks.

 You can also go online to access the Response Log.

Finding Courage   1

Notice & Note

READING MODEL

For more information on these and other signposts to Notice & Note, visit the **Reading Studio**.

When you read a scene between a main character and someone older or more experienced, pause to see if it's a **Words of the Wiser** signpost.

from THE BREADWINNER

You are about to read an excerpt from the novel *The Breadwinner*. In it, you will notice and note signposts that offer clues about the novel's setting and characters. Here are three key signposts to look for as you read this excerpt and other works of fiction.

▶ **Words of the Wiser** It can be easy to give advice, but much harder to take it. How do you feel when someone—especially someone older than you—makes a suggestion? Do you listen to the advice of the older or more experienced people in your life?

When a wise character in a work of fiction offers advice or a solution to a problem, it's worth listening. As a reader, paying attention to **Words of the Wiser** can:

- offer insight into the current dilemma or situation
- help you make predictions about what happens next
- reveal more about the main character
- hint at the theme or lesson of the story

In this example from *The Breadwinner,* a student has marked some Words of the Wiser spoken to a girl named Parvana:

> 1   They were going to turn her into a boy.
> 2   "As a boy, you'll be able to move in and out of the market, buy what we need, and no one will stop you," Mother said.
> 3   "It's a perfect solution," Mrs. Weera said.
> 4   "You'll be our cousin from Jalalabad," Nooria said, "come to stay with us while our father is away."

Anchor Question
When you notice this signpost, ask: What's the lesson for the character?

What solution to a problem is introduced?	To be able to shop in the market and buy things for her family, Parvana can pretend to be a boy.
Why do you think this advice is important to the story?	Even though it will be hard for Parvana to pretend to be a boy, she may learn some important lessons.

2   Unit 1

▶ **Aha Moment** Have you ever looked in the mirror and been surprised at how totally different you look with a new hairstyle or new glasses? An **Aha Moment** is when you realize something that changes your understanding of yourself, others, or the world around you. In a story, Aha Moments allow characters the chance to reexamine themselves and their world. A character experiencing an **Aha Moment** may:

- change the way she feels about herself or others
- take a step toward solving a problem or reach a new understanding

Here's an example of a student finding and marking an Aha Moment in *The Breadwinner*:

> 7 "But no one will ask about you."
>
> 8 At these words, Parvana turned her head sharply to glare at her sister. If ever there was a time to say something mean, this was it, but she couldn't think of anything. <u>After all, what Nooria said was true.</u>

When you see a phrase like one of these, pause to see if it's an **Aha Moment**:

That's when I knew . . .

For the first time . . .

And just like that . . .

I suddenly realized . . .

Anchor Question
When you notice this signpost, ask: How might this change things?

What word(s) tell you something has changed?	"After all, what Nooria said was true."
What might this realization tell you about Parvana?	Parvana may be beginning to accept her family's plans for her.

▶ **Contrasts and Contradictions** You probably pay close attention when a friend says or does something unexpected. If a character says or does something you haven't expected, you should pay attention, too. **Contrasts and Contradictions** like these can give you a deeper understanding of a character. If action and dialogue surprise you, take a minute to consider the meaning.

In this example, a student marked a Contrast and Contradiction:

> 5 Parvana stared at the three of them. It was as though they were speaking a foreign language, and <u>she didn't have a clue what they were saying.</u>

Anchor Question
When you notice this signpost, ask: Why did the character act or feel this way?

What contradiction is expressed here?	Even though Parvana speaks the same language as her family, she can't understand what they're telling her.
What does this moment tell us about Parvana?	Parvana cannot stand the thought of doing what they're asking.

ANALYZE & APPLY

from THE BREADWINNER

Novel by **Deborah Ellis**

? ESSENTIAL QUESTION:

How do you find courage in the face of fear?

GET READY

QUICK START

In a small group, discuss what you know about stories set in different cultures or time periods. How do those stories differ from stories about your own culture and times? What do those differences reveal?

ANALYZE HOW CHARACTER DEVELOPS PLOT

A fictional **character** is any person, animal, or imaginary creature who takes part in the action of a work of literature. Characters take part in a series of events that make up the **plot.** Both character and plot are essential to fiction because they work together to tell a good story. Here are some ways that character and plot interact:

- Authors use a character's personality and circumstances to help set the plot in motion.
- Characters respond to events of the plot in external ways (their own actions and their interactions with other characters) and internal ways (their inner thoughts and feelings).
- Characters' responses to events, in turn, shape the plot as it develops.

GENRE ELEMENTS: HISTORICAL FICTION

- includes the basic elements of fiction: setting, character, plot, conflict, and theme
- is set in the past and includes real places and real events of historical importance
- is a type of realistic fiction, in which fictional characters behave like real people and use human abilities to cope with life's challenges

ANALYZE SETTING AND CHARACTER

Historical fiction is set in the past and uses cultural elements of a particular time and place to tell the story. The **setting,** or the time and place in which the action occurs, influences **character development,** or how characters change throughout the story. In *The Breadwinner,* the setting—Afghanistan during a time of harsh rule—influences how the characters develop.

As you read *The Breadwinner,* note how the characters respond to the cultural setting of Afghanistan, including its rules for how men and women should dress and behave. Use a chart like the one below.

Character	Features of Setting	Character's Response	My Ideas About the Character
Parvana			
Nooria			
Mother			

The Breadwinner 5

GET READY

CRITICAL VOCABULARY

| solution | responsibility | stammer | fume |

To see how many Critical Vocabulary words you already know, use them to complete the sentences.

1. It was her _____ to walk the dog twice a day.

2. The insult made her _____ each time she remembered it.

3. Eating a healthy snack is a good _____ when you feel low on energy.

4. He had a tendency to _____ when he was speaking in front of large groups of people.

LANGUAGE CONVENTIONS

Capitalization of Proper Nouns A **common noun** is a general name for a person, place, thing, or idea. A **proper noun** names a specific person, place, thing, or idea. Proper nouns, including abbreviations (a shortened form of a word), acronyms (words whose letters stand for other words), initials, and organizations, should be capitalized.

"You'll be our cousin from ==Jalalabad==," ==Nooria== said.

==She dreamed of working for the== ==ICRC==, ==the International Committee of the Red Cross==, to help war refugees.

ANNOTATION MODEL   NOTICE & NOTE

As you read, notice and note signposts, including **Words of the Wiser**, **Aha Moments**, and **Contrasts and Contradictions**. Here is an example of how one reader responded to the beginning of *The Breadwinner*.

> 6 "If anybody asks about you, <u>we'll say that you have gone to stay with an aunt in Kunduz</u>," Mother said.
>
> 7 "But no one will ask about you."
>
> 8 At these words, Parvana turned to glare at her sister.

That's odd. The mother wants everyone to lie about Parvana. Why? That contradicts what I think most parents would tell their children.

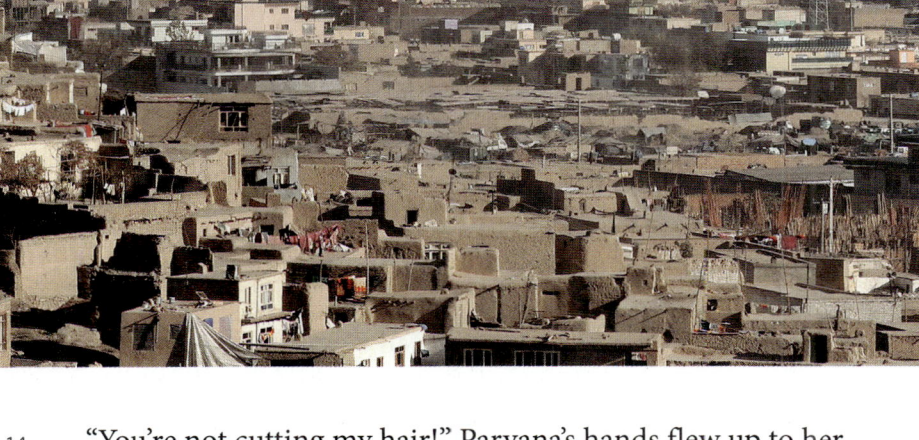

14 "You're not cutting my hair!" Parvana's hands flew up to her head.

15 "How else will you look like a boy?" Mother asked;

16 "Cut Nooria's hair! She's the oldest! It's her responsibility to look after me, not my **responsibility** to look after her!"

17 "No one would believe me to be a boy," Nooria said calmly, looking down at her body. Nooria being calm just made Parvana madder.

18 "I'll look like that soon," Parvana said.

19 "You wish."

20 "We'll deal with that when the time comes," Mother said quickly, heading off the fight she knew was coming. "Until then, we have no choice. Someone has to be able to go outside, and you are the one most likely to look like a boy."

21 Parvana thought about it. Her fingers reached up her back to see how long her hair had grown.

22 "It has to be your decision," Mrs. Weera said. "We can force you to cut off your hair, but you're still the one who has to go outside and act the part. We know this is a big thing we're asking, but I think you can do it. How about it?"

23 Parvana realized Mrs. Weera was right. They could hold her down and cut off her hair, but for anything more, they needed her cooperation. In the end, it really was her decision.

24 Somehow, knowing that made it easier to agree.

25 "All right," she said. "I'll do it."

26 "Well done," said Mrs. Weera. "That's the spirit."

27 Nooria snapped the scissors again. "I'll cut your hair," she said.

responsibility
(rĭ-spŏn´sə-bĭl´ĭ-tē) *n*. A *responsibility* is a duty, obligation, or burden.

NOTICE & NOTE

WORDS OF THE WISER

Notice & Note: What insight does Mrs. Weera offer Parvana? Mark this detail.

Cite Evidence: How does Parvana come to the realization that Mrs. Weera is right?

NOTICE & NOTE

LANGUAGE CONVENTIONS

When the word *mother* is used as a proper noun to name a specific person it is capitalized throughout the excerpt. Explain why the word *mother's* is not capitalized in paragraph 34.

CONTRASTS AND CONTRADICTIONS

Notice & Note: What contrasting feelings does Parvana experience in paragraph 34? Mark each of her feelings.

Cause/Effect: What causes Parvana to change her feelings about her hair?

AHA MOMENT

Notice & Note: What is Parvana's realization in paragraph 40? Mark her realization.

Analyze: How might Parvana's realization change the way she feels about her disguise?

28 "I'll cut it," Mother said, taking the scissors away. "Let's do it now, Parvana. Thinking about it won't make it any easier."

29 Parvana and her mother went into the washroom where the cement floor would make it easier to clean up the cut-off hair. Mother took Hossain's clothes in with them.

30 "Do you want to watch?" Mother asked, nodding toward the mirror.

31 Parvana shook her head, then changed her mind. If this was the last she would see of her hair, then she wanted to see it for as long as she could.

32 Mother worked quickly. First she cut off a huge chunk in a straight line at her neck. She held it up for Parvana to see.

33 "I have a lovely piece of ribbon packed away," she said. "We'll tie this up with it, and you can keep it."

34 Parvana looked at the hair in her mother's hand. While it was on her head, it had seemed important. It didn't seem important any more.

35 "No, thanks," said Parvana. "Throw it away."

36 Her mother's lips tightened. "If you're going to sulk about it," she said, and she tossed the hair down to the floor.

37 As more and more hair fell away, Parvana began to feel like a different person. Her whole face showed. What was left of her hair was short and shaggy. It curled in a soft fringe around her ears. There were no long parts to fall into her eyes, to become tangled on a windy day, to take forever to dry when she got caught in the rain.

38 Her forehead seemed bigger. Her eyes seemed bigger, too, maybe because she was opening them so wide to be able to see everything. Her ears seemed to stick out from her head.

39 They look a little funny, Parvana thought, but a nice sort of funny.

40 I have a nice face, she decided.

41 Mother rubbed her hands brusquely[2] over Parvana's head to rub away any stray hairs.

42 "Change your clothes," she said. Then she left the washroom.

43 All alone, Parvana's hand crept up to the top of her head. Touching her hair gingerly[3] at first, she soon rubbed the palm of her hand all over her head. Her new hair felt both bristly and soft. It tickled the skin on her hand.

---

[2] **brusquely** (brŭsk´lē): abruptly or curtly.
[3] **gingerly** (jĭn´jər-lē): cautiously or carefully.

BACKGROUND

Deborah Ellis (b. 1960) wrote The Breadwinner after interviewing Afghan women and girls in a refugee camp in Pakistan. In this excerpt, 11-year-old Parvana lives with her family in Kabul, Afghanistan, in the 1990s. Parvana's family, like others, has suffered under harsh government rule. Parvana's father has been imprisoned and her older brother, Hossain, has been killed. With no men to help, Parvana's family must find a way to survive.

from
THE BREADWINNER
Novel by Deborah Ellis

SETTING A PURPOSE

As you read, pay attention to any changes in the way the main character, Parvana, perceives herself and her role within her family. Note details that help you understand her character, the setting, and the conflict she faces.

1 They were going to turn her into a boy.

2 "As a boy, you'll be able to move in and out of the market, buy what we need, and no one will stop you," Mother said.

3 "It's a perfect **solution**," Mrs. Weera said.

4 "You'll be our cousin from Jalalabad," Nooria said, "come to stay with us while our father is away."

5 Parvana stared at the three of them. It was as though they were speaking a foreign language, and she didn't have a clue what they were saying.

6 "If anybody asks about you, we'll say that you have gone to stay with an aunt in Kunduz,"[1] Mother said.

---

[1] **Kunduz** (ko͞on´do͞oz): the capital city of Kunduz Province in northern Afghanistan, situated north of Kabul.

Notice & Note

Use the side margins to notice and note signposts in the text.

solution
(sə-lo͞o´shən) n. A solution is a way of handling a problem.

NOTICE & NOTE

ANALYZE SETTING AND CHARACTER

Annotate: Mark details in paragraph 8 that describe the cultural setting in which Parvana lives.

Infer: How might this setting affect the story's characters?

CONTRASTS AND CONTRADICTIONS

Notice & Note: What opposing thoughts does Parvana express in paragraph 11? Mark these details.

Draw Conclusions: Why is Parvana not ready to "give in"?

ANALYZE HOW CHARACTER DEVELOPS PLOT

Annotate: In paragraphs 12–16, mark Parvana's reaction to the idea that she should disguise herself as a boy.

Analyze: How might Parvana's reaction affect the plot?

7   "But no one will ask about you."

8   At these words, Parvana turned her head sharply to glare at her sister. If ever there was a time to say something mean, this was it, but she couldn't think of anything. After all, what Nooria said was true. None of her friends had seen her since the Taliban closed the schools. Her relatives were scattered to different parts of the country, even to different countries. There was no one to ask about her.

9   "You'll wear Hossain's clothes." Mother's voice caught, and for a moment it seemed as though she would cry, but she got control of herself again.

10 "They will be a bit big for you, but we can make some adjustments if we have to." She glanced over at Mrs. Weera. "Those clothes have been idle long enough. It's time they were put to use."

11 Parvana guessed Mrs. Weera and her mother had been talking long and hard while she was asleep. She was glad of that. Her mother already looked better. But that didn't mean she was ready to give in.

12 "It won't work," she said. "I won't look like a boy. I have long hair."

13 Nooria opened the cupboard door, took out the sewing kit and slowly opened it up. It looked to Parvana as if Nooria was having too much fun as she lifted out the scissors and snapped them open and shut a few times.

8   Unit 1

44 I like it, she thought, and she smiled.

45 She took off her own clothes and put on her brother's. Hossain's shalwar kameez[4] was pale green, both the loose shirt and the baggy trousers. The shirt hung down very low, and the trousers were too long, but by rolling them up at the waist, they were all right.

46 There was a pocket sewn into the left side of the shirt, near the chest. It was just big enough to hold money and maybe a few candies, if she ever had candies again. There was another pocket on the front. It was nice to have pockets. Her girl clothes didn't have any.

47 "Parvana, haven't you changed yet?"

48 Parvana stopped looking at herself in the mirror and joined her family.

49 The first face she saw was Maryam's. Her little sister looked as if she couldn't quite figure out who had walked into the room.

50 "It's me, Maryam," Parvana said.

51 "Parvana!" Maryam laughed as she recognized her.

52 "Hossain," her mother whispered.

53 "You look less ugly as a boy than you do as a girl," Nooria said quickly. If Mother started remembering Hossain, she'd just start crying again.

54 "You look fine," said Mrs. Weera.

55 "Put this on." Mother handed Parvana a cap. Parvana put it on her head. It was a white cap with beautiful embroidery all over it. Maybe she'd never wear her special red shalwar kameez again, but she had a new cap to take its place.

ANALYZE HOW CHARACTER DEVELOPS PLOT

Annotate: In paragraph 53, circle what Nooria says in response to Parvana's disguise. Underline what Nooria is thinking.

Infer: What do you learn about Nooria here?

---

4 **shalwar kameez** (shäl´vär kə-mēz´): a type of long, loose shirt and pants, worn by both men and women.

NOTICE & NOTE

ANALYZE SETTING AND CHARACTER

Annotate: Mark the words in paragraphs 56–59 that refer to the story's cultural setting.

Synthesize: How do you explain the relationship between the cultural setting and Parvana's reaction in paragraph 59?

56   "Here's some money," her mother said. "Buy what you were not able to buy yesterday." She placed a pattu[5] around Parvana's shoulder. It was her father's. "Hurry back."

57   Parvana tucked the money into her new pocket. She slipped her feet into her sandals, then reached for her chador.[6]

58   "You won't be needing that," Nooria said.

59   Parvana had forgotten. Suddenly she was scared. Everyone would see her face! They would know she wasn't a boy!

60   She turned around to plead with her mother. "Don't make me do this!"

61   "You see?" Nooria said in her nastiest voice. "I told you she was too scared."

62   "It's easy to call someone else scared when you're safe inside your home all the time!" Parvana shot back. She spun around and went outside, slamming the door behind her.

---

[5] **pattu** (pə´tōō): a gray or brown woolen shawl worn by Afghan men and boys.

[6] **chador** (chä-dôr´): a cloth worn by women and girls to cover their hair and shoulders.

NOTICE & NOTE

63   Out on the street, she kept waiting for people to point at her and call her a fake. No one did. No one paid any attention to her at all. The more she was ignored, the more confident she felt.

64   When she had gone into the market with her father, she had kept silent and covered up her face as much as possible. She had tried her best to be invisible. Now, with her face open to the sunshine, she was invisible in another way. She was just one more boy on the street. She was nothing worth paying attention to.

65   When she came to the shop that sold tea, rice and other groceries, she hesitated for a slight moment, then walked boldly through the door. I'm a boy, she kept saying to herself. It gave her courage.

66   "What do you want?" the grocer asked.

67   "Some . . . some tea," Parvana **stammered** out.

68   "How much? What kind?" The grocer was gruff, but it was ordinary bad-mood gruff, not gruff out of anger that there was a girl in his shop.

ANALYZE HOW CHARACTER DEVELOPS PLOT

Annotate: Mark the words in paragraph 65 that show what Parvana is feeling or thinking.

Draw Conclusions: What does the author reveal about Parvana's character in this paragraph?

stammer
(stăm´ər) v. To *stammer* is to speak with involuntary pauses or repetitions.

The Breadwinner   13

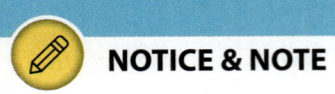

NOTICE & NOTE

AHA MOMENT

Notice & Note: What does Parvana suddenly realize in paragraph 73? Mark her realization.

Infer: How does Parvana feel about herself at this moment, and how might it affect her future and the future of her family?

WORDS OF THE WISER

Notice & Note: What advice does Nooria give Parvana in paragraphs 85–87? Mark Nooria's advice.

Evaluate: What do you think about Nooria's advice? What are the consequences for Parvana and Mother?

69   Parvana pointed to the brand of tea they usually had at home. "Is that the cheapest?"

70   "This one is the cheapest." He showed her another one.

71   "I'll take the cheapest one. I also need five pounds of rice."

72   "Don't tell me. You want the cheapest kind. Big spender."

73   Parvana left the shop with rice and tea, feeling very proud of herself. "I can do this!" she whispered.

74   Onions were cheap at the vegetable stand. She bought a few.

75   "Look what I got!" Parvana exclaimed, as she burst through the door of her home. "I did it! I did the shopping, and nobody bothered me."

76   "Parvana!" Maryam ran to her and gave her a hug. Parvana hugged her back as best she could with her arms full of groceries.

77   Mother was back on the toshak,[7] facing the wall, her back to the room. Ali sat beside her, patting her and saying, "Ma-ma-ma," trying to get her attention.

78   Nooria took the groceries from Parvana and handed her the water bucket.

79   "As long as you've got your sandals on," she said.

80   "What's wrong with Mother now?"

81   "Shhh! Not so loud! Do you want her to hear you? She got upset after seeing you in Hossain's clothes. Can you blame her? Also, Mrs. Weera went home, and that's made her sad. Now, please go and get water."

82   "I got water yesterday!"

83   "I had a lot of cleaning to do. Ali was almost out of diapers. Would you rather wash diapers than fetch the water?"

84   Parvana fetched the water.

85   "Keep those clothes on," Nooria said when Parvana returned. "I've been thinking about this. If you're going to be a boy outside, you should be a boy inside, too. What if someone comes by?"

86   That made sense to Parvana. "What about Mother? Won't it upset her to see me in Hossain's clothes all the time?"

87   "She'll have to get used to it."

88   For the first time, Parvana noticed the tired lines on Nooria's face. She looked much older than seventeen. "I'll help you with supper," she offered.

89   "You? Help? All you'd do is get in my way."

---

[7] **toshak** (tō´shŏk): a narrow mattress used in many Afghan homes instead of chairs or beds.

90   Parvana **fumed**. It was impossible to be nice to Nooria!

91   Mother got up for supper and made an effort to be cheerful. She complimented Parvana on her shopping success, but seemed to have a hard time looking at her.

92   Later that night, when they were all stretched out for sleep, Ali fussed a little.

93   "Go to sleep, Hossain," Parvana heard her mother say. "Go to sleep, my son."

NOTICE & NOTE

fume
(fyo͞om) *v.* To *fume* about something is to feel or show displeasure or resentment.

CHECK YOUR UNDERSTANDING

Answer these questions before moving on to the **Analyze the Text** section on the following page.

1. Which of the following sentences best shows the problem that Parvana's family is trying to solve?

    A There was no one to ask about Parvana.

    B Someone has to go to the market to buy food and supplies.

    C Hossain's clothes do not fit Parvana.

    D Mother misses her son Hossain.

2. In paragraphs 37–40, the writer describes Parvana's experience of the haircut in order to —

    F show how Nooria is envious of Parvana

    G describe a traumatic event

    H give directions on how to cut hair

    J show how Parvana's changing appearance is beginning to affect her outlook

3. Which one of the following ideas is true?

    A Parvana feels proud that she bought food at the market.

    B Mother is delighted that Parvana reminds her of Hossain.

    C The family forces Parvana to disguise herself as a boy.

    D Parvana treasures her long hair after Mother cuts it off.

RESPOND

ANALYZE THE TEXT

Support your responses with evidence from the text. **NOTEBOOK**

1. **Analyze** What methods does the author use to describe elements of both culture and setting in paragraphs 64–72?

2. **Compare** Think about Parvana's character at the beginning of the excerpt (paragraphs 1–16) and near the end (paragraphs 85–88). What changes do you notice about Parvana over this time, and how do they affect the plot?

3. **Evaluate** How effectively has the author used setting to develop Parvana and other characters?

4. **Interpret** Review paragraphs 91–93 at the end of the excerpt. What does the author reveal about Mother, and how might this information affect the plot?

5. **Notice & Note** Review Parvana's observations about appearing in public in paragraphs 63–65. In your own words, describe what she realizes in this moment. How might this understanding help her in the future?

RESEARCH

RESEARCH TIP
Many well-known authors have their own websites. Visit Deborah Ellis's website to find out more about her and the humanitarian causes she supports.

Deborah Ellis, the author of *The Breadwinner,* has donated money from her book sales to help fund humanitarian efforts, including education projects for Afghan women and children. Research at least two aid organizations, which may include those shown below. Begin by generating questions that will guide your research. Record what you learn in the chart.

ORGANIZATION	RESEARCH QUESTION/ANSWER
Doctors Without Borders	
International Committee of the Red Cross (ICRC)	

Extend Deborah Ellis has written many books for young people. With a partner, find out about some of Ellis's other titles. Are there more books like *The Breadwinner*?

RESPOND

CREATE AND PRESENT

Write a Letter Compose a formal business letter to one of the aid organizations you researched, requesting more information about the organization's mission.

- ❏ Follow the structure of a formal letter by including the date and the organization's name and address before the salutation and body of the letter.
- ❏ Keep the tone of your writing formal. Request information in a courteous and respectful way. Include your name and address at the end of the letter.
- ❏ You may wish to send your letter via email. Check the organization's website for an email address.

Go to **Writing Arguments: Formal Style** in the **Writing Studio** for more on formal style.

Give a Multimodal Presentation Give a presentation that uses both text and visual elements to share what you learned about the organization with your class.

- ❏ Make sure your presentation is organized so that your audience can easily understand the information.
- ❏ Pay attention to your speaking rate, enunciation, and volume.
- ❏ Maintain eye contact with the audience. Use natural gestures while you speak. When you are finished, ask classmates if they have any questions about your presentation.

 Go to **Giving a Presentation** in the **Speaking and Listening Studio** for help with giving a presentation.

RESPOND TO THE ESSENTIAL QUESTION

 How do you find courage in the face of fear?

Gather Information Review your annotations and notes on *The Breadwinner*. Then, add relevant details to your Response Log. As you determine which information to include, think about:

- the kinds of fears people face
- how people are willing to face fear to help those they love
- how people can overcome fear

At the end of the unit, use your notes to write an informational essay.

ACADEMIC VOCABULARY

As you write and discuss what you learned from the novel excerpt, be sure to use the Academic Vocabulary words. Check off each of the words that you use.

- ❏ evident
- ❏ factor
- ❏ indicate
- ❏ similar
- ❏ specific

RESPOND

WORD BANK
solution
responsibility
stammer
fume

CRITICAL VOCABULARY

Practice and Apply Mark the letter of the better answer to each question.

1. Which of the following is most likely to cause someone to **fume**?
   a. an act of kindness
   b. an insulting comment

2. Which of the following is an example of a **responsibility**?
   a. feeding a pet
   b. playing a game

3. Which of the following is likely to need a **solution**?
   a. a problem
   b. an airplane

4. Which of the following is an example of a **stammer**?
   a. speaking with repetitive sounds and pauses
   b. walking with uneven steps

VOCABULARY STRATEGY:
Parts of Speech

For a clear understanding of a word's meaning, determine the word's **part of speech,** or the function it performs in a sentence. Parts of speech and their dictionary abbreviations include noun (*n.*), pronoun (*pron.*), verb (*v.*), adjective (*adj.*), and adverb (*adv.*).

Review paragraphs 89–90 to see how the word *fume* is used in the selection. Parvana *fumed* after Nooria said something unkind. Here, the word's part of speech is a verb. If you look up *fume* in a dictionary, you will see that it can also be used as a noun, meaning "gas" or "smoke." For words with **multiple meanings,** such as *fume,* compare the word's usage in context to the various dictionary definitions and their corresponding parts of speech to determine the correct meaning.

Practice and Apply Work with a partner to determine the meanings of *responsibility, solution,* and *stammer* in *The Breadwinner.* Together, use a dictionary to determine each word's part of speech and its meaning. Finally, write original sentences for *fume, responsibility, solution,* and *stammer.*

 Go to the **Vocabulary Studio** for more on using resources.

RESPOND

LANGUAGE CONVENTIONS:
Capitalization of Proper Nouns

Proper nouns name a specific person, place, thing, or idea. Proper nouns are capitalized to help distinguish them from common nouns, which serve as general names for people, places, things, or ideas. In *The Breadwinner* proper nouns are used in the following ways.

- To name specific people

    Parvana realized Mrs. Weera was right.

- To name specific places, such as cities

    "You'll be our cousin from Jalalabad," said Nooria, "come to stay with us while our father is away."

- To name a specific thing, in this case, the title of the novel

    The Breadwinner

Practice and Apply Write your own sentences using capitalized proper nouns, following the examples from *The Breadwinner*. Your sentences can be about how Parvana faces challenges or ways in which you or someone else found courage in the face of fear. When you have finished, share your sentences with a partner. Check each other's work to see whether proper nouns have been capitalized and common nouns have been written in lowercase letters.

> Go to the **Grammar Studio** for more on capitalization and proper nouns.

ANALYZE & APPLY

LIFE DOESN'T FRIGHTEN ME

Poem by **Maya Angelou**

ESSENTIAL QUESTION:

How do you find courage in the face of fear?

GET READY

QUICK START

The poem you are about to read explores both real and imaginary fears that we all face as we grow up. Make notes about both real and imaginary fears that you have now or have had in the past. After you read the poem, you'll write your own poem about facing fear.

REAL FEARS	IMAGINARY FEARS

ANALYZE SPEAKER

"Life Doesn't Frighten Me" is a **lyric poem.** Lyric poetry is a form of poetry in which a single speaker expresses his or her personal ideas and feelings. Lyric poetry can take many forms and can address all types of topics, including complex ideas or everyday experiences.

The **speaker** in any type of poetry is the voice that "talks" to the reader. The speaker may be the poet or a fictional character. Lyric poems are usually written from a first-person perspective, using the pronoun *I* or *me*. However, use of first-person pronouns does not mean that the poet is the speaker. Clues in the title and individual lines can help you determine the speaker and identify his or her situation. As you read the lyric poem, use a chart like this to help you make inferences about the poem's speaker.

GENRE ELEMENTS: LYRIC POETRY
- usually short to convey emotional intensity
- usually written in first-person point of view to express the speaker's thoughts and feelings
- often uses repetition, refrain, and rhyme to create a melodic quality
- includes many forms, such as sonnets, odes, and elegies

MY QUESTIONS	EVIDENCE FROM THE POEM
Who is speaking? How do I know?	
What ideas and feelings does the speaker communicate? Why?	

Life Doesn't Frighten Me 21

GET READY

ANALYZE REFRAIN

Poets use structure and poetic elements to create mood and reinforce meaning. Often a poet will repeat certain words, sounds, or even syllables in a poem. This device is called **repetition.** In many types of poetry, including lyric poems, poets use repetition to emphasize important ideas, to convey the speaker's attitude toward a subject or the audience, to reveal the author's purpose, and to give the poem a musical quality. One kind of repetition is **refrain**—a phrase, line, or set of phrases or lines repeated regularly throughout the poem at intervals, often at the end of a stanza.

Here is an example of a refrain from the narrative poem "Annabel Lee" by Edgar Allan Poe. Find the refrain and mark it.

> It was many and many a year ago,
>   In a kingdom by the sea,
> That a maiden there lived whom you may know
>   By the name of Annabel Lee…
>
> *I* was a child and *she* was a child,
>   In this kingdom by the sea,
> But we loved with a love that was more than love—
>   I and my Annabel Lee…

As you read the lyric poem "Life Doesn't Frighten Me," listen for the refrain, and think about how it conveys information about the speaker's voice and the poem's mood and message.

ANNOTATION MODEL

NOTICE & NOTE

As you read, note clues about the poem's speaker, and examine how the poet uses a refrain to convey a message. This model shows one reader's notes about the beginning of "Life Doesn't Frighten Me."

> Shadows on the wall
> Noises down the hall
> Life doesn't frighten (me) at all
> Bad dogs barking loud
> 5 Big ghosts in a cloud
> <u>Life doesn't frighten me at all.</u>

The poem uses the pronoun "me," but the speaker might not be the poet.

This line is repeated, so it must be a refrain.

BACKGROUND

Maya Angelou (1928–2014) was born Marguerite Annie Johnson in St. Louis, Missouri. Though a childhood trauma led her to stop speaking for five and a half years, Angelou grew up to pursue a career as a singer and actor. She later turned to writing as her main form of expression, and in 1970, her best-selling autobiography *I Know Why the Caged Bird Sings* made her an international literary star. She is widely admired as a fearless and inspiring voice.

LIFE DOESN'T FRIGHTEN ME

Poem by Maya Angelou

SETTING A PURPOSE

As you read, pay attention to the details that explain the nature of fear and how fear can affect everyday life, both physically and emotionally.

> Shadows on the wall
> Noises down the hall
> Life doesn't frighten me at all
> Bad dogs barking loud
> 5 Big ghosts in a cloud
> Life doesn't frighten me at all.
>
> Mean old Mother Goose
> Lions on the loose
> They don't frighten me at all
> 10 Dragons breathing flame
> On my counterpane[1]
> That doesn't frighten me at all.

---

[1] **counterpane:** a bedspread.

Notice & Note

Use the side margins to notice and note signposts in the text.

ANALYZE SPEAKER

Annotate: Circle words and phrases in lines 1–12 that give you clues about the identity of the speaker.

Infer: Who do you think the speaker is in this poem? Why?

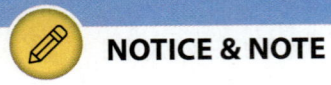

NOTICE & NOTE

ANALYZE REFRAIN

Annotate: In lines 13–21, mark the phrase that is repeated in most of the stanzas.

Interpret: What is the purpose of the repeated phrase? What idea does it emphasize?

I go boo
Make them shoo
15 I make fun
Way they run
I won't cry
So they fly
I just smile
20 They go wild
Life doesn't frighten me at all.

Tough guys in a fight
All alone at night
Life doesn't frighten me at all.

25 Panthers in the park
Strangers in the dark
No, they don't frighten me at all.

That new classroom where
Boys all pull my hair
30 (Kissy little girls
With their hair in curls)
They don't frighten me at all.

Don't show me frogs and snakes
And listen for my scream,
35 If I'm afraid at all
It's only in my dreams.

I've got a magic charm
That I keep up my sleeve,
I can walk the ocean floor
40 And never have to breathe.

Life doesn't frighten me at all
Not at all
Not at all.
Life doesn't frighten me at all.

> **AGAIN AND AGAIN**
>
> **Notice & Note:** What lines are repeated in the last stanza? Mark the lines.
>
> **Interpret:** Why do you think the speaker repeats those lines?

CHECK YOUR UNDERSTANDING

Answer these questions before moving on to the **Analyze the Text** section on the following page.

1 The speaker in the poem confronts fears by —

　A screaming at scary things

　B pulling classmates' hair

　C smiling and making fun

　D reading nursery rhymes

2 The lines "If I'm afraid at all / It's only in my dreams" emphasize that the speaker is —

　F brave in the face of danger

　G scared of waking up

　H brave only when asleep

　J tired and needs to rest

3 What is an important topic in the poem?

　A Going to school every day

　B Being afraid of animals

　C Using your imagination

　D Getting enough sleep

RESPOND

ANALYZE THE TEXT

Support your responses with evidence from the text. **NOTEBOOK**

1. **Draw Conclusions** Review lines 1–9 and lines 37–40. What conclusions can you draw about the speaker's age and personality?

2. **Analyze** Reread lines 1–21. Which scary things are clearly imaginary? Which are possibly real? What effect does this variety of scary things create in the poem?

3. **Evaluate** Read aloud lines 1–24. Notice the change to shorter line lengths in the third stanza. What effect does this change have on your reading?

4. **Synthesize** Explain how the poet uses the refrain "Life doesn't frighten me at all" to help convey the meaning of the poem. Do you think the speaker of the poem is truly unafraid? Why or why not?

5. **Notice & Note** Review all the things that the speaker claims not to be afraid of. What is the effect of naming them?

RESEARCH

RESEARCH TIP
When you conduct online research, evaluate the credibility of websites. Web addresses ending in .gov, .edu, or .org may be expertly reviewed more frequently, but you should always read critically. Look for an About section to help identify who created the website.

With a partner, research the poem that Maya Angelou delivered at the 1993 presidential inauguration. Listen to or watch Angelou delivering the poem. Use what you learn to answer these questions.

QUESTION	ANSWER
Who was the new president inaugurated in 1993?	
What poem did Maya Angelou recite at the inauguration?	
What award did Angelou win for her reading of the inaugural poem?	

Extend How is the poem Maya Angelou delivered at the 1993 presidential inauguration similar to "Life Doesn't Frighten Me"? Discuss with your partner what the two poems have in common.

RESPOND

CREATE AND PRESENT

Write a Poem Write a poem in which you employ a young speaker to express fears, both real and imaginary. Review your notes on the Quick Start activity before you begin.

❑ Decide if you want your poem to be humorous or serious.
❑ Choose examples of fears that create the most vivid picture in your mind or evoke the strongest feelings.
❑ Include a refrain to emphasize the meaning of the poem.

Present a Poem Different people can read the same poem aloud in very different ways. With a partner, prepare a choral reading of "Life Doesn't Frighten Me."

❑ Decide who will read which lines or stanzas of the poem.
❑ Practice reading the poem, adjusting the rhythm and pacing of your reading according to different line lengths in the poem.
❑ Make eye contact with your audience, and use facial expressions and natural gestures to convey the meaning of the poem.
❑ Practice your choral reading until you can present the poem smoothly. Then, read it aloud to a small group or the class.

Go to the **Writing Studio** for more on the writing process.

Go to the **Speaking and Listening Studio** for more on giving a presentation.

RESPOND TO THE ESSENTIAL QUESTION

? How do you find courage in the face of fear?

Gather Information Review your annotations and notes on "Life Doesn't Frighten Me." Then, add relevant details to your Response Log. As you determine which information to include, think about:

- the difference between real and imaginary fears
- how the kinds of things you fear change as you grow up
- the best way to face fear

At the end of the unit, use your notes to write an informational essay.

ACADEMIC VOCABULARY

As you write and discuss what you learned from the poem, be sure to use the Academic Vocabulary words. Check off each of the words that you use.

❑ evident
❑ factor
❑ indicate
❑ similar
❑ specific

Life Doesn't Frighten Me

ANALYZE & APPLY

FEARS AND PHOBIAS

Informational Text by **kidshealth.org**

? ESSENTIAL QUESTION:

How do you find courage in the face of fear?

GET READY

QUICK START

The fear of heights is called *acrophobia*. How do you feel when you see a rollercoaster like the one on the previous page?

CITE EVIDENCE

To support analysis of any text that you read, you need to be able to **cite evidence,** or provide specific information from the text. Evidence can include details, facts, statistics, quotations, and examples.

- ❑ To gather support for an inference or conclusion, mark significant words and details throughout the text.
- ❑ To summarize the main idea and details, cite details from different sections of the text, in the correct order.
- ❑ To analyze how a text is organized, mark words that signal a pattern of organization, such as *because* or *as a result* for cause-and-effect organization.

GENRE ELEMENTS: INFORMATIONAL TEXT
- provides factual information
- includes evidence to support ideas
- contains text features
- includes many forms, such as news articles and essays

ANALYZE STRUCTURE

Text features are design elements that highlight the organization and important details in an informational text.

TEXT FEATURE	EXAMPLE
A **heading** or **subheading** indicates the beginning of a new topic or section.	**What Is Fear?** Fear is one of the most basic human emotions. It is programmed into the nervous system and works like an instinct. From the time we're infants. . . .
A **sidebar,** or **boxed feature,** contains information related to a main topic set in a box alongside or within an article.	*Some people find the rush of fear exciting. They might seek out the thrill of extreme sports and savor the scariest horror flicks. Others do not like the experience of feeling afraid or taking risks.*
Colored type is used to emphasize an important term or idea.	A tiny brain structure called the **amygdala** (pronounced: uh-mig-duh-luh) keeps track of experiences that trigger strong emotions.

You can use text features to get an idea of the topics in a text. They can also help you locate the controlling idea, or thesis statement, and its supporting evidence. As you read, you will note the author's use of text features.

Fears and Phobias

GET READY

CRITICAL VOCABULARY

activate   turbulence   trigger   immaturity

To see how many Critical Vocabulary words you already know, use them to complete the sentences.

1. A frightening sound can _____ a fear response.

2. _____ might cause a child to act carelessly around danger.

3. Remember to _____ your device in case you need to contact a friend.

4. The flight was calm until _____ caused the plane to rock.

LANGUAGE CONVENTIONS

Dashes In this lesson, you will learn about the effective use of dashes in writing. Dashes are used to set off phrases that are added to sentences or that interrupt them:

Feeling afraid is very natural—and helpful—in some situations.

A dash is made with two unspaced hyphens. As you read "Fears and Phobias," note the author's use of dashes.

ANNOTATION MODEL

NOTICE & NOTE

As you read, note the author's use of text features to organize the article. You can also mark up evidence that supports your own ideas. In the model, you can see one reader's notes about "Fears and Phobias."

What Is Fear?

2   Fear is one of the most basic human emotions. It is programmed into the nervous system and works like an instinct. From the time we're infants, we are equipped with the survival instincts necessary to respond with fear when we sense danger or feel unsafe.

3   Fear helps protect us. It makes us alert to danger and prepares us to deal with it. Feeling afraid is very natural—and helpful—in some situations. Fear can be like a warning, a signal that cautions us to be careful.

subheading—introduces a new topic

important ideas about fear

These details tell me fear can be helpful.

BACKGROUND

Most people experience fear now and then; fear is an ordinary part of life. Some fears may be overcome quickly; others may continue, in varying degrees, for a lifetime. Science explains why we experience fear and why sometimes our fears seem out of control. Whether it is a fear of spiders, a fear of the dark, or a fear of flying, using science to understand our responses to fear is the first step toward conquering it.

FEARS AND PHOBIAS
Informational Text by kidshealth.org

SETTING A PURPOSE

As you read, pay attention to the details that explain the nature of fear and how fear can affect everyday life, both physically and emotionally.

1   The roller coaster hesitates for a split second at the peak of its steep track after a long, slow climb. You know what's about to happen—and there's no way to avoid it now. It's time to hang onto the handrail, palms sweating, heart racing, and brace yourself for the wild ride down.

What Is Fear?

2   Fear is one of the most basic human emotions. It is programmed into the nervous system and works like an instinct. From the time we're infants, we are equipped with the survival instincts necessary to respond with fear when we sense danger or feel unsafe.

3   Fear helps protect us. It makes us alert to danger and prepares us to deal with it. Feeling afraid is very natural—

NOTICE & NOTE

Notice & Note

Use the side margins to notice and note signposts in the text.

ANALYZE STRUCTURE

Annotate: Mark the first subheading in the article. Then, mark two details in paragraphs 2–4 that answer the question it asks.

Analyze: Does the writer suggest that fear is mostly helpful or unhelpful? Cite evidence in your answer.

NOTICE & NOTE

and helpful—in some situations. Fear can be like a warning, a signal that cautions us to be careful.

4   Like all emotions, fear can be mild, medium, or intense, depending on the situation and the person. A feeling of fear can be brief or it can last longer.

How Fear Works

5   When we sense danger, the brain reacts instantly, sending signals that **activate** the nervous system. This causes physical responses, such as a faster heartbeat, rapid breathing, and an increase in blood pressure. Blood pumps to muscle groups to prepare the body for physical action (such as running or fighting). Skin sweats to keep the body cool. Some people might notice sensations in the stomach, head, chest, legs, or hands. These physical sensations of fear can be mild or strong.

6   This response is known as "fight or flight" because that is exactly what the body is preparing itself to do: fight off the danger or run fast to get away. The body stays in this state of fight-flight until the brain receives an "all clear" message and turns off the response.

7   Sometimes fear is **triggered** by something that is startling or unexpected (like a loud noise), even if it's not actually dangerous. That's because the fear reaction is activated instantly—a few seconds faster than the thinking part of the brain can process or evaluate what's happening. As soon as the brain gets enough information to realize there's no danger ("Oh, it's just a balloon bursting—whew!"), it turns off the fear reaction. All this can happen in seconds.

Fear or Fun?

Some people find the rush of fear exciting. They might seek out the thrill of extreme sports and savor the scariest horror flicks. Others do not like the experience of feeling afraid or taking risks. During the scariest moments of a roller coaster ride one person might think, "I'll never get on this thing again—that is, if I make it out alive!" while another person thinks, "This is awesome! As soon as it's over, I'm getting back on!"

---

activate
(ăk´tə-vāt´) *v.* To *activate* something means to cause it to start working.

trigger
(trĭg´r) *v.* To *trigger* something means to cause it to begin.

ANALYZE STRUCTURE
Annotate: Mark the most important idea in the boxed feature "Fear or Fun?"

Connect: How does the information in this feature relate to what you have read so far?

Fears People Have

8   Fear is the word we use to describe our emotional reaction to something that seems dangerous. But the word "fear" is used in another way, too: to name something a person often feels afraid of.

9   People fear things or situations that make them feel unsafe or unsure. For instance, someone who isn't a strong swimmer might have a fear of deep water. In this case, the fear is helpful because it cautions the person to stay safe. Someone could overcome this fear by learning how to swim safely.

10   A fear can be healthy if it cautions a person to stay safe around something that could be dangerous. But sometimes a fear is unnecessary and causes more caution than the situation calls for.

11   Many people have a fear of public speaking. Whether it's giving a report in class, speaking at an assembly, or reciting lines in the school play, speaking in front of others is one of the most common fears people have.

12   People tend to avoid the situations or things they fear. But this doesn't help them overcome fear—in fact, it can be the reverse. Avoiding something scary reinforces a fear and keeps it strong.

13   People can overcome unnecessary fears by giving themselves the chance to learn about and gradually get used to the thing or situation they're afraid of. For example, people

CITE EVIDENCE

Annotate: In paragraphs 8–13, mark an example of a healthy fear and an example of an unnecessary fear.

Compare: How are healthy fears different from unnecessary fears?

NOTICE & NOTE

turbulence
(tûr´byə-ləns) *n*. In flying, *turbulence* is an interruption in the flow of wind that causes planes to rise, fall, or sway in a rough way.

LANGUAGE CONVENTIONS
Dashes can be used to show an interruption of thought, to include an additional detail, or to emphasize an idea. Explain how the writer uses a dash in paragraph 14.

who fly despite a fear of flying can become used to unfamiliar sensations like takeoff or **turbulence**. They learn what to expect and have a chance to watch what others do to relax and enjoy the flight. Gradually (and safely) facing fear helps someone overcome it.

Fears During Childhood

14 Certain fears are normal during childhood. That's because fear can be a natural reaction to feeling unsure and vulnerable—and much of what children experience is new and unfamiliar.

15 Young kids often have fears of the dark, being alone, strangers, and monsters or other scary imaginary creatures. School-aged kids might be afraid when it's stormy or at a first sleepover. As they grow and learn, with the support of adults, most kids are able to slowly conquer these fears and outgrow them.

16 Some kids are more sensitive to fears and may have a tough time overcoming them. When fears last beyond the expected age, it might be a sign that someone is overly fearful, worried, or anxious. People whose fears are too intense or last too long might need help and support to overcome them.

Phobias

17 A phobia is an intense fear reaction to a particular thing or a situation. With a phobia, the fear is out of proportion to the potential danger. But to the person with the phobia, the danger feels real because the fear is so very strong.

18 Phobias cause people to worry about, dread, feel upset by, and avoid the things or situations they fear because the physical sensations of fear can be so intense. So having a phobia can interfere with normal activities. A person with a phobia of dogs might feel afraid to walk to school in case he or she sees a dog on the way. Someone with an elevator phobia might avoid a field trip if it involves going on an elevator.

19 A girl with a phobia of thunderstorms might be afraid to go to school if the weather forecast predicts a storm. She might feel terrible distress and fear when the sky turns cloudy. A guy with social phobia experiences intense fear of public speaking or interacting, and may be afraid to answer questions in class, give a report, or speak to classmates in the lunchroom.

20 It can be exhausting and upsetting to feel the intense fear that goes with having a phobia. It can be disappointing to miss out on opportunities because fear is holding you back. And it can be confusing and embarrassing to feel afraid of things that others seem to have no problem with.

21 Sometimes, people get teased about their fears. Even if the person doing the teasing doesn't mean to be unkind and unfair, teasing only makes the situation worse.

What Causes Phobias?

22 Some phobias develop when someone has a scary experience with a particular thing or situation. A tiny brain structure called the **amygdala** (pronounced: uh-mig-duh-luh) keeps track of experiences that trigger strong emotions. Once a certain thing or situation triggers a strong fear reaction, the amygdala warns the person by triggering a fear reaction every time he or she encounters (or even thinks about) that thing or situation.

23 Someone might develop a bee phobia after being stung during a particularly scary situation. For that person, looking at a photograph of a bee, seeing a bee from a distance, or even walking near flowers where there *could* be a bee can all trigger the phobia.

24 Sometimes, though, there may be no single event that causes a particular phobia. Some people may be more sensitive

---

NOTICE & NOTE

CITE EVIDENCE

Annotate: In paragraph 17, mark the definition of *phobia*.

Connect: How might a phobia affect someone? Cite evidence from paragraphs 18–21 in your response.

WORD GAPS

Notice & Note: Mark clues in paragraph 22 that help you understand the word in purple type.

Infer: Why does the author introduce the word *amygdala* in this section of the article?

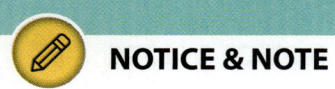

NOTICE & NOTE

immaturity
(ĭm´ə-tyo͝or´ĭ-tē) *n. Immaturity* is the state of not being fully developed or grown.

CITE EVIDENCE

Annotate: Mark details in paragraph 26 that explain how someone may overcome a phobia.

Interpret: Choose one of the strategies for overcoming fear discussed in paragraphs 27–32. Then, explain whether it seems effective, citing text evidence in your response.

to fears because of personality traits they are born with, certain genes[1] they've inherited, or situations they've experienced. People who have had strong childhood fears or anxiety may be more likely to have one or more phobias.

25   Having a phobia isn't a sign of weakness or **immaturity**. It's a response the brain has learned in an attempt to protect the person. It's as if the brain's alert system triggers a false alarm, generating intense fear that is out of proportion to the situation. Because the fear signal is so intense, the person is convinced the danger is greater than it actually is.

Overcoming Phobias

26 People can learn to overcome phobias by gradually facing their fears. This is not easy at first. It takes willingness and bravery. Sometimes people need the help of a therapist[2] to guide them through the process.

27   Overcoming a phobia usually starts with making a long list of the person's fears in least-to-worst order. For example, with a dog phobia, the list might start with the things the person is least afraid of, such as looking at a photo of a dog. It will then work all the way up to worst fears, such as standing next to someone who's petting a dog, petting a dog on a leash, and walking a dog.

28   Gradually, and with support, the person tries each fear situation on the list—one at a time, starting with the least fear. The person isn't forced to do anything and works on each fear until he or she feels comfortable, taking as long as needed.

29   A therapist could also show someone with a dog phobia how to approach, pet, and walk a dog, and help the person to try it, too. The person may expect terrible things to happen when near a dog. Talking about this can help, too. When people find that what they fear doesn't actually turn out to be true, it can be a great relief.

30   A therapist might also teach relaxation practices such as specific ways of breathing, muscle relaxation training, or soothing self-talk. These can help people feel comfortable and bold enough to face the fears on their list.

31   As somebody gets used to a feared object or situation, the brain adjusts how it responds and the phobia is overcome.

---

[1] **genes** (jēnz): the parts of cells that give a living thing its physical characteristics and make it grow and develop; a person's genes come from his or her parents and other blood relatives.

[2] **therapist** (thĕr´ə-pĭst): a person who is skilled in treating mental or physical illness.

32   Often, the hardest part of overcoming a phobia is getting started. Once a person decides to go for it—and gets the right coaching and support—it can be surprising how quickly fear can melt away.

CHECK YOUR UNDERSTANDING

Answer these questions before moving on to the **Analyze the Text** section on the following page.

1 The author included the section "What Causes Phobias?" to —
   A express that it is important to overcome fears
   B explain that getting stung by a bee is dangerous
   C convince readers that there's nothing wrong with a phobia
   D describe what happens when people become afraid

2 In paragraph 27, the writer includes specific information on dog phobias to —
   F describe a physical reaction to fear
   G persuade readers to seek help for their fears
   H give a specific example of how a fear can be overcome
   J show that some fears can be unnecessary

3 Which idea is supported by information throughout the selection?
   A Adults enjoy the excitement that fear provides.
   B Fears can be overcome with help and support.
   C Phobias are the result of a single event.
   D Children are frightened by unfamiliar things.

RESPOND

ANALYZE THE TEXT

Support your responses with evidence from the text. 📓 **NOTEBOOK**

1. **Cause/Effect** Examine paragraphs 5–7 and identify examples of cause-and-effect relationships.

2. **Cite Evidence** What causes phobias? Cite evidence from the text that explains where phobias come from.

3. **Draw Conclusions** Review paragraphs 26–32. What factors help people overcome phobias? Explain whether the author believes it is worthwhile to try to overcome phobias and why.

4. **Interpret** What additional information does the boxed feature provide? How does it add to your understanding of the article?

5. **Notice & Note** What does the term "fight-flight" refer to? How do the clues in paragraph 6 help you figure out the meaning of the term?

RESEARCH

Well-known people have not allowed phobias to prevent them from accomplishing great things. Research these well-known figures who have suffered from a phobia. Record what you learn in the chart.

RESEARCH TIP
The best search terms are very specific. Along with the well-known person's name, you will want to include a word such as *phobia* or *fear* to make sure you get the information you need.

WELL-KNOWN PEOPLE	PHOBIA
George Washington	
Oprah Winfrey	
Winston Churchill	

Connect In paragraph 26, the writer states that "People can learn to overcome phobias by gradually facing their fears." With a small group, and with this informational text in mind, discuss how these well-known people may or may not have overcome their fears.

CREATE AND PRESENT

Write an Informational Essay Write a three- to four-paragraph essay in which you compare and contrast fears and phobias.

- ❑ Introduce the topic and express your controlling idea on fears and phobias.
- ❑ Then, tell about similarities and differences between fears and phobias. Include details from the text to support your ideas. Use transitions as you move from point to point.
- ❑ In your final paragraph, state your conclusion.

Discuss with a Small Group Hold a small group discussion about whether the information in "Fears and Phobias" can help someone overcome a fear.

- ❑ As a group, review the text and decide which information is relevant to the discussion. Use the subheadings to help you locate information.
- ❑ Have group members take notes on ideas and details that relate to the topic.
- ❑ Together, review the ideas and suggest which ones can help someone overcome a fear. Listen respectfully to all ideas and identify points on which group members agree or disagree.

RESPOND

 Go to **Writing Informative Texts** in the **Writing Studio** for help writing an informational essay.

 Go to **Participating in Collaborative Discussions** in the **Speaking and Listening Studio** for help with having a group discussion.

RESPOND TO THE ESSENTIAL QUESTION

? How do you find courage in the face of fear?

Gather Information Review your annotations and notes on "Fears and Phobias." Then, add relevant details to your Response Log. As you determine which information to include, think about:

- the kinds of fears people face
- what happens to people when they face a specific fear
- how people can overcome a specific fear

At the end of the unit, use your notes to write an informational essay.

ACADEMIC VOCABULARY

As you write and discuss what you learned from the text, be sure to use the Academic Vocabulary words. Check off each of the words that you use.

- ❑ evident
- ❑ factor
- ❑ indicate
- ❑ similar
- ❑ specific

Fears and Phobias 39

RESPOND

WORD BANK
activate
trigger
turbulence
immaturity

CRITICAL VOCABULARY

Practice and Apply Choose the better answer to each question. Then, explain your response.

1. Which of the following is an example of **immaturity**?
   a. explaining why you are upset
   b. crying when you don't get your way

2. Which of the following is an example of **activate**?
   a. unplugging a computer
   b. pressing the power button

3. Which canoe trip involves **turbulence**?
   a. canoeing on a calm lake
   b. canoeing on a rushing river

4. Which of these is more likely to **trigger** an allergy?
   a. getting stung by a bee
   b. reading about bees

VOCABULARY STRATEGY:
Prefixes That Mean "Not"

A **prefix** is a word part that appears at the beginning of a base word to form a new word. Many prefixes that mean "not" come from Latin, the language of ancient Rome. One example appears in the vocabulary word *immaturity* (im + maturity). Other prefixes that mean "not" include *in–*, *mis–*, *non–*, and *un–*. Many base, or root, words also come from Latin and Greek, such as *dem–*, meaning people.

Go to the **Vocabulary Studio** for more on prefixes.

Practice and Apply First, identify the prefix that means "not" in each boldface word. Then, state the meaning of the boldface word in your own words.

1. Not having Sunday hours at the library is **inconvenient** for people who work during the week.

   _____

2. A **nonviolent** protest would help the group avoid a confrontation.

   _____

3. Denying a citizen the right to vote is **undemocratic**.

   _____

4. The careless reporter **misquoted** the mayor's remarks.

LANGUAGE CONVENTIONS:
Dashes

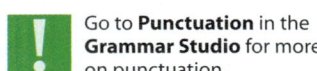

Go to **Punctuation** in the **Grammar Studio** for more on punctuation.

Writers use dashes to interrupt their thoughts abruptly or to emphasize important ideas. A stylistic choice—used in both literary and informational texts—dashes add variety and voice.

In "Fears and Phobias" dashes are used in the following ways:

- to set off emphatic and abrupt interruptions

    Feeling afraid is very natural—and helpful—in some situations.

- to mark sharp turns in thought

    But this doesn't help them overcome fear—in fact, it can be the reverse.

- to enclose added elements that give greater emphasis

    Once a person decides to go for it—and gets the right coaching and support—it can be surprising how quickly fear can melt away.

- to set off an expression that summarizes or illustrates a statement that precedes it

    That's because the fear reaction is activated instantly—a few seconds faster than the thinking part of the brain can process or evaluate what's happening.

Practice and Apply Write your own sentences with dashes using the examples from "Fears and Phobias" as models. Your sentences can be about your own fears and phobias or those of someone you know. When you have finished, share your sentences with a partner and compare your use of dashes.

ANALYZE & APPLY

MEDIA
WIRED FOR FEAR

Video by the **California Science Center**

> **? ESSENTIAL QUESTION:**
>
> How do you find courage in the face of fear?

QUICK START

Think about a time you were frightened or startled. Did your heart start racing? Did you start sweating? Describe to a partner what frightened you and how your body reacted to it.

ANALYZE DIGITAL TEXT

The **purpose,** or intent, of any video or digital text is usually to inform, entertain, persuade, or express the feelings or thoughts of the creator. To meet the purpose, the video's creator uses words as well as visual and sound elements to convey information.

Visual elements, or images, can help viewers understand **technical terms,** which are the words and phrases used in a particular profession or field of study.

GENRE ELEMENTS: MEDIA
- conveys a message
- targets a specific audience
- is created for a specific purpose
- includes TV broadcasts, videos, newspapers, magazines, and the Internet

STILLS	images that are motionless, such as illustrations or photographs
ANIMATION	images that appear to move and seem alive; created through drawings, computer graphics, or photographs

Sound elements include what you hear in a video:

MUSIC	sounds created by singing, playing instruments, or using computer-generated tones; creates a mood
NARRATION	the words as well as the expression and quality of voice used by the narrator

42 Unit 1

GET READY

BACKGROUND

"Fear is a full-body experience." This is how the website Goose Bumps! The Science of Fear introduces its topic "Fear and the Brain." This website includes a collection of videos, articles, and images about sensory information (what we see, hear, taste, smell, touch) that alerts us to what might be harmful to us. The section of the website titled "Wired for Fear" includes a video that provides an animated version of how the brain processes fear reactions.

SETTING A PURPOSE

As you view the animated video, consider how the information is presented. Notice how the video introduces and explains new terms and ideas using text, sound, and visuals. **NOTEBOOK**

To view the video, log in online and select **"WIRED FOR FEAR"** from the unit menu.

As needed, pause the video to make notes about what impresses you or about ideas you might want to talk about later. Replay or rewind so that you can clarify anything you do not understand.

Wired for Fear

RESPOND

ANALYZE MEDIA

Support your responses with evidence from the video. NOTEBOOK

1. **Summarize** Describe how the video explains what the hiker experiences.

2. **Cause/Effect** Review the sequence that uses the animated model. What are some ways our bodies respond when the amygdala senses danger? What parts of the brain activate these responses?

3. **Analyze** Explain the title "Wired for Fear." Why does the video use flashing lights and graphics that show movement in the animated model of how the brain processes potential danger?

4. **Interpret** Describe the music used in the video. In what ways does it support the purpose of the video?

5. **Critique** Think about the purpose of the video. Consider the techniques that are used to support the information presented. Do you think "Wired for Fear" is an effective informational video? Why or why not?

RESEARCH

As you've learned from the video, fear can have a dramatic impact on the body. In fact, there are many accounts of people performing superhuman feats of strength when faced with fear, such as lifting a car off someone after an accident. With a partner, do some research to find such a story and share it with the class.

RESEARCH TIP
Information on the Internet is not always accurate; a search on a topic such as this one could result in some wildly exaggerated and undocumented stories. Be sure to use only reputable sources, such as *Scientific American*, *National Geographic*, or similar sources.

EVENT	DETAIL

Connect Consider what you learned about using visual and sound elements in a video to achieve a specific purpose. What kind of video would you create to present the event you just researched? With your partner, sketch out the sound and visual elements you would include to convey the event.

RESPOND

CREATE AND PRESENT

Write a Narrative Write a story about a time you were frightened.

- ❏ Establish the situation by introducing the event. Where did it take place? Were other people there?
- ❏ Describe the sequence of events in a logical order.
- ❏ Include dialogue and vivid images to convey the experience.
- ❏ Review your story to add or clarify details of the event.

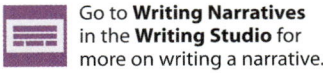

Go to **Writing Narratives** in the **Writing Studio** for more on writing a narrative.

Produce a Podcast With a partner, create an audio recording for a podcast review of the video "Wired for Fear."

- ❏ Make notes about visual and sound elements in the video that made both positive and negative impressions.
- ❏ Explain how each element you have chosen clarifies the topic, using examples from the video. Present ideas for additional information that could have been included to improve the video, drawing on other videos or sources as needed.
- ❏ Create the recording of your review with a partner, using a conversational approach and clear enunciation. Share your podcast with a larger group.

Go to **Analyzing and Evaluating Presentations** in the **Speaking and Listening Studio** for help with reviewing a presentation.

RESPOND TO THE ESSENTIAL QUESTION

 How do you find courage in the face of fear?

Gather Information Review your annotations and notes on "Wired for Fear." Then, add relevant details to your Response Log. As you determine which information to include, think about why fear is a necessary emotion.

At the end of the unit, use your notes to write an informational essay.

ACADEMIC VOCABULARY

As you write and discuss what you learned from the video, be sure to use the Academic Vocabulary words. Check off each of the words that you use.

- ❏ evident
- ❏ factor
- ❏ indicate
- ❏ similar
- ❏ specific

COLLABORATE & COMPARE

INFORMATIONAL TEXT
EMBARRASSED?
Blame Your Brain
by **Jennifer Connor-Smith**
pages 49–53

COMPARE THEME AND MAIN IDEA

As you read these texts, notice how their ideas relate to your own experiences, as well as how those ideas relate to the experiences of other young people. Then, look for ways that the ideas in the two texts relate to each other. After you read both selections, you will collaborate with a small group on a final project.

? ESSENTIAL QUESTION:

How do you find courage in the face of fear?

SHORT STORY
THE RAVINE
by **Graham Salisbury**
pages 61–71

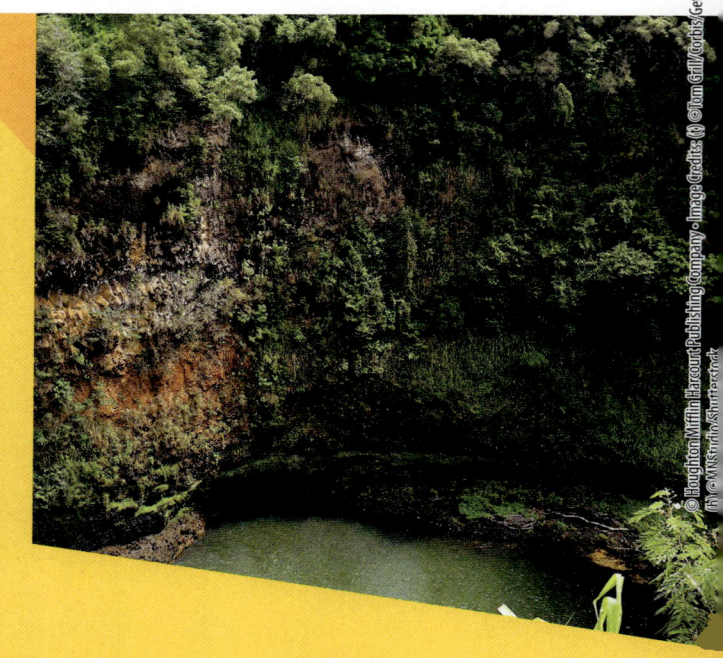

GET READY

Embarrassed?

QUICK START

Disappointing someone or feeling embarrassed won't cause physical pain or permanent damage, so why fear either one? With a group, discuss how fear of embarrassment can affect how we behave.

MAKE PREDICTIONS

You make **predictions,** reasonable guesses based on what you know from experience, all the time. Then, as you gain additional information, you either confirm that a prediction is correct or revise it if it happens to be wrong. You can also make and confirm predictions as you read.

Use the following aspects of informational texts to help you predict the topics, ideas, and evidence an author discusses.

- **Text Features:** Subheadings, boldfaced words, and graphics point out important ideas that you can use to make your predictions.
- **Text Structure:** The way a text is organized helps you take in new information and predict what the author will explain next.

ANALYZE ORGANIZATIONAL PATTERNS

To help you understand ideas that may be new to you, authors of informational texts organize facts and examples carefully. Here are some common organizational patterns.

ORGANIZATIONAL PATTERN	WHAT IT DOES
Definition	explains a topic or idea by identifying its key characteristics and/or distinguishing it from similar or related topics or ideas
Classification	organizes objects, ideas, or information into groups, or classes, based on common characteristics
Advantage and Disadvantage	evaluates a topic or proposal by analyzing both its positive and negative aspects

As you read "Embarrassed? Blame Your Brain," note how the author uses a variety of organizational patterns to help you better understand the text's topic and key ideas.

GENRE ELEMENTS: INFORMATIONAL TEXT
- provides factual information
- uses evidence to support ideas
- contains text features
- includes many forms, such as news articles and essays

Embarrassed? Blame Your Brain 47

GET READY

CRITICAL VOCABULARY

essential   amplify   generate   humiliation

To preview the Critical Vocabulary words, complete each of the following sentences with the correct vocabulary word.

1. It is necessary, or _____ , to bring water on a long hike.

2. Stereo speakers _____ music.

3. We used social media to _____ interest in our event.

4. No one likes to experience _____ or embarrassment.

LANGUAGE CONVENTIONS

Commas Among their other uses, **commas** help set off introductory words, phrases, or clauses in sentences. Read the sentence below. Notice the introductory element and the comma that follows it.

These days, you flood with embarrassment if your dad sings in front of your friends or you drop a tray in the cafeteria.

As you read, look for sentences with introductory elements and commas.

ANNOTATION MODEL

NOTICE & NOTE

Here is an example of how one reader made predictions while reading.

It's All in Your Head

3   Sometime during middle school, changes in brain activity transform how we see the world. Spending time with other kids becomes a top priority. Hormones power up the brain's reward system, making hanging out with friends more fun than ever before. But these changes come with a downside. Fitting in becomes essential. Threat-detection systems focus on what other people think and scan for any hints of disapproval. Hormones push the brain's shame and self-consciousness systems into overdrive.

The subhead tells me that this section will talk about something imagined, or not real.

My prediction is almost correct— the author is talking about how our brains affect what we experience.

The author started out discussing advantages of hormones. The word "But" tells me that she'll now switch to explaining disadvantages.

BACKGROUND

We've all been in situations in which we've based a decision less on rational, logical thinking than on social pressure. Psychological research reveals that these snap decisions can have complex, confusing roots. In the following article, science writer and clinical psychologist **Jennifer Connor-Smith** *explains why teenagers naturally develop a strong and sometimes overwhelming fear of embarrassment.*

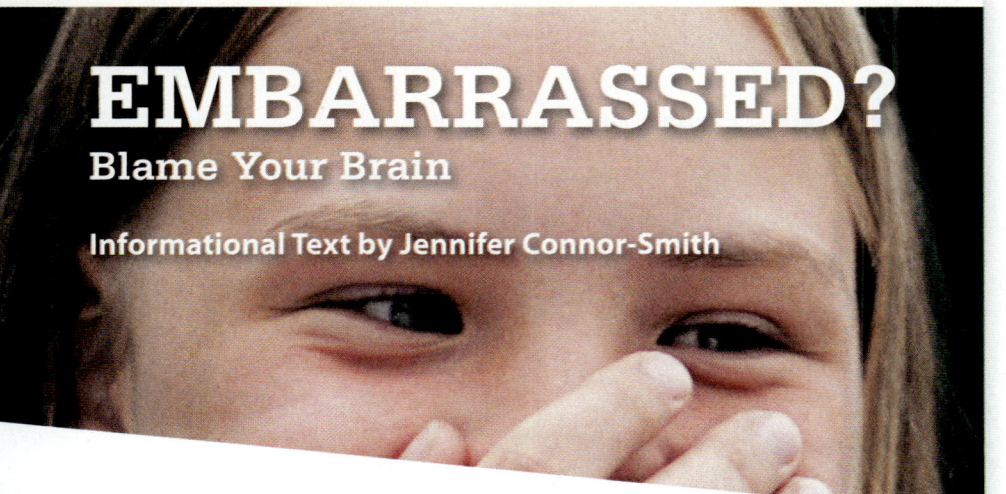

EMBARRASSED?
Blame Your Brain

Informational Text by Jennifer Connor-Smith

PREPARE TO COMPARE

As you read, make note of how fear of embarrassment can drive people's actions. This information will help you compare the ideas of this text with ideas in "The Ravine," which follows it.

1   Remember when you could pick your nose in public or run outside in your underpants without a second thought? These days, you flood with embarrassment if your dad sings in front of your friends or you drop a tray in the cafeteria.

2   What changed? Not the rules about nose picking or your father's singing voice, but your brain.

It's All in Your Head

3   Sometime during middle school, changes in brain activity transform how we see the world. Spending time with other kids becomes a top priority. Hormones[1] power up the brain's reward system, making hanging out with friends more fun

---

[1] **hormones:** chemical messengers that travel through the blood.

NOTICE & NOTE

Notice & Note

Use the side margins to notice and note signposts in the text.

MAKE PREDICTIONS
Annotate: Mark the subheading.
Predict: What do you think this section will be about?

NOTICE & NOTE

essential
(ĭ-sĕn´shəl) *adj.* Something *essential* is so important that you can't do without it.

than ever before. But these changes come with a down side. Fitting in becomes **essential**. Threat-detection systems focus on what other people think and scan for any hints of disapproval. Hormones push the brain's shame and self-consciousness systems into overdrive.

4   Because of these brain changes, teens start reacting more strongly to social problems. Scientists don't know this *just* from surviving middle school—they have evidence from laboratory research. During a challenge like giving a speech, teens release

FEELINGS CENTRAL

A Quick Tour of Key Brain Regions Certain feelings and reactions take place in specific brain regions. Here are some regions associated with the emotional highs and lows of our social lives.

dACC The dorsal anterior cingulate cortex (dACC) and anterior insula comprise the brain's "Ow!" system that reacts to both physical and social pain.

Lateral Prefrontal Cortex Adults activate the lateral prefrontal cortex to help defend against hurt feelings. Something to look forward to?

Prefrontal Cortex

Anterior Insula
Septal Nuclei
Hypothalamus
Amygdala
Hippocampus
VTA

Limbic System The limbic system is where fight-or-flight reactions to stress or fear take place. Along with the ventral tegmental area (VTA), the limbic system is also involved in the brain's reward circuit.

more stress hormones and have higher blood pressure than kids or adults. Teens don't even have to tackle a challenge to feel stressed. Even being watched over a video monitor makes teens sweat more than adults.

Words Do Hurt Like Sticks and Stones

5   Why do we use pain words, like "hurt feelings" and "broken hearted," to talk about problems with other people? Maybe because our brains react to physical pain and social rejection in the same way. Psychologists explore this connection between physical and social pain by measuring brain activity while people play a computer game called Cyberball.

6   In Cyberball, research participants play a game of catch online with two other players. At least, that's what they believe is happening. In reality, the other "players" are fake, just part of the game's programming. The game starts fair, with the players programmed to share the ball with the research participant. Then, with no warning, the players start throwing the ball only to each other, leaving the research participant out completely.

7   No big surprise—teens in these Cyberball experiments feel sad and rejected. The surprising part? Rejection activates the same brain systems that physical pain triggers. Brain scans show that rejection fires up the "Ow!" part of our brain that makes pain upsetting. Without this pain-response system, we would recognize physical pain, but it wouldn't bother us. This physical pain system also responds to many kinds of social pain, like thinking about a breakup or being called boring.

8   Some people have especially reactive pain-response systems. A stronger "Ow!" brain response in the lab translates to people feeling more rejected, self-conscious, and sad in real life. Differences in pain-system reactivity may help explain why rejection hurts teenagers more than young kids. In Cyberball experiments comparing children to teens, teens activate brain systems related to pain and sadness more strongly.

Embarrassment Has an Unfair Advantage

9   Our thoughts and feelings depend on the balance between many different brain systems. Activity in one system can **amplify** or cancel out activity in another. Because our brains take more than two decades to develop, some brain systems come online sooner than others. Unfortunately, the systems that trigger embarrassment and fear of rejection fire up years before the systems that tame bad feelings.

NOTICE & NOTE

ANALYZE ORGANIZATIONAL PATTERNS

Annotate: Mark the subhead.

Analyze: Which main organizational pattern is the author using? How can you tell?

LANGUAGE CONVENTIONS
Remember that a comma may be used to set off an introductory element in a sentence. In paragraph 8, mark an example of an introductory element and its comma.

amplify
(ăm´plə-fī) v. To *amplify* something is to make it stronger or more intense.

NOTICE & NOTE

generate
(jĕn´ə-rāt´) *v*. To *generate* is to create and develop something.

CONTRASTS AND CONTRADICTIONS

Notice & Note: In paragraphs 12-13, mark examples of the negative effects of a fear of rejection. Then, mark examples of its positive effects.

Analyze: Why does the article note both the positive and negative effects of a fear of rejection? Is that fear good for us? Why or why not?

humiliation
(hyōō-mĭl´ē-ā´shən) *n*. A feeling of *humiliation* is even more intense than a feeling of embarrassment.

ANALYZE ORGANIZATIONAL PATTERNS

Annotate: Mark the two steps listed in the boxed feature on this page and the next.

Analyze: How does numbering these steps help you better understand the text?

10   Imagine a tug-of-war with fear of rejection, the desire to fit in, and self-consciousness all pulling on the same side. With nothing pulling against them, they easily drag in all sorts of bad feelings. This imbalance means even small problems, like tripping in the hallway, can trigger a wave of embarrassment.

11   Brain scans reveal that adults unleash a powerful defender to pull the brain back into balance. Adult brains quickly fire up systems to soothe anxiety and **generate** positive thoughts. These systems help balance out concern about what other people think, so adults feel less hurt and embarrassed by rejection.

12   Wouldn't it be better if we could just turn off hurt feelings, embarrassment, and the desire to fit in? Probably not. Before modern society, people needed to belong to a group to survive. Without a group, people couldn't find enough food or protect themselves. Fear of rejection forced people to behave well enough for the community to keep them around.

13   Our lives don't depend on social acceptance anymore, but social pain is still helpful. Fear of rejection pulls on the right side in the tug-of-war against mean or selfish behavior. Shame punishes us for lying or cheating, even if we don't get caught. Social pain hurts, but it also makes us nicer. Brain scans show that teens with strong pain-response systems give more support to other kids.

14   Unfortunately, knowing the benefits of social pain won't save you from a flash of **humiliation** when your mom reminds you to take a "potty break" in front of your friends. But you can take comfort in reminding yourself that the pain makes you a better person. Maybe even one less likely to embarrass your own kids someday.

NEED HELP?

Your heart pounds, your face flames red, and your stomach feels like you've swallowed a live octopus. Meltdown mode doesn't come with an off switch—you need to hack your brain. Here are two steps you can take.

1. **Deactivate the alarm.** Your brain treats social slipups like a threat to survival, preparing your body to fight. You can't directly shut down this threat alert system, but you can trick your brain into doing it. Slow, deep breathing informs your brain the emergency has passed. Just relax your shoulders, fill your lungs completely, and exhale slowly. Your brain will respond by slowing your heart and reducing stress hormones.

2. **Disagree with yourself.** Stress floods your brain with negative thoughts. Imagining awful possibilities is your brain's attempt to protect you. The solution? Don't believe everything you think. If you wouldn't say it to a friend, find something more reasonable to say to yourself. In the moment, this boosts your mood. Over time, it rewires your brain. Brain cells forge new connections each time you talk back to negative thoughts. Eventually, realizing problems aren't so bad becomes automatic, just like riding a bike.

CHECK YOUR UNDERSTANDING

Answer these questions before moving on to the **Analyze the Text** section on the following page.

1 This article is mostly about —

   A situations that are embarrassing to teenagers

   B why teenagers are so sensitive to social pressure

   C how to avoid feeling embarrassed

   D the benefits of embarrassment

2 How does the author mainly support her ideas?

   F With references to other information sources

   G With experts' opinions

   H With funny anecdotes

   J With scientific evidence

3 What information does the section at the end of the article provide?

   A It tells who you should call if you need help.

   B It gives tips for handling the stress of embarrassment.

   C It defines important vocabulary words.

   D It summarizes the most important ideas in the article.

RESPOND

ANALYZE THE TEXT

Support your responses with evidence from the text. 📓 NOTEBOOK

1. **Compare** Why is fear of embarrassment worse for teenagers than for younger children and adults, according to the article?

2. **Critique** Why does the author consider fear of embarrassment as at least somewhat positive? Do you agree with this view?

3. **Predict** Review the subheading "Words Do Hurt Like Sticks and Stones." What would you predict this section to be about? Summarize the section and explain whether your prediction was accurate.

4. **Analyze** Review the graphic on page 50. How does the text that accompanies the graphic help you predict what the graphic will show?

5. **Notice & Note** Reread paragraphs 9–11 and notice the word *anxiety*. Using clues from the text, provide your own definition of *anxiety* and give an example of when someone might experience it.

RESEARCH TIP

If you have a two-word search term, enclosing both words within quotation marks (for example, "Cyberball experiment") will help you target your search. The quotation marks around the term will find only examples that use both words together.

RESEARCH

Find out more about the Cyberball study the author discusses in the text. Keep track of your sources in a chart like the one shown. Remember to use quotation marks around text taken word-for-word from a source.

URL/SOURCE	PARAPHRASED OR QUOTED INFORMATION

Connect Share what you learned in a panel discussion or brief presentation. Provide the source for each piece of information you use.

RESPOND

CREATE AND DISCUSS

Write an Advertisement Use what you've learned from the selection to create an advertisement for a service that helps young people overcome their fear of embarrassment.

- ❏ Start with an attention-getting slogan or question.
- ❏ Then, include bulleted statements summarizing how your service works. Support your statements with text evidence.
- ❏ End with a call to action that encourages young people to hire you.

Go to the **Writing Studio** for more on writing informative texts.

Discuss with a Small Group As you discuss how fear drives people's actions, take notes, ask for and discuss ideas from group members, and identify points of agreement and disagreement. Use ideas from your advertisements to inform your discussion. Discuss these ideas:

- ❏ Is there a difference between how you might respond to a genuine danger and how you might respond to the possibility of embarrassing yourself?
- ❏ What is going on in your brain when you're in a potentially embarrassing situation?

Go to the **Speaking and Listening Studio** for help with having a group discussion.

RESPOND TO THE ESSENTIAL QUESTION

? How do you find courage in the face of fear?

Gather Information Review your annotations and notes on "Embarrassed?" and highlight those that help answer the Essential Question. Then, add relevant details to your Response Log.

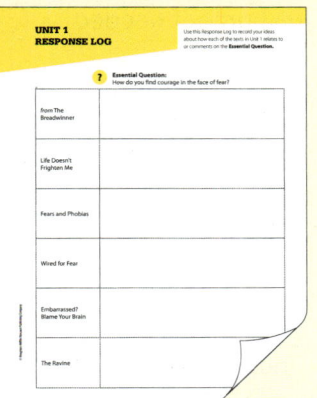

ACADEMIC VOCABULARY

As you write and discuss what you learned from the article, be sure to use the Academic Vocabulary words. Check off each of the words that you use.

- ❏ evident
- ❏ factor
- ❏ indicate
- ❏ similar
- ❏ specific

RESPOND

WORD BANK
amplify generate
essential humiliation

CRITICAL VOCABULARY

Practice and Apply Answer each question using the Critical Vocabulary word in a complete sentence.

1. What is an **essential** part of your morning routine?
_____

2. Why would a band playing outdoors need to **amplify** their instruments? _____

3. What is a good way to **generate** ideas for a weekend activity?
_____

4. How does **humiliation** make someone feel?
_____

VOCABULARY STRATEGY:
Synonyms and Antonyms

A **synonym** has the same meaning as another word. An **antonym** has the opposite or nearly the opposite meaning of a word. For example, a synonym of *amplify* is *enlarge*; an antonym of *amplify* is *reduce*. Identifying synonyms and antonyms can help clarify and expand your understanding of a word.

Write a synonym and an antonym for each of the following words in the space provided. *Amplify* is used as an example. Use a print or online resource, if needed.

Go to **Synonyms and Antonyms** in the **Vocabulary Studio** for more on synonyms and antonyms.

WORD	SYNONYM	ANTONYM
amplify	enlarge	reduce
essential		
generate		
humiliation		

Practice and Apply Write a sentence of your own, using a synonym or an antonym, for each of the following words used in the article.

1. reactive (paragraph 8: synonym)

2. imbalance (paragraph 10: antonym)

3. rewires (Need Help? section: synonym)

RESPOND

LANGUAGE CONVENTIONS:
Commas after Introductory Elements

An **introductory element** is a clause, phrase, or word that sets the stage for the main idea of the sentence. **Commas** are used after an introductory element to help make the meaning clearer.

These examples from the article show how commas are used with the different types of introductory elements.

1. <u>Because of these brain changes</u>, teens start reacting more strongly to social problems. (introductory clause)

2. <u>In Cyberball</u>, research participants play a game of catch online with two other players. (introductory phrase)

3. <u>Unfortunately</u>, the systems that trigger embarrassment and fear of rejection fire up years before the systems that tame bad feelings. (introductory word)

Practice and Apply Write three or four sentences summarizing the article, using different types of introductory elements and commas.

> Go to **Punctuation: End Marks and Commas** in the **Grammar Studio** for more on using commas.

COLLABORATE & COMPARE

SHORT STORY
THE RAVINE
by **Graham Salisbury**
pages 61–71

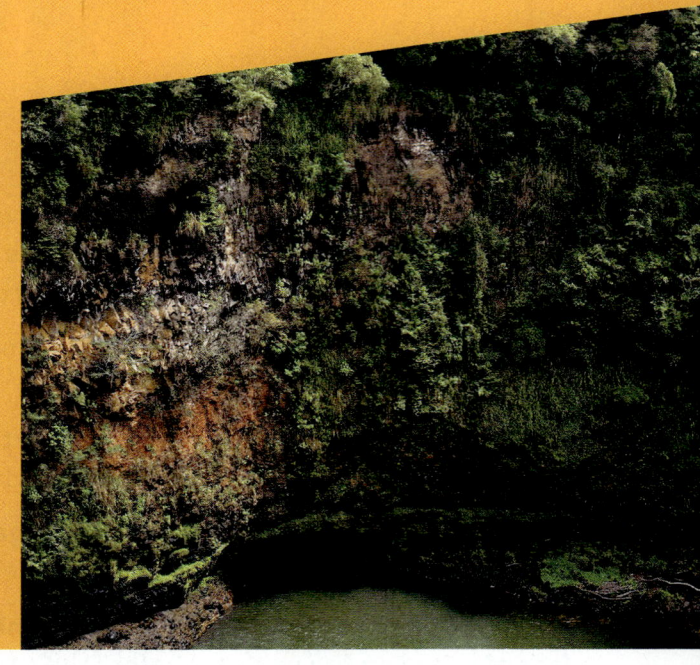

COMPARE THEMES AND MAIN IDEAS

Now that you've read "Embarrassed? Blame Your Brain," read "The Ravine" and explore how this short story connects to some of the same ideas. As you read, notice how the ideas in both texts relate to your own experiences and how the ideas in the two texts relate to each other. After you have read both selections, you will collaborate with a small group on a final project that involves an analysis of both texts.

 ESSENTIAL QUESTION:

How do you find courage in the face of fear?

INFORMATIONAL TEXT
EMBARRASSED?
Blame Your Brain
by **Jennifer Connor-Smith**
pages 49–53

The Ravine

QUICK START

Sometimes it's difficult to do something you're afraid to do—just because you're embarrassed to let other people know you're afraid. List "smart" reasons to overcome a fear. Then list "silly" reasons. Discuss your reasons with a partner.

MAKE INFERENCES

An **inference** is a logical guess based on facts and one's own knowledge and experience. To support an inference, **cite evidence**, or provide examples from the text. Here is one way you might make an inference about Joe-Boy, a character in "The Ravine."

EVIDENCE FROM THE STORY	MY OWN KNOWLEDGE	INFERENCE
Joe-Boy is Vinny's "best friend." He teases Vinny for being afraid.	Sometimes friends tease each other in a friendly way, but Joe-Boy's teasing seems mean.	They may be friends, but Joe-Boy may be unkind—or even mean.

ANALYZE CHARACTERS AND SETTINGS

In realistic fiction, characters—like real people—have personalities and motivations and experience life-changing events. The **setting**, or the time and place in which the action occurs, often helps draw attention to the traits, motivations, and development of the characters.

- **Character traits** are the qualities shown by a character, such as physical traits (tall with brown eyes) or expressions of personality (kind or anxious).
- **Character motivations** are the reasons a character acts, feels, or thinks in a certain way.
- **Character development** is how a character changes over the course of a story.

As you read "The Ravine," note how the story's characters respond to events, the setting, and each other.

GET READY

GENRE ELEMENTS: SHORT STORY
- includes the basic elements of fiction—setting, characters, plot, conflict, and theme
- may center on one particular moment or event
- can be read in one sitting

GET READY

CRITICAL VOCABULARY

murky   rivulet   cascade   precipice

To preview the Critical Vocabulary words, replace each boldfaced word with a different word or words that have the same meaning.

1. He dropped his watch into the (**murky**) _____ water and watched it disappear.

2. She hopped over a thin (**rivulet**) _____ of the stream.

3. The river's frightening (**cascade**) _____ into the canyon roared ahead of them.

4. When they arrived at the top, no one wanted to step any closer to the (**precipice**) _____ .

LANGUAGE CONVENTIONS

Subordinating Conjunctions In this lesson, you will learn about forming **complex sentences** by using **subordinating conjunctions**, which introduce adverb clauses, to connect ideas. As you read "The Ravine," watch for subordinating conjunctions, such as *because, if, since, until, when,* and *where,* and notice how they connect ideas.

Example:

          1ˢᵗ Idea   2ⁿᵈ Idea
They took their time (because) the hand and footholds were slimy with moss.

ANNOTATION MODEL

NOTICE & NOTE

As you read, note how each character responds to the setting and other characters. Consider what these responses tell you about the character's traits and motivations. You can also mark up evidence that supports your own ideas. In the model, you can see one reader's notes about a character's response to the setting in "The Ravine."

38 The fifteen-foot ledge was not the problem. 39 It was the one above it, the one you had to work up to, the big one, where you had to take a deadly zigzag trail that climbed up and away from the waterfall, then cut back and forth to a foot-wide ledge something more like fifty feet up. 40 That was the problem.	Vinny's thoughts—his internal response to the setting—reveal something about him. He's afraid to climb to the higher ledge, "the problem." He also may not want his friends to know that he's afraid.

BACKGROUND

Graham Salisbury (b. 1944) was born in Pennsylvania but grew up in Hawaii. His father was killed in World War II. Raised by a distant mother, Salisbury lacked guidance. His characters explore choices similar to those he faced—making and keeping friends and learning honesty and courage. Their struggles, like Salisbury's, also take place in a Hawaiian setting. Among his many writing awards are the Boston Globe/Horn Book award and a School Library Journal Best Book of the Year award.

THE RAVINE

Short Story by Graham Salisbury

PREPARE TO COMPARE

As you read, pay attention to Vinny's struggles with fear and his desire to please and impress his friends. Note details that help you understand what he's like, his motivations, and the conflict he faces.

1   When Vinny and three others dropped down into the ravine,[1] they entered a jungle thick with tangled trees and rumors of what might have happened to the dead boy's body.

2   The muddy trail was slick and, in places where it had fallen away, flat-out dangerous. The cool breeze that swept the Hawaiian hillside pastures above died early in the descent.

3   There were four of them—Vinny; his best friend, Joe-Boy; Mo, who was afraid of nothing; and Joe-Boy's *haole*[2] girlfriend, Starlene—all fifteen. It was a Tuesday in July, two weeks and a day after the boy had drowned. If, in fact, that's what had happened to him.

---

[1] **ravine** (rə-vēn´): a deep, narrow valley made by running water.
[2] **haole** (hou´lē): in Hawaii, a white person or non-native Hawaiian.

Notice & Note

Use the side margins to notice and note signposts in the text.

MAKE INFERENCES

Annotate: Mark details in paragraphs 1–3 that hint that this setting is frightening.

Infer: What might lead four teens to venture into a setting like this?

NOTICE & NOTE

ANALYZE CHARACTERS AND SETTINGS

Annotate: In paragraphs 5–12, mark each of Vinny's reactions to what Joe-Boy says.

Infer: What do Vinny's reactions tell you about him? What is he afraid to admit to Joe-Boy? How do you know?

MEMORY MOMENT

Notice & Note: What does Vinny remember about events following the boy's disappearance? Mark details in paragraph 17 about the search for the missing boy.

Analyze: How might the memory of these details affect Vinny?

4   Vinny slipped, and dropped his towel in the mud. He picked it up and tried to brush it off, but instead smeared the mud spot around until the towel resembled something someone's dog had slept on. "Tst," he said.

5   Joe-Boy, hiking down just behind him, laughed. "Hey, Vinny, just think, that kid walked where you walking."

6   "Shuddup," Vinny said.

7   "You prob'ly stepping right where his foot was."

8   Vinny moved to the edge of the trail, where the ravine fell through a twisted jungle of gnarly trees and underbrush to the stream far below. He could see Starlene and Mo farther ahead, their heads bobbing as they walked, both almost down to the pond where the boy had died.

9   "Hey," Joe-Boy went on, "maybe you going be the one to find his body."

10 "You don't cut it out, Joe-Boy, I going . . . I going . . ."

11 "What, cry?"

12 Vinny scowled. Sometimes Joe-Boy was a big fat babooze.

13 They slid down the trail. Mud oozed between Vinny's toes. He grabbed at roots and branches to keep from falling. Mo and Starlene were out of sight now, the trail ahead having cut back.

14 Joe-Boy said, "You going jump in the water and go down and your hand going touch his face, stuck under the rocks. *Ha ha ha . . . a ha ha ha!*"

15 Vinny winced. He didn't want to be here. It was too soon, way too soon. Two weeks and one day.

16 He saw a footprint in the mud and stepped around it.

17 The dead boy had jumped and had never come back up. Four search and rescue divers hunted for two days straight and never found him. Not a trace. Gave Vinny the creeps. It didn't make sense. The pond wasn't that big.

18 He wondered why it didn't seem to bother anyone else. Maybe it did and they just didn't want to say.

19 Butchie was the kid's name. Only fourteen.

20 Fourteen.

21 Two weeks and one day ago he was walking down this trail. Now nobody could find him.

22 The jungle crushed in, reaching over the trail, and Vinny brushed leafy branches aside. The roar of the waterfall got louder, louder.

23 Starlene said it was the goddess that took him, the one that lives in the stone down by the road. She did that every now and then, Starlene said, took somebody when she got lonely. Took him and kept him. Vinny had heard that legend before, but he'd never believed in it.

62 Unit 1

24 Now he didn't know what he believed.

25 The body had to be stuck down there. But still, four divers and they couldn't find it?

26 Vinny decided he'd better believe in the legend. If he didn't, the goddess might get mad and send him bad luck. Or maybe take *him*, too.

27 *Stopstopstop! Don't think like that.*

28 "Come on," Joe-Boy said, nudging Vinny from behind. "Hurry it up."

29 Just then Starlene whooped, her voice bouncing around the walls of the ravine.

30 "Let's go," Joe-Boy said. "They there already."

31 Moments later, Vinny jumped up onto a large boulder at the edge of the pond. Starlene was swimming out in the brown water. It wasn't **murky** brown, but clean and clear to a depth of maybe three or four feet. Because of the waterfall you had to yell if you wanted to say something. The whole place smelled of mud and ginger and iron.

32 Starlene swam across to the waterfall on the far side of the pond and ducked under it, then climbed out and edged along the rock wall behind it, moving slowly, like a spider. Above, sun-sparkling stream water spilled over the lip of a one-hundred-foot drop.

NOTICE & NOTE

ANALYZE CHARACTERS AND SETTINGS

Annotate: Mark each of Vinny's thoughts in paragraphs 24–28.

Describe: What do his thoughts indicate about what he's like? How would you describe Vinny to a friend?

murky
(mur´kē) *adj.* Something *murky* is dark, obscure, and gloomy.

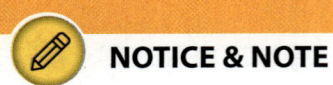

NOTICE & NOTE

33 Mo and Joe-Boy threw their towels onto the rocks and dove into the pond. Vinny watched, his muddy towel hooked around his neck. Reluctantly, he let it fall, then dove in after them.

34 The cold mountain water tasted tangy. Was it because the boy's body was down there decomposing?[3] He spit it out.

35 He followed Joe-Boy and Mo to the waterfall and ducked under it. They climbed up onto the rock ledge, just as Starlene had done, then spidered their way over to where you could climb to a small ledge about fifteen feet up. They took their time because the hand and footholds were slimy with moss.

36 Starlene jumped first. Her shriek echoed off the rocky cliff, then died in the dense green jungle.

37 Mo jumped, then Joe-Boy, then Vinny.

38 The fifteen-foot ledge was not the problem.

39 It was the one above it, the one you had to work up to, the big one, where you had to take a deadly zigzag trail that climbed up and away from the waterfall, then cut back and forth to a foot-wide ledge something more like fifty feet up.

40 That was the problem.

41 That was where the boy had jumped from.

42 Joe-Boy and Starlene swam out to the middle of the pond. Mo swam back under the waterfall and climbed once again to the fifteen-foot ledge.

43 Vinny started to swim out toward Joe-Boy but stopped when he saw Starlene put her arms around him. She kissed him. They sank under for a long time, then came back up, still kissing.

44 Vinny turned away and swam back over to the other side of the pond, where he'd first gotten in. His mother would kill him if she ever heard about where he'd come. After the boy drowned, or was taken by the goddess, or whatever happened to him, she said never to come to this pond again. Ever. It was off-limits. Permanently.

45 But not his dad. He said, "You fall off a horse, you get back on, right? Or else you going be scared of it all your life."

46 His mother scoffed and waved him off. "Don't listen to him, Vinny, listen to me. Don't go there. That pond is haunted." Which had made his dad laugh.

47 But Vinny promised he'd stay away.

MAKE INFERENCES

Annotate: Reread paragraphs 43–44, marking each of Vinny's responses to Joe-Boy and Starlene.

Infer: Why might Vinny respond as he does?

ANALYZE CHARACTERS AND SETTINGS

Annotate: In paragraphs 46–47, mark what Vinny's mother says about the setting of the pond.

Analyze: How might what Vinny's mother has said influence Vinny?

---

[3] **decomposing** (dē´kəm-pōz´ĭng): starting to decay and fall apart.

48 But then Starlene and Joe-Boy said, "Come with us anyway. You let your mommy run your life, or what?" And Vinny said, "But what if I get caught?" And Joe-Boy said, "So?"

49 Vinny mashed his lips. He was so weak. Couldn't even say no. But if he'd said, "I can't go, my mother won't like it," they would have laughed him right off the island. No, he had to go. No choice.

50 So he'd come along, and so far it was fine. He'd even gone in the water. Everyone was happy. All he had to do now was wait it out and go home and hope his mother never heard about it.

51 When he looked up, Starlene was gone.

52 He glanced around the pond until he spotted her starting up the zigzag trail to the fifty-foot ledge. She was moving slowly, hanging on to roots and branches on the upside of the cliff. He couldn't believe she was going there. He wanted to yell, *Hey, Starlene, that's where he* died!

53 But she already knew that.

54 Mo jumped from the lower ledge, yelling, "Banzaiiii!" An explosion of coffee-colored water erupted when he hit.

55 Joe-Boy swam over to where Starlene had gotten out. He waved to Vinny, grinning like a fool, then followed Starlene up the zigzag trail.

56 Now Starlene was twenty-five, thirty feet up. Vinny watched her for a while, then lost sight of her when she slipped behind a wall of jungle that blocked his view. A few minutes later she popped back out, now almost at the top, where the trail ended, where there was nothing but mud and a few plants to grab on to if you slipped, plants that would rip right out of the ground, plants that wouldn't stop you if you fell, nothing but your screams between you and the rocks below.

57 Vinny's stomach tingled just watching her. He couldn't imagine what it must feel like to be up there, especially if you were afraid of heights, like he was. *She has no fear*, Vinny thought, *no fear at all. Pleasepleaseplease, Starlene. I don't want to see you die.*

58 Starlene crept forward, making her way to the end of the trail, where the small ledge was.

59 Joe-Boy popped out of the jungle behind her. He stopped, waiting for her to jump before going on.

60 Vinny held his breath.

NOTICE & NOTE

LANGUAGE CONVENTIONS
Subordinating conjunctions are used to connect ideas in a complex sentence. Circle the word *until* in the first sentence of paragraph 52. What does the subordinating conjunction *until* suggest about Vinny's glance around the pond?

MAKE INFERENCES
Annotate: In paragraph 57, underline Vinny's descriptions of what Starlene is like. Then, circle the thoughts that show his worry.

Infer: How does Vinny feel about Starlene?

NOTICE & NOTE

ANALYZE CHARACTERS AND SETTINGS

Annotate: In paragraphs 61–69, mark each description of Starlene's actions.

Analyze: Based on her actions, how would you describe Starlene? How accurate is Vinny's view of her?

61 Starlene, in her cutoff jeans and soaked T-shirt, stood perfectly still, her arms at her sides. Vinny suddenly felt like hugging her. Why, he couldn't tell. *Starlene, please.*

62 She reached behind her and took a wide leaf from a plant, then eased down and scooped up a finger of mud. She made a brown cross on her forehead, then wiped her muddy fingers on her jeans.

63 She waited.

64 Was she thinking about the dead boy?

65 She stuck the stem end of the leaf in her mouth, leaving the rest of it to hang out. When she jumped, the leaf would flap up and cover her nose and keep water from rushing into it. An old island trick.

66 She jumped.

67 Down, down.

68 Almost in slow motion, it seemed at first, then faster and faster. She fell feetfirst, arms flapping to keep balance so she wouldn't land on her back, or stomach, which would probably almost kill her.

69 Just before she hit, she crossed her arms over her chest and vanished within a small explosion of rusty water.

70 Vinny stood, not breathing at all, praying.

71 Ten seconds. Twenty, thirty . . .

72 She came back up, laughing.

73 *She shouldn't make fun that way*, Vinny thought. It was dangerous, disrespectful. It was asking for it.

74 Vinny looked up when he heard Joe-Boy shout, "Hey, Vinny, watch how a man does it! Look!"

75 Joe-Boy scooped up some mud and drew a stroke of lightning across his chest. When he jumped, he threw himself out, face and body parallel to the pond, his arms and legs spread out. *He's crazy*, Vinny thought, *absolutely insane*. At the last second Joe-Boy folded into a ball and hit. *Ca-roomp!* He came up whooping and yelling, "*Wooo!* So *good*! Come on, Vinny, it's hot!"

76 Vinny faked a laugh. He waved, shouting, "Naah, the water's too cold!"

77 Now Mo was heading up the zigzag trail—Mo, who hardly ever said a word and would do anything anyone ever challenged him to do. *Come on, Mo, not you, too.*

78 Vinny knew then that he would have to jump.

79 Jump, or never live it down.

80 Mo jumped in the same way Joe-Boy had, man-style, splayed out in a suicide fall. He came up grinning.

81 Starlene and Joe-Boy turned toward Vinny.

82 Vinny got up and hiked around the edge of the pond, walking in the muddy shallows, looking at a school of small brown-backed fish near a ginger patch.

83 Maybe they'd forget about him.

84 Starlene torpedoed over, swimming underwater. Her body glittered in the small amount of sunlight that penetrated the trees around the rim of the ravine. When she came up, she broke the surface smoothly, gracefully, like a swan. Her blond hair sleeked back like river grass.

85 She smiled a sweet smile. "Joe-Boy says you're afraid to jump. I didn't believe him. He's wrong, right?"

86 Vinny said quickly, "Of course he's wrong. I just don't want to, that's all. The water's cold."

87 "Naah, it's nice."

88 Vinny looked away. On the other side of the pond Joe-Boy and Mo were on the cliff behind the waterfall.

89 "Joe-Boy says your mom told you not to come here. Is that true?"

90 Vinny nodded. "Yeah. Stupid, but she thinks it's haunted."

91 "She's right."

92 "What?"

93 "That boy didn't die, Vinny. The stone goddess took him. He's in a good place right now. He's her prince."

MAKE INFERENCES

Annotate: Circle Vinny's description of Mo in paragraphs 77–79.

Infer: Why might Vinny feel that he'll have to jump if Mo jumps? What would make him feel that he would "never live it down" if he doesn't jump?

ANALYZE CHARACTERS AND SETTINGS

Annotate: In paragraphs 85–96, mark what Starlene says to Vinny.

Analyze: What do Starlene's words say about her? What do Vinny's responses tell you about him?

The Ravine 67

NOTICE & NOTE

94   Vinny scowled. He couldn't tell if Starlene was teasing him or if she really believed that. He said, "Yeah, prob'ly."

95   "Are you going to jump, or is Joe-Boy right?"

96   "Joe-Boy's an idiot. Sure I'm going to jump."

97   Starlene grinned, staring at Vinny a little too long. "He is an idiot, isn't he? But I love him."

98   "Yeah, well . . ."

99   "Go to it, big boy. I'll be watching."

100   Starlene sank down and swam out into the pond.

101   *Ca-ripes.*

102   Vinny ripped a hank[4] of white ginger from the ginger patch and smelled it, and prayed he'd still be alive after the sun went down.

103   He took his time climbing the zigzag trail. When he got to the part where the jungle hid him from view, he stopped and smelled the ginger again. So sweet and alive it made Vinny wish for all he was worth that he was climbing out of the ravine right now, heading home.

104   But of course, there was no way he could do that.

105   Not before jumping.

106   He tossed the ginger onto the muddy trail and continued on. He slipped once or twice, maybe three times. He didn't keep track. He was too numb now, too caught up in the insane thing he was about to do. He'd never been this far up the trail before. Once he'd tried to go all the way, but couldn't. It made him dizzy.

107   When he stepped out and the jungle opened into a huge bowl where he could look down, way, way down, he could see their three heads in the water, heads with arms moving slowly to keep them afloat, and a few bright rays of sunlight pouring down onto them, and when he saw this, his stomach fluttered and rose. Something sour came up and he spit it out.

108   It made him wobble to look down. He closed his eyes. His whole body trembled. The trail was no wider than the length of his foot. And it was wet and muddy from little **rivulets** of water that bled from the side of the cliff.

109   The next few steps were the hardest he'd ever taken in his life. He tried not to look down, but he couldn't help it. His gaze was drawn there. He struggled to push back an urge to fly, just jump off and fly. He could almost see himself spiraling down like a glider, or a bird, or a leaf.

ANALYZE CHARACTERS AND SETTINGS
Annotate: In paragraphs 107–110, mark descriptions of the story's setting.

Infer: What do Vinny's responses to the setting tell you about him?

rivulet
(rĭv´yə-lĭt) *n.* A *rivulet* is a small brook or stream.

---
[4] **hank** (hăngk): a coiled or looped bundle of something, such as rope or yarn.

NOTICE & NOTE

110 His hands shook as if he were freezing. He wondered, *Had the dead boy felt this way?* Or had he felt brave, like Starlene or Joe-Boy, or Mo, who seemed to feel nothing.

111 Somebody from below shouted, but Vinny couldn't make it out over the waterfall, roaring down just feet beyond the ledge where he would soon be standing, **cascading** past so close its mist dampened the air he breathed.

112 *The dead boy had just come to the ravine to have fun*, Vinny thought. Just a regular kid like himself, come to swim and be with his friends, then go home and eat macaroni and cheese and watch TV, maybe play with his dog or wander around after dark.

113 But he'd done none of that.

114 Where was he?

115 Inch by inch Vinny made it to the ledge. He stood, swaying slightly, the tips of his toes one small movement from the **precipice**.

116 Far below, Joe-Boy waved his arm back and forth. It was dreamy to see—back and forth, back and forth. He looked so small down there.

117 For a moment Vinny's mind went blank, as if he were in some trance, some dream where he could so easily lean out and fall, and think or feel nothing.

118 A breeze picked up and moved the trees on the ridge-line, but not a breath of it reached the fifty-foot ledge.

119 Vinny thought he heard a voice, small and distant. Yes. Something inside him, a tiny voice pleading, *Don't do it. Walk away. Just turn and go and walk back down.*

120 " . . . I can't," Vinny whispered.

121 *You can, you can, you can. Walk back down.*

122 Vinny waited.

123 And waited.

124 Joe-Boy yelled, then Starlene, both of them waving.

125 Then something very strange happened.

126 Vinny felt at peace. Completely and totally calm and at peace. He had not made up his mind about jumping. But something else inside him had.

127 Thoughts and feelings swarmed, stinging him: *Jump! Jump! Jump! Jump!*

128 But deep inside, where the peace was, where his mind wasn't, he would not jump. He would walk back down.

cascade
(kăs-kād´) *v.* Something that can *cascade* will fall, pour, or rush in stages, like a waterfall over steep rocks.

precipice
(prĕs´ə-pĭs) *n.* A *precipice* is an overhanging or extremely steep area of rock.

ANALYZE CHARACTERS AND SETTINGS
Annotate: In paragraphs 119–130, underline each thought that encourages Vinny not to jump. Then, circle evidence of the feelings created by those thoughts.

Analyze: What fear is Vinny overcoming? What does this tell you about him?

The Ravine   69

NOTICE & NOTE

MAKE INFERENCES

Annotate: In paragraphs 132–133, mark words that indicate how the group leaves the ravine.

Infer: What does this suggest about the group and how they feel about Vinny?

AHA MOMENT

Notice & Note: What does Vinny suddenly realize in paragraph 133? Mark this detail.

Infer: What does this tell you about how Vinny feels about his choice?

129   *No! No, no, no!*

130   Vinny eased down and fingered up some mud and made a cross on his chest, big and bold. He grabbed a leaf, stuck it in his mouth. *Be calm, be calm. Don't look down.*

131   After a long pause he spit the leaf out and rubbed the cross to a blur.

132   They walked out of the ravine in silence, Starlene, Joe-Boy, and Mo far ahead of him. They hadn't said a word since he'd come down off the trail. He knew what they were thinking. He knew, he knew, he knew.

133   At the same time the peace was still there. He had no idea what it was. But he prayed it wouldn't leave him now, prayed it wouldn't go away, would never go away, because in there, in that place where the peace was, it didn't matter what they thought.

134   Vinny emerged from the ravine into a brilliance that surprised him. Joe-Boy, Starlene, and Mo were now almost down to the road.

135   Vinny breathed deeply, and looked up and out over the island. He saw, from there, a land that rolled away like honey,

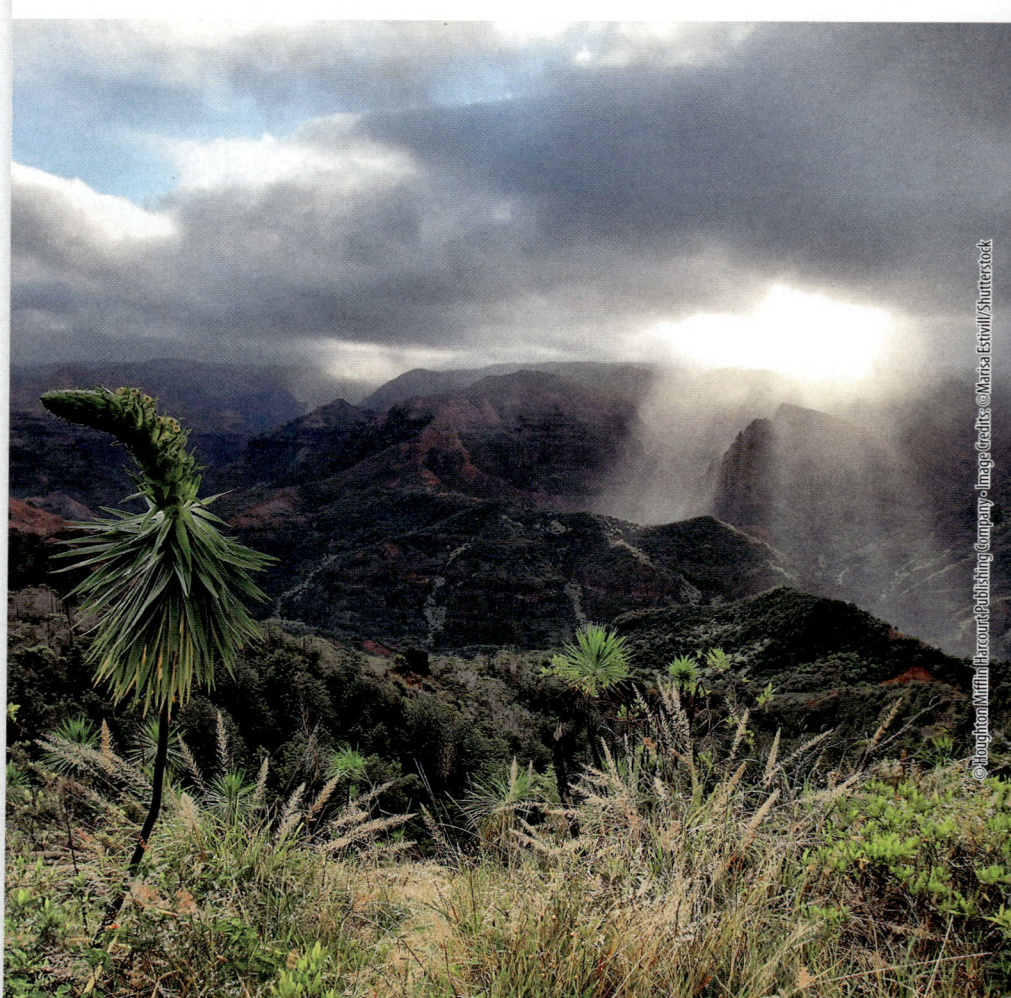

easing down a descent of rich Kikuyu grass pasture-land, flowing from there over vast highlands of brown and green, then, finally, falling massively to the coast and flat blue sea. He'd never seen anything like it.

136   Had it always been here? This view of the island?
137   He stared and stared, then sat, taking it in.
138   He'd never seen anything so beautiful in all his life.

CHECK YOUR UNDERSTANDING

Answer these questions before moving on to the **Analyze the Text** section on the following page.

1 Which of the following is not true?

   A Vinny's father encourages him to go back to the pond.

   B Starlene, Joe-Boy, and Mo jump from the fifty-foot ledge.

   C Butchie and Vinny had been close friends for many years.

   D Vinny tries to avoid jumping by claiming that the water is too cold.

2 Which of the following sentences shows that Starlene suspects that Vinny is afraid?

   F "Are you going to jump, or is Joe-Boy right?"

   G "Come with us anyway. You let your mommy run your life, or what?"

   H *Her shriek echoed off the rocky cliff, then died in the dense green jungle.*

   J *Starlene said it was the goddess that took him, the one that lives in the stone by the road.*

3 As the story concludes —

   A the four friends walk home together

   B readers know that the group found Butchie

   C Joe-Boy, Starlene, and Mo leave Vinny behind

   D Vinny feels embarrassed by his decision not to jump

The Ravine

RESPOND

ANALYZE THE TEXT

Support your responses with evidence from the text. 📓 **NOTEBOOK**

1. **Summarize** Review paragraphs 23–27. In your own words, summarize the legend about the goddess. Explain how this aspect of the story's cultural setting influences Vinny.

2. **Draw Conclusions** Review paragraphs 31–39. What are some examples of language the author uses to describe the setting? Why is the setting important to the story?

3. **Make Inferences** Before jumping, the characters perform certain rituals. Reread paragraphs 61–80 to review how they prepare to jump. What inferences can you make about the characters' feelings and their reasons for these rituals?

4. **Analyze** Consider Vinny's feelings and actions throughout the story. How is Vinny different by the end of the story? How is he the same?

5. **Notice & Note** What does Vinny suddenly realize in paragraphs 51–53? Why is this realization a problem for Vinny?

RESEARCH

RESEARCH TIP
It's always easier to begin a research project by creating a research plan. First, identify exactly what you want to learn. Then, create a step-by-step plan to guide your research.

Hawaii is known not only for its beautiful beaches, volcanoes, and waterfalls, but also for the culture of its people. Do some research to explore the history of a few sports played in Hawaii. Make sure your sources are reliable and credible, such as a respected university or an established media outlet.

SPORT	INFORMATION ABOUT THE SPORT AND ITS SIGNIFICANCE
lele kawa (diving)	
he'e nalu (surfing)	
he'e hōlua (mountain surfing)	
'o'o ihe (spear throwing)	

Extend Explain why each sport is significant to Hawaiian culture. What do these activities tell you about native Hawaiians?

RESPOND

CREATE AND DISCUSS

Write a Compare and Contrast Essay Write a three- or four-paragraph essay in which you compare and contrast Vinny with one of the other characters in "The Ravine." Review your notes and annotations before you begin.

- ❏ Introduce your essay by describing the character traits of Vinny and the other character you have selected.
- ❏ Then, explain similarities and differences between the two characters. Include details from the text about the characters' actions and motivations to support your ideas.
- ❏ In your final paragraph, state your conclusion about the two characters.

Share and Discuss With a small group, discuss your opinions about Vinny's actions in "The Ravine." Can Vinny be characterized as a coward, a hero, or something else?

- ❏ Review the story with your group to identify the thoughts and actions that help you understand Vinny.
- ❏ Then, discuss Vinny's motivations and what those motivations reveal. As you discuss, listen closely, ask each other questions to help clarify ideas, and take notes.
- ❏ Finally, end your discussion by listing the conclusions of each member of your group.

Go to the **Writing Studio** for more on planning and drafting essays.

 Go to the **Speaking** and **Listening Studio** for help with having a group discussion.

RESPOND TO THE ESSENTIAL QUESTION

 How do you find courage in the face of fear?

Gather Information Review your annotations and notes on "The Ravine." Consider how Vinny found the courage to face a fear. Think about his actions, motivations, and traits as you respond. Then, add relevant details to your Response Log.

At the end of the unit, use your notes to write an informational essay.

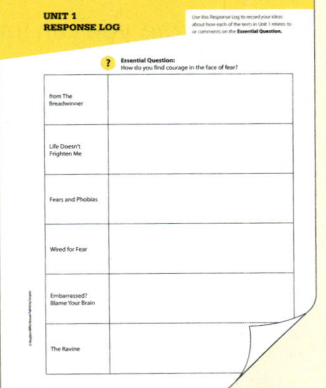

ACADEMIC VOCABULARY

As you write and discuss what you learned from "The Ravine," be sure to use the Academic Vocabulary words. Check off each of the words that you use.

- ❏ evident
- ❏ factor
- ❏ indicate
- ❏ similar
- ❏ specific

RESPOND

CRITICAL VOCABULARY

WORD BANK
murky   cascade
rivulet   precipice

Practice and Apply With a partner, discuss and write down an answer to each of the following questions. Then work together to write a sentence for each vocabulary word.

1. Which vocabulary word goes with *cloudy* and *dark*? Why?
   _____

2. Which vocabulary word goes with *edge*? Why?
   _____

3. Which vocabulary word goes with *trickle*? Why?
   _____

4. Which vocabulary word goes with *pouring*? Why?
   _____

VOCABULARY STRATEGY:
Context Clues

 Go to the **Vocabulary Studio** for more on context clues.

When you encounter an unfamiliar word, one way to figure out the meaning is to use **context clues,** or hints about meaning that may be found in the words, phrases, sentences, and paragraphs that surround that unknown word. Look at the following example from the text:

> **And it was wet and muddy from little rivulets of water that bled from the side of the cliff.**

To figure out the meaning of *rivulets*, look for clues in the surrounding words and ideas in the sentence. The sentence says that the rivulets of water "bled" from the cliff. This helps you imagine water flowing from the cliff in the same way that blood flows from a cut or scrape on your arm; the blood looks like a running stream. Combining this image with the word *little*, you can imagine that rivulets might be little streams. Then use a dictionary to confirm your guess: A rivulet is "a small brook or stream."

Practice and Apply Review "The Ravine" and find the following words. Look at the surrounding words and sentences for clues to each word's meaning. Fill out this chart.

WORD	LOCATION OF CONTEXT CLUES	MY GUESSED DEFINITION	DICTIONARY DEFINITION
winced	(paragraphs 14–15)		
scoffed	(paragraphs 45–46)		
parallel	(paragraph 75)		

LANGUAGE CONVENTIONS:
Subordinating Conjunctions

A **simple sentence** expresses a single, complete thought: *They took their time. The hand and footholds were slimy with moss.* However, you can use connecting words and phrases called **subordinating conjunctions** to connect and clarify ideas, forming **complex sentences.** Complex sentences include answers to questions such as *How? Where? When? Why? For how long? How much? To what extent?* and *Under what condition?*

Why did Joe-Boy, Mo, and Vinny take their time?

They took their time *because* the hand and footholds were slimy with moss. (paragraph 35)

> **RESPOND**
>
> Go to **Conjunctions and Interjections** in the **Grammar Studio** for more on using subordinating conjunctions.

COMMON SUBORDINATING CONJUNCTIONS

after	as long as	because	in order that	though	whenever
although	as much as	before	since	unless	where
as	as soon as	how	so that	until	wherever
as if	as though	if	than	when	while

The writer of "The Ravine" clarifies descriptions by creating complex sentences that answer questions such as these:

- Where? Where is the edge of the trail?

    Vinny moved to the edge of the trail, *where* the ravine fell through a twisted jungle of gnarly trees and underbrush to the stream far below. (paragraph 8)

- Under what condition? Under what condition would Vinny's mother get angry?

    His mother would kill him *if* she ever heard about where he'd come. (paragraph 44)

- When? When did the water erupt?

    An explosion of coffee-colored water erupted *when* he hit. (paragraph 54).

Practice and Apply Write three pairs of related simple sentences. Then, use a subordinating conjunction to connect the sentences in each pair. When you have finished, share your new complex sentences with a partner and work together to create a few more complex sentences.

RESPOND

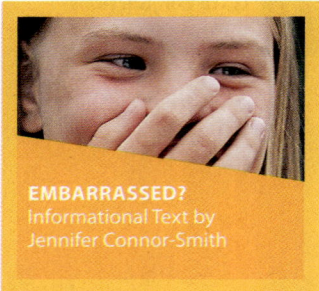

EMBARRASSED?
Informational Text by
Jennifer Connor-Smith

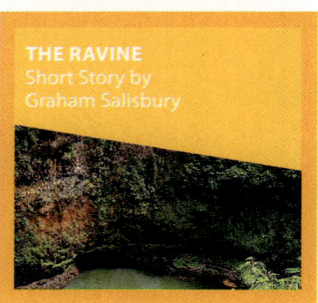

THE RAVINE
Short Story by
Graham Salisbury

Collaborate & Compare

COMPARE TEXTS

When you compare two or more texts on the same topic, you **synthesize** the information, making connections and building your understanding of key ideas. It's often easy to synthesize information when the texts you're comparing are the same **genre,** or type of writing. However, you can often gain a more thorough understanding of a topic by comparing texts from different genres—like an informational text and a short story.

In a small group, complete the Venn diagram with similarities and differences in what you learned about responses to the fear of embarrassment in the two texts. Think about the themes and main ideas shared by the texts. One example is completed for you.

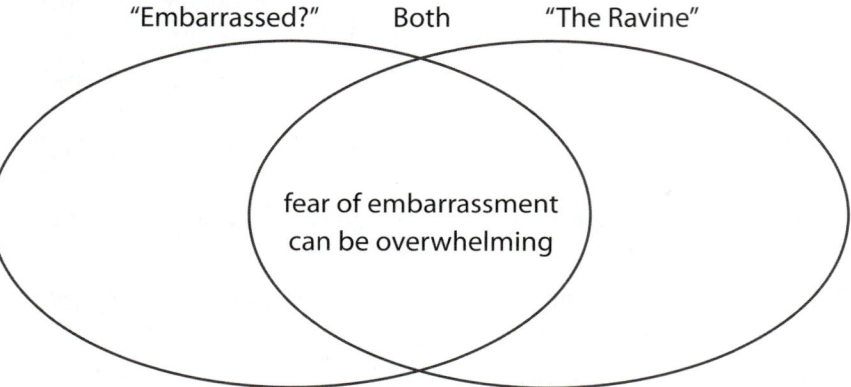

ANALYZE THE TEXTS

Discuss these questions in your group.

1. **Connect** What similar ideas about fear of embarrassment do the article and the short story share? Cite evidence in your anwer.

2. **Contrast** What differences are there between the choice Vinny makes and what you would expect him to do, based on the article?

3. **Infer** Why does Vinny make the choice that he does? What is happening in his brain as he makes this choice, based on the article?

4. **Synthesize** What theme or message about how young people approach fear can you synthesize from the two texts? What theme or message do they share?

RESPOND

RESEARCH AND SHARE

Now your group can continue exploring the main ideas in these texts by collaborating to present research in a panel discussion. Follow these steps:

1. **Develop Research Questions** In your group, brainstorm questions you'd like answered about young peoples' fear of embarrassment. Make sure that everyone contributes ideas to the list. Circle the most interesting questions. Then, assign each of the circled questions to group members for research. When those questions have been answered, your group will have gathered plenty of information to present in a panel discussion.

2. **Gather the Information** As you begin to research your individual question or questions from the list, check that your sources are reliable and credible.
   - A **reliable** source comes from an expert on the topic or someone with firsthand experience of the topic.
   - A **credible** source presents ideas fairly and accurately, avoiding bias (unfairly favoring one view), hyperbole (exaggeration), and stereotype (overgeneralizing a characteristic, such as saying that all teenagers are reckless).

   Take notes from two or more sources for each question, paraphrasing and summarizing key information that provides an answer. You can use this framework to synthesize what you learn:

RESEARCH TIP
To find strong sources, begin with the suggestions for Independent Reading at the end of this unit.

My Question:	
Source 1 information:	Source 2 information:
Ideas the two sources share that answer my question:	

3. **Share What You Learn** Once research is complete, everyone in your group will have become an expert on a different aspect of the topic. Gather together and share what you have learned. Listen to what others have to say, ask questions to request and clarify information, and build on the ideas of others as you discuss the topic. Use your research notes to back up your views with text evidence.

Collaborate & Compare

INDEPENDENT READING

? ESSENTIAL QUESTION:

How do you find courage in the face of fear?

Reader's Choice

Setting a Purpose Select one or more of these options from your eBook to continue your exploration of the Essential Question.
- Read the descriptions to see which text grabs your interest.
- Think about which genres you enjoy reading.

Notice & Note

In this unit, you practiced noticing and noting three signposts: **Words of the Wiser, Aha Moment,** and **Contrasts and Contradictions.** As you read independently, these signposts and others will aid your understanding. Below are the anchor questions to ask when you read literature and nonfiction.

Reading Literature: Stories, Poems, and Plays		
Signpost	**Anchor Question**	**Lesson**
Contrasts and Contradictions	Why did the character act that way?	p. 3
Aha Moment	How might this change things?	p. 3
Tough Questions	What does this make me wonder about?	p. 172
Words of the Wiser	What's the lesson for the character?	p. 2
Again and Again	Why might the author keep bringing this up?	p. 92
Memory Moment	Why is this memory important?	p. 93

Reading Nonfiction: Essays, Articles, and Arguments		
Signpost	**Anchor Question(s)**	**Lesson**
Big Questions	What surprised me? What did the author think I already knew? What challenged, changed, or confirmed what I already knew?	p. 246 p. 420 p. 332
Contrasts and Contradictions	What is the difference, and why does it matter?	p. 247
Extreme or Absolute Language	Why did the author use this language?	p. 247
Numbers and Stats	Why did the author use these numbers or amounts?	p. 333
Quoted Words	Why was this person quoted or cited, and what did this add?	p. 333
Word Gaps	Do I know this word from someplace else? Does it seem like technical talk for this topic? Do clues in the sentence help me understand the word?	p. 421

INDEPENDENT READING

You can preview these texts in Unit 1 of your eBook.

Then, check off the text or texts that you select to read on your own.

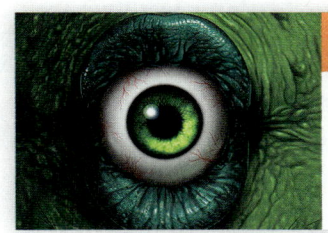

POEM

Horrors
Lewis Carroll

What are those terrible things that go bump in the night?

SHORT STORY

Vanquishing the Hungry Chinese Zombie
Claudine Gueh

A girl faces terror to protect her parents and the family store.

NARRATIVE NONFICTION

Running into Danger on an Alaskan Trail
Cinthia Ritchie

A long-distance runner has a terrifying encounter with a bear.

INFORMATIONAL TEXT

Face Your Fears: Choking Under Pressure Is Every Athlete's Worst Nightmare
Dana Hudepohl

How do athletes handle fear and stress while dealing with the pressure to succeed at competitive sports?

Collaborate and Share Find a partner to discuss what you learned from at least one of your independent readings.

- Give a brief synopsis or summary of the text.
- Describe any signposts that you noticed in the text and explain what they revealed to you.
- Describe what you most enjoyed or found most challenging about the text. Give specific examples.
- Decide whether you would recommend the text to others. Why or why not?

 Go to the **Reading Studio** for more resources on **Notice & Note.**

Independent Reading 79

WRITING TASK

Write an Informational Essay

This unit focuses on fear and the ways it can shape and alter our lives. For this writing task, you will write an informational essay on a topic related to fear and how people respond to it. Review the article "Fears and Phobias" to see an example of a well-written informational selection that you can use as a mentor text.

As you write your essay, you can use the notes from your Response Log, which you filled out after reading each text in this unit.

Go to the **Writing Studio** for help writing an informational essay.

Writing Prompt

Read the information in the box below.

> Fear can prevent you from achieving your goals, deciding something important, or fully enjoying your life.

This is the topic or context for your essay.

Think carefully about the following question.

> How do you find courage in the face of fear?

This is the essential question for the unit. How would you answer this question, based on the readings in this unit?

Write an essay explaining how people find the courage to face their fears.

Now mark the words that identify exactly what you are being asked to produce.

Be sure to—

- ❏ provide an introduction that catches the reader's attention, clearly states the topic, and includes a clear controlling idea or thesis statement
- ❏ support main ideas with evidence from sources
- ❏ organize information in a logical way
- ❏ connect related ideas effectively
- ❏ use appropriate word choice
- ❏ end by summarizing ideas or drawing an overall conclusion

Review these points as you write and again when you finish. Make any needed changes.

WRITING TASK

Plan

Before you start writing, plan your essay. First, choose a topic and appropriate genre. For this writing task, you already know that the topic relates to how people find the courage to face their fears, and you know that the genre is an informational essay. Next, identify your purpose and audience. Then, use a range of strategies to determine the ideas you'd like to include in your essay. These strategies may include discussing the topic with your classmates, doing some background reading, or thinking about how your own personal interests and experiences relate to the topic. Use the table below to assist you in planning your draft.

Go to **Writing Informative Texts: Developing a Topic** for help planning your essay.

Notice & Note
From Reading to Writing

As you plan your informational essay, apply what you've learned about signposts to your own writing. Remember that writers use common features, called signposts, to help convey their message to readers. Think about how you can incorporate **Quoted Words** into your essay.

 Go to the **Reading Studio** for more resources on Notice & Note.

Informational Essay Planning Table	
Topic	How people find the courage to face fear
Genre	Informational essay
Purpose	
Audience	
Ideas from discussion with classmates	
Ideas from background reading	
Personal interests related to topic	

Use the notes from your Response Log as you plan your essay.

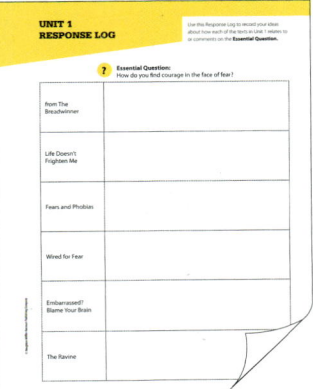

Background Reading Review the notes you took in your Response Log after reading the texts in this unit. Your notes will guide your review of the texts, and will help you carry out the background reading that will assist you as you formulate the key ideas of your essay.

Write an Informational Essay   81

WRITING TASK

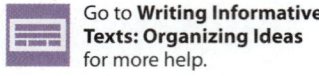 Go to **Writing Informative Texts: Organizing Ideas** for more help.

Organize Your Ideas Part of planning is organizing the ideas and information you have gathered. The process of organizing helps you decide on a logical order of information as you draft your essay. You can use the chart below to make an outline of the ideas you will cover. You can also use the chart to record the evidence that will support your ideas.

Main Topic: Finding Courage in the Face of Fear		
Kinds of fears people face	**How people respond to fear**	**How people find courage when facing fear**
Supporting Details	Supporting Details	Supporting Details

② Develop a Draft

 You might prefer to draft your essay online.

Once you have completed your planning activities, you will be ready to draft your informational essay. As you draft, refer to your graphic organizer and the outline you have created, as well as to any notes you took on the texts in the unit. Write an introduction, a main body of paragraphs that connect logically and reflect depth of thought, and then write a conclusion.

Using a word processor or online writing application makes it easier to make changes or move sentences around later when you are ready to revise your first draft.

WRITING TASK

Use the Mentor Text

Author's Craft
Your introduction is your first chance to capture the reader's attention. In addition to your controlling idea or thesis statement, your introduction should include something that gets your reader interested in reading your essay. Note the way the writer captures the reader's attention in "Fears and Phobias."

The roller coaster hesitates for a split second at the peak of its steep track after a long, slow climb. You know what's about to happen—and there's no way to avoid it now. It's time to hang onto the handrail, palms sweating, heart racing, and brace yourself for the wild ride down.	The writer uses a vivid description of riding a roller coaster to convey the fear that some people feel during this experience.

Apply What You've Learned To capture your reader's attention, you might include a surprising fact, a famous quotation, or a personal anecdote related to the topic.

Supporting Details
Supporting details are words, phrases, or sentences that tell more about a central idea. Notice how the author of "Fears and Phobias" uses the following example to support a key idea about one cause of phobias.

Someone might develop a bee phobia after being stung during a particularly scary situation. For that person, looking at a photograph of a bee, seeing a bee from a distance, or even walking near flowers where there *could* be a bee can all trigger the phobia.	The author provides an example as a supporting detail to help explain how fright and pain can cause a phobia.

Apply What You've Learned The details you include in your own informational essay should be clearly related to your ideas about how people find courage to face fear. Some types of details you can use to support your ideas are facts, examples, and quotations.

Write an Informational Essay   83

WRITING TASK

③ Revise

Go to **Writing Informative Texts: Precise Language and Vocabulary** for help revising your essay.

On Your Own Once you have written your draft, go back and look for ways to improve it. As you reread and revise it, think about whether you have achieved your purpose. The Revision Guide will help you focus on specific elements to make your writing stronger.

Revision Guide

Ask Yourself	Tips	Revision Techniques
1. Does my introduction grab a reader's attention?	**Mark** the introduction.	**Add** an interesting fact, example, or quotation that illustrates the topic or central point.
2. Does my introduction clearly state the purpose?	**Mark** the controlling idea or thesis statement.	**Add** a sentence that clearly states your controlling idea.
3. Are my main ideas organized in a clear and logical way?	**Circle** each main idea. **Underline** transitions from one idea to the next.	**Reorder** ideas so that each one flows easily to the next. **Add** appropriate transitions to connect ideas and clarify the organization.
4. Do I support each main idea with evidence?	**Mark** each supporting fact, definition, example, or quotation.	**Add** facts, details, examples, or quotations to support ideas.
5. Do I use compound and complex sentences to make relationships between ideas clear?	**Mark** each compound and complex sentence.	**Combine** some simple sentences to form compound and complex sentences.
6. Does my conclusion support the topic?	**Mark** the conclusion.	**Add** a statement that summarizes the main ideas.

ACADEMIC VOCABULARY

As you conduct your **peer review,** be sure to use these words.

❑ evident
❑ factor
❑ indicate
❑ similar
❑ specific

With a Partner Once you and your partner have worked through the Revision Guide on your own, exchange papers and evaluate each other's drafts in a **peer review.** Focus on providing revision suggestions for at least three of the items mentioned in the chart. Explain why you think your partner's draft should be revised and what your specific suggestions are.

When receiving feedback from your partner, listen attentively and ask questions to make sure you fully understand the suggested revisions.

WRITING TASK

4 Edit

Once you have addressed the organization, development, and flow of ideas in your essay, you can improve the finer points of your draft. Edit for the proper use of standard English conventions and make sure to correct any misspellings or grammatical errors.

Language Conventions

Compound and Complex Sentences Using too many simple sentences can make it difficult for readers to recognize how details are connected. You can clarify your ideas by including a variety of sentence structures in your writing.

- A **compound sentence** consists of two or more independent clauses. The clauses in compound sentences are connected with commas or dashes and coordinating conjunctions (*and, but, or, nor, yet, for, so*).
- A **complex sentence** consists of one independent clause and at least one dependent clause. Many dependent clauses start with words such as *when, until, who, where, because,* and *so that*.

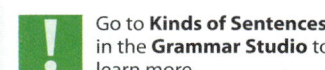

Go to **Kinds of Sentences** in the **Grammar Studio** to learn more.

The chart contains examples of simple, compound, and complex sentences from "Fears and Phobias."

Sentence Type	Example
Simple Sentence	Fear is one of the most basic human emotions.
Compound Sentence	You know what's about to happen—and there's no way to avoid it now.
Complex Sentence	As they grow and learn, with the support of adults, most kids are able to slowly conquer these fears and outgrow them.

5 Publish

After you give your essay its finishing touches, choose a way to share it with your audience. Consider these options:

- Present your essay as a speech to the class.
- Post your essay as a blog on a classroom or school website.

WRITING TASK

Use the scoring guide to evaluate your essay.

	Writing Task Scoring Guide: Informational Essay		
	Organization/Progression	**Development of Ideas**	**Use of Language and Language Conventions**
4	• The organization is effective and appropriate to the purpose. • All ideas are focused on the topic specified in the prompt. • Transitions clearly show the relationship among ideas.	• The introduction catches the reader's attention, clearly identifying the topic. • The essay contains a clear, concise, and well-defined controlling idea or thesis statement. • The topic is well developed with clear main ideas, supported by specific and well-chosen facts, details, examples, etc. • The conclusion effectively summarizes the information presented.	• Language and word choice is purposeful and precise. • A variety of simple, compound, and complex sentences is used to show how ideas are related. • Spelling, capitalization, and punctuation are correct. • Grammar, usage, and mechanics are correct. • Research sources are cited correctly.
3	• The organization is, for the most part, effective and appropriate to the purpose. • Most ideas are focused on the topic specified in the prompt. • A few more transitions are needed to show the relationship among ideas.	• The introduction could be more engaging. The topic is identified. • The essay contains a clear controlling idea or thesis statement. • The development of ideas is clear because the writer uses specific and appropriate facts, details, examples, and quotations. • The conclusion summarizes the information presented.	• Language is for the most part specific and clear. • Sentences vary somewhat in structure. • Some spelling, capitalization, and punctuation mistakes are present. • Some grammar and usage errors occur. • Research sources are cited with some formatting errors.
2	• The organization is evident but is not always appropriate to the purpose. • Only some ideas are focused on the topic specified in the prompt. • More transitions are needed to show the relationship among ideas.	• The introduction is only partly informative; the topic is unclear. • The controlling idea or thesis statement does not express a clear point. • The development of ideas is minimal. The writer uses facts, details, examples, etc., that are inappropriate or ineffective. • The conclusion is only partially effective.	• Language is often vague and general. • Compound and complex sentences are hardly used. • Spelling, capitalization, and punctuation are often incorrect but do not make reading difficult. • Grammar and usage errors are frequent, but ideas are still clear. • Only one or two research sources are cited, using incorrect format.
1	• The organization is not appropriate to the purpose. • Ideas are not focused on the topic specified in the prompt. • No transitions are used, making the essay difficult to understand.	• The introduction is missing or confusing. • The controlling idea or thesis statement is missing. • The development of ideas is weak. Supporting facts, details, examples, or quotations are unreliable, vague, or missing. • The conclusion is missing.	• Language is inappropriate for the text or is vague and confusing. • There is no sentence variety. • Many spelling, capitalization, and punctuation errors are present, making reading difficult. • Many grammatical and usage errors confuse the writer's ideas. • Research sources are not cited.

Give a Presentation

You will now adapt your informational essay for presentation to your classmates. You also will listen to their presentations, ask questions to better understand their ideas, and help them improve their work.

Go to **Giving a Presentation** in the **Speaking and Listening Studio** to learn more.

1 Adapt Your Essay for Presentation

Review your informational essay, and use the chart below to guide you as you adapt your essay and create a script and presentation materials.

Presentation Planning Chart		
Title and Introduction	How will you revise your title and introduction to capture your listener's attention? Is there a more concise way to state your controlling idea or thesis?	
Audience	What information will your audience already know? What information can you exclude? What information should you add?	
Effective Language and Organization	Which parts of your essay should be simplified? Where can you add transitions such as *first, second,* and *finally*?	
Visuals	What images or graphics would help clarify ideas or add interest? What text should appear on screen?	

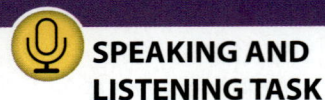

SPEAKING AND LISTENING TASK

2 Practice with a Partner or Group

Once you've completed your draft, practice with a partner or group to improve both the presentation and your delivery.

Practice Effective Verbal Techniques

- ❏ **Enunciation** Replace words that you stumble over, and rearrange sentences so that your delivery is smooth.
- ❏ **Voice Modulation and Pitch** Use your voice to display enthusiasm and emphasis.
- ❏ **Speaking Rate** Speak slowly enough that listeners understand you. Pause now and then to let them consider important points.
- ❏ **Volume** Remember that listeners at the back of the room need to hear you.

Practice Effective Nonverbal Techniques

- ❏ **Eye Contact** Try to let your eyes rest on each member of the audience at least once.
- ❏ **Facial Expression** Smile, frown, or raise an eyebrow to show your feelings or to emphasize points.
- ❏ **Gestures** Stand tall and relaxed, and use natural gestures—shrugs, nods, or shakes of your head—to add meaning and interest to your presentation.

Provide and Consider Advice for Improvement

As a listener, pay close attention. Take notes about ways that presenters can improve their presentations and more effectively use verbal and nonverbal techniques. Paraphrase and summarize each presenter's key ideas and main points to confirm your understanding, and ask questions to clarify any confusing ideas.

As a presenter, listen closely to questions and consider ways to revise your presentation to make sure your points are clear and logically sequenced. Remember to ask for suggestions about how you might change onscreen text or images to make your presentation clearer and more interesting.

3 Deliver Your Presentation

Use the advice you received during practice to make final changes to your presentation. Then, using effective verbal and nonverbal techniques, present it to your classmates.

As you work to improve your presentation, be sure to follow discussion rules:

- ❏ Listen closely to each other.
- ❏ Don't interrupt.
- ❏ Stay on topic.
- ❏ Ask relevant questions.
- ❏ Provide clear, thoughtful, and direct answers.

REFLECT

Reflect on the Unit

By completing your informational essay, you have created a writing product that pulls together and expresses your thoughts about the reading you have done in this unit. Now is a good time to reflect on what you have learned.

Reflect on the Essential Question

- How do you find courage in the face of fear? How has your answer to this question changed since you first considered it when you started this unit?

- What are some examples from the texts you've read that show how people find the courage to face their fears?

Reflect on Your Reading

- Which selections were the most interesting or surprising to you?

- From which selection did you learn the most about how people face their fears?

Reflect on the Writing Task

- What difficulties did you encounter while working on your informational essay? How might you avoid them next time?

- What parts of the essay were the easiest and hardest to write? Why?

Reflect on the Speaking and Listening Task

- What was the most significant change you made when you adapted your essay for oral presentation?

- How did you decide on which visuals to use? Which were effective?

- Public speaking is a common fear. How were your own feelings about public speaking affected by the knowledge you gained?

UNIT 1 SELECTIONS
- *The Breadwinner*
- "Life Doesn't Frighten Me"
- "Fears and Phobias"
- "Wired for Fear"
- "Embarrassed? Blame Your Brain"
- "The Ravine"

UNIT 2

THROUGH AN ANIMAL'S EYES

? ESSENTIAL QUESTION:

What can you learn by seeing the world through an animal's eyes?

" I have wished that I could . . . look out onto the world through the eyes, with the mind, of a chimpanzee. "

Jane Goodall

UNIT 2

ACADEMIC VOCABULARY

Academic Vocabulary words are words you use when you discuss and write about texts. In this unit, you will learn and practice using five words.

✓ **benefit**   ❑ **distinct**   ❑ **environment**   ❑ **illustrate**   ❑ **respond**

Study the Word Network to learn more about the word **benefit.**

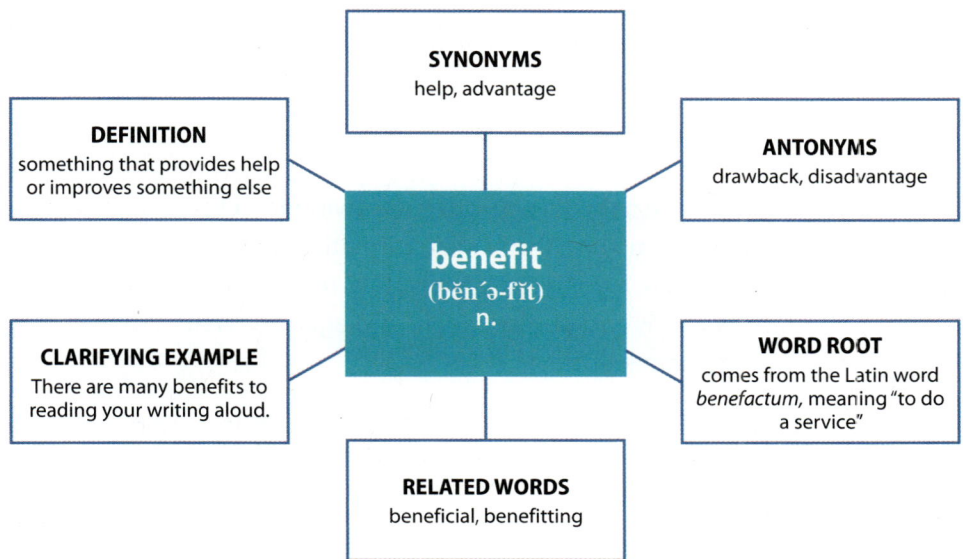

Write and Discuss Discuss the completed Word Network with a partner, making sure to talk through all of the boxes until you both understand the word, its synonyms, antonyms, and related forms. Then, fill out Word Networks for the remaining four words. Use a dictionary or online resource to help you complete the activity.

 Go online to access the Word Networks.

RESPOND TO THE ESSENTIAL QUESTION

In this unit, you will explore what can be learned by seeing the world through an animal's eyes. As you read, you will revisit the **Essential Question** and gather your ideas about it in the **Response Log** that appears on page R2. At the end of the unit, you will write an **argument** about what you can learn by seeing the world from an animal's perspective. You will also **present an argument.** Filling out the Response Log will help you prepare for these tasks.

 You can also go online to access the Response Log.

Through an Animal's Eyes 91

Notice & Note
READING MODEL

from PAX

You are about to read an excerpt from the novel *Pax*. In it, you will notice and note signposts that will give you clues about the novel's characters and themes. Here are three key signposts to look for as you read this excerpt and other works of fiction.

 For more information on these and other signposts to Notice & Note, visit the **Reading Studio.**

Again and Again When you're reviewing for a test, you have a good reason for studying the same information again and again. In fiction, authors have a good reason for using repetition, too. Authors may repeat words and phrases again and again, as well as repeat images, actions, and events.

When you read and encounter repeated use of the following, pause to see whether it's an **Again and Again** signpost:

- an unusual word or phrase
- an image or symbol
- a behavior
- an action or event

If you notice an author repeatedly using certain images, words, or actions in a work of fiction, pay attention. An **Again and Again** signpost may:

- suggest a theme or lesson of the text
- reveal an important symbol in the text
- explain a character's motivations or behaviors
- signal developments in a conflict and plot

In this example, a student underlined an instance of Again and Again.

Anchor Question
When you notice this signpost, ask: Why might the author keep bringing this up?

> 1 <u>By the vibrations, he learned</u> also that the road had grown coarser. He stretched up from his boy's lap and <u>sniffed at threads of scent</u> leaking in through the window, <u>which told him</u> they were now traveling into woodlands.

What behavior is being repeated?	The character frequently uses his senses to get information.
Why is this repeated behavior important?	The use of senses and sensory information (sight, hearing, taste, smell, and touch) may reveal something about the character.

92 Unit 2

▶ **Memory Moment** Do you ever find yourself remembering important past events when you're experiencing new situations? Recalling a past event—whether it's happy, ordinary, or upsetting—can help you understand the past, and it can shape your response in the present.

When a fictional character pauses to remember a moment from the past, stop to think about the **Memory Moment**. A Memory Moment can:

- explain or provide insight into the current situation
- reveal something that's bothering or motivating a character
- hint at the theme or lesson of the text

Read this part of *Pax* to see a student's annotation of a Memory Moment.

> 3   The boy's anxiety surprised the fox. <u>The few times they had traveled in the car before</u>, the boy had been calm or even excited.

Anchor Question
When you notice this signpost, ask: Why is this memory important?

What moment is remembered here?	The boy felt calm on other car trips.
Why do you think this memory is important?	The memory of the boy's feelings contrasts with his feelings now. Something changed; something is bothering the boy.

▶ **Contrasts and Contradictions** What if your best friend texted you every day and then one day suddenly didn't text you? You'd probably wonder what was going on: Is he mad at me? Is he not feeling well?

Sudden differences in fiction can grab your attention in the same way. **Contrasts and Contradictions** often help the reader better understand a character or the conflict of the story.

Here's an example of a student marking an instance of Contrasts and Contradictions.

> 3   <u>The fox nudged</u> his muzzle into the glove's webbing, <u>although he hated the leather smell</u>. His boy always laughed when he did this.

When you see a phrase like any of those below, pause to see if it's a **Contrasts and Contradictions** signpost:

I don't know why I did it . . .

But this was different . . .

Even though . . .

What contradiction is expressed here?	The fox is putting his nose near a smell that he hates.
Why do you think the fox is behaving this way?	The fox may be trying to get the boy to laugh. Maybe the fox is trying to help the boy feel happy again.

ANALYZE & APPLY

from PAX
Novel by **Sara Pennypacker**

? ESSENTIAL QUESTION:

What can you learn by seeing the world through an animal's eyes?

GET READY

QUICK START

People can develop strong bonds with cats, dogs, and other pets. What bonds can we form with animals that are usually found in the wild? Discuss the topic with classmates.

ANALYZE POINT OF VIEW

Point of view is the vantage point, or perspective, from which a story is told. The author's choice of **narrator**—the voice that tells the story—depends on whose perspective the author wants to show. In a work told from the **first-person point of view,** the narrator is a character in the story. In a work told from the **third-person point of view,** the narrator is not a character in the story. Third-person narrators may be **omniscient,** knowing everything, or **limited,** knowing only certain aspects of the story. Use the diagram below as you read to help you determine which third-person point of view is used in *Pax*.

GENRE ELEMENTS: NOVEL
- includes the basic elements of fiction—plot, characters, conflict, setting, and theme
- is longer than a short story or novella and is often organized into chapters
- provides authors with the length to develop plot and characters (who may or may not be human) more thoroughly

Third-Person Limited Point of View
Narrator knows and describes the thoughts and feelings of just one character, usually the main character.

Narrator is an outside observer, not a character.
Narrator tells the story using third-person pronouns *she/he, her/him, they. I* and *we* are used only in dialogue.

Third-Person Omniscient Point of View
Narrator knows and describes the thoughts and feelings of all characters.

ANALYZE VOICE

Authors use key details and specific language to develop the **voice**—the unique personality or sensibility—of a character or a narrator.

- Voice helps readers "hear" a character's personality.
- Voice can reflect an attitude or way of seeing the world and can help set the **mood**—the feeling or atmosphere—of the work.
- Voice is developed through an author's choice of words and phrases, and may be revealed in thoughts, descriptions, and dialogue.

As you read, note specific details that help create the voice of the excerpt's main character.

Pax 95

GET READY

CRITICAL VOCABULARY

sensitive   anxiety   injury   displease

To see how many Critical Vocabulary words you already know, use them to complete the sentences below.

1. It takes a while for an _____ to heal.
2. _____ can cause a person to feel nervous about the future.
3. A cat has _____ whiskers that help it feel vibrations.
4. It may _____ your teacher if you forget to do your homework.

LANGUAGE CONVENTIONS

Complex Sentences Writers use different sentence structures to connect ideas. A **complex sentence** includes one independent clause and one or more subordinate clauses. An **independent clause** has both a subject and verb and can stand alone as a complete sentence. A **subordinate clause**—also called a dependent clause—has a subject and verb but cannot stand alone as a sentence. Subordinate clauses start with such words as *when, until, who, where, because,* and *so that*.

When I get a good night's sleep, I wake up feeling refreshed.

In the above complex sentence, *When I get a good night's sleep* is a subordinate clause. It cannot stand alone. *I wake up feeling refreshed* is an independent clause, or a complete sentence that can stand alone. Note the author's use of complex sentences as you read *Pax*.

ANNOTATION MODEL

NOTICE & NOTE

As you read, notice and note signposts, including **Again and Again, Memory Moments,** and **Contrasts and Contradictions.** The following example shows how one reader responded to the opening of *Pax*.

> 1 The fox felt the car slow before the boy did, as he felt everything first. Through the pads of his paws, along his spine, in the sensitive whiskers at his wrists. By the vibrations, he learned also that the road had grown coarser. He stretched up from his boy's lap and sniffed at threads of scent leaking in through the window, which told him they were now traveling into woodlands.

I see lots of description of what the fox senses here.

The narrator repeatedly describes what the fox senses through touch and smell.

BACKGROUND

Sara Pennypacker *(b. 1951) recalls feeling very shy as a child. She spent her time making art and reading and writing stories—activities she still enjoys as an adult. She is the author of many books, including the* Clementine *series and* Summer of the Gypsy Moths. *Honors for her books include a Golden Kite Award and a Christopher's Medal.*

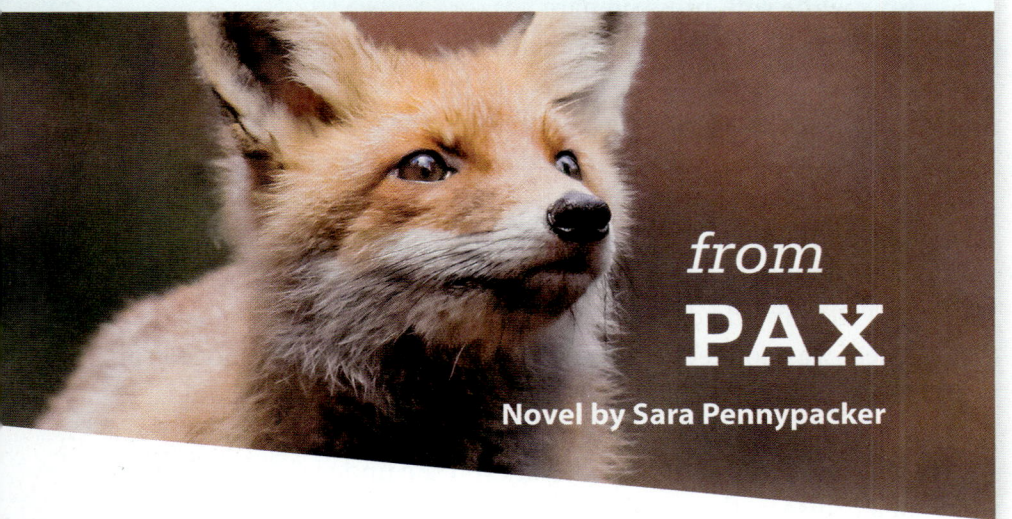

from PAX

Novel by Sara Pennypacker

SETTING A PURPOSE

As you read, pay attention to the ways in which the fox and the boy experience the world. Notice how the author uses sensory details to tell the story.

1. The fox felt the car slow before the boy did, as he felt everything first. Through the pads of his paws, along his spine, in the **sensitive** whiskers at his wrists. By the vibrations, he learned also that the road had grown coarser. He stretched up from his boy's lap and sniffed at threads of scent leaking in through the window, which told him they were now traveling into woodlands. The sharp odors of pine—wood, bark, cones, and needles—slivered through the air like blades, but beneath that, the fox recognized softer clover and wild garlic and ferns, and also a hundred things he had never encountered before but that smelled green and urgent.

2. The boy sensed something now, too. He pulled his pet back to him and gripped his baseball glove more tightly.

NOTICE & NOTE

Notice & Note

Use the side margins to notice and note signposts in the text.

sensitive
(sĕn´sĭ-tĭv) *adj.* Something *sensitive* is able to perceive small differences or changes in the environment.

ANALYZE POINT OF VIEW
Annotate: Mark the pronouns that the narrator uses in paragraphs 1 and 2.

Interpret: In addition to telling you about thoughts and feelings, what do these pronouns tell you about the point of view used here?

Pax 97

NOTICE & NOTE

anxiety
(ăng-zī´ĭ-tē) *n.* Anxiety is a feeling of uneasiness, fear, or worry.

CONTRASTS AND CONTRADICTIONS

Notice & Note: What unexpected thing does the fox notice about the boy in paragraph 5? Mark what the fox notices.

Analyze: How does this event affect the fox?

injury
(ĭn´jə-rē) *n.* An *injury* is damage or harm done to a person or a thing.

AGAIN AND AGAIN

Notice & Note: Which of the five senses is repeatedly mentioned in paragraph 7? Mark the sensory details.

Infer: What do these references tell you about what is important to the fox and what is important to the boy?

3   The boy's **anxiety** surprised the fox. The few times they had traveled in the car before, the boy had been calm or even excited. The fox nudged his muzzle into the glove's webbing, although he hated the leather smell. His boy always laughed when he did this. He would close the glove around his pet's head, play-wrestling, and in this way the fox would distract him.

4   But today the boy lifted his pet and buried his face in the fox's white ruff, pressing hard.

5   It was then that the fox realized his boy was crying. He twisted around to study his face to be sure. Yes, crying— although without a sound, something the fox had never known him to do. The boy hadn't shed tears for a very long time, but the fox remembered: always before he had cried out, as if to demand that attention be paid to the curious occurrence of salty water streaming from his eyes.

6   The fox licked at the tears and then grew more confused. There was no scent of blood. He squirmed out of the boy's arms to inspect his human more carefully, alarmed that he could have failed to notice an **injury,** although his sense of smell was never wrong. No, no blood; not even the under-skin pooling of a bruise or the marrow leak of a cracked bone,[1] which had happened once.

7   The car pulled to the right, and the suitcase beside them shifted. By its scent, the fox knew it held the boy's clothing and the things from his room he handled most often: the photo he kept on top of his bureau and the items he hid in the bottom drawer. He pawed at a corner, hoping to pry the suitcase open enough for the boy's weak nose to smell these favored things and be comforted. But just then the car slowed again, this time to a rumbling crawl. The boy slumped forward, his head in his hands.

8   The fox's heartbeat climbed and the brushy hairs of his tail lifted. The charred[2] metal scent of the father's new clothing was burning his throat. He leaped to the window and scratched at it. Sometimes at home his boy would raise a similar glass wall if he did this. He always felt better when the glass wall was lifted.

9   Instead, the boy pulled him down onto his lap again and spoke to his father in a begging tone. The fox had learned the meaning of many human words, and he heard him use one

---

[1] **marrow leak of a cracked bone:** *marrow* is the thick, dark substance at the core of a bone, which is exposed when a bone is broken or cracked open.

[2] **charred** (chärd): burned or scorched.

NOTICE & NOTE

of them now: "NO." Often the "no" word was linked to one of the two names he knew: his own and his boy's. He listened carefully, but today it was just the "NO," pleaded to the father over and over.

10   The car juddered[3] to a full stop and tilted off to the right, a cloud of dust rising beyond the window. The father reached over the seat again, and after saying something to his son in a soft voice that didn't match his hard lie-scent,[4] he grasped the fox by the scruff of the neck.

11   His boy did not resist, so the fox did not resist. He hung limp and vulnerable[5] in the man's grasp, although he was now frightened enough to nip. He would not **displease** his humans today. The father opened the car door and strode over gravel and patchy weeds to the edge of a wood. The boy got out and followed.

12   The father set the fox down, and the fox bounded out of his reach. He locked his gaze on his two humans, surprised to notice that they were nearly the same height now. The boy had grown very tall recently.

13   The father pointed to the woods. The boy looked at his father for a long moment, his eyes streaming again. And then he dried his face with the neck of his T-shirt and nodded. He reached into his jeans pocket and withdrew an old plastic soldier, the fox's favorite toy.

14   The fox came to alert, ready for the familiar game. His boy would throw the toy, and he would track it down—a feat the boy always seemed to find remarkable. He would retrieve the toy and wait with it in his mouth until the boy found him and took it back to toss again.

15   And sure enough, the boy held the toy soldier aloft and then hurled it into the woods. The fox's relief—they were only here to play the game!—made him careless. He streaked toward the woods without looking back at his humans. If he had, he would have seen the boy wrench away from his father and cross his arms over his face, and he would have returned. Whatever his boy needed—protection, distraction, affection—he would have offered.

16   Instead, he set off after the toy. Finding it was slightly more difficult than usual, as there were so many other, fresher odors

ANALYZE POINT OF VIEW
Annotate: Mark the narrator's description of the father's words and actions in paragraph 10.

Evaluate: What effect on the reader does the third-person limited point of view have here?

displease
(dĭs-plēz´) *v.* To *displease* someone is to cause annoyance or irritation.

ANALYZE VOICE
Annotate: Mark the words in paragraph 15 that help show the fox's personality and attitude toward the boy.

Analyze: How do the author's word choices contribute to mood and voice?

---

[3] **juddered** (jŭd´ərd): to shake or vibrate rapidly.
[4] **lie-scent:** the smell that the fox detects of the father's insincerity.
[5] **vulnerable** (vŭl´nər-ə-bəl): open to harm.

Pax

NOTICE & NOTE

ANALYZE VOICE

Annotate: Mark the words and details that help establish mood and voice in paragraph 17.

Compare: How have voice and mood changed since paragraph 15?

in the woods. But only slightly—after all, the scent of his boy was also on the toy. That scent he could find anywhere.

17   The toy soldier lay facedown at the burled root of a butternut tree, as if he had pitched himself there in despair. His rifle, its butt pressed tirelessly against his face, was buried to the hilt in leaf litter. The fox nudged the toy free, took it between his teeth, and rose on his haunches[6] to allow his boy to find him.

18   In the still woods, the only movements were bars of sunlight glinting like green glass through the leafy canopy. He stretched higher. There was no sign of his boy. A prickle of worry shivered up the fox's spine. He dropped the toy and barked. There was no response. He barked again, and again was answered by only silence. If this was a new game, he did not like it.

19   He picked up the toy soldier and began to retrace his trail. As he loped out of the woods, a jay streaked in above him, shrieking. The fox froze, torn.

20   His boy was waiting to play the game. But birds! Hours upon hours he had watched birds from his pen, quivering at the sight of them slicing the sky as recklessly as the lightning he often saw on summer evenings. The freedom of their flights always mesmerized[7] him.

MEMORY MOMENT

Notice & Note: What does the fox recall in paragraph 20? Mark this memory.

Compare: How does this memory differ from other moments the fox has recalled? What does this memory reveal about the fox?

---

[6] **haunches** (hôn′chĕz): the lower body and legs of an animal.

[7] **mesmerized** (mĕz′mə-rīzd): held fixed in attention as though hypnotized.

21   The jay called again, deeper in the forest now, but answered by a chorus of reply. For one more moment the fox hesitated, peering into the trees for another sight of the electric-blue wedge.

22   And then, behind him, he heard a car door slam shut, and then another. He bounded at full speed, heedless of the briars that tore at his cheeks. The car's engine roared to life, and the fox skidded to a stop at the edge of the road.

23   His boy rolled the window down and reached his arms out. And as the car sped away in a pelting spray of gravel, the father cried out the boy's name, *"Peter!"* And the boy cried out the only other name the fox knew.

24   *"Pax!"*

LANGUAGE CONVENTIONS
Complex sentences combine subordinate clauses with independent clauses. Mark the word *as* in paragraph 23; then mark the independent clause and the subordinate clause. What does this complex sentence tell the reader about what is happening in this moment?

CHECK YOUR UNDERSTANDING

Answer these questions before moving on to the **Analyze the Text** section on the following page.

1 Which idea is not supported by information in the selection?

   A The fox likes and trusts the boy's father.

   B The fox and the boy share a close bond.

   C The fox is curious about the smells and sounds of nature.

   D The fox is confused by the boy's behavior.

2 Which of the following sentences suggests that the boy feels anxious?

   F *The fox felt the car slow before the boy did, as he felt everything first.*

   G *The boy sensed something now, too.*

   H *He pulled his pet back to him and gripped his baseball glove more tightly.*

   J *His boy did not resist, so the fox did not resist.*

3 What happens at the end of the selection?

   A The boy and the fox go home together.

   B The father takes the boy shopping for a dog.

   C The boy jumps out of the car and runs after the fox.

   D The fox is left at the edge of the road as the car speeds away.

RESPOND

ANALYZE THE TEXT

Support your responses with evidence from the text. 📓 **NOTEBOOK**

1. **Evaluate** Review paragraph 1. What details does the author use to describe key ideas about the fox?

2. **Cite Evidence** Cite evidence from the text that indicates the narrator's point of view. What is the specific purpose or benefit of using this point of view in *Pax*?

3. **Summarize** Review paragraphs 7–9. What is the mood of this passage? Explain how the author's use of language contributes to the mood.

4. **Interpret** Review paragraph 18, especially the last sentence of the paragraph. How does point of view contribute to the character's voice?

5. **Notice & Note** Review paragraph 3. What do the fox's memories suggest about the relationship between the boy and the fox?

RESEARCH

RESEARCH TIP
Consider searching for magazines or websites for children. Popular general-interest magazines, especially those for children, often include stories about pets and animals.

What kinds of bonds do people have with their pets? Research at least two true stories that illustrate the special bond between humans and pets. If you'd like, you may include one story of your own pet or of the pets of people you know. Record what you learn in the chart.

PERSON AND PET	DETAILS ABOUT THEIR BOND

Connect In paragraph 16, the fox is certain he can fetch a toy that holds the boy's scent because "that scent he could find anywhere." With your classmates, discuss how an animal's sense of smell is important in the stories you have researched.

RESPOND

CREATE AND PRESENT

Write a Story Write a fictional narrative from the point of view of an animal or an object.

- ❏ Think about what and how your character sees, hears, touches, smells, and tastes.
- ❏ Incorporate the elements of fiction: setting, character, plot, conflict, and theme.
- ❏ Include complex sentences, checking to make sure that you've used them correctly. If the subject of a sentence is singular, make sure that the verb is singular; if the subject is plural, make sure that the verb is plural.

Go to **Writing Narratives** in the **Writing Studio** for more on writing a story, or narrative.

Create a Multimodal Presentation Present your narrative, using both text and visual features.

- ❏ Keep the point of view you used in your narrative.
- ❏ Use images or video to help show your character's perspective.
- ❏ When you share your presentation with the class, communicate your ideas effectively by maintaining eye contact and speaking at an appropriate rate and volume.

Go to **Using Media in a Presentation** in the **Speaking and Listening Studio** for help with using media in presentations.

RESPOND TO THE ESSENTIAL QUESTION

 What can you learn by seeing the world through an animal's eyes?

Gather Information Review your annotations and notes on *Pax*. Then, add relevant details to your Response Log. As you decide which information to include, think about:

- how animals sense their surroundings
- how animals and people communicate
- what animals can teach humans

At the end of the unit, use your notes to write an argument.

ACADEMIC VOCABULARY

As you write and discuss what you learned from the selection, be sure to use the Academic Vocabulary words. Check off each of the words that you use.

- ❏ benefit
- ❏ distinct
- ❏ environment
- ❏ illustrate
- ❏ respond

RESPOND

WORD BANK
sensitive
anxiety
injury
displease

CRITICAL VOCABULARY

Practice and Apply Use your understanding of the vocabulary words to answer each question.

1. Does someone experiencing **anxiety** feel happy or upset? Why?
   _____

2. Which is more likely to **displease** someone, a gift or an insult? Why?
   _____

3. If you had an **injury** would you need a doctor or a teacher? Why?
   _____

4. Can a **sensitive** scientific instrument detect small changes? Why?
   _____

Go to **Understanding Word Origins** in the **Vocabulary Studio** for more on Greek and Latin roots.

VOCABULARY STRATEGY:
Greek and Latin Roots

A **root** is a word part that contains the core meaning of a word, so knowing its meaning can help you understand a word. Roots are often combined with word parts such as prefixes or suffixes to form words. Many English words contain roots and other word parts from older languages, including Greek and Latin. For example, the word *injury* contains the Latin root *jur* plus the prefix *in-*. The root *jur* or *jus* or *jud* means "justice" or "law," and the prefix *in-* means "not," so you can guess that *injury* sometimes means "unlawful physical or emotional harm."

Practice and Apply Find the word that contains the Latin root *jur* or *jus* or *jud* in each sentence. Use context clues and the root's meaning to write a definition of the word. Then use a dictionary to check your definition.

1. A judge was appointed to oversee the trial.
   _____

2. A jury of twelve people was chosen to decide guilt or innocence.
   _____

3. She had to justify to her mother that she needed a cell phone.
   _____

RESPOND

LANGUAGE CONVENTIONS:
Complex Sentences

Writers use **complex sentences** to connect related ideas and to make their writing flow more smoothly. Complex sentences can make your writing more expressive, as well as more formal.

 Go to **Complex Sentences** in the **Grammar Studio** for more on complex sentences.

As you practice writing complex sentences, make sure that you follow the rules of good grammar. Here are some mistakes to look out for.

- Comma splices (independent clauses joined by a comma alone)
   Incorrect: The fox felt the car slow before the boy did, he felt everything first.

   Correct: The fox felt the car slow before the boy did, as he felt everything first.

- Run-on sentences (two or more sentences written as though they were one)
   Incorrect: The fox licked at the tears and then grew more confused there was no scent of blood.

   Correct: The fox licked at the tears and then grew more confused. There was no scent of blood.

- Sentence fragments (a group of words that is only part of a sentence)
   Incorrect: The boy slumped forward. His head in his hands.

   Correct: The boy slumped forward, his head in his hands.

Practice and Apply Work independently to create your own complex sentences written from the point of view of the fox. Imagine what the fox experienced after the car drove away, and then describe it in your sentences. Share your sentences with a classmate, checking for use of complex sentences and correct grammar.

ANALYZE & APPLY

ZOO

Science Fiction by **Edward Hoch**

? ESSENTIAL QUESTION:

What can you learn by seeing the world through an animal's eyes?

GET READY

QUICK START

What do you think and feel when you see an animal at the zoo for the first time? What might the zoo experience be like for the animals themselves? Discuss your answers with classmates.

INFER MULTIPLE THEMES

A story's **theme** is its message about life or human nature. Stories often have multiple themes. For example, a story about a teenager who gets lost in the wilderness might include themes about the power of nature as well as the endurance of the human spirit.

Authors use narration, dialogue, details, characterization, and text structure to convey theme. Themes can be stated **explicitly** (in an outright way) or may be conveyed **implicitly** (indirectly) through repeated ideas, words, and imagery. As you read, use this chart to record evidence from the story that conveys theme. To **infer** the story's multiple themes, use your notes to help you make logical guesses based on evidence and your own knowledge and experience.

GENRE ELEMENTS: SCIENCE FICTION
- combines scientific information and the author's imagination to create unexpected possibilities
- often makes a statement about human nature or the human experience
- is usually set in the future
- may have a surprise ending
- includes such forms as short stories and novels

EVIDENCE FROM THE STORY	INFERENCE	POSSIBLE THEMES

ANALYZE POINT OF VIEW

Point of view refers to the perspective from which a story is told.

- In a story told from the **first-person point of view,** the narrator is a character in the story and uses first-person pronouns such as *I, me,* and *we.* The reader sees only what that character sees.

- In a story told from the **third-person point of view,** the narrator is not a character in the story and uses the pronouns *he, she,* and *they.* A third-person narrator who reveals what all the characters think and feel is said to be **omniscient.**

- As you read this story, note how its omniscient point of view affects the information you receive and helps convey the story's theme.

Zoo 107

GET READY

CRITICAL VOCABULARY

| interplanetary | constantly | microphone | embrace |

To see how many Critical Vocabulary words you already know, use them to complete the sentences below.

1. The father wrapped his child in a warm _____ .

2. She used a _____ so that everyone could hear her speech.

3. The sounds of traffic _____ zooming by made sleep difficult.

4. Astronauts of the future may conduct _____ travel throughout the solar system.

LANGUAGE CONVENTIONS

Verb Tenses Notice the verbs in the following sentence from "Zoo." A **verb** expresses an action, condition, or a state of being. The **tense** of a verb shows the time of the action. The tenses of verbs and verb phrases describe present, past, and future events.

The crowd's noise died down and he continued.

Both *died* and *continued* are verb forms describing actions that have taken place in the past. They also help express the sequence of events. As you read "Zoo," notice how the author's use of verb tenses clarifies when events occur.

ANNOTATION MODEL

NOTICE & NOTE

As you read, note how the author's use of verb tense helps you understand when the action takes place. In the model, you can see one reader's notes about "Zoo."

1. The children <u>were</u> always good during the month of August, especially when it <u>began</u> to get near the twenty-third. It <u>was</u> on this day that Professor Hugo's Interplanetary Zoo <u>settled</u> down for its annual six-hour visit to the Chicago area.

The verbs are in the past tense. These sentences describe events that have happened repeatedly in the past.

108 Unit 2

BACKGROUND

Edward Hoch *(1930–2008) is best known for his crime fiction and mysteries, having published more than 900 mystery stories. In this science fiction story, Hoch imagines a surprising, futuristic zoo. Throughout the history of zoos, most animals were exhibited in cages. However, zookeepers today have a greater understanding of animals' needs. Many modern zoo enclosures replicate animals' natural habitats, with the intent of making zoo animals healthier and more comfortable.*

ZOO
Science Fiction by Edward Hoch

SETTING A PURPOSE
Read this short story to discover one writer's ideas about zoos of the future and the animals those zoos might display.

1   The children were always good during the month of August, especially when it began to get near the twenty-third. It was on this day that Professor Hugo's **Interplanetary** Zoo settled down for its annual six-hour visit to the Chicago area.

2   Before daybreak the crowds would form, long lines of children and adults both, each one clutching his or her dollar and waiting with wonderment to see what race of strange creatures the professor had brought this year.

3   In the past they had sometimes been treated to three-legged creatures from Venus, or tall, thin men from Mars, or even snakelike horrors from somewhere more distant. This year, as the great round ship settled slowly to Earth in the huge tri-city parking area just outside of Chicago, they watched with awe[1] as the sides slowly slid up to reveal

---
[1] **awe** (ô): a feeling of fear and wonder.

Notice & Note

Use the side margins to notice and note signposts in the text.

interplanetary
(ĭn´tər-plăn´ĭ-tĕr´ē) *adj.*
Interplanetary means existing or occurring between planets.

INFER MULTIPLE THEMES
Annotate: Mark the words and phrases used to describe the zoo animals in paragraph 3.

Analyze: What do the descriptions reveal about the humans' feelings toward the zoo animals?

Zoo   109

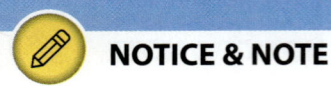

NOTICE & NOTE

constantly
(kŏn´stənt-lē) *adv. Constantly* means something that is regularly occurring.

microphone
(mī´krə-fōn´) *n.* A *microphone* is an instrument that is often used to amplify the voice.

LANGUAGE CONVENTIONS
Writers use consistent **verb tenses** so that readers know when the action takes place. Mark the verbs and verb phrases used in paragraph 5. What generalization can you make about the use of verb tenses in this paragraph?

ANALYZE POINT OF VIEW
Annotate: Mark each noun and pronoun in paragraph 7.

Analyze: Is the narrator a character in the story? From what point of view is this story told? Explain.

embrace
(ĕm-brās´) *v.* To *embrace* someone is to hug or hold the person close.

the familiar barred cages. In them were some wild breed of nightmare—small, horselike animals that moved with quick, jerking motions and **constantly** chattered in a high-pitched tongue. The citizens of Earth clustered around as Professor Hugo's crew quickly collected the waiting dollars, and soon the good professor himself made an appearance, wearing his many-colored rainbow cape and top hat. "Peoples of Earth," he called into his **microphone**.

4   The crowd's noise died down and he continued. "Peoples of Earth, this year you see a real treat for your single dollar—the little-known horse-spider people of Kaan—brought to you across a million miles of space at great expense. Gather around, see them, study them, listen to them, tell your friends about them. But hurry! My ship can remain here only six hours!"

5   And the crowds slowly filed by, at once horrified and fascinated by these strange creatures that looked like horses but ran up the walls of their cages like spiders. "This is certainly worth a dollar," one man remarked, hurrying away. "I'm going home to get the wife."

6   All day long it went like that, until ten thousand people had filed by the barred cages set into the side of the spaceship. Then, as the six-hour limit ran out, Professor Hugo once more took the microphone in hand. "We must go now, but we will return next year on this date. And if you enjoyed our zoo this year, telephone your friends in other cities about it. We will land in New York tomorrow, and next week on to London, Paris, Rome, Hong Kong, and Tokyo. Then on to other worlds!"

7   He waved farewell to them, and as the ship rose from the ground, the Earth peoples agreed that this had been the very best Zoo yet. . . .

8   Some two months and three planets later, the silver ship of Professor Hugo settled at last onto the familiar jagged rocks of Kaan, and the odd horse-spider creatures filed quickly out of their cages. Professor Hugo was there to say a few parting words, and then they scurried[2] away in a hundred different directions, seeking their homes among the rocks.

9   In one house, the she-creature was happy to see the return of her mate and offspring.[3] She babbled a greeting in the strange tongue and hurried to **embrace** them. "It was a long time you were gone! Was it good?"

---

[2] **scurry** (skûr´ē): to run with light steps; scamper.
[3] **offspring** (ôf´sprĭng): a child or children.

10   And the he-creature nodded. "The little one enjoyed it especially. We visited eight worlds and saw many things."

11   The little one ran up the wall of the cave. "On the place called Earth it was the best. The creatures there wear garments over their skins, and they walk on two legs."

12   "But isn't it dangerous?" asked the she-creature.

13   "No," her mate answered. "There are bars to protect us from them. We remain right in the ship. Next time you must come with us. It is well worth the nineteen commocs it costs."

14   And the little one nodded. "It was the very best Zoo ever. . . ."

> **AGAIN AND AGAIN**
>
> **Notice & Note:** What phrase from earlier in the story is repeated in the final paragraph of the text? Who said it the first time? Who said it the second time? Mark each time the phrase is repeated.
>
> **Analyze:** Why does the author repeat this sentence? How does the repetition help you understand one theme of the story?

CHECK YOUR UNDERSTANDING

Answer these questions before moving on to the **Analyze the Text** section on the following page.

1   In the first sentence of the story, the narrator tells us that *the children were always good during the month of August* to —

   A   explain that they have a calendar similar to ours

   B   let the reader know that children are the story's focus

   C   build suspense as the reader wonders why the children are good

   D   describe the importance of good and evil in the story

2   Which of the following excerpts from the story suggests that humans are a lot like other animals?

   F   *"I'm going home to get the wife."*

   G   *"But hurry! My ship can remain here only six hours!"*

   H   *the Earth peoples agreed that this had been the very best Zoo yet. . . .*

   J   *In one house, the she-creature was happy to see the return of her mate and offspring.*

3   What is an important theme in the selection?

   A   People don't see themselves as others do.

   B   Fear is good because it can keep you safe.

   C   Professor Hugo is a brilliant man.

   D   Everyone loves going to the zoo.

Zoo   111

RESPOND

ANALYZE THE TEXT

Support your responses with evidence from the text. 📓 **NOTEBOOK**

1. **Compare** How is Professor Hugo's Interplanetary Zoo like zoos that exist in our world? How does his zoo differ from ours? What do these similarities and differences help the author reveal?

2. **Infer** How does the author describe the animals in the Interplanetary Zoo? How do the zoo animals describe humans? How can you use these observations to make an inference about the story's themes?

3. **Evaluate** Review paragraphs 1–2 and 8–14. From which point of view is the story told? How do you know? Why do you think the author chose to tell the story this way?

4. **Draw Conclusions** Compare paragraphs 7 and 14. How does the author's use of repetition ("the very best Zoo yet"/"the best Zoo ever") affect the story?

5. **Notice & Note** Notice the author's repeated references to money, both in a familiar currency (dollars) and an unfamiliar currency ("commocs"). Why do you think the author mentions money more than once?

RESEARCH

RESEARCH TIP
Choosing effective search terms will make your research more productive. Use specific words and phrases to pinpoint results. For example: *best new science fiction* or *science fiction reviews*.

Investigate reviews of recent science fiction works (including novels, short stories, movies, or television) to identify several common messages revealed through science fiction. Record what you learn in the chart.

TITLE OF WORK	MESSAGE OR MESSAGES

Extend Works of science fiction typically present a theme, or message about life and human nature. What might the stories you researched have to say about human nature?

RESPOND

CREATE AND PRESENT

Create a Storyboard Work in a small group to create a storyboard for a "Zoo" movie. Create futuristic illustrations of scenes and costumes suited to a science fiction story.

❏ Discuss ways to convert "Zoo" into a movie. Create a storyboard for the movie — a visual map that illustrates significant moments in each scene of the movie.

❏ Sketch set designs that highlight the interplanetary travels of Dr. Hugo. Be sure viewers will recognize that the movie is set in the future.

❏ Include sketches of costumes for different characters in the story.

Present and Discuss As a small group, present and discuss your storyboard with the class.

❏ Explain your group's storyboard to the class. Ask for questions from the class about your storyboard.

❏ Do your best to respond to questions and comments fully. Defend your group's decisions, but acknowledge suggestions for improvements.

❏ As a class, discuss and compare the strengths of each group's storyboard. Identify points of agreement and disagreement in your discussion.

Go to the **Writing Studio** for more on creating narratives.

Go to the **Speaking and Listening Studio** for help with participating in a group discussion.

RESPOND TO THE ESSENTIAL QUESTION

❓ What can you learn by seeing the world through an animal's eyes?

Gather Information Review your annotations and notes on "Zoo." Then, add relevant details to your Response Log. As you determine which information to include, think about:

• how people relate to animals
• how people relate to others
• how people are fascinated by or fearful of the unknown

At the end of the unit, use your notes to write an argument.

ACADEMIC VOCABULARY

As you write and discuss what you learned from the story, be sure to use the Academic Vocabulary words. Check off each of the words that you use.

❏ benefit
❏ distinct
❏ environment
❏ illustrate
❏ respond

Zoo 113

RESPOND

WORD BANK
interplanetary
constantly
microphone
embrace

CRITICAL VOCABULARY

Practice and Apply Circle the letter of the best answer to each question.

1. Which of the following is a **constantly** heard sound?
   a. the hum of an engine
   b. the ring of a doorbell

2. Which of the following is most likely to **embrace**?
   a. a dog and a cat
   b. a parent and a child

3. Which of the following is an example of **interplanetary** travel?
   a. travel among planets
   b. travel on a planet

4. Which of the following is an example of a **microphone**?
   a. a device used to make phone calls
   b. a device used to make the voice louder

VOCABULARY STRATEGY:
Greek Roots

A **root** is a word part that contains the core meaning of a word. Many English words contain roots that come from older languages, such as Greek and Latin. Knowing the meaning of a word's root can help you determine the word's meaning.

For example, in *microphone,* the base word—a word part that by itself is also a word—is *phone*. The word *phone* comes from a Greek root meaning "sound." The prefix *micro-* comes from another Greek root meaning "small."

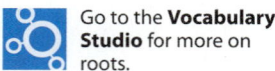
Go to the **Vocabulary Studio** for more on roots.

Practice and Apply Use your understanding of *micro* and *phone*, as well as context clues, to choose the word that best completes each sentence. Then write the meaning of each word under each sentence.

symphony   cacophony   micromanaged

1. He _____ the project by questioning every tiny detail.

   _____

2. Students in the school _____ made music together.

   _____

3. The blaring car horns created a _____.

   _____

114 Unit 2

RESPOND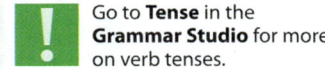

LANGUAGE CONVENTIONS:
Verb Tenses

A **verb** expresses an action, a condition, or a state of being. Helping verbs such as *is, could, has,* and *might* can be combined with verbs to form **verb phrases**. The **tense** of a verb shows the time of the action. The tenses of verbs and verb phrases allow you to describe present, past, and future events. Using verb tenses consistently and appropriately helps the reader understand when events in a story occur.

In "Zoo," verb tenses are used in the following ways.

- To narrate past events

  In the past they had sometimes been treated to three legged creatures from Venus. . . .

- To show that the action is consistently happening in the past

  And the he-creature nodded. "The little one enjoyed it especially. We visited eight worlds and saw many things."

- To make a distinction between past-tense narration and direct quotes spoken in the present tense

  "This is certainly worth a dollar," one man remarked, hurrying away. "I'm going home to get the wife."

Practice and Apply Write your own sentences using past and present verb tenses consistently to describe when action takes place. Your sentences can be about animals, or you can write your own imagined scene to add to "Zoo." When you have finished, share your sentences with a partner and compare your use of verb tenses.

> Go to **Tense** in the **Grammar Studio** for more on verb tenses.

ANALYZE & APPLY

from ANIMAL SNOOPS: THE WONDROUS WORLD OF WILDLIFE SPIES

Informational Text by **Peter Christie**

? ESSENTIAL QUESTION:

What can you learn by seeing the world through an animal's eyes?

GET READY

QUICK START

Have you ever had a sneaking suspicion that your family pet or the pet of someone you know has been spying on you or listening in on your conversations? Share your experience with the class.

ANALYZE TEXT STRUCTURE

An **anecdote** is a short account of an event that is usually intended to entertain or make a point. Authors use anecdotes to introduce or illustrate important ideas in a way that is easy to understand and remember. As you read the following informational text, note how the author uses anecdotes to structure and present his ideas. Think about how the anecdotes help explain those ideas in a humorous and entertaining way.

DETERMINE KEY IDEAS

To develop and deepen your understanding of what you read, you need to be able to determine key ideas and evaluate details of the text. A **key idea** is a very important idea about a topic in the text. As you read, write down key ideas of the text in the graphic organizer below. Include important details from the text that support each key idea.

GENRE ELEMENTS: INFORMATIONAL TEXT
- provides factual information
- includes evidence to support ideas
- often contains text features
- includes many forms, such as news articles and essays
- includes science writing, which explains complex scientific topics in language that is easy to understand

KEY IDEA	SUPPORTING DETAILS

Animal Snoops: The Wondrous World of Wildlife Spies

GET READY

CRITICAL VOCABULARY

eavesdrop   foil   predator   stake   intercept

To see how many Critical Vocabulary words you already know, use them to complete the sentences.

1. A younger sibling might _____ on his older sibling's conversations.

2. A _____ such as the lion is a fierce hunter.

3. She knew what would be at _____ if she lost the important document.

4. The football player was able to _____ the pass; it was an incredible play.

5. The superhero attempted to _____ the villain's evil plan.

LANGUAGE CONVENTIONS

Capitalization Proper nouns name specific people, places, and things. Each word in a proper noun begins with a capital letter. **Proper adjectives** are formed from proper nouns. They are always capitalized and often end in the letters *n, an, ian, ese,* or *ish*. In the following sentence from *Animal Snoops,* note how the proper adjective is capitalized:

The tall grasses of the East African savannah surrounded him like a curtain. . . .

As you read *Animal Snoops,* note the capitalization of proper nouns and proper adjectives.

ANNOTATION MODEL   NOTICE & NOTE

As you read, note the author's use of text features and anecdotes to structure the text. In the model, you can see one reader's notes about *Animal Snoops.*

Deep Secrets Overheard

Tick, tick, creak.

27 In the eerie, deep-water gloom off the coast of Norway, an enormous sperm whale makes mysterious noises before it abruptly rakes its toothy mouth through a school of swimming squid.

The subheading introduces a new topic by using a sound effect, and it is followed by an anecdote about a whale.

118 Unit 2

BACKGROUND

Peter Christie (b. 1962) loved exploring nature in the fields and streams of his native Canada as a child. As a freelance science author and editor, he enjoys writing for young people because they are naturally curious. Young people also love a good story, and for Christie, the best science writing is about telling a story. In his explorations of animal behavior and intelligence, Christie continues to find many stories to tell.

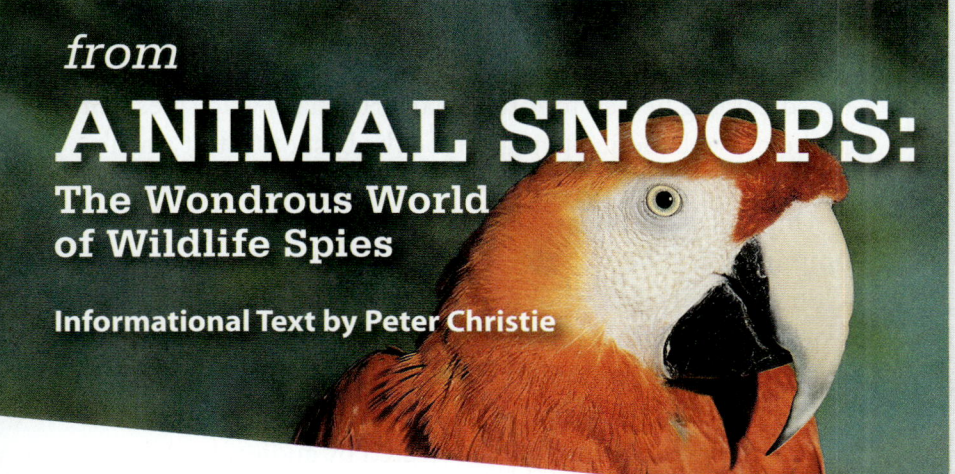

from ANIMAL SNOOPS: The Wondrous World of Wildlife Spies

Informational Text by Peter Christie

SETTING A PURPOSE

As you read, pay attention to the distinct ways animals snoop and spy on other animals in their environment, and note the reasons they do.

Presenting: The Bird-Brained Burglar Bust

1. The house in Memphis, Tennessee, sat empty: the coast was clear for a robbery. Quickly and secretively, the three young burglars checked the windows and doors and found a way in. They piled up computers, DVD players, and other electronic equipment.

2. The thieves talked as they worked, paying no attention to the parrot, nearly motionless in its cage. Only when the crooks were ready to make their getaway did the bird finally pipe up. "JJ," it said plainly. "JJ, JJ."

3. Marshmallow—a six-year-old green parrot—had been quietly **eavesdropping**. And the private-eye parrot had learned a thing or two, including the nickname of one of the robbers: JJ.

NOTICE & NOTE

Notice & Note

Use the side margins to notice and note signposts in the text.

ANALYZE TEXT STRUCTURE
Annotate: Mark the subhead.
Predict: What do you think this section will discuss?

eavesdrop
(ēvz´drŏp´) *intr.v.* To *eavesdrop* is to listen secretly to others' private conversations.

NOTICE & NOTE

4   The burglars fled but soon realized that the parrot knew too much. "They were afraid the bird would stool[1] on them," said Billy Reilly, a local police officer. When the thieves returned to the crime scene to nab the bird, police captured them.

5   The Memphis crooks hadn't counted on Marshmallow's talents as an eavesdropper. Why would they? Few people imagine that animals can be highly skilled spies and snoops. Yet nature is filled with them.

6   More and more, scientists are discovering that creatures—from bugs to baboons—are experts at watching, listening, and prying into the lives of other animals. While Marshmallow's eavesdropping helped to **foil** human criminals, wild spies work for their own benefit. Spying can be the best or fastest way to find food or a mate, or get early warning of a **predator**.

7   Until recently, researchers preferred to think of communication between animals as similar to two people talking privately. But wildlife sounds and signals are often loud or bright enough that it is easy for others to listen in. It's like having conversations on social media that every one of your friends—and maybe some of your enemies—can read.

8   Animal messages are often detected by audiences that were not meant to get wind of[2] them. Hungry gopher snakes, for example, use foot-drumming signals between kangaroo rats to locate a snaky snack. Female chickadees listen in on singing contests of territorial[3] males when choosing a mate.

9   Biologists call it eavesdropping. It sounds sneaky, but it works well. And some animals are doubly sneaky, changing their behavior when they expect to be overheard. The animal communication network is far more complicated than researchers used to believe.

10 The **stakes** in wild spy games are high. Eavesdropping can determine whether animals mate, find a home, or enjoy a sneaky life instead of meeting sudden death. It can reveal whom they should trust and even affect the evolution of songs and signals.

DETERMINE KEY IDEAS
Annotate: Circle a key idea of the text in paragraph 5.
Cite Evidence: As you read, mark details in the text that support this idea.

foil
(foil) *v.* If you *foil* someone, you stop that person from being successful at something.

predator
(prĕd´ə-tər) *n.* A *predator* is an animal that survives by eating other animals.

stake
(stāk) *n.* A *stake* is something that can be gained or lost in a situation, such as money, food, or life.

---

[1] **stool:** a slang term meaning to tell on someone else, especially to spy on someone or to inform the police; to be a stool pigeon.
[2] **get wind of:** to learn of or find out about.
[3] **territorial** (tĕr´ĭ-tôr´ē-əl): displaying the behavior of defending a territory, or area, from other animals.

11   Naturally clever secret agents learn things from snooping that help them survive and pass their genes to the next generation. It's one more tool that crafty creatures use to understand the world around them.

The Hungry Spy: Spying and Prying Predators

12   The path home was one the eastern chipmunk had traveled a hundred times before: under the ferns to the narrow tunnel into his burrow. The small animal ran briskly through the quiet Pennsylvania forest.

13   Suddenly, a flash and a sting. The startled chipmunk jumped. Dried leaves scattered. A sharp pain seared his haunches.[4] Scrambling away, he glimpsed the motionless length of a timber rattlesnake.

DETERMINE KEY IDEAS
Annotate: Mark details in paragraphs 13–16 that describe how the snake hunts its prey.

Identify Patterns: How does the snake use its senses to hunt?

14   The ambush had succeeded. The deadly serpent had lain coiled and still for many hours, waiting. Even now, after striking, the snake was in no hurry. She would track down the chipmunk's lifeless body after her venom had done its work.

15   Patience is among the most practiced skills of a rattlesnake. Snooping is another. Before choosing an ambush site, timber rattlesnakes study the habits of their prey. Using their highly sensitive, flickering tongues, the snakes use scent clues to reveal the routines of rodents and other tasty animals.

---

[4] **haunches** (hônch´əz): the hips, buttocks, and upper thighs of an animal.

Animal Snoops: The Wondrous World of Wildlife Spies   121

NOTICE & NOTE

16   Their tongues are so remarkable that they also pry into the hunting habits of other rattlesnakes. Scenting the difference between a recently fed rattlesnake and a hungry one, they use the clues to hide where another snake has dined and the hunting is likely to be successful.

17   For many animals, snooping and spying can mean the difference between a full stomach and starvation. Some creatures, like the rattlesnake, spy on the habits of their prey. Others **intercept** private communication—and think of the signals as a call to supper.

18   *Photinus* fireflies, for instance, broadcast their mating messages with a light show. These plant-eating beetles flash luminescent[5] abdomens to wow potential mates on warm North American summer nights.

19   A bigger relative is named *Photuris.* They also blink biological tail lights during courtship, but are not always looking for a mate. These fireflies are predators that eat their smaller *Photinus* cousins. They spy on their blinking prey and follow the flashing beacon to a nighttime meal.

intercept
(ĭn´tər-sĕpt´) *v.* To *intercept* is to stop or interrupt something.

LANGUAGE CONVENTIONS
Proper nouns and proper adjectives should begin with a capital letter. Circle the proper noun and underline the proper adjectives in paragraph 18.

A flashing **Photinus** *firefly* looks good to his mate—but he looks delicious to his **Photuris** cousin!

20   In the still-frigid early spring of northern Europe, a male moor frog begins his tuneless chorus: *Waug, waug, waug.*

21   Not minding that the ice has barely loosed its grip on the pond edge, the frog has emerged from wintering beneath marsh-bottom muck. He's all set to attract female moor frogs the moment they wake from chilly months of sleep.

ANALYZE TEXT STRUCTURE
Annotate: Mark the sound effects in paragraphs 20–22. What do these effects convey?

Evaluate: How does this anecdote use humor to help you understand the text's important ideas?

---

[5] **luminescent** (lōō´mə-nĕs´ənt): brightly lit up.

NOTICE & NOTE

22   *Waug, waug, waug...* **WHAM!**

23   With a lightning strike, the long, lance-like bill of a white stork jabs through the marsh grass and snatches up the singing frog. In an instant, the tireless music-maker becomes the dinner of a spy.

24   White storks are master eavesdroppers. They rely on the songs of moor frogs to guide them when they're hunting. The birds are so skillful that they can stealthily follow frog sounds to within two or three strides of an unsuspecting singer.

25   Some spies can intercept signals sent by plants. Bright flowers invite bees and other animals to come for a meal of pollen or nectar (and to pollinate the plants at the same time). Scientists believe that the most symmetrical flowers—where each half mirrors the other like two sides of a face—help bees and birds recognize them as healthy, with top-quality pollen and nectar.

26   But crab spiders are deadly spies: they love to eat honeybees and know all about this flower-bee communication system. These sneaky spiders build their bee-trapping webs next to good-looking, symmetrical blooms that bees are more likely to visit.

DETERMINE KEY IDEAS

Annotate: Mark the definition of *symmetrical* in paragraph 25.

Summarize: Summarize how crab spiders use symmetrical flowers to hunt honeybees.

Animal Snoops: The Wondrous World of Wildlife Spies   123

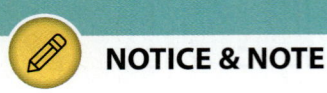

NOTICE & NOTE

Deep Secrets Overheard

Tick, tick, creak.

27 In the eerie, deep-water gloom off the coast of Norway, an enormous sperm whale makes mysterious noises before it abruptly rakes its toothy mouth through a school of swimming squid.

28 Scientists believe the whale is using echolocation[6]—in the same way bats use echoes of their ultrasonic[7] chirps to "see" in the dark. The whale's ticks and creaks help it zero in on prey.

29 But the sounds may also help distant sperm whales to find a good meal. The whales' echolocation sounds travel far, farther than the length of Manhattan Island. Sly sperm whales may eavesdrop to learn where another whale is hunting successfully, and drop by for lunch.

Live and Let Die: Spying and Prying to Stay Alive

30 The tiny antelope jerked his head up to listen.

31 He was a Gunther's dik-dik, a miniature antelope no larger than a Labrador dog. The tall grasses of the East African savannah[8] surrounded him like a curtain: he was well hidden from leopards and hyenas, but predators were also concealed from him. Through the chattering of birds and insects, the dik-dik recognized a familiar sound: *Gwaa, gwaa, gwaa.*

32 The insistent cry had an electric effect on the dik-dik. He leaped and bolted through the grass. The fleeing animal glimpsed the source of the sound—on a nearby tree sat a white-bellied go-away bird, sentinel of the savannah. Beyond it, barely visible above the grass, were the large black ears of a hunting wild dog.

33 Go-away birds are known for their noisy alarm call; the *gwaa* is thought by some to sound like a person shouting "g'away." These social birds feed together in chattering groups. A loud, urgent *gwaa* cry is a signal to other go-away birds that an eagle, wild dog, or other predator has been spotted nearby.

NUMBERS AND STATS

Notice & Note: Mark the two animals in paragraph 31 whose sizes are compared.

Infer: Why might the author use comparison to describe the size of the Gunther's dik-dik and not numbers, such as its weight?

DETERMINE KEY IDEAS

Annotate: In paragraph 33, circle the bird sound and underline its purpose.

Summarize: Review paragraph 33; then, explain why the dik-dik eavesdrops on the go-away bird.

---

[6] **echolocation** (ĕk´ō-lō-kā´shən): a system used by some animals to locate objects around them; the animals produce high-pitched sounds and "listen" for the sounds to come back.

[7] **ultrasonic** (ŭl´trə-sŏn´ĭk): not able to be heard by humans; above the range of sound waves that humans can hear.

[8] **savannah** (sə-văn´ə): a flat grassland environment located in or near the tropics.

124 Unit 2

34 Many of these dangerous hunters also eat dik-diks. The wary antelopes use every trick in the book to avoid becoming a meal—including eavesdropping on go-away bird communication. Unable to see far on the grassy savannah, dik-diks rely on the birds, which spot approaching predators from treetop lookouts.

35 For many animals, spying is a life-and-death business. Creatures that catch warning signals meant for others may stay one step ahead of enemies.

CHECK YOUR UNDERSTANDING

Answer these questions before moving on to the **Analyze the Text** section on the following page.

1 The author includes information about animal eavesdropping to —

   A explain that it is important to understand animal skills

   B inform readers about how this skill helps animals survive

   C convince readers that they should become animal scientists

   D give a funny example of how a parrot solved a crime

2 In paragraphs 20–24, the author includes an anecdote to —

   F show how eavesdropping provides an animal with prey

   G persuade readers to learn more about white storks

   H give a specific example of how animal sounds work

   J describe the mating rituals of moor frogs

3 Which idea is supported by information throughout the selection?

   A Animal eavesdropping is a real scientific term.

   B Animal sounds are for communication within the same species.

   C Animal spying is a fun game that only happens in the wild.

   D Animal snooping can determine life or death for animals.

RESPOND

ANALYZE THE TEXT

Support your responses with evidence from the text. 📓 NOTEBOOK

1. **Analyze** The author opens the text with an anecdote about a pet parrot. Explain the author's purpose for including this anecdote.

2. **Summarize** Review paragraphs 6–9. Summarize key ideas from this section of the text.

3. **Infer** The author refers to the animals in the text as spies and snoops. What does he mean by this?

4. **Synthesize** What important idea does the photograph and caption of the firefly following paragraph 19 help you understand?

5. **Notice & Note** Reread paragraph 29 and note how the author describes how far a whale's echolocation sound travels. Why does the author describe distance this way? Make a generalization about how science writing communicates facts.

RESEARCH

The author presents many different types of animals in the text. Choose one of the text's animals that interests you and find additional information about that animal. Use the chart below to help you begin your research. Use the questions you'd like to have answered to guide you as you gather information about your animal.

RESEARCH TIP
The best search terms are very specific. In your search, you will want to include the animal's name and a term related to it. For example, search for *white stork* and *hunting* to make sure you get the information you need.

Which animal interests me?	I remember this animal from the article because …	Questions I'd like to have answered …

Extend In a small group, share your research about the animal you selected. Work together to compare and contrast the information from your research with the information provided in *Animal Snoops*.

RESPOND

CREATE AND DISCUSS

Write an Informational Essay Write a three- to four-paragraph essay about the animal you selected to research.

- ❏ Introduce the topic and end your first paragraph with a thesis statement, or a sentence that provides your controlling idea.
- ❏ Choose a way to organize your essay, such as gathering similar information into topic paragraphs. Include details from your research to support your ideas.
- ❏ Include transition words and phrases, such as *because, therefore,* and *for that reason,* to clarify ideas and to make connections among ideas.
- ❏ In your final paragraph, state your conclusion about your animal.

Discuss with a Small Group Work with a small group to discuss the behaviors of familiar animals, including pets and wildlife. What conclusions about animal intelligence can you draw based on the animal behaviors you have discussed? Use the following points to help you in discussion:

- ❏ Review the ideas together and ask questions of each other.
- ❏ Listen attentively to all ideas.
- ❏ Identify points of agreement and disagreement and discuss them respectfully.

Go to the **Writing Studio** for help writing informational texts.

Go to the **Speaking and Listening Studio** for more on participating in discussions.

RESPOND TO THE ESSENTIAL QUESTION

 What can you learn by seeing the world through an animal's eyes?

Gather Information Review your annotations and notes on *Animal Snoops*. Then, add relevant details to your Response Log. As you determine which information to include, think about:

- how animals pay close attention to their surroundings
- why animals observe their surroundings so closely
- what behaviors show animal intelligence

At the end of the unit, use your notes to write an argument.

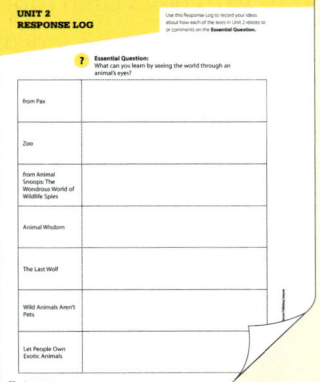

ACADEMIC VOCABULARY

As you write and discuss what you learned from the text, be sure to use the Academic Vocabulary words. Check off each of the words that you use.

- ❏ benefit
- ❏ distinct
- ❏ environment
- ❏ illustrate
- ❏ respond

Animal Snoops: The Wondrous World of Wildlife Spies

RESPOND

WORD BANK
eavesdrop
foil
predator
stake
intercept

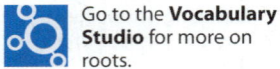
Go to the **Vocabulary Studio** for more on roots.

CRITICAL VOCABULARY

Practice and Apply Describe what is alike and different about the two words in each pair.

1. *eavesdrop* and *listen* _____
2. *stake* and *reward* _____
3. *foil* and *intercept* _____
4. *predator* and *enemy* _____

VOCABULARY STRATEGY:
Latin Roots

Sometimes you can figure out the meaning of an unfamiliar word by examining its root. A **root** is a word part that contains the core meaning of the word. For example, *-cept* comes from a Latin root meaning "to take." You can use the meaning of the root to figure out that *intercept* describes the action of taking, or stopping, someone or something on the way from one place to another.

Creating a word family is another way to use a Latin root to determine the meaning of an unfamiliar word. Thinking of other words that include the same root can help you recognize their related meanings and arrive at a meaning for an unfamiliar word. A word family that includes the same root as *intercept* would include words such as *reception, accept,* and *receptacle.*

Practice and Apply Think of words related to the word *predatory*. This word has a Latin root suffix, which comes at the end of the word. The suffixes *-tory* or *-ory* mean "relating to" or "having a place for." Fill in the word web with words that have these suffixes.

128 Unit 2

LANGUAGE CONVENTIONS:
Capitalization

Many proper adjectives describe cultural references or locations. The chart below shows two types of proper adjectives that require capitalization.

TYPE	EXAMPLES
cultural references	The Chinese dumplings were delicious. Erin is taking West African dance lessons.
location	We live close to the Canadian border. During our trip we visited many Midwestern cities.

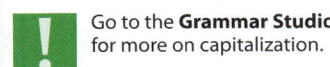

Go to the **Grammar Studio** for more on capitalization.

Practice and Apply Mark the proper nouns and proper adjectives that should be capitalized in each sentence.

1. My sister and I love italian cooking.
2. Jamaica was formerly a british colony, a region ruled by the united kingdom, or uk.
3. The pacific northwest region of the united states has many national forests.
4. We visited the english countryside.
5. We enjoyed strolling through the quaint austrian village.

COLLABORATE & COMPARE

POEM
ANIMAL WISDOM
by **Nancy Wood**
pages 133–135

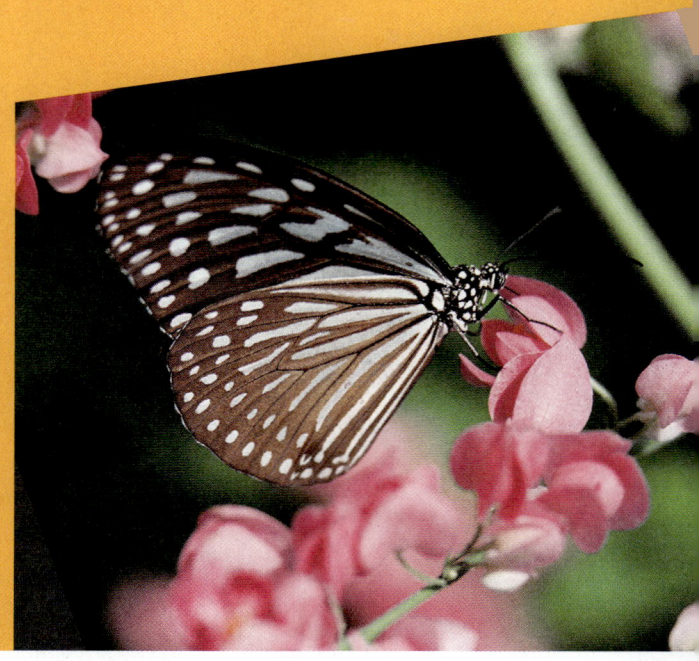

COMPARE THEMES

As you read, focus on discovering themes, or messages about life or human nature, that both poems share. What ideas are communicated by each poem? Which ideas do they have in common?

 ESSENTIAL QUESTION:

What can you learn by seeing the world through an animal's eyes?

POEM
THE LAST WOLF
by **Mary TallMountain**
pages 136–137

GET READY

QUICK START

People and animals constantly interact with each other. Can you think of a time when you had an interaction in which an animal showed its intelligence? Think about why the interaction left an impression on you. Discuss your experience with your group.

ANALYZE PERSONIFICATION AND IMAGERY

Figurative language is language that has meaning beyond the literal meaning of the words. **Personification,** one type of figurative language, uses words to describe an object or animal as if it has human characteristics. Authors might use personification to emphasize an idea or create an emotional effect. For example, in "Animal Wisdom," a turtle is described as if it were human, talking the way a person would.

GENRE ELEMENTS: POETRY
- may use figurative language, including personification
- often includes imagery that appeals to the five senses
- expresses a theme, or a "big idea" message about life

"ANIMAL WISDOM" EXAMPLE	PERSONIFICATION
Turtle crawled up on land. He said: What's missing is the ability to find contentment in a slow-paced life.	The author uses personification to express an idea about what might be missing from the world.

Imagery is the use of words and phrases in a way that allows readers to experience, or imagine, how something looks, feels, sounds, smells, or tastes. To find imagery in a piece of writing, ask yourself, "What details help me experience what the author is describing? What sensory language helps me do that?" In "The Last Wolf," the author uses imagery to describe a wolf entering the city.

"THE LAST WOLF" EXAMPLE	IMAGERY
and I heard his baying echoes down the steep smashed warrens of Montgomery Street and past the few ruby-crowned highrises left standing	The sensory details in these lines help the reader imagine the sounds of the wolf and view what it sees.

As you read "Animal Wisdom" and "The Last Wolf," analyze the authors' use of imagery and personification to determine their specific reasons for using these techniques.

GET READY

PARAPHRASE

Paraphrasing is restating text in your own words, which can help you **monitor comprehension** and ensure that you understand the text as you're reading. A paraphrase is written in simpler language and is about the same length as the original text, and an accurate paraphrase must keep the logical order and meaning of the original text. The chart below shows a paraphrase of a section of "The Last Wolf."

ORIGINAL TEXT	PARAPHRASE
he laid his long gray muzzle on the spare white spread and his eyes burned yellow his small dotted eyebrows quivered	The wolf put his head on the bed and stared with intense emotion.

Be sure your paraphrase accurately reflects the meaning of the original text, but avoid using the exact wording, or even the same sentence structure, of the text you are paraphrasing. If you do include exact words in your paraphrase, enclose those words in quotation marks.

ANNOTATION MODEL

NOTICE & NOTE

As you read, note examples of imagery and personification that move or surprise you. You can also paraphrase difficult passages in the side margin. In the model, you can see how one reader marked the first stanza of "Animal Wisdom" and made notes.

At first, the wild creatures were too busy
to explore their natural curiosity until
Turtle crawled up on land. He said:
What's missing is the ability
5   to find contentment in a slow-paced life.

A turtle talking! I wonder why?

Paraphrase: The animals did not take time to discover the world around them until turtle pointed it out to them.

BACKGROUND

People and animals are in constant interaction with each other. It is not surprising, then, that animals have long been a favorite focus of poets and storytellers such as **Nancy Wood** *(1936–2013). In particular, Native American literature and culture express a strong reverence for animals and the land, air, and water they share with us. Nancy Wood was a poet, novelist, and photographer who lived in Colorado and New Mexico, where she was inspired by Native American culture and the wilderness.*

ANIMAL WISDOM

Poem by Nancy Wood

PREPARE TO COMPARE

As you read, note the ways the different animals in Wood's poem demonstrate their intelligence. Think about the speaker's view of nature and what it suggests about seeing the world through an animal's eyes.

At first, the wild creatures were too busy
to explore their natural curiosity until
Turtle crawled up on land. He said:
What's missing is the ability
5 to find contentment in a slow-paced life.

Notice & Note

Use the side margins to notice and note signposts in the text.

NOTICE & NOTE

ANALYZE PERSONIFICATION

Annotate: Mark an example of personification in lines 6–11.

Infer: What can you infer about the bear through the poet's use of personification?

AHA MOMENT

Notice & Note: What does Eagle realize about the animals? Mark what Eagle says.

Describe: What does Eagle recognize about disagreement? How might his recognition help others?

ANALYZE IMAGERY

Annotate: Mark two examples of imagery related to the natural world in lines 23–34.

Interpret: What ideas about nature does the poet convey through these images?

PARAPHRASE

Annotate: Mark the final thought expressed in the poem.

Interpret: Restate the final thought in your own words.

As the oceans receded, fish sprouted whiskers.
Certain animals grew four legs and were able
to roam from shore to shore. Bear stood
upright and looked around. He said:
10 What's missing is devotion
to place, to give meaning to passing time.

Mountains grew from fiery heat, while
above them soared birds, the greatest
of which was Eagle, to whom penetrating
15 vision was given. He said: What's missing
is laughter so that arguments
can be resolved without rancor.[1]

After darkness and light settled their
differences
20 and the creatures paired up,
people appeared in all the corners of
the world. They said: What's missing
is perception.[2] They began to notice
the beauty hidden
25 in an ordinary stone,
the short lives of snowflakes,
the perfection of bird wings, and
the way a butterfly speaks
through its fragility.[3] When they realized

30 they had something in common with animals,
people began saying the same things.
They defended the Earth together,
though it was the animals who insisted
on keeping their own names.

---

[1] **rancor** (răng´kər): long-lasting resentment or anger.
[2] **perception** (pər-sĕp´shən): the ability to understand something, usually through the senses; also insight, intuition.
[3] **fragility** (frə-jĭl´ĭ-tē): easily broken, damaged, or destroyed; frail.

NOTICE & NOTE

CHECK YOUR UNDERSTANDING

Answer these questions about "Animal Wisdom" before moving on to the next poem.

1 The imagery in the poem suggests the animals are —

   A silly

   B angry

   C tired

   D curious

2 Which of the following is an example of personification?

   F *above them soared birds*

   G *animals were able to roam from shore to shore*

   H *as the oceans receded*

   J *darkness and light settled their differences*

3 An important message in "Animal Wisdom" is that —

   A animals understand the earth

   B people know more than animals

   C eagles have excellent vision

   D animals have many names

NOTICE & NOTE

BACKGROUND
Mary TallMountain *(1918–1994) was born in a small village along the Yukon River in Alaska. After her Athabaskan mother became seriously ill, TallMountain was adopted and taken away from her village. Living far from her family and home, TallMountain felt like an outsider. Many of her poems and stories reflect her struggles to reconnect with nature and her lost home. Her writing is highly praised as part of the renaissance of Native American literature during the last few decades of the 20th century.*

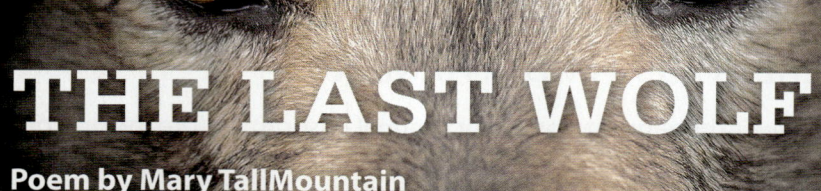

THE LAST WOLF
Poem by Mary TallMountain

Notice & Note
Use the side margins to notice and note signposts in the text.

PREPARE TO COMPARE
As you read, look for details and ideas that illustrate the speaker's perspective on wild animals and the environment.

    the last wolf hurried toward me
    through the ruined city
    and I heard his baying echoes
    down the steep smashed warrens[1]
5   of Montgomery Street and past
    the few ruby-crowned highrises
    left standing
    their lighted elevators useless

    passing the flickering red and green
10 of traffic signals
    baying his way eastward
    in the mystery of his wild loping gait
    closer the sounds in the deadly night
    through clutter and rubble of quiet blocks

PARAPHRASE
Annotate: Mark any unfamiliar words and phrases in lines 1–8. Use a dictionary to determine their meanings.

Interpret: Restate lines 1–8 in your own words. Remember to maintain the order and meaning of the original text.

---
[1] **warrens** (wôr´ənz): overcrowded living areas.

15 I heard his voice ascending[2] the hill
    and at last his low whine as he came
    floor by empty floor to the room
    where I sat
    in my narrow bed looking west, waiting
20 I heard him snuffle[3] at the door and
    I watched
    he trotted across the floor
    he laid his long gray muzzle
    on the spare white spread
25 and his eyes burned yellow
    his small dotted eyebrows quivered

    Yes, I said.
    I know what they have done.

---

[2] ascending (ə-sĕn´dĭng): rising up.
[3] snuffle (snŭf´əl): sniff.

ANALYZE IMAGERY
Annotate: Mark striking examples of imagery used to describe the wolf in lines 15–26.

Infer: What does this use of imagery suggest about how the last wolf feels?

CHECK YOUR UNDERSTANDING

Answer these questions about "The Last Wolf" before moving on to the **Analyze the Texts** section.

1 In "The Last Wolf," what has happened to the city?

   A Animals have attacked it.

   B People have ruined it.

   C A big storm has destroyed it.

   D It is being rebuilt.

2 Which line in "The Last Wolf" appeals to the sense of sight?

   F *and I heard his baying echoes*

   G *in the mystery of his wild loping gait*

   H *and at last his low whine as he came*

   J *I heard him snuffle at the door and*

3 The line "their lighted elevators useless" emphasizes —

   A the emptiness and ruin of the city

   B the height of the buildings

   C the size of the wolf

   D the darkness of the city

RESPOND

ANALYZE THE TEXTS

Support your responses with evidence from the texts. **NOTEBOOK**

1. **Cite Evidence** Reread lines 1–17 of "Animal Wisdom." How does the use of personification affect the way you perceive the animals? Cite text evidence in your response.

2. **Interpret** Paraphrase lines 29–34 of "Animal Wisdom." Why do you think the animals "insisted on keeping their own names"?

3. **Analyze** Reread lines 1–8 of "The Last Wolf." What mood or feeling does the imagery in these lines create?

4. **Evaluate** Reread lines 9–26 of "The Last Wolf." How does the poet's use of figurative language and details suggest that the wolf is intelligent? Is this use effective? Cite text evidence.

5. **Notice & Note** State in your own words the meaning of the last two lines of "The Last Wolf." How do these lines reflect a change in the speaker of the poem? How might the lines affect a reader?

RESEARCH

The action of Mary TallMountain's poem takes place in a "ruined city," which is not a place one would expect to find a wolf. Do research and complete the chart below, providing details about wolves in your answers. Be sure to add your own questions and answers to the chart.

RESEARCH TIP
Consider using your textbooks from other subject areas as a source of information. For instance, you can search the index or table of contents of your science textbook to see whether it contains information about wolves.

QUESTIONS	ANSWERS
What is a wolf's natural habitat? Where do wolves usually live?	
What do wolves eat?	
My own questions:	

Connect In "The Last Wolf," the author presents the wolf outside its natural environment. What is TallMountain suggesting about humanity's relationship to the natural world? What other texts do you know that feature wolves, and how do those texts differ from "The Last Wolf"?

138 Unit 2

RESPOND

CREATE AND PRESENT

Discuss the Poems Hold a group discussion on how the different animals in the poems demonstrate their intelligence and what this suggests about each poet's view of wildlife.

- ❏ Discuss how the poets present the animals' intelligence in each poem. Support your ideas with details from the poems.
- ❏ Take notes about your ideas and other students' thoughts.
- ❏ As a group, identify points of agreement or disagreement, and then draw a conclusion on how each poet feels about wildlife.

Present Imagery With your group, create a poster on which you share your interpretation of key images from the poems.

- ❏ With your group, choose three images from the poems that struck you as especially memorable. Illustrate and display the examples of imagery on a board for your class to see.
- ❏ Indicate the sense to which each image appeals.
- ❏ Note the meaning conveyed by each image.
- ❏ Explain why the images you chose are memorable to you.

Go to the **Speaking and Listening Studio** for more on holding a discussion.

RESPOND TO THE ESSENTIAL QUESTION

What can you learn by seeing the world through an animal's eyes?

Gather Information Review your annotations and notes on "Animal Wisdom" and "The Last Wolf." Then, add relevant details to your Response Log. As you determine which information to include, think about:

- what the imagery suggests about the animals
- how animals and humans relate in the poems
- how the writers portray the animals in the poems

At the end of the unit, use your notes to write an argument.

ACADEMIC VOCABULARY

As you discuss and present your ideas about the poems, be sure to use the Academic Vocabulary words. Check off each of the words that you use.

- ❏ benefit
- ❏ distinct
- ❏ environment
- ❏ illustrate
- ❏ respond

Animal Wisdom / The Last Wolf

RESPOND

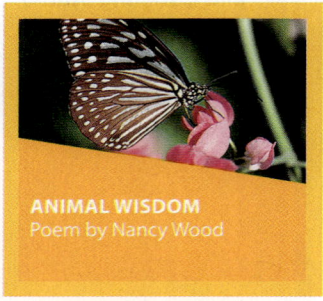

ANIMAL WISDOM
Poem by Nancy Wood

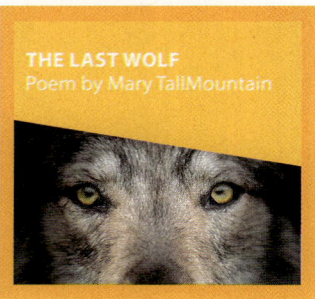

THE LAST WOLF
Poem by Mary TallMountain

Collaborate & Compare

COMPARE THEMES

"Animal Wisdom" and "The Last Wolf" are poems about animals, nature, and human beings. Although the poems share similar topics, they may express different themes. A poem's **theme** is its "big picture" idea, or its message about life or human nature. When you ask what a poem means, you are asking about theme.

Poets do not generally state themes directly. It is up to you to **infer** a theme based on a poem's significant details. As you review the poems for details that hint at a theme, you might consider:

- ❏ key statements that the speaker or characters may make
- ❏ significant events that occur in the poem
- ❏ memorable images that describe the characters or setting

With your group, complete a chart with details from both poems.

	ANIMAL WISDOM	**THE LAST WOLF**
Key Statements		
Significant Events		
Memorable Images		

ANALYZE THE TEXTS

Discuss answers to these questions with your group.

1. **Compare** With your group, review the images that you cited in your chart. In what ways are the images similar? In what ways are they different? Explain.

2. **Infer** Both poems contain themes about the way humans relate to the natural world. Compare these themes. Cite text evidence in your discussion.

3. **Evaluate** In "Animal Wisdom," the animal characters speak as humans do. In "The Last Wolf," the wolf communicates without speaking. Discuss which portrayal you find more effective. Why?

4. **Interpret** Reflect on how human beings benefit from the wisdom of animals. Listen and learn from others in your group, and adjust your opinion, if needed.

RESPOND

COMPARE AND PRESENT

Now your group can continue exploring the ideas in these texts by identifying and comparing their themes. Follow these steps:

1. **Decide on the most important details.** With your group, review your chart to identify the most important details from each poem. Identify points you agree on, and resolve disagreements through discussion, basing your decisions on evidence from the texts.

2. **Create theme statements.** State a theme for each poem, using complete sentences. Remember, it is up to you and your group to infer the themes based on details. You can use a chart like the one shown here to determine the theme each writer suggests.

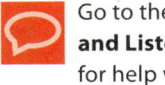

Go to the **Speaking and Listening Studio** for help with giving a presentation.

DETAIL	DETAIL	DETAIL

THEME

3. **Compare and contrast themes.** With your group, discuss similarities and differences in the themes of the poems. Listen actively to the members of your group, take notes, and ask the group to clarify any points you do not understand. Identify points of agreement or disagreement before you present your ideas.

4. **Present to the class.** Now it is time to present your ideas. State your conclusions about the themes of the poems. Discuss points of similarity and difference in themes. You may adapt the charts you created or use other visuals to help convey your ideas and information to the class.

Collaborate & Compare 141

COLLABORATE & COMPARE

ARGUMENT
WILD ANIMALS AREN'T PETS
by **USA TODAY**
pages 145–147

COMPARE ARGUMENTS

As you read, focus on the evidence used to support the claims in the arguments "Wild Animals Aren't Pets" and "Let People Own Exotic Animals." Think about which points in each selection make sense to you and which do not. Then, consider the strength of the evidence presented to support each point.

 ESSENTIAL QUESTION:

What can you learn by seeing the world through an animal's eyes?

ARGUMENT
LET PEOPLE OWN EXOTIC ANIMALS
by **Zuzana Kukol**
pages 148–151

GET READY

QUICK START

People everywhere have a fascination for wild, exotic animals. Do you think people should be allowed to keep these creatures as pets? Write down two reasons why or why not.

IDENTIFY CLAIMS IN ARGUMENTS

The selections "Wild Animals Aren't Pets" and "Let People Own Exotic Animals" present opposing arguments. A written **argument** expresses a position, or makes a claim about an issue or problem, and supports that position with reasons and evidence. The **claim,** or the writer's position, is often stated early in the argument, such as in the introductory paragraph or even in the title. A claim may be stated more than one time and in more than one way; often, a claim will be restated in the conclusion.

As you read the following texts, use a chart like the following to identify each argument's claim.

GENRE ELEMENTS: ARGUMENT
- makes a claim or takes a position on an issue
- supports its claim with reasons and evidence (facts, statistics, quotations, and examples)
- presents counterarguments to address objections
- uses logic or emotion to persuade readers

TITLE	CLAIM	LOCATION(S) IN THE TEXT
"Wild Animals Aren't Pets"		
"Let People Own Exotic Animals"		

ANALYZE EVIDENCE

Evidence is a specific piece of information that an author gives to support a claim. Evidence can include facts, quotations, examples, statistics, or even personal experiences. As you read each text, look for the specific types of evidence provided by the author.

To evaluate how convincing and accurate an author's evidence is, distinguish between **fact** and **opinion.** Facts are statements that can be proven, observed, or measured. Opinions are personal beliefs that may or may not be supported by facts. As you read each article, look for fact-based evidence and opinions.

Wild Animals Aren't Pets / Let People Own Exotic Animals   143

GET READY

CRITICAL VOCABULARY

exotic   dictate   exempt   regulate

To preview the Critical Vocabulary words, replace the boldfaced word or words in parentheses with a vocabulary word with a similar meaning.

1. We want the city council to (**control**) _____ the amount of pollution that factories release into the air.
2. The (**unusual, foreign**) _____ plant looked like a creature from another planet.
3. Our leader's new orders (**command, require**) _____ what we should do next.
4. I was (**excused**) _____ from the test because I was sick.

LANGUAGE CONVENTIONS:
Words Spelled Correctly

To avoid confusion in your writing, it is important to use and spell words correctly. Many common words have similar spellings or sound alike but have different meanings. Here is an example from the text.

> **With animals running <u>loose</u> and darkness closing in, authorities arrived with no good choices to protect the public.**

The word *loose* is commonly misspelled as *lose*, which is a different word with a different meaning. *Lose* means "fail to win." If the writer had misspelled *loose* as *lose*, readers would have been confused and distracted. In this lesson, you will learn about other words that are commonly mistaken for each other and are often misspelled.

ANNOTATION MODEL

NOTICE & NOTE

As you read, note the author's use of emotion to convince readers to agree with the claim. In the model, you can see one reader's notes about the use of emotion at the beginning of "Wild Animals Aren't Pets."

> 2   Until recently, though, few people knew how easy it is to own a wild animal as a pet. Or how potentially (tragic).
> 3   But just as a 2007 raid on property owned by football star Michael Vick laid bare the little known and (cruel) world of dogfighting, a story that unfolded in a small Ohio city recently opened the public's eyes to the little known, (distressing) world of "exotic" pets.

strong words for negative emotions

144 Unit 2

BACKGROUND

Wild animals are animals that live in nature. They can be as rare as a snow leopard or as common as a tree squirrel. Although many states have laws that prohibit owning a wild animal, thousands of people in the United States keep animals, such as wolves, pythons, crocodiles, and bears, as pets. Some people want to make it illegal to have these kinds of pets. They argue that these animals pose a safety and health risk to people and the environment.

WILD ANIMALS AREN'T PETS

Argument by USA TODAY

PREPARE TO COMPARE

As you read, focus on the facts the author uses to support the claim.

1   In many states, anyone with a few hundred dollars and a yen[1] for the unusual can own a python, a black bear or a big cat as a "pet." For $8,000 a baby white tiger can be yours. Sometimes, wild animals are even offered free: "Siberian tigers looking for a good home," read an ad in the *Animal Finder's Guide.*

2   Until recently, though, few people knew how easy it is to own a wild animal as a pet. Or how potentially tragic.

3   But just as a 2007 raid on property owned by football star Michael Vick laid bare the little known and cruel world of dogfighting, a story that unfolded in a small Ohio city recently opened the public's eyes to the little known, distressing world of **"exotic"** pets. We're not suggesting that people who own these animals are cruel. Many surely love them. But public safety, common sense and compassion for animals all **dictate** the same conclusion: Wild animals are not pets.

---

[1] **yen** (yĕn): a strong desire or inclination.

NOTICE & NOTE

Use the side margins to notice and note signposts in the text.

IDENTIFY CLAIMS IN ARGUMENTS

Annotate: Mark the claim in the title.

Analyze: Do you think it's effective to state the claim in this location? Why or why not?

exotic
(ĭg-zŏt´ĭk) *adj.* Something that is *exotic* is from another part of the world.

dictate
(dĭk´tāt´) *v.* To *dictate* something is to require that it be done or decided.

NOTICE & NOTE

EXTREME OR ABSOLUTE LANGUAGE

Notice & Note: What extreme or absolute language is used in paragraph 4? Mark the language used to describe the actions of the authorities.

Analyze: Why do you think the author chose these words?

LANGUAGE CONVENTIONS

Annotate: In paragraph 7, mark the word *too*.

Compare: What are two common misspellings of this word? What is the meaning of each of the three words?

ANALYZE EVIDENCE

Annotate: In paragraph 9, mark the states that do not have rules about keeping wild animals as pets.

Analyze: Does the evidence the author provides about state regulation support the claim? Explain.

exempt
(ĭg-zĕmpt´): *adj.* A person who is *exempt* is freed or excused from following a law or duty others must obey.

4   If that weren't already obvious, it became more so when collector Terry Thompson opened the cages on his Zanesville farm, springing dozens of lions, tigers, bears and other wild creatures before killing himself. With animals running loose and darkness closing in, authorities arrived with no good choices to protect the public. They shot all but a handful of the animals as the nation watched, transfixed[2] and horrified.

5   Owners of "exotic" animals claim they rarely maim or kill. But is the death rate really the point?

6   In 2009, a 2-year-old Florida girl was strangled by a 12-foot-long Burmese python, a family pet that had gotten out of its aquarium. That same year, a Connecticut woman was mauled and disfigured by a neighbor's pet chimp. Last year, a caretaker was mauled to death by a bear owned by a Cleveland collector. In Zanesville, it was the animals themselves, including 18 rare Bengal tigers, who became innocent victims.

7   Trade in these beautiful creatures thrives in the USA, where thousands are bred and sold through classified ads or at auctions centered in Indiana, Missouri and Tennessee. There's too little to stop it.

8   A 2003 federal law, which forbids the interstate transport of certain big cats, has stopped much of the trade on the Internet, according to the Humane Society of the U.S. But monkeys, baboons and other primates were left out, and measures to plug that hole have twice stalled in Congress.

9   Only collectors who exhibit animals need a federal license. Those, such as Thompson, who keep the animals as "pets" are left alone, unless states intervene.[3] And many do not. Eight—Alabama, Idaho, Ohio, Nevada, North Carolina, South Carolina, West Virginia and Wisconsin—have no rules, and in 13 others the laws are lax,[4] according to Born Free USA, which has lobbied for years for stronger laws.

10   After the Cleveland bear-mauling, then-Ohio Gov. Ted Strickland issued an emergency order to ban possession of wild animals. While it **exempted** current owners, Thompson might have been forced to give up his menagerie[5] because he had been cited for animal cruelty. We'll never know. Strickland's successor, John Kasich, let the order expire.

---

[2] **transfixed** (trăns-fĭkst´): motionless, as with terror, amazement, or other strong emotion.
[3] **intervene** (ĭn´tər-vēn´): to come between so as to block or change an action.
[4] **lax** (lăks): not rigorous, strict, or firm.
[5] **menagerie** (mə-năj´ə-rē): a collection of live wild animals, often kept for showing to the public.

146   Unit 2

NOTICE & NOTE

CHECK YOUR UNDERSTANDING

Answer these questions about "Wild Animals Aren't Pets" before moving on to the next selection.

1 What is the claim of the argument "Wild Animals Aren't Pets"?

   A Ownership of wild animals should be regulated.

   B Wild animals should not be kept as pets.

   C Owning a wild animal is not easy.

   D More needs to be done to prohibit the breeding of wild animals.

2 What point is supported by the author's evidence that wild animals in private ownership cause harm?

   F People who own wild animals are cruel.

   G Only wealthy people can afford to buy wild animals.

   H Ownership of wild animals can hurt the animals, humans, or both.

   J It is easy to own a wild animal.

3 Which sentence from the text suggests that the author will offer a counterargument to an opposing claim?

   A *Owners of "exotic" animals claim they rarely maim or kill.*

   B *Until recently, though, few people knew how easy it is to own a wild animal as a pet.*

   C *Only collectors who exhibit animals need a federal license.*

   D *We're not suggesting that people who own these animals are cruel.*

NOTICE & NOTE

BACKGROUND

Some people claim that private citizens have no business keeping wild and exotic animals as pets. Others disagree, claiming that with proper care, captivity is a safe place for animals. In 2012, in Zanesville, Ohio, Terry Thompson set free his collection of exotic animals. Most of them had to be killed on sight to protect nearby residents. In the aftermath of this tragedy, **Zuzana Kukol** *wrote this commentary, maintaining that private owners, through captive breeding, provide one of the most effective ways to save threatened species. "Tigers," Kukol has said, "are better than dogs. They don't bark."*

LET PEOPLE OWN EXOTIC ANIMALS

Argument by Zuzana Kukol

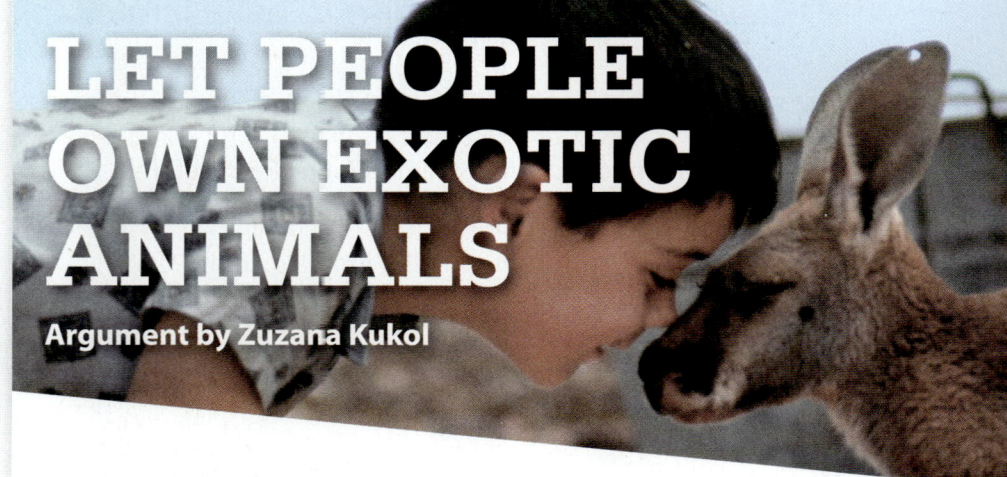

PREPARE TO COMPARE

As you read, look for ways the author supports her claim and addresses counterarguments. Do you agree with her claim? Why or why not?

Notice & Note
Use the side margins to notice and note signposts in the text.

IDENTIFY CLAIMS IN ARGUMENTS
Annotate: Mark the author's claim in the second paragraph.

Interpret: In your own words, give the reasons the author presents to support the claim.

regulate
(rĕg´yə-lāt´) *v.* If you *regulate* something, you control or direct it according to a rule, principle, or law.

1 The recent tragedy in Zanesville, Ohio brought back the question of whether private ownership of wild and exotic animals should be legal.

2 The simple answer is yes. Responsible private ownership of exotic animals should be legal if animal welfare is taken care of. Terry Thompson didn't represent the typical responsible owner. He had a criminal record and animal abuse charges. What Thompson did was selfish and insane; we cannot **regulate** insanity.

148   Unit 2

3   People keep exotic animals for commercial[1] reasons and as pets. Most exotic animals—such as big cats, bears or apes—are in commercial, federally inspected facilities. These animals are born in captivity, and not "stolen" from the wild. Captive breeding eliminates the pressure on wild populations, and also serves as a backup in case the animals go extinct.[2]

4   Dangers from exotic animals are low. On average in the United States, only 3.25 people per year are killed by captive big cats, snakes, elephants and bears. Most of these fatalities are owners, family members, friends and trainers voluntarily on the property where the animals were kept. Meanwhile, traffic accidents kill about 125 people per day.

ANALYZE EVIDENCE
Annotate: Mark the evidence the author provides to support her claim in paragraphs 4 and 5.

Compare: How are the two examples of evidence alike? How are they different?

---

[1] **commercial** (kə-mûr′shəl): of or relating to commerce or trade.
[2] **extinct** (ĭk-stĭngkt′): no longer existing or living.

NOTICE & NOTE

LANGUAGE CONVENTIONS

Annotate: Mark the word *choose* in paragraph 5.

Compare: What is a common misspelling of *choose*? What does each word mean?

5   If we have the freedom to choose what car to buy, where to live, or what domestic animal to have, why shouldn't we have the same freedom to choose what species of wild or exotic animal to own and to love?

6   Would the Ohio situation be any different if the animals were owned by a government and their caretaker released them? Is this really about private ownership, or is it about certain people's personal issues with exotics in captivity?

7   If society overreacts and bans exotics because of actions of a few deranged[3] individuals, then we need to ban kids, as that is the only way to totally stop child abuse, and we need to ban humans, because that is the only way to stop murder. Silly, isn't it?

---

[3] **deranged** (dĭ-rānjd): mentally unbalanced; insane.

CHECK YOUR UNDERSTANDING

Answer these questions before moving on to the **Analyze the Text** section on the following page.

1 What is the claim presented in the commentary "Let People Own Exotic Animals"?

   A   Ownership of exotic animals should be regulated.

   B   Exotic animals make good pets.

   C   Captive breeding helps save wild populations.

   D   Responsible private ownership of exotic pets should be permitted if the animals are properly cared for.

2 Which sentence or phrase from the text is a fact that supports the claim?

   F   *We cannot regulate insanity.*

   G   *On average in the United States, only 3.25 people per year are killed by captive big cats, snakes, elephants and bears.*

   H   *Captive breeding eliminates the pressure on wild populations. . . .*

   J   *Terry Thompson didn't represent the typical responsible owner.*

3 Which sentence or phrase from the text uses strong, emotional language to support the claim?

   A   *Terry Thompson didn't represent the typical responsible owner.*

   B   *Dangers from exotic animals are low.*

   C   *People keep exotic animals for commercial reasons and as pets.*

   D   *. . . why shouldn't we have the same freedom to choose what species or exotic animal to own and to love?*

RESPOND

ANALYZE THE TEXT

Support your responses with evidence from the text. 📓 **NOTEBOOK**

1. **Identify** What is the claim of each article and how do they differ?

2. **Summarize** Reread paragraph 3 in "Let People Own Exotic Animals." According to the writer, where are most exotic animals kept and what is the benefit of breeding them?

3. **Analyze** Reread paragraph 4 in "Wild Animals Aren't Pets." What specific evidence does the writer use to support the argument that people should not be allowed to own exotic animals? Explain how the evidence is or is not directly related to the claim.

4. **Analyze** Review paragraph 4 in "Let People Own Exotic Animals." What specific evidence does the writer use to support the argument that people should be allowed to own exotic animals? Explain how the evidence is or is not directly related to the claim.

5. **Notice & Note** Find examples of extreme or absolute language in "Wild Animals Aren't Pets" or "Let People Own Exotic Animals." Do you think the author's word choice exaggerates or overstates the author's points? Explain.

RESEARCH

RESEARCH TIP
The best search terms are very specific. Along with the animal's name, you will want to include terms such as *diet, protected species,* or *regulations*.

Investigate an exotic animal that you are interested in. What are the pros and cons of owning the animal as a pet? Generate questions about the needs of this animal. Then, gather information from a variety of sources and record what you learn in the chart.

EXOTIC ANIMAL:	
PROS OF OWNING AS A PET	**CONS OF OWNING AS A PET**

Connect In "Let People Own Exotic Animals," the writer states, "Captive breeding eliminates the pressure on wild populations, and also serves as a backup in case the animals go extinct." With a small group, discuss whether your research uncovered any evidence to support this idea.

RESPOND

CREATE AND PRESENT

Write an Argument Take a position, pro or con, about owning the exotic animal you researched. Then, write a formal letter to a government official, supporting your position.

- ❏ Use appropriate vocabulary and a formal tone in your letter.
- ❏ Clearly state your argument's claim in the opening paragraph.
- ❏ In the next paragraphs, provide reasons and evidence that support your claim.
- ❏ In your final paragraph, state your conclusion about owning the exotic animal.

Create and Present a Public Service Announcement (PSA) Take the argument you have developed about owning the exotic animal you investigated and create a PSA poster supporting your position.

- ❏ Present your PSA poster to your group. Make eye contact with your audience and use an appropriate speaking rate and volume.
- ❏ Ask group members to respond to your ideas by suggesting ways that you might improve your PSA.
- ❏ Work together to identify steps you might take to further educate people about your position. Listen closely and respectfully to all ideas.

Go to the **Writing Studio** for more on writing an argument.

Go to the **Speaking and Listening Studio** for help giving a presentation.

RESPOND TO THE ESSENTIAL QUESTION

 What can you learn by seeing the world through an animal's eyes?

Gather Information Review your annotations and notes on "Wild Animals Aren't Pets" and "Let People Own Exotic Animals." Then, add relevant details to your Response Log. As you determine what points to include, think about the reasons people want to own exotic animals and the pros and cons of owning exotic animals.

At the end of the unit, you will use your notes to write an argument.

ACADEMIC VOCABULARY
As you write and discuss what you learned from the texts, be sure to use the Academic Vocabulary words. Check off each of the words that you use.

- ❏ benefit
- ❏ distinct
- ❏ environment
- ❏ illustrate
- ❏ respond

RESPOND

WORD BANK
exotic exempt
dictate regulate

CRITICAL VOCABULARY

Practice and Apply Choose the correct response to each question.

1. Which of the following could be described as **exotic**?
   a. a pair of sneakers
   b. a rare type of flower

2. Which of the following is something a school might **dictate**?
   a. students' hobbies
   b. the length of recess

3. What might cause someone to be **exempt** from soccer practice?
   a. a previous absence
   b. an injury

4. Which of the following might a government **regulate**?
   a. how fast people drive
   b. what people eat for dinner

VOCABULARY STRATEGY:
Word Origins

Knowing the origin and historical development of a word, also known as its **etymology,** gives you a deeper understanding of the word. When you study a word's history and origin, you can find out when, where, and how the word came to be.

 Go to **Understanding Word Origins** and **Using Reference Resources** the **Vocabulary Studio** for more on word origins and resources.

Practice and Apply Using print and online resources, look up each Critical Vocabulary word and complete the chart below. Use these resources to determine each word's syllabication and pronunciation, and then identify its etymology and current meaning.

WORD	SYLLABICATION / PRONUNCIATION	ETYMOLOGY / CURRENT MEANING
dictate		
exempt		
exotic		
regulate		

RESPOND

LANGUAGE CONVENTIONS:
Words Spelled Correctly

Many common words with similar spellings and pronunciations are easily confused. Here are some examples.

advice/advise
lie/lay
passed/past
than/then
two/too/to
their/there/they're

Knowing which word is correct in a particular situation is critical for clear communication—as a writer and as a reader.

Practice and Apply Choose the word that correctly completes each sentence. You may use a dictionary if you'd like.

1. Gena did not (accept/except) Mindy's offer of a ride to school.
2. I will not discuss this any (farther/further) until I speak to my family.
3. A lawyer will (advice/advise) you of your rights.
4. The old bridge did not look like it could (bare/bear) the weight of the truck.
5. Russell slammed his foot on the (brake/break) to avoid hitting the ducks crossing the road in front of him.
6. The judge's ruling today will have a significant (affect/effect) on similar cases waiting to be heard.
7. Malia (passed/past) by the library on her way to the store.
8. We would rather see a movie (than/then) go to the park.

RESPOND

Collaborate & Compare

COMPARE ARGUMENTS

When you **compare and contrast** two arguments on the same issue, you analyze how each argument is presented. First, you trace and evaluate each argument: identify its claim, follow its support and reasoning, and decide whether it is convincing. Then, you determine how each author's viewpoint or attitude toward the issue differs.

As a group, fill in the key points and evidence from both texts.

❏ Look at the evidence each writer provides as support—facts, reasons, examples, and statistics. Does the evidence support the claim in a logical way?

❏ Look for persuasive language—words with strong positive or negative connotations. Are the writers trying to be persuasive by appealing to your emotions, to your logic, or to both?

WILD ANIMALS AREN'T PETS
Argument by USA TODAY

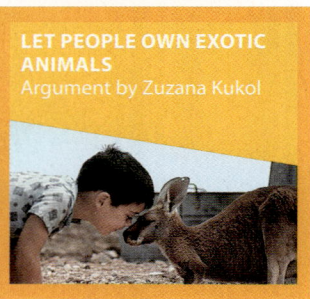

LET PEOPLE OWN EXOTIC ANIMALS
Argument by Zuzana Kukol

	WILD ANIMALS AREN'T PETS	LET PEOPLE OWN EXOTIC ANIMALS
Claim		
Evidence and Reasoning		
Persuasive Language		
Why/Why Not Convincing?		

ANALYZE THE TEXTS

Discuss these questions in your group.

1. **Compare** Compare each writer's claim and the kinds of evidence that support it. Does each author include enough evidence to support the claim?

2. **Evaluate** Examine each text and identify words that have a strong impact. For each text, tell whether the author's word choices are effective and why.

3. **Evaluate** Identify examples of the author's opinion in each text. Do these opinions strengthen or weaken the argument?

4. **Critique** Which argument seems more authoritative? Why?

RESPOND

RESEARCH AND DEBATE

Plan a **debate**—an organized exchange of opinions on an issue—about whether people should be permitted to sell exotic animals to private owners. Follow these steps to hold a fair, productive debate.

1. **Assign Roles** Select one person to be the **moderator,** who presents the topic and goals of the debate, keeps track of the time, and introduces and thanks the participants. Choose another person to be the **note taker,** who keeps track of points made during the debate.

2. **Form Two Teams** One team will argue the affirmative side of the issue (pro), and the other team will argue the negative side (con). Within your team, assign roles to each member.
   - ❏ One member of each team will introduce the team's claim and supporting evidence.
   - ❏ One member will respond to questions and opposing claims in an exchange with a member of the opposing team.
   - ❏ One member will present a strong closing argument.

3. **Research and Prepare Notes** Search the texts you've read as well as print and online sources for valid reasons and evidence to support your claim. Anticipate possible opposing claims and gather evidence to counter those claims.

4. **Hold the Debate** The moderator begins by stating the topic or issue and introducing the participants. The moderator tells participants whose turn it is to speak and how much time each speaker has.

EVALUATE DEBATE PERFORMANCE
Use this checklist to evaluate participants, including yourself.
- ❏ was well prepared with notes from research on topic
- ❏ presented claim and evidence effectively
- ❏ argued convincingly to support team's argument
- ❏ argued convincingly to rebut opposing team's argument
- ❏ used formal tone and appropriate vocabulary
- ❏ observed proper debate etiquette
- ❏ remained polite and did not interrupt
- ❏ presented a strong closing argument

SPEAKER	TASK	TIME
Affirmative Speaker 1	Present the claim and supporting evidence for the affirmative (pro) side of the argument.	5 minutes
Negative Speaker 1	Ask questions that will prompt the other team to address flaws in its argument.	3 minutes
Affirmative Speaker 2	Respond to the questions posed by the opposing team and counter any concerns.	3 minutes
Negative Speaker 2	Present the claim and supporting evidence for the negative (con) side of the argument.	5 minutes
Affirmative Speaker 2	Ask questions that will prompt the other team to address flaws in its argument.	3 minutes
Negative Speaker 1	Respond to the questions posed by the opposing team and counter any concerns.	3 minutes
Affirmative Speaker 3	Summarize the claim and evidence for the affirmative side and explain why your reasoning is more valid than that of the opposing team.	3 minutes
Negative Speaker 3	Summarize the claim and evidence for the negative side and explain why your reasoning is more valid than that of the opposing team.	3 minutes

Collaborate & Compare   157

INDEPENDENT READING

? ESSENTIAL QUESTION:

What can you learn by seeing the world through an animal's eyes?

Reader's Choice

Setting a Purpose Select one or more of these options from your eBook to continue your exploration of the Essential Question.
- Read the descriptions to see which text grabs your interest.
- Think about which genres you enjoy reading.

Notice & Note

In this unit, you practiced noticing and noting three signposts: **Again and Again, Memory Moment,** and **Contrasts and Contradictions.** As you read independently, these signposts and others will aid your understanding. Below are the anchor questions to ask when you read literature and nonfiction.

Reading Literature: Stories, Poems, and Plays		
Signpost	**Anchor Question**	**Lesson**
Contrasts and Contradictions	Why did the character act that way?	p. 3
Aha Moment	How might this change things?	p. 3
Tough Questions	What does this make me wonder about?	p. 172
Words of the Wiser	What's the lesson for the character?	p. 2
Again and Again	Why might the author keep bringing this up?	p. 92
Memory Moment	Why is this memory important?	p. 93

Reading Nonfiction: Essays, Articles, and Arguments		
Signpost	**Anchor Question(s)**	**Lesson**
Big Questions	What surprised me? What did the author think I already knew? What challenged, changed, or confirmed what I already knew?	p. 246 p. 420 p. 332
Contrasts and Contradictions	What is the difference, and why does it matter?	p. 247
Extreme or Absolute Language	Why did the author use this language?	p. 247
Numbers and Stats	Why did the author use these numbers or amounts?	p. 333
Quoted Words	Why was this person quoted or cited, and what did this add?	p. 333
Word Gaps	Do I know this word from someplace else? Does it seem like technical talk for this topic? Do clues in the sentence help me understand the word?	p. 421

INDEPENDENT READING

You can preview these texts in Unit 2 of your eBook.

Then, check off the text or texts that you select to read on your own.

POEM

The Caterpillar
Robert Graves

A poet sees the world through the eyes of a caterpillar.

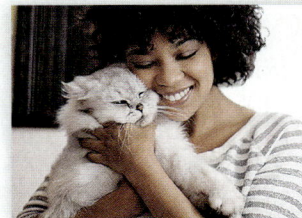

POEM

The Flying Cat
Naomi Shihab Nye

What happens when a pet owner prepares to take her cat on a plane?

SHORT STORY

The Pod
Maureen Crane Wartski

A teenager recovering from a serious accident discovers empathy for a stranded animal.

SPEECH

Tribute to the Dog
George Graham Vest

A famous speech wins a case for a sheep farmer whose dog was shot and killed.

ARGUMENTS

Views on Zoos

What's your position on whether zoos should exist?

Collaborate and Share Get with a partner to discuss what you learned from at least one of your independent readings.

- Give a brief synopsis or summary of the text.
- Describe any signposts that you noticed in the text and explain what they revealed to you.
- Describe what you most enjoyed or found most challenging about the text. Give specific examples.
- Decide if you would recommend the text to others. Why or why not?

Go to the **Reading Studio** for more resources on **Notice & Note**.

Independent Reading 159

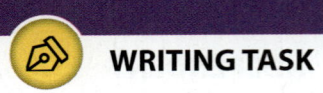

WRITING TASK

Go to the **Writing Studio** for help writing an argument.

Write an Argument

This unit focuses on what we can learn by seeing the world through the eyes of animals. For this writing task, you will write an argumentative essay on a topic related to seeing the world from the perspective of an animal. For examples of arguments that you can use as mentor texts, review "Wild Animals Aren't Pets" and "Let People Own Exotic Animals."

As you write your argument, use the notes from your Response Log, which you filled out after reading the texts in this unit.

Writing Prompt

Read the information in the box below.

> Considering a perspective other than your own can help you broaden your understanding of how the world works.

This is the topic or context for your argument.

Think carefully about the following question.

> What can you learn by seeing the world through an animal's eyes?

This is the Essential Question for the unit. How would you answer this question, based on the texts in the unit?

Write an argument defending your ideas about what you can learn by seeing the world from an animal's perspective.

Now mark the words that identify exactly what you are being asked to produce.

Be sure to—

- ❏ provide an introduction that clearly states your claim
- ❏ support your claim with logical reasons and relevant text evidence
- ❏ organize information with a purposeful structure
- ❏ use correct subject-verb agreement
- ❏ use persuasive language
- ❏ address counterarguments
- ❏ conclude by effectively summarizing your claim

Review these points as you write and again when you finish. Make any needed changes.

WRITING TASK

1 Plan

Before you start writing, plan your argument. Decide on a claim you will make about the topic. Your claim is the opinion, or stance, that you will take, support, and persuasively defend against counterarguments. In an argumentative essay, the claim is the thesis statement. First, write your claim. Then use the charts below to help you plan your argument. Next, consider how to effectively refute counterarguments.

My Claim: _____

_____

Reasons and Text Evidence
Reason: Evidence from text:
Reason: Evidence from text:
Reason: Evidence from text:

Opposing Claim	My Response

Background Reading Review the notes you have taken in your Response Log after reading the texts in this unit. These texts are the background reading that you will use to formulate the key ideas in your argument.

Go to **Writing Arguments: Building Effective Support** in the **Writing Studio** for help planning your argument.

Notice & Note
From Reading to Writing

As you plan your argument, apply what you've learned about signposts to your own writing. Remember that writers use common features, called signposts, to help convey their message to readers.

Think about how you can incorporate **Numbers and Stats** into your essay.

Use the notes from your Response Log as you plan your argument.

Write an Argument 161

WRITING TASK

Go to **Writing Arguments: Creating a Coherent Argument** in the **Writing Studio** for help organizing your ideas.

Organize Your Ideas Part of planning is organizing the information you have gathered to draft your argument. How will you capture the reader's attention in your introduction? What is the best order to present your reasons? Which counterarguments will you refute? Use the chart below to make notes. An effective tactic is to lead and conclude with your strongest reasons and evidence; include one or two related reasons in between. Then, summarize your claim and reasons in a persuasive conclusion.

Organizing My Argument	
Introduction/Claim	
1st Reason and Evidence	
2nd Reason and Evidence	
3rd Reason and Evidence	
Counterarguments to Address	
Conclusion	

You might prefer to draft your essay online.

❷ Develop a Draft

Once you have completed your planning activities, you will be ready to begin drafting your argument. Refer to the planning work you did, as well as to any notes you took as you studied the texts in the unit. These will provide a kind of map for you to follow as you write. Using a word processor or online writing application makes it easier to make changes or move sentences around later, when you are ready to revise your first draft.

WRITING TASK

Use the Mentor Texts

Persuasive Language

Writers use different techniques to persuade readers. Using persuasive language is one technique. Persuasive language includes words with strong negative and positive connotations, which are the ideas and feelings attached to the words.

> **Terry Thompson didn't represent the typical responsible owner. He had a criminal record and animal abuse charges. What Thompson did was selfish and insane; we cannot regulate insanity.**

The writer of "Let People Own Exotic Animals" uses words with strong negative connotations, like "selfish" and "insane," to make her point that typical exotic animal owners are not like Terry Thompson.

Apply What You've Learned Review your argument for words that you can replace with persuasive language. Consider whether the words you choose have positive or negative connotations.

Author's Craft

Writers often build interest and show the importance of their topic with well-chosen references to familiar stories and events. By citing examples that are relevant to their claims, writers find common ground with their readers—an important step in the process of persuasion.

> **But just as a 2007 raid on property owned by football star Michael Vick laid bare the little known and cruel world of dogfighting, a story that unfolded in a small Ohio city recently opened the public's eyes to the little known, distressing world of "exotic" pets.**

The writer of "Wild Animals Aren't Pets" builds anticipation and foreshadows a similar sense of public outrage by referring to the 2007 Michael Vick dogfighting story.

Apply What You've Learned To help persuade your readers to agree with your claim, use the strategy of bringing up a well-known story that will influence their reaction to the evidence you cite.

Write an Argument 163

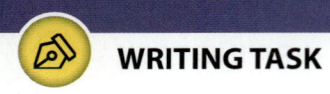

WRITING TASK

Go to **Writing Arguments: Formal Style** in the **Writing Studio** for help revising your argument.

3 Revise

On Your Own Once you have written your draft, go back and look for ways to improve your argument. As you reread and revise, think about whether you have achieved your purpose. The Revision Guide will help you focus on specific elements to make your writing stronger.

Revision Guide

Ask Yourself	Tips	Revision Techniques
1. Does my introduction create interest and clearly state a claim?	**Underline** the claim and **circle** the attention-getting opening.	**Add** a clear claim, and **add** a relevant attention-getting detail.
2. Are my reasons and evidence organized logically and linked with transitions?	**Underline** the reasons and text evidence. **Circle** transitional words and phrases.	**Reorder** reasons and evidence in a logical sequence, and **add** transitions to link reasons and evidence.
3. Are counterarguments expressed and addressed effectively?	**Mark** counterarguments and sentences that address or refute those views.	**Edit** sentences that refute a counterargument to clarify valid reasons.
4. Is there subject-verb agreement in my sentences?	**Underline** subjects and **circle** verbs.	**Replace** subjects and verbs that don't agree.
5. Do I use strong persuasive language?	**Mark** stated reasons and evidence.	**Add** persuasive language to emphasize points.
6. Does my conclusion summarize my claim?	**Mark** the conclusion.	**Add** a statement that summarizes the claim.

ACADEMIC VOCABULARY

As you conduct your **peer review,** be sure to use these words.

- ❑ benefit
- ❑ distinct
- ❑ environment
- ❑ illustrate
- ❑ respond

With a Partner Once you and your partner have worked through the Revision Guide on your own, exchange papers and evaluate each other's draft in a **peer review.** Focus on providing revision suggestions for at least three of the items mentioned in the chart. Explain why you think your partner's draft should be revised and what your specific suggestions are.

When receiving feedback from your partner, listen attentively and ask questions to make sure you fully understand the revision suggestions.

164 Unit 2

4 Edit

Once you have addressed the organization, development, and flow of ideas in your argument, you can work on improving the finer points of your draft. Edit for the proper use of standard English conventions and correct any misspellings or grammatical errors.

Language Conventions

Verb Tenses It's important to maintain consistency in verb tenses, both within a paragraph and across paragraphs. For example, if the beginning paragraph uses the present tense, the other paragraphs should, too.

Also, look for intervening phrases and clauses, and make sure that they do not affect subject-verb agreement in your sentences.

- An **intervening phrase** or **clause** is a group of words that comes between the subject and the verb.
- A singular subject should have a singular verb, and a plural subject should have a plural verb, even if there is an intervening phrase or clause between the subject and verb.

> Go to **Subject-Verb Agreement** in the **Grammar Studio** to learn more.

The chart contains examples of intervening phrases and clauses in sentences from "Wild Animals Aren't Pets."

Sentence	Intervening Phrase or Clause	Subject and Verb
A 2003 federal law, which forbids the interstate transport of certain big cats, has stopped much of the trade on the Internet, according to the Humane Society of the U.S.	which forbids the interstate transport of certain big cats	Subject: law [singular] Verb: has stopped [singular, present tense]
Only collectors who exhibit animals need a federal license.	who exhibit animals	Subject: collectors [plural] Verb: need [plural, present tense]

5 Publish

After you give your argument its finishing touches, choose a way to share it with your audience. Consider these options:

- Present your argument as a speech to the class.
- Post your argument as a blog on a classroom or school website.

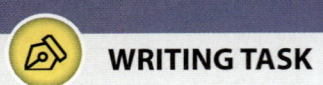 **WRITING TASK**

Use the scoring guide to evaluate your argument.

Writing Task Scoring Guide: Argument			
	Organization/Progression	**Development of Ideas**	**Use of Language and Conventions**
4	• The introduction is highly engaging and clearly states a claim. • Reasons and evidence are well organized and persuasive. • The claim is well supported and summarized in the conclusion.	• Counterarguments are addressed and well refuted. • Coherence occurs within and across the paragraphs. • Transitions clearly show the relationship between ideas.	• Language and word choice are purposeful and persuasive. • Verb tenses are used consistently and appropriately. • Spelling, punctuation, grammar, usage, and mechanics are correct.
3	• The introduction is engaging and states a claim. • Reasons and evidence are organized and somewhat persuasive. • The claim is supported and summarized in the conclusion.	• Counterarguments are addressed and refuted. • Coherence occurs within and across most paragraphs. • Transitions show the relationship between ideas.	• Language and word choice are often purposeful and persuasive. • Most verb tenses are used consistently and correctly. • Some mistakes occur in spelling, punctuation, grammar, usage, or mechanics.
2	• The introduction has a topic but no clearly stated claim. • Reasons and evidence are disorganized and not persuasive. • The claim is not well supported or not addresssed in the conclusion.	• Counterarguments are not addressed logically. • There is little coherence within and across paragraphs. • Transitions are ineffective or confusing.	• Language is often vague and too general. • Verb tenses are not always used consistently or correctly. • Spelling, punctuation, grammar, usage, and mechanics are often incorrect.
1	• The introduction does not include a claim. • Reasons and evidence are disorganized or missing. • The claim is not supported and the conclusion is missing.	• Counterarguments are not addressed. • The argument is incoherent. • Transitions are nonexistent or are unclear.	• Language is inappropriate for an argument. • Verb tenses are incorrect. • Language is vague and confusing. • Many errors occur in spelling, punctuation, grammar, mechanics, and usage.

Present an Argument

You will now adapt your argument to create a video presentation for your classmates. You will also listen to their presentations, ask questions to better understand their ideas, and help them improve their work.

SPEAKING AND LISTENING TASK

Go to **Giving a Presentation** in the **Speaking and Listening Studio** to learn more.

1 Adapt Your Argument for Presentation

Use the chart below to guide you as you create a script for a video "news editorial" based on your argument, with you as the speaker.

Presentation Planning Chart		
Title and Introduction	• How will you revise your title and introduction to capture the listener's attention? • Is there a way to state your claim aloud that is more engaging for video?	
Audience	• Who is your audience? What do you want them to understand? • Are your tone, word choices, and visual elements or graphics appropriate for persuading this audience?	
Effective Language and Organization	• Is your script logically organized? Is it interesting to listen to? Should parts be rearranged or excluded? • Where can you add evidence, persuasive language, or interesting examples to strengthen your argument? • Do you address a counterargument?	
Visuals	• What type of media or visual elements will you use? • What type of audio elements will you use? What text will appear on screen?	

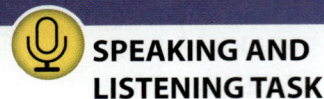

SPEAKING AND LISTENING TASK

As you work on improving your presentations, be sure to follow discussion rules:

❏ Listen closely to each other.
❏ Don't interrupt.
❏ Stay on topic.
❏ Ask only helpful, relevant questions.
❏ Provide clear, thoughtful, and direct responses.

2 Practice with a Partner or Group

Once you've completed a first draft of your video script, practice with a partner or group to gather feedback and make improvements. Consider both verbal and nonverbal techniques while practicing your presentation and creating a draft recording.

Practice Your Presentation

❏ Begin with an attention-grabbing statement. Then, clearly state your argument's claim.
❏ Don't just read the script. Speak with enthusiasm and conviction.
❏ Replace words that you stumble over and rearrange sentences so that your delivery is smooth.
❏ Use your voice effectively, varying your pitch and tone. Pause now and then to let the audience consider important points.
❏ Avoid using slang. Use formal language that shows the importance of your topic and vocabulary that is persuasive.
❏ Look directly at the camera frequently to give the impression that you are directly addressing individuals in your audience.
❏ Use gestures and facial expressions to emphasize ideas and express emotion. Smile, frown, or raise an eyebrow to show your feelings or emphasize a point. Stay calm and relaxed.

Provide and Consider Advice for Improvement

As a listener, pay close attention. Take notes about ways that presenters can improve their presentations. Paraphrase each presenter's key ideas and main points to confirm your understanding, and ask questions to clarify any confusing ideas.

As a presenter, listen closely to questions and consider ways to revise your presentation to make sure your points are clear and logically sequenced. Remember to ask for suggestions about how you might change onscreen text, images, or audio to make your presentation more interesting and persuasive.

3 Deliver Your Presentation

Use the advice you received to make changes. Then, record a final version, and show it to your classmates.

Reflect on the Unit

By completing your argument, you have created a writing product that pulls together and expresses your thoughts about the reading you have done in this unit. Now is a good time to reflect on what you have learned.

Reflect on the Essential Question

- What can you learn by seeing the world through an animal's eyes? How has your answer to this question changed since you first considered it?

- What are some examples from the texts you've read that show what you can learn by seeing the world through an animal's eyes?

Reflect on Your Reading

- Which selections presented viewpoints with which you agreed or disagreed?

- If you were to recommend one selection to a friend, which would it be? Why?

Reflect on the Writing Task

- What was challenging about writing your argument? Based on your experience, how might you change the way you plan and organize your work the next time you write an essay?

- What were the hardest and easiest parts of writing a claim?

- What improvements did you make during revision? Why did you make them?

Reflect on the Speaking and Listening Task

- What changes did you make to adapt your essay to a video news editorial?

- What was challenging about video production? What did you enjoy about it?

UNIT 2 SELECTIONS
- *Pax*
- "Zoo"
- *Animal Snoops: The Wondrous World of Wildlife Spies*
- "Animal Wisdom"
- "The Last Wolf"
- "Wild Animals Aren't Pets"
- "Let People Own Exotic Animals"

UNIT 3

SURVIVING THE UNTHINKABLE

ESSENTIAL QUESTION:

What does it take to be a survivor?

"Through every kind of disaster and setback and catastrophe. We are survivors."

Robert Fulghum

UNIT 3

ACADEMIC VOCABULARY

Academic Vocabulary words are words you use when you discuss and write about texts. In this unit, you will practice and learn five words.

✓ **circumstance**   ☐ **constraint**   ☐ **impact**   ☐ **injure**   ☐ **significant**

Study the Word Network to learn more about the word **circumstance**.

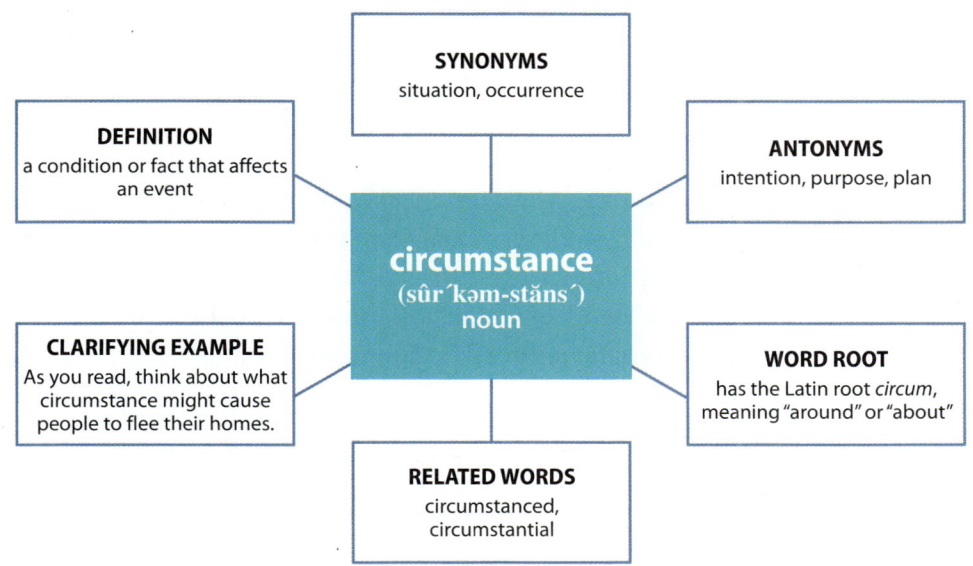

SYNONYMS: situation, occurrence
ANTONYMS: intention, purpose, plan
DEFINITION: a condition or fact that affects an event
CLARIFYING EXAMPLE: As you read, think about what circumstance might cause people to flee their homes.
WORD ROOT: has the Latin root *circum*, meaning "around" or "about"
RELATED WORDS: circumstanced, circumstantial

circumstance (sûr´kəm-stăns´) *noun*

Write and Discuss Discuss the completed Word Network with a partner, making sure to talk through all of the boxes until you both understand the word, its synonyms, antonyms, and related forms. Then, fill out Word Networks for the remaining four words. Use a dictionary or online resource to help you complete the activity.

 Go online to access the Word Networks.

RESPOND TO THE ESSENTIAL QUESTION

In this unit, you will read about people who overcome great obstacles to survive truly difficult situations. As you read, you will revisit the **Essential Question** and gather your ideas about it in the **Response Log** that appears on page R3. At the end of the unit, you will have the opportunity to write your own **nonfiction narrative** about an event in your life or the life of someone you know that shows what it takes to be a survivor. Filling out the Response Log will help you prepare for this writing task.

 You can also go online to access the Response Log.

Surviving the Unthinkable

Notice & Note

READING MODEL

from A LONG WALK TO WATER

 For more information on these and other signposts to Notice & Note, visit the **Reading Studio**.

You are about to read an excerpt from the novel *A Long Walk to Water*. In the excerpt, you will notice and note signposts that give you clues about the novel's characters and themes. Here are three key signposts to look for as you read this excerpt and other works of fiction.

When you read and encounter an expression of doubt like these, pause to see if it's a **Tough Questions** signpost:

I couldn't understand how this happened . . .

I couldn't imagine why she . . .

It was so confusing . . .

▶ **Tough Questions** *Why didn't I stick up for my friend? Why did I pass up that opportunity? Whom should I turn to for advice?* Sometimes the most difficult questions we ask ourselves have answers that are hard for us to accept. In a work of fiction, a setting or set of extreme circumstances may force a character to ask Tough Questions.

When a character expresses doubt and confusion about an issue, it's usually for a good reason. Paying attention to **Tough Questions** can:

- reveal a character's internal conflict
- offer insight into the theme of the work
- help you, the reader, think about the answers to the questions
- show how the author develops the character

Here's an example of a student finding and marking a pair of Tough Questions asked by Salva Dut, the main character in *A Long Walk to Water*:

Anchor Question
When you notice this signpost, ask: What does this make me wonder about?

> 16 Some of the rebels then joined the back of the line; now the villagers were surrounded.
> 17 *What are they going to do to us? Where is my family?*

What Tough Questions are asked?	What are they going to do to us? Where is my family?
What doubt or confusion do the questions convey?	Salva feels confused about what the rebels may want, and he has doubts about his own safety.

172 Unit 3

▶ **Again and Again** When an author repeats words, images, or events throughout a literary work, he or she is calling attention to elements important to understanding the text. **Again and Again** signposts can help the reader understand plot, setting, symbolism, theme, character development, and conflict.

When you notice a recurring word, phrase, image, or event, think about what it means. In this part of *A Long Walk to Water*, a student has underlined an example of Again and Again:

> 5   He ran until he could not run anymore. Then he walked. For hours, until the sun was nearly gone from the sky.
> 6   Other people were walking, too.

Anchor Question
When you notice this signpost, ask: Why might the author keep bringing this up?

What words or images are used repeatedly?	The text repeats words and images related to running and walking.
Why do you think the author repeats these words and images?	The repetition shows something about Salva's character; he runs until he's exhausted, so he begins walking for hours. He refuses to give up.

▶ **Aha Moment** During certain points in a work of fiction, a character may come to a sudden realization that changes his understanding of himself, others, and the world around him.

A character experiencing an **Aha Moment** may:

- suddenly understand something
- discover a way to solve a problem
- reach a broader understanding about life

Aha Moments help further the plot and help develop characters. In this example, an Aha Moment is underlined:

When you see a phrase like one of these, pause to see if it's an **Aha Moment**:

That's when I knew . . .

Finally, I understood . . .

Everything was clear . . .

I realized . . .

All of a sudden . . .

> 3   In the smoke and dust, he couldn't see the school building anymore. He tripped and almost fell. No more looking back; it slowed him down.

Anchor Question
When you notice this signpost, ask: How might this change things?

What realization does Salva have?	He can't look back any more. Looking back slows him down and may cost him his life.
What might this realization reveal about Salva's character?	Salva may have to give up his old life. He may be facing a dramatic change in his life, testing his character.

Notice & Note

ANALYZE & APPLY

from A LONG WALK TO WATER

Novel by **Linda Sue Park**

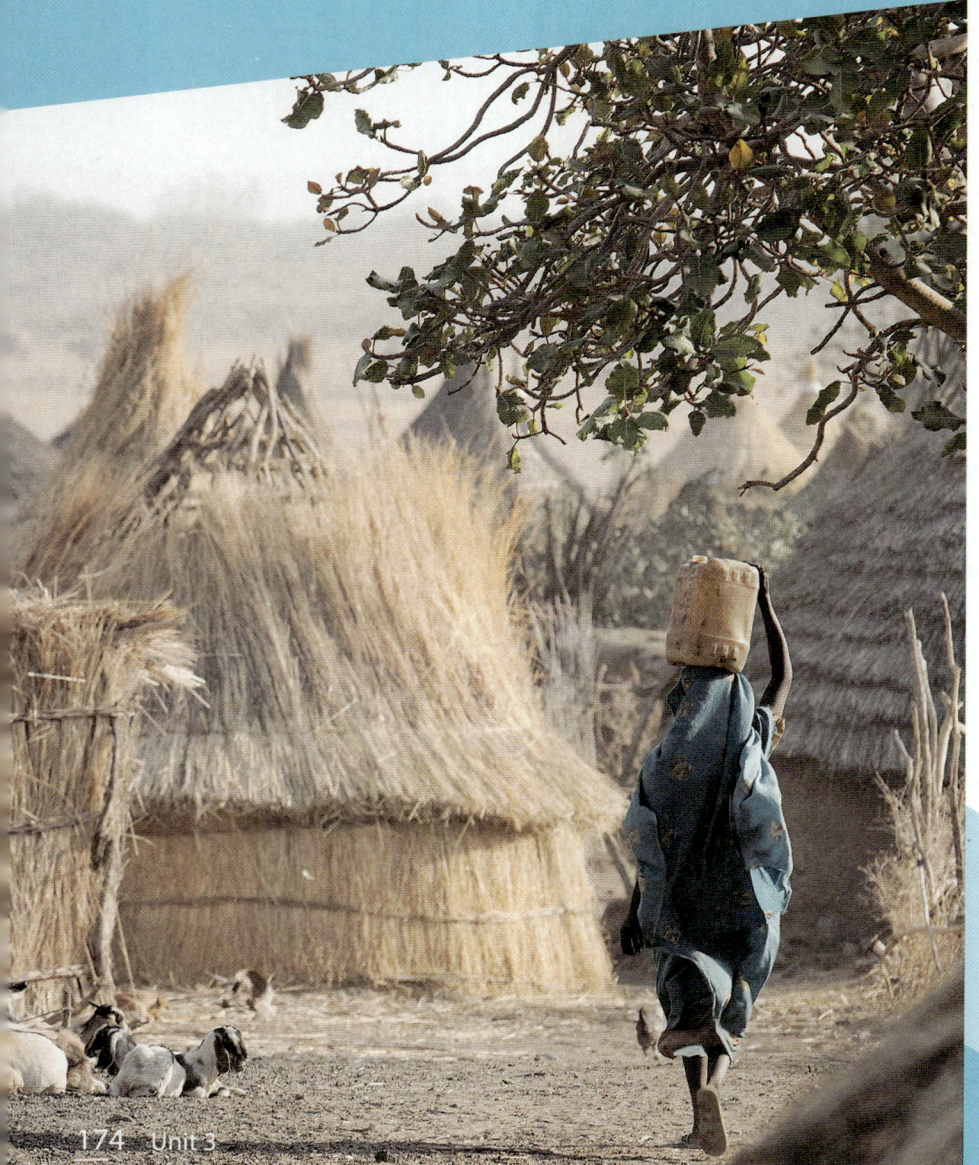

ESSENTIAL QUESTION:

What does it take to be a survivor?

GET READY

QUICK START

How would you feel if you had to leave your home, family, and community without any warning? What might you miss the most? Discuss your thoughts with a partner.

ANALYZE SETTING AND CHARACTER

A **character** is a person, animal, or imaginary creature who takes part in the action of a work of literature. In realistic fiction, characters—like real people—have personalities and motivations; they experience life-changing events. The **setting,** or the time and place in which the action occurs, influences the development of the characters. Elements of setting include geographic location, historical period, season, time of day, and culture.

- To understand historical setting, find the setting's geographic location on a map, and read to learn about the time period.
- To analyze character, annotate and compare passages that describe the character's thoughts or actions at the beginning, middle, and end of the work.
- To understand how setting affects character, note how characters respond to historical and cultural events.

GENRE ELEMENTS: HISTORICAL FICTION

- has the basic features of fiction, including plot, characters, conflict, setting, and theme
- is set in the past and includes real places and real events of historical importance
- may be based on actual people who lived during the work's historical and cultural setting and who dealt with the setting's challenges in remarkable ways

MONITOR COMPREHENSION

Readers sometimes finish a section of text without fully understanding it. Perhaps your attention drifted while reading, or you hurried through a key passage too quickly. When you **monitor comprehension,** you use different strategies to check your understanding as you read. If you are confused after reading a passage, use any of the techniques below to help you understand the text.

MONITORING STRATEGY	BENEFIT
Question	Develop and ask questions as you read to clarify understanding.
Connect	Use background knowledge to connect with the text, including any background information provided with the selection.
Reread	Reread passages you don't understand—even out loud or extra slowly—to aid comprehension.
Annotate	Mark specific words that will help you understand plot, conflict, character development, and other elements of fiction.

A Long Walk to Water

GET READY

CRITICAL VOCABULARY

veer   hesitate   collapse   scurry   shoulder

See which Critical Vocabulary words you already know. Complete each sentence in a way that shows the meaning of the vocabulary word.

1. A building might **collapse** if _____.
2. Someone might **hesitate** to join a swim team because _____.
3. A mouse may **scurry** when _____.
4. When hiking, travelers might **shoulder** _____.
5. If you were riding a bicycle that began to **veer,** you might _____.

LANGUAGE CONVENTIONS

Prepositions and Prepositional Phrases A **preposition** is a word that relates one word to another word. The words *around, at, by, for, from, in, of, over, to, under,* and *with* are examples of prepositions. Prepositions are useful for expressing where, when, and how words and ideas relate to one another.

> Salva hestitated <u>for</u> a moment.
> Salva took a few steps <u>toward</u> the men.

A **prepositional phrase** consists of a preposition, its object, and any modifiers of the object.

> The soldier was holding the gun <u>with only one hand</u>.

As you read, look for prepositions and prepositional phrases.

ANNOTATION MODEL   **NOTICE & NOTE**

As you read, notice and note signposts, including **Tough Questions, Again and Again,** and **Aha Moments.** In the model, you can see how one reader responds to *A Long Walk to Water.*

---

1   *BOOM!*

2   Salva turned and looked. Behind him, <u>a huge black cloud of smoke rose</u>. <u>Flames darted out of its base.</u> Overhead, <u>a jet plane veered</u> away like a sleek evil bird.

3   In the <u>smoke and dust</u>, he couldn't see the school building anymore.

Where is the sound coming from?

Repeated images describe an explosion. The details are related to violence, and the jet suggests that this may be a wartime bombing.

BACKGROUND

Linda Sue Park (b. 1960) has written several books for young people. *A Long Walk to Water* is historical fiction based on the story of Salva Dut, who fled his home in Sudan in 1985 during a civil war. He, like many boys, was separated from his family. Eventually, he found refuge in the United States and later returned to what is now the country of South Sudan. To aid the people of his homeland, he formed an organization that drills wells, which provide clean water.

from A LONG WALK TO WATER
Novel by Linda Sue Park

SETTING A PURPOSE

War and violence can lead to anxiety, panic, and confusion. As you read, consider how the main character, Salva, is affected by the wartime setting.

Notice & Note

Use the side margins to notice and note signposts in the text.

1   B*OOM!*

2   Salva turned and looked. Behind him, a huge black cloud of smoke rose. Flames darted out of its base. Overhead, a jet plane **veered** away like a sleek evil bird.

3   In the smoke and dust, he couldn't see the school building anymore. He tripped and almost fell. No more looking back; it slowed him down.

4   Salva lowered his head and ran.

5   He ran until he could not run anymore. Then he walked. For hours, until the sun was nearly gone from the sky.

6   Other people were walking, too. There were so many of them that they couldn't all be from the school village; they must have come from the whole area.

veer
(vîr) *v.* Something that can *veer* will swerve, or suddenly change course or direction.

A Long Walk to Water   177

NOTICE & NOTE

TOUGH QUESTIONS

Notice & Note: In paragraph 7, Salva seems concerned and confused. Mark the questions Salva asks.

Analyze: What do Salva's questions tell you about his internal conflict?

7   As Salva walked, the same thoughts kept going through his head in rhythm with his steps. *Where are we going? Where is my family? When will I see them again?*

8   The people stopped walking when it grew too dark to see the path. At first, everyone stood around uncertainly, speaking in tense whispers or silent with fear.

Map of Sudan, 1985

178   Unit 3

NOTICE & NOTE

9   Then some of the men gathered and talked for a few moments. One of them called out, "Villages—group yourselves by villages. You will find someone you know."

10 Salva wandered around until he heard the words "Loun-Ariik! The village of Loun-Ariik, here!"

11 Relief flooded through him. That was his village! He hurried toward the sound of the voice.

12 A dozen or so people stood in a loose group at the side of the road. Salva scanned their faces. There was no one from his family. He recognized a few people—a woman with a baby, two men, a teenage girl—but no one he knew well. Still, it was comforting to see them.

13 They spent the night right there by the road, the men taking shifts to keep watch.[1] The next morning, they began walking again. Salva stayed in the midst of the crowd with the other villagers from Loun-Ariik.

14 In the early afternoon, he saw a large group of soldiers up ahead.

---

[1] **taking shifts to keep watch:** the men take turns watching for dangerous wild animals, including lions, as well as dangerous people, such as fighters with weapons.

ANALYZE SETTING AND CHARACTER

Annotate: Circle the words in paragraphs 9–11 related to setting, and underline words that describe Salva's thoughts and actions.

Connect: Think about how it might feel to be lost. How does Salva's reaction to the setting help you understand his character?

LANGUAGE CONVENTIONS

In paragraph 13, circle the prepositions and underline the prepositional phrases in the sentence that begins, "Salva stayed. . . ." How do these prepositions and prepositional phrases help you understand what is happening?

A Long Walk to Water   179

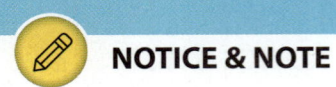 **NOTICE & NOTE**

15   Word passed through the crowd: "It's the rebels." The rebels—those who were fighting against the government.[2]

16   Salva passed several rebel soldiers waiting by the side of the road. Each of them held a big gun. Their guns were not pointed at the crowd, but even so, the soldiers seemed fierce and watchful. Some of the rebels then joined the back of the line; now the villagers were surrounded.

17   *What are they going to do to us? Where is my family?*

AGAIN AND AGAIN

Notice & Note: In paragraph 17, mark each question. Which question has Salva asked before?

Evaluate: Why does the author repeat Salva's question? Is it reasonable for Salva to ask this at this point of the novel? Why?

hesitate
(hĕz´ĭ-tāt´) *v.* To *hesitate* is to pause or wait in uncertainty.

18   Late in the day, the villagers arrived at the rebel camp. The soldiers ordered them to separate into two groups—men in one group, women and children and the elderly in the other. Teenage boys, it seemed, were considered men, for boys who looked to be only a few years older than Salva were joining the men's group.

19   Salva **hesitated** for a moment. He was only eleven, but he was the son of an important family. He was Salva Mawien Dut Ariik, from the village named for his grandfather. His father always told him to act like a man—to follow the example of his older brothers and, in turn, set a good example for Kuol.[3]

20   Salva took a few steps toward the men.

21   "Hey!"

22   A soldier approached Salva and raised his gun.

23   Salva froze. All he could see was the gun's huge barrel, black and gleaming, as it moved toward his face.

24   The end of the barrel touched his chin.

25   Salva felt his knees turn to water. He closed his eyes.

26   *If I die now, I will never see my family again.*

27   Somehow, this thought strengthened him enough to keep him from **collapsing** in terror.

collapse
(kə-lăps´) *v.* When something is said to *collapse*, it falls down.

28   He took a deep breath and opened his eyes.

29   The soldier was holding the gun with only one hand. He was not *aiming* it; he was using it to lift Salva's chin so he could get a better look at his face.

30   "Over there," the soldier said. He moved the gun and pointed it toward the group of women and children.

---

[2] **those who were fighting against the government:** in Sudan's civil war, government soldiers fought against opposition groups who wanted to seize control of territory and take over the Sudanese government.
[3] **Kuol:** Salva's younger brother.

31   "You are not a man yet. Don't be in such a hurry!" He laughed and clapped Salva on the shoulder.

32   Salva **scurried** over to the women's side.

33   The next morning, the rebels moved on from the camp. The village men were forced to carry supplies: guns and mortars, shells, radio equipment.[4] Salva watched as one man protested that he did not want to go with the rebels. A soldier hit him in the face with the butt of a gun.[5] The man fell to the ground, bleeding.

34   After that, no one objected. The men **shouldered** the heavy equipment and left the camp.

scurry
(skûr´ē) *v.* Something that can *scurry* will run with quick, light steps.

MONITOR COMPREHENSION
Annotate: Mark the words in paragraph 33 related to war and violence.

Analyze: Use background knowledge and information provided in the footnotes to help you understand the setting. How would you describe the setting to a friend?

shoulder
(shōl´dər) *v.* To *shoulder* something is to carry it on one's shoulders.

[4] **guns and mortars, shells, radio equipment:** mortars are large, portable weapons that fire explosive bombs, called *shells*; radio equipment is used to communicate, often in remote areas.

[5] **butt of a gun:** the thicker end of a gun, which is held in the hand, or in the case of a rifle, held up against the shoulder while firing.

NOTICE & NOTE

35   Everyone else began walking again. They went in the opposite direction from the rebels, for wherever the rebels went, there was sure to be fighting.

36   Salva stayed with the group from Loun-Ariik. It was smaller now, without the men. And except for the infant, Salva was the only child.

37   That evening they found a barn in which to spend the night. Salva tossed restlessly in the itchy hay.

38   *Where are we going? Where is my family? When will I see them again?*

39   It took him a long time to fall asleep.

AHA MOMENT

Notice & Note: What has Salva realized in paragraphs 40–46? Mark the words that show what he suddenly realizes.

Draw Conclusions: Why might Salva's fellow villagers have done this?

40   Even before he was fully awake, Salva could feel that something was wrong. He lay very still with his eyes closed, trying to sense what it might be.

41   Finally, he sat up and opened his eyes.

42   No one else was in the barn.

43   Salva stood so quickly that for a moment he felt dizzy. He rushed to the door and looked out.

44   Nobody. Nothing.

45   They had left him.

46   He was alone.

CHECK YOUR UNDERSTANDING

Answer these questions before moving on to the **Analyze the Text** section on the following page.

1. Which of the following is not true about the selection?

    A Salva is a rebel who battles the Sudanese government.

    B The setting is Sudan during a civil war in 1985.

    C Salva is fleeing from wartime violence.

    D Many people have left their villages.

2. In paragraph 4, Salva "lowered his head and ran" because —

    F he was late and he had to get home

    G it was beginning to thunderstorm

    H he heard and saw what seemed to be an explosion

    J he heard that a famous storyteller was coming to his village

3. When Salva awakens at the end of the selection he —

    A realizes he is abandoned and alone

    B discovers the other villagers have taken his food

    C realizes that his fear and confusion were part of a dream

    D smells breakfast cooking

RESPOND

ANALYZE THE TEXT

Support your responses with evidence from the text. **NOTEBOOK**

1. **Interpret** How does the background information that precedes the selection help you understand what is happening in the selection's opening scene (paragraphs 1–4)?

2. **Evaluate** Review paragraphs 37–39. Identify details that describe the setting. How might Salva's surroundings affect his thoughts and actions?

3. **Draw Conclusions** Review paragraphs 31–34. What might Salva have felt after he went to the women's side? How might Salva's feelings have changed after witnessing what happened to the man who did not want to go with the rebels? Explain.

4. **Predict** Review paragraph 40 to the end of the excerpt. What questions can you ask to monitor your comprehension and help you predict what will happen next?

5. **Notice & Note** Review paragraphs 3–4. What does the phrase *No more looking back* mean? How might this realization affect Salva as the novel continues?

RESEARCH

RESEARCH TIP
Reputable websites often link to other reliable sites offering more information on the subject. Following links such as these can offer more in-depth information and insights.

A Long Walk to Water is based on the true story of a Sudanese boy named Salva Dut. As an adult, Dut founded the organization Water for South Sudan which drills wells to supply water to the people of his homeland. Use multiple sources to conduct your own research on Water for South Sudan. Use the chart to record what the organization does, how it raises money, what challenges it faces, and how well it has succeeded.

WATER FOR SOUTH SUDAN	
Research Question	Answer/Source

Connect Salva Dut's difficult journey inspired him to work to improve and transform the lives of others. With a small group, discuss any moments in *A Long Walk to Water* that help you understand the real-life Salva Dut who you learned about in your research.

RESPOND

CREATE AND DISCUSS

Write an Informational Essay Write an essay explaining how the setting of *A Long Walk to Water* shapes Salva's experience and character.

- ❑ Review the selection's background information, graphics, and footnotes about Sudan.
- ❑ Review annotations you made during reading that relate to setting and character, and find a cause-and-effect relationship between the novel's setting and Salva's character.
- ❑ As you write, use prepositions and prepositional phrases to help express relationships between ideas.
- ❑ Make sure your essay is guided by a thesis statement or a clear controlling idea, and be sure to support your thesis with explicit and implicit evidence from the text.

Discuss with a Small Group Have a discussion about the challenges Salva faces and what character traits would be required to meet these challenges.

- ❑ As a group, review the text and make a list of each challenge. Review the ending and make predictions about the challenges Salva may face later.
- ❑ Have group members volunteer character traits, such as independence, perseverance, or kindness, that would be helpful in meeting each challenge.
- ❑ Draw upon personal experience and ideas in other texts to inform your thinking and responses.

Go to the **Writing Studio** for more on writing informative texts.

Go to the **Speaking and Listening Studio** for help with having a group discussion.

GROUP WORK CHECKLIST

Follow these guidelines when working in groups:

- ❑ Listen actively.
- ❑ Ask specific questions.
- ❑ Respond respectfully.
- ❑ Consider all ideas.
- ❑ Take notes about important points.
- ❑ Adjust your responses as new evidence is discovered.

RESPOND TO THE ESSENTIAL QUESTION

 What does it take to be a survivor?

Gather Information Review your annotations and notes on *A Long Walk to Water*. Then, add relevant details to your Response Log. As you determine which information to include, think about:

- the significant challenges Salva faces
- how characters respond to the setting
- what Salva must do to survive

At the end of the unit, use your notes to write a nonfiction narrative.

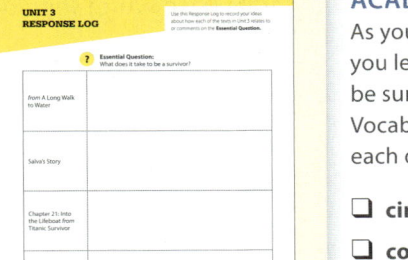

ACADEMIC VOCABULARY

As you write and discuss what you learned from the selection, be sure to use the Academic Vocabulary words. Check off each of the words that you use.

- ❑ circumstance
- ❑ constraint
- ❑ impact
- ❑ injure
- ❑ significant

A Long Walk to Water

RESPOND

WORD BANK
veer
hesitate
collapse
scurry
shoulder

CRITICAL VOCABULARY

Practice and Apply Choose the letter of the better answer to each question.

1. Which of the following is an example of **collapse**?
   a. a falling tower   b. a stack of paper

2. Which of the following would cause most people to **hesitate**?
   a. skydiving   b. knitting

3. Which of the following is an example of **scurry**?
   a. a brown bear sitting down   b. a running squirrel

4. Which of the following would someone **shoulder**?
   a. a heavy package   b. a baseball

5. Which of the following is an example of **veer**?
   a. a car quickly changing direction   b. a thin coat of paint

VOCABULARY STRATEGY: Vocabulary Resources

 Go to the **Vocabulary Studio** for more on vocabulary resources.

A print or online dictionary is a useful tool for determining the meaning of a word. Many words have multiple meanings, and some words can be used as different parts of speech. A dictionary includes every meaning of a word, as well as its syllabication (how it breaks into syllables), pronunciation, part of speech, and word origin.

Practice and Apply Look up *shouldered* in a dictionary by searching for its base word, *shoulder,* and then answer the questions.

1. What parts of speech are listed for *shoulder?*
   _____

2. Review the use of *shouldered* in paragraph 34. According to its context and suffix and the dictionary, what part of speech is *shouldered?*
   _____

3. How many syllables do *shoulder* and *shouldered* have?
   _____

4. What is the word origin and dictionary meaning of *shoulder* as it is used in the selection?
   _____

RESPOND

LANGUAGE CONVENTIONS:
Prepositions and Prepositional Phrases

Writers use **prepositions** and **prepositional phrases** to express where, when, and how words and ideas are related. When inserting prepositional phrases between a subject and a verb, be sure to correctly identify the subject and verb so that they agree. If the sentence has a singular subject, it should have a singular verb. If the sentence has a plural subject, it should have a plural verb.

In the following sentence, *the villagers* is the subject, and *in the text* is a prepositional phrase. The subject is plural, so the verb must also be plural.

The villagers in the text seems/seem frightened.

The verb *to be* presents special problems in agreement. This verb does not follow the usual patterns. Study the sentence below to determine which form of *to be* is correct. First identify the subject of the sentence, and then mark the correct verb.

Each of the students is/are required to attend.

Each is the subject of the sentence, while *of the students* is a prepositional phrase that modifies *each*. Because *each* is singular, use *is*, the singular form of the verb *to be*.

Practice and Apply Write your own sentences about Salva's response when he discovers that he has been left alone. Use prepositions and prepositional phrases. When you have finished writing, compare your use of prepositions and prepositional phrases with a partner. Check your partner's work for subject-verb agreement.

Go to the **Grammar Studio** for more on prepositions and prepositional phrases.

ANALYZE & APPLY

MEDIA

SALVA'S STORY

Documentary by **POVRoseMedia**

ESSENTIAL QUESTION:

What does it take to be a survivor?

QUICK START

Why might someone choose to return to a place where he or she had once undergone great suffering? Discuss your ideas with a partner.

ANALYZE CHARACTERISTICS OF DIGITAL TEXT

A **documentary** is a nonfiction film or video that tells about important people, historic places, or significant events. A documentary's purpose is often to inform or explain. Filmmakers gather information about a topic and present the material in an engaging way. They do this by incorporating some of the following features in their work.

GENRE ELEMENTS: DOCUMENTARY
- highlights a person, place, event, or cause
- targets a specific audience
- is created for a specific purpose
- includes TV broadcasts, videos, newspapers, magazines, and the Internet

FEATURE OF A DOCUMENTARY	HOW THE FEATURE MIGHT BE USED
animated graphics, such as maps and charts	to provide visual support for complex ideas
voice-over narration, or the voice of an unseen speaker	to summarize key scenes or events; to provide background information
primary sources, such as recordings from an event	to show real-life experiences and historical details
footage, such as reenactments or film clips	to bring a topic to life

188 Unit 3

GET READY

BACKGROUND

During a long and brutal civil war in Sudan, thousands of children fled on foot to neighboring countries. Along the way, many died. Salva Dut was one of the children, called the Lost Boys, who survived. For almost six years, he lived in a refugee camp with nearly 100,000 other refugees. In 1996, he became one of the first Lost Boys to resettle in the United States. Dut founded the organization Water for South Sudan. The group drills wells and provides clean water to villages in South Sudan. The book A Long Walk to Water *is based on Salva Dut's life story.*

SETTING A PURPOSE

As you view the short documentary, consider how the information about Salva Dut is presented. Notice how different features help to engage the viewer.

As needed, pause the video to make notes about what impresses you or ideas you might want to talk about later. Replay or rewind so that you can clarify anything you do not understand.

Salva's Story

RESPOND

ANALYZE MEDIA

Support your responses with evidence from the video. **NOTEBOOK**

1. **Summarize** Describe the purpose of the voice-over narration in *Salva's Story*.

2. **Critique** Think about the purpose of the map of Sudan, Ethiopia, and Kenya. Do you think the graphic was effective? Why or why not?

3. **Analyze** Review the scenes that show Salva Dut in his former village. What effect is achieved by showing footage of him in that environment?

4. **Interpret** Why do you think the filmmakers chose to use footage depicting people walking through a desert and children clamoring for food?

5. **Connect** Why did Dut tell the filmmakers the story of visiting his father when he was ill? How did that experience shape decisions Dut made afterward?

RESEARCH

RESEARCH TIP
When you research a specific group of people, consider visiting sites of established organizations that support or represent that group. The International Rescue Committee and UNICEF are two organizations that work with the Lost Boys of Sudan.

The video provides a brief explanation about who the Lost Boys of Sudan are and what they experienced. Consider other information you would like to know about the Lost Boys. Identify one research question that you would like to have answered, and then use reputable sources to find the answer. Use more than one source.

RESEARCH QUESTION	NOTES AND SOURCES

Extend Consider what you learned in your research. Would *Salva's Story* be improved if it included this information? Why or why not? If you were one of the filmmakers, which features or techniques might you use to incorporate the information?

RESPOND

CREATE AND PRESENT

Write a Summary Write a summary of the main events described in *Salva's Story*.

- ❏ Review *Salva's Story* and take notes on the events described in the video. Make sure to jot down dates when they are provided.
- ❏ If necessary, review the video several times to make sure your notes are accurate.
- ❏ Create a simple timeline to help you organize the main events in chronological order—the order in which they occurred.
- ❏ Write your summary using your own words. To create a concise summary, only include the main events described in the video.
- ❏ Refer to the timeline you created as you write.

Go to the **Writing Studio: Summarizing, Paraphrasing, and Quoting** in the **Writing Studio** for more on writing a summary.

Analyze and Evaluate the Video With a small group, closely examine the effectiveness of the features in *Salva's Story*.

- ❏ As a group, make a chart listing the features used in the video, such as voice-over narration and footage.
- ❏ Review the video on your own. Then, using a rating system from 1 to 5, score the effectiveness of each feature.
- ❏ Gather as a group again and discuss your evaluations. Share the reasons for the scores that you gave. Consider group members' positions that are different from your own, and adjust your scores as appropriate.

Go to **Participating in Collaborative Discussions** in the **Speaking and Listening Studio** for help with having a small group discussion.

GROUP WORK CHECKLIST

- ❏ Listen actively.
- ❏ Ask specific questions.
- ❏ Respond respectfully.
- ❏ Consider group members' suggestions.
- ❏ Take notes about important points.
- ❏ Use the Academic Vocabulary words in your discussion.
  - ❏ **circumstance**
  - ❏ **constraint**
  - ❏ **impact**
  - ❏ **injure**
  - ❏ **significant**

RESPOND TO THE ESSENTIAL QUESTION

 What does it take to be a survivor?

Gather Information Review your notes on *Salva's Story*. Then, add relevant details to your Response Log. As you determine which information to include, think about what it takes to be a survivor.

At the end of the unit, use your notes to write a nonfiction narrative.

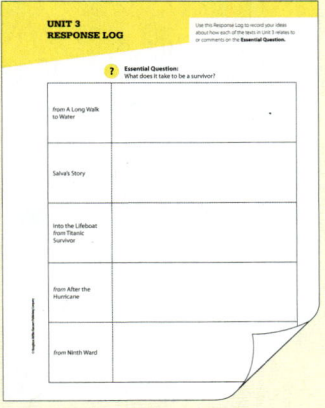

Salva's Story 191

ANALYZE & APPLY

INTO THE LIFEBOAT
from **TITANIC SURVIVOR**

Memoir by **Violet Jessop**

? ESSENTIAL QUESTION:

What does it take to be a survivor?

GET READY

QUICK START

What do you know about the *Titanic?* Where did you get your information about the ship? Discuss your answers with a partner.

EXPLAIN AUTHOR'S PURPOSE AND MESSAGE

To explain the **author's purpose,** begin by asking why the author wrote the text. In the case of a memoir, the genre offers clues to the author's purpose. Memoirs are first-person accounts of historical events or moments in a person's life that are especially meaningful. The purpose is to recreate a moment in the author's own experience and enable the reader to understand that moment's significance.

The **author's message** is what the author wants you to take away—an insight, a personal connection, a deeper understanding. To explain the author's message within a text, think about the following:

- What does the author want the reader to feel?
- What main idea or theme is the author presenting?

To see if your ideas about the author's purpose and message are on the right track, find evidence in the text. Text evidence supports your ideas and refines your understanding of the author's purpose and message.

CREATE MENTAL IMAGES

Authors choose words that create mental images to establish a text's setting, action, and characters. Vivid descriptions help readers "see" pictures in their minds. Creating mental images as you read will help you understand the author's purpose and message as well as identify the evidence to support your ideas. Look at the examples below.

GENRE ELEMENTS: MEMOIR

- is a form of autobiographical writing
- includes the writer's personal experiences and observations of significant events or people
- often has an informal or intimate tone
- presents insights into the impact of historical events on people's lives

DESCRIPTIVE LANGUAGE	MENTAL IMAGE
A tiny breeze, the first we had felt on this calm night, blew an icy blast across my face. . . .	The words *breeze* and *calm* are opposites of *icy blast*, creating tension and a sense of sudden danger.
. . . as the ship seemed to right herself like a hurt animal with a broken back.	Similes are a kind of comparison. This simile compares the ship to an injured animal. Readers can imagine a creature, too injured to survive, that nevertheless fights to live.

Into the Lifeboat 193

GET READY

CRITICAL VOCABULARY

| reluctance | illuminate | unrestrainedly |
| reassure | fascinate | agonizing |

See which Critical Vocabulary words you know by choosing the better answer.

1. If you do something with **reluctance,** you are _____.
   a. unwilling   b. excited

2. If you are _____, you want someone to **reassure** you.
   a. unsure   b. confident

3. When street lights **illuminate** a highway, they _____ the road.
   a. hide   b. brighten

4. If books **fascinate** you, they _____ you.
   a. interest   b. bore

5. If a person behaves **unrestrainedly,** he or she acts _____.
   a. without control   b. with interest

6. If you are **agonizing** about a test, you are _____ about it.
   a. really confident   b. extremely worried

LANGUAGE CONVENTIONS

Commas In this lesson, you will learn about the correct use of commas in complex sentences, transitions, and introductory elements. Commas set dependent clauses and phrases off so that a reader can quickly grasp a sentence's meaning. The following example from the text shows comma use in a complex sentence:

Fascinated, my eyes never left the ship, as if by looking I could keep her afloat.

As you read the selection, note the author's use of commas.

ANNOTATION MODEL

NOTICE & NOTE

As you read, note the author's word choices and imagery. In the model, you can see one reader's notes about mental images.

1 You could almost imagine this a scene of (busily curious) people (with not very much to do.) True, there were officers and men (briskly getting lifeboats) ready to lower, their (tense faces) strangely in contrast to the (well ordered groups) wandering about.

These words give me a mental image of people trying not to panic.

194 Unit 3

BACKGROUND

Violet Jessop *(1887–1971) was a stewardess on board the* Titanic *for its first and only voyage in 1912. Because of its state-of-the-art construction, the luxurious* Titanic *was considered practically unsinkable—so it didn't carry enough lifeboats for all of its passengers. When the ship sank, Jessop, along with most of the women and children, was rescued on one of the lifeboats. Despite surviving two other disasters aboard ships, she continued to work aboard them until 1950.*

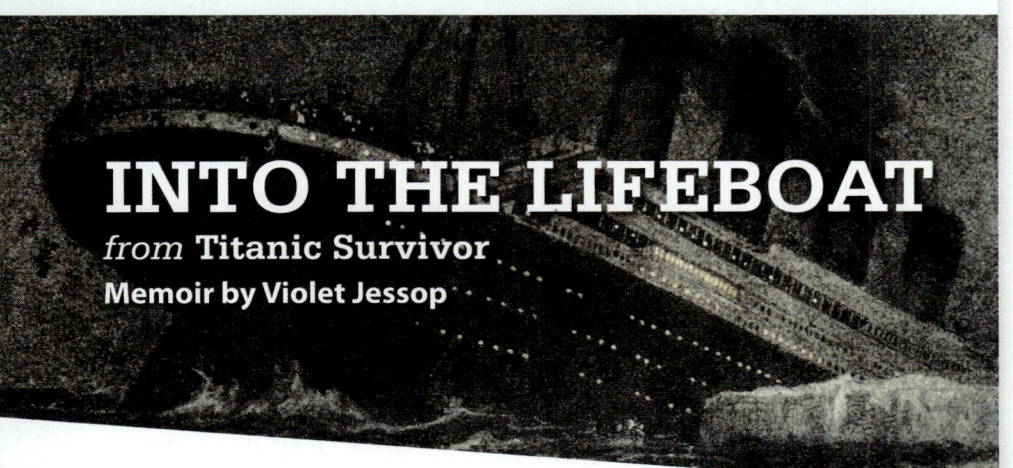

INTO THE LIFEBOAT
from Titanic Survivor
Memoir by Violet Jessop

SETTING A PURPOSE

As you read, note the author's word choice and use of imagery. Be aware of the mental images they create in your mind. Think about how these images enrich the experience of reading this selection.

Notice & Note

Use the side margins to notice and note signposts in the text.

1   You could almost imagine this a scene of busily curious people with not very much to do. True, there were officers and men briskly getting lifeboats ready to lower, their tense faces strangely in contrast to the well ordered groups wandering about. I felt chilly without a coat, so I went down again for something to cover my shoulders and picked up a silk eiderdown[1] from the first open cabin I came to. How strange it was to pass all those rooms lit up so brilliantly, their doors open and contents lying around in disorder. Jewels sparkled on dressing tables and a pair of silver slippers were lying just where they had been kicked off.

---

[1] **silk eiderdown** (sĭlk ī´dər-doun´): a quilt stuffed with the down, or feathers, of the eider duck; this luxurious item would have been considered inappropriate for a stewardess to wear while at work.

Into the Lifeboat   195

NOTICE & NOTE

CONTRASTS AND CONTRADICTIONS

Notice & Note: What surprises Jessop in paragraph 3? Mark something unexpected.

Infer: What could be Jessop's purpose for including this observation?

EXPLAIN AUTHOR'S PURPOSE

Annotate: Reread paragraphs 4–5. Mark who was allowed to get into the lifeboats first.

Evaluate: Why would this be an important point for the author to present early in the text?

reluctance
(rĭ-lŭk′təns) *n.* Showing *reluctance* to do something means you are unwilling.

reassure
(rē′ə-shoŏr′) *v.* To *reassure* someone is to give comfort or confidence to that person.

2   I gathered my eiderdown and went up. On my way **I passed a group of officers, still in their mess jackets,[2] hands in pockets, chatting quietly on the companion square as men do who are waiting for something. They smiled at me and I waved back.**

3   As I turned I ran into Jock, the bandleader and his crowd with their instruments. "Funny, they must be going to play," thought I, and at this late hour! Jock smiled in passing, looking rather pale for him, remarking, "Just going to give them a tune to cheer things up a bit," and passed on. Presently the strains of the band reached me faintly as I stood on deck watching a young woman excitedly remonstrating[3] with an embarrassed young officer. He wanted her to get into the lifeboat he was trying to fill but she refused to go without her father.

4   "He must wait," responded the officer, "till the decks are cleared of women and children."

5   Out on deck, the first arguments started over who would and who wouldn't go into the boats which appeared to be suspended miles above the yawning blackness below.

6   Nobody was anxious to move; *Titanic* seemed so steady. To justify their **reluctance**, some pointed to a light on the horizon: another ship's lights![4] People were **reassured,** content to bide their time.[5]

---

[2] **mess jacket:** a man's short, close-fitting jacket worn by the military or as part of a uniform for officers, waiters, etc.

[3] **remonstrating** (rĭ-mŏn′strāt′ĭng): to say or plead in protest or objection.

[4] **another ship's lights:** two ships were nearby, the *Carpathia* and the *Californian*; the *Carpathia* was more than 50 miles away, and the *Californian* was about 20 miles away.

[5] **bide their time:** to wait in a patient way for further developments.

7   One boat was already being lowered with very few people in it. When this was pointed out as a shining example for backward souls by the officer near me, he got a rather alarming response as the crowd surged forward to embark. The boat was lowered very full, almost too full this time; and so on. Always, some held back in need of coaxing while a few were too eager.

8   A steward stood waiting with his back to the bulkhead,[6] hands in his pockets. It struck me forcibly as the first time I had ever seen a steward stand thus amid a group of distinguished guests.

9   A woman standing near me gave an approving glance as John Jacob Astor handed his wife into a boat, waving encouragingly to her as he stepped back into an ever-increasing crowd of men.

10   Ann Turnbull,[7] still silent and unmoved, dragged a little behind me. I suggested we keep together and we stood awhile to watch. There was nothing else we could do. Dimly I heard a shot.

11   Glancing forward I caught my breath as a white rocket shot up,[8] then another. Distress rockets! They went very high with great noise. The lights on the horizon seemed to come nearer. That cheered up the group about us, who had slowly started to fill a boat. Young officers urged them to greater speed, showing unlimited patience, I thought. Another rocket went up into the night.

12   A few women near me started to cry loudly when they realized a parting had to take place, their husbands standing silently by. They were Poles[9] and could not understand a word of English. Surely a terrible plight, to be among a crowd in such a situation and not be able to understand anything that is being said.

13   Boats were now being lowered more rapidly and a crowd of foreigners was brought up by a steward from the third class. They dashed eagerly as one man over to a boat, almost more than the officer could control. But he regained order and managed to get the boat away. It descended slowly, uncertainly

---

NOTICE & NOTE

CONTRASTS AND CONTRADICTIONS

Notice & Note: In paragraph 7, mark people's contrasting reactions to getting into the lifeboats.

Cause/Effect: What caused these different responses to leaving the *Titanic*?

LANGUAGE CONVENTIONS
Annotate: In paragraphs 10–12, mark commas that set off introductory elements at the beginning of sentences.

CREATE MENTAL IMAGES
Annotate: Mark the author's word choices in paragraph 11 that create mental images.

Connect: How do these images help develop the scene and show the author's feelings about the situation?

---

[6] **bulkhead:** a supporting barrier or wall dividing a ship into compartments that prevents leaks and fires.
[7] **Ann Turnbull:** another stewardess aboard the *Titanic* and a friend to Jessop.
[8] **a white rocket shot up:** a large Roman candle that indicated a ship's identity and condition to other ships; at the time, it was a way to communicate over long distances.
[9] **Poles:** people from Poland.

Into the Lifeboat   197

NOTICE & NOTE

at first, now one end up and then the other; the falls were new and difficult to handle.[10] Some men nearby were throwing things over the side—deck chairs, rafts or any wooden thing lying nearby.

14   Suddenly, the crowd of people beside me parted. A man dashed to the ship's side, and before anyone could stop him, hurled himself into the descending boat. There was a murmur of amazement and disapproval.

15   I turned to say something to Ann. Looking along the length of the ship, I noticed the forward part of her was lower now, much lower! For a fraction of a second, my heart stood still, as is often the case when faith, hitherto unshaken faith, gets its first setback.

16   One of the mailmen from our sorting office joined us. His work was finished, he remarked unemotionally. "The mail is floating up to F-deck with the water," he told us.

17   I tried not to hear what he said, not wanting to believe what he accepted so stoically.[11] Instead, I listened to the faint sounds of music from Jock's men. They were playing *Nearer My God to Thee.*[12]

18   My arm was suddenly jerked and I turned to see young Mason who had been busy filling a boat. His face looked weary and tired, but he gave a bright smile as he ordered my group into the boat, calling out "Good luck!" as we stepped in, helped by his willing, guiding hand. I nearly fell over the tackle and oars[13] as I tried to assist Ann in beside me. She was suffering with her feet, I could see, and found her lifebelt got in the way of moving freely.

19   Before I could do anything, young Mason hailed me and held up something, calling as he prepared to throw it, "Look after this, will you?" and I reached out to receive somebody's forgotten baby in my arms.

20   It started to whimper as I pressed it to me, the hard cork surface of the lifebelt being anything but a comfort, poor mite. The boat was full now, full of people with dull, inquiring faces. I spoke to one woman but she shook her head, not understanding a word I said.

EXPLAIN AUTHOR'S MESSAGE

Annotate: Mark details in paragraphs 19–23 related to the baby Jessop holds in the lifeboat.

Explain: What message is conveyed through the use of details about the baby?

---

[10] **the falls were new and difficult to handle:** lifeboat "falls" are the ropes and blocks used with a crane to lower the boat.
[11] **stoically** (stō´ĭk-ə-lē): enduring pain and hardship without showing feelings or complaining.
[12] **playing *Nearer My God to Thee*:** a 19th-century Christian hymn popularly believed to have been played as the *Titanic* sank.
[13] **tackle and oars:** lifeboat equipment and paddles.

198   Unit 3

21   Groaning, the boat descended a fearful distance into that inky blackness beneath, intensified as the lights fell on it occasionally.

22   "Surely it is all a dream," I thought as I looked up the side of the ship, beautifully **illuminated**, each deck alive with lights; the dynamos were on the top deck.[14] I tried to make myself believe it could not be true, all this. I even noticed a few people leaning over the rail, watching in an unconcerned manner; perhaps they too were persuading themselves it was a bad dream!

23   We touched the water with a terrific thud, a bone-cracking thud which started the baby crying in earnest. Somebody in the forepart ordered oars out and we slowly pulled away from

illuminate
(ĭ-lōō´mə-nāt´) v. To *illuminate* means to brighten or give light.

---

[14] **the dynamos were on the top deck:** dynamos were electric generators on the ship; their location helps explain why the lights remained on.

NOTICE & NOTE

the side of the ship. I noticed one of the few men in the boat rowing; he was a fireman who had evidently just come up from the stokehold,[15] his face still black with coal dust and eyes red-rimmed, wearing only a thin singlet[16] to protect him from the icy cold.

fascinate
(făs´ə-nāt´) v. To *fascinate* someone means to capture the interest or attention of that person.

24   **Fascinated,** my eyes never left the ship, as if by looking I could keep her afloat. I reflected that but four days ago I had wished to see her from afar, to be able to admire her under way; now there she was, my *Titanic,* magnificent queen of the ocean, a perfection of man's handiwork, her splendid lines outlined against the night, every light twinkling.

25   I started unconsciously to count the decks by the rows of lights. One, two, three, four, five, six; then again—one, two, three, four, five. I stopped. Surely I had miscounted. I went over them again more carefully, hushing the whimpering baby meanwhile.

26   No, I had made no mistake. There were only five decks now; then I started all over again—only four now. She was getting lower in the water, I could not any longer deny it.

unrestrainedly
(ŭn´rĭ-strā´nĭd-lē) adv. Doing something *unrestrainedly* means doing it without control.

27   As if all could read my mind, the women in the boat started to weep, some silently, some **unrestrainedly.** I closed my eyes and prayed, prayed for one and all but dared not think of anyone in particular. I dared not visualize those people I had just left, warm and alive as I was. I tried to busy myself with the baby, but could not refrain from looking up again. Only three decks now, and still not a list to one side or the other.[17]

28   Desperately, I turned to where that other ship's lights shone on the horizon; surely they should be getting nearer by now. It was such a long, long time since we had first seen their comforting glow. They should be with us by now, taking off those patient waiting people over there. But no, she did not seem nearer, in fact, she seemed further away. Strange!

CREATE MENTAL IMAGES
Annotate: Mark the figurative language in paragraph 29.

Infer: Discuss the mental images invoked by this language.

29   A tiny breeze, the first we had felt on this calm night, blew an icy blast across my face; it felt like a knife in its penetrating coldness. I sat paralyzed with cold and misery, as I watched *Titanic* give a lurch forward. One of the huge funnels toppled off[18] like a cardboard model, falling into the sea with a fearful roar. A few cries came to us across the water, then silence, as the ship seemed to right herself like a hurt animal with a

---

[15] **stokehold:** the area or compartment into which a ship's furnaces or boilers open.
[16] **thin singlet:** a sleeveless, tight-fitting undershirt or athletic shirt.
[17] **not a list to one side or the other:** no tilt of the ship.
[18] **One of the huge funnels toppled off:** a smokestack fell off.

NOTICE & NOTE

broken back. She settled for a few minutes, but one more deck of lighted ports disappeared. Then she went down by the head with a thundering roar of underwater explosions, our proud ship, our beautiful *Titanic* gone to her doom.

30   One awful moment of empty, misty blackness enveloped us in its loneliness, then an unforgettable, **agonizing** cry went up from 1500 despairing throats, a long wail and then silence and our tiny craft tossing about at the mercy of the ice field.

agonizing
(ăg´ə-nīz´ĭng) *adj.* To be in an *agonizing* state means to feel great mental suffering and worry.

CHECK YOUR UNDERSTANDING

Answer these questions before moving on to the **Analyze the Text** section on the following page.

1 The author wrote this text to —

   A express her opinion about a time in history

   B explain exactly why the *Titanic* sank

   C inform readers about how she survived the *Titanic*

   D describe what daily life was like for her on the *Titanic*

2 The author includes information about what others were doing before she got on the lifeboat in order to —

   F describe how everyone was worried about their clothes

   G show how many didn't realize the ship would sink

   H give a specific example of how to get on a lifeboat

   J entertain readers with interesting facts

3 Why does the author describe how she counted the rows of deck lights when she was in the lifeboat?

   A To show how she realized that the ship was truly sinking

   B To prove that she was right in a conversation with another passenger

   C To show that she wanted to soothe the baby she was holding

   D To explain that the deck lights were on as a signal for help

Into the Lifeboat   201

RESPOND

ANALYZE THE TEXT

Support your responses with evidence from the text. **NOTEBOOK**

1. **Analyze** What mental image does the author's choice of words create in the passage "... his face still black with coal dust and eyes red-rimmed, wearing only a thin singlet to protect him from the icy cold" (paragraph 23)?

2. **Compare** Compare the author's use of the phrase "yawning blackness below" in paragraph 5 with her reference to "that inky blackness beneath" in paragraph 21. What does the author convey about the characters' feelings by returning to this image?

3. **Evaluate** Consider the author's purpose in paragraph 22. Does she communicate that purpose effectively? Cite evidence to support your claim.

4. **Draw Conclusions** Which characters in the text does the author admire? Cite evidence to support your claim.

5. **Notice & Note** How do the author's thoughts and observations about the *Titanic* in paragraph 24 help readers understand the author's purpose? Cite evidence to support your claim.

RESEARCH TIP
The best search terms are very specific. Think about your topic and come up with key words or phrases. For example, a key phrase could be "names of *Titanic* survivors." Using quotation marks around your search phrase often yields more targeted results.

RESEARCH

Look up *Titanic* survivors other than author Violet Jessop, and choose one to investigate. First, use the chart below to make a list of survivors. Then, choose one person to research further, using multiple sources. What happened to that person at the time of the ship's sinking? What happened afterward?

SURVIVOR'S NAME	AGE, GENDER	NOTES

Connect With a small group, discuss the survivor you researched. Then, learn about the survivors others researched. Are there any similarities in the way these survivors described their experiences? Synthesize the information you have uncovered in your research.

RESPOND

CREATE AND PRESENT

Write a Friendly Letter Write a letter to a friend describing a crowded or disorganized situation that you've seen or experienced recently. It could be at a sports event, in the cafeteria, on the bus, or another place. Follow the instructions and format below to compose your letter.

❏ Use the letter conventions, such as a date at the top, a greeting, and a closing, that are appropriate for a letter to a friend.
❏ Write in the informal, familiar tone you would use with a friend.
❏ Help the reader imagine what it was like to be at the scene by using vivid descriptions to create mental images.
❏ When revising, check for correct use of commas.

Go to **Task, Purpose, and Audience** in the **Writing Studio** for more on tone and style.

CREATE A MULTIMEDIA PRESENTATION

Gather video clips and images to create a short multimedia presentation about Violet Jessop. Decide whether you want your presentation to be a video or a slideshow. Follow these steps:

❏ Review Jessop's story and decide which parts you want to focus on in your presentation.
❏ Search for images and video that you can use.
❏ Develop a clear narrative by making connections between the different media sources you've chosen.
❏ Revise drafts before deciding on a final sequence.
❏ Practice your presentation in order to express your ideas effectively.

Go to **Using Media in a Presentation** in the **Speaking and Listening Studio** for help creating a multimedia presentation.

REVIEW PRESENTATIONS
Evaluate yourself and your classmates using this checklist.
❏ makes eye contact
❏ speaks at an appropriate rate and volume
❏ enunciates clearly
❏ uses natural gestures

RESPOND TO THE ESSENTIAL QUESTION

 What does it take to be a survivor?

Gather Information Review your annotations and notes on "Into the Lifeboat." Add relevant details to your Response Log. Think about the author's:

- detailed observations
- experience as a survivor
- contribution to understanding what it takes to be a survivor

At the end of the unit, use your notes to write a nonfiction narrative.

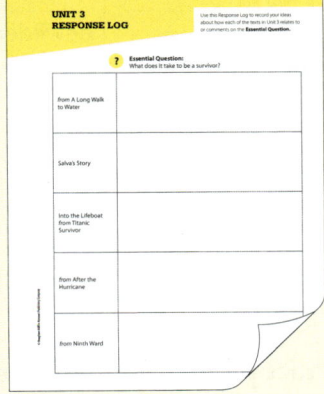

ACADEMIC VOCABULARY
As you write and discuss what you learned from the memoir, be sure to use the Academic Vocabulary words. Check off each of the words that you use.

❏ **circumstance**
❏ **constraint**
❏ **impact**
❏ **injure**
❏ **significant**

Into the Lifeboat 203

RESPOND

WORD BANK
reluctance
reassure
illuminate
fascinate
unrestrainedly
agonizing

CRITICAL VOCABULARY

Practice and Apply Fill in the blank with the correct Critical Vocabulary word from the Word Bank.

1. The sound of crying from the sinking ship was _____ to hear.

2. Volcanoes and tsunamis _____ me.

3. _____ , she splashed paint all over the canvas.

4. The lights _____ the football field for the night game.

5. With _____ , he turned in his incomplete test.

6. The coach takes time to _____ players before a game.

VOCABULARY STRATEGY: Context Clues

 Go to the **Vocabulary Studio** for more on context clues.

To figure out what an unfamiliar word in a text means, look for **context clues.** Context clues are words or phrases that provide hints about the meaning of a word that you don't know. The following are two types of context clues: analogies and definitions.

UNFAMILIAR WORD	CONTEXT CLUE	TYPE OF CLUE	POSSIBLE MEANING
Like a bear cub losing sight of its mother, Laura was **reluctant** to part with her rescuer.	like a bear cub about to lose sight of its mother	analogy—a pair of items that are related in some way	resisting or not wanting something to happen
He felt **confounded,** or bewildered, when he learned that the ship had sunk.	bewildered	definition— words in the text define the unfamiliar word	greatly confused

Once you think you understand a new term, confirm your definition by checking a dictionary.

Practice and Apply Locate the following words in the selection: *hailed* (paragraph 19) and *whimper* (paragraph 20). Mark context clues, and then write definitions for the words. Use a dictionary to check your definitions.

LANGUAGE CONVENTIONS: Commas

Commas help communicate and clarify ideas by grouping words together to form units of meaning in a sentence.

In "Into the Lifeboat" commas are used in the following ways:

- to set off dependent clauses (groups of words that contain a verb and its subject but cannot stand alone) in complex sentences

   A few women near me started to cry loudly when they realized a parting had to take place, their husbands standing silently by.

- to set off transitions that link different words and phrases

   Fascinated, my eyes never left the ship, as if by looking I could keep her afloat.

- to set off introductory elements

   Instead, I listened to the faint sounds of music from Jock's men.

Using commas or other punctuation incorrectly causes confusion and misunderstanding. For example, comma splices incorrectly connect two independent clauses without a conjunction, such as *and* or *but*.

Incorrect: She agonized over leaving the ship, she eventually did go.
Correct: She agonized over leaving the ship, but she eventually did go.

In a run-on sentence, punctuation might be missing altogether.

Incorrect: The steward did not smile he served the musicians.
Correct: The steward did not smile. He served the musicians.

Practice and Apply Write your own sentences about the selection, using commas. Use the examples from "Into the Lifeboat" as models. When you have finished, share your sentences with a partner and explain each comma you used. Then, work together to identify places that a comma might make a sentence clearer. Revise your sentences as needed for clarity.

 RESPOND

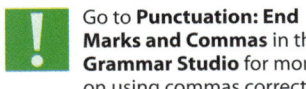 Go to **Punctuation: End Marks and Commas** in the **Grammar Studio** for more on using commas correctly.

COLLABORATE & COMPARE

POEM

from
AFTER THE HURRICANE
by **Rita Williams-Garcia**
pages 209–217

COMPARE ACROSS GENRES

As you read, notice how both texts tell about young peoples' experiences with the same natural disaster, Hurricane Katrina. Look for ideas in the two texts that are similar or related. After you read both selections, you will collaborate with a small group on a final project.

 ESSENTIAL QUESTION:

What does it take to be a survivor?

NOVEL

from
NINTH WARD
by **Jewell Parker Rhodes**
pages 223–227

206   Unit 3

from After the Hurricane

QUICK START

Read the title of the poem. What do you predict it will be about?

ANALYZE THE EFFECTS OF STRUCTURE AND METER

A poem's **form,** or **structure,** is the way its words and lines are arranged on a page. Some forms are also defined by poetic devices, such as rhyme, repetition, and rhythm. Many traditional forms of poetry use regular patterns of stressed and unstressed syllables to establish a regular rhythm, or **meter.** Paying attention to a poem's structure and meter can help you determine a poem's meaning, message, and theme.

Free verse is a form of poetry with no regular patterns of line length, rhyme, or rhythm. In free verse, poets use poetic devices such as repetition, word choice, catalogs (lists of related words and ideas), and alliteration (the repetition of consonant sounds at the beginning of words) to create rhythm and express ideas. Although free verse does not have a set structure, you can understand the organization of a free verse poem by analyzing its basic structural elements.

STRUCTURAL ELEMENT	DEFINITION
line	any text appearing on one line—a sentence, a phrase, or a single word
line break	the place where a line of poetry ends; may be used to add emphasis to certain words and phrases
stanza	a group of two or more lines that form a unit in a poem to express related ideas—as a paragraph functions in prose

To analyze free verse, pay attention to line breaks and groupings of lines, and note the effects these choices have on the sound and feel of the poem. Ask and answer these questions as you read.
- What ideas are expressed in particular lines and stanzas, and in the entire poem?
- How does the use of free verse support the poem's ideas?
- What rhythms are created by repetition or line lengths?
- How do poetic devices work to create structure and organization?
- How do poetic devices contribute to the poem's message or theme?

GET READY

GENRE ELEMENTS: FREE VERSE POETRY
- lacks regular patterns of rhyme, rhythm, or line length
- captures the sounds and rhythms of ordinary speech
- varies line length to call attention to words and ideas
- includes poetic devices—alliteration, figurative language, imagery, and rhythm

GET READY

DESCRIBE AN AUTHOR'S USE OF FIGURATIVE LANGUAGE

Figurative language is language that communicates meanings beyond the literal meanings of words. Authors use figurative language to create effects, to emphasize ideas, and to evoke emotions. Personification, simile, and metaphor are types of figurative language.

Personification is a type of figurative language in which an animal, object, or idea is given human qualities. A **simile** uses the words *like* or *as* to make a comparison between two essentially unlike things. A **metaphor** compares two unlike things without using *like* or *as*. An **extended metaphor** compares two unlike things at length and in several ways.

To identify and analyze figurative language in a poem, ask:
- Does the poet portray animals, objects, or ideas with human characteristics? Why? What is the effect of the personification?
- Does the poet use simile or metaphor to make comparisons? What things are being compared? What message or emotion is the poet trying to convey through the comparison?
- How might the poet's use of figurative language connect to the theme or message of the poem?

ANNOTATION MODEL

NOTICE & NOTE

As you read, note elements of free verse and examples of figurative language. Mark evidence that suggests theme, plus any words that make you pause to think. Here are one reader's notes about "After the Hurricane."

> this could be a disaster movie with
>
> helicopters whipping up sky overhead,
>
> Special Effects brought in to create Lake George
>
> 10   and not the great Mississippi
>
> meeting Lake Ponchartrain.

The disaster movie metaphor gives me a strong image of the scene. The helicopters and special effects make an extended metaphor. I should look up Lake George.

There are 3 references to water. I wonder if they are hints about the theme.

BACKGROUND

Rita Williams-Garcia (b. 1957) draws on her own experiences to write about issues that urban teenagers face today. The following poem focuses on one young person's experience with Hurricane Katrina. On August 29, 2005, Hurricane Katrina ripped through the Gulf Coast, causing massive damage along the coast. In the city of New Orleans, thousands of people were left homeless, almost 2,000 people lost their lives, and hundreds more were missing. Years later, parts of the city have still not been rebuilt.

from AFTER THE HURRICANE
Poem by Rita Williams-Garcia

PREPARE TO COMPARE

As you read, pay attention to the events that take place and how the speaker reacts to them. These observations will help you compare the poem with the selection that follows.

> If toilets flushed,
> if babies slept,
> if faucets ran,
> old bodies didn't die in the sun,
> 5 if none of it were real,
> if we weren't in it,
> this could be a disaster movie with
> helicopters whipping up sky overhead,
> Special Effects brought in to create Lake George
> 10   and not the great Mississippi
>   meeting Lake Pontchartrain.
> Out-of-work waiters would pose as policemen,
> locals as extras paid in box lunches.
> For set design, dump raw sewage, trash everywhere,
> 15 news trucks, patrol cars, army tanks, Humvees.

Notice & Note

Use the side margins to notice and note signposts in the text.

ANALYZE THE EFFECTS OF STRUCTURE AND METER

Annotate: Mark the use of repetition in lines 1–6.

Identify Patterns: How does repetition and line length affect the poem's rhythm?

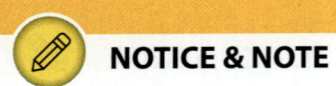

NOTICE & NOTE

If none of it were real,
if we weren't in it,
this could be a big-budget disaster flick
King, Jasper, and I'd rent
20   after band practice
like we did last Tuesday watching *Titanic* on Grandmama's
sofa.
That Jasper could *laaaugh* at all the actors drowning
while the band played—*glub, glub, glub*—to the death.

25   But this ain't that. We're waist high in it.
Camera crews bark, "Big Mike! Get this, over here!"
"Roll tape."
"Got that?"
"Good God!"
30   "Shut it down."
This ain't hardly no picture.
We're not on location.
We're herded. Domed in,
feels like for good
35   unless you caught a bus like Ma
or Jasper's family (save Jasper).
I still want to smash a camera,
break a lens, make them stop shooting.
But King says, "No, Freddie. Gotta show it.
40   Who'd believe it without film?"

AGAIN AND AGAIN

Notice & Note: Why is water so significant to the speaker? Mark words used to describe water in lines 41–65.

Infer: What does the repetition of *water* and the way it is described tell you about its importance to the speaker?

Still no running water, no food, no power, no help.
The world is here but no one's coming.
The Guard[1] is here with rifles pointed.
The Red Cross got their tables set up.
45   Weathermen, anchors,[2] reporters, meteorologists,
a fleet of black Homeland SUVs.
The world is here
but where is the water? The food? The power?
The way to Ma or Jasper's people.
50   They just herd us, split us, film us, guard us.

---

[1] **The Guard:** the National Guard of the United States, units of reserve soldiers that are controlled by each state. The National Guard responds to both the federal (national) and state governments for a variety of emergencies, both in this country and abroad.

[2] **anchors** (ăng´kərs): people who organize and read the news on media newscasts (television, radio, online); they work with a team that includes reporters and camera operators to report the news.

No one said feed us. No one brought water.
The world is here but no one's coming.
Helicopters overhead beat up on our skies.

⁂

Miracle One.
55 King noses around the news guys,
runs back to Jasper and me.
"There's water trucks held up on the highway.
Gallons, girl! Water by the gallons.
Fresh drinking water.
60 Clean shower water.
See that, Freddie. The water company loves us.
Somebody thought to send us water."
Even with our trumpets drowned, King's chest swells.
He booms, "Brass Crew, are you with me?
65 Let's get outta here, bring back some water."

How can I leave TK and Grandmama?
How can I leave, and be happy to leave?
Watch me. Just watch me
high step on outta here
70 for the water I say I'll bring back.
Honest to God, I heard "Brass Crew" and was gone.
I heard *Elbows up,*
natural breath!
That was enough.
75 How can I leave, and be happy to leave?
Easy. As needing to breathe new air.

King's got a First Trumpet stride. Jasper walks.
I lick the salt off my bare arms,
turn to look back at the people
80 held up by canes, hugging strollers, collapsible
black and newly colored people,
women with shirts for head wraps.
Salt dries my tongue.
I turn my eyes from them and walk.
85 I don't have to tell myself
it's not a school project for Ms. LeBlanc,

NOTICE & NOTE

DESCRIBE AN AUTHOR'S USE OF FIGURATIVE LANGUAGE

Annotate: In lines 60–65, mark the use of personification.

Interpret: Why did the poet use personification here?

▸ **TOUGH QUESTIONS**

Notice & Note: What are the questions asked by the speaker in lines 66–76? Mark the repeated questions.

Draw Conclusions: What conflict is revealed by these questions and their answers?

DESCRIBE AN AUTHOR'S USE OF FIGURATIVE LANGUAGE

Annotate: Mark the words making comparisons to "Freddie's Diorama" in lines 85–101.

Evaluate: What is the effect of the speaker saying that all of these images are "not a school project"?

After the Hurricane

NOTICE & NOTE

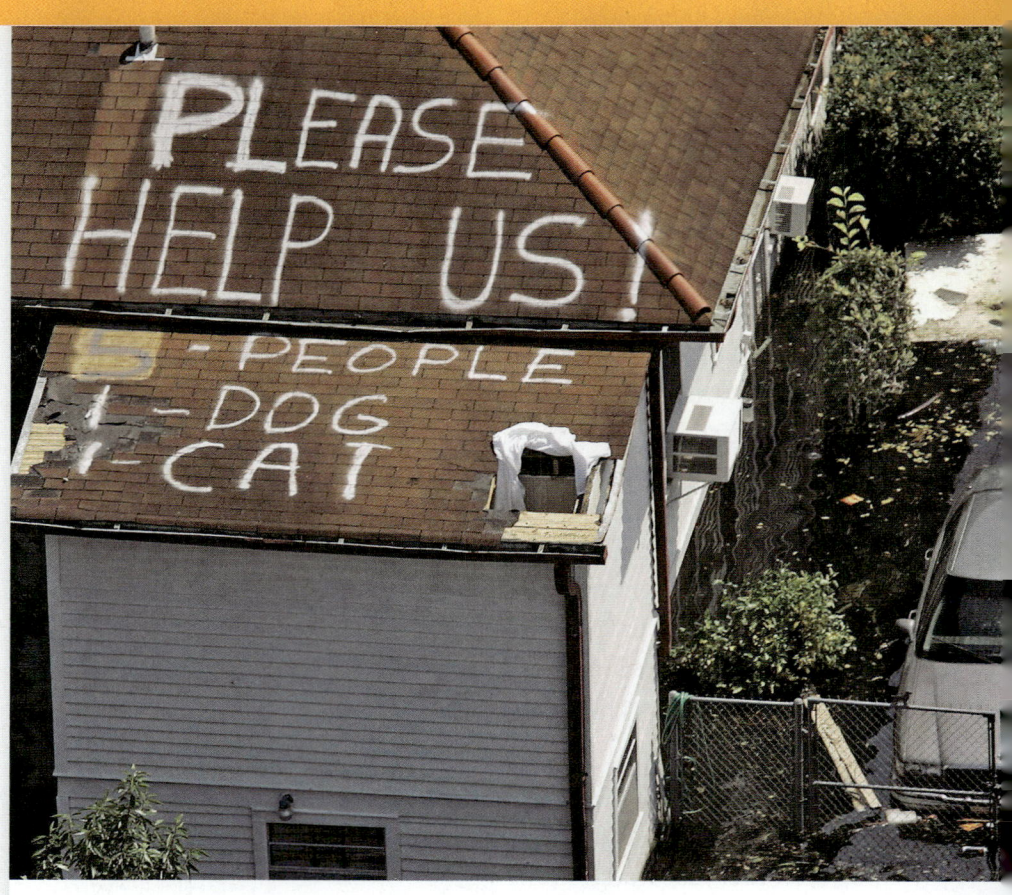

"The Colored Peoples of Freddie's Diorama."³
Green pasted just so, around the huts just so.
The despair just right.
90 It's not my social studies diorama
depicting "Over There," across the Atlantic,
the Pacific. Bodies of water.
Way, way over there.
The refugees of the mudslides,
95 refugees of the tsunami,
refugees of Rwanda.
No. It is US. In state. In country.
Drowned but not separated by
bodies of water or by spoken language.
100 The despair is just right, no translation needed.
We are not the refugees in my social studies diorama.
We are 11th graders,
a broken brass line,
old homeowners, grandmamas, head chefs, street

ANALYZE THE EFFECTS OF STRUCTURE AND METER

Annotate: Catalogs, or lists of related words, give structure and rhythm to free verse. Mark the catalog in lines 102–114.

Analyze: Identify how the words in the list are related. What effect does this catalog have on the poem's structure and meter? What effect does it have on the poem's meaning?

---

³ **diorama** (dī´ə-răm´ə): a three-dimensional scene in which models of people, animals, or other objects are arranged in natural poses against a painted background.

105 performers, a saxophonist mourning the loss of his Selmer
horn of 43 years and wife of 38 years. We are aunties,
dry cleaners, cops' daughters, deacons, cement mixers,
auto mechanics, trombonists without trombones, quartets
scattered, communion servers, stranded freshmen, old
110 nuns, X-ray technicians, bread bakers, curators,[4] diabetics,
shrimpers,[5] dishwashers, seamstresses, brides-to-be, new
daddies, taxi drivers, principals, Cub Scouts crying, car
dealers, other dealers, hairstylists, too many babies, too
many of us to count.
115 Still wearing what we had on when it hit.
When we fled,
or were wheeled, piggybacked, airlifted, carried off.
Citizens herded.
We are Ms. LeBlanc, social studies teacher, a rag wrapped
120 around her head,
And Principal Canelle. He missed that last bus.

* * *

Minor Miracle.
We walk past the Guard.
You'd think they'd see us
125 marching on outta here.
You'd think they'd stop us. Keep us domed.
But we're on the march, a broken brass line.
King, Jasper, and me, Fredericka.
King needs to lead; I need to leave.
130 Been following his lead since
band camp. Junior band. Senior band.
Box formations, flying diamonds, complicated transitions.
Jasper sticks close. A horn player, a laugher. Not a talker.
See anything to laugh about?
135 Jasper sticks close. Stays quiet. Maybe a nod.

Keeping step I would ask myself,
Aren't you ashamed? No.
Of band pride? No.
You band geek. So.
140 Aren't you ashamed? No.
You want to parade? So.
Raise your trumpet? So.

---

[4] **curators** (kyoŏ-rā′tərz): people who manage and oversee; most often describes those who manage a museum and its collection of art.

[5] **shrimpers** (shrĭmp′ərz): people who catch shrimp—small edible sea animals with a semihard outer shell.

DESCRIBE AN AUTHOR'S USE OF FIGURATIVE LANGUAGE

Annotate: Mark the language in lines 123–133 that compares the speaker and her friends to part of a school band.

Analyze: How does the speaker use the metaphor of a school band to develop an idea?

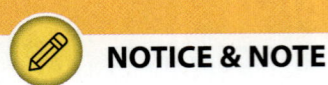

NOTICE & NOTE

ANALYZE THE EFFECTS OF STRUCTURE AND METER

Annotate: Read lines 136–161 aloud and mark repeated words and phrases.

Analyze: How do elements of structure and meter—including line breaks, repetition, and rhythm—help convey the speaker's feelings at this point in the poem?

Aren't you ashamed? No.
To praise Saint Louis?
145 "Oh, when the saints go marching in?"
Aren't you ashamed? No.
Of strutting krewe[6]
On Mardi Gras? The Fourth of July?
These very streets
150 Purple and gold, bop
Stars and Stripes, bop
Aren't you ashamed?
To shake and boogie?
Aren't you ashamed?
155 To enjoy your march,
while Grandmama suffers
and no milk for TK?
Tell the truth. Aren't you ashamed?
No. I'm not ashamed.
160 I step high, elbows up.
Band pride.

King asks, "Freddie, what you thinking?"
I say, "I'm not thinking, King."
But I'm dried out on the inside.
165 Hungry talks LOUD, you know.
"Let's try the Beauxmart. The Food Circle. Something."

King knows better. He doesn't say.
Still, we go and find (no surprise)
the Beauxmart's been hit. Stripped. Smashed.
170 Forget about Food Circle and every corner grocery.
Nothing left but rotten milk,
glass shards.[7] Loose shopping carts.
Jasper sighs. Grabs a cart.

Stomach won't shut up.
175 Talking. Knotting. Cramping. I whine,
"Let's go to Doolie's."
Again, King knows better. Still, we go,
almost passed right by. Didn't see it until
Jasper points. King sighs.

---

[6] **krewe** (kroō): any of several groups of people who organize and participate in the annual Mardi Gras carnival in New Orleans.
[7] **shards** (shärdz): small pieces of something that has been broken.

214 Unit 3

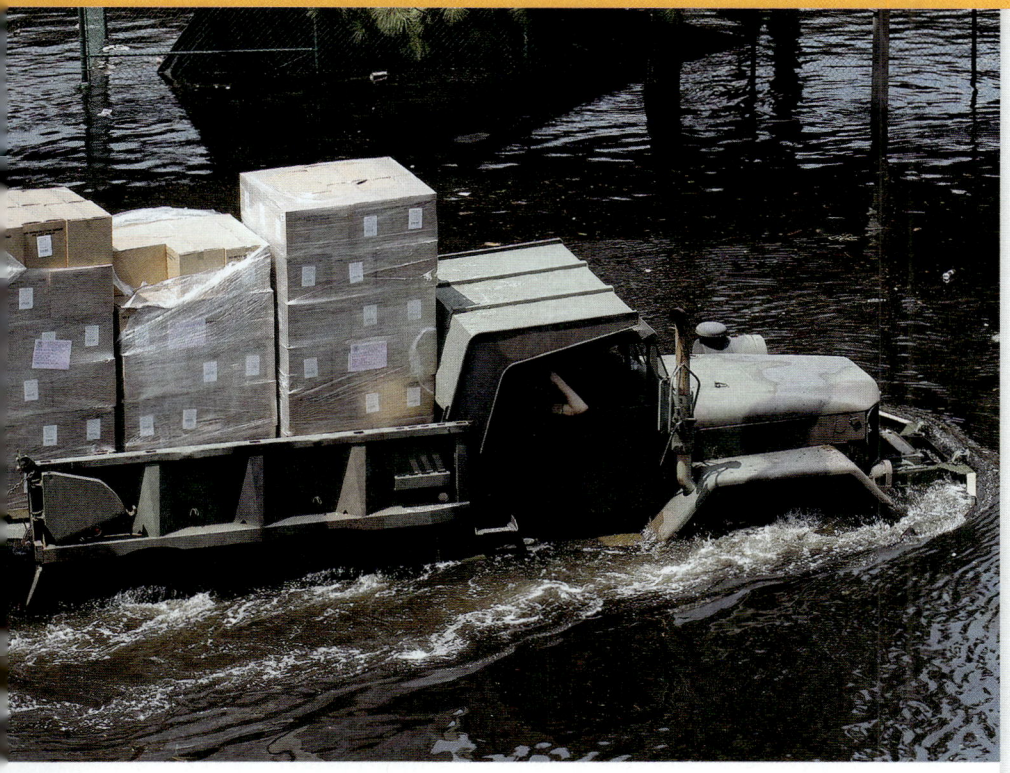

180 Check out the D in Doolie's, blown clear off.
The outside boarded up, chained up, locked.
Black and red spray-painted:
LOOTERS WILL BE SHOT.
I can't believe it.
185 Doolie who buys block tickets to home games
Doolie who sponsors our team bus
Band instruments, uniforms (all underwater),
Chicken bucket championships. The band eats half-price.
My eyes say, *Freddie, believe the spray paint:*
190 *Big Sean Doolie will shoot the looters.*
Yeah. Big Sean Doolie.
Believe.

King (First Trumpet) was right,
he doesn't make me (Second) like I'm second.
195 A simple, "Come on, Brass. Let's get this water."
I follow King. Jasper pushes the cart.
First, Second, Third. No bop step,
high step, no feather head shake,
no shimmy[8] front, boogie back.
200 Just walk.

> **AHA MOMENT**
>
> **Notice & Note:** What does the speaker realize in lines 184–192? Mark the words that indicate that the speaker's view of her world is changing.
>
> **Cite Evidence:** What evidence in the stanza shows the speaker has come to realize something? Why is this realization important?

---

[8] **shimmy** (shĭm´ē): to do the shimmy, a dance involving rapid shaking of the body.

NOTICE & NOTE

ANALYZE THE EFFECTS OF STRUCTURE AND METER

Annotate: In lines 201–208, mark repeated phrases and examples of alliteration.

Draw Conclusions: How do these elements help convey the speaker's feelings at the end of the poem?

"Hear that?"
Another helicopter overhead.
Another chopper stirring up the Big Empty.
Wide blades good for nothing but whirling up
205 heavy heat, heavy stink on empty streets
full of ghosts and mosquitoes.
Swat all you want. Look around.
Nothing here but us in Big Empty.

NOTICE & NOTE

CHECK YOUR UNDERSTANDING

Answer these questions before moving on to the **Analyze the Text** section on the following page.

1. In lines 5–7, the speaker in the poem says *if none of it were real* to —

   A express that the hurricane never happened, and that it is as fictional as a disaster movie

   B express a dislike for disaster movies

   C express that the disaster is very real, but she wishes it was fictional, like a disaster movie

   D suggest that the story of the hurricane would never make a good disaster movie

2. In lines 136–146, the speaker's questions and answers show that —

   F she is writing a journal entry to remember her experience

   G she dislikes the experiences she has had in the school band

   H she will stay inside the shelter because it is the right thing to do

   J despite her doubts, she is determined to leave the shelter because it is the right thing to do

3. Which idea expresses how the speaker feels by the end of the poem?

   A She feels relieved that the helicopter is there to help them.

   B She feels dismayed and stranded in the devastation.

   C She is happy that they will soon find some water.

   D She has come to love the sound of the helicopters.

After the Hurricane 217

RESPOND

ANALYZE THE TEXT

Support your responses with evidence from the text. 📓 **NOTEBOOK**

1. **Summarize** How does the poet use figurative language in lines 50–53 to convey meaning or ideas?

2. **Infer** Identify examples of repetition in lines 66–76. How might the poet's use of repetition point to a theme in the poem?

3. **Analyze** Reread lines 155–166 aloud. How do elements of free verse contribute to the pace and rhythm of the poem?

4. **Draw Conclusions** Identify the examples of figurative language in lines 174–175. What idea might the poet be trying to express by using this figurative language?

5. **Notice & Note** Identify ways in which water is mentioned throughout the poem. What ideas are conveyed by water images in the poem?

RESEARCH

"After the Hurricane" describes the speaker's experience following Hurricane Katrina, revealing how a group of students responds to the disaster. The poem's speaker criticizes some of the responses of others—including the media and aid organizations—to the disaster.

In a small group, choose and research a more recent natural disaster to identify volunteers, professionals, and organizations that responded to that disaster. Generate questions about the responders, such as *What did they do? Who did they help? How effective were they?* Then, conduct research to answer your questions.

RESEARCH TIP
Reviewing video clips and news reports that followed the disaster your group selects may help you identify organizations involved in relief efforts.

RESPONDER	QUESTION	ANSWER

Connect How does the experience of the poem's speaker compare to any disasters experienced by members of your group, class, or someone you know or have heard about? With your group, discuss ways in which the poem does or does not reflect personal experiences.

218   Unit 3

RESPOND

CREATE AND PRESENT

Write a Poem Using "After the Hurricane" as a model, write a narrative poem describing an event that you have experienced or witnessed. Your poem can be about a disaster, an important milestone or achievement, or another experience that made an impression on you.

- ❏ Write a quick sketch or description of your experience.
- ❏ Use everyday speech to expand your description of the experience into a poem.
- ❏ Vary the length and grouping of your lines to change the rhythm and meter of your poem.
- ❏ Incorporate elements of free verse in your poem, such as catalogs, alliteration, and repetition.
- ❏ Include poetic devices, such as simile, metaphor, and extended metaphor.

Go to the **Writing Studio** for more on writing narratives.

Poetry Jam A poetry jam is a way to share poetry in an informal atmosphere. Hold a poetry jam to present your poem to a small group or to the entire class.

- ❏ Maintain eye contact as much as possible when presenting.
- ❏ Speak clearly, at a rate and volume that allows everyone to hear you. Speak at a pace that emphasizes the rhythm of your poem.
- ❏ Use an appropriate stance and gestures while speaking.
- ❏ Listen actively to each presenter and ask questions to help clarify understanding. Offer constructive advice where helpful.

Go to the **Speaking and Listening Studio** for help with having a group discussion.

RESPOND TO THE ESSENTIAL QUESTION

 What does it take to be a survivor?

Gather Information Review your annotations and notes on the poem. Then, add relevant details to your Response Log. As you determine which information to include, think about the needs of the people in the poem and how they responded to obstacles and challenges.

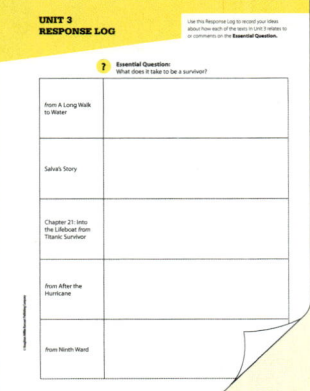

At the end of the unit, use your notes to write a nonfiction narrative.

ACADEMIC VOCABULARY
As you write and discuss what you learned about "After the Hurricane," be sure to use the Academic Vocabulary words. Check off the words that you use.

- ❏ circumstance
- ❏ constraint
- ❏ impact
- ❏ injure
- ❏ significant

COLLABORATE & COMPARE

NOVEL
from
NINTH WARD
by **Jewell Parker Rhodes**
pages 223–227

COMPARE ACROSS GENRES

Now that you've read "After the Hurricane," read an excerpt from *Ninth Ward* to see how this work of historical fiction tells another story of survival related to Hurricane Katrina. As you read, think about how the author uses setting and language to describe the narrator's experience. After you read, you will collaborate with a small group on a final project.

? ESSENTIAL QUESTION:

What does it take to be a survivor?

POEM
from
AFTER THE HURRICANE
by **Rita Williams-Garcia**
pages 209–217

220 Unit 3

GET READY

from Ninth Ward

QUICK START

What do you say to yourself when the going gets tough? What if you had to coach a friend or a sibling through a difficult time? Write three encouraging things you would say.

ANALYZE HISTORICAL AND CULTURAL SETTING

The **setting** of a work of literature is the time and place of the action. In historical fiction, the time period and culture play a significant role in both plot and characterization. This selection's setting is one area of New Orleans during the aftermath of Hurricane Katrina. As the text's fictional characters respond to the setting, the author reveals the characters' important qualities and values.

- Setting can influence characters' values, beliefs, and emotions.
- Setting can affect how characters act and interact with others.
- Characters develop as they respond to historical and cultural elements throughout the story. Their response may suggest the story's theme.

GENRE ELEMENTS: HISTORICAL FICTION

- is set in the past
- includes real places and real events of historical importance
- can be a short story or a novel
- has the basic features of realistic fiction, including plot, characters, conflict, setting, and theme

ANALYZE AUTHOR'S USE OF LANGUAGE

Mood is the feeling or atmosphere that a writer creates for the reader. Descriptive words, imagery, and figurative language all influence the mood of a work. *Ninth Ward* is a first-person narrative, so the mood created by the narrator's voice can reveal something about the main character. As you read, note how language helps create the mood of the text, and what the mood reveals about the text's characters and theme. Use a chart like the one below.

TEXT	MOOD	MY IDEAS ABOUT CHARACTER AND THEME
TaShon lifts his head and wipes his eyes. He looks far-off.	expectant	TaShon is someone who takes time to think before speaking.

Ninth Ward

GET READY

CRITICAL VOCABULARY

fortitude   endure   horizon   angular   focus

To see how many Critical Vocabulary words you already know, use them to complete the sentences.

1. Happy memories gave them _____ to survive the challenge.
2. The performer had to _____ his attention to walk on the tightrope.
3. Sharp, straight lines meet to create a/an _____ pattern.
4. The setting sun slipped beneath the _____ .
5. He could not _____ walking against the icy cold wind.

LANGUAGE CONVENTIONS

Pronouns A **pronoun** is a word that takes the place of a noun or another pronoun. **Personal pronouns,** such as *I, me, he, she, we, us, you,* and *it,* refer to the person making a statement, the person(s) being addressed, or the person(s) or thing(s) the statement is about.

The helicopter doesn't seem to see us. It keeps flying.

The personal pronoun *us* refers to the narrator, Lanesha, and her neighbor TaShon. *It* refers to an object, the helicopter. As you read, notice the author's use of pronouns.

ANNOTATION MODEL

NOTICE & NOTE

As you read, note words the author uses to indicate setting. Notice the effect of the author's use of language on the mood and characterization, and how mood may indicate theme. You can also mark evidence that supports your own ideas. In the model, you can see one reader's notes about *Ninth Ward*.

1 No land. Only sky and dirty water.	Sounds bleak. I wonder where they are.
2 TaShon has his head buried in Spot's fur. He's crying full-out—sobbing like the world has ended and Noah hasn't landed his ark.	More details about water, and also sadness. Maybe they are stranded or surrounded by water.

BACKGROUND

Jewell Parker Rhodes (b. 1954) loved to read and write as a child. Ninth Ward is her first published book for young people. The Ninth Ward is one of seventeen wards, or administrative districts, in New Orleans. The largest and easternmost ward, the Ninth Ward is divided by a shipping channel and another waterway. When Hurricane Katrina struck New Orleans in 2005, the Ninth Ward received the greatest damage. Many residents lost their lives and homes in the hurricane.

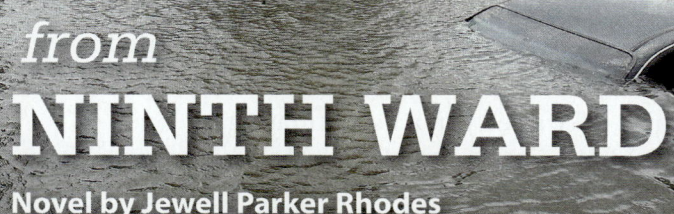

from NINTH WARD

Novel by Jewell Parker Rhodes

PREPARE TO COMPARE

As you read, pay attention to the selection's mood and setting. Note how characters respond to events. Think about how these elements may help you recognize the selection's theme, or message.

Notice & Note

Use the side margins to notice and note signposts in the text.

ANALYZE HISTORICAL AND CULTURAL SETTING

Annotate: Mark words in paragraphs 1–3 that show the setting.

Identify: Which elements tell you about the place and time? Are there any elements that tell you about the cultural setting?

1 No land. Only sky and dirty water.

2 TaShon has his head buried in Spot's fur. He's crying full-out—sobbing like the world has ended and Noah hasn't landed his ark.[1]

3 I want to sit and cry, too. But it's almost dawn, and I think when there's light, someone will surely find us. I also think, still dark, I've got to make sure TaShon doesn't fall off the roof into the water.

---

[1] **Noah hasn't landed his ark:** in the biblical flood story, Noah builds an ark, or large boat, to save his family and animals of every kind from a flood.

Ninth Ward 223

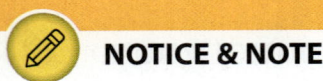

NOTICE & NOTE

fortitude
(fôr´tĭ-tōōd) *n.* To have *fortitude* is to show strength of mind and face difficulty with courage.

endure
(ĕn-dŏŏr´) *v.* To *endure* is to carry on despite difficulty or suffering.

ANALYZE AUTHOR'S USE OF LANGUAGE

Annotate: Mark the words in paragraph 8 that help establish the mood of this scene.

Analyze: How would you describe the mood here?

LANGUAGE CONVENTIONS

Mark the pronouns in the first sentence of paragraph 12. Who are the pronouns referring to?

horizon
(hə-rī´zən) *n.* The *horizon* is the intersection of the earth and sky.

angular
(ăng´gyə-lər) *adj.* Something that is *angular*, such as a peaked roof, has two sides that form an angle.

4   I feel tired, sad. Even though I expect to see her as a ghost, I know I'll still miss the flesh and blood Mama Ya-Ya.[2] The warm hands. Her making breakfast. And me resting my head upon her shoulder. I'll miss talking to her. Listening to her stories.

5   TaShon lifts his head and wipes his eyes. He looks far-off. For a minute, I think he's going to be his quiet old self, and pretend to disappear. Then, he says softly, "**Fortitude**."

6   "Strength to **endure**."

7   "That's right. We're going to show fortitude."

8   TaShon and I scoot closer, our arms and legs touching. I put my arms around him; he puts his arms around me. Neither of us moves. I know we are both thinking, murmuring in our minds, over and over again, "Fortitude. Fortitude. Fortitude."

9   Sunrise. As far as my eye can see, there is water.

10 The Mississippi is brown, filled with leaves, branches, and pieces of folks' lives. I see a plastic three-wheeler tangled in algae. I see a picture frame with a gap-toothed boy smiling in black and white. I see a red car, a Ford, floating.

11 Overhead, I hear a helicopter. It sounds like a lawn mower in the sky.

12 Me and TaShon start yelling, waving our hands. "Here, over here." The helicopter doesn't seem to see us. It keeps flying south. Its big bird wings circling and the roar of its engine getting softer.

13 TaShon is cursing now. I haven't the heart to say, "Watch your mouth." I'm positive the 'copter man saw us. How come he didn't stop? Lift us in the air with rope?

14 I start trembling and look around my neighborhood. The **horizon** is like none I've seen before. Just tips of houses. Tops or halves of trees. Lampposts hacked off by water. Rooftops—some flat, some **angular**—most, empty.

15 Far left, I see a man and woman sitting on a roof, their feet in the water. Two blocks east, I see what I think is an entire family. Five, six people, all different sizes, waving white sheets.[3] I hear them screaming, calling for help.

16 Where are the others? At the Superdome? Safe in Baton Rouge?[4]

---

[2] **Mama Ya-Ya:** Lanesha's elderly caretaker who has died during the water's rise.

[3] **waving white sheets:** in wartime, soldiers wave white flags to signal their willingness to surrender to the enemy.

[4] **At the Superdome? Safe in Baton Rouge?:** the Superdome is the name of the stadium in New Orleans that sheltered Katrina refugees. Baton Rouge is Louisiana's capital, and the city to which thousands of New Orleans residents fled to escape Hurricane Katrina.

17   TaShon says softly, "At least we made it out of the attic, didn't we, Lanesha?"

18   I look at TaShon. I should've known better. Should've known that there was more to see about TaShon than he ever let show. He's a butterfly, too.

19   "Yes, we did," I say. "We made it out."

20   No one is coming. All day and all night, we waited. Spot panted, slept. TaShon swatted at mosquitoes and his feet turned itchy red after he left them in the water to cool off. We are both sunburned. Funny, I didn't think black folks sunburned. But all day in the sun, no shade, has made me and TaShon red faced. My cheeks and shoulders hurt like someone touched them with a hot iron.

21   I keep **focused** on the horizon. Above it, I search for helicopters. Below it, I search for signs of my neighbors.

22   I used to think the Mississippi was beautiful. Not anymore. Up close, it is filled with garbage; clothes and furniture, ugly catfish and eels.

23   My lips are cracked. I'm hungry. Thirsty. Tired. I tell TaShon a hundred different Bible stories—all about hope. I tell him about Moses, David and Goliath, and Noah's ark.[5] "Someone's coming," I insist. "People know we're here." But I feel Spot, if he could talk, would say, "That's a lie," then blink his big brown eyes.

24   The moon is high. TaShon is feverish and asleep. His legs, up to his knees, are bright red. His face is peeling.

25   I haven't seen any ghosts either. Are they scared?

26   I murmur, "Mama Ya-Ya, help me. Momma, help me." But the night doesn't answer. Nothing shimmers. There's no message from another world.

27   Day two since the flood. Day three since the hurricane.

28   No one has come to our rescue. There's no TV. No radio. No news from anywhere. The family that has been hollering for help is quiet now.

29   I can't make the Mississippi disappear. I can't make food and water appear. But we're going to go stir-crazy, get more and more miserable.

30   I press my head to my hand. I feel dizzy.

---

[5] **Moses, David and Goliath, and Noah's ark:** in a set of stories from the Bible, Moses is directed by God to lead the Israelites out of Egypt; David is a boy who killed Goliath, a giant warrior; and Noah's ark is the large boat Noah built to save his family and animals from a flood.

NOTICE & NOTE

AHA MOMENT

Notice & Note: What does Lanesha realize about TaShon in paragraphs 16–19? Mark the words that show Lanesha is realizing something about TaShon's character.

Interpret: What does Lanesha mean when she compares TaShon to a butterfly?

focus
(fō´kəs) v. When you *focus* on something, you keep attention fixed on it.

ANALYZE AUTHOR'S USE OF LANGUAGE

Annotate: Mark the words in paragraph 23 that help show mood.

Infer: What does the mood suggest about the kind of person the narrator is?

NOTICE & NOTE

ANALYZE HISTORICAL AND CULTURAL SETTING

Annotate: Mark the details in paragraphs 34–40 that help describe the scene.

Predict: What do these details reveal about the challenges Lanesha and TaShon now face?

31   TaShon's itching, rubbing his left foot against his right leg. "Look. A rowboat."

32   I exhale. "Mr. Henri's! He liked catfish. He always gave some to Mama Ya-Ya."

33   TaShon's eyes are bright.

34   I move to the left—careful not to slip in the water, my feet angling on the roof. It's slippery. Water is in my tennis shoes. The shingles are slick with oil and gunk.

35   I can barely see the house next door. Most of it is covered with water. But a rowboat is floating, caught between our two houses and a bigger willow tree that kept it from floating down the street. It is maybe six, seven feet away. It's south, *perpendicular* to both our houses. "A sharp right angle." If it'd been parallel, it might've floated out—at least on the north side. But the angle kept it safe.

36   "Do you think we can reach it?" asks TaShon. "The boat?"

37   I squint. The boat's rope must be floating deep, loose inside the water.

38   My arms aren't long enough to push the boat free and I'm not sure I can doggy-paddle to it.

39   "The angle's all wrong."

40   Well, right and wrong, I think. Right, 'cause being perpendicular, it didn't get swept away in the storm. Wrong, 'cause being perpendicular, it needs to be unstuck.

41   I see TaShon's shoulders sagging. Giving up.

42   How can I rescue a rowboat?

43   EVERYTHING IS MATH. Think, Lanesha.

44   I look about. There are all kinds of pieces of wood, trees floating in the water. I see a long, thin trunk floating.

45   "TaShon. We've got to catch that tree." It looks like a young willow. Just a few years old.

46   I'm sure my hands can fit around its trunk. With effort, I can hold it like a stick.

47   I lie down on my stomach, shouting, "Come on, come on!" like a lunatic to the tree. It bobs left, then right. Then turns sideways.

48   "We've got to grab it, TaShon!"

49   TaShon lies beside me on his stomach, too. We flap our hands in the water, trying to make it draw near. Trying to create another current in the muddy tide.

50   "It's coming," hollers TaShon. "It's coming."

51   "Brace yourself." Though the tree is moving slow, it'll be heavy. "Don't fall! Don't fall in."

52   I stretch my arms wide, clawing at the water, trying to move the trunk closer. I strain, feeling the pull in my shoulders. Water is lapping, almost to my chin.

53   I clutch bark. A piece cracks away in my hand.

54   "Get it, get it," TaShon screams. His arms are too short. The trunk is floating by.

55   I inch my body further, my hips and legs still touching the roof. Inhaling, I plunge forward. My arms are around the tree.

CHECK YOUR UNDERSTANDING

Answer these questions before moving on to the **Analyze the Text** section on the following page.

1 Which sentence from the text suggests that Lanesha and TaShon want to be rescued?

   A *The horizon is like none I've seen before.*

   B *I see a red car, a Ford, floating.*

   C *I think when there's light, someone will surely find us.*

   D *"Yes, we did," I say. "We made it out."*

2 In paragraph 2, the narrator says, "Noah hasn't landed his ark" to —

   F introduce another character in the story

   G show that the story is set in the time of the Bible

   H show that TaShon enjoys Bible stories

   J show that the land has been covered by floodwater

3 Which idea is supported by information at the conclusion of the selection?

   A Lanesha has faith that Spot will help them escape.

   B Lanesha is determined to save them.

   C Lanesha no longer enjoys telling Bible stories.

   D Lanesha is very certain that they will be rescued.

RESPOND

ANALYZE THE TEXT

Support your responses with evidence from the text. 📓 NOTEBOOK

1. **Analyze** Reread paragraphs 1–3 and note details about setting and character traits. How is the historical setting related to the characters?

2. **Draw Conclusions** Review the author's use of language in paragraph 8. How do mood and characterization suggest the text's theme?

3. **Summarize** Review paragraphs 9–11. How does the text help you understand the novel's cultural setting?

4. **Compare** Review paragraphs 3 and 13. How would you compare the narrator's attitude in the two passages? Explain how Lanesha's character has changed over time.

5. **Notice & Note** Review paragraphs 36–48. What does Lanesha realize about their situation? Explain how Lanesha uses this realization to help TaShon overcome his sense of hopelessness.

RESEARCH

The city of New Orleans is divided into areas called "wards." The Ninth Ward suffered badly from Hurricane Katrina. Investigate the history of the Ninth Ward, from the time before Hurricane Katrina to the present. Use a chart like the one shown to record relevant information from reliable sources.

RESEARCH TIP
Use the search words "image of _____" to find photographs of an event. Type "map of _____" to help you understand the geography of an area. Try the search words "history of Ninth Ward" to find websites about the Ninth Ward. Evaluate your search results by looking for information about the organization that runs the site.

NINTH WARD	
FACT	SOURCE

Connect Is there information online about the history of your own city or neighborhood? Many areas have local historical societies that also maintain websites. Go online to find information about your community's history.

RESPOND

CREATE AND PRESENT

Write Live Posts What would the narrator of *Ninth Ward* have posted on social media if she had had a smartphone? Imagine you are Lanesha, looking out from her rooftop describing the setting surrounding her. Write a sequence of social media posts from Lanesha's point of view, directed at a friend far away.

❏ Use what you know about the character of Lanesha, including her voice, personality traits, and relationship to TaShon, to describe what she sees, thinks, and feels.
❏ Follow spelling and grammar conventions.
❏ Make sure you use pronouns correctly. Check to see if they agree with the nouns to which they refer.

Create a Poster In the beginning of the selection, the characters reflect on the importance of fortitude. In a small group, work together to write your own definition of *fortitude*. Then, gather images from magazines or the Internet, or make your own drawings, to represent fortitude. Design your poster around the images you have selected. Present your poster to the class and explain the images you chose. When listening to other groups' presentations, take notes and ask questions respectfully.

 Go to **The Language of Narrative** in the **Writing Studio** for more on descriptive writing.

Go to **Giving a Presentation: Delivering Your Presentation** in the **Speaking and Listening Studio** for help presenting your ideas.

PRESENTATION CHECKLIST
❏ **Maintain eye contact.**
❏ **Speak at a natural rate.**
❏ **Be loud and clear.**
❏ **Point to different parts of your poster as you speak.**

RESPOND TO THE ESSENTIAL QUESTION

 What does it take to be a survivor?

Gather Information Review your annotations and notes on *Ninth Ward* and highlight those that help answer the Essential Question. Then, add relevant details to your Response Log.

At the end of the unit, use your notes to write a nonfiction narrative.

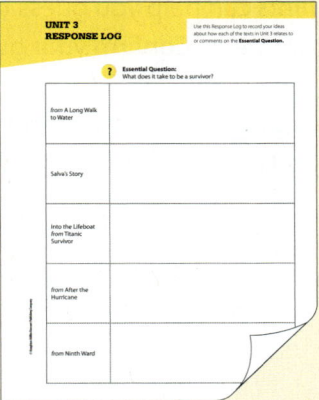

ACADEMIC VOCABULARY
As you write and discuss what you learned from the selections, be sure to use the Academic Vocabulary words. Check off each of the words that you use.

❏ circumstance
❏ constraint
❏ impact
❏ injure
❏ significant

RESPOND

WORD BANK
fortitude
endure
horizon
angular
focus

Go to the **Vocabulary Studio** for more on context clues.

CRITICAL VOCABULARY

Practice and Apply Explain which vocabulary word is most closely related to another word you know.

1. Which vocabulary word goes with *sunset*? Why?
2. Which vocabulary word goes with *strength*? Why?
3. Which vocabulary word goes with *lasting*? Why?
4. Which vocabulary word goes with *concentrate*? Why?
5. Which vocabulary word goes with *pointed*? Why?

VOCABULARY STRATEGY: Context Clues

Context clues are the words and phrases surrounding a word that provide hints about its meaning. Sometimes, you may find a context clue in the same sentence as an unfamiliar word. The whole sentence can also be a good clue. In *Ninth Ward,* the meaning of *horizon* is suggested by its context.

I keep focused on the horizon. Above it, I search for helicopters. Below it, I search for signs of my neighbors.

If you didn't know what *horizon* means, the words "above it" and "below it" are clues. Reread the whole paragraph for another context clue: above the horizon she looks for helicopters (in the sky); below it, she looks for people (on the ground or in the water). Together these hints can help you guess that *horizon* is "the place where the earth and sky meet." Confirm your guess by checking a print or online dictionary.

Practice and Apply Find context clues for each of the following words and guess the word's meaning. Then, check your definition.

WORD	CONTEXT CLUES	GUESSED DEFINITION	DEFINITION
fortitude (paragraph 5)			
endure (paragraph 6)			
angular (paragraph 14)			

230 Unit 3

LANGUAGE CONVENTIONS:
Pronouns

Pronouns are words used in place of a noun or another pronoun.

In *Ninth Ward,* the author uses both **personal pronouns** (including *I, me, my, we, us, our, you, yours, she, he, it, they, them,* and *theirs*) and **indefinite pronouns** (including *both, all, most, many, anyone, everybody, several,* and *none*).

In *Ninth Ward,* personal pronouns are used in the following ways:
- To refer to a person making a statement
  My lips are cracked. I'm hungry.

- To refer to the person being addressed
  TaShon has his head buried in Spot's fur. He's crying full out.

- To refer to the people the statement is about
  TaShon says softly, "At least we made it out of the attic, didn't we, Lanesha?"

The selection also uses **indefinite pronouns** to refer to one or more persons or things not specifically mentioned.

But it's almost dawn, and I think when there's light, someone will surely find us.

Someone refers to the unknown people that Lanesha hopes will rescue them.

Practice and Apply Write your own sentences with personal and indefinite pronouns, using the examples from *Ninth Ward* as models. Your sentences can be about your own survival under difficult circumstances or about another topic. When you have finished, share your sentences with a partner and compare your use of pronouns.

RESPOND

Go to the **Grammar Studio** for more on pronouns.

RESPOND

Collaborate & Compare

COMPARE TEXTS

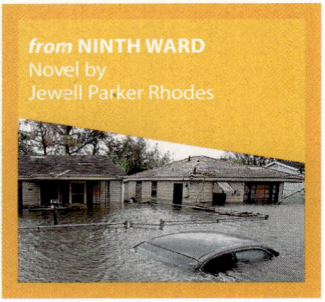

from **AFTER THE HURRICANE**
Poem by
Rita Williams-Garcia

from **NINTH WARD**
Novel by
Jewell Parker Rhodes

"After the Hurricane" and *Ninth Ward* use different **genres,** or types of writing, to explore the effects of Hurricane Katrina on residents of New Orleans. Even though the works are about a similar topic, they may express different themes. **Theme** is a message about life or human nature. Comparing texts from different genres—like poetry and historical fiction—can give you a deeper understanding of the topic.

Often, writers do not state themes directly. Instead, readers must **infer** themes based on information from the text and their own knowledge. This information may include key statements, significant events, and memorable images or symbols.

With your group, complete the chart by citing text evidence from the selections.

	"AFTER THE HURRICANE"	NINTH WARD
Key Statements		
Significant Events		
Memorable Images		

ANALYZE THE TEXTS

Discuss these questions in your group.

1. **Identify** How are the speaker in "After the Hurricane" and the narrator in *Ninth Ward* similar?

2. **Compare** How are the circumstances faced by the poem's speaker and the novel's narrator different? How are their responses to their circumstances different?

3. **Infer** Think about the image of helicopters in both selections. What ideas does this image suggest in each selection?

4. **Draw Conclusions** What have you learned from these selections about what it takes to be a survivor?

RESPOND

RESEARCH AND SHARE

Continue exploring the ideas in the texts by developing your own guidelines for how an organization can provide help in a natural disaster. Follow these steps:

1. **Develop a Question** In your group, brainstorm questions about how government and volunteer organizations help victims of natural disasters. Make sure that everyone contributes ideas to the list. Circle the most interesting questions, and then decide which group member or members will research each question.

2. **Gather Information** As you begin to research your assigned question, avoid plagiarism by properly citing your sources.
   - ❑ **Plagiarism** is the unauthorized use of someone else's words or ideas. Plagiarism is not honest.
   - ❑ You can avoid plagiarism by including a proper **citation** for each source you use.
   - ❑ To **cite print or digital sources,** include author, title, and publication information, according to the style guide your teacher prefers.

As you take notes on your research, be sure to record information about your sources. Take notes from two or more sources, paraphrasing and summarizing key information that answers your question.

RESEARCH TIP
When using a search engine for Internet research, don't automatically click on the first result that comes up. Sometimes, the topmost results are paid ads. Make sure the search result doesn't say "Ad" before the link. Read the summaries for each result, determine which ones are best for your search, and choose two or three to click on.

GROUP WORK CHECKLIST
- ❑ Contribute your own ideas.
- ❑ Consider the ideas of others.
- ❑ Ask clarifying questions.
- ❑ Take notes as necessary.
- ❑ When presenting, maintain eye contact.
- ❑ Speak at a natural rate.
- ❑ Be loud and clear.
- ❑ Gesture naturally.

MY QUESTION:

Source 1 Information:	Source 2 Information:
Citation:	Citation:

Ideas from the sources that answer my question:

3. **Develop and Share Instructions** Share and discuss your research with your group. Use everyone's research to help develop a set of guidelines that describe how an organization can help victims of a natural disaster. Present your guidelines to the class, and include your citations.

Collaborate & Compare 233

INDEPENDENT READING

ESSENTIAL QUESTION:

What does it take to be a survivor?

Reader's Choice

Setting a Purpose   Select one or more of these options from your eBook to continue your exploration of the Essential Question.

- Read the descriptions to see which text grabs your interest.
- Think about which genres you enjoy reading.

Notice & Note

In this unit, you practiced noticing and noting three signposts: **Tough Questions, Again and Again,** and **Aha Moment.** As you read independently, these signposts and others will aid your understanding. Below are the anchor questions to ask when you read literature and nonfiction.

Reading Literature: Stories, Poems, and Plays		
Signpost	**Anchor Question**	**Lesson**
Contrasts and Contradictions	Why did the character act that way?	p. 3
Aha Moment	How might this change things?	p. 3
Tough Questions	What does this make me wonder about?	p. 172
Words of the Wiser	What's the lesson for the character?	p. 2
Again and Again	Why might the author keep bringing this up?	p. 92
Memory Moment	Why is this memory important?	p. 93

Reading Nonfiction: Essays, Articles, and Arguments		
Signpost	**Anchor Question(s)**	**Lesson**
Big Questions	What surprised me? What did the author think I already knew? What challenged, changed, or confirmed what I already knew?	p. 246 p. 420 p. 332
Contrasts and Contradictions	What is the difference, and why does it matter?	p. 247
Extreme or Absolute Language	Why did the author use this language?	p. 247
Numbers and Stats	Why did the author use these numbers or amounts?	p. 333
Quoted Words	Why was this person quoted or cited, and what did this add?	p. 333
Word Gaps	Do I know this word from someplace else? Does it seem like technical talk for this topic? Do clues in the sentence help me understand the word?	p. 421

234   Unit 3

INDEPENDENT READING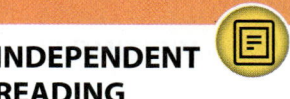

You can preview these texts in Unit 3 of your eBook.
Then, check off the text or texts that you select to read on your own.

☐
POEM
Watcher: After Katrina, 2005
Natasha D. Trethewey

In the weeks following a devastating hurricane, what might you observe?

☐
SHORT STORY
The Day I Didn't Go to the Pool
Leslie J. Wyatt

An older brother must think fast in order to save his siblings.

☐
SHORT STORY
Tuesday of the Other June
Norma Fox Mazer

Relentless bullying affects all aspects of a girl's life.

☐
SPEECH
In Event of Moon Disaster
Bill Safire

What speech would the president have given if the first moon landing had ended in disaster?

☐
INFORMATIONAL TEXT
Ready: Preparing Your Pets for Emergencies Makes Sense
Ready.gov

A practical guide prepares pet owners for an emergency.

Collaborate and Share Find a partner to discuss what you learned from at least one of your independent readings.

- Give a brief synopsis or summary of the text.
- Describe any signposts that you noticed in the text and explain what they revealed to you.
- Describe what you most enjoyed or found most challenging about the text. Give specific examples.
- Decide if you would recommend the text to others. Why or why not?

 Go to the **Reading Studio** for more resources on **Notice & Note**.

Independent Reading 235

WRITING TASK

Write a Nonfiction Narrative

Go to the **Writing Studio** for help writing narratives.

This unit focuses on what it takes to be a survivor. For this writing task, you will write a nonfiction narrative about the qualities of a survivor, about what it takes to survive a disaster or a difficult event. For an example of a nonfiction narrative you can use as a mentor text, review the memoir "Into the Lifeboat."

As you write your nonfiction narrative, you can use the notes from your Response Log, which you filled out after reading each text in this unit.

Writing Prompt

Read the information in the box below.

> The instinct to survive is powerful: you do what you must in order to stay alive, and you help others do the same.

This is the topic or context for your nonfiction narrative.

Think carefully about the following question.

> What does it take to be a survivor?

This is the unit's Essential Question. How would you answer this question, based on the texts in this unit?

Write a nonfiction narrative or memoir about what it took for you or someone you know to survive a disaster or difficult event.

Now mark the words that identify exactly what you are being asked to produce.

Be sure to—

- ☐ establish a situation that introduces real people, places, and events, using specific details and strong imagery
- ☐ organize an event sequence that unfolds naturally and logically
- ☐ include elements such as setting, pacing, conflict, and dialogue
- ☐ use precise words and sensory language, and maintain a consistent style and tone
- ☐ develop a mood
- ☐ provide a conclusion that follows from and reflects on the events

Review these points as you write and again when you finish. Make any needed changes.

236 Unit 3

WRITING TASK

 Plan

Before you start writing, plan your nonfiction narrative. First, decide which experience you are going to write about. Next, choose your narrator, who can be someone in the narrative or an observer. Then consider whether using sources such as news articles, emails, and texts will add interest and credibility to your narrative. Finally, think about setting and mood. Where and when will your narrative take place? What mood would you like to establish? Take notes in the chart below to help you plan your nonfiction narrative.

Go to **Writing Narratives: Introduction** for help planning your narrative.

Nonfiction Narrative Planning Chart	
Subject of my narrative	
Narrator and point of view	
Main event and characters	
Setting	
Mood	
Sources of information	
Conclusion reflecting on the event	

Background Reading Review the notes you have taken in your Response Log after reading the texts in this unit. These texts are the background reading that will help you formulate the key ideas that will inform your narrative.

Notice & Note

From Reading to Writing

As you plan your nonfiction narrative, apply what you've learned about signposts to your own writing. Remember that writers use common features, called signposts, to help convey their message to readers. Think about how you can incorporate **Contrasts and Contradictions** into your narrative.

Go to the **Reading Studio** for more resources on Notice & Note.

Use the notes from your Response Log as you plan your nonfiction narrative.

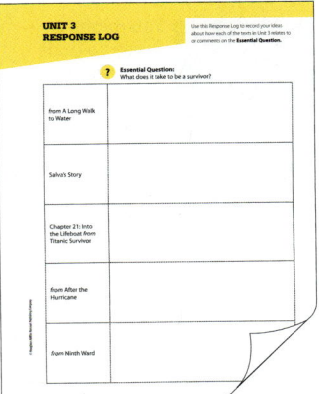

Write a Nonfiction Narrative   237

WRITING TASK

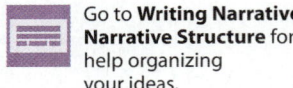
Go to **Writing Narratives: Narrative Structure** for help organizing your ideas.

Organize Your Ideas Planning includes organizing your ideas in an order that will help your reader understand your narrative. In a nonfiction narrative, the story is often told in chronological order, or the sequence in which the events took place. Use a graphic organizer like the one below to organize your narrative's events in chronological order.

EVENTS IN MY NARRATIVE

② Develop a Draft

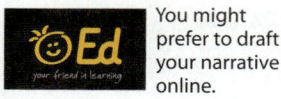
You might prefer to draft your narrative online.

Once you have completed your planning activities, you will be ready to begin drafting your narrative. Refer to the planning chart and graphic organizer you have created, as well as to any notes you took as you studied the texts in the unit. These will provide a kind of map for you to follow as you write. Using a word processor or online writing application makes it easier to make changes or move sentences around later when you are ready to revise your first draft.

Use the Mentor Text

Setting and Mood
Using descriptive language and sensory details can help establish the setting and mood of your narrative. Specific details, thoughtful word choice, and clear imagery will help your reader form mental images of the events and characters you write about, giving the reader a deeper sense of the experience.

> **How strange it was to pass all those rooms lit up so brilliantly, their doors open and contents lying around in disorder. Jewels sparkled on dressing tables and a pair of silver slippers were lying just where they had been kicked off.**

The author uses vivid imagery to establish the luxurious setting and a dreamlike mood. The glamorous scene contrasts with the unfolding tragedy and shows that people had left everything behind.

Apply What You've Learned Review your narrative and find scenes that you can enhance using descriptive and sensory language. Identify places in your narrative where you can add more detail.

Sequence
Describing events in chronological order pulls readers into the story as if they were experiencing it along with the narrator. Words signaling time, such as *first, then, next, at last,* and *finally,* mark the sequence. The pace at which events unfold—anywhere from slow and dreamy to fast and furious—helps set the tone.

> **I started unconsciously to count the decks by the rows of lights. One, two, three, four, five, six; then again— one, two, three, four, five. I stopped. Surely I had miscounted. I went over them again more carefully, hushing the whimpering baby meanwhile. No, I had made no mistake. There were only five decks now; then I started all over again—only four now. She was getting lower in the water, I could not any longer deny it.**

The author relates the order of events chronologically—and the steady, solemn pace reflects the tragic sinking of the majestic ship, deck by deck, right before her eyes.

Apply What You've Learned Events in your narrative should be told in the order they occurred to reveal how the experience took place in real life. Review your narrative and look for ways to make the sequence clear.

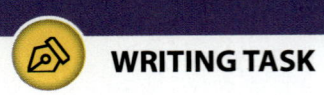
WRITING TASK

3 Revise

On Your Own Once you have written your draft, go back and look for ways to improve your nonfiction narrative. As you reread and revise, think about whether you have achieved your purpose of fully capturing the experience of a survivor. The Revision Guide will help you focus on specific elements to make your writing stronger.

Go to **The Language of Narrative** in the **Writing Studio** for help revising your narrative.

Revision Guide		
Ask Yourself	**Tips**	**Revision Techniques**
1. Do I use narrative elements such as setting, conflict, and dialogue?	**Mark** details that show when and where the experience happened.	**Add** details about setting and conflict. Include dialogue.
2. Do I maintain a clear and consistent point of view?	**Mark** pronouns such as *I*, *my*, *he*, and *she*.	**Change** pronouns that cause a shift in the point of view.
3. Do I tell events in chronological order?	**Mark** words that show time order.	**Connect** events with words and phrases that show the order in time.
4. Do I use sensory language to develop events and characters?	**Mark** words and phrases that appeal to the senses.	**Add** words and phrases that describe sights, sounds, and feelings.
5. Do I use verbs and verb phrases to tell when events occurred?	**Mark** verbs and verb phrases.	**Add** verbs and verb phrases that describe when the action takes place, keeping verb tense consistent.
6. Does my conclusion reflect on the event?	**Mark** the conclusion.	**Add** a sentence that reflects on the event.

ACADEMIC VOCABULARY

As you conduct your **peer review,** be sure to use these words.

☐ circumstance
☐ constraint
☐ impact
☐ injure
☐ significant

With a Partner Once you and your partner have worked through the Revision Guide on your own, exchange papers and evaluate each other's draft in a **peer review**. Focus on providing revision suggestions for at least three of the items in the chart. Explain why you think your partner's draft should be revised and what your specific suggestions are.

When receiving feedback from your partner, listen attentively and ask questions to make sure you fully understand the revision suggestions.

4 Edit

Once you have addressed the organization, development, and flow of ideas in your narrative, you can improve the finer points of your draft. Edit for the proper use of standard English conventions and correct any misspellings or grammatical errors.

Language Conventions

Consistent Verb Tense A **verb** expresses an action, a condition, or state of being. Helping verbs such as *is*, *could*, *has*, and *might* can be combined with verbs to form **verb phrases.** For example, adding the helping verb *was* to the verb *run* makes the verb phrase *was running*. The **tense** of a verb or verb phrase shows the time of action: present, past, or future. Keeping the verb tense consistent is important, but there are instances in which prepositions or prepositional phrases can "interrupt" or affect a verb tense. In the excerpt below, the verb tense remains consistently past tense (yellow highlight), except for in the dialogue, which is in future tense (blue highlight).

> As I turned I ran into Jock, the bandleader and his crowd with their instruments. "Funny, they must be going to play," thought I. . . .

! Go to the **Grammar Studio** to learn more about using verbs.

Look at the examples in the chart below.

Verb or Phrase	Verb Tense	Example Sentence
Verbs: was, seemed	past	Nobody **was** anxious to move; *Titanic* **seemed** so steady.
Verb Phrase: could keep	past	Fascinated, my eyes never left the ship, as if by looking I **could keep** her afloat.
Interrupting Prepositional Phrase	past and present	Violet Jessop climbed awkwardly into the lifeboat and, **in an act that demonstrates the desperate nature of the moment,** reached up to catch a bundle that turned out to be a baby.

5 Publish

After you give your nonfiction narrative its finishing touches, choose a way to share it with your audience. Consider these options:

- Present your nonfiction narrative as a speech to the class.
- Post your nonfiction narrative as a blog on a classroom or school website.

WRITING TASK

Use the scoring guide to evaluate your nonfiction narrative.

	Writing Task Scoring Guide: Nonfiction Narrative		
	Organization/Progression	**Development of Ideas**	**Use of Language and Conventions**
4	• The organization is effective and logical; events are organized chronologically. • The introduction identifies the subject and creates a strong impression. • Transitions clearly connect events. • Pacing skillfully builds anticipation. • The conclusion reflects on the significance of the experience and leaves the reader with new insight.	• Background information helps to explain events. • Descriptions effectively establish the setting and set the mood. • Use of dialogue and conflict create a strong sense of the characters. • The narrative depicts what it takes to be a survivor.	• Point of view, style, and tone are consistent and effective. • Sensory language and details vividly reveal characters, places, and events. • Sentences are varied and have a rhythmic flow. • Tense in verbs and verb phrases are used correctly and clarify the sequence of events. • Spelling, grammar, usage, and mechanics are correct.
3	• The organization is generally logical; the sequence of events is confusing in a few places. • The introduction identifies the subject. • More transitions would make the sequence of events clearer. • Pacing is somewhat effective. • The conclusion reflects on the experience.	• Background information mostly helps to explain events. • Descriptions mostly establish the setting and set the mood. • Use of dialogue and conflict mostly help to develop the characters. • The narrative mostly addresses the topic of what it takes to be a survivor.	• Point of view, style, and tone are occasionally inconsistent. • Some sensory language is used to reveal characters, places, and events. • Sentences are somewhat varied. • Some errors in the use of tense in verbs and verb phrases occur. • Some spelling, grammar, usage, and mechanics errors occur.
2	• The organization is confusing; missing or extraneous events are distracting. • The introduction briefly mentions the subject. • Few transitions are used throughout. • Pacing is choppy and ineffective. • The conclusion only hints at the significance of the experience.	• More background is needed throughout. • More descriptions are needed to establish the setting and set the mood. • Inadequate use of dialogue and conflict contribute to weak character development. • The narrative vaguely indicates what it might take to be a survivor.	• Point of view, style, and tone are inconsistent. • Sensory language and details are lacking. • Sentences hardly vary; fragments or run-on sentences are present. • The use of tense in verbs and verb phrases is inconsistent. • Multiple spelling, grammar, usage, or mechanics errors occur.
1	• There is no evident organization or sequence of events. • The introduction does not identify the subject. • There is no evident pacing of events. • Transitions are not used, making the narrative difficult to understand. • There is no conclusion.	• Necessary background is missing. • Descriptions needed to establish the setting and set the mood are lacking. • Character development is lacking. • The narrative does not provide a sense of what it takes to be a survivor.	• Point of view, style, and tone are never established. • Sensory language is not used. • Sentences do not vary; several fragments and run-on sentences are present. • Incorrect use of tense in verbs and verb phrases makes the sequence of events confusing. • Spelling, grammar, usage, or mechanics errors create confusion.

REFLECT

Reflect on the Unit

By completing your nonfiction narrative, you have created a writing product that pulls together and expresses your thoughts about the reading you have done in this unit. Now is a good time to reflect on what you have learned.

Reflect on the Essential Question

- What do you think it takes to be a survivor? How has your answer to this question changed since you first considered it when you started this unit?

- What are some examples from the texts you've read that show how people survived a catastrophic event?

Reflect on Your Reading

- Which selections gave you the strongest sense of what it would be like to experience a particular disaster?

- From which selection did you learn the most about what it takes to be a survivor?

Reflect on the Writing Task

- What did you learn about yourself or others as you wrote about what it takes to be a survivor?

- Which writing skills did you strengthen as you drafted and edited your narrative?

UNIT 3 SELECTIONS
- *A Long Walk to Water*
- *Salva's Story*
- "Into the Lifeboat" from *Titanic Survivor*
- "After the Hurricane"
- *Ninth Ward*

UNIT 4

DISCOVERING YOUR VOICE

? ESSENTIAL QUESTION:

What are the ways you can make yourself heard?

" When I speak, the words come pouring out of me. "

Jacqueline Woodson

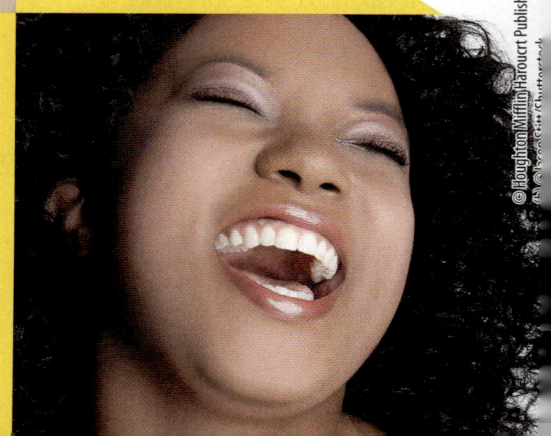

UNIT 4

ACADEMIC VOCABULARY

Academic Vocabulary words are words you use when you discuss and write about texts. In this unit, you will practice and learn five words.

✓ appropriate ☐ authority ☐ consequence ☐ element ☐ justify

Study the Word Network to learn more about the word **appropriate**.

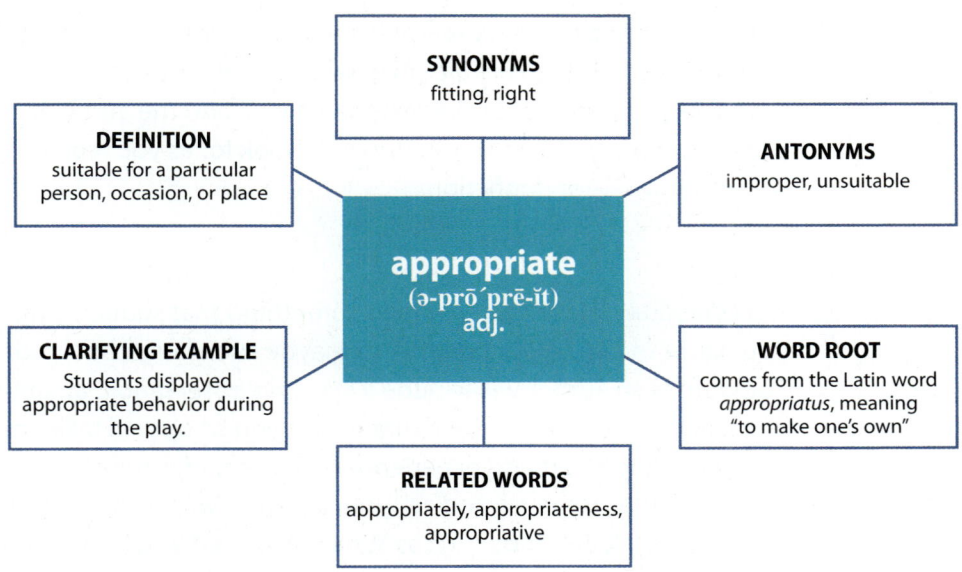

Write and Discuss Discuss the completed Word Network with a partner, making sure to talk through all of the boxes until you both understand the word, its synonyms, antonyms, and related forms. Then, fill out Word Networks for the remaining four words. Use a dictionary or online resource to help you complete the activity.

 Go online to access the Word Networks.

RESPOND TO THE ESSENTIAL QUESTION

In this unit, you will read about the different ways that people find their voices and express their ideas. As you read, you will revisit the **Essential Question** and gather your ideas about it in the **Response Log** that appears on page R4. At the end of the unit, you will have the opportunity to create a **multimodal argument** about your favorite way to express yourself. You will gather graphics and images that help support your argument. Filling out the **Response Log** will help you prepare for this task.

 You can also go online to access the Response Log.

Discovering Your Voice 245

Notice & Note

READING MODEL

from SELFIE: THE CHANGING FACE OF SELF-PORTRAITS

You are about to read an excerpt from the multimodal text *Selfie: The Changing Face of Self-Portraits*. In it, you will notice and note signposts that give you clues about the text's main idea and the author's purpose. Here are three key signposts to look for as you read this text and other works of nonfiction.

For more information on these and other signposts to Notice & Note, visit the **Reading Studio**.

Big Questions Have you ever read something that suddenly made you pause to catch your breath—or maybe even laugh out loud? Sometimes an author will include a startling observation, an unusual fact, or an unexpected phrase that makes you sit up and take notice. If you're reading a text and experience a moment of astonishment, then it's a good idea to pause and ask yourself what was so surprising about it. Asking **Big Questions** such as **What surprised you?** can clarify information that you did not already know and lead you to ask and answer more questions as you read.

When you are surprised by something you read, pause and ask yourself if you should apply the **Big Questions** strategy. Then, do the following:

Identify words or phrases that surprised you.

Ask yourself why the author included this surprising element.

Continue to look for and clarify surprising information as you read.

Read this part of *Selfie: The Changing Face of Self-Portraits* to see a student's annotation of a Big Question:

> 4   Take Vincent van Gogh, who cut off a piece of his ear, but still thought it would make a nice picture.

What surprised you?	I didn't know Vincent van Gogh cut off a piece of his ear! It surprised me that he did this and then painted a picture of himself afterwards.
What is the author's purpose in including this detail?	The text is about self-portraits, and this would be an example of a very unusual self-portrait. Why would he paint something like that?

▶ **Extreme or Absolute Language** Have you ever caught yourself exaggerating when you tell a friend a story? The story itself may be true, but the details may be overstated for the sake of effect. **Hyperbole** is a figure of speech in which the truth is exaggerated for emphasis or humorous effect. In nonfiction, writers sometimes use hyperbole and other types of extreme or absolute language to make a point.

Extreme or Absolute Language includes words that indicate certainty (*all, none, everyone, no one, always, never, totally*) without supporting evidence, as well as statements that appear exaggerated or express a rigid position.

Here is an example of a student finding and marking instances of Extreme or Absolute Language:

> 3 . . . but most of all <u>they let us look right inside the minds</u> of the brilliant (<u>and sometimes a bit bonkers</u>) people who created them.

When you read a phrase like these, pause to see if it's an **Extreme or Absolute Language** signpost:

We must all agree . . .

Everyone knows . . .

Nothing in the universe . . .

You will never believe . . .

Anchor Question
When you notice this signpost, ask: Why did the author use this language?

What is extreme or absolute about this language?	Use of hyperbole: self-portraits don't literally show us the inside of a person's mind. Bonkers is a slang word meaning "crazy," which seems extreme or exaggerated.
What might be the author's purpose in using this language?	The author may be using exaggeration and humor to help explain and emphasize the point about what self-portraits reveal.

▶ **Contrasts and Contradictions** The writer of this selection compares artists of the past to the selfie-snapping smart-phone users of today. In this example, a student underlined a **Contrast and Contradiction.**

> 1 They <u>never saw a smartphone, or the Internet,</u> and most of them <u>couldn't even tell you what a camera was.</u> But <u>they did all know about selfies!</u>

Anchor Question
When you notice this signpost, ask: What is the difference, and why does it matter?

What contrast or contradiction is shown here?	People in the past didn't have Internet, smart phones, or even cameras. But they did have selfies, like we do today.
Why did the author include this contrast or contradiction?	The contrast shows that while technology may have changed over time, what people actually do with technology has not.

Notice & Note   247

ANALYZE & APPLY

from SELFIE:
THE CHANGING FACE OF SELF-PORTRAITS

Multimodal Text by **Susie Brooks**

? ESSENTIAL QUESTION:

What are the ways you can make yourself heard?

GET READY

QUICK START

Some of the world's most famous "selfies" have been displayed in art museums around the world. What do you think it would take for one of your own selfies to be exhibited in a museum? Discuss your response with the class.

ANALYZE MULTIMODAL TEXTS

The multimodal selection you are about to read conveys ideas through text and visual details. To find the key ideas in this multimodal text, follow these steps:

- Identify the specific topic of each paragraph or section.
- Examine all the details the author provides, including details found in text, illustrations, images, and graphic features.
- Reread the text after studying the artwork, synthesizing information from both. This will reinforce key ideas the author is trying to convey.

ANALYZE PRINT AND GRAPHIC FEATURES

Print features are elements of text design, such as boldface type, headings, captions, and fonts. **Graphic features** are visual elements that help call attention to information, such as charts, diagrams, graphs, photographs, maps, and art. Together, print and graphic features present information, create interest, and guide readers through a text. You can **skim**—quickly read or view—these features before a close reading to help you **predict** what the text will be about and set a purpose for reading. As you read, note how print and graphic features help convey information. These features can also help you quickly locate topics or ideas after reading.

GENRE ELEMENTS: MULTIMODAL INFORMATIONAL TEXT

- provides factual information
- includes evidence to support ideas
- uses more than one mode of communication: text, art, sound, video, and so on
- includes many forms, such as picture books, websites, and digital media

PRINT FEATURES	GRAPHIC FEATURES
A **heading** or **subheading** indicates the beginning of a new topic or section. New sections may begin with a **drop cap**, or a large capital letter at the beginning of a paragraph.	**Color effects,** such as highlighted text, doodles, and colored backgrounds, can organize and call attention to information.
A **caption** contains information about an image or illustration.	A box, speech balloon, or other shape may be used to display information about an image or to call attention to additional information.

Selfie: The Changing Face of Self-Portraits 249

GET READY

CRITICAL VOCABULARY

| portrait | etch | reflection | span |

To see how many Critical Vocabulary words you already know, use them to complete the sentences.

1. Their trip around the world will _____ at least six months.
2. A _____ of the president is in the hall.
3. His _____ in the mirror smiled back at him.
4. In art class, we learned how to _____ drawings into wood.

LANGUAGE CONVENTIONS

Commas can clarify the meaning of sentences by separating certain words, phrases, or clauses. In this lesson, you will learn how to use commas to set off introductory elements. An **introductory element** is a word, phrase, or dependent clause that appears at the beginning of a sentence.

By the end of his life, Rembrandt was an expert in capturing character.

In the sentence above, a comma separates the introductory phrase *By the end of his life* from the independent clause that completes the sentence. The comma makes the sentence easier to understand.

ANNOTATION MODEL

NOTICE & NOTE

As you read, notice and note signposts, including **Big Questions, Extreme or Absolute Language,** and **Contrasts and Contradictions.** In the model shown, you can see how one reader responded to the opening of *Selfie: The Changing Face of Self-Portraits*.

> 1 <u>You can probably do it with your eyes closed</u>: point your phone camera at your face; press the shutter button and bingo—a selfie! But <u>next time you smile/hug a celebrity and post the pic</u>, spare a thought for Rembrandt van Rijn and Vincent van Gogh, among others.

Why would I take a picture of myself with my eyes closed?

These are exaggerations, but they grabbed my attention!

BACKGROUND

Does it surprise you to learn that selfies actually have a long history in art? Children's author and art historian **Susie Brooks** *explains how even before the invention of photography, the Internet, and the smart phone, people throughout history have longed to put their best face forward and share their images with the world.*

from
SELFIE:
THE CHANGING FACE OF SELF-PORTRAITS

Multimodal Text by Susie Brooks

SETTING A PURPOSE

As you read, pay attention to how the multimodal elements of the text, including images, and print and graphic features, work together to convey topics and key ideas.

NOTICE & NOTE

Notice & Note

Use the side margins to notice and note signposts in the text.

All By Your Selfie

1   You can probably do it with your eyes closed: point your phone camera at your face; press the shutter button and bingo—a selfie! But next time you smile/hug a celebrity and post the pic, spare a thought for Rembrandt van Rijn and Vincent van Gogh, among others. They never saw a smartphone, or the Internet, and most of them couldn't even tell you what a camera was. But they did all know about selfies!

2   Back in the old days, selfies were more commonly known as self-portraits. Before photography was invented, people who wanted pictures of themselves (and could afford it) commissioned artists to paint their **portraits**. If you were

LANGUAGE CONVENTIONS

In paragraph 2, how are commas used to set off introductory elements? What effect do the commas have on the sentences?

portrait
(pôr´trĭt) *n.* A *portrait* is a person's likeness, especially one showing the face, which may be painted, photographed, or otherwise represented.

Selfie: The Changing Face of Self-Portraits   251

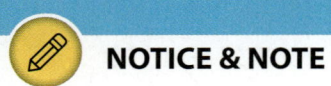

NOTICE & NOTE

an artist it was even easier—you just looked in the mirror and painted what you saw!

3   Self-portraits can often tell us about the clothing of a particular time, about art material and styles, and how old or rich or handsome the artist was or is—but most of all they let us look right inside the minds of the brilliant (and sometimes a bit bonkers) people who created them.

4   Take Vincent van Gogh, who cut off a piece of his ear, but still thought it would make a nice picture. Rembrandt drew, painted and **etched** his own **reflection** so many times we can see almost every stage of his life!

Albrecht Dürer

5   Dürer looks haughty[1] and confident, with a stiff but elegant pose. His clothing is expensive, extravagant and Italian in style.

etch
(ĕch) v. To *etch* is to cut or carve a drawing into a surface such as wood or metal.

reflection
(rĭ-flĕk´shən) n. A *reflection* is an image shown back, as from a mirror.

Born: 1471 in Germany
Died: 1528, aged 56

Self-Portrait, 1500

ANALYZE PRINT AND GRAPHIC FEATURES

Annotate: Mark information included in the caption for the Dürer painting.

Compare: How can you distinguish the caption from other print features, such as headings? What is the purpose of the caption?

---
[1] **haughty** (hô´tē): scornfully proud or arrogant.

6   We all want to look good in a selfie—and 500 years ago it was the same. Albrecht Dürer dressed up in fancy clothes for this self-portrait, announcing to the world that he was rich and grand.

7   Dürer was 26 when he painted this and already a leading artist, best known for his woodcut prints. On a trip to Italy, he noticed that great artists had a higher social status than they did at home in Germany. Dürer wanted to be treated like that too! After Dürer's death, admirers cut locks of his hair to remember him by. You can still see some at the Academy of Fine Arts in Vienna, Austria.

Rembrandt van Rijn

8   Rembrandt was the biggest selfie maker of his time, creating nearly 100 self-portraits that **spanned** 40 years of his life. They track his changing appearance, as well as his developing painting style.

9   Rembrandt pictured himself in all sorts of poses, outfits and moods. As a young man, he often appeared in fine clothing, perhaps in the style of the rich people whose portraits he painted. Sometimes his scenes were theatrical, like the one he painted at the age of 29 with his wife Saskia sitting on his knee.

NOTICE & NOTE

ANALYZE PRINT AND GRAPHIC FEATURES

Annotate: Mark the print and graphic features on this page, such as headings, captions, and images. Then, predict what this section will be about.

Analyze: How does each feature help organize and present the information in an effective way?

span
(spăn) v. To *span* is to extend over a period of time.

Born: 1606 in the Netherlands
Died: 1669, aged 63

Self-Portrait as a Young Man, 1634

Self-Portrait with Saskia, 1636

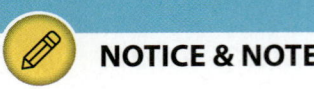

NOTICE & NOTE

CONTRASTS AND CONTRADICTIONS

Notice & Note: Do you agree with the author's description of Rembrandt's last self-portrait? Mark the description and study the image to see if you agree.

Connect: How does Rembrandt's final "selfie" surprise you? Would you choose to take a picture of yourself that didn't show you looking your best? Why or why not?

10   By the end of his life, Rembrandt was an expert at capturing character. He stripped away all the fancy dress and showed us simply Rembrandt the person. In his last self-portrait aged 63, he seems sad yet calm and dignified. We see him inside and out, with every lump, sag and wrinkle on display.

11   When experts examined his painting under X-ray, they discovered that the artist had made some changes. Originally his hat was much bigger and all white, and his hands had held a paintbrush. Rembrandt painted over this detail, bringing all our attention back to his face.

Self-Portrait at the Age of 63, 1669

Born: 1755 in France
Died: 1842, aged 86

Self-Portrait in a Straw Hat, 1782

Elizabeth Vigée Le Brun

12   This lady looks pretty in her straw hat and pink dress. She has a gentle smile and a friendly and welcoming gaze. Vigée Le Brun wanted people to like her in this selfie—and they did.

13   In the 18th century, female artists had to work hard to be taken seriously. Traditionally, painting was something that women did mostly as a hobby. Vigée Le Brun was extremely talented and she also sold her skills well. Self-portraits like this one were a way to attract attention and win people's hearts.

14   Elizabeth looks natural and relaxed in the painting. She seems comfortable with her palette and brushes, but they aren't the focus of the scene.

NOTICE & NOTE

ANALYZE MULTIMODAL TEXTS

Annotate: In paragraphs 12–14, mark the descriptions of the painting.

Summarize: Use details in the text to explain how Vigée Le Brun used her self-portraits to help promote her work.

Selfie: The Changing Face of Self-Portraits   255

NOTICE & NOTE

CONTRASTS AND CONTRADICTIONS

Notice & Note: How does Ducreux's painting contrast with other self-portraits you have learned about? Mark how the author describes Ducreux's self-portrait.

Infer: What might the artist wish to reveal about himself in this portrait?

Joseph Ducreux

15   These days, funny faces in selfies are nothing unusual, but in the 1700s people tended to be more straight-faced.[2] Most self-portraits avoided any strong feeling of being happy, cross or tired. It was different for the artists on these pages, though!

16   Joseph Ducreux found traditional portraiture[3] too prim and proper. Instead, he tried to capture the personalities of everyone he painted. In this self-portrait, he caught himself in the middle of a yawn. There's nothing shy or self-conscious about it—he pushes out his belly and opens his mouth wide, in a way that makes us want to yawn too.

Born: 1735 in France
Died: 1802, aged 67

Self-Portrait, Yawning, 1783

---

[2] **straight-faced:** showing no sign of emotion.
[3] **portraiture** (pôr´trĭ-choŏr´): the practice of creating portraits.

Born: 1853 in Netherlands
Died: 1890, aged 37

Self-Portrait with Bandaged Ear, 1889

Vincent van Gogh

17 You might take a selfie when something unusual happens to you. Van Gogh made this one after he cut a piece from his ear following an argument with his friend and fellow artist, Gauguin.

18 Can you see the bandage on the side of van Gogh's head? The unlucky ear was actually the left one, but he was looking in a mirror when he painted this. Rather than hiding his injury, he made it the focus of the picture. His face looks as if he's lost in thought.

19 Notice how van Gogh used big, thick brushstrokes. They bring out the different textures of his clothes, fur cap, bandage and bony face. Sometimes he squeezed paint straight from the tube onto the canvas, and it would take weeks and weeks to dry! Behind the artist we can see a Japanese print. Van Gogh was fascinated by Japanese art. He loved its bold outlines, flat colours and shapes, and did his best to use them in his own work.

20 When he painted this selfie, van Gogh was mentally ill. After cutting the chunk off his ear, he gave it to a woman as a "gift." He was taken into a hospital and a few months later checked into an asylum.

NOTICE & NOTE

ANALYZE PRINT AND GRAPHIC FEATURES

Annotate: Mark the graphic features used in the Vincent Van Gogh section.

Summarize: What effect do the graphic features have on the presentation of the author's ideas?

▶ **BIG QUESTIONS**

Notice & Note: Mark the words in paragraph 20 that may come as a surprise to many readers.

Draw Conclusions: Why might the author have included this detail?

Selfie: The Changing Face of Self-Portraits

NOTICE & NOTE

EXTREME OR ABSOLUTE LANGUAGE

Notice & Note: What examples of absolute language occur in paragraph 21? Mark examples of hyperbole in the paragraph.

Analyze: What is the effect of the author's use of hyperbole? What is she trying to convey?

Selfies Today

21   Selfies today are everywhere! With digital cameras and smartphones, anyone can snap themselves in an instant and share the picture with their friends or the world. Celebrities are doing it. Politicians are doing it. Will the selfie craze ever end?

22   2013 was the year that "#selfie" took off. More than 17 million people were posting a selfie on social media every week. In 2014, the word "selfie" made it into the Oxford Dictionary and was approved for the board game Scrabble! Technologies such as front-facing cameras, selfie sticks and hand-gesture sensors have made selfie-snapping easier than ever before.

23   In 2013, Pope Francis went viral in the first "Papal selfie," taken with young fans at the Vatican.

24   When you post a selfie, you're displaying a view of yourself that you want other people to see. When artists make self-portraits, it's the same! So next time you pose, remember you have something in common with every famous face in this book!

Selfie with Pope Francis

NOTICE & NOTE

CHECK YOUR UNDERSTANDING

Answer these questions before moving on to the **Analyze the Text** section on the following page.

1 The author included the section "All By Your Selfie" to —

   A teach the reader how to take a selfie

   B introduce the reader to the selection's topic

   C discuss female artists who made self-portraits

   D show that selfies are unique to modern times

2 In the section on artist Elizabeth Vigée Le Brun, the author includes a portrait by the artist to show that she —

   F considered painting just a hobby

   G made copies of her work for admirers

   H lived long ago

   J used self portraits to attract attention

3 Which idea is not supported by information throughout the selection?

   A Selfies and self-portraits have a lot in common.

   B Self-portraits offer information about the past.

   C Only wealthy, famous artists could create self-portraits.

   D Self-portraits can express personality and feeling.

Selfie: The Changing Face of Self-Portraits

RESPOND

ANALYZE THE TEXT

Support your responses with evidence from the text. 📓 **NOTEBOOK**

1. **Summarize** Review the last two paragraphs of the section about Rembrandt. How did Rembrandt evolve as a portrait painter over time, and how is it apparent in his final self-portrait?

2. **Analyze** In the section about Vincent van Gogh, how does the author use writing and visual modes of communication to communicate key ideas?

3. **Draw Conclusions** Review the section "Selfies Today," and note the selfie of Pope Francis. How does this selfie support the author's ideas about selfies and self-portraits?

4. **Critique** Review the way headings and graphics are presented throughout the selection. How effectively do the print and graphic features of the selection contribute to its overall structure?

5. **Notice & Note** Identify an idea in the text that surprised you. What about the idea was surprising?

RESEARCH

With a partner, research one of the artists mentioned in the text. Use more than one source, and guide your research with *who, what, where, when, how,* and *why* questions, like those below.

RESEARCH TIP
When you conduct research online, make sure that your sources are reliable. For biographical information on artists, consider using art museum websites or a trusted online encyclopedia.

QUESTIONS	ANSWERS
Who was this artist, and when did he or she live?	
What was the artist's style and medium?	
Where did the artist work?	
How was his/her artwork viewed during his/her lifetime?	
Why is this artist remembered today?	

Extend Identify an artist alive today who is known for creating self-portraits. Share images of the artist's work with the class.

RESPOND

CREATE AND DISCUSS

Summarize Key Ideas Write a summary of the key ideas in the selection. Use evidence from the text and the images to support the ideas you identify. Your summary should:

❏ Clearly state the key ideas presented in the selection.
❏ Support the ideas with evidence from the text, including print and graphic features.
❏ Use commas correctly, especially after introductory elements.

Critique with a Small Group Review the selection's headings and other graphic features. Discuss the purpose and effectiveness of each element. Then create new graphic features for the selection.

❏ As you review, have a group member create a list of the selection's graphic features.
❏ As you discuss the selection's features, analyze the strengths and weaknesses of each.
❏ Work together to create new heading designs and add other graphic features to help organize the selection.

Go to **Using Textual Evidence: Summarizing, Paraphrasing, and Quoting** in the **Writing Studio** for more on using textual evidence in a summary.

 Go to **Participating in Collaborative Discussions** in the **Speaking and Listening Studio** for help with having a group discussion.

RESPOND TO THE ESSENTIAL QUESTION

 What are the ways you can make yourself heard?

Gather Information Review your annotations and notes on *Selfie: The Changing Face of Self-Portraits*. Then, add relevant details to your Response Log. As you determine which information to include, think about the ways that people express themselves and how self-expression communicates ideas about the individual.

At the end of the unit, use your notes to write a multimodal argument.

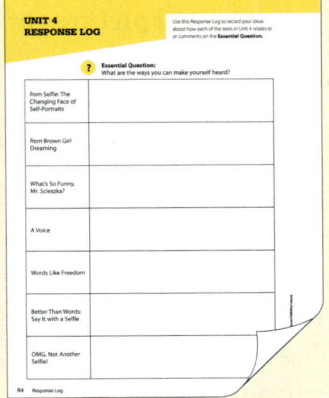

ACADEMIC VOCABULARY

As you write about and discuss what you learned from the selection, be sure to use the Academic Vocabulary words. Check off each of the words that you use.

❏ appropriate
❏ authority
❏ consequence
❏ element
❏ justify

RESPOND

WORD BANK
portrait
etch
reflection
span

CRITICAL VOCABULARY

Practice and Apply Complete each sentence in a way that shows the meaning of the Critical Vocabulary word.

1. The art teacher showed the class how to **etch** by _____.

2. A **portrait** is a type of painting that shows _____.

3. The **reflection** in the car's rear-view mirror showed _____.

4. The **span** of one year is equal to _____.

VOCABULARY STRATEGY:
Context Clues

When you come across an unfamiliar word in your reading, one way to determine its meaning is to use **context clues.** Context clues are hints about the meaning of an unknown word that may be found in the words, phrases, sentences, and paragraphs that surround that unknown word. Sometimes you can find a definition of an unknown word within the text. At other times, you can use surrounding words and phrases to infer the meaning of that word. Look at the following example:

> Before photography was invented, people who wanted pictures of themselves (and could afford it) commissioned artists to paint their portraits. If you were an artist it was even easier—you just looked in the mirror and painted what you saw!

If the meaning of *portraits* is unclear, look for clues to its meaning nearby. Notice how the sentence that follows *portraits* hints at the word's meaning. It says that artists who wanted to paint their own portraits "just looked in the mirror and painted" what they saw. This clue allows you to infer that *portrait* means "the painted likeness of a person's face."

Practice and Apply Working with a partner, use context clues to determine the meaning of *commissioned* in the previous example. Write a definition for the word. Finally, look up *commission* in a print or an online dictionary. Compare your definition to the dictionary definition. Discuss the similarities and differences with your partner.

Go to the **Vocabulary Studio** for more on context clues.

RESPOND

LANGUAGE CONVENTIONS:
Commas After Introductory Elements

An **introductory element** is a word, phrase, or dependent clause used to begin a sentence. A **phrase** is a group of related words that does not contain a subject and a predicate but functions in a sentence as a single part of speech. A **dependent clause** is a group of words containing a subject and predicate, but it cannot stand alone as a sentence. These introductory elements modify and clarify the ideas they precede. Writers place commas after introductory elements to make their sentences easier to understand.

In *Selfie: The Changing Face of Self-Portraits,* commas are used in the following ways:

 Go to **Punctuation: End Marks and Commas** in the **Grammar Studio** for more on using commas.

- to set off an introductory word

   Instead, he tried to capture the personalities of everyone he painted.

- to set off an introductory phrase

   On a trip to Italy, he noticed that great artists had a higher social status than they did at home in Germany.

- to set off a dependent clause used as an introductory element

   When he painted this selfie, van Gogh was mentally ill.

Practice and Apply Write your own sentences with commas that set off introductory words, phrases, and dependent clauses. Your sentences can express your observations about the self-portraits shown in the selection, or they can be about your own experiences with selfies. When you have finished, share your sentences with a partner and compare your use of commas.

ANALYZE & APPLY

from BROWN GIRL DREAMING

Memoir in Verse by **Jacqueline Woodson**

? ESSENTIAL QUESTION:

What are the ways you can make yourself heard?

GET READY

QUICK START

Look at the titles of the poems in this selection. What do you think you will learn about the author and her life? Share your thoughts with the class.

ANALYZE TEXT STRUCTURE AND PURPOSE

Poems, rather than chapters, create the **structure** for *Brown Girl Dreaming*, Jacqueline Woodson's memoir in verse. The word *memoir* comes from French, meaning "memory." Memoirs are written from the first-person point of view, detailing a writer's observations about significant events and people in the writer's life. Memoirs also may inform readers about historical events and their effects on the writer. While most memoirs are written in prose, Jacqueline Woodson structured her memoir as verse. Her poems contain all of the elements of a memoir.

Why might Woodson have used this particular style to write her memoir? As you read the excerpt from *Brown Girl Dreaming*, take notes on the elements of memoir and consider how they connect to the **author's purpose**—the main reason for writing the text.

GENRE ELEMENTS: MEMOIR IN VERSE

- is a personal narrative told from first-person point of view
- includes the writer's own experiences and observations of significant events or people
- has an informal or even intimate tone
- presents insights into the impact of historical events on people's lives, particularly the writer's
- tells the story through a series of poems

ELEMENTS OF A MEMOIR	AUTHOR'S PURPOSE

Brown Girl Dreaming 265

GET READY

MAKE CONNECTIONS

The full text of *Brown Girl Dreaming* presents events from Woodson's life along with her family's stories, drawing on a history from periods of enslavement to the civil rights era to Woodson's childhood in the 1970s. Her approach allows readers to connect their personal experiences to hers, as well as to connect her ideas to society and other texts. As you read, use a web diagram like the one below to organize your connections between *Brown Girl Dreaming* and your own experiences and ideas, and between the memoir and other texts.

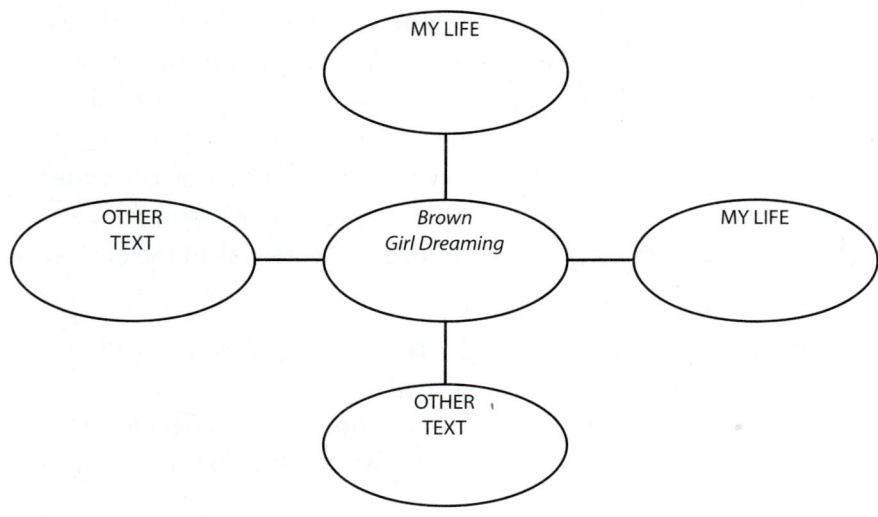

ANNOTATION MODEL

NOTICE & NOTE

As you read, note clues that reveal the author's purpose and examine how she uses text structure to convey a message. This model shows one reader's notes from the beginning of the excerpt from *Brown Girl Dreaming*.

writing #1

It's easier to make up stories

than it is to write them down. When I speak,

the words come pouring out of me. <u>The story</u>

<u>wakes up and walks all over the room. Sits in a chair,</u>

5   <u>crosses one leg over the other, says,</u>

<u>*Let me introduce myself*.</u> Then just starts going on and on.

Does #1 mean it's the first poem about writing? Maybe there will be more poems about writing later.

She personifies "story," as if it's a close friend talking to her. It feels very personal.

BACKGROUND

Jacqueline Woodson *(b. 1963), who had difficulty reading when she was young, has written more than 30 books. She wrote* Brown Girl Dreaming *to learn about her family and to discover what led her to become a writer. She says her memoir is a series of poems "because memories come to people in small bursts."* Brown Girl Dreaming *won the National Book Award in 2014, and Woodson was named National Ambassador for Young People's Literature for 2018–2019.*

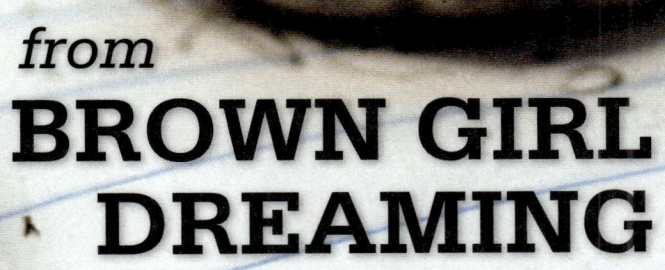

from BROWN GIRL DREAMING

Memoir in Verse by Jacqueline Woodson

SETTING A PURPOSE

As you read, notice how Woodson uses elements of poetry, including repetition, line breaks, and imagery, to describe events.

writing #1

It's easier to make up stories
than it is to write them down. When I speak,
the words come pouring out of me. The story
wakes up and walks all over the room. Sits in a chair,
5   crosses one leg over the other, says,
Let me introduce myself. Then just starts going on and on.
But as I bend over my composition notebook,
only my name
comes quickly. Each letter, neatly printed
10 between the pale blue lines. Then white
space and air and me wondering, *How do I
spell introduce?* Trying again and again
until there is nothing but pink
bits of eraser and a hole now.
15 where a story should be.

Notice & Note

Use the side margins to notice and note signposts in the text.

ANALYZE TEXT STRUCTURE AND PURPOSE

Annotate: Mark the result of the author not being able to spell *introduce*.

Infer: What might this reveal about the author's purpose?

NOTICE & NOTE

MEMORY MOMENT

Notice & Note: What does the author remember writing on the board? Mark what she writes and then mark why she writes it.

Analyze: Why might this memory be important to the author? Is she able to "make herself heard"?

late autumn

Ms. Moskowitz calls us one by one and says,
Come up to the board and write your name.
When it's my turn, I walk down the aisle from
my seat in the back, write *Jacqueline Woodson*—
20 the way I've done a hundred times, turn back
toward my seat, proud as anything
of my name in white letters on the dusty blackboard.
But Ms. Moskowitz stops me, says,
In cursive too, please. But the *q* in Jacqueline is too hard
25 so I write *Jackie Woodson* for the first time. Struggle
only a *little* bit with the *k*.

Is that what you want us to call you?

I want to say, *No, my name is Jacqueline*
but I am scared of that cursive *q*, know
30 I may never be able to connect it to *c* and *u*
so I nod even though
I am lying.

the other woodson

Even though so many people think my sister and I
are twins,
35 I am the other Woodson, following behind her each year
into the same classroom she had the year before. Each
teacher smiles when they call my name. *Woodson,* they
say. *You must be Odella's sister.* Then they nod
slowly, over and over again, call me Odella. Say,
40 *I'm sorry! You look so much like her and she is SO brilliant!*
then wait for my brilliance to light up
the classroom. Wait for my arm to fly into
the air with every answer. Wait for my pencil
to move quickly through the too-easy math problems
45 on the mimeographed sheet.[1] Wait for me to stand
before class, easily reading words even high school
students stumble over. And they keep waiting.
And waiting
and waiting
50 and waiting

until one day, they walk into the classroom,
almost call me Odel—then stop

remember that I am the other Woodson

and begin searching for brilliance

55 at another desk.

---

[1] **mimeographed sheet** (mĭm´ē-ə-grăft´ shēt): a page from a duplicating machine, which makes copies of written, drawn, or typed material by pressing ink through a stencil on to paper.

MAKE CONNECTIONS

Annotate: Mark comparisons other people make about the author and her sister.

Connect: Have you ever been compared to someone else? How did it make you feel?

NOTICE & NOTE

reading

I am not my sister.
Words from the books curl around each other
make little sense
until
60 I read them again
and again, the story
settling into memory. *Too slow*
the teacher says.
Read faster.
65 *Too babyish,* the teacher says.
Read older.
But I don't want to read faster or older or
any way else that might
make the story disappear too quickly from where it's settling
70 inside my brain,
slowly becoming
a part of me.
A story I will remember
long after I've read it for the second, third,
75 tenth, hundredth time.

MEMORY MOMENT

Notice & Note: Why does the author reread books? Mark the memory the narrator describes.

Infer: Why might this memory be important to the development of the author's writing?

stevie and me

Every Monday, my mother takes us
to the library around the corner. We are allowed
to take out seven books each. On those days,
no one complains
80 that all I want are picture books.

Those days, no one tells me to read faster
to read harder books
to read like Dell.

No one is there to say, *Not that book,*
85 when I stop in front of the small paperback
with a brown boy on the cover.
Stevie.

I read:
One day my momma told me,
90 *"You know you're gonna have*
a little friend come stay with you."
And I said, "Who is it?"

If someone had been fussing with me
to read like my sister, I might have missed
95 the picture book filled with brown people, more
brown people than I'd ever seen
in a book before.

The little boy's name was Steven but
his mother kept calling him Stevie.
100 *My name is Robert but my momma don't*
call me Robertie.

If someone had taken
that book out of my hand
said, *You're too old for this*
105 maybe
I'd never have believed
that someone who looked like me
could be in the pages of the book
that someone who looked like me
110 had a story.

ANALYZE TEXT STRUCTURE AND PURPOSE

Annotate: Mark the type of library books the author likes.

Analyze: How might the books relate to the author's purpose for writing about this memory?

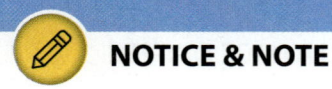

NOTICE & NOTE

MAKE CONNECTIONS

Annotate: Mark the italicized phrases.

Connect: How do these messages compare to ones you have heard from adults in your life? Recall another text in which a character was given conflicting messages about adult life. How does it compare to Woodson's memory?

when i tell my family

When I tell my family
I want to be a writer, they smile and say,
We see you in the backyard with your writing.
They say,
115 *We hear you making up all those stories.*
And,
We used to write poems.
And,
It's a good hobby, we see how quiet it keeps you.
120 They say,
But maybe you should be a teacher,
a lawyer,
do hair . . .

I'll think about it, I say.

125 And maybe all of us know

this is just another one of my
stories.

272   Unit 4

CHECK YOUR UNDERSTANDING

Answer these questions before moving on to the **Analyze the Text** section on the following page.

1 The poems reveal that as a child the author struggled with —

   A listening to her mother

   B reading and writing

   C going on family outings

   D playing and practicing sports

2 The book *Stevie* is important to the author because —

   F it has people of color in it

   G it is the first library book she checks out

   H it has a character in it who is a writer

   J it is the first book she can read

3 Which phrase best fits the author's description of her older sister?

   A Helpful and kind

   B Competitive and ambitious

   C Protective and watchful

   D Intelligent and studious

RESPOND

ANALYZE THE TEXT

Support your responses with evidence from the text. 📓 **NOTEBOOK**

1. **Connect** Choose a few lines from the selection that connect to another text you have read. What is the connection? Explain.

2. **Draw Conclusions** Review the titles of the verses in this excerpt. What do the titles have in common? How do you think this feature relates to the author's overall purpose in writing the memoir?

3. **Analyze** Review the italicized words throughout the selection. Why do you think the author italicized these words? Cite evidence in your answer.

4. **Summarize** Review and summarize the first poem, "writing #1." How do the first two lines provide structure and meaning?

5. **Notice & Note** Review lines 124–127. What do you think the author is trying to say here? Why did she include this memory?

RESEARCH

Use multiple sources to research and answer questions about the author Jacqueline Woodson. Ask your own questions about Woodson and her work, and then find the answers.

RESEARCH TIP
You can research authors online. Authors often host their own websites with information on their lives, their books, and their writing process. Publishers may post interviews, video clips, and photos.

QUESTION	ANSWER
What helped Woodson most as she learned to write?	
How did "lying" influence her writing?	
What did her teachers think of her writing?	
What are some fun facts about Woodson?	
My question(s):	

Connect Consider what you've learned about Jacqueline Woodson in your research. Discuss the information you've discovered with a partner. Does the information you learned clarify any questions you had about *Brown Girl Dreaming*?

RESPOND

CREATE AND PRESENT

Describe a Connection Write a brief, formal letter or email to Jacqueline Woodson. Describe a meaningful connection you found between your life and an aspect or event in her memoir.

- ❏ Include the date and the name of the person your letter is for.
- ❏ Write the body of your letter, describing the connection.
- ❏ What aspects or events in the selection moved you or brought meaning to your life? Provide details about your life that will help Woodson understand the connection.
- ❏ Remember to sign your letter.

Go to **Writing Informative Texts: Formal Style** in the **Writing Studio** for more on styles of writing.

Compose and Present a Biographical Poem Choose an event that affected your life. Write a free verse or formal poem about that event.

- ❏ Choose an event to write about and the poetic form that best conveys your experience, either free verse or formal. Write your poem.
- ❏ Practice reading your poem aloud and present it to a small group or to the class.
- ❏ Make eye contact with your audience and use pacing, tone, and voice to help convey your poem's meaning.
- ❏ Answer questions about your poem, and ask questions about the purpose and message of the poems of other students.

 Go to **Giving a Presentation: Delivering Your Presentation** in the **Speaking and Listening Studio** for more on presenting your work.

RESPOND TO THE ESSENTIAL QUESTION

 What are the ways you can make yourself heard?

Gather Information Review your annotations and notes from *Brown Girl Dreaming*. Then, add relevant details to your Response Log. As you determine what information to include, think about:

- how the author expresses herself
- how verse can be used to express oneself
- what kinds of things are important to express

At the end of the unit, use your notes to create a multimodal argument.

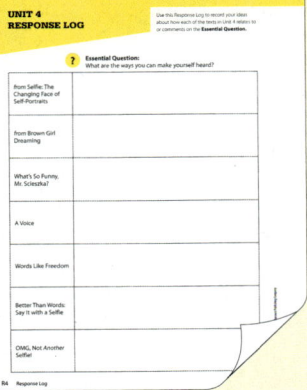

ACADEMIC VOCABULARY

As you write and discuss what you learned from the poems, be sure to use the Academic Vocabulary words. Check off each of the words that you use.

- ❏ appropriate
- ❏ authority
- ❏ consequence
- ❏ element
- ❏ justify

ANALYZE & APPLY

WHAT'S SO FUNNY, MR. SCIESZKA?

Humor by **Jon Scieszka**

ESSENTIAL QUESTION:

What are the ways you can make yourself heard?

GET READY

QUICK START

Have you ever had to make an on-the-spot choice that could change your life forever? Think of a big choice you made and how it has changed your life. Write down your thoughts.

MAKE INFERENCES ABOUT AUTHOR'S PURPOSE AND MESSAGE

An **author's purpose** is the main reason for writing the text. The purpose may be to inform, entertain, persuade, or express thoughts and feelings. Most writers do not state a purpose directly, but suggest it through the information they present and the text's tone and structure. Structural elements include how sentences and paragraphs are organized, as well as how the text presents ideas or describes events.

An **author's message** is the main idea of a particular work. Often, the author doesn't explicitly state a message. Readers must **infer** or discover that message as they read.

To make an inference about an author's purpose and message, make a logical guess based on facts and clues in the text, combined with your own knowledge and experience. Support your inference with evidence from the text, and confirm or revise your inference as you read.

Here is an inference, based on evidence from the text, about the message of "What's So Funny, Mr. Sciezska?"

GENRE ELEMENTS: HUMOR
- may include exaggeration
- often uses double meanings
- relies on amusing descriptions
- may incorporate comic irony
- often includes witty or funny dialogue

INFERENCE ABOUT THE MESSAGE	EVIDENCE FROM THE TEXT
At times you are faced with making a choice that can alter the course of your life.	That day I reached a life-choice fork in the road. I saw two life paths laid out clearly before me.

ANALYZE AUTHOR'S USE OF LANGUAGE

Writers use descriptive words, imagery, and figurative language to create a feeling, or **mood**. A mood might be tense, creepy, or peaceful, for example. Writers also use language to create **voice**, or the distinct personality readers hear as they read a text.

- To analyze how the author uses language to create mood, mark figurative language, imagery, and word choices, noting their effects.
- To determine voice, mark significant words that capture personality.

GET READY

CRITICAL VOCABULARY

| apology | history | terror | pause |

To see how many Critical Vocabulary words you already know, use them to complete the sentences.

1. _____ between key points when speaking to an audience.
2. The newspaper issued a/an _____ for printing misinformation.
3. The soldier recounted the _____ of the frightening battle.
4. Do you have records of your family's _____?

LANGUAGE CONVENTIONS

Pronouns A pronoun is a word used in place of a noun or another pronoun, such as *he*, *she*, or *it*. The word or word group to which a pronoun refers is its **antecedent**. If an antecedent is singular, use a singular pronoun. If an antecedent is plural, use a plural pronoun.

> My friend and back-row pal, Tim K. had just told me the funniest joke I had ever heard. The fact that he had told it while Sister Mary Margaret was droning on . . . only made it funnier.

The singular pronoun *it* relates to the singular noun *joke*. The singular pronoun *he* refers to the singular *Tim K*.

> Sister Mary Margaret's eyes were wider than I had ever seen them.

The plural pronoun *them* relates to the plural antecedent *eyes*.

As you read the text, notice the pronouns and antecedents.

ANNOTATION MODEL

NOTICE & NOTE

As you read, mark descriptive words, figurative language, and imagery to understand mood and voice. In the model, you can see how one reader responded to a passage in "What's So Funny, Mr. Scieszka?"

1 The voice flew across the room and nailed me to the back of my seat.

2 "What's so funny, Mr. Scieszka?"

3 The voice belonged to Sister Margaret Mary. And it had just flown across our fifth-grade religion class at St. Luke's Elementary School to find me in what I had thought was the safety of the back row.

This figurative language makes me feel the harshness of Sister Margaret Mary's voice. The mood seems tense.

BACKGROUND

Jon Scieszka *(b. 1954) grew up in Flint, Michigan, with five brothers, who provided plenty of material for writing funny stories. Scieszka's* The Stinky Cheese Man and Other Fairly Stupid Tales *won a Caldecott Honor medal. In 2008, the Library of Congress appointed Scieszka the first Ambassador for Young People's Literature. "What's So Funny, Mr. Scieszka?" is from* Knucklehead, *a humorous memoir about his rambunctious childhood.*

WHAT'S SO FUNNY, MR. SCIESZKA?

Humor by Jon Scieszka

SETTING A PURPOSE

Humor can be an effective way to make your voice heard. In this story, the author uses humor to describe a choice he made as a child that had life-changing consequences. The choice is between playing it safe or taking a leap and making himself heard.

1   The voice flew across the room and nailed me to the back of my seat.

2   "What's so funny, Mr. Scieszka?"

3   The voice belonged to Sister Margaret Mary.[1] And it had just flown across our fifth-grade religion class at St. Luke's Elementary School to find me in what I had thought was the safety of the back row.

4   "What's so funny?" I repeated, trying desperately to stop laughing.

5   I knew the correct answer to this question was, "Nothing, Sister."

6   "I'm sorry, Sister," was also a very good reply.

---

[1] **Sister Margaret Mary:** the nun teaching religion class; Sister is the form of address for a nun.

Notice & Note

Use the side margins to notice and note signposts in the text.

ANALYZE AUTHOR'S USE OF LANGUAGE

Annotate: Reread paragraphs 1–3. Mark examples of descriptive words and imagery.

Infer: How does this language create the mood and voice of the story?

NOTICE & NOTE

ANALYZE AUTHOR'S USE OF LANGUAGE

Annotate: Read paragraphs 7–8. Mark instances of extreme language or exaggeration.

Infer: Why do you think the author uses extreme language and exaggeration?

TOUGH QUESTIONS

Notice & Note: How does the author describe the two life paths he sees before him? Mark the author's two choices in paragraph 10.

Evaluate: What do you think the long-term consequences of each choice might be?

AHA MOMENT

Notice & Note: Mark the author's realization in paragraphs 11–12.

Infer: Why is this a crucial moment for him?

apology
(ə-pŏl´ə-jē) n. An *apology* is an expression of regret or a request for forgiveness.

7 And nine times out of ten, ninety-nine times out of a hundred, I would have used one of those answers. But that day in fifth-grade religion class, something happened. That day I reached a life-choice fork in the road.[2]

8 My friend and back-row pal, Tim K. had just told me the funniest joke I had ever heard. The fact that he had told it while Sister Margaret Mary was droning on about our future place in heaven or hell only made it funnier.

9 Now I was called out.

10 I saw two life paths laid out clearly before me. Down the one path of the quick **apology** lay a good grade for religion class, a spot in heaven, maybe even sainthood if things worked out later in life. Down the other path lay the chance of a very big laugh . . . though mixed with punishment, maybe a note to my parents, quite possibly one mad God and forever in hell.

11 A good grade in religion class is always a good thing in Catholic school. I knew that. But I also knew this was a really funny joke. I was torn between going for the A and heaven, and

[2] **fork in the road:** a metaphor referring to a moment in life when you have to make a big choice.

280 Unit 4

going for the laugh with a chance of hell. Both were right in front of me.

12   So when Sister Margaret Mary asked her next question, "Would you like to share it with the rest of the class?" I chose my life's path.

13   "Well, there's this guy who wants to be a bell ringer,"³ I begin. "But he doesn't have any arms."

14   Sister Margaret Mary's eyes pop open wider than I have ever seen them. The whole class turns to look at me and the train wreck about to happen. Even my pal Tim K. is shaking his head. Nobody in the **history** of St. Luke's Elementary School has ever chosen to "share it with the rest of the class." But I feel it. I have to do it. It is my path.

15   "The priest who is looking for a good bell ringer says, 'You can't ring the bells. You don't have any arms.' "

16   The faces of my fellow fifth-graders are looking a bit wavy and blurry. " 'I don't need arms,' says the bell-ringing guy. 'Watch this.' And he runs up the bell tower and starts bouncing his face off the bells and making beautiful music."

17   Half of the class laughs. I'm not sure if it's out of nervousness or pity. But it's a lot of laughs.

18   Sister Margaret Mary's eyes open impossibly wider.

19   Light floods the classroom. I can't really see anybody now. I can only feel the punch line building. I head toward the light.

20   "So the bell-ringing guy goes to finish his song with one last smack of his face, but this time he misses the bell and falls right out of the tower. He lands on the ground and is knocked out. A whole crowd gathers around him."

21   The whole fifth-grade religion class has gathered around me. It is a feeling of unbelievable power mixed with **terror** for a low-profile⁴ fifth-grader like myself.

22   " 'Who is this guy?' the villagers ask."

23   I feel the whole world **pause** for just a single beat, like it always does before a good punch line.

NOTICE & NOTE

MAKE INFERENCES ABOUT AUTHOR'S PURPOSE AND MESSAGE

Annotate: Reread paragraphs 12–23. Mark the sequence of events as they occur in chronological order.

Infer: How do you think the way the text is structured supports the author's main purpose for writing the text?

history
(hĭs´tə-rē) *n. History* is a chronological record of events of a person or institution.

ANALYZE AUTHOR'S USE OF LANGUAGE

Annotate: Reread paragraphs 14–21. Mark descriptive words and imagery that create a distinct mood.

Infer: What do you think Scieszka is feeling as he tells the joke? What do you think Sister Margaret Mary and the class are feeling?

terror
(tĕr´ər) *n. Terror* is extreme fear of something.

pause
(pôz) *v.* To *pause* is to hesitate or suspend action.

---

³ **bell ringer:** a person who rings the bells of a church or tower, usually by pulling on a rope.
⁴ **low profile:** subdued or modest behavior to avoid attracting attention.

NOTICE & NOTE

MAKE INFERENCES ABOUT AUTHOR'S PURPOSE AND MESSAGE

Annotate: Reread the last paragraph. Mark words or phrases that help identify the author's message.

Infer: What is the author's message in this story?

LANGUAGE CONVENTIONS

It is used several times in paragraph 25. Mark each instance of the pronoun *it*, and indicate the antecedent for each one.

24 " 'I don't know his name,' says the priest. 'But his face rings a bell.' "

25 I don't remember the grade I got in fifth-grade religion class. But I do remember the laugh I got. It was huge. It was the whole class (except Sister Margaret Mary). It was out-of-control hysterical. It was glorious. And it set me on my lifelong path of answering that classic question, "What's so funny, Mr. Scieszka?"

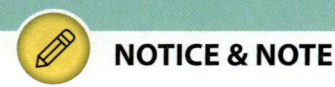

282   Unit 4

NOTICE & NOTE

CHECK YOUR UNDERSTANDING

Answer these questions before moving on to the **Analyze the Text** section on the following page.

1 The author's purpose for writing this humorous narrative is most likely to —

   A make people tell jokes

   B describe a life-changing moment in his life

   C explain why he didn't get a good grade in religion class

   D describe what it's like to go to Catholic school

2 In what way does the structure of the text contribute to its effectiveness?

   F It builds momentum to keep the reader engaged until the end.

   G The sequence of events takes the reader into the past.

   H The structure tells the reader that this is a kind of memoir.

   J The structure supports the purpose of the article.

3 Which sentence from the text best relates to the message of the story?

   A *I knew the correct answer to this question was, "Nothing, Sister."*

   B *That day I reached a life-choice fork in the road.*

   C *A good grade in religion class is always a good thing in Catholic school.*

   D *The whole class turns to look at me and the train wreck about to happen.*

RESPOND

ANALYZE THE TEXT

Support your responses with evidence from the text. **NOTEBOOK**

1. **Evaluate** Review paragraphs 10–14. How would you describe the voice of the narrator? Cite evidence from the text to support your description.

2. **Analyze** How does the text structure contribute to the author's purpose? Support your reasoning with evidence from the text.

3. **Evaluate** Review paragraphs 13–23. What was Mr. Scieszka feeling as he repeated the joke in front of the class? Cite examples of the language the author uses to convey his experience.

4. **Draw Conclusions** Is the author usually someone who seeks attention or who likes to perform? Cite evidence from the text to support your answer.

5. **Notice & Note** Find examples of extreme or absolute language in "What's So Funny, Mr. Scieszka?" Explain how this language contributes to the mood and voice of the story.

RESEARCH

RESEARCH TIP
The best search terms are very specific. Along with the humorist's name, include the books, TV shows, or movies with which he or she is associated.

Conduct research into your favorite childhood humorist. Identify what inspired that person to become a humorist, and why that person considers humor important. What does your research reveal about his or her purpose? Record what you learn in the chart.

NAME OF HUMORIST:	
Inspiration for Becoming a Humorist	
Why Humor Is Important	
Humorist's Purpose	

Extend Conduct research on Jon Scieszka, the author of "What's So Funny, Mr. Scieszka?" Find out more about what inspired him to become a humorist and why he thinks humor is important. What else has he written or produced? Share the results of your research with a partner.

RESPOND

CREATE AND PRESENT

Analyze Author's Purpose and Message Review your notes and annotations from the reading. Then, write a three- to four-paragraph analysis of Scieszka's purpose. Why does he tell this story? What is his purpose and message? Follow these steps:

❑ Include a controlling idea or thesis about the author's purpose.
❑ Provide text evidence to support your ideas.
❑ Make pronouns clearly identify and agree with their antecedents.

Explain the Steps for Telling a Joke Discuss with a small group what you know about how to deliver a silly joke to someone much younger than you.

❑ Select a joke that is appropriate for a younger audience. Remember to consider suggestions from all group members.
❑ Outline the steps for telling the joke successfully to a younger audience. Include how you say the joke, what facial expressions and gestures to use, what tone of voice to use, when to pause, and how often to make eye contact.
❑ Deliver your joke to the class, following the steps in your outline. After you tell the joke, explain the steps in your outline.

 Go to **Writing Informative Texts** in the **Writing Studio** for more on writing an analysis.

 Go to **Participating in Collaborative Discussions** in the **Speaking and Listening Studio** for help with having a group discussion.

RESPOND TO THE ESSENTIAL QUESTION

? What are the ways you can make yourself heard?

Gather Information Review your annotations and notes on "What's So Funny, Mr. Scieszka?" Then, add relevant details to your Response Log. As you determine which information to include, think about:

- the kinds of choices people make in life
- what happens when people must make quick decisions
- how humor can help people cope with challenging situations

At the end of the unit, use your notes to write a multimodal argument.

ACADEMIC VOCABULARY

As you discuss what you learned from the text, be sure to use the Academic Vocabulary words. Check off each of the words that you use.

❑ appropriate
❑ authority
❑ consequence
❑ element
❑ justify

RESPOND

WORD BANK
apology
history
terror
pause

CRITICAL VOCABULARY

Practice and Apply With a partner, discuss and write down an answer to each of the following questions. Then work together to write a sentence for each vocabulary word.

1. Which vocabulary word goes with *fright?* Why?
2. Which vocabulary word goes with *wait?* Why?
3. Which vocabulary word goes with *the past?* Why?
4. Which vocabulary word goes with *regret?* Why?

VOCABULARY STRATEGY:
Resources

You can often determine the meaning of an unfamiliar word by examining its root. A **root** is a word part that contains the core meaning of the word. For example, *tech* comes from a Greek root that can mean "art," "skill," or "craft." You can find this root in the word *technician;* you can use the root to figure out that *technician* refers to someone who has a specific skill.

Practice and Apply Using dictionaries and online resources, determine the origin and source of meaning for each Critical Vocabulary word. Then build related words from each word, emphasizing the role of the Greek or Latin root.

 Go to **Using Reference Resources** in the **Vocabulary Studio** for more on how to determine origins and sources of meanings.

WORD	ORIGIN/MEANING	ROOT	RELATED WORDS FROM SAME ROOT
apology	a thoughtful reply or response (as a defending speech in court)	from *apologiā* apo- (off) + logo (speech)	apologist apologize apologetic
history			
terror			
pause			

286 Unit 4

LANGUAGE CONVENTIONS: Pronouns

A **pronoun** is a word used in place of a noun or another pronoun. The word or group that the pronoun refers to is its **antecedent.**

Personal, indefinite, and relative pronouns are three common types of pronouns. **Personal pronouns** may replace nouns representing people. **Indefinite pronouns** refer to one or more persons or things not specifically mentioned and usually have no antecedents. **Relative pronouns** relate, or connect, adjective clauses to the words they modify in sentences. Look at these examples:

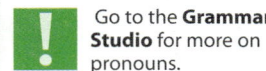

Go to the **Grammar Studio** for more on pronouns.

PERSONAL	INDEFINITE	RELATIVE
I, you, we, they, me, ours, she, it, my, us	another, anybody, both, all, none, most, no one	who, which, that, whose, whom
Maria is tall; she is taller than I am.	No one is taking the bus today.	The author, who wrote my favorite book, will speak here next week.

Pronoun-Antecedent Agreement To make sure a personal pronoun agrees with its antecedent, ask yourself: "Which noun is this pronoun replacing?" Read the following two sentences. Which one is correct?

- The little girl fed the cat; she was kind to animals.
- The little girl fed the cat; they were kind to animals.

The first sentence is correct. The noun being replaced is *girl*. The personal pronoun *she* agrees with the antecedent because it is singular and feminine. In the second sentence, *they* is plural and does not agree with the antecedent.

Practice and Apply Write two humorous sentences for each type of pronoun—personal, indefinite, and relative. Don't use the same pronoun twice.

COLLABORATE & COMPARE

POEM
A VOICE
by **Pat Mora**
pages 291–293

COMPARE POEMS

As you read, notice the use of figurative language and identify details that help you understand each poem's speaker and tone. After you read both poems, you will collaborate with a small group on a final project.

 ESSENTIAL QUESTION:

What are the ways you can make yourself heard?

POEM
WORDS LIKE FREEDOM
by **Langston Hughes**
pages 294–295

GET READY

QUICK START

Make a list of what you think about when you hear the words *freedom* and *liberty*. Discuss your list with classmates.

ANALYZE FIGURATIVE LANGUAGE

Poets use **figurative language,** such as simile and metaphor, to express ideas in an imaginative way. A **simile** is a comparison of two unlike things using the words *like* or *as*. A **metaphor** is a comparison of two unlike things that have some qualities in common, but a metaphor does not use *like* or *as*. The poem "A Voice" opens with a simile:

> Even the <u>lights on the stage</u> unrelenting as <u>the desert sun</u> couldn't hide the other students . . .

The simile compares the stage lights to a desert sun, emphasizing how unforgiving and severe the lights seem. When analyzing simile and metaphor, ask yourself: What two things is the poet comparing? Why? What feelings and attitudes does the simile or metaphor help explain?

Personification is a type of figurative language in which an object, animal, or idea is given human qualities. Poets use personification to emphasize an idea or to create an emotional effect. The poem "Words Like Freedom" contains personification:

> On my heartstrings <u>freedom</u> <u>sings</u>

Here, the poet gives the abstract idea of freedom the human ability to sing. When analyzing personification, ask yourself: What nonhuman things are given human qualities? Why? What is the effect of the personification?

As you read "A Voice" and "Words Like Freedom," use a chart like the following to analyze each poet's use of figurative language.

GENRE ELEMENTS: POETRY

- uses sound devices, imagery, and figurative language, such as simile, metaphor, and personification, to express ideas and emotions
- includes rhyme or rhythm to emphasize the musical quality of language
- arranges words and lines in different ways to produce an effect

EXAMPLE	TYPE OF FIGURATIVE LANGUAGE	WHAT IS THE POET TELLING ME?
Their eyes were pinpricks	metaphor	Their stares were painful.

A Voice / Words Like Freedom

GET READY

MAKE INFERENCES

When you make an **inference** about a literary work, you use evidence from the text and your own knowledge and experience to make a logical guess. Readers can identify and put together clues, such as a poet's choice of words and images, to make inferences about a poem.

The **tone** of a literary work expresses the writer's voice and attitude toward his or her subject, helping to communicate **mood.** Words such as *angry*, *playful*, or *mocking* can be used to describe different tones. Writers establish tone through images and descriptions. Tone is very closely linked to the **speaker** in a poem. The speaker is the voice that "talks" to the reader.

Read these lines from "A Voice":

> **In your house that smelled like
> rose powder, you spoke Spanish formal . . .**

These lines provide a clue about the home of the person in the poem. From this, readers can infer that the poem's speaker has a deep understanding of this person's home life. The speaker's tone can be described here as *understanding* or *intimate*. The following checklist will help you make inferences about speaker and tone:

❏ Identify the topic of the poem.
❏ Pay attention to images and descriptions. Are they serious, silly, happy, or sad?
❏ Decide how the speaker feels about the topic. Does he or she feel happy, sad, proud, or angry?

ANNOTATION MODEL

NOTICE & NOTE

As you read, note inferences about the poem and the speaker of the poem. In the model, you can see one reader's notes about the first stanza of "A Voice."

1 Even the lights on the stage unrelenting

   as the desert sun couldn't hide the other

   students, their eyes also unrelenting,

Interesting! The speaker compares lights on a stage to the desert sun. I wonder why.

290 Unit 4

BACKGROUND

Pat Mora *(b. 1942) was born in El Paso, Texas, to a Mexican-American family that spoke both English and Spanish. Mora grew up speaking both languages, and today she writes in English and in Spanish. When not writing, Mora spends much of her time encouraging children of all languages to read books. In 1996, she founded a holiday called "El día de los niños/El día de los libros," or "Children's Day/Book Day."*

A VOICE
by Pat Mora

PREPARE TO COMPARE

As you read, note how figurative language and tone help you understand the special relationship between the poem's speaker and her Mexican-American mother.

> 1 Even the lights on the stage unrelenting[1]
>   as the desert sun couldn't hide the other
>   students, their eyes also unrelenting,
>   students who spoke English every night
>
> 5 as they ate their meat, potatoes, gravy.
>   Not you. In your house that smelled like
>   rose powder, you spoke Spanish formal
>   as your father, the judge without a courtroom
>
>   in the country he floated to in the dark
> 10 on a flatbed truck. He walked slow
>   as a hot river down the narrow hall
>   of your house. You never dared to race past him,

---

[1] **unrelenting** (ŭn′rĭ-lĕn′tĭng): steady and persistent; continuing on without stopping.

Notice & Note

Use the side margins to notice and note signposts in the text.

MAKE INFERENCES

Annotate: In lines 1–8, mark the differences between the students who spoke English and the person in the poem referred to as "you."

Compare: What does this comparison tell you about the speaker of the poem and her subject, "you"?

NOTICE & NOTE

MAKE INFERENCES

Annotate: In lines 13–16, mark how the speaker describes her subject's ability to learn English and how English is viewed in her home.

Evaluate: How does this description help you understand the speaker's tone?

MEMORY MOMENT

Notice & Note: What does the memory in lines 25–29 reveal? Mark the speaker's memory.

Infer: What does this memory help explain about the present moment?

ANALYZE FIGURATIVE LANGUAGE

Annotate: Mark the figurative language in lines 30–34.

Interpret: How do these comparisons express the emotions of the poem's subject?

---

to say, "Please move," in the language
you learned effortlessly, as you learned to run,
15 the language forbidden at home, though your mother
said you learned it to fight with the neighbors.

You liked winning with words. You liked
writing speeches about patriotism and democracy.
You liked all the faces looking at you, all those eyes.
20 "How did I do it?" you ask me now. "How did I do it

when my parents didn't understand?"
The family story says your voice is the voice
of an aunt in Mexico, spunky² as a peacock.
Family stories sing of what lives in the blood.

25 You told me only once about the time you went
to the state capitol, your family proud as if
you'd been named governor. But when you looked
around, the only Mexican in the auditorium,

you wanted to hide from those strange faces.
30 Their eyes were pinpricks,³ and you faked
hoarseness. You, who are never at a loss
for words, felt your breath stick in your throat

like an ice-cube. "I can't," you whispered.
"I can't." Yet you did. Not that day but years later.
35 You taught the four of us to speak up.
This is America, Mom. The undo-able is done

in the next generation.⁴ Your breath moves
through the family like the wind
39 moves through the trees.

---

² **spunky** (spŭng′kē): spirited, plucky; having energy and courage.
³ **pinpricks** (pĭn′prĭkz′): small wounds or punctures made by, or as if by, a pin.
⁴ **generation** (jĕn′ə-rā′shən): people at the same stage of descent from a common ancestor; grandparents, parents, and children represent three different generations.

CHECK YOUR UNDERSTANDING

Answer these questions about "A Voice" before moving on to the next poem.

1 What language did the speaker's mother primarily use at home?

   A Spanish

   B English

   C an unknown language

   D an ancient language

2 Which of the following is an example of a simile?

   F *their eyes also unrelenting*

   G *He walked slow / as a hot river*

   H *country he floated to in the dark*

   J *You liked writing speeches*

3 "A Voice" makes the statement that —

   A learning a new language is difficult

   B family stories should only be spoken in native languages

   C people should memorize family stories

   D family stories communicate a family's history

NOTICE & NOTE

BACKGROUND

Langston Hughes *(1902–1967) began writing poetry as a child, but he didn't gain fame until he met a famous poet in a restaurant where Hughes was working. Hughes left several of his poems at the poet's table; the poet was impressed and helped introduce Hughes to a wider audience. Hughes became one of the most important voices in the Harlem Renaissance. Much of his work focuses on the experiences of his fellow African Americans who lived around him in Harlem.*

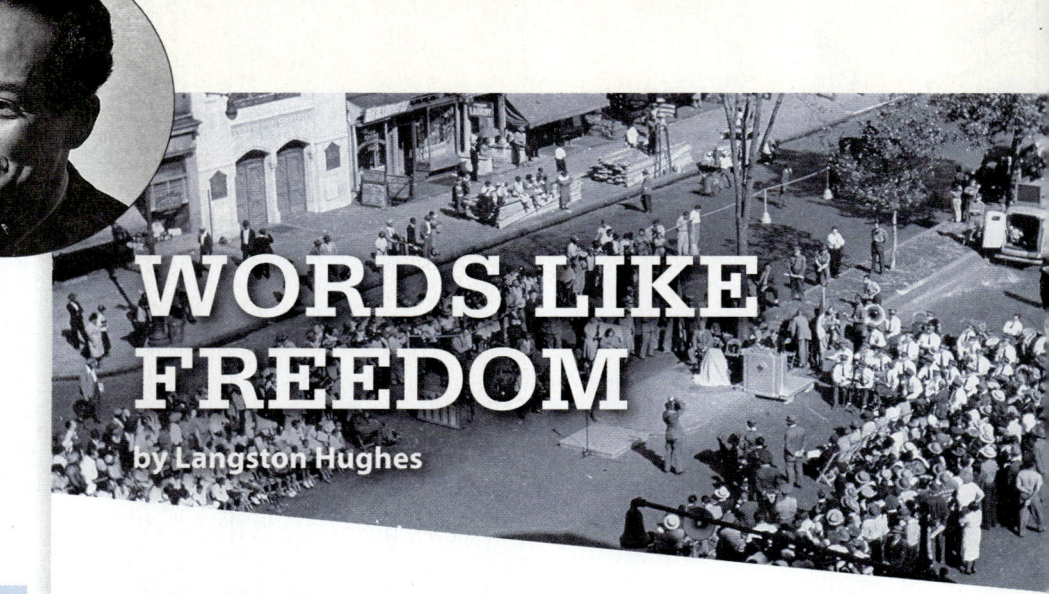

WORDS LIKE FREEDOM
by Langston Hughes

PREPARE TO COMPARE

As you read, note the poet's use of figurative language and identify details that help you make inferences about the speaker and that speaker's tone.

There are words like *Freedom*
Sweet and wonderful to say.
On my heartstrings freedom sings
All day everyday.

5 There are words like *Liberty*
That almost make me cry.
If you had known what I know
You would know why.

Notice & Note

Use the side margins to notice and note signposts in the text.

ANALYZE FIGURATIVE LANGUAGE

Annotate: Mark the figurative language the speaker uses to describe freedom in line 3.

Analyze: What emotional effect does this figurative language create?

MAKE INFERENCES

Annotate: In line 6, mark the speaker's reaction to the word *liberty*.

Compare: How has the tone changed from the first to the second stanza? What does this change tell you about the speaker's feelings?

CHECK YOUR UNDERSTANDING

Answer these questions about "Words Like Freedom" before moving on to the **Analyze the Texts** section on the following page.

1. In "Words Like Freedom," which two feelings are expressed?

    A courage and wonder

    B happiness and pride

    C sadness and frustration

    D joy and sadness

2. Which line in "Words Like Freedom" suggests the speaker has experienced hardships?

    F *All day everyday.*

    G *There are words like* Liberty

    H *If you had known what I know*

    I *Sweet and wonderful to say.*

3. In the poem, the words *freedom* and *liberty* are italicized and capitalized to emphasize —

    A the importance of these ideals

    B the fact that they are proper nouns

    C their place in the U.S. Constitution

    D how often they are misunderstood

RESPOND

ANALYZE THE TEXTS

Support your responses with evidence from the texts. 📓 **NOTEBOOK**

1. **Infer** Reread lines 7–14 of "A Voice," in which the speaker describes her grandfather. What is the simile in these lines? What inferences can you make about the relationship between the speaker's mother and her father?

2. **Interpret** Reread lines 17–18 of "A Voice." What do the lines tell you about the speaker's view of her mother and the overall tone of the poem? What word would you use to describe the mood?

3. **Analyze** Identify the figurative language in line 3 of "Words Like Freedom." What tone is expressed through this use of figurative language?

4. **Analyze** Describe how and why the tone changes through "Words Like Freedom." How would you describe the poem's mood?

5. **Notice & Note** Reread lines 20–24 of "A Voice." How does the speaker's memory about the family story connect to lines 35–39?

RESEARCH

RESEARCH TIP
General search terms such as "Harlem Renaissance artists" will bring up many artists to choose from. To find information on a specific artist, search using the artist's name.

The Harlem Renaissance was a movement in the 1920s and 1930s centered in Harlem in New York. African American poets, writers, artists, and musicians gathered in Harlem to create art and press for civil rights. Research three artists active during the Harlem Renaissance. Write a short description of the type of art they created and the message they wanted to express through their art.

ARTISTS OF THE HARLEM RENAISSANCE		
NAME	**ART FORM**	**DESCRIPTION/MESSAGE**
	literature	
	painting	
	music	

Extend Pick one individual you researched and share your favorite example of his or her artwork, music, or writing with a small group. Discuss the ideas the work conveys.

RESPOND

CREATE AND PRESENT

Characterize the Speaker Write a brief informational essay describing the speaker of one or both poems. Cite evidence from the poem or poems to support your description.

❏ Review what you've learned about tone and speaker.
❏ Develop a clear controlling idea or thesis statement.
❏ Make inferences about the speaker(s) based on textual evidence and your own experiences.

Discuss and Analyze Figurative Language With a group, use the checklist below to discuss and analyze figurative language in the poems.

❏ Review and share your notes and annotations.
❏ Identify each use of figurative language in "A Voice" and "Words Like Freedom."
❏ Identify what is being compared or given human characteristics, and analyze the effect of the figurative language.
❏ Explain what the figurative language suggests about each poem's speaker and ideas.

Go to the **Writing Studio** for more on writing informational texts.

Go to the **Speaking and Listening Studio** for help with having a group discussion.

RESPOND TO THE ESSENTIAL QUESTION

 What are the ways you can make yourself heard?

Gather Information Review your annotations and notes on "A Voice" and "Words Like Freedom." Then, add relevant details to your Response Log. As you determine which information to include, think about:

- Why it is important to speak out
- How tone expresses feelings and attitudes about certain subjects
- How poetry can bring out strong emotions in readers

At the end of the unit, you will use your notes to write a multimodal argument.

ACADEMIC VOCABULARY

As you write and discuss what you learned from the poems, be sure to use the Academic Vocabulary words. Check off each of the words that you use.

❏ appropriate
❏ authority
❏ consequence
❏ element
❏ justify

RESPOND

Collaborate & Compare

MAKE CONNECTIONS TO SPEAKERS

The **speaker** in a poem is the voice that "talks" to the reader, similar to the narrator in fiction. The speaker of a poem may be the poet or a fictional character. You can use details in the text to draw conclusions about the speaker of a poem. As you review the poems to compare the speakers of "A Voice" and "Words Like Freedom," consider the following:

- who the speaker of the poem is
- how figurative language and word choice help you determine the tone(s) of the poem
- how tone helps you understand the attitude of the speaker or the poet toward the subject

With your group, complete the chart.

A VOICE
Poem by Pat Mora

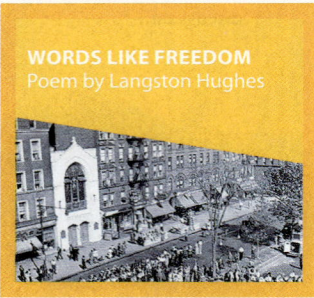

WORDS LIKE FREEDOM
Poem by Langston Hughes

	SPEAKER	TOPIC OR SUBJECT OF THE POEM	TONE OF THE POEM
A Voice			
Words Like Freedom			

ANALYZE THE TEXTS

Discuss these questions in your group.

1. **Evaluate** Why might a poet choose to convey multiple tones within the same poem? Explain.

2. **Synthesize** Is the speaker in each poem the same person as the poet? Explain.

3. **Compare** Do these poems share the same topic or subject matter? Explain your reasoning.

4. **Infer** Based on your analysis of the poems' speakers, what themes, or messages about life, are the speakers trying to convey? Cite text evidence in your discussion.

RESPOND

DISCUSS CONNECTIONS TO SPEAKERS

Compare the poems' speakers and discuss your own reactions and connections to the speakers. Follow these steps.

1. **Discuss and identify similarities.** With your group, review your work and identify the speakers' shared thoughts or attitudes. Find points you agree on, and resolve disagreements through discussion based on evidence from the poems.

2. **Record the similarities.** Fill in the chart below to record similarities, and provide evidence from the poems.

3. **Connect.** Make connections and discuss how your thoughts, experiences, and attitudes are similar to and different from the thoughts, experiences, and attitudes of the speakers in the poems.

Go to the **Speaking and Listening Studio** for help with group discussions.

GROUP WORK CHECKLIST
- ❏ Listen actively.
- ❏ Ask specific questions.
- ❏ Respond respectfully.
- ❏ Consider group members' suggestions.
- ❏ Take notes about important points.

SPEAKERS' SIMILARITIES	EVIDENCE FROM THE POEMS	HOW I AM SIMILAR AND DIFFERENT

Collaborate & Compare

COLLABORATE & COMPARE

ARGUMENT
BETTER THAN WORDS:
SAY IT WITH A SELFIE
by **Gloria Chang**
pages 303–307

COMPARE ARGUMENTS

As you read the arguments, focus on the reasons and evidence used to support the claims. Think about which points seem convincing to you and which do not; then, consider why.

? ESSENTIAL QUESTION:

What are the ways you can make yourself heard?

ARGUMENT
OMG, NOT ANOTHER SELFIE!
by **Shermakaye Bass**
pages 308–313

GET READY

QUICK START

Why do people take selfies? Do they take them for good reasons? For bad reasons? Write down two good reasons for taking a selfie; then, write down two bad reasons.

ANALYZE RHETORICAL DEVICES

In arguments, writers use **rhetorical devices,** or techniques for convincing readers to agree with a claim. These include **parallelism** (repeating similar grammatical structures), **hyperbole** (exaggerating the truth for effect), and **repetition** (repeating a word, phrase, or line).

During an analysis, you may suspect that something is wrong with an argument. This may be because the argument contains faulty reasoning or a **logical fallacy,** an error in logic. As you read, distinguish between rhetorical devices used for effect and fallacies. Recognizing fallacies will help you explain why an argument is unconvincing.

Analyzing a writer's argument will help you draw conclusions about the writer's reliability, credibility, and bias (the side of the argument the writer favors). Look for these and other types of misleading techniques:

GENRE ELEMENTS: ARGUMENT

- states a position or makes a claim about a topic
- includes evidence—facts, statistics, quotations, examples, or personal experience—to support the position
- uses logic or emotion, as well as rhetorical devices, to persuade readers

FALLACY	DEFINITION	EXAMPLE
Personal attack or name-calling (ad hominem)	An attempt to discredit an idea by attacking the character of a person or group associated with the idea	Only immature people like Frank enjoy video games.
Overgeneralization, or sweeping generalization	A generalization that is too broad; uses words such as *all, everyone, every time, no one,* and *none*	They make bad choices all the time.
Stereotyping	Broad statements about people based on gender, age, ethnicity, race, or other qualities	Boys are better at sports than girls.

IDENTIFY AN ARGUMENT'S AUDIENCE

How a writer presents and supports an argument depends on the intended audience of readers. For example, some audiences may be persuaded by statistics and factual evidence. Other audiences may respond more strongly to evidence that focuses on personal experience. Analyze types of evidence to help you identify the intended audience. As you read, ask yourself: To whom might this type of evidence appeal? To students? Teachers? Parents? Others?

GET READY

CRITICAL VOCABULARY

saturated   indulgent   narcissist   intimacy
passion   eternity   celebrity

To preview the words, replace the boldfaced word(s) in parentheses with a vocabulary word that has a similar meaning.

1. The Olympic athlete is a/an (**star**) _____ .
2. It took a/an (**long time**) _____ for the bus to arrive.
3. She has a/an (**enormous enthusiasm**) _____ for skiing.
4. I don't know a single (**self-obsessed person**) _____.
5. Eating candy all the time is (**excessively permissive**) _____.
6. Good friends often share a/an (**closeness**) _____ .
7. The ground was (**drenched**) _____ with rain.

LANGUAGE CONVENTIONS

Many common words have similar spellings or sound the same but have different meanings. Watch out for **commonly confused words**. Here is an example from "Better Than Words: Say It with a Selfie":

<u>**It's**</u> **easy to create a self-portrait with a smart phone and** <u>**its**</u> **filters.**

The word *its* is commonly misspelled as *it's*. *It's* is the contraction for "it is" or "it has." The word *its* is the possessive form of the pronoun *it*. In this lesson, you will learn about other commonly confused words.

ANNOTATION MODEL

NOTICE & NOTE

As you read, note ways in which the writer tries to persuade the reader. In the model, you can see one reader's notes about hyperbole in "Better Than Words: Say It with a Selfie."

> 1 <u>Everyone everywhere</u> owns and uses a smart phone, and, with <u>at least a million</u> different social platforms available, you'd have to live in a cave not to take part in and appreciate this form of communication.

Examples of hyperbole, or exaggeration. Not everyone owns and uses a smart phone. There aren't really one million social platforms.

BACKGROUND

Today, people of all ages—young and old—use smart phones. Children grow up sending photos and making video calls to grandparents. Students use phones to carry out research for school and to connect with friends, and, though the word selfie only entered our vocabulary in the early 2000s, people know all about them. With the rise in popularity, people have developed strong opinions about selfies. As you read this writer's argument, consider your own opinion.

BETTER THAN WORDS:
Say It with a Selfie
Argument by Gloria Chang

PREPARE TO COMPARE

As you read, identify the writer's claim and the evidence she uses to support that claim. Pay attention to how the writer's persuasive techniques affect your thoughts about selfies. Who do you think her audience is?

Notice & Note

Use the side margins to notice and note signposts in the text.

ANALYZE RHETORICAL DEVICES

Annotate: Mark an example of repetition in paragraph 1.

Connect: What is the purpose of this repetition? What effect does the use of this rhetorical device have on you as a reader?

1   In our digital age, the selfie is the best way to express oneself, empower oneself, and even surround oneself with friends. Everyone everywhere owns and uses a smart phone, and, with at least a million different social media platforms available, you'd have to live in a cave not to take part in and appreciate this form of communication. Sure, there are critics who say that selfies are taken only by narcissists[1] craving attention, but those critics really do live in caves—and they certainly have no friends.

---

[1] **narcissists** (när´sĭ-sĭstz): people who are preoccupied with their looks. From the Greek myth of Narcissus, a young man who fell in love with his own reflection in a pool of water.

NOTICE & NOTE

saturated
(săch´ə-rāt´əd) *adj.* Something that is *saturated* is filled until it is unable to hold or contain more.

passion
(păsh´ən) *n. Passion* means boundless enthusiasm.

EXTREME OR ABSOLUTE LANGUAGE

Notice & Note: Why do you think the writer uses extreme or absolute language to describe photographers and their work? Mark extreme or absolute language used in paragraph 4.

Analyze: What bias does this language reveal?

Selfies are about art and about life.

2 In a society **saturated,** stuffed to the brim, with social media, selfies are an artistic form of self-expression. Humans, since the beginning of time, have used self-portraits to express themselves. From ancient Egypt to the early Greeks to famous painters such as Rembrandt and Van Gogh,[2] people have expressed themselves artistically through self-portraits.

3 The only difference between the artists of old and modern selfie-takers is that technology now allows anyone and everyone to be an artist, and a "self-portrait" is now called a "selfie." It's easy to create a "self-portrait" with a smart phone and its filters. You don't need to know how to draw or paint when you have a cell phone!

Selfies are about self discovery.

4 Selfies allow people to show different parts of themselves. Maybe it's their artistic side, maybe it's their silly side, or maybe it's to show an interest or **passion,** such as a love of certain foods. Whatever that side may be, by showing the selfie-taker's interests, selfies become more real than any boring photographer's work. Photographers don't care if they show who you truly are in those boring photos; they're interested only in making sure you are in focus. They don't know what you are like. How can they? None of us even know ourselves until we experiment with different views, explore different interests, and discover the things that influence us.

5 In this way, selfies—unlike past self-portraits that weren't taken on handy mobile devices—allow us an easier and better way to find out who we are. Just like trying on different clothes to find what works best for our personalities, taking selfies is an excellent way to test how we look and feel in certain outfits, poses, and places. Our own reactions to these pictures, along with the reactions of friends and strangers, help us figure out what works for us as unique individuals.

Selfies are about self-expression.

6 Taking a selfie is like saying to the world, "this is me, right now, right here!" And a selfie does a better job of communicating this who, when, and where than spoken or written words can. After all, the human brain, as science shows, is hard-wired to

---
[2] **Rembrandt and Van Gogh:** Rembrandt van Rijn (rěm´ brănt´ văn rīn´) (1606–1669) and Vincent van Gogh (văn gō´) (1853–1890) were Dutch painters known for their self-portraits.

recognize faces. In other words, we naturally recognize things and people visually. The effect is more immediate. The objects, people, and background in a selfie can show what a selfie-taker likes, hates, admires, or aspires to.[3] The taker's attitude will naturally affect his or her facial expressions. As they say, a picture is worth a thousand words.

7   Even museums and art galleries know that selfies can be an artistic means of self-expression. They encourage visitors to take selfies with works of art to share as art. One gallery in London even held an international selfie competition for people to submit the most artistic selfies.

8   But don't just trust the artists and everyone who takes selfies. Trust science. One scientist who studied the motivation for taking selfies found that we take selfies as a form of self-expression, not to be narcissistic. So don't assume that you're a narcissist; don't assume that it's all about you.

Selfies are about self-confidence.

9   Selfies empower us because they fulfill our need for validation from friends, family, and the rest of the world. If you don't believe it, try it. Science has shown, once again, that taking selfies makes you more confident, especially kids. We all know it. Some people are not allowed to say positive things about themselves because other people will say that they are full of themselves. But a selfie is a photo, so it's acceptable for those people to show what they're proud of.

10   Sure, people may get fixated on selfies being about physical things, but that doesn't mean the selfie has to be about how someone looks. Everything in a selfie can tell you about a person. For example, a selfie can show that someone may be the next celebrity chef because that person always posts selfies of himself or herself cooking and eating at different places in the world.

11   Selfies also empower us because they make us happy. In two studies, researchers discovered that people who took selfies and people who didn't both thought pictures taken by themselves (those are selfies!) made them more attractive and likable. If you like photos of yourself, taking them boosts your confidence. In another study, scientists had college students take selfies and share them. This made them more confident and comfortable with their smiling faces. It may not even be possible to take too many selfies.

---

[3] **aspires to:** strives toward, wants to be like.

NOTICE & NOTE

LANGUAGE CONVENTIONS
Annotate: Mark the words *effect* and *affect* in paragraph 6.
Identify: Explain each word's part of speech and meaning.

IDENTIFY AN ARGUMENT'S AUDIENCE
Annotate: Mark the evidence or support the writer provides in paragraph 8 to support her claim.
Draw Conclusions: Who do you think the writer's audience is?

NOTICE & NOTE

ANALYZE RHETORICAL DEVICES

Annotate: Mark examples of stereotyping and name-calling in paragraph 12.

Draw Conclusions: How do these examples affect the writer's credibility?

12 In short, taking and sharing selfies boosts both self-confidence and self-esteem. People who say otherwise are like cavemen. They're probably people who've never taken selfies, so they probably don't have any self-confidence whatsoever. They probably hate people who do have self-confidence.

Selfies are about making connections.

13 The best part of taking selfies is that they're a great way to connect with friends or even make new friends. Since we all have smart phones and social media is everywhere and here to stay, we stay in touch with friends by taking selfies. It's like sending a letter in past times. But selfies are faster and are sent with a phone instead of a horse. By taking and sharing a selfie, you can share what you are thinking, feeling, or doing with your friends. Social media is made for others to give feedback so friends can tell you what they are thinking, feeling, or doing. They can do this by sending their favorite emoticons[4] or posting comments or sending a selfie of themselves back to you.

IDENTIFY AN ARGUMENT'S AUDIENCE

Annotate: Mark evidence the writer uses to support her claim in paragraph 14.

Analyze: Who might this type of evidence appeal to? Who is the intended audience of the argument?

14 Selfies are all about online social networks and social networks lead to better relationships. Teens especially say they have more positive experiences than negative ones when using social media. Selfies may have been around for only about a dozen years, but they're today's way to connect with other people.

Selfies are about making memories.

15 Selfies also help us create special memories. By posing with friends or at special events or places, we create snapshots that we can look back on with fond feelings. Obviously, taking selfies helps create memories because people naturally take selfies when something is happening right there close to them. They also take selfies when visiting places they like or think are funny or strange or interesting.

---

[4] **emoticons:** emojis, or icons used to express an emotion in text messages or online.

16   There are even "relfies," where couples take photos of themselves. Did you know that couples who take and show more relfies are more satisfied with and committed to their relationships than people who don't? And there are "groupies," selfies that include the selfie-taker and friends or family or even celebrities. They make the best memories since they include people we want to remember.

Selfies really are better than words.

17   Whether by ourselves, or with our favorite things, places, or people, selfies obviously say it better than words.

18   They express who we are and what matters most to us.

NOTICE & NOTE

CHECK YOUR UNDERSTANDING

Answer these questions before moving on to the next selection.

1   What is the primary claim the writer makes about the role of selfies today?

   A   People who take selfies are healthier than people who don't.

   B   Photographers don't know how to take good selfies.

   C   Selfies are the most effective tool for expressing ourselves.

   D   Everyone needs a cell phone to survive.

2   What point is the writer trying to make by saying that anyone who doesn't take or appreciate selfies must live in a cave?

   F   People who don't take selfies are likely to be alone.

   G   Anyone who does not like selfies is isolated from society and living in the past.

   H   People who don't take selfies don't have cellular service.

   J   The only way to have friends today is to take and share selfies.

3   How does the writer mainly support her ideas?

   A   with direct quotations from other informational sources

   B   with experts' opinions

   C   with anecdotes and personal experience

   D   with statistics from scientific studies

NOTICE & NOTE

BACKGROUND

Most people have friends or family members who love to post their pictures of meals, sporting events, vacations, outfits, and pets to social media. Sometimes we may wonder if some of our friends spend every waking hour on their phones. Is there such a thing as sharing too many photos? The author of this argument takes a stand.

OMG, NOT ANOTHER SELFIE!

Argument by Shermakaye Bass

PREPARE TO COMPARE

As you read, pay attention to the rhetorical devices the writer uses to enhance her argument and persuade her audience. Can you identify any logical fallacies or faulty reasoning?

Notice & Note

Use the side margins to notice and note signposts in the text.

1 "Hey, guys—look! Look at me! Here I am on summer vacation at the beach. Oh, and here I am with my bestie at the soccer game! And check this out: Me doing duck face. And, oh, here I am with this morning's . . . pancakes."

2 Those lines might have been spoken by any one of us who's caught up in the selfie craze these days. Social media sites are filled with the selfie-**indulgent,** people who've given in to the desire to be seen. But do people really want to see what you had for breakfast? And do you really want to see how much "fun" other people are having? Especially if their lives seem so much cooler than yours?

3 The answer is probably "no," yet most of us do look at our friends' selfies, and most of us do post selfies ourselves. In fact, one search engine giant has found that almost 24 billion selfies were uploaded through its online photo application in 2015.

indulgent
(ĭn-dŭl´jənt) adj. *Indulgent* means excessively permissive. *Self-indulgent* is when one is overly permissive with oneself. The pun *selfie-indulgent* means that a person indulges in taking many selfies.

308 Unit 4

That number doesn't even include those uploaded to popular social media sites.

4   We take selfies without even thinking. We strike a favorite pose. We click. We tap a couple of times. We share. This allows the rest of the world to see us as we'd like to be seen; however, it's not as we usually look in person.

5   One problem with this selfie mania is that once you've posted a picture of yourself you can't take it back, even if you decide that it's not quite your best shot. It's out there. For as many years as there are stars in the sky or grains of sand in the Sahara.[1] For all of **eternity**.

6   The only cure for a bad selfie is to take another one and post *it*, but you know what happens next: this reposting and re-snapping and reposting and re-snapping and reposting can go on and on and on, creating a cycle of frustration and wounded confidence! That cycle, inspired by the desire to control and "improve" our own images can lead to some serious psychological trouble, especially for young people. Selfies can be downright bad for us—bad for our self esteem and body image, bad for our productivity and our schoolwork, even bad for our friendships. If we're too selfie obsessed, we start to look as foolishly self-centered and shallow as poor old Narcissus[2] as he sat there falling madly in love with his own reflection. And no one wants to sit in the school cafeteria with a known **narcissist,** anyway, right? After all, selfie takers are *so* in love with themselves!

7   The truth is that taking selfies may seem harmless and fun, but more and more research shows that this fad can confuse a person's sense of identity, and it may even fiddle with his or her sense of reality. We might start to think that we look better than we actually do. That wouldn't be so terrible. But we also might start comparing ourselves to others too often. We might start believing negative things like, "I'll never be as cute as my best friend," or "I'll never be as popular as the new kid," or "I'll never have that much fun. Ever."

8   On the other hand, we may continue to think that "if I can just make myself look good enough and cool enough, I'll get more 'likes,' which means I'll get more friends. Then people will like me for real. Then, one day I'll become a real

eternity
(ĭ-tûr´nĭ-tē) *n.* Eternity refers to infinite time, without beginning or end.

ANALYZE RHETORICAL DEVICES
Annotate: Mark the overgeneralization about people who take selfies in the last sentence of paragraph 6.

Evaluate: How does the writer's use of this rhetorical device affect her credibility?

narcissist
(när´sĭ-sĭst´) *n.* A person who is preoccupied with his or her looks is a *narcissist*.

---

[1] **grains of sand in the Sahara:** the Sahara is a desert in Africa that covers an area the size of the United States.

[2] **Narcissus** (när-sĭs´əs): in Greek mythology, Narcissus was a young man who fell in love with his own reflection in a pool of water.

NOTICE & NOTE

celebrity
(sə-lĕb′rĭ-tē) *n.* A *celebrity* is a famous person.

LANGUAGE CONVENTIONS
Annotate: Mark the word *sense* in paragraph 11.

Summarize: Explain the meaning of the word. What word is it commonly confused with?

celebrity." However, selfies can put distance between us and the people we care about; they can sometimes create jealousy and competition. That's certainly no way to become a star.

9   Selfies can even have the opposite effect of what we'd hoped. Recent studies show that the selfie process not only has become oddly addictive and dangerous, but it can even set up the selfie-taker for ridicule. Some people will spend hours taking photos of themselves, trying for that perfect shot, and still wind up disappointed. Their thinking is that if they can just find the right "capture," they'll be popular, pretty—a somebody.

10 Of course, this is not true. Therefore, when we take certain actions (posting selfie after selfie) expecting certain results (fame and friendship) and then don't get those results, we get hurt feelings instead. We feel rejected, as if we don't matter. And that's a sure-fire formula for low self-esteem: "I posted this picture of myself and nobody has liked it," we think, "so I must be a nobody."

11 "One of the reasons kids take selfies is to post those pictures online. And the purpose of posting online often is to get 'likes,'" affirms author and former teacher Katie Schumacher, who launched the "Don't Press Send Campaign" in 2013. "If you post something and get a lot of 'likes,' it reinforces the feeling of importance and the sense of approval from others," Mrs. Schumacher says in a 2016 *ParentCo* story, "The Dangers of the Selfie and How You Can Help Your Kids."

12   "The 'like' is the reward. But if you don't get enough 'likes,' you will keep trying to get a better picture from a different angle or with someone more popular," Mrs. Schumacher says.

13   On top of hunting for "likes," young people often take selfies hoping to impress or catch the attention of someone in particular. Maybe it's someone they have a crush on or someone who's bullied them. Maybe they want that person to have a better opinion of them. If that someone doesn't notice the post or makes a negative comment, then the selfie-taker can feel worse than if he or she had never posted at all!

14   Dr. Allison Chase, a psychologist and behavior specialist in Austin, Texas, also has weighed in. "This is particularly challenging for kids and teens, as they are trying to figure out who they are and what their identity is." In that 2016 *ParentCo* article, Dr. Chase warns about getting caught in the trap of worrying too much about appearances and approval.

15   She warns against believing that posting and sharing and liking creates actual friendship and **intimacy**. As Dr. Chase says, we "create the illusion of feeling more connected and more 'liked' in a way that is controllable and oftentimes, staged. The end result is a competitive environment with increased self-focus, less true connection and, more often than not, increased self-criticism."

16   That, as you now know, can lead to more selfie sessions and even deeper disappointment. We begin to think that if we could only catch that perfect angle, or frame the picture to disguise our braces or acne or big nose, we'd be more popular. But, seeing all these selfies of cool kids in cool places with cool parents and friends, we wonder, "How can I possibly compete?"

17   Still, all dangers aside, the selfie has grown to be as much a part of our culture as the Declaration of Independence or our Constitution.[3] And the person who invented the selfie stick—Wayne Fromm, who patented a version in 2005—is probably pretty rich by now. But believe it or not, the term "selfie" wasn't even used until 2002, when the word first entered our vocabulary, according to Merriam-Webster's Dictionary. Now, more than 15 years later, we've turned it into a verb ("I'm going to selfie on my new kick-scooter!"). And in 2013, a national news agency reported that the Oxford Dictionaries had chosen "selfie" as its Word of the Year, claiming that the use of the word had grown by 17,000 percent between 2012 and 2013!

---

[3] **Declaration of Independence or our Constitution:** foundational documents of the United States.

> **NOTICE & NOTE**
>
> **IDENTIFY AN ARGUMENT'S AUDIENCE**
> **Annotate:** Mark the name and professional background of the person quoted in paragraph 14. Underline the quotation from this person and its source.
>
> **Draw Conclusions:** How does the quote help you understand who the audience is? How does the use of this quotation affect the credibility of the writer?
>
> **intimacy**
> (ĭn′tə-mə-sē) *n. Intimacy* means close friendship and familiarity.

NOTICE & NOTE

ANALYZE RHETORICAL DEVICES

Annotate: In paragraph 19, mark repeated phrases.

Respond: What effect does the writer achieve by repeating these phrases?

18   Wow.

19   Don't let all the hoopla fool you, though. The reality—the "real" reality—is that spending too much time taking our own pictures or focusing on how we look or spending too much time on other people's selfies can be more harmful than helpful to our tender egos. Selfies are carefully posed and selected images that present us at our best (we think). They're images that literally put our best face forward (we think!). But that's not actually so.

20   Selfies don't represent reality, and they certainly don't represent who we truly are.

NOTICE & NOTE

CHECK YOUR UNDERSTANDING

Answer these questions before moving on to the **Analyze the Texts** section on the following page.

1. What is the writer's position on selfies?

    A Taking too many selfies can be bad for a person's self-esteem.

    B If you take enough selfies, your self-esteem will eventually improve.

    C People who take selfies can only be friends with other people who take selfies.

    D People who take lots of selfies are the best photographers.

2. Which group is most likely the writer's intended audience?

    F Narcissists

    G Shy people

    H Psychologists

    J Parents and their children

3. The writer mainly supports her claim with —

    A funny stories and personal experiences

    B experts' opinions

    C interviews with celebrities

    D scientific data and charts

RESPOND

ANALYZE THE TEXTS

Support your responses with evidence from the text. 📓 NOTEBOOK

1. **Evaluate** Find an instance of parallelism in either argument and evaluate its impact on the argument. Does the use of this rhetorical device make the argument stronger? Explain.

2. **Critique** Find an example of stereotyping in either argument. Explain how stereotyping affects the writer's credibility and the effectiveness of her argument.

3. **Compare** Reread paragraph 11 in "Better Than Words: Say It with a Selfie" and paragraph 11 in "OMG, Not *Another* Selfie!" Both writers use experts to back up their claims. What specific evidence does each writer use to support her argument? Explain which writer's evidence you think is more persuasive and credible and why.

4. **Analyze** Review paragraph 13 in "Better Than Words: Say It with a Selfie." Find an example of a logical fallacy and explain how it shows an error in the writer's logic.

5. **Notice & Note** Find and then list an example of extreme or absolute language in either argument. Why do you think the writer chose these words?

RESEARCH TIP
Before researching, consider the best search terms to use. For general information, try "photography and history." Try "early selfies" to find out about early self-portrait photography.

RESEARCH

Conduct research into the first use of photography to take self-portraits. Use multiple sources to investigate early photographers, types of cameras, and technical breakthroughs. Then fill in the chart.

QUESTION	ANSWER
Who is credited with taking the first self-portrait with a camera?	
What early portable camera led to self-portraiture becoming widespread?	
What technical breakthrough in the 1880s made it easier to create self-portraits?	
When and in what country did the term *selfie* originate?	

Connect Consider what you learned about early pioneers in self-portraiture. Why did people first take self-portraits? Compare the reasons to what motivates people to take selfies today. Discuss your answers with a small group.

314 Unit 4

CREATE AND PRESENT

Compose an Argument Take a position—pro or con—about whether the use of cell phones should be permitted in movie theaters or at the dinner table, and write a three- or four-paragraph argument.

- ❏ Select an audience likely to disagree with your claim.
- ❏ Clearly state your claim in the opening paragraph. Use vocabulary appropriate to your audience.
- ❏ Use at least one rhetorical device to enhance your argument and help persuade your audience.
- ❏ Provide evidence that supports your claim and use sound reasoning that appeals to your audience. Do not use faulty reasoning or include logical fallacies.
- ❏ In your final paragraph, state your conclusion.
- ❏ Check your spelling to ensure that you have correctly used any confusing words, such as *its/it's, affect/effect,* and *their/there/they're.*

Go to the **Writing Studio** for more on writing an argument.

Create and Present "The Perfect Selfie" In a small group, discuss how to explain the "perfect selfie" to someone who has never taken one and doesn't want to. Work with your group to identify the qualities that make a perfect selfie. Then write a short speech explaining the perfect selfie to your audience.

- ❏ Discuss what to include in your speech to persuade a person who doesn't want to take a selfie that there might be some benefit to taking one.
- ❏ Anticipate your audience's opposing viewpoint and identify evidence to help overcome your audience's objections.
- ❏ Listen closely and respectfully to all speakers in your group.

Go to the **Speaking and Listening Studio** for help with creating and presenting a speech.

RESPOND TO THE ESSENTIAL QUESTION

 What are the ways you can make yourself heard?

Gather Information Review your annotations and notes on the selections. Then, add relevant details to your Response Log. As you determine what points to include, think about the pros and cons of selfies as a form of self-expression. At the end of the unit, you will use your notes to create a multimodal argument.

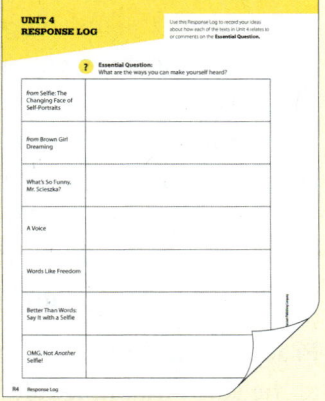

ACADEMIC VOCABULARY

As you write and discuss what you learned from the selections, be sure to use the Academic Vocabulary words. Check off the words that you use.

- ❏ **appropriate**
- ❏ **authority**
- ❏ **consequence**
- ❏ **element**
- ❏ **justify**

RESPOND

WORD BANK
- saturate
- passion
- indulgent
- eternity
- narcissist
- celebrity
- intimacy

CRITICAL VOCABULARY

Practice and Apply Use what you know about the vocabulary words to answer these questions.

1. Which of the following is an example of **indulgent**?
   a. eating three desserts   b. eating one dessert

2. Which of these is more likely to be **saturated**?
   a. a sponge   b. a waterproof jacket

3. Which of the following is the better example of **intimacy**?
   a. a close friendship   b. a new acquaintance

4. Which of the following is an example of **passion**?
   a. quiet laughter   b. a strong emotion

5. Which of the following is an example of a **narcissist**?
   a. someone who loves flowers   b. someone who loves only himself

6. Which of the following is most similar to **eternity**?
   a. the future   b. forever

7. Which of the following is an example of a **celebrity**?
   a. a favorite teacher   b. a TV star

Go to the **Vocabulary Studio** for more on context clues.

VOCABULARY STRATEGY:
Context Clues

When you encounter an unfamiliar word, one way to figure out its meaning is to use **context clues,** or hints about meaning found in the text surrounding the unfamiliar word. Here is an example:

> There are critics who say that selfies are taken only by narcissists[1] craving attention.

To figure out the meaning of *narcissists,* note the words *craving attention* that appear after the unfamiliar word. These words hint that narcissists are people who crave attention. Also note that the word is footnoted. A footnote gives information about an unfamiliar word. Here, the footnote reads "people who are preoccupied with their looks. From the Greek myth of Narcissus, a young man who fell in love with his own reflection in a pool of water." This confirms that a *narcissist* is someone obsessed with his or her appearance.

Practice and Apply Find an unfamiliar word in each of the texts. Look at the surrounding text for clues to help you determine each word's meaning. Check your guesses in a dictionary.

RESPOND

LANGUAGE CONVENTIONS:
Commonly Confused Words

The main reason for writing is to communicate ideas with others. Therefore, to avoid creating confusion, it is extremely important for writers to use and spell words correctly. Many common English words, such as *its* and *it's,* are spelled similarly but have different meanings. Remember that *it's* is the contraction of "it is" or "it has," and the word *its* is the possessive form of the pronoun *it*. Other commonly confused words include *effect/affect, there/their/they're,* and *to/two/too.* Study how these words are used correctly in the selections.

> Go to **A Glossary of Usage** in the **Grammar Studio** for more on commonly confused words.

The effect is more immediate. (noun)

The taker's attitude will naturally affect his or her facial expressions. (verb)

People naturally take selfies when something is happening right there close to them. (adverb describing location)

This made them more confident and comfortable with their smiling faces. (adjective, possessive form of *they*)

They're probably people who've never taken selfies. (contraction of "they are")

In two studies, researchers discovered that people who took selfies. . . . (the number 2)

It may not even be possible to take too many selfies. (part of verb *to take;* adverb meaning "more than enough" or "very")

Practice and Apply Choose the word that correctly completes each sentence.

1. My mom comes in to say goodnight when (its/it's) bedtime.
2. Jerome decided not to use the black-and-white (affect/effect) on his photograph.
3. (There/Their/They're) all obsessed with playing the latest computer game.
4. Andrea was (to/two/too) tired to wake up when her alarm rang.
5. My cousins gave me a ride (to/two/too) (there/their/they're) house.
6. What time will you be (there/their/they're)?
7. How much you study may (affect/effect) your grade on the test.

RESPOND

Collaborate & Compare

COMPARE AND EVALUATE ARGUMENTS

BETTER THAN WORDS: SAY IT WITH A SELFIE
Argument by Gloria Chang

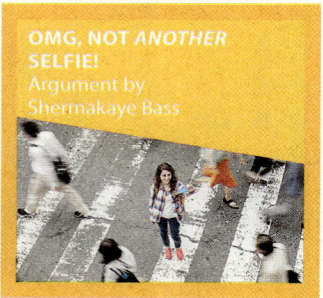

OMG, NOT *ANOTHER* SELFIE!
Argument by Shermakaye Bass

When you **compare and evaluate** two arguments on the same topic, you analyze how each argument is presented and decide how effective each argument is. First, determine the claim of each argument. Then, examine the strength of the evidence and the sources cited. Does the evidence effectively support the claim? Finally, identify flaws in the argument, including examples of logical fallacies. How do these flaws weaken the argument?

As a group, complete a chart like the one below. As you discuss, ask questions to help clarify group members' positions. Notice points on which you agree and disagree. Then, reach a group consensus about which text you think presents its argument more effectively.

	"BETTER THAN WORDS: SAY IT WITH A SELFIE"	"OMG, NOT *ANOTHER* SELFIE!"
Claim		
Evidence and Support		
Sources		
Flaws in the Argument		

ANALYZE THE TEXTS

Discuss these questions in your group.

1. **Compare** Do you think the two writers are addressing the same audience? How do you know?

2. **Synthesize** Both texts offer explanations about why people take selfies. Explain what each writer states is the purpose of the selfie.

3. **Critique** Which argument do you think provides the strongest evidence to support its claim? Explain.

4. **Evaluate** Which rhetorical device does each argument use most effectively? Explain.

318 Unit 4

RESEARCH AND DISCUSS

How have cell phones changed since they were first invented? With your group, briefly discuss how cell phones have changed since you—or your parents or grandparents—first began using them. Then, research developments and advancements in cell phone technology.

1. **Develop Questions** What would you like to know about the history of cell phones? As a group, brainstorm questions you would like to research. Then, decide who in your group is going to research which questions.

2. **Gather Information** As you research, make sure your sources are reliable and credible. Take notes from two or more sources, paraphrasing and summarizing key information to avoid plagiarism (the unauthorized use of someone else's words), and keep track of your sources. Use the checklist in the margin to help you identify information to include for each source. Cite those sources, following the format your teacher prefers.

3. **Share What You Learn** As a group, discuss your research. Listen closely to what others say, ask questions to request and clarify information, and build on the ideas of others as you examine the history of cell phones. Use your research notes to back up your ideas with text evidence.

4. **Prepare a Presentation** Use the information you gathered with your group to create an informational presentation that describes major events in the history of the cell phone. Consider using a sequence chart like the one below to help you organize important events in the development of the cell phone.

TRACKING SOURCES
❏ Author(s) name
❏ Article title
❏ Source or publisher
❏ Name of site
❏ Publication date

GROUP WORK CHECKLIST
❏ Listen actively.
❏ Ask specific questions.
❏ Respond respectfully.
❏ Consider group members' suggestions.
❏ Take notes about important points.

History of the Cell Phone

5. **Practice and Share Your Presentation** Decide who in your group will be responsible for sharing the different parts of your presentation with the class. Make sure all members participate. Practice your presentation and identify areas that need improvement. Finally, deliver your presentation to the class. As you present, make sure to make eye contact with the class, speak at a comfortable rate, enunciate clearly, and use natural gestures.

INDEPENDENT READING

ESSENTIAL QUESTION:

What are the ways you can make yourself heard?

Reader's Choice

Setting a Purpose Select one or more of these options from your eBook to continue your exploration of the Essential Question.

- Read the descriptions to see which text grabs your interest.
- Think about which genres you enjoy reading.

Notice & Note

In this unit, you practiced asking **Big Questions** and noticing and noting two signposts: **Extreme or Absolute Language** and **Contrasts and Contradictions**. As you read independently, these signposts and others will aid your understanding. Below are the anchor questions to ask when you read literature and nonfiction.

Reading Literature: Stories, Poems, and Plays

Signpost	Anchor Question	Lesson
Contrasts and Contradictions	Why did the character act that way?	p. 3
Aha Moment	How might this change things?	p. 3
Tough Questions	What does this make me wonder about?	p. 172
Words of the Wiser	What's the lesson for the character?	p. 2
Again and Again	Why might the author keep bringing this up?	p. 92
Memory Moment	Why is this memory important?	p. 93

Reading Nonfiction: Essays, Articles, and Arguments

Signpost	Anchor Question(s)	Lesson
Big Questions	What surprised me? What did the author think I already knew? What challenged, changed, or confirmed what I already knew?	p. 246 p. 420 p. 332
Contrasts and Contradictions	What is the difference, and why does it matter?	p. 247
Extreme or Absolute Language	Why did the author use this language?	p. 247
Numbers and Stats	Why did the author use these numbers or amounts?	p. 333
Quoted Words	Why was this person quoted or cited, and what did this add?	p. 333
Word Gaps	Do I know this word from someplace else? Does it seem like technical talk for this topic? Do clues in the sentence help me understand the word?	p. 421

INDEPENDENT READING

You can preview these texts in Unit 4 of your eBook.
Then, check off the text or texts that you select to read on your own.

POEM

I Was a Skinny Tomboy Kid
Alma Luz Villanueva

As a tomboy grows up, her self-perception shifts.

POEM

Words are Birds
Francisco X. Alarcón

A poet imagines words having the qualities and characteristics of birds.

SHORT STORY

Eleven
Sandra Cisneros

Can you be eleven but still feel ten, eight, or even two years old?

SHORT STORY

On Dragonwings
Lucy D. Ford

If you saw dragons in the night sky, would your life change?

INFORMATIONAL TEXT

Carved on the Walls
Judy Yung

A discovery on the walls of an immigration detainment center reveals a painful history.

Collaborate and Share Find a partner to discuss what you learned from at least one of your independent readings.

- Give a brief synopsis or summary of the text.
- Describe any signposts that you noticed in the text and explain what they revealed to you.
- Describe what you most enjoyed or found most challenging about the text. Give specific examples.
- Decide if you would recommend the text to others. Why or why not?

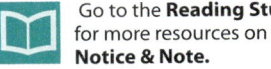

Go to the **Reading Studio** for more resources on **Notice & Note**.

Independent Reading 321

WRITING TASK

Create a Multimodal Argument

Go to the **Writing Studio** for help writing your argument.

This unit focuses on the different ways people express themselves. Whether it's fine art, graphic design, photography, video, poetry, or comedy, there are many ways to make your unique voice heard. Select your favorite mode of self-expression, and write an argument explaining why that medium is effective. Include graphics or images to support your ideas. For an example of an engaging argument, review "OMG, Not *Another* Selfie!"

As you create your multimodal argument, use the notes from your Response Log, which you filled out after reading the texts in this unit.

Writing Prompt

Read the information in the box below.

This is the topic or context for your essay.

> There are many creative options for discovering your voice and making yourself heard.

Think carefully about the following question.

Based on the texts you read in this unit, how would you answer this question?

> What are the ways you can make yourself heard?

Write an argument explaining why your favorite type of self-expression is effective. Include images or graphics to support your ideas.

Now mark the words that identify exactly what you are being asked to produce.

Be sure to—

- ❑ clearly state the argument's claim in your introduction
- ❑ support your claim with text evidence, sound reasoning, and relevant graphics or images
- ❑ organize information with a purposeful structure
- ❑ use words and a tone appropriate for your audience
- ❑ use appropriate rhetorical devices
- ❑ use correct pronoun-antecedent agreement
- ❑ conclude by effectively summarizing the claim

Review these points as you write and again when you finish. Make any needed changes.

WRITING TASK

1 Plan

Use the charts below to help you plan your argument. A strong argument states a clear claim and supports it with sound reasons and evidence. Who is your audience and what do these readers already know about your topic? What graphics and images will you use to support your claim? Think about images that represent your favorite type of self-expression. For example, if you're writing about photography, choose favorite photographs that express the power of the medium. Be creative and selective with your choices.

Go to **Writing Arguments: What is a Claim?** for help planning your argument.

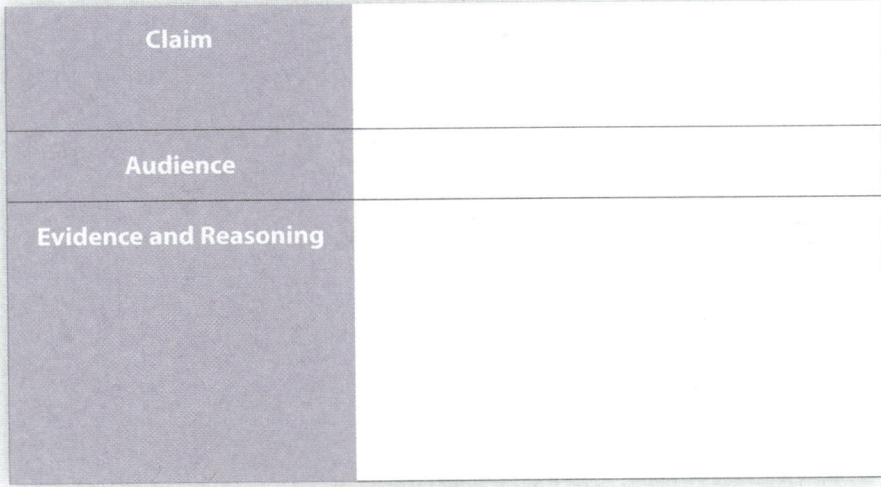

Claim	
Audience	
Evidence and Reasoning	

Notice & Note

From Reading to Writing

As you plan your multimodal argument, apply what you've learned about signposts to your own work. Remember that writers use common features, called signposts, to help convey their message to readers.

Think about how you can incorporate **Quoted Words** into your argument.

 Go to the **Reading Studio** for more resources on Notice & Note.

Graphics and Images	How They Support the Argument

Background Reading Review the notes you have taken in your Response Log after reading the texts in this unit. These texts provide background reading that will help you formulate the key ideas you will include in your argument.

Use the notes from your **Response Log** as you plan your multimodal argument.

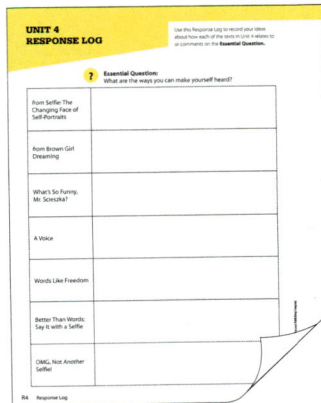

Create a Multimodal Argument 323

WRITING TASK

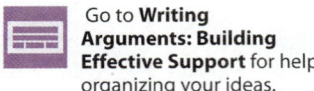 Go to **Writing Arguments: Building Effective Support** for help organizing your ideas.

Organize Your Ideas After you have gathered reasons, text evidence, and images to support your claim, organize the information. This will help you draft your argument. How will you capture the reader's attention in your introduction? What is your strongest evidence? Where will you insert images that support your argument? What information is important to include in the captions? How will you summarize your claim in a persuasive conclusion? Use the chart below to make notes about the elements of your multimodal argument.

Organizing My Multimodal Argument	
Introduction and claim	
Reason/Evidence	
Reason/Evidence	
Reason/Evidence	
Images and graphics with captions	
Conclusion	

② Develop a Draft

 You might prefer to draft your argument online.

Once you have completed your planning activities, you will be ready to begin drafting your argument. Refer to your charts and the outline you have created, as well as to any notes you took as you studied the texts in the unit. These will provide a kind of map for you to follow as you write. Using a word processor or online writing application makes it easier to make changes or move sentences around later when you are ready to revise your first draft.

WRITING TASK

Use the Mentor Text

Audience

Authors consider their **audience** when they decide what words and tone to use. For example, a formal **tone** may be appropriate in an essay addressing government leaders, but it wouldn't be the best choice in an essay addressing teens. Note the way the author of "OMG, Not *Another* Selfie!" uses specific language to "speak" to her audience.

"Hey, guys — look! Look at me! Here I am on summer vacation at the beach. Oh, and here I am with my bestie at the soccer game! And check this out: me doing duck face. And, oh, here I am with this morning's . . . pancakes."	The author uses a conversational tone and words like "bestie," "guys," and "check this out" to appeal to an audience of young people.

Apply What You've Learned Think about phrases and expressions that are appropriate for your audience. Use terms that will make your audience feel as if you are speaking directly to them.

Rhetorical Devices

Rhetorical devices are techniques writers use to enhance their arguments and communicate more effectively. They include parallelism, emotional appeals, and repetition. Notice how the author of "OMG, Not *Another* Selfie!" uses repetition and parallelism in the following passage.

We take selfies without even thinking. We strike a favorite pose. We click. We tap a couple of times. We share.	The author repeats "we" in a series of short, parallel sentences. The rhetorical devices stress the idea that taking selfies is something that people do with little thought or consideration.

Apply What You've Learned Consider using repetition to emphasize one of your points. Experiment with repeating a word or phrase to capture the reader's attention and strengthen your argument.

Create a Multimodal Argument

WRITING TASK

Go to **Writing Arguments: Creating a Coherent Argument** for help revising your argument.

3 Revise

On Your Own Once you have written your draft, go back and look for ways to improve your multimodal argument. As you reread and revise, think about whether you have achieved your purpose. The Revision Guide will help you focus on specific elements to make your writing stronger.

Revision Guide

Ask Yourself	Tips	Revision Techniques
1. Does my introduction create interest and clearly state a claim?	**Underline** the claim and **circle** the attention-getting opening.	**Add** a clear claim, and **add** a relevant, attention-getting detail.
2. Are my reasons and evidence organized logically?	**Mark** the reasons and evidence.	**Reorder** reasons and evidence in a logical sequence.
3. Do my images and graphics support my claim?	**Mark** images and graphics.	**Revise** captions to clarify the connection between the claim and the images and graphics.
4. Is there pronoun-antecedent agreement in my sentences?	**Underline** pronouns and **circle** antecedents.	**Replace** pronouns and antecedents that don't agree.
5. How well have I used persuasive language and rhetorical devices?	**Mark** persuasive language and rhetorical devices.	**Add** persuasive language or strengthen a rhetorical device to emphasize a point.
6. Does my conclusion summarize my claim?	**Mark** the conclusion.	**Add** a statement that summarizes the claim.

ACADEMIC VOCABULARY

As you conduct your **peer review,** be sure to use these words.

- ❑ appropriate
- ❑ authority
- ❑ consequence
- ❑ element
- ❑ justify

With a Partner Once you and your partner have worked through the Revision Guide on your own, exchange papers and evaluate each other's draft in a **peer review.** Focus on providing revision suggestions for at least three of the items mentioned in the chart. Explain why you think your partner's draft should be revised and what your specific suggestions are.

When receiving feedback from your partner, listen attentively and ask questions to make sure you fully understand the revision suggestions.

WRITING TASK

4 Edit

Once you have addressed the organization, development, and flow of ideas in your argument, improve the finer points of your draft. Edit for the proper use of standard English conventions and correct any misspellings or grammatical errors.

> ! Go to the **Grammar Studio** to learn more about pronouns.

Language Conventions

A **pronoun** is a word that is used in place of a noun or another pronoun. The word that the pronoun refers to is its **antecedent**. Pronouns should always agree in number with their antecedents.

To make sure a pronoun agrees with its antecedent, ask yourself, "Which noun is this pronoun replacing?"

In the sentence below, the pronoun "them" replaces the noun "phones."

Please turn your *phones* off, and keep *them* off during the movie.

As you edit, stay aware of personal, indefinite, and relative pronouns.

- **Personal pronouns** express person or thing, number, gender, and case. Singular examples include *I, you, she, he, it*; plural examples are *we, you,* and *they*.

- **Indefinite pronouns** refer to one or more persons or things not specifically mentioned. They usually have no antecedents. Indefinite pronouns include: *another, anybody, no one, neither, both, many, none, more, most, some, any*.

- **Relative pronouns** relate, or connect, adjective clauses to the words they modify in sentences. They include *who, whom, which, what,* and *that*.

In the chart below, pronouns are underlined and antecedents are circled.

PRONOUN TYPE	EXAMPLE
Personal	(Selfies) don't represent reality, and they don't capture people realistically, either.
Indefinite	And no one wants to sit in the school cafeteria with a known narcissist, right?
Relative	And the person who invented the selfie stick—(Wayne Fromm,) who patented his selfie stick in 2005—is probably pretty rich by now.

5 Publish

Finalize your argument and choose a way to share it with your audience. Consider these options:

- Post your argument as a blog on a classroom or school website.
- Publish your essay in the school newsletter.

Create a Multimodal Argument 327

WRITING TASK

Use the scoring guide to evaluate your essay.

	Writing Task Scoring Guide: Multimodal Argument		
	Organization/Progression	**Development of Ideas**	**Use of Language and Conventions**
4	• The reasons, evidence, images, and graphics are organized logically and consistently to persuasive effect. • Coherence occurs within and across the paragraphs.	• The introduction skillfully pulls the reader in; the writer clearly states a claim about the topic. • The claim is convincingly supported by logical reasons, relevant text evidence, and appropriate images and graphics. • The conclusion effectively summarizes the claim.	• Language and word choice is purposeful and persuasive. • Pronouns are used correctly. • Spelling, capitalization, and punctuation are correct. • Grammar, usage, and mechanics are correct.
3	• The organization of reasons, evidence, images, and graphics is confusing in a few places. • Coherence occurs within and across most paragraphs.	• The introduction is somewhat engaging; the writer states a claim about the topic. • Most reasons, evidence, and images and graphics support the claim. • The conclusion restates the claim.	• Language and word choice is often purposeful and persuasive. • Pronouns are used correctly in most instances. • Some spelling, capitalization, and punctuation mistakes are present. • Some grammar and usage errors occur.
2	• The organization of reasons, evidence, images, and graphics is confusing in many places. • There is little coherence within and across paragraphs.	• The introduction is incomplete; the writer identifies a topic, but the claim is not clearly stated. • The reasons, evidence, and images and graphics are not always logical or relevant. • The conclusion includes an incomplete summary of the claim.	• Language is often vague and unpersuasive. • Pronouns are often incorrectly used. • Spelling, capitalization, and punctuation are often incorrect but do not make reading difficult. • Grammar and usage errors make the writing difficult to understand in some places.
1	• The organization is not logical; reasons, evidence, images, and graphics are presented randomly. • A lack of coherence within and across paragraphs makes the argument difficult to understand.	• The introduction does not include a claim. • Supporting reasons, evidence, images, and graphics are missing. • The conclusion is missing.	• Language is inappropriate for the text. • Language is vague and confusing. • Pronouns are used incorrectly most of the time. • Many spelling, capitalization, and punctuation errors are present. • Many grammatical and usage errors confuse the writer's ideas.

Reflect on the Unit

By completing your multimodal argument, you have created a writing product that pulls together and expresses your thoughts about the reading you have done in this unit. Now is a good time to reflect on what you have learned.

Reflect on the Essential Question

- What are the ways you can make yourself heard? How has your answer to this question changed since you first considered it when you started this unit?

- From the texts you've read, what are some examples of ways to make yourself heard?

Reflect on Your Reading

- Which selections were the most interesting or surprising to you?

- From which selection did you learn the most about how people make their voices heard?

Reflect on the Writing Task

- What difficulties did you encounter while working on your multimodal argument? How might you avoid them next time?

- Which image or graphic do you think adds the most value to your argument? Why do you think so?

- What improvements did you make to your argument as you were revising?

UNIT 4 SELECTIONS
- *Selfie: The Changing Face of Self-Portraits*
- *Brown Girl Dreaming*
- "What's So Funny, Mr. Scieszka?"
- "A Voice"
- "Words Like Freedom"
- "Better Than Words: Say It with a Selfie"
- "OMG, Not *Another* Selfie!"

UNIT 5

NEVER GIVE UP

ESSENTIAL QUESTION:

What keeps people from giving up?

> "Even if you are not ready for day / it cannot always be night."
>
> — Gwendolyn Brooks

UNIT 5

ACADEMIC VOCABULARY

Academic Vocabulary words are words you use when you discuss and write about texts. In this unit you will practice and learn five words.

☑ achieve ☐ individual ☐ instance ☐ outcome ☐ principle

Study the Word Network to learn more about the word **achieve**.

Write and Discuss Discuss the completed Word Network with a partner, making sure to talk through all of the boxes until you both understand the word, its synonyms, antonyms, and related forms. Then, fill out Word Networks for the remaining four words. Use a dictionary or online resource to help you complete the activity.

 Go online to access the Word Networks.

RESPOND TO THE ESSENTIAL QUESTION

In this unit, you will read about the different ways people succeed and thrive in the face of adversity or difficulties. As you read, you will revisit the **Essential Question** and gather your ideas about it in the **Response Log** that appears on page R5. At the end of the unit, you will have the opportunity to write a **biographical report**. The report will be based on your research on a well-known person who refused to give up. Filling out the Response Log will help you prepare for this writing task.

 You can also go online to access the Response Log.

Never Give Up 331

Notice & Note
READING MODEL

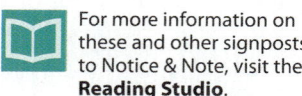 For more information on these and other signposts to Notice & Note, visit the **Reading Studio**.

A SCHOOLGIRL'S DIARY from I AM MALALA

You are about to read an excerpt from the autobiographical memoir *I Am Malala*. In it, you will notice and note signposts that will give you clues about the writer's thoughts and feelings, important events in the writer's life, and her purpose for writing. Here are three key signposts to look for as you read this selection and other works of nonfiction.

Big Questions When you are reading something that confirms what you already know, you might find yourself nodding your head as you read, as if to say, "Yes, I know exactly what that's like." At other times, writing casts a light on something that is totally unfamiliar—challenging our assumptions, surprising us, or changing our beliefs.

As you compare what you're reading to your own experiences, take a moment and reflect on the ideas the author is presenting. Ask yourself **Big Questions** such as the following:

- What confirms what I already know?
- What challenges what I already know?
- What changes what I already know?

Read this paragraph from *I Am Malala* and notice how a student annotated text associated with two Big Questions.

> 47   I had never written a diary before and didn't know how to begin, so the BBC correspondent said he would help me. He had to call me on my mother's phone because, even though we had a computer, there were frequent power cuts and few places in Mingora with Internet access.

What confirms something that you may already know?	It can be difficult to start a new writing project, especially when you've never tried that writing form.
What challenges or changes something you may have known?	I know that not everyone has their own computer, but I didn't know that some places in the world have frequent power cuts or no Internet access at all.

▶ **Numbers and Stats** When an author writes that he walked five miles to the closest market, readers learn about more than just the distance. The author may be explaining the setting (perhaps it's rural), economic conditions (poverty may prevent the construction of roads), or personality (perhaps he's stubborn). When an author provides **Numbers and Stats,** think about why this information is included. In this example, a student marked a few Numbers and Stats.

> 13   We piled inside, <u>twenty girls</u> and <u>two teachers</u> crammed into the <u>three rows of benches</u> stretching down the length of the *dyna.*

Anchor Question
When you notice this signpost, ask: Why did the author use these numbers or amounts?

How are numbers or statistics used here?	They show how many people have to fit into the vehicle and how much seating is available.
Why do you think the author included numbers here?	The numbers emphasize how crowded it is; the author may be showing that the school is poor.

▶ **Quoted Words** In autobiography and memoir, authors may use quotations to express the personal perspective of friends or family members, or to highlight the words of other significant persons in the author's life. When you encounter **Quoted Words,** ask yourself how the words may support the author's point of view and purpose. In this example, a student marked an instance of Quoted Words.

> 25   "<u>After the fifteenth of January, no girl, whether big or little, shall go to school. Otherwise, you know what we can do. And the parents and the school principal will be responsible.</u>"
> 26   That was the news that came over Radio Mullah in late December 2008. . . .

Anchor Question
When you notice this signpost, ask: Why was this person quoted or cited and what did this add?

Who said the quoted words and what do they mean?	The words came from a radio station. They mean that no girls can go to school, and they hint that something bad will happen if they do go.
Why did the author include the quoted words?	Using quoted words adds credibility to the author's description; the threat sounds very real.

Notice & Note   333

ANALYZE & APPLY

A SCHOOLGIRL'S DIARY
from I AM MALALA

Memoir by **Malala Yousafzai** with **Patricia McCormick**

? ESSENTIAL QUESTION:

What keeps people from giving up?

GET READY

QUICK START

Which right do you value the most? Freedom of thought or expression? Access to education? How would you react if you were told suddenly that this right was being taken away because of who you are? Share your thoughts with the class.

ANALYZE CHARACTERISTICS AND FEATURES OF INFORMATIONAL TEXTS

The following selection is an excerpt from the book *I Am Malala*, which is a **memoir,** or a form of autobiography in which a writer shares his or her personal experiences and observations. A memoir shows how the writer remembers his or her own life and may focus on a specific period in the writer's life.

As you read the selection, pay attention to characteristics and features this selection shares with other informational texts.

- A **prologue,** or preface, is an introduction that helps provide readers with background information about the text. It may describe the text's setting or an important event, or the writer may use the prologue to tell readers why he or she decided to write the memoir.
- A **map** is a graphic feature that shows where events in the text take place.
- A **controlling idea** is the main point the author wants to convey in the writing. In a memoir, the controlling idea may be tied to the author's purpose for writing the work.

GENRE ELEMENTS: MEMOIR
- told in the first-person point of view from the writer's own perspective
- includes descriptions of people and events that have influenced the writer
- expresses the writer's personal thoughts and feelings, often using an informal or intimate tone

GENERATE QUESTIONS

Readers improve their understanding of a text when they generate, or produce, questions before, during, and after they read. As you read the selection, monitor your comprehension and deepen your understanding of the text by asking *who, what, when, where, why,* and *how* questions.

GENERATE QUESTIONS	TRY THIS
Set a purpose **before** reading. By asking yourself what you expect to learn from the text, you'll be ready to find the answers as you read.	Preview the text by scanning background information, headings, maps, etc. **Ask:** Why am I reading this text? What do I know about the subject already? What am I going to learn?
Monitor comprehension **during** reading. Ask questions as you read, pause to reread, and confirm your understanding.	Reread words, sentences, and paragraphs as needed to clarify understanding. **Ask:** Why did the author add this detail? What idea does the author want to share?
Identify or confirm the controlling idea **after** reading. The questions you ask yourself will help you understand the work as a whole.	Take time to think about what you just read. Review the key ideas. **Ask:** Did I learn what I thought I would? What was the author's purpose in writing?

A Schoolgirl's Diary *from* I Am Malala

GET READY

CRITICAL VOCABULARY

| debate | edict | defy | pseudonym | anonymous |

To see how many Critical Vocabulary words you already know, use them to complete the sentences.

1. The class held a/an _____ to address the issue's pros and cons.

2. I gave a/an _____ donation to keep my identity secret.

3. It is natural for toddlers to _____ their parents.

4. The spy used a/an _____ instead of her real name.

5. The commander gave a/an _____ describing the new rules.

LANGUAGE CONVENTIONS

Capitalization In this lesson, you will learn about the capitalization of proper nouns. A **proper noun** names a specific person, place, thing, or idea.

<u>**Haji Baba Road**</u> **was a jumble of brightly colored rickshaws, women in flowing robes, men on scooters. . . .**

As a proper noun, *Haji Baba Road* is capitalized because it names a specific place and thing. As you read the selection, notice how the author uses capitalization to distinguish proper nouns.

ANNOTATION MODEL

NOTICE & NOTE

As you read, notice and note signposts, including **Big Questions, Numbers and Stats,** and **Quoted Words.** Here is an example of how one reader responded to the opening paragraphs of the selection.

2 It was the most ordinary of days. I was fifteen, in grade nine, and I'd stayed up far too late the night before, studying for an exam.

3   I'd already heard the rooster crow at dawn but had fallen back to sleep. I'd heard the morning call to prayer from the mosque nearby but managed to hide under my quilt. And I'd pretended not to hear my father come to wake me.

I stay up late a lot, too. I also pretend to be asleep!

I know about morning prayers, but I've never heard a "call." I wonder where she lives.

BACKGROUND

In 2007, an extreme militant group took control of the area of Pakistan where **Malala Yousafzai's** (b. 1997) family lived. The group banned girls from attending school. Yousafzai publicly supported girls' education, and in 2012 she was attacked. Her family moved to England, where she continued to advocate for girls' rights. In 2014 she became the youngest recipient of the Nobel Peace Prize. This selection is from the Young Readers Edition of her memoir, I Am Malala, published in 2014.

A SCHOOLGIRL'S DIARY
from I AM MALALA

Memoir by Malala Yousafzai with Patricia McCormick

SETTING A PURPOSE

As you read, pay attention to the details the author includes to convey ideas about her life at home, at school, and in her community. Use these details to help you answer these questions: What kind of person is Malala? What is most important to her?

DEDICATION

1 To those children all over the world who have no access to education, to those teachers who bravely continue teaching, and to anyone who has fought for their basic human rights and education.

PROLOGUE

2 It was the most ordinary of days. I was fifteen, in grade nine, and I'd stayed up far too late the night before, studying for an exam.

3 I'd already heard the rooster crow at dawn but had fallen back to sleep. I'd heard the morning call to prayer from the mosque nearby but managed to hide under my quilt. And I'd pretended not to hear my father come to wake me.

Notice & Note

Use the side margins to notice and note signposts in the text.

ANALYZE CHARACTERISTICS AND FEATURES OF INFORMATIONAL TEXTS

Annotate: Mark details in paragraphs 2–3 that help set the scene of the prologue.

Identify: What does this background information reveal about the author?

NOTICE & NOTE

QUOTED WORDS

Notice & Note: What can you tell from the author's use of quoted words? Mark the quoted words in paragraph 4.

Draw Conclusions: What do these words suggest about Malala's relationship to her mother?

4   Then my mother came and gently shook my shoulder. "Wake up, *pisho*," she said, calling me *kitten* in Pashto, the language of the Pashtun people. "It's seven thirty and you're late for school!"

5   I had an exam on Pakistani studies. So I said a quick prayer to God. *If it is your will, may I please come in first?* I whispered. *Oh, and thank you for all my success so far!*

Map of Swat, Pakistan, and surrounding areas

6   I gulped down a bit of fried egg and chapati[1] with my tea. My youngest brother, Atal, was in an especially cheeky mood that morning. He was complaining about all the attention I'd received for speaking out about girls getting the same education as boys, and my father teased him a little at the breakfast table.

7   "When Malala is prime minister[2] someday, you can be her secretary," he said.

8   Atal, the little clown in the family, pretended to be cross. "No!" he cried. "She will be *my* secretary!"

9   All this banter nearly made me late, and I raced out the door, my half-eaten breakfast still on the table. I ran down the lane just in time to see the school bus crammed with other girls on their way to school. I jumped in that Tuesday morning and never looked back at my home.

———

10   The ride to school was quick, just five minutes up the road and along the river. I arrived on time, and exam day passed as it always did. The chaos of Mingora city surrounded us with its honking horns and factory noises while we worked silently, bent over our papers in hushed concentration. By day's end I was tired but happy; I knew I'd done well on my test.

11   "Let's stay on for the second trip," said Moniba, my best friend. "That way we can chat a little longer." We always liked to stay on for the late pickup.

12   When our bus was called, we ran down the steps. As usual, Moniba and the other girls covered their heads and faces before we stepped outside the gate and got into the waiting *dyna*,[3] the white truck that was our Khushal School "bus." And, as usual, our driver was ready with a magic trick to amuse us. That day, he made a pebble disappear. No matter how hard we tried, we couldn't figure out his secret.

GENERATE QUESTIONS
Annotate: In paragraph 9, mark details that lead you to pause and ask questions.

Draw Conclusions: What questions can you ask at this point in the text? Look for the answers as you continue to read.

---

[1] **chapati** (chə-pä´tē): a flat, circular bread common in Pakistan and northern India.
[2] **prime minister:** in Pakistan, the prime minister is the head of government.
[3] **dyna** (dĭn´ə): a small, bus-like truck with a roof, sides, an open back, and benches for seats.

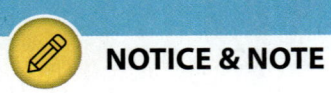

NOTICE & NOTE

BIG QUESTIONS

Notice & Note: Mark the words in paragraph 14 that challenge, change, or confirm what you already know.

Analyze: What questions can you ask yourself about this passage? Why did the author include this information?

13   We piled inside, twenty girls and two teachers crammed into the three rows of benches stretching down the length of the *dyna*. It was hot and sticky, and there were no windows, just a yellowed plastic sheet that flapped against the side as we bounced along Mingora's crowded rush-hour streets.

14   Haji Baba Road was a jumble of brightly colored rickshaws,[4] women in flowing robes, men on scooters, honking and zigzagging through the traffic. We passed a shopkeeper butchering chickens. A boy selling ice-cream cones. A billboard for Dr. Humayun's Hair Transplant Institute. Moniba and I were deep in conversation. I had many friends, but she was the friend of my heart, the one with whom I shared everything. That day, when we were talking about who would get the highest marks[5] this term, one of the other girls started a song, and the rest of us joined in.

15   Just after we passed the Little Giants snack factory and the bend in the road not more than three minutes from my house, the van slowed to a halt. It was oddly quiet outside.

16   "It's so calm today," I said to Moniba. "Where are all the people?"

17   I don't remember anything after that, but here's the story that's been told to me:

18   Two young men in white robes stepped in front of our truck.

19   "Is this the Khushal School bus?" one of them asked.

20   The driver laughed. The name of the school was painted in black letters on the side.

21   The other young man jumped onto the tailboard and leaned into the back, where we were all sitting.

22   "Who is Malala?" he asked.

23   No one said a word, but a few girls looked in my direction. He raised his arm and pointed at me. Some of the girls screamed, and I squeezed Moniba's hand.

24   Who is Malala? I am Malala, and this is my story.

---

[4] **rickshaws** (rĭk´shôz): in Pakistan, a small motorized vehicle that carries passengers.
[5] **marks:** school grades.

NOTICE & NOTE

My friends keep a chair in class for me (far right) at the Khushal School.

A Schoolgirl's Diary

25 "After the fifteenth of January, no girl, whether big or little, shall go to school. Otherwise, you know what we can do. And the parents and the school principal will be responsible."

26 That was the news that came over Radio Mullah[6] in late December 2008. At first, I thought it was just one of his crazy pronouncements. It was the twenty-first century! How could one man stop more than fifty thousand girls from going to school?

27 I am a hopeful person—my friends may say too hopeful, maybe even a little crazy. But I simply did not believe that this man could stop us. School was our right.

28 We **debated** his **edict** in class. "Who will stop him?" the other girls said. "The Taliban[7] have already blown up hundreds of schools, and no one has done anything."

29 "We will," I said. "We will call on our government to come and end this madness."

30 "The government?" one girl said. "The government can't even shut down Fazlullah's radio station!"[8]

---

[6] **Radio Mullah:** the on-air name for radio broadcaster Maulana Fazlullah, who spread his radical beliefs that girls should not go to school and encouraged violence.
[7] **Taliban** (tăl´ə-băn´): a group of militant Islamic fundamentalists. The name comes from *Talib*, which means "religious student."
[8] **Fazlullah's radio station:** Maulana Fazlullah, the voice of Radio Mullah (see footnote 6). Fazlullah became head of the Taliban in Pakistan.

debate
(dĭ-bāt´) v. To *debate* is to discuss opposing points or ideas.

edict
(ē´dĭkt´) n. An *edict* is a command or pronouncement enforced as law.

NOTICE & NOTE

31   The debate went round and round. I didn't give in. But even to me, my argument sounded a bit thin.

32   One by one, girls stopped coming to school. Their fathers forbade them. Their brothers forbade them.

33   Within days we had gone from twenty-seven girls in our grade to ten.

34   I was sad and frustrated—but I also understood. In our culture, girls do not **defy** the males in their families. And I realized that the fathers and brothers and uncles who made my friends stay home were doing so out of concern for their safety. It was hard not to feel a bit depressed sometimes, not to feel as though the families who kept their girls at home were simply surrendering to Fazlullah. But whenever I'd catch myself giving in to a feeling of defeat, I'd have one of my talks with God. *Help us appreciate the school days that are left to us, God, and give us the courage to fight even harder for more.*

---

defy
(dĭ-fī´) *v.* To *defy* someone is to oppose or refuse to cooperate with that person.

NUMBERS AND STATS

Notice & Note: Why does Malala include numbers and dates in paragraphs 33 and 35? Mark where numbers are used.

Infer: What is the importance of understanding these details?

35   School had been due to end the first week of January for our usual winter break, so my father decided to postpone the holiday. We would remain in classes through 14 January. That way we could squeeze in every minute left to us. And the ten remaining girls in my class lingered in the courtyard every day after school in case these were our last chances to be together.

36   At home in the evenings I wondered what I would do with my life if I couldn't go to school. One of the girls at school had gotten married off before Fazlullah's edict. She was twelve. I knew my parents wouldn't do that to me, but I wondered, what *would* I do? Spend the rest of my life indoors, out of sight, with no TV to watch and no books to read? How would I complete my studies and become a doctor, which was my greatest hope at the time? I played with my shoebox dolls and thought: *The Taliban want to turn the girls of Pakistan into identical, lifeless dolls.*

37   While we girls savored the days until January 15, Fazlullah struck again and again. The previous year had been hard, but the days of January 2009 were among the darkest of our lives. Every morning, someone arrived at school with a story about another killing, sometimes two, sometimes three a night. Fazlullah's men killed a woman in Mingora because they said she was "doing *fahashi*," or being indecent, because she was a

dancer. And they killed a man in the valley because he refused to wear his pants short the way the Taliban did. And now, we would be forbidden from going to school.

38   One afternoon I heard my father on the phone. "All the teachers have refused," he said. "They are too afraid. But I will see what I can do." He hung up and rushed out of the house.

39   A friend who worked at the BBC, the powerful British Broadcasting Corporation network, had asked him to find someone from the school to write a diary about life under the Taliban for its Urdu[9] website—a teacher or an older student. All the teachers had said no, but Maryam's younger sister Ayesha, one of the older girls, had agreed.

40   The next day, we had a visitor: Ayesha's father. He would not allow his daughter to tell her story. "It's too risky," he said.

41   My father didn't argue with him. The Taliban were cruel; but even *they* wouldn't hurt a child, he wanted to say. But he respected Ayesha's father's decision and prepared to call the BBC with the bad news.

42   I was only eleven, but I said, "Why not me?" I knew he'd wanted someone older, not a child.

43   I looked at my father's hopeful—nervous—face. He had been so brave for speaking out. It was one thing to talk to national and local media, but this diary might be read by people outside Pakistan. It was the BBC, after all. My father had always stood by me. Could I stand by him? I knew without even thinking that I could. I would do anything to be able to continue going to school. But first we went to my mother.

44   If she was afraid, I wouldn't do it. Because if I didn't have her support, it would be like speaking with only half my heart.

45   But my mother agreed. She gave us her answer with a verse from the Holy Quran.[10] "Falsehood has to die," she said. "And truth has to come forward." God would protect me, she said, because my mission was a good one.

46   Many people in Swat[11] saw danger everywhere they looked. But our family didn't look at life that way. We saw possibility. And we felt a responsibility to stand up for our homeland. My father and I are the starry-eyed ones. "Things have to get better," we always say. My mother is our rock. While our heads are in the sky, her feet are on the ground. But we all believed

ANALYZE CHARACTERISTICS AND FEATURES OF INFORMATIONAL TEXTS

Annotate: In paragraph 45, mark the term that is footnoted.

Analyze: How does the footnote help you understand the reason that Malala's mother agrees to the decision?

---

[9] **Urdu** (ûr´dōō): Pakistan's national language.
[10] **Quran** (kə-rän´): the sacred book of the religion of Islam, also spelled Koran.
[11] **Swat:** the Swat Valley of northwest Pakistan and the town of Mingora is where the memoir's narrative takes place.

NOTICE & NOTE

Students outside during a science fair at the Khushal School.

LANGUAGE CONVENTIONS

Proper nouns are capitalized, as are their abbreviations. Explain how each instance of capitalization is used in paragraph 47.

pseudonym
(sōōd´n-ĭm´) n. A *pseudonym* is a fictitious name, particularly a pen name.

in hope. "Speaking up is the only way things will get better," she said.

47   I had never written a diary before and didn't know how to begin, so the BBC correspondent said he would help me. He had to call me on my mother's phone because, even though we had a computer, there were frequent power cuts and few places in Mingora with Internet access. The first time he called, he told me he was using his wife's phone because his own phone had been bugged[12] by the intelligence services.

48   He suggested that I use a fake name so the Taliban wouldn't know who was writing the diary. I didn't want to change my name, but he was worried about my safety. That is why he chose a **pseudonym** for me: Gul Makai, which means "cornflower" and is the name of a heroine in a Pashtun folk story.

49   My first diary entry appeared on 3 January 2009, about two weeks before Fazlullah's deadline. The title was "I Am Afraid." I wrote about how hard it was to study or to sleep at night with the constant sounds of fighting in the hills outside town. And I

---

[12] **bugged:** equipped with a concealed listening device to overhear private conversations.

described how I walked to school each morning, looking over my shoulder for fear I'd see a Talib following me.

50   I was writing from the privacy of my bedroom, using a secret identity, but thanks to the Internet, the story of what was happening in Swat was there for the whole world to see. It was as if God had at long last granted my wish for that magic pencil.

51   In my next entry, I wrote about how school was the center of my life and about how proud I was to walk the streets of Mingora in my school uniform.

52   As exciting as it was to be Gul Makai, it was hard not to tell anyone—especially at school. The diary of this **anonymous** Pakistani schoolgirl was all anyone talked about. One girl even printed it out and showed it to my father.

53   "It's very good," he said with a knowing smile.

---

54   With the threat of school closing quickly becoming a reality, I appreciated going even more. In the days leading up to the last one, it was decided that wearing our uniforms was too dangerous, so we were told to dress in our everyday clothes. I decided I wasn't going to cower in fear of Fazlullah's wrath. I would obey the instruction about the uniform, but that day I chose my brightest pink *shalwar kamiz*.[13]

55   As soon as I left the house, I thought for a second about turning back. We'd heard stories of people throwing acid in the faces of girls in Afghanistan. It hadn't happened here yet, but with everything that *had* happened, it didn't seem impossible. But somehow my feet carried me forward, all the way to school.

56   What a peculiar place Mingora had become. Gunfire and cannons as background noise. Hardly any people in the streets. (And if you did see anyone, you couldn't help but think, *This person could be a terrorist*.) And a girl in a pink *shalwar kamiz* sneaking off to school.

---

anonymous
(ə-nŏn´ə-məs) *adj.* Someone who is *anonymous* has an undisclosed or unknown name.

ANALYZE CHARACTERISTICS AND FEATURES OF INFORMATIONAL TEXTS

Annotate: Underline words in paragraph 54 that convey facts. Circle words that convey thoughts and feelings.

Synthesize: How does the author use facts, thoughts, and feelings to convey an idea in the paragraph? What is that idea?

---

[13] **shalwar kamiz** (shäl´vär kə-mēz´): a type of long, loose shirt and pants, worn by both men and women.

NOTICE & NOTE

57   The BBC correspondent asked for more news from Swat for the next diary post. I didn't know what to tell him. He asked me to write about the killings. It seemed so obvious to him that this was news. But to me, what you experience every day is no longer news.

58   It was as if I had become immune to fear. Until one day, on my way home from school, I heard a man behind me say, "I will kill you." My heart stopped, but somehow my feet kept going. I quickened my pace until I was far ahead of him. I ran home, shut the door, and, after a few seconds, peeked out at him. There he was, oblivious to me, shouting at someone on his phone.

59   I laughed a bit at myself. "Malala," I told myself, "there are real things to be afraid of. You don't need to imagine danger where there is none."

60   The real worry, it seemed to me, was being found out. And, of course, it was Moniba who was first to guess the identity of Gul Makai. "I read a diary in the newspaper," she told me one day at recess, "and the story sounded like our story, what happens in our school. It's you, isn't it?" she said.

61   I could not lie, not to Moniba. But when I confessed, she became more angry than ever. "How can you say you're my best friend when you're keeping such an important secret from me?" She turned on her heel and left. And yet I knew, as angry as she was, she wouldn't reveal my secret.

62   It was my father who did that. By accident, of course. He was telling a reporter how terrifying it was for children just to walk to and from school. His own daughter, he said, thought a man on his phone had threatened to kill her. Just about everyone recognized the story from the diary, and by April, my days as Gul Makai, the secret diarist, would be over.

63   But the diary had done its job. Now a number of reporters were following the story of Fazlullah's attempt to shut down the girls' schools of Pakistan, including a man from the *New York Times*.

GENERATE QUESTIONS

Annotate: Mark any words in paragraphs 62 and 63 that lead you to ask questions.

Predict: What questions do you have at the end of the excerpt? Based on what you have read, what do you predict will happen to Malala next?

NOTICE & NOTE

CHECK YOUR UNDERSTANDING

Answer these questions before moving on to the **Analyze the Text** section on the following page.

1 Which of the following expresses Malala's ideas about the importance of education?

   A *I'd already heard the rooster crow at dawn but had fallen back asleep.*

   B *I had an exam on Pakistani studies.*

   C *"After the fifteenth of January, no girl, whether big or little, shall go to school."*

   D *How would I complete my studies and become a doctor, which was my greatest hope at the time?*

2 The author wrote her diary entries under a false name mainly because —

   F she feared that her father would punish her if she used her real name

   G she feared that the Taliban would punish her for speaking out

   H she was too modest to use her real name

   J she did not want her friends to be envious of her

3 Which of the following is not true?

   A Malala's father wanted her to go to school.

   B Malala and her best friend, Moniba, wrote the diary entries.

   C Education is very important to Malala.

   D Malala is a spiritual person who says prayers regularly.

RESPOND

ANALYZE THE TEXT

Support your responses with evidence from the text. 📓 **NOTEBOOK**

1. **Analyze** Review paragraph 2 and paragraphs 10–11. What question can you ask about Malala's life that is answered in paragraphs 10–11? Why do you think the author includes these details? What is her purpose?

2. **Predict** Review paragraphs 23 and 55. What question might you ask when you read paragraph 23? Using information from paragraph 55, what prediction can you make about what happened to Malala on the bus?

3. **Evaluate** Review the title of the memoir and paragraphs 22–24. How has the author used the statement "I am Malala" to communicate an idea? Is it an effective way to communicate her idea?

4. **Cite Evidence** Review paragraphs 61–63. How does the author use characteristics common to a memoir to convey key ideas?

5. **Notice & Note** What quoted words does the author use in paragraphs 58–59? How do these quotations help you understand Malala's character and her purpose for writing?

RESEARCH TIP
Malala Yousafzai has won several important awards. Check sites of organizations that have honored her work to find biographical information you can use in your research.

RESEARCH

When the selection ends, the reader does not know what happens to Malala Yousafzai, her family, and her friends. Generate questions you can use to research how her life unfolds after this excerpt ends. Use the book *I Am Malala* or other sources to answer your questions. Record your findings in a table like this one.

RESEARCH QUESTION	ANSWER AND SOURCE

Extend In paragraph 57, the author writes, "But to me, what you experience every day is no longer news." Using a print or online newspaper, find stories on topics that may be everyday experiences for some people, but seem newsworthy to you. Discuss your findings in a small group.

RESPOND

CREATE AND DISCUSS

Write a Formal Letter Should the British Broadcasting Corporation (BBC) have asked Malala, or any student, to report on news under dangerous conditions, such as those faced by Pakistani schoolchildren? Compose a business letter that reflects your opinion on the topic, addressed to a news organization. Be sure to capitalize proper nouns. Include these features:

- ❏ **Heading:** your name and address at the top of the page
- ❏ **Date:** the date of your letter
- ❏ **Address:** the name and address of the person and company who will receive your letter
- ❏ **Salutation:** a greeting, such as *To Whom It May Concern,* or, if you are writing to a specific person, *Dear Mr./Ms.* _____; end the greeting with a colon.
- ❏ **Body:** Include an introduction, then state your point, and finish with a concluding sentence or two. Keep your communication brief, polite, and clear. Be sure to capitalize proper nouns.
- ❏ **Closing and Signature:** *Sincerely,* followed by a space for your signature, and then your full name

Discuss with a Small Group Freewrite in response to this question: What would you do with your time if you couldn't go to school? Share your response with a small group. Discuss whether you would be happy or satisfied not going to school and what you think the long-term consequences would be.

Go to **Writing Arguments: Formal Style** in the **Writing Studio** for more on writing in a formal style.

Go to **Participating in Collaborative Discussions** in the **Speaking and Listening Studio** for help with having a group discussion.

GROUP WORK CHECKLIST
- ❏ Listen actively.
- ❏ Ask specific questions.
- ❏ Respond respectfully.
- ❏ Consider group members' suggestions.
- ❏ Take notes about important points.

RESPOND TO THE ESSENTIAL QUESTION

 What keeps people from giving up?

Gather Information Review your annotations and notes on the selection. Then, add relevant details to your Response Log. As you determine which information to include, think about what Malala values and how others can learn from her example.

At the end of the unit, use your notes to write a biographical report.

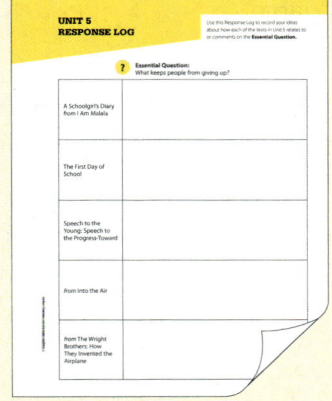

ACADEMIC VOCABULARY

As you write and discuss what you learned from the selection, be sure to use the Academic Vocabulary words. Check off each of the words that you use.

- ❏ achieve
- ❏ individual
- ❏ instance
- ❏ outcome
- ❏ principle

A Schoolgirl's Diary from I Am Malala

RESPOND

WORD BANK
debate
edict
defy
pseudonym
anonymous

CRITICAL VOCABULARY

Practice and Apply Use what you know about the Critical Vocabulary words to answer these questions.

1. How would you know that an article was written by an **anonymous** author?

   _____

2. Do you like to **debate?** Why or why not?

   _____

3. What kind of **edict** might you **defy?** Why?

   _____

4. If you wanted to use a **pseudonym,** what would you choose? Why?

   _____

VOCABULARY STRATEGY:
Greek and Latin Roots

Many English words contain Greek or Latin roots. A **root** is a word part that contains the core meaning of the word. Knowing the origin and meaning of roots and affixes can help you determine the meaning of an unfamiliar word.

Remember that a **prefix** is an affix that appears at the beginning of a word and a **suffix** is an affix that appears at the end of a word. For example, the word *pseudonym* contains the Greek prefix *pseudo-*, meaning "false," and *nym*, which comes from a Greek root meaning "name."

Use an online or print dictionary to check the meaning and origins of words, word roots, and affixes. Your dictionary may also have a section about word roots, which will offer additional information on meaning.

Go to **Analyzing Word Structure** in the **Vocabulary Studio** for more on Greek and Latin roots.

Practice and Apply Work in small groups to determine the origin and meaning of the word parts in *anonymous, debate, defy,* and *edict*. Use a dictionary to look up entire words as well as roots, prefixes, and affixes.

LANGUAGE CONVENTIONS:
Capitalization

Writers capitalize proper nouns to distinguish them from common nouns. Recall that a **proper noun** names a particular person, place, thing, or idea; a **common noun** is a general name for a person, place, thing, or idea. Proper nouns include languages, cities, ethnicities, school names, brands, titles, organizations and their abbreviations, initials that stand for someone's name, and acronyms (words formed by combining the initial letters of a series of words). In the selection, capitalization is used in the following ways.

Go to the **Grammar Studio** for more on capitalization.

CATEGORY OF PROPER NOUN	EXAMPLE
Names of schools	the Khushal School bus
Titles used before a name, names of people, and names of businesses	Dr. Humayun's Hair Transplant Institute
Organizations and their acronyms	British Broadcasting Corporation BBC
Countries	Pakistan
Ethnicities	Pashtun
Languages	Urdu, Pashto
Titles of books, chapters, published works, and newspapers	Quran "A Schoolgirl's Diary" "I Am Afraid" New York Times
Days of the week, months of the year	Tuesday October

Practice and Apply Write your own sentences with proper nouns, using the examples from *I Am Malala* as models. Your sentences can be about Malala Yousafzai or your own experiences with challenges and persistence. When you have finished, share your sentences with a partner and compare your work.

ANALYZE & APPLY

THE FIRST DAY OF SCHOOL

Short Story by **R. V. CASSILL**

? ESSENTIAL QUESTION:

What keeps people from giving up?

GET READY

QUICK START

How much do you know about the historical practice of segregation in U.S. public schools? List three facts about segregation and three questions you have about it.

ANALYZE ELEMENTS OF PLOT

The series of events in a work of fiction is called the **plot.** The plot usually centers on a conflict, or struggle, faced by the main character. Most plots have the following five stages: exposition, rising action, climax, falling action, and resolution:

Climax is the point of greatest tension in the work. Here, the conflict is resolved and the outcome becomes clear.

Rising action introduces or develops the conflict. Events occur that make the conflict get more complicated and build toward the climax.

Falling action is the stage in which the story begins to draw to a close. Events show the results of the important decision or action that happened at the climax.

Exposition provides background information and introduces the setting, characters, and sometimes the conflict.

Resolution is the final outcome of the story.

Sometimes authors use **nonlinear elements,** including flashbacks, to provide a better understanding of a character or of the plot's action. A **flashback** is an interruption of the plot that presents events that took place at an earlier time. As you read, consider what a flashback reveals about the characters and how it fits into the story's structure.

ANALYZE INFLUENCE OF SETTING ON PLOT AND CHARACTER

In "The First Day of School," the characters are fictional, but the historical events described are not. As you read, note how the story's historical and cultural setting influences its characters and plot development. Read the background information and look for clues about the time and place of the story as you read. Ask yourself, how does the setting help create and reveal the conflicts of the plot?

GENRE ELEMENTS: SHORT STORY

- is a work of short fiction that centers on a single idea and can be read in one sitting
- usually includes one main conflict that involves the characters and keeps the story moving
- includes the basic elements of fiction—plot, character, setting, and theme
- may be based on real people and historical events

GET READY

CRITICAL VOCABULARY

resentment   lament   stealthily   linger   serene   poised

Use the Critical Vocabulary words to complete the sentences.

1. The cat crept _____ through the bushes, stalking a bird.
2. I decided to _____ in bed for a few minutes of extra sleep.
3. In the portrait, the woman looked relaxed and _____ .
4. I feel _____ when my sister gets to stay up later than me.
5. I will _____ going to the movies if you can't come too!
6. He appeared _____ and confident in front of the class.

LANGUAGE CONVENTIONS

Sentence patterns include simple, compound, complex, and compound-complex sentences. The following is an example of a compound sentence from "The First Day of School."

He heard the tap of heels on the stairs, and his sister came down into the kitchen.

A comma is used to separate the two independent clauses joined by the coordinating conjunction *and*. As you read the selection, pay attention to the variety of sentence patterns and how commas are used in each.

ANNOTATION MODEL   NOTICE & NOTE

As you read, note the stages of plot and instances of flashback. You can also mark details that help you understand the setting of the story. In the model, you can see one reader's notes about "The First Day of School."

> 13   He heard the tap of heels on the stairs, and his sister came down into the kitchen. <u>She looked fresh and cool in her white dress.</u> Her lids looked heavy. She must have slept all right—and for this John felt both envy and a faint **resentment**. <u>He had not really slept since midnight.</u> The heavy traffic in town, the long wail of horns as somebody raced in on the U.S. highway holding the horn button down, and the restless murmur, like the sound of a celebration down in the courthouse square, had kept him awake after that.

This description of getting ready for school shows that this day seems different.

This is the start of a flashback. The setting is tense and unsettled.

354 Unit 5

BACKGROUND

In 1954, the United States Supreme Court ruled that segregation in public schools (the practice of having "separate but equal" schools for whites and blacks) was unconstitutional. This decision meant that schools had to begin integrating students at all levels. Schoolchildren, particularly in the southern United States, prepared to face the anger, hatred, and often violence of those who opposed this policy. In 1958, in the midst of this difficult time, **R. V. Cassill** (1919–2002) wrote this story.

THE FIRST DAY OF SCHOOL

Short Story by R. V. Cassill

SETTING A PURPOSE

As you read, pay close attention to details about the setting and the clues that indicate what is significant about this first day of school.

1   Thirteen bubbles floated in the milk. Their pearl transparent hemispheres[1] gleamed like souvenirs of the summer days just past, rich with blue reflections of the sky and of shadowy greens. John Hawkins jabbed the bubble closest to him with his spoon, and it disappeared without a ripple. On the white surface there was no mark of where it had been.

2   "Stop tooling[2] that oatmeal and eat it," his mother said. She glanced meaningfully at the clock on the varnished cupboard. She nodded a heavy, emphatic affirmation[3] that now the clock was boss. Summer was over, when

---

[1] **hemispheres** (hĕmʹĭ-sfîrzʹ): halves of a sphere, which is a three-dimensional circular, or ball, shape.
[2] **tooling** (to͞oʹlĭng): working with something, as with a tool such as a spoon.
[3] **affirmation** (ăfʹər-māʹshən): positive, strong support of the truth of something.

Notice & Note

Use the side margins to notice and note signposts in the text.

ANALYZE INFLUENCE OF SETTING ON PLOT AND CHARACTER

Annotate: In paragraph 2, mark details of setting.

Analyze: What does the setting reveal about this stage of the plot?

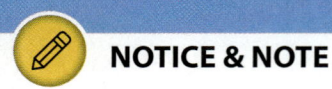

NOTICE & NOTE

ANALYZE ELEMENTS OF PLOT

Annotate: In paragraphs 3–12, mark the details that show you John is worried and upset about something.

Analyze: What is the conflict that is introduced here? What stage of the plot is this?

LANGUAGE CONVENTIONS

Authors vary their sentence patterns to make their writing smooth, clear, and interesting to read. Explain the effect of the author's use of varying sentence patterns and commas in paragraph 13.

resentment
(rĭ-zĕnt´mənt) *n.* If you feel *resentment,* you feel anger or irritation.

the gracious oncoming of morning light and the stir of early breezes promised that time was a luxury.

3 "Audrey's not even down yet," he said.

4 "Audrey'll be down."

5 "You think she's taking longer to dress because she wants to look nice today?"

6 "She likes to look *neat*."

7 "What I was thinking," he said slowly, "was that maybe she didn't feel like going today. Didn't feel *exactly* like it."

8 "Of course she'll go."

9 "I meant she might not want to go until tomorrow, maybe. Until we see what happens."

10 "Nothing's going to happen," his mother said.

11 "I know there isn't. But what if it did?" Again John swirled the tip of his spoon in the milk. It was like writing on a surface that would keep no mark.

12 "Eat and be quiet. Audrey's coming, so let's stop this here kind of talk."

13 He heard the tap of heels on the stairs, and his sister came down into the kitchen. She looked fresh and cool in her white dress. Her lids looked heavy. She must have slept all right—and for this John felt both envy and a faint **resentment**. He had not really slept since midnight. The heavy traffic in town, the long wail of horns as somebody raced in on the U.S. highway holding the horn button down, and the restless murmur, like the sound of a celebration down in the courthouse square, had kept him awake after that. Each time a car had passed their house his breath had gone tight and sluggish. It was better to stay awake and ready, he had told himself, than to be caught asleep.

14 "Daddy gone?" Audrey asked softly as she took her place across the table from her brother.

15 "He's been gone an hour," their mother answered. "*You* know what time he has to be at the mine."

16 "She means, did he go to work today?" John said. His voice had risen impatiently. He met his mother's stout[4] gaze in a staring contest, trying to make her admit by at least some flicker of expression that today was different from any other day. "I thought he might be down at Reverend Specker's," John said. "Cal's father and Vonnie's and some of the others are going to be there to wait and see."

17 Maybe his mother smiled then. If so, the smile was so faint that he could not be sure. "You know your father isn't much of a hand for waiting," she said. "Eat. It's a quarter past eight."

---

[4] **stout** (stout): bold, brave, determined.

356 Unit 5

NOTICE & NOTE

18 As he spooned the warm oatmeal into his mouth he heard the rain crow calling again from the trees beyond the railroad embankment. He had heard it since the first light came before dawn, and he had thought, Maybe the bird knows it's going to rain, after all. He hoped it would. *They won't come out in the rain,* he had thought. Not so many of them, at least. He could wear a raincoat. A raincoat might help him feel more protected on the walk to school. It would be a sort of disguise, at least.

19 But since dawn the sun had lain across the green Kentucky trees and the roofs of town like a clean, hard fire. The sky was as clear as fresh-washed window glass. The rain crow was wrong about the weather. And still, John thought, its **lamenting**, repeated call must mean something.

lament
(lə-mĕnt´) *v.* If you *lament,* you are wailing or crying as a way of expressing grief.

20 His mother and Audrey were talking about the groceries she was to bring when she came home from school at lunch time. A five-pound bag of sugar, a fresh pineapple, a pound of butter . . .

21 "Listen!" John said. Downtown the sound of a siren had begun. A volley of automobile horns broke around it as if they meant to drown it out. "*Listen* to them."

22 "It's only the National Guard, I expect," his mother said calmly. "They came in early this morning before light. And it may be some foolish kids honking at them, the way they would. Audrey, if Henry doesn't have a good-looking roast, why then let it go, and I'll walk out to Weaver's this afternoon and get one there. I wanted to have something a little bit special for our dinner tonight."

23 So . . . John thought . . . she wasn't asleep last night either. Someone had come **stealthily** to the house to bring his parents word about the National Guard. That meant they knew about the others who had come into town, too. Maybe all through the night there had been a swift passage of messengers through the neighborhood and a whispering of information that his mother meant to keep from him. Your folks told you, he reflected bitterly, that nothing is better than knowing. Knowing whatever there is in this world to be known. That was why you had to be one of the half dozen kids out of some nine hundred colored of school age who were going today to start classes at Joseph P. Gilmore High instead of Webster. Knowing and learning the truth were worth so much they said—and then left it to the hooting rain crow to tell you that things were worse than everybody had hoped.

stealthily
(stĕl´thə-lē) *adv.* To do something *stealthily* means doing it quietly and secretly so no one notices.

ANALYZE INFLUENCE OF SETTING ON PLOT AND CHARACTER
Annotate: Mark details in paragraph 23 that help you better understand the setting of the story.

Analyze: How does the cultural and historical setting of the story affect John and lead to the conflict?

NOTICE & NOTE

ANALYZE INFLUENCE OF SETTING ON PLOT AND CHARACTER

Annotate: In paragraph 25, mark details about who will walk to school with John and his sister.

Draw Conclusions: Why is it necessary that the children are walked to school by adults?

linger
(lĭng′gər) *v.* To *linger* means to leave slowly and reluctantly, not wanting to go.

24   Something had gone wrong, bad enough wrong so the National Guard had to be called out.

25   "It's eight twenty-five," his mother said. "Did you get that snap sewed on right, Audrey?" As her experienced fingers examined the shoulder of Audrey's dress they **lingered** a moment in an involuntary, sheltering caress. "It's all arranged," she told her children, "how you'll walk down to the Baptist Church and meet the others there. You know there'll be Reverend Chader, Reverend Smith, and Mr. Hall to go with you. It may be that the white ministers will go with you, or they may be waiting at school. We don't know. But now you be sure, don't you go farther than the Baptist Church alone." Carefully she lifted her hand clear of Audrey's shoulder. John thought, Why doesn't she hug her if that's what she wants to do?

26   He pushed away from the table and went out on the front porch. The dazzling sunlight lay shadowless on the street that swept down toward the Baptist Church at the edge of the colored section. The street seemed awfully long this morning, the way it had looked when he was little. A chicken was

clucking contentedly behind their neighbor's house, feeling the warmth, settling itself into the sun-warmed dust. Lucky chicken.

27   He blinked at the sun's glare on the concrete steps leading down from the porch. He remembered something else from the time he was little. Once he had kicked Audrey's doll buggy down these same steps. He had done it out of meanness—for some silly reason he had been mad at her. But as soon as the buggy had started to bump down, he had understood how terrible it was not to be able to run after it and stop it. It had gathered speed at each step and when it hit the sidewalk it had spilled over. Audrey's doll had smashed into sharp little pieces on the sidewalk below. His mother had come out of the house to find him crying harder than Audrey. "Now you know that when something gets out of your hands it is in the Devil's hands," his mother had explained to him. Did she expect him to forget—now—that that was always the way things went to smash when they got out of hand? Again he heard the siren and the hooting, mocking horns from the center of town. Didn't his mother think *they* could get out of hand?

28   He closed his eyes and seemed to see something like a doll buggy bump down long steps like those at Joseph P. Gilmore High, and it seemed to him that it was not a doll that was riding down to be smashed.

29   He made up his mind then. He would go today, because he had said he would. Therefore he had to. But he wouldn't go unless Audrey stayed home. That was going to be his condition. His bargaining looked perfect. He would trade them one for one.

30   His mother and Audrey came together onto the porch. His mother said, "My stars, I forgot to give you the money for the groceries." She let the screen door bang as she went swiftly back into the house.

31   As soon as they were alone, he took Audrey's bare arm in his hand and pinched hard. "You gotta stay home," he whispered. "Don't you know there's thousands of people down there? Didn't you hear them coming in all night long? You slept, didn't you? All right. You can hear them now. Tell her you're sick. She won't expect you to go if you're sick. I'll knock you down, I'll smash you if you don't tell her that." He bared his teeth and twisted his nails into the skin of her arm. "Hear them horns," he hissed.

32   He forced her halfway to her knees with the strength of his fear and rage. They swayed there, locked for a minute. Her knee

---

NOTICE & NOTE

ANALYZE ELEMENTS OF PLOT

Annotate: In paragraph 27, underline the words that show a flashback is beginning. Circle the words that signal the flashback has ended.

Analyze: How does the flashback help you understand John's character?

NOTICE & NOTE

AHA MOMENT

Notice & Note: What new information does Audrey provide in paragraph 33? Mark the new information.

Analyze: What does John learn about his sister and his family? How does this information help you better understand Audrey's character and her relationship to her brother?

serene
(sə-rēn´) *adj.* If you are *serene*, you are calm and unflustered.

poised
(poizd) *adj.* To be poised means to be calm and assured, showing balanced feeling and action.

ANALYZE ELEMENTS OF PLOT

Annotate: Mark details in paragraphs 40–44 that contribute to the resolution of the story.

Summarize: What is the resolution, or final outcome, of the story?

dropped to the porch floor. She lowered her eyes. He thought he had won.

33   But she was saying something and in spite of himself he listened to her almost whispered refusal. "Don't you know anything? Don't you know it's harder for them than us? Don't you know Daddy didn't go to the mine this morning? They laid him off on account of us. They told him not to come if we went to school."

34   Uncertainly he relaxed his grip. "How do you know all that?"

35   "I listen," she said. Her eyes lit with a sudden spark that seemed to come from their absolute brown depths. "But I don't let on all I know the way you do. I'm not a . . ." Her last word sunk so low that he could not exactly hear it. But if his ear missed it, his understanding caught it. He knew she had said "coward."

36   He let her get up then. She was standing beside him, **serene** and prim when their mother came out on the porch again.

37   "Here, child," their mother said to Audrey, counting the dollar bills into her hand. "There's six, and I guess it will be all right if you have some left if you and Brother get yourselves a cone to lick on the way home."

38   John was not looking at his sister then. He was already turning to face the shadowless street, but he heard the unmistakable **poised** amusement of her voice when she said, "Ma, don't you know we're a little too old for that?"

39   "Yes, you are," their mother said. "Seems I had forgotten that."

40   They were too old to take each other's hand, either, as they went down the steps of their home and into the street. As they turned to the right, facing the sun, they heard the chattering of a tank's tread on the pavement by the school. A voice too distant to be understood bawled a military command. There were horns again and a crescendo[5] of boos.

41   Behind them they heard their mother call something. It was lost in the general racket.

42   "What?" John called back to her. "What?"

43   She had followed them out as far as the sidewalk, but not past the gate. As they hesitated to listen, she put her hands to either side of her mouth and called to them the words she had so often used when she let them go away from home.

44   "Behave yourselves," she said.

---

[5] **crescendo** (krə-shĕn´dō): a slow, gradual increase in volume, intensity, or force.

CHECK YOUR UNDERSTANDING

Answer these questions before moving on to the **Analyze the Text** section on the following page.

1 John Hawkins is upset with his mother because —

   A she acts as if this morning is like any other day

   B she gives grocery money to his sister and not to him

   C she makes him eat his breakfast even though he is ill

   D she doesn't take his father to work

2 The author includes details about the National Guard to —

   F describe the work that they do

   G add tension to the situation and complicate the plot

   H give a side detail that doesn't add much to plot

   J describe the characters in vivid details

3 Why does John tell his sister to pretend to be sick?

   A He likes to tell his little sister what to do.

   B He believes she is ill and pretending to be well.

   C He knows that is what his mother really wants.

   D He does not want either of them to face danger at school.

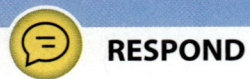

RESPOND

ANALYZE THE TEXT

Support your responses with evidence from the text. 📓 NOTEBOOK

1. **Identify** What are three details in the story that help you understand the text's historical and cultural setting?

2. **Infer** Reread paragraphs 18–19. How does the setting reveal, contribute to, and create conflict in the story?

3. **Analyze** Reread paragraphs 27–29. What is the connection between what John remembers and what is happening in the story now? Describe what you learn about John and how the flashback moves the plot of the story forward.

4. **Interpret** What is the climax of the story? Explain.

5. **Notice & Note** Review paragraphs 33–36. Summarize what John realizes about other members of his family. How does this help him resolve his own internal conflict?

RESEARCH

RESEARCH TIP
To begin online research about the historical and cultural setting of the story, use "Little Rock Nine" or "*Brown v. Board of Education*" as your search terms.

The short story "The First Day of School" is based on events surrounding the 1954 Supreme Court ruling known as *Brown v. Board of Education* and the actions of a group of students in Little Rock, Arkansas, known as the Little Rock Nine. In a small group, brainstorm several questions about the historical and cultural setting of the story. After your discussion, work individually to research and answer one or more of your questions. Use the chart below to take notes.

QUESTION	ANSWER

Extend In 1999, the Little Rock Nine were honored with Congressional Gold Medals. Research why this award is given and who other recipients are. Share your findings with the class.

362 Unit 5

RESPOND

CREATE AND DISCOVER

Write an Analytical Essay Write a one-page essay that explains John's feelings and actions on the morning of his first day of school. Focus on how the historical setting of the story motivates him. Include the following in your essay:

- ❏ Introduce a controlling idea about how John feels about going to school on this day.
- ❏ Discuss how the historical and cultural setting of the story affects John.
- ❏ Show how John's response to events in his past affects his actions in the present.
- ❏ Sum up your ideas with a concluding statement.
- ❏ Remember to use transitions to connect ideas, vary your sentence patterns, and punctuate your sentences correctly.

Go to **Writing Informative Texts** in the **Writing Studio** for more on developing a topic and organizing ideas.

Compare and Contrast with a Small Group Have a discussion about the story's historical context, based on your research and the setting of the text. Compare and contrast that context with your own experiences on a typical first day of school. Use the following approaches to help with the discussion:

- ❏ Encourage everyone to participate and listen actively.
- ❏ Take notes.
- ❏ Respectfully consider other viewpoints.
- ❏ Identify points of agreement and disagreement.

Go to **Participating in Collaborative Discussions: Speaking Constructively** in the **Speaking and Listening Studio** for help with having a group discussion.

RESPOND TO THE ESSENTIAL QUESTION

? What keeps people from giving up?

Gather Information Review your annotations and notes on "The First Day of School." Then, add relevant details to your Response Log. As you determine which information to include, think about:

- the kinds of hardships people face
- what keeps people going during hard times
- how this story is an example of not giving up

At the end of the unit, use your notes to write a biographical report.

ACADEMIC VOCABULARY

As you write and discuss what you learned from the short story, be sure to use the Academic Vocabulary words. Check off each of the words that you use.

- ❏ achieve
- ❏ individual
- ❏ instance
- ❏ outcome
- ❏ principle

RESPOND

WORD BANK
resentment
lament
stealthily
linger
serene
poised

CRITICAL VOCABULARY

Practice and Apply Answer these questions.

1. Does a **serene** sky indicate stormy or sunny weather? Explain.
   _____

2. Why are you likely to **linger** at the end of a school dance?
   _____

3. Does a **poised** person appear calm or appear nervous? Explain.
   _____

4. How can you tell if a teammate is **lamenting** the score?
   _____

5. Describe what **resentment** feels like.
   _____

6. Describe the behavior of an animal that moves **stealthily**.
   _____

VOCABULARY STRATEGY: Thesaurus

A **thesaurus** is a reference book of synonyms, or words that have nearly the same meaning. As with a dictionary, words are listed alphabetically. Each word has a list of synonyms and often a list of antonyms, or words with opposite meanings, as well. To use an online thesaurus:

- Look for the search box and type in your word.
- Click on the onscreen icon, such as a magnifying glass, and the thesaurus will display the word's meaning and synonyms.
- You also may be able to click an icon to hear a pronunciation.

Go to the **Vocabulary Studio** for more on using resources.

Practice and Apply Use a thesaurus to select a synonym for each vocabulary word. Then use the synonym in a sentence that shows its meaning, as in the example below for *resentment*.

WORD	SYNONYM	SENTENCE
resentment	animosity	My opponent scowled after I beat him; I could sense his *animosity*.
lament		
stealthily		
linger		

RESPOND

LANGUAGE CONVENTIONS:
Sentence Patterns

Authors use a variety of sentence patterns to make their writing smooth, clear, and interesting to read. Review the sentence patterns and examples from "The First Day of School" in the chart. Note how commas are used to separate clauses and make the sentences easier to read.

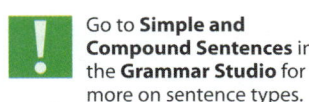

Go to **Simple and Compound Sentences** in the **Grammar Studio** for more on sentence types.

SENTENCE PATTERN	DESCRIPTION AND EXAMPLE
Simple	one independent clause **She looked fresh and cool in her white dress.**
Compound	two or more independent clauses joined with a coordinating conjunction, such as *and, or, but, not, yet, so* **He heard the tap of heels on the stairs, and his sister came down into the kitchen.**
Complex	one independent clause and one or more subordinate, or dependent, clauses **Summer was over, when the gracious oncoming of morning light and the stir of early breezes promised that time was a luxury.**
Compound-Complex	two or more independent clauses and one or more subordinate clauses **It had gathered speed at each step and when it hit the sidewalk it had spilled over.**

Practice and Apply Change the sentence pattern of each sentence or group of sentences. First, identify the original pattern used in each sentence. Then revise, using a different sentence pattern.

1. John hadn't slept very well the night before because the sounds of car horns and loud voices kept him awake.

   _____

2. Audrey came down the stairs. She acted prim. The dress she had chosen looked fresh and cool.

   _____

3. Their mother came onto the porch. She called to them. She followed them down the street.

   _____

The First Day of School 365

ANALYZE & APPLY

SPEECH TO THE YOUNG: SPEECH TO THE PROGRESS-TOWARD

Poem by **Gwendolyn Brooks**

ESSENTIAL QUESTION:

What keeps people from giving up?

GET READY

QUICK START

What kind of advice have you been given by the adults in your life? Have you found this advice helpful or not? Explain your thoughts to a partner.

ANALYZE THE EFFECTS OF METER AND STRUCTURAL ELEMENTS

"Speech to the Young: Speech to the Progress-Toward" is a **free verse poem,** which means that it does not follow a specific rhyming pattern or metrical form. It does use other elements of poetry to convey meaning and ideas, including:

- ❏ **Line breaks** and different line lengths to create effects and emphasis
- ❏ **Repetition,** or repeated sounds, words, phrases, or lines, to reinforce meaning and create an appealing rhythm, emphasis, or sense of unity
- ❏ **Rhythm,** or the pattern of stressed and unstressed syllables in a line, to bring out the musical quality of language, create mood, and emphasize ideas
- ❏ **Alliteration,** or the repetition of the consonant sounds at the beginning of words, to contribute to and create rhythm in a poem

As you read the poem, use a chart like this to help you analyze what the poetic elements reveal.

GENRE ELEMENTS: POETRY

- may include rhyme, rhythm, and meter
- features line breaks and the use of white space for effects and meaning
- may use repetition and rhyme to create a melodic quality
- often contains figurative language and literary devices such as alliteration, consonance, and assonance

POETIC ELEMENT	EXAMPLE IN POEM	EFFECT
Line break		
Repetition		
Rhythm		
Alliteration		

GET READY

MAKE INFERENCES ABOUT THEME AND AUTHOR'S PURPOSE

Poets use structure and poetic elements to create mood and communicate meaning and themes. A **theme** is a message about life or human nature that a writer shares with readers. Often, especially with shorter poems, the metrical and structural elements express theme and purpose indirectly. Many times readers must **infer,** or form a logical opinion, about what the writer's message may be. When making inferences, readers need to support their ideas with evidence from the text and use personal experience or knowledge to inform their inferences.

Using a graphic organizer like the one below can help guide your thoughts when making inferences about the theme and the author's purpose.

Theme:
Author's Purpose:

Structural or Metrical Elements:

Other Evidence:

ANNOTATION MODEL

NOTICE & NOTE

As you read, note clues about the poem's theme and author's purpose, and examine how the poet uses poetic elements to convey a message. This model shows one reader's notes about the beginning of "Speech to the Young: Speech to the Progress-Toward."

> Say to them,
> say to the <u>down-keepers</u>,
> the <u>sun-slappers</u>,
> the <u>self-soilers</u>,
> 5 the <u>harmony-hushers</u>,
> "Even if you are not ready for day
> It cannot always be night."

The poet uses "er" words to describe people who put down or criticize other people or other people's ideas.

368 Unit 5

BACKGROUND

Gwendolyn Brooks (1917–2000) published more than twenty books of poetry and several books of prose. Her writing portrays African Americans in daily life and relies on a number of poetic devices and forms. In 1950, for her book of poetry *Annie Allen,* she became the first African American to win a Pulitzer Prize. The longtime Chicago resident became Poet Laureate of Illinois in 1968. In 1985, she became the first African American woman to become Poet Laureate of the United States.

SPEECH TO THE YOUNG: SPEECH TO THE PROGRESS-TOWARD

Poem by Gwendolyn Brooks

SETTING A PURPOSE

As you read, pay attention to repeated words and sounds and think about how they add to the meaning of the poem. Note the effect of Brooks' use of line breaks and line length to create rhythm and emphasis.

Say to them,
say to the down-keepers,
the sun-slappers,
the self-soilers,
5   the harmony-hushers,
"Even if you are not ready for day
it cannot always be night."

MAKE INFERENCES ABOUT THEME AND AUTHOR'S PURPOSE

Annotate: Mark the quotation in the poem.

Infer: Why do you think these lines are in quotes, and what is the meaning of these lines?

NOTICE & NOTE

ANALYZE THE EFFECTS OF METER AND STRUCTURAL ELEMENTS

Annotate: Mark lines in the poem that give direct advice.

Analyze: How do these lines contribute to the rhythm of the poem?

WORDS OF THE WISER

Notice & Note: What words of the wiser are being communicated to readers? Mark repeated and rhyming words in lines 10–13.

Draw Conclusions: What message does Brooks express in these last lines of the poem?

You will be right.
For that is the hard home-run.

10 Live not for battles won.
Live not for the-end-of-the-song.
Live in the along.

CHECK YOUR UNDERSTANDING

Answer these questions before moving on to the **Analyze the Text** section on the following page.

1 The speaker in the poem is talking to —

   A her country

   B her family

   C newborns

   D young people

2 The repetition of the word *Live* in the second stanza emphasizes the author's message about —

   F being brave in the face of danger

   G being present and aware during one's life

   H being awake during the day, not at night

   J being ready for the next competition

3 Which phrase describes the poem's message?

   A advice from the speaker

   B correction for the reader

   C sadness from the speaker

   D insulting for the reader

RESPOND

ANALYZE THE TEXT

Support your responses with evidence from the text. 📓 **NOTEBOOK**

1. **Infer** What conclusions can you draw about the meaning of the phrase "self-soilers" in line 4?

2. **Analyze** Reread lines 5-9. Where are there instances of alliteration in those lines? What emphasis does this poetic device create?

3. **Cite Evidence** What theme is the author conveying through this poem? How does she express this theme? Cite evidence to support your inference.

4. **Synthesize** Explain the author's purpose in using the word "speech" twice in the long title, yet making the poem itself very brief.

5. **Notice & Note** What lesson or message is the speaker conveying, and what is meant by the phrase "progress-toward" in the title? Cite evidence to support your response.

RESEARCH TIP
When you conduct online research, evaluate the credibility of websites. Web addresses ending in .gov, .edu, or .org may be reviewed more frequently, but always read critically. Look for an About section to help identify who created the website.

RESEARCH

Research the life and career of poet Gwendolyn Brooks. Use the graphic organizer below to guide your research.

KEY LIFE EVENTS	KEY CAREER EVENTS	IMPORTANCE OF HER POETRY

Extend Find another poem by Gwendolyn Brooks. With your partner, discuss the effects that rhythm, line breaks, and other devices create.

RESPOND

CREATE AND PRESENT

Write a Short Poem Write a short poem in the spirit of "Speech to the Young: Speech to the Progress-Toward." Craft your own inspirational "speech" to a student, relative, or friend who is younger than you are.

❑ Choose a theme and message that you want to communicate.

❑ Choose points of advice and think of creative ways to express them.

❑ Include poetic elements, such as alliteration, repetition, rhythm, rhyme, and thoughtful line breaks.

Record Your Poem Record your poem to present to your class as a video or audio podcast.

❑ Practice reading the poem, adjusting the rhythm of your reading according to different line lengths in the poem.

❑ Practice your reading until you can present the poem as if you were in front of an audience. Rehearse making eye contact and using natural facial expressions and gestures, speaking clearly, and using proper pacing and volume to help convey the meaning of your poem.

❑ Record your poem.

Go to the **Writing Studio** for more on the writing process.

Go to **Producing and Publishing with Technology: Writing for the Internet** in the **Speaking and Listening Studio** for more on online writing and podcasts.

RESPOND TO THE ESSENTIAL QUESTION

? What keeps people from giving up?

Gather Information Review your annotations and notes on "Speech to the Young: Speech to the Progress-Toward." Then, add relevant details to your Response Log. As you determine which information to include, think about:

- how the poet conveys her purpose
- how poetic devices and elements influence theme in a poem
- how advice can help us make choices

At the end of the unit, use your notes to write a biographical report.

ACADEMIC VOCABULARY

As you write and discuss what you learned from the poem, be sure to use the Academic Vocabulary words. Check off each of the words that you use.

❑ achieve
❑ individual
❑ instance
❑ outcome
❑ principle

Speech to the Young: Speech to the Progress-Toward   373

COLLABORATE & COMPARE

GRAPHIC BIOGRAPHY
from
INTO THE AIR
by **Robert Burleigh**
illustrated by **Bill Wylie**
pages 377–385

COMPARE PRESENTATIONS

As you read each selection, look for the key ideas each author wants the reader to understand about similar events. Notice the ways in which elements of each genre are used to present those ideas. After you read both selections, you will collaborate with a small group on a final project.

 ESSENTIAL QUESTION:

What keeps people from giving up?

BIOGRAPHY
from
THE WRIGHT BROTHERS:
HOW THEY INVENTED THE AIRPLANE
by **Russell Freedman**
pages 393–399

GET READY

from Into the Air

QUICK START

Have you ever built something or assembled a complicated toy from a kit? Would you rather do it alone, or with a partner? Share your thoughts with the class.

ANALYZE CHARACTERISTICS OF MULTIMODAL TEXTS

Multimodal texts present information through multiple modes, or ways of expression. The graphic biography you are about to read uses both written text and comic-book style illustrations to tell a biographical story. These print and graphic features work together to organize information, deliver ideas, and guide readers through the text. Look for these features as you read:

MULTIMODAL FEATURE	DESCRIPTION
caption	a text box that provides narration; text may be set in all capital letters
speech balloon	a balloon-shaped graphic with a pointer containing dialogue—what a character says aloud
thought bubble	a cloud-shaped graphic that tells what a character is thinking
image panel	an illustration, often set within a border or frame

DETERMINE KEY IDEAS IN MULTIMODAL TEXTS

In a graphic biography, details in print and graphic features convey the text's **key ideas,** or important points. You can use key ideas to make inferences about a text's **controlling idea,** or thesis statement. Look for a summary of key ideas in the **afterword,** a section sometimes found at the end of a text that offers more information about the biographical subject. To find key ideas in a graphic biography:

- Examine details in each print feature.
- Study illustrations that accompany the text; then, reread the text.
- Use details from the text and illustrations to make inferences about key ideas.

GENRE ELEMENTS: GRAPHIC BIOGRAPHY

- uses illustrations and text to present information
- includes the basic elements of biography—a true account of someone's life—as told by another person; usually written from a third-person point of view
- includes facts and descriptions of events, people, and experiences that shape subjects' lives.

Into the Air

GET READY

CRITICAL VOCABULARY

| discourage | incorrect | prepare |
| defeat | preserve | demonstration |

To see how many Critical Vocabulary words you already know, use them to complete the sentences.

1. We were able to _____ our opponents by six points.
2. _____ for your road trip by planning a route.
3. Don't let a few minor setbacks _____ you.
4. After finishing a test, check for any _____ answers.
5. _____ a long-term friendship by being a good listener.
6. We watched a cooking _____ on using spices correctly.

LANGUAGE CONVENTIONS: Adverbs and Adverb Clauses

Adverbs modify, or describe, verbs, adjectives, or other adverbs. Adverbs are often formed by adding the suffix -*ly* to an adjective. For example: *slow + -ly = slowly*. An **adverb clause** is a subordinate clause that functions as an adverb. Adverb clauses answer questions of *When? Where? How? Why? How often? How long? Under what condition? To what extent?* or *How much?*

>   <u>As the fan blows air through the tunnel</u>, the brothers <u>carefully</u> note how each kind of wing works.

The adverb clause describes when the brothers make notes; the adverb describes how they make notes.

ANNOTATION MODEL

NOTICE & NOTE

As you read, note how multimodal text features communicate key ideas. You can also mark up evidence that supports your own ideas. In the model, you can see one reader's notes about *Into the Air*.

> Day after difficult day, <u>discouraged</u> but not <u>defeated</u>, the Wrights carry the damaged glider back to the campsite, repair it, and <u>try again</u>.

I see ideas about facing challenges without giving up, about trying again and again. These details tell me that the Wrights refused to give up.

BACKGROUND

As boys, brothers Orville and Wilbur Wright were fascinated by flight. In the late 1800s, they honed their mechanical skills at their bicycle sales and repair shop in Ohio, and later studied the work of Otto Lilienthal, who had built a glider with bat-like wings. The following excerpt, by author **Robert Burleigh** and illustrator **Bill Wylie**, begins in 1901, as the Wrights try to build a glider for longer flights—an important step toward powered flight.

from
INTO THE AIR

**Graphic Biography by Robert Burleigh
illustrated by Bill Wylie**

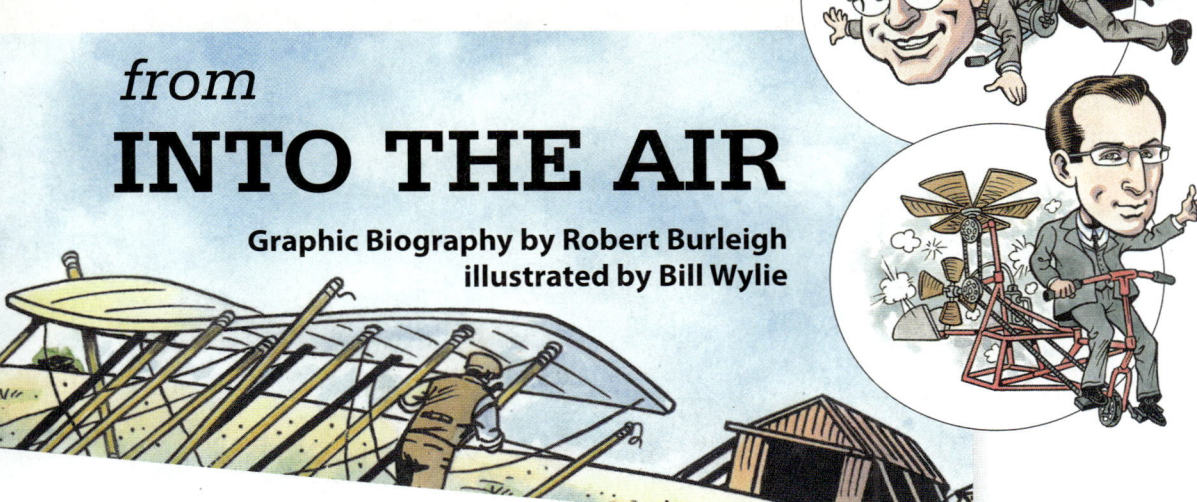

PREPARE TO COMPARE

As you read, note how the Wright brothers are able to pursue their dreams despite difficult challenges. This information will help you compare *Into the Air* with the biography of the Wright brothers that follows.

Notice & Note

Use the side margins to notice and note signposts in the text.

NOTICE & NOTE

discourage
(dĭ-skûr´ĭj) v. To *discourage* is to take away hope or confidence.

defeat
(dĭ-fēt´) v. To *defeat* a person or his or her efforts is to prevent his or her success.

ANALYZE CHARACTERISTICS OF MULTIMODAL TEXTS

Annotate: Mark the print features on this page.

Identify: Name the types of print features and explain the purpose of each.

---

[1] **glider:** an aircraft that relies on gravity and air currents, rather than an engine, for flight; early experiments in glider flight were essential to developing motorized aircraft.

[2] **Lilienthal's air-pressure tables:** a set of calculations produced by German aviation pioneer Otto Lilienthal used in the design of aircraft wings.

NOTICE & NOTE

incorrect
(ĭn´kə-rĕkt´) *adj.* Something *incorrect* is faulty or wrong.

DETERMINE KEY IDEAS IN MULTIMODAL TEXTS
Annotate: Mark details in the text and illustrations that express any doubts the brothers share.

Infer: How do these details work together to express an idea?

Into the Air   379

NOTICE & NOTE

ANALYZE CHARACTERISTICS OF MULTIMODAL TEXTS

Annotate: Study the two illustration panels on this page. Mark the background illustration and the inset illustration.

Compare: How do the illustrations work together and on their own to tell this part of the story?

[3] **hit rock bottom:** to reach the most bleak and hopeless moment.

NOTICE & NOTE

DETERMINE KEY IDEAS IN MULTIMODAL TEXTS

Annotate: Mark the print and graphic details on this page that refer to asking and answering questions.

Draw Conclusions: What inferences can you make from these details?

Into the Air 381

NOTICE & NOTE

LANGUAGE CONVENTIONS

Adverbs modify verbs, adjectives, or other adverbs. Mark the adverb in the caption that begins "As the fan blows." What does this adverb reveal about how the brothers work?

preserve
(prĭ-zûrv´) v. To *preserve* something is to keep it or save it.

NOTICE & NOTE

ANALYZE CHARACTERISTICS OF MULTIMODAL TEXTS

Annotate: Mark the details that help describe the brothers' new glider design.

Analyze: How do the print and graphic features work together to help you understand the design?

prepare
(prĭ-pâr´) v. To *prepare* is to get ready for an event or an occasion.

Into the Air 383

NOTICE & NOTE

BIG QUESTIONS

Notice & Note: Mark the places in the text that confirm what you may have already known about the Wright brothers.

Analyze: How did the writer reveal new information while discussing known facts?

AFTERWORD

1   The Wright brothers' story did not end at Kitty Hawk. As the brothers well knew, there was more work to be done on the airplane. Some of the problems still to be resolved included making the takeoff simpler, learning to execute complete turns in the air, and designing the plane so that the pilot could fly sitting up. In 1904 and 1905, the brothers used an empty pasture near their home in Dayton for many additional experiments and tests.

384 Unit 5

NOTICE & NOTE

2   Meanwhile, only slowly did people in the United States and abroad become aware of the Wright brothers and the importance of their invention. For several years, the American government showed no interest in the Wrights' flying machine. Finally, in 1908, the brothers were able to convince the government that flight was possible and useful. During the same year, Wilbur went to Europe and gave a series of flying **demonstrations** that made him and Orville instant celebrities.

3   Wilbur died of an illness in 1912. But Orville, who died in 1948, lived to see "the age of flight" expand in ways that he and his brother never foresaw. Today there is a sixty-foot high monument to the Wright brothers at Kill Devil Hills, North Carolina. But perhaps the real monuments to the vision, courage, and dedication of Wilbur and Orville Wright are the airplanes you see above you, flying back and forth across the country, every day.

demonstration
(dĕm´ən-strā´shən) *n.* A *demonstration* is a presentation meant to show how something works.

CHECK YOUR UNDERSTANDING

Answer these questions before moving on to the **Analyze the Text** section on the following page.

1   The selection includes illustrations of the Wright brothers' experiments to —

   A   show that testing ideas was important to their work

   B   make us think the Wright brothers were intelligent

   C   show how they were always doubting themselves

   D   help describe outdated technology

2   The Wright brothers invented a box-shaped wind tunnel to —

   F   earn money by selling it to other inventors

   G   answer their questions about wing design

   H   use as a model for a much larger tunnel they would build later

   J   use in a flight demonstration

3   Which of the following is not true about *Into the Air*?

   A   The brothers did not like to give up.

   B   The brothers were always successful.

   C   The brothers sometimes felt discouraged.

   D   The brothers asked and answered questions to develop their ideas.

RESPOND

ANALYZE THE TEXT

Support your responses with evidence from the text. 📓 **NOTEBOOK**

1. **Summarize** Review the print and graphic features on the first page of the selection. What do these elements tell you about the Wright brothers at this point in the story?

2. **Evaluate** Review the caption that begins, "Late into the nights" on the second page of the selection. What is the caption's purpose, and how effectively does it communicate an idea?

3. **Infer** Review the speech balloons appearing in the train illustration on the third page of the selection. What might be the author's purpose in including this dialogue?

4. **Compare** Review the illustrations in the last three pages of the selection; then, compare them to the illustrations on the first three pages. How do the illustrations convey a change in mood?

5. **Notice & Note** Reread the afterword. How does the information presented in the afterword challenge, change, or confirm what you knew about the Wright brothers before reading this selection?

RESEARCH TIP
Follow links from reliable web sites about the Wright brothers to other sites that provide information about later pioneers of flight, such as Louis Bleriot, Charles Lindbergh, Harriet Quimby, and Amelia Earhart.

RESEARCH

At the end of this excerpt, the Wright brothers have yet to achieve their ultimate goal of powered flight (motor-driven aircraft). One of the Wright brothers' biggest achievements was to inspire other people to make flight discoveries. Investigate advances in flight that followed the work of the Wright brothers. Who made these advances? Why were they important? Record what you learn in the chart.

FLIGHT PIONEERS	ACHIEVEMENTS AND THEIR IMPORTANCE

Connect Choose one of the aviation pioneers you learned about in your research. Share what you've learned with a small group.

386 Unit 5

RESPOND

CREATE AND DISCUSS

Write a Summary Write a three- to four-paragraph objective summary of *Into the Air*.

- ❏ Use your own words to paraphrase the selection's print and graphic content.
- ❏ Use your annotations and analysis of the selection to make inferences about the selection's main or controlling idea, or thesis statement.
- ❏ Include details and evidence that support the controlling idea.
- ❏ Use adverbs and adverbial clauses in your summary.

 Go to **Using Textual Evidence: Summarizing, Paraphrasing, and Quoting** in the **Writing Studio** for more on summarizing and paraphrasing texts.

Discuss with a Small Group With a group, discuss the purpose of each type of print and graphic feature in the selection, including captions, speech balloons, thought bubbles, and illustrations.

- ❏ Review the table of print and graphic features.
- ❏ Discuss how each element contributes to your understanding of the historical and biographical information in the selection.
- ❏ Check off each item on the table after it has been discussed.
- ❏ Take notes on your discussion; then, compare your notes with those of other members in the group.
- ❏ Participate actively: listen closely, pose and answer questions, and ask others for their opinions.

 Go to **Participating in Collaborative Discussions** in the **Speaking and Listening Studio** for help with having a group discussion.

RESPOND TO THE ESSENTIAL QUESTION

 What keeps people from giving up?

Gather Information Review your annotations and notes on *Into the Air*. Then, add relevant details to your Response Log. As you determine which information to include, consider how people solve problems and think about failure and success.

At the end of the unit, use your notes to write a biographical report.

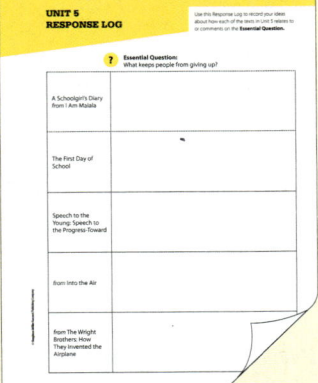

ACADEMIC VOCABULARY
As you write and discuss what you learned from the article, be sure to use the Academic Vocabulary words. Check off each of the words that you use.

- ❏ achieve
- ❏ individual
- ❏ instance
- ❏ outcome
- ❏ principle

RESPOND

WORD BANK
discourage
defeat
incorrect
preserve
prepare
demonstration

CRITICAL VOCABULARY

Practice and Apply Complete each sentence in a way that shows the meaning of the Vocabulary word.

1. You might **prepare** for a bicycle ride by _____.
2. If your answer is **incorrect,** return to the text and _____.
3. He gave a **demonstration** of his new invention so _____.
4. The weather might **defeat** the campers if _____.
5. She tried to **discourage** the puppy from _____.
6. The museum worked to **preserve** the artwork so that _____.

VOCABULARY STRATEGY:
Affixes

 Go to the **Vocabulary Studio** for more on roots, base words, and affixes.

Adding an **affix**—a prefix or a suffix—to a base word forms a new word. A **prefix** appears at the beginning of a base or root word to form a new word. A **suffix** is added to the end of a base or root word to form a new word. Knowing the meaning of common affixes can help you determine the meaning of some unfamiliar words.

PREFIX	MEANING	SUFFIX	EFFECT OR MEANING
dis-	"deprive of"	-d, -ed, -ing	to change verb tense
in-	"not"	-s, -es	to change the number of a noun
pre-	"earlier, before"	-ation	"action, or process"

Practice and Apply Use the chart above to determine the meaning of the prefix and/or affix in each of the following words: *discouraged, defeated, incorrect, preserved, preparing, demonstrations*. With a partner, write a definition for each word and determine its part of speech. Check your work in a dictionary.

LANGUAGE CONVENTIONS:
Adverbs and Adverb Clauses

Recall that **adverbs** can modify verbs, adjectives, or other adverbs. Writers use adverbs and adverb clauses to tell more about the time, manner, place, or cause of an event. A **conjunctive adverb** is an adverb that is used to connect ideas. Here are a few examples of conjunctive adverbs:

however	meanwhile	nonetheless
therefore	moreover	then
finally	furthermore	otherwise

Here is an example of the conjunctive adverb *meanwhile* as used in *Into the Air*:

> <u>Meanwhile</u>, only slowly did people in the United States and abroad become aware of the Wright brothers. . . .

Notice how the conjunctive adverb *meanwhile* introduces the main clause and that a comma is used to separate the conjunctive adverb from the rest of the sentence. Note also how the adverb *slowly* modifies the verb phrase *did become*.

Practice and Apply Write your own sentences using the examples from *Into the Air* as models. Your sentences can be about what kept the Wright brothers from giving up, or they can include your own advice on how to persist in the face of challenges. When you have finished, share your sentences with a partner and compare your use of adverbs, adverb clauses, and conjunctive adverbs.

RESPOND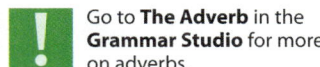

! Go to **The Adverb** in the **Grammar Studio** for more on adverbs.

COLLABORATE & COMPARE

BIOGRAPHY

from
THE WRIGHT BROTHERS:
HOW THEY INVENTED THE AIRPLANE

by **Russell Freedman**

pages 393–399

COMPARE PRESENTATIONS

Now that you have read *Into the Air*, read *The Wright Brothers: How They Invented the Airplane* to see how this selection presents some of the same ideas as it describes similar events. As you read, think about your own experiences with problem solving and persevering. After you are finished, you will collaborate with a small group on a final project analyzing the two texts.

ESSENTIAL QUESTION:

What keeps people from giving up?

GRAPHIC BIOGRAPHY

from
INTO THE AIR

by **Robert Burleigh**
illustrated by **Bill Wylie**

pages 377–385

390 Unit 5

from The Wright Brothers

QUICK START

Would you like to build and test your own flying machine? Why or why not? Discuss your answers with a partner.

ANALYZE CHARACTERISTICS OF INFORMATIONAL TEXTS

Informational texts present facts, events, and ideas in an organized way so that they make sense to the reader. Recognizing a **pattern of organization**—the way ideas and information are arranged in a nonfiction text—will help you better understand the information. As you read, note examples of organizational patterns listed below.

ORGANIZATIONAL PATTERNS	
definition	defines new terms or technical language within the text
classification	sorts ideas into groups and then describes characteristics
chronological order	relates information in time-order sequence
cause and effect	explains a cause-and-effect relationship
advantage and disadvantage	presents the pros and cons of an issue to clarify ideas
key idea and supporting details	establishes a key idea and supports it with details as evidence

DETERMINE KEY IDEAS

Key ideas are important ideas the author wants readers to understand. As you read, look for the text's main idea, as well as key ideas in each paragraph. Sometimes these ideas are not stated directly, but are implied, or suggested by details. As you read, determine key ideas by following these steps:

- Identify the topic of each paragraph or section.
- Note details, including descriptions, facts, and quotations.
- Ask yourself what key idea the details convey about the topic.

GET READY

GENRE ELEMENTS: BIOGRAPHY

- uses text and sometimes photographs or illustrations to tell a true-life story about a person or group of people
- usually written in third-person but may include direct quotations, including the words of the subject or subjects
- includes facts and descriptions of events, people, and experiences that shaped the subject or subjects

The Wright Brothers: How They Invented the Airplane   391

GET READY

CRITICAL VOCABULARY

experiment   prediction   accurate   calculate   apparatus

To see how many Critical Vocabulary words you already know, use them to complete the sentences.

1. We should _____ how long it will take us to drive 500 miles.

2. We conducted the _____ in our new laboratory.

3. A wheelchair is a/an _____ that increases a person's mobility.

4. Make a/an _____ about what will happen in the story.

5. She took careful and _____ measurements.

LANGUAGE CONVENTIONS

Commas help clarify the meaning of sentences by separating certain words or phrases. Commas also set off transitions. **Transitions** such as *because* and *for that reason* clarify relationships between ideas.

To begin with, they were very cautious.

In the above example, "to begin with" links ideas about time with how the Wright brothers acted—with caution. As you read the text, note the author's use of commas after transitions.

ANNOTATION MODEL

NOTICE & NOTE

As you read, note the organizational patterns that are used to present key ideas and structure the text. You can also mark up evidence that supports your own ideas. In the model, you can see one reader's notes about the beginning of *The Wright Brothers*:

> 1   The brothers <u>returned</u> to Kitty Hawk on <u>July 10, 1901</u>. <u>This year</u> they wanted to be closer to their launching site at Kill Devil Hills, so they loaded their camping equipment, glider parts, and some lumber into a beach cart, drove it 4 miles south, and set up camp a few hundred feet from the bottom of Big Hill.

Details about time tell me that the Wright Brothers have been to Kitty Hawk before.

BACKGROUND

Russell Freedman *(b. 1929) specializes in nonfiction storytelling, especially biographies. He has written numerous works for young people, including* Freedom Walkers: The Story of the Montgomery Bus Boycott *and* Becoming Ben Franklin: How a Candle-Maker's Son Helped Light the Flame of Liberty. *He won a Newbery Medal—a prize seldom given for nonfiction—for his 1988 biography of Abraham Lincoln,* Lincoln: A Photobiography.

from
THE WRIGHT BROTHERS:
HOW THEY INVENTED THE AIRPLANE
Biography by Russell Freedman

PREPARE TO COMPARE

As you read, note times when the Wright brothers could have given up on their dream, but did not. Look for details that show how they worked together to overcome obstacles.

1   The brothers returned to Kitty Hawk on July 10, 1901. This year they wanted to be closer to their launching site[1] at Kill Devil Hills, so they loaded their camping equipment, glider parts, and some lumber into a beach cart, drove it 4 miles south, and set up camp a few hundred feet from the bottom of Big Hill. Again they lived in a tent, but they also put up a large wooden shed to use as a workshop and hangar[2] for the new glider. This year they would share their camp with visitors. Their friend Octave Chanute and two associates joined the Wrights for a few days to observe their **experiments** and to test a new glider that Chanute had recently designed.

---

[1] **site:** the place or setting where something happens.
[2] **hangar:** a shelter for storing aircraft.

NOTICE & NOTE

Notice & Note

Use the side margins to notice and note signposts in the text.

ANALYZE CHARACTERISTICS OF INFORMATIONAL TEXTS
Annotate: Mark any references to chronology, or the sequence in which events occur, in paragraph 1.

Analyze: How do references to time help you understand the text?

experiment
(ĭk-spĕr´ə-mənt) *n.* An *experiment* is a test to determine if an idea is true or to see if a device works.

NOTICE & NOTE

2 Once again, Wilbur acted as pilot. Some of his glides were as good or better than the year before, and yet one problem after another cropped up.³ They had designed the glider's wings according to air-pressure tables published by Otto Lilienthal, but the wings didn't have nearly the lifting power⁴ the Wrights had expected. To make matters worse, the forward elevator, controlling up-and-down movements, wasn't as effective as they had hoped.

3 Puzzled and dejected, they closed their camp at the end of August, sooner than they had planned, and went back to Dayton.

4 "We doubted that we would ever resume our experiments," Wilbur wrote later. "When we looked at the time and money which we had expended, and considered the progress made and the distance yet to go, we considered our experiments a failure. At this time I made the **prediction** that man would sometime fly, but that it would not be in our lifetime."

5 The experiments that Wilbur and Orville had carried out with their latest glider in 1901 were far from encouraging. Reflecting on their problems, Wilbur observed: "We saw that the calculations upon which all flying machines had been based were unreliable,⁵ and that all were simply groping in the dark.⁶

prediction
(prĭ-dĭk´shən) *n.* When someone makes a *prediction*, they make a guess about something that has not yet happened.

ANALYZE CHARACTERISTICS OF INFORMATIONAL TEXTS
Annotate: Mark the words in paragraph 5 that refer to the disadvantages of the existing data.

Cause and Effect: What decision did the Wright brothers make about data, and why did they make it?

---

³ **cropped up:** happened suddenly or unexpectedly.
⁴ **lifting power:** the force that holds the glider in the air; most of the lift is produced by airflow over the wings.
⁵ **calculations . . . unreliable:** a reference to the data in the air-pressure tables produced by German aviation pioneer Otto Lilienthal. The Wrights had used this data to design the wings of their glider.
⁶ **groping in the dark:** looking for answers without much guidance.

Having set out with absolute faith in the existing scientific data, we were driven to doubt one thing after another, till finally, after two years of experiment, we cast it all aside, and decided to rely entirely on our own investigations."

6   In the gaslit workroom[7] behind their bicycle shop, Wilbur and Orville began to compile their own data. They wanted to test different types of wing surfaces and obtain **accurate** air-pressure tables. To do this, they built a wind tunnel—a wooden box 6 feet long with a glass viewing window on top and a fan at one end. It wasn't the world's first wind tunnel, but it would be the first to yield valuable results for the construction of a practical airplane.

7   The materials needed to make model wings, or *airfoils*, and the tools to shape them were right at hand. Using tin shears, hammers, files, and a soldering iron, the brothers fashioned as many as two hundred miniature wings out of tin, galvanized iron, steel, solder, and wax. They made wings that were thick or thin, curved or flat, wings with rounded tips and pointed tips, slender wings and stubby wings. They attached these experimental airfoils to balances made of bicycle spokes and old hacksaw blades. Then they tested the wings in their wind tunnel to see how they behaved in a moving airstream.

8   For several weeks they were absorbed in painstaking and systematic lab work—testing, measuring, and **calculating** as they tried to unlock the secrets of an aircraft wing. The work was tedious. It was repetitious. Yet they would look back on that winter as a time of great excitement, when each new day promised discoveries waiting to be made. "Wilbur and I could hardly wait for morning to come," Orville declared, "to get at something that interested us. *That's* happiness."

9   The Wrights knew that they were exploring uncharted territory with their wind-tunnel tests. Each new bit of data jotted down in their notebooks added to their understanding of how an airfoil works. Gradually they replaced the calculations of others with facts and figures of their own. Their doubts vanished, and their faith in themselves grew. When their lab tests were finally completed, they felt confident that they could calculate in advance the performance of an aircraft's wings with far greater accuracy than had ever before been possible.

---

[7] **gaslit workroom:** indoor lighting came from gas-fueled lamps, which were dimmer than the electric lights used today.

NOTICE & NOTE

accurate
(ăk´yər-ĭt) *adj.* Something *accurate* is correct.

DETERMINE KEY IDEAS
Annotate: Mark the key idea of paragraph 8.
Analyze: How do details found in the paragraph support this key idea?

calculate
(kăl´kyə-lāt´) *v.* To *calculate* is to figure out an answer by using math.

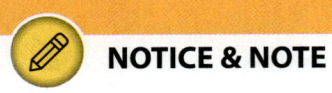

NOTICE & NOTE

NUMBERS AND STATS

Notice & Note: What does the numeric information in paragraph 10 reveal? Mark the places where the author provides numeric information.

Draw Conclusions: What is the purpose of including these numbers?

10   Armed with this new knowledge, they designed their biggest glider yet. Its wings, longer and narrower than before, measured 32 feet from tip to tip and 5 feet from front to rear. For the first time, the new glider had a tail—two 6-foot-high vertical fins, designed to help stabilize the machine during turns. The hip cradle[8] developed the year before to control wing warping[9] was retained. The craft weighed just under 120 pounds.

11   With growing anticipation, Wilbur and Orville prepared for their 1902 trip to the Outer Banks. "They really ought to get away for a while," Katharine wrote to her father. "Will is thin and nervous and so is Orv. They will be all right when they get down in the sand where the salt breezes blow. . . . They think that life at Kitty Hawk cures all ills, you know."

12   "The flying machine is in process of making now. Will spins the sewing machine around by the hour while Orv squats around marking the places to sew [the cotton wing covering]. There is no place in the house to live but I'll be lonesome enough by this time next week and wish I could have some of their racket around."

13   The brothers reached the Outer Banks at the end of August with their trunks, baggage, and crates carrying the glider parts.

14   By the middle of September they had assembled their new glider and were ready to try it out. This year they took turns in the pilot's position, giving Orville a chance to fly for the first time. To begin with, they were very cautious. They would launch the machine from the slope on Big Hill and glide only a short distance as they practiced working the controls. Steering to the right or left was accomplished by warping the wings, with the glider always turning toward the lower wing. Up-and-down movements were controlled by the forward elevator.

15   In a few days they made dozens of short but successful test glides. At this point, things looked more promising than ever. The only mishap occurred one afternoon when Orville was at the controls. That evening he recorded the incident in his diary:

16   "I was sailing along smoothly without any trouble . . . when I noticed that one wing was getting a little too high and that the machine was slowly sliding off in the opposite direction. . . . The next thing I knew was that the wing was very high in the air, a great deal higher than before, and I thought I must have worked the twisting **apparatus** the wrong

apparatus
(ăp´ə-rătˊəs) *n.* An *apparatus* is a piece of equipment.

---

[8] **hip cradle:** a device that allowed the pilot to lie down and use hip movement to control the rudder and wings.

[9] **wing warping:** the Wright Brothers' discovery of how they could twist the ends of the wings in order to balance and control the aircraft.

way. Thinking of nothing else . . . I threw the wingtips to their greatest angle. By this time I found suddenly that I was making a descent backwards toward the low wing, from a height of 25 or 30 feet. . . . The result was a heap of flying machine, cloth and sticks in a heap, with me in the center without a bruise or scratch. The experiments thereupon suddenly came to a close till repairs can be made. In spite of this sad catastrophe we are tonight in a hilarious mood as a result of the encouraging performance of the machine."

17   A few days' labor made the glider as good as new. It wasn't seriously damaged again during hundreds of test glides, and it repeatedly withstood rough landings at full speed. Wilbur and Orville became more and more confident. "Our new machine is a very great improvement over anything we had built before and over anything anyone has built," Wilbur told his father. "Everything is so much more satisfactory that we now believe that the flying problem is really nearing its solution."

18   And yet the solution was not yet quite at hand. As they continued their test flights, a baffling new problem arose. On most flights, the glider performed almost perfectly. But every so often—in about one flight out of fifty—it would spin out of control as the pilot tried to level off after a turn.

LANGUAGE CONVENTIONS

Writers use commas to make the meaning of their sentences clear. Mark the commas in the second and third sentences in paragraph 18. Then, read the sentences aloud, pausing after each comma. Finally, read the sentences without the pauses. Which is easier to understand? Why?

NOTICE & NOTE

DETERMINE KEY IDEAS
Annotate: Mark the words in paragraph 19 that suggest the key idea of the paragraph.

Summarize: Use your own words to restate the key idea of paragraph 19. How do details support this idea?

19   Lying in bed one sleepless night, Orville figured out what the problem was. The fixed tail worked perfectly well most of the time. During some turns, however—when the airspeed was low and the pilot failed to level off soon enough—pressure was built up on the tail, throwing the glider off balance and into a spin. That's just what happened to Orville the day of his accident. The cure was to make the tail movable—like a ship's rudder or a bird's tail.

20   The next morning at breakfast, Orville told Wilbur about his idea. After thinking it over for a few minutes, Wilbur agreed. Then he offered an idea of his own. Why not connect the new movable tail to the wing-warping wires? This would allow the pilot to twist the wings and turn the tail at the same time, simply by shifting his hips. With the wings and tail coordinated, the glider would always make a smooth banked turn.

QUOTED WORDS
Notice & Note: What does the quotation in paragraph 21 reveal? Mark the quotation.

Analyze: What was likely the author's purpose for including this quotation?

21   They removed the original tail and installed a movable single-vaned tail[10] 5 feet high. From then on, there were no more problems. The movable tail rudder finally gave the Wright brothers complete control of their glider. "With this improvement our serious troubles ended," wrote Wilbur, "and thereafter we devoted ourselves to the work of gaining skill by continued practice."

---

[10] **single-vaned tail:** the one-piece plate that extends from the back end of the aircraft for stability and control.

22   Wilbur and Orville made hundreds of perfectly controlled glides in 1902. They proved that their laboratory tests were accurate. The next step was to build a powered airplane. "Before leaving camp," Orville wrote, "we were already at work on the general design of a new machine which we proposed to propel with a motor."

CHECK YOUR UNDERSTANDING

Answer these questions before moving on to the **Analyze the Text** section on the following page.

1 What is the main subject of this biography?

   A All early aviators

   B Aviation pioneers Orville and Wilbur Wright

   C The entire Wright family

   D The correct way to design a motor-powered airplane

2 How does the author mainly support his ideas?

   F With facts, quotations, and historical information

   G With historians' and engineers' opinions

   H With illustrations, photographs, and tables

   J With references to websites

3 Which idea is supported by information throughout the selection?

   A The Wright brothers were more interested in bicycles than airplanes.

   B The Wright brothers did not believe in building on the work of other pioneers.

   C The Wright brothers used science and creativity to solve the puzzle of flight.

   D The Wright brothers relied mostly on inspiration to solve the puzzle of flight.

RESPOND

ANALYZE THE TEXT

Support your responses with evidence from the text. 📓 NOTEBOOK

1. **Analyze** Review paragraph 6. How does the author define *wind tunnel*? How does the description of a wind tunnel affect your understanding of the text?

2. **Cause and Effect** Review paragraph 9. What effect did the wind tunnel tests have on the Wright brothers and their work?

3. **Identify Patterns** Review paragraph 18. What pattern of organization is used to structure the paragraph's information? How does the organization add to your understanding of the selection?

4. **Cite Evidence** Review paragraphs 19–21. What details does the author provide about how the brothers work together? What key idea do these details suggest?

5. **Notice & Note** Review the use of direct quotations throughout the selection. How do the quotations help you understand the key ideas in the selection?

RESEARCH TIP
Specific search terms will give you the best results. If you want to find out more about the Wrights' test flights, try *Wright brothers Kitty Hawk*. If you want to learn what the Wright brothers were working on at a specific time, add the year to your search words. For example, *Wright brothers Kitty Hawk 1903*.

RESEARCH

At the end of this excerpt, the Wrights plan to use what they have learned about creating a successful glider to build a motorized airplane. Work individually to investigate what steps the Wrights took toward achieving their final goal of powered flight. Note the successes and failures they experienced along the way. Use multiple sources, and record what you learn in the following table.

AIRCRAFT DESIGN CHANGES	RESULTS

Extend The selection mentions the work of German flight pioneer Otto Lilienthal. Research Lilienthal's life and achievements to find out how his work inspired others to make advances in flight.

RESPOND

CREATE AND DISCUSS

Write a Summary Review paragraphs 13–22; then, write a three-paragraph summary of that section.

- ❏ State key ideas and supporting details found in the section.
- ❏ Paraphrase ideas by stating them in your own words.
- ❏ Use transitions and introductory elements.
- ❏ Use Critical Vocabulary words when appropriate.

Hold a Small Group Discussion Have a group discussion to determine a possible central or main idea for the selection.

- ❏ Remind group members that you are not looking for a topic. Instead, you are looking for a message that is central to the text.
- ❏ Provide support for your ideas by citing text evidence.
- ❏ Review the ideas together. Listen closely and actively to each other.
- ❏ Ask questions to clarify points. Respond appropriately.

Go to **Using Textual Evidence: Summarizing, Paraphrasing, and Quoting** in the **Writing Studio** for more on summarizing and paraphrasing.

 Go to **Participating in Collaborative Discussions: Listening and Responding** in the **Speaking and Listening Studio** for help with having a group discussion.

RESPOND TO THE ESSENTIAL QUESTION

? What keeps people from giving up?

Gather Information Review your annotations and notes on *The Wright Brothers: How They Invented the Airplane*. Then, add relevant details to your Response Log. As you determine which information to include, think about how the Wright brothers faced challenges and how readers might follow their example.

At the end of the unit, use your notes to write a biographical report.

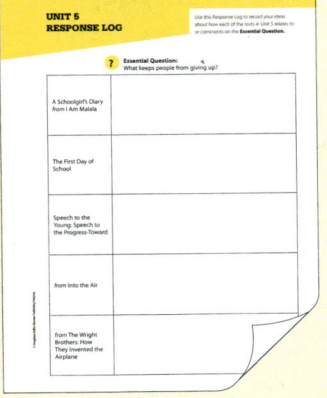

ACADEMIC VOCABULARY

As you write and discuss what you learned from the selection, be sure to use the Academic Vocabulary words. Check off the words that you use.

- ❏ achieve
- ❏ individual
- ❏ instance
- ❏ outcome
- ❏ principle

RESPOND

WORD BANK
experiment
prediction
accurate
calculate
apparatus

CRITICAL VOCABULARY

Practice and Apply Use what you know about the Vocabulary words to answer these questions.

1. Why is it important to be **accurate** when you **calculate** how much water to bring on a trip through the desert?

2. What type of **apparatus** could be used to measure weight?

3. What is one possible purpose of an **experiment**?

4. Why is it useful to make a **prediction** before taking a risk?

VOCABULARY STRATEGY:
Resources

In *The Wright Brothers: How They Invented the Airplane,* the author uses technical and scientific language to describe how the Wrights developed their glider. Sometimes, writers provide definitions or context clues to help readers determine the meaning of technical terms. But if you need more help to understand a technical term or subject in your reading, turn to online and print resources for additional information.

A **standard dictionary** will tell you a word's definitions, pronunciation, syllabication, parts of speech, history, and origin. A **specialized dictionary** focuses on terms related to a particular field of study or work. An **encyclopedia** includes facts and background information on many subjects. Finally, many professional and technical organizations host websites that may be useful in defining terminology.

Practice and Apply Use context clues in the selection, as well as online and print resources, to define these terms: *air pressure* (paragraphs 2 and 6), *forward elevator* (paragraphs 2 and 14), and *airfoil* (paragraphs 7 and 9). Cite the resources you used to write your definition. Share your definitions with a classmate and compare results.

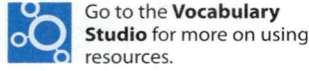 Go to the **Vocabulary Studio** for more on using resources.

RESPOND

LANGUAGE CONVENTIONS:
Commas and Sentence Types

As you have learned, writers use commas to make the meaning of their sentences clear. In addition to setting off introductory elements and transition words, commas are used in a variety of sentence types. Commas are useful in **compound sentences,** or sentences that consist of two or more independent clauses. They are also needed to clarify **complex sentences,** sentences that combine an independent clause with one or more dependent clauses.

The selection uses commas in the following ways:

- To separate independent clauses in a compound sentence

   Their doubts vanished, and their faith in themselves grew.

- To separate a dependent clause from an independent clause in a complex sentence

   When their lab tests were finally completed, they felt confident that they could calculate in advance the performance of an aircraft's wings with far greater accuracy than had ever before been possible.

- To set off a transitional phrase that clarifies sequence

   At this point, things looked more promising than ever.

Practice and Apply Write your own sentences with commas, using the examples from the selection as models. Your sentences can be about how your own work habits are similar to or different from those of the Wright brothers, or your sentences may be about some other topic related to the Wright brothers. When you have finished, share your sentences with a partner and compare your use of commas.

> Go to **Commas with Compound Sentences** in the **Grammar Studio** for more on commas and sentence types.

RESPOND

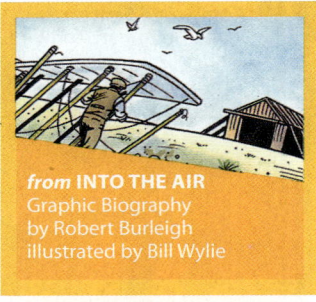

from **INTO THE AIR**
Graphic Biography
by Robert Burleigh
illustrated by Bill Wylie

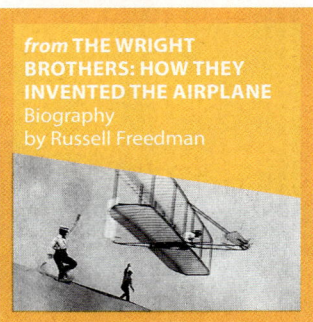

from **THE WRIGHT BROTHERS: HOW THEY INVENTED THE AIRPLANE**
Biography
by Russell Freedman

Collaborate & Compare

INFER AND SYNTHESIZE KEY IDEAS WITHIN AND ACROSS TEXTS

The two selections you have read focus on some of the same events in the lives of Wilbur and Orville Wright. You will now review and compare the **key ideas** you have found in these texts and **synthesize** the information to determine a key idea that the two texts share.

In this task, you will need to make inferences to determine the messages that the authors have not stated outright. An **inference** is a logical guess based on facts and your own knowledge and experience. Evidence from the text should support an inference.

In a small group, complete a chart like the one below. Analyze each scene or event listed in the first column, and infer the key ideas in each selection.

Scene/Event	Key Ideas from *Into the Air*	Key Ideas from *The Wright Brothers*
Summer 1901		
Wind Tunnel Experiments		
Fall 1902		

ANALYZE THE TEXTS

Discuss these questions in your group.

1. **Compare** Think about the Wright brothers' quotations and dialogue in each text. How are these words presented in each biography? Describe similarities and differences.

2. **Infer** What do the frustrations experienced by the brothers in the summer of 1901 say about what they were like and what was important to them? Use evidence to explain your response.

3. **Evaluate** Between the two selections, which is more effective in communicating facts? Ideas? Moods and emotions? Explain.

4. **Synthesize** What have you learned from these sources about the importance of trying hard and not giving up?

RESPOND

COMPARE KEY IDEAS

Now, your group can continue exploring the ideas in these texts by collaborating on a presentation to give to your class. Follow these steps:

1. **Gather Information** In your group, review and then list the key events that appear in both texts.

2. **Discuss** Examine the similarities and differences in how each event is presented in the texts. Ask:
   ❏ How do the authors use **text** to describe this event?
      ❏ Between the two selections, how is the text similar?
      ❏ Between the two selections, how is the text different?

   ❏ How do the authors use **images** to describe this event?
      ❏ Between the two selections, how are the images similar?
      ❏ Between the two selections, how are the images different?

   ❏ What is the **key idea** of this event, as presented in each selection?
      ❏ Between the two selections, how are the ideas similar?
      ❏ Between the two selections, how are the ideas different?

As you discuss, remember to listen to what others say, to ask questions to request and clarify information, and to build on the ideas of others. Use the chart below to take notes. As a group, determine what you think is the main idea shared by the two selections.

Scene/Event:	
Similarities:	Differences:
Key Idea:	Key Idea:

3. **Share What You Learn** Now you can share your group's findings with the rest of the class. Begin by stating what your group thinks is the main idea expressed by the two selections. Use your notes to remember important points to talk about. Speak clearly and loudly enough for others to hear. Remember to invite the class to ask questions. Answer questions respectfully.

Collaborate & Compare   405

INDEPENDENT READING

 ESSENTIAL QUESTION:

What keeps people from giving up?

Reader's Choice

Setting a Purpose Select one or more of these options from your eBook to continue your exploration of the Essential Question.

- Read the descriptions to see which text grabs your interest.
- Think about which genres you enjoy reading.

Notice & Note

In this unit, you practiced asking **Big Questions** and noting two signposts: **Numbers and Stats** and **Quoted Words.** As you read independently, these signposts and others will aid your understanding. Below are the anchor questions to ask when you read literature and nonfiction.

Reading Literature: Stories, Poems, and Plays		
Signpost	**Anchor Question**	**Lesson**
Contrasts and Contradictions	Why did the character act that way?	p. 3
Aha Moment	How might this change things?	p. 3
Tough Questions	What does this make me wonder about?	p. 172
Words of the Wiser	What's the lesson for the character?	p. 2
Again and Again	Why might the author keep bringing this up?	p. 92
Memory Moment	Why is this memory important?	p. 93

Reading Nonfiction: Essays, Articles, and Arguments		
Signpost	**Anchor Question(s)**	**Lesson**
Big Questions	What surprised me? What did the author think I already knew? What challenged, changed, or confirmed what I already knew?	p. 246 p. 420 p. 332
Contrasts and Contradictions	What is the difference, and why does it matter?	p. 247
Extreme or Absolute Language	Why did the author use this language?	p. 247
Numbers and Stats	Why did the author use these numbers or amounts?	p. 333
Quoted Words	Why was this person quoted or cited, and what did this add?	p. 333
Word Gaps	Do I know this word from someplace else? Does it seem like technical talk for this topic? Do clues in the sentence help me understand the word?	p. 421

INDEPENDENT READING

You can preview these texts in Unit 5 of your eBook.

Then, check off the text or texts that you select to read on your own.

☐

POEM

Paul Revere's Ride
Henry Wadsworth Longfellow

Paul Revere gallops through villages all night, alerting settlers of the coming attack by the British.

☐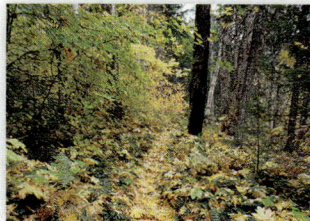

POEM

The Road Not Taken
Robert Frost

How do you choose between two unknowns?

☐

DRAMA

Damon and Pythias
dramatized by Fan Kissen

In prison, Damon waits for his best friend to return to face the consequences.

☐

SPEECH

Education First
from **Malala's Speech to the United Nations**
Malala Yousafzai

A near fatal gunshot wound makes Malala even more committed to speaking up for change.

Collaborate and Share With a partner discuss what you learned from at least one of your independent readings.

- Give a brief synopsis or summary of the text.
- Describe any signposts that you noticed in the text and explain what they revealed to you.
- Describe what you most enjoyed or found most challenging about the text. Give specific examples.
- Decide if you would recommend the text to others. Why or why not?

 Go to the **Reading Studio** for more resources on **Notice & Note**.

Independent Reading 407

WRITING TASK

Write a Biographical Report

Go to **Conducting Research** in the **Writing Studio** for help researching and writing a report.

This unit focuses on what makes people persist, or keep trying, despite struggle and hardship. For this writing task, you will research and write a biographical report explaining why a well-known person from history refused to give up when faced with a crisis or difficult problem to solve. For an example of a well-written biography, review the mentor text from *The Wright Brothers: How They Invented the Airplane*.

As you write your report, use the notes from your Response Log, which you filled out after reading the texts in this unit.

Writing Prompt

Read the information in the box below.

This is the topic or context for your report.

> The human spirit is capable of profound resilience and a powerful drive to never give up in the face of adversity.

Think carefully about the following question.

This is the Essential Question for the unit. How would you answer this question, based on the texts in this unit?

> What keeps people from giving up?

Write a biographical report explaining why a well-known person from history refused to give up.

Now mark the words that identify exactly what you are being asked to produce.

Be sure to—

❑ write an engaging introduction that clearly states the topic and highlights a controlling idea or thesis statement
❑ use primary and secondary sources in your research
❑ avoid plagiarism; cite and use source materials ethically
❑ organize information in a logical way
❑ connect related ideas effectively
❑ use appropriate word choice and a formal voice and tone
❑ end by summarizing ideas or drawing an overall conclusion

Review these points as you write and again when you finish. Make any needed changes.

WRITING TASK

1 Plan

Before you start writing, plan your biographical report. Which well-known historical person will you write about? Follow these preliminary steps and use a table like the one below to keep research notes.

☐ Think of questions you have about this person, related to the topic of never giving up; focus your research on answering these questions.

☐ Conduct research, using primary and secondary sources. Keep track of where you get your information so that you can cite it correctly.

Research Notes
Questions I have about this person:
Source: title; author; page number; date; url, if source is online
Notes:
Source: title; author; page number; date; url, if source is online
Notes:
Source: title; author; page number; date; url, if source is online
Notes:

List your sources at the end of the report or cite them in footnotes, using the style your teacher prefers. If you quote directly from a source, cite it in the report and use quotation marks. Otherwise, put information in your own words, paraphrasing to avoid plagiarism.

Background Reading Review the notes you took in your Response Log after reading the texts in this unit. These texts are the background reading that will help you formulate the key ideas you will include in your biographical report.

Go to **Conducting Research: Introduction** for help planning your research.

PRIMARY SOURCES
- letters and diaries
- autobiographies
- eyewitness accounts

SECONDARY SOURCES
- biographies
- news articles
- textbooks
- encyclopedias

Notice & Note
From Reading to Writing

As you plan your report, apply what you've learned about signposts to your own writing. Remember that writers use common features, called signposts, to help convey their message to readers. Think about how you can incorporate **Numbers and Stats** into your report.

Go to the **Reading Studio** for more resources on **Notice & Note**.

Use the notes from your **Response Log** as you plan your report.

Write a Biographical Report 409

WRITING TASK

 Go to the **Using Textual Evidence: Writing an Outline** in the **Writing Studio** for help organizing your ideas.

Organize Your Ideas The next step in planning is to create an outline. The outline helps you organize the information you have collected and prepares you for writing your rough draft. Since you are writing a biographical report, organize your notes chronologically—the order in which events took place. Use the table below to help you plan your draft.

Biographical Report Outline	
Purpose of report; audience	
Introduction: background on subject and controlling idea or thesis	
Childhood and early life related to controlling idea or thesis	
Main events, struggles	
Accomplishments and ideas from background reading	
Conclusion	

2 Develop a Draft

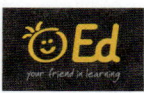 You might prefer to draft your biographical report online.

Once you have completed your planning activities, you will be ready to write the rough draft of your biographical report. Refer to your research notes and the outline you have created, as well as to any notes you took as you studied the texts in the unit. These will provide a kind of map for you to follow as you write. Using a word processor or online writing application makes it easier to make changes or move sentences around later when you are ready to revise your first draft.

WRITING TASK

Use the Mentor Text

Author's Craft
Authors use descriptive language and details to chronicle the steps leading up to a major accomplishment, including struggles and obstacles faced along the way. This method is an effective way to communicate what it means to never give up and to achieve something important or overcome a crisis.

> Using tin shears, hammers, files, and a soldering iron, the brothers fashioned as many as two hundred miniature wings out of tin, galvanized iron, steel, solder, and wax.

Specific details create a vivid sense of how the Wright brothers struggled to find the right design.

Apply What You've Learned To hold your reader's attention, use descriptive details to communicate how the subject of your report overcame obstacles on the way to achieving success.

Primary and Secondary Sources
Writers of biographies and other nonfiction texts depend on reliable primary, or firsthand, and secondary, or secondhand, sources for their information. Readers have confidence that the text is accurate when writers cite their sources. Readers also refer to these sources if they want more information about a topic or if they want proof that a source is dependable.

> With growing anticipation, Wilbur and Orville prepared for their 1902 trip to the Outer Banks. "They really ought to get away for a while," Katharine wrote to her father.

The writer paraphrases, or puts in his own words, information in the first sentence. He quotes a letter, which is a primary source, in the second sentence.

Apply What You've Learned. When you copy text from a source exactly as it's written, put it in quotes. Otherwise, readers will think you wrote it yourself, and that is plagiarism. Most of the time you will restate information and put it in your own words. Whether you are quoting directly or paraphrasing, cite and list your sources according to the style your teacher prefers.

Write a Biographical Report 411

WRITING TASK

Go to **Using Textual Evidence: Attribution** in the **Writing Studio** the for help with citing sources.

3 Revise

On Your Own Once you have written your draft, go back and look for ways to improve your biographical report. As you reread and revise, think about whether you have achieved your purpose. The Revision Guide focuses on specific elements to make your writing stronger.

Revision Guide		
Ask Yourself	**Tips**	**Revision Techniques**
1. Does my introduction describe the subject's background?	**Mark** the introduction.	**Add** an interesting fact, example, or quotation that describes the subject's background.
2. Do I use descriptive details and relevant, interesting facts?	**Mark** each descriptive detail and fact.	**Replace** words and phrases with more vivid details and interesting facts.
3. Are events arranged in chronological order?	**Mark** each event.	**Reorder** events if necessary.
4. Do I use transitions between ideas effectively so that events are connected?	**Mark** transitional words and phrases.	**Include** appropriate transitional words to smooth and clarify the flow of information.
5. Do I cite sources correctly and use source materials ethically?	**Mark** facts, examples, and quotations.	**Add** academic citations according to your teacher's preference, indicating the source for each piece of information.
6. Does my conclusion convey how never giving up was the key to the subject's accomplishments?	**Mark** the conclusion.	**Add** a reflection on why never giving up was pivotal to the subject's success.

ACADEMIC VOCABULARY

As you conduct your **peer review,** be sure to use these words.

❏ achieve
❏ individual
❏ instance
❏ outcome
❏ principle

With a Partner Once you and your partner have worked through the Revision Guide on your own, exchange papers and evaluate each other's draft in a **peer review.** Focus on providing revision suggestions for at least three of the items mentioned in the chart. Explain why you think your partner's draft should be revised and what your specific suggestions are.

When receiving feedback from your partner, listen attentively and ask questions to make sure you fully understand the revision suggestions.

WRITING TASK

4 Edit

Once you have addressed the organization, development, and flow of ideas in your draft, you are ready to improve its finer points. Edit for the proper use of standard English conventions and correct any misspellings or grammatical errors. Ensure that the tone of your report is formal.

Language Conventions

Adverbs describe verbs, adjectives, and other adverbs by telling *where, when, how,* or *to what extent*. Examples of adverbs include *very, now,* and *slowly*.

Conjunctive adverbs often connect two independent clauses to show that the second clause relates to the first. They can also be used in a single clause (sentence). *Conjunctive* means joining or connecting. Examples of conjunctive adverbs include *consequently, finally, then, furthermore, however,* and *nevertheless*. Punctuation sets conjunctive adverbs off: a semicolon before and a comma after when connecting two independent clauses, and a comma before and after when used within a single clause. Here are some examples:

- **Single clause:** The manager, **however,** maintains that he kept his promise to stay within the budget.
- **Two independent clauses:** The pepperoni pizza was the best I've ever had; **nevertheless,** I like plain cheese pizza even more.

Writers use adverbs and conjunctive adverbs to add variety and nuance, or shades of meaning, to their sentences.

The chart shows examples from *The Wright Brothers: How They Invented the Airplane*.

	Example
Adverb	<u>Gradually</u> they replaced the calculations of others with their own.
Conjunctive Adverb	"With this improvement our serious troubles ended . . . <u>thereafter</u>, we devoted ourselves to the work of gaining skill by continued practice."

> Go to **Adverbs** in the **Grammar Studio** to learn more about adverbs.

5 Publish

After you have given your biographical report its finishing touches, choose a way to share it with your audience. Options include presenting your report as a speech to the class, or posting it as a blog on a classroom or school website.

Write a Biographical Report

WRITING TASK

Use the scoring guide to evaluate your biographical report.

	Writing Task Scoring Guide: Biographical Report		
	Organization/Progression	**Development of Ideas**	**Use of Language and Conventions**
4	• The organization is smooth, effective and logical; events are organized chronologically. • All ideas are focused on the topic specified in the prompt. • Background information helps identify an individual and explain events. • Transitions logically connect events in sequence. • All research sources are cited correctly.	• The introduction catches the reader's attention and clearly identifies the historical figure/subject. • The report contains a clear, concise, and well-defined thesis statement or controlling idea. • The events are supported by specific and well-chosen facts, details, quotations, etc. • The conclusion reflects on the significance of never giving up as a key factor in the historical figure's accomplishments.	• Tone is appropriately formal. • Descriptive language and varied sentence structures make the report appealing and interesting. • Spelling, grammar, usage, and mechanics are correct. • Adverbs and conjunctive adverbs are used correctly and effectively.
3	• The organization is appropriate to the purpose; events are organized chronologically. • Most ideas are focused on the topic specified in the prompt. • More background information would help identify the individual and explain events. • A few more transitions are needed to logically connect events. • Most research sources are cited correctly.	• The introduction could be more engaging. The historical figure/subject is identified. • The report contains a clear thesis statement or controlling idea. • The events are supported by facts, details, quotations, etc. • The conclusion indicates the role of never giving up in the historical figure's accomplishments.	• Tone is usually appropriate and formal. • Language is usually descriptive and there is some variation in sentence structure. • Spelling, grammar, usage, and mechanics are mostly correct. • Adverbs and conjunctive adverbs are correctly used most of the time.
2	• The organization is confusing; missing or extraneous events are distracting. • Only some ideas are focused on the topic specified in the prompt. • Not enough background information is given to explain events. • More transitions are needed to logically connect events. • Not all research sources are cited.	• The introduction is not engaging and does not provide a clear picture of the historical figure. • The thesis statement or controlling idea is unclear. • The events are not well supported by facts, details, quotations, etc. • The conclusion is only partially effective.	• Tone is inconsistent and sometimes too casual. • Language is not descriptive and sentence structure lacks variation. • Spelling, grammar, usage, and mechanics are not always correct. • Adverbs and conjunctive adverbs are not always used correctly.
1	• Events are out of sequence and disorganized. • Ideas are not focused on the topic specified in the prompt. • Background information is nonexistent. • No transitions are used, making the report difficult to understand. • Research sources are not cited.	• The introduction is confusing. • The thesis statement or controlling idea is missing. • Supporting facts, details, examples, or quotations are unreliable, vague, or missing. • The conclusion does not connect never giving up to the historical person's accomplishments.	• Tone is inappropriate and too casual. • Language is vague and confusing. • Many spelling, capitalization, and punctuation errors are present. • Many grammatical and usage errors confuse the writer's ideas. • Adverbs and conjunctive adverbs are misused or missing.

SPEAKING AND LISTENING TASK

Produce and Present a Podcast

You will now turn your biographical report into an audio podcast to present to your classmates. You will also listen to their podcasts, ask questions, and help them make improvements.

Go to the **Speaking and Listening Studio: Using Media in a Presentation** for help planning and crafting your podcast.

1 Develop a Script

First, craft a script from your biographical report. You want to make the same points, but your script will be shorter than your report, so choose facts and details that will be interesting to hear, rather than read.

2 Plan Your Podcast

Use the planning chart below to write a script based on your biographical report and to record an engaging audio podcast.

Podcast Planning Chart		
Write a Script	How will you write your script to appeal to listeners? How will you repurpose the report to sound natural and convincing when you read your script aloud?	
Audience	In a spoken medium, you reach your audience in a more personal way than in a report. How will you connect with your listeners?	
Effective Language and Organization	Which parts of your report can be simplified for your podcast? How should the descriptions change for reading aloud and creating impressions through your voice?	
Practice and Revise	Do you sound natural and knowledgeable? Practice reading your script aloud; revise until you are satisfied with how it sounds.	

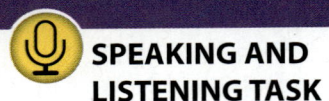

SPEAKING AND LISTENING TASK

As you work to improve your podcast, follow discussion rules:
- ❏ listen closely to each other
- ❏ don't interrupt
- ❏ stay on topic
- ❏ ask only helpful, relevant questions
- ❏ provide only clear, thoughtful, and direct answers

③ Practice with a Partner or Group

Once you've completed a satisfactory draft of your script, practice it aloud with a partner or group to improve it. Consider the following points to create an engaging podcast.

Effective Script-Writing Techniques

- ❏ **Outline** Create an outline to help you organize the events and key information in your script.
- ❏ **Spoken Word** A script is different from a report or essay in that it is spoken aloud. Keep your sentences conversational, as if you are talking to a friend, using appropriate language.
- ❏ **Transitions** Remember to use transitional words such as *first, next, consequently,* and *finally,* to make your script flow naturally between ideas and events.
- ❏ **Tell a Story** A good script tells a story that entertains and engages your audience.

Effective Verbal Techniques

- ❏ **Enunciation** Replace words that you stumble over, and rearrange sentences so that your delivery is smooth.
- ❏ **Voice Modulation and Pitch** Use your voice to display enthusiasm and emphasis.
- ❏ **Speaking Rate** Speak slowly enough that listeners understand you. Pause now and then to let them consider important points.
- ❏ **Volume** Remember to maintain a volume that is loud enough for listeners to hear every word easily.

Provide and Consider Advice for Improvement

As a listener, pay close attention. Take notes about ways that presenters can improve their scripts and more effectively use verbal techniques. Paraphrase and summarize each presenter's key ideas and main points to confirm your understanding, and ask questions to clarify any confusing ideas.

As a presenter, listen closely to questions and consider ways to revise your script to make sure your points are clear and logically sequenced. Remember to ask for suggestions about how you might change your script to make your podcast clearer and more interesting.

④ Record and Present Your Podcast

Use the advice you received during practice and record your podcast. Then, play your finished podcast for your classmates.

Reflect on the Unit

By completing your biographical report, you have created a writing product that pulls together and expresses your thoughts about the reading you have done in this unit. Now is a good time to reflect on what you have learned.

Reflect on the Essential Question

- How did the people you read about in this unit shed light on why people don't give up? What did they have in common, and how are they different in the way they handled adversity and crisis?

- What are some examples from the texts you've read that show what keeps people from giving up?

Reflect on Your Reading

- Of the people you read about in this unit, who inspired you the most, and why?

- Consider one of the texts you read. If you had been in the situation described in the text, would you have persisted or would you have given up? Explain your answer.

Reflect on the Writing Task

- How did you choose a person from history to write about?

- What was your strategy for conveying this person's story as effectively as possible?

- What was challenging about using primary and secondary sources?

Reflect on the Speaking and Listening Task

- What did you change about your report to turn it into a script?

- What qualities do the best podcasts share?

UNIT 5 SELECTIONS
- "A Schoolgirl's Diary" from *I Am Malala*
- "The First Day of School"
- "Speech to the Young: Speech to the Progress-Toward"
- *Into the Air*
- *The Wright Brothers: How They Invented the Airplane*

UNIT 6

HIDDEN TRUTHS

ESSENTIAL QUESTION:

What hidden truths about people and the world are revealed in stories?

> "The destiny of the world is determined less by battles that are lost and won than by the stories it loves and believes in."
>
> — Harold Goddard

UNIT 6

ACADEMIC VOCABULARY

Academic Vocabulary words are words you use when you discuss and write about texts. In this unit you will practice and learn five words.

✓ emphasize   ☐ occur   ☐ period   ☐ relevant   ☐ tradition

Study the Word Network to learn more about the word **emphasize**.

Write and Discuss Discuss the completed Word Network with a partner, making sure to talk through all of the boxes until you both understand the word, its synonyms, antonyms, and related forms. Then, fill out Word Networks for the remaining four words. Use a dictionary or online resource to help you complete the activity.

 Go online to access the Word Networks.

RESPOND TO THE ESSENTIAL QUESTION

In this unit, you will read stories about behaviors and traits common in people the world over. As you read, you will revisit the **Essential Question** and gather your ideas about it in the **Response Log** that appears on page R6. At the end of the unit, you will have the opportunity to write a **short story** or **folktale** that communicates a message about life or human nature. Filling out the Response Log will help you prepare for this writing task.

 You can also go online to access the Response Log.

Hidden Truths 419

Notice & Note

READING MODEL

from STORYTELLING

You are about to read the introduction to the nonfiction book *Storytelling*. As you read, you will notice and note signposts that will give you clues about the author's ideas and purpose for writing. Here are three key signposts to look for as you read this introduction and other works of nonfiction.

 For more information on these and other signposts to Notice & Note, visit the **Reading Studio.**

Whenever you read nonfiction, remember to ask yourself these **Big Questions:**

What did the author think I already knew?

What challenged, changed, or confirmed what I already knew?

What surprised me?

Big Questions Have you ever walked into the classroom while your teacher was in the middle of explaining a lesson? Maybe what he or she said mostly made sense, but you probably didn't understand everything. Sometimes you can get that same feeling while you're reading. Even when you've read every word, you may get the feeling that you've missed something.

If you feel lost or confused while reading, it's time to stop and ask yourself, **What did the author think I already knew?** By asking yourself this Big Question, you can clarify the point the author is trying to make and decide what to look for as you continue reading. In this example, a student underlined challenging phrases in *Storytelling*:

> 2 <u>The pull of the story is universal.</u> There is no known culture without some form of storytelling, and <u>the craving to know "what comes next"</u> has been felt by every human being, regardless of age, gender, culture, or century.

Which words or phrases are confusing?	The pull of the story is universal. the craving to know "what comes next"
What did the author think I already knew?	The author thought I already knew what "the pull of the story" means and that I've felt a strong desire to know what comes next in a story.

Word Gaps It doesn't matter how old you are or how strong a reader you are—authors sometimes use words and phrases that you don't understand. When you come across **Word Gaps,** or words that are unfamiliar to you, pause to clarify their meaning. Ask:

- Do I know this word from someplace else? Does the word have another meaning that is familiar to me?
- Does the word seem like technical talk related to this topic or like special vocabulary used when writing about this topic?
- Can I find clues in the context to help me understand the word?

By taking the time to fill in those gaps, you will gain a deeper understanding of the text. Here, a student annotated a Word Gap:

> 4   Every conversation is rife with information-packed stories of what the teller has been doing recently.

Anchor Question
When you notice this signpost, ask: Do context clues in the sentence help me understand the word?

What is the unfamiliar word?	rife
Do context clues in the sentence help me understand the word?	The clue "information-packed" makes me think the word "rife" may mean "a lot of something" or "abundant." I'll check a dictionary to find out if I'm right.

Quoted Words Have you noticed that nonfiction authors sometimes quote or paraphrase the words of experts on a topic? Quotations from authorities help support the author's ideas. If you spot quotation marks or someone's name, title, and credentials (information about their area of study or professional background), pause to consider this evidence. **Quoted Words** often direct readers to important ideas. This example shows a student's annotation of Quoted Words:

> 6   The Liberian storyteller Won-Ldy Paye related how Anansi spider stories have been used to "say without saying" in front of a chief.

Anchor Question
When you notice this signpost, ask: Why was this person quoted or cited and what does this add?

What clues tell you that someone has been quoted or cited?	Name and credentials (Liberian storyteller Won-Ldy Paye), plus quotation marks
Why was this person quoted?	She must have knowledge about the topic.

Notice & Note

ANALYZE & APPLY

from STORYTELLING

Book Introduction by **Josepha Sherman**

? ESSENTIAL QUESTION:

What hidden truths about people and the world are revealed in stories?

GET READY

QUICK START

Imagine you wanted to persuade someone to read a book that you really enjoyed. What might you say to introduce the book and explain its importance? Discuss your ideas with the class.

ANALYZE CHARACTERISTICS OF INFORMATIONAL TEXTS

Nonfiction writers organize and present facts and ideas in a variety of ways. Recognizing **structural elements** and **organizational patterns** will help deepen your understanding of a work and its controlling idea.

The selection you are about to read is the introduction to a book about storytelling. An **introduction** is a feature that provides background information about the text's subject, often offering the writer's point of view on that subject. As you read the introduction, look for the ways that the author presents and organizes information.

GENRE ELEMENTS: BOOK INTRODUCTION
- appears before the main text
- introduces readers to the author's ideas and the purpose of the main text
- includes ideas and supporting evidence

ORGANIZATIONAL PATTERN	DESCRIPTION
Definition/Description	states, explains, and describes new terms or ideas
Cause and Effect	explains a cause-and-effect relationship between events and ideas
Classification	presents information by topic or type of idea
Key Ideas and Supporting Details	establishes ideas and supports them with evidence

MAKE INFERENCES ABOUT KEY IDEAS

Key ideas are important ideas that an author wants readers to understand. Authors may state these ideas **explicitly,** or directly. However, some ideas are stated **implicitly,** or indirectly. In such cases, readers must make inferences about implied ideas. An **inference** is a logical guess based on evidence from the text as well as prior knowledge. Making inferences about key ideas will help you identify and understand an author's **controlling idea**—the main point of the text.

As you read, look for explicit and implicit ideas. Use text evidence and your knowledge of the structure of the text, as well as your personal knowledge, to make inferences about the author's key ideas.

Storytelling

GET READY

CRITICAL VOCABULARY

universal	invariably	nurture	adversity
integral	trance	chastise	

To see how many Critical Vocabulary words you already know, use them to complete the sentences.

1. _____ experiences are those shared by all humanity.

2. _____ , most of us face stress and _____ .

3. Weekly practice is a/an _____ part of the team's training.

4. A coach may _____ a team for laziness and _____ the team with encouragement.

5. The dance seemed to put the audience into a/an _____ .

LANGUAGE CONVENTIONS

Complex Sentences In a **complex sentence**, an independent clause is combined with one or more dependent clauses. An **independent clause** expresses a complete thought and can stand alone. A **dependent clause** cannot stand alone. In the complex sentence below, the dependent clause is "where remarkable things happen."

The teller takes the listener to distant places where remarkable things happen.

As you read the selection, look for the ways in which the author uses complex sentences to combine ideas.

ANNOTATION MODEL

NOTICE & NOTE

As you read, notice and note the signposts **Big Questions, Word Gaps,** and **Quoted Words**. Here is an example of how one reader responded to unfamiliar ideas in the selection:

> 2   Once a story has begun, there is something deep within the human psyche that must hear what will happen next. The pull of the story is universal. There is no known culture without some form of storytelling, and the craving to know "what comes next" has been felt by every human being, regardless of age, gender, culture, or century.

What is the psyche? What is the "pull of the story"? What does the author think I already know?

BACKGROUND

Author and folklore expert **Josepha Sherman** (1946–2012) became interested in folktales at an early age. She loved to compare and retell folktales from around the world. Her works include Trickster Tales: Forty Folk Stories from Around the World and The Shining Falcon, which is based on Russian folklore and was awarded the 1990 Compton Cook Award for best fantasy fiction. The excerpt you are about to read is from the introduction to an encyclopedia of mythology and folklore that Sherman edited.

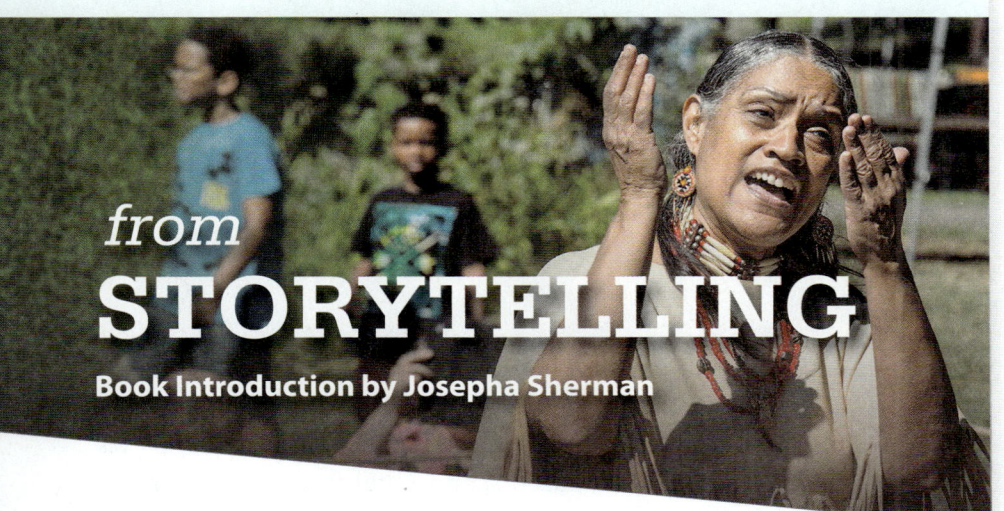

from STORYTELLING
Book Introduction by Josepha Sherman

SETTING A PURPOSE

As you read, study the organizational patterns in the text as well as the details about the importance of storytelling to understand why the author wrote this introduction.

Once Upon a Time . . .

1   . . . there was a story. Story openings take a number of forms: "once there was," "once there was not," "once, in the long ago days," and many others. But no matter what shape the opening words take, the result is always the same—listeners are hooked.

2   Once a story has begun, there is something deep within the human psyche[1] that must hear what will happen next. The pull of the story is **universal**. There is no known culture without some form of storytelling, and the craving[2] to know "what comes next" has been felt by every human being, regardless of age, gender, culture, or century.

---

[1] **psyche** (sī´kē): the spirit or soul.
[2] **craving** (krā´vĭng): an overwhelming urge or desire.

NOTICE & NOTE

Notice & Note

Use the side margins to notice and note signposts in the text.

ANALYZE CHARACTERISTICS OF INFORMATIONAL TEXTS

Annotate: Mark cause-and-effect words in paragraphs 1–2.

Summarize: What idea is the author sharing here?

LANGUAGE CONVENTIONS

Complex sentences combine dependent and independent clauses to clarify ideas. Explain how the writer uses a complex sentence to connect ideas in paragraph 2.

universal
(yoo´nə-vûr´-səl) *adj.* Something that is *universal* affects every member of a group.

Storytelling   425

NOTICE & NOTE

integral
(ĭn-tĕ´grəl) *adj*. Something that is *integral* is necessary or essential for completeness.

invariably
(ĭn-vâr´ē-ə-blē) *adv*. Something that happens *invariably* occurs again and again or constantly.

WORD GAPS

Notice & Note: Mark any Word Gaps in paragraphs 4 and 5.

Analyze: What questions can you ask yourself to understand the meaning of the words? Why do you think the author chose to use these words?

3   Storytelling is present in many aspects of human life. Stories are told by grandparents, parents, and other family members. Professional storytellers share their tales at fairs, festivals, schools, libraries, and other sites. Stories are **integral** to the mediums of television, film, opera, and theater, and storytelling sessions sometimes take place in the business world at special meetings. Campfire tales are meant to make campers shiver. And urban legends, contemporary folktales that usually are attributed to a "friend of a friend," are told and retold. No matter how unlikely the tale may be, the teller **invariably** insists, "It's *true!*"

Why Tell Stories?

4   The real question may be how can one *not* tell stories? Every conversation is rife[3] with information-packed stories of what the teller has been doing recently. People share stories they have heard from others, retell stories they have read, and even rehash things they have seen on television. Anyone who chooses to formalize this sharing takes on the role of the "storyteller."

5   The most wonderful gift of story is the bonding of a group. Held close under the spell of a story, the group breathes as one. The shared experience softens the edges between

---
[3] **rife** (rīf): prevalent or in widespread use.

individuals and brings everyone closer in the warmth of the moment. Together, the members of the group enter a "story **trance**." Storytellers benefit, in turn, as they experience the heartwarming feeling of holding the audience's attention and **nurturing** the group by sharing a beloved tale.

6   Many stories also serve the community in a broader sense. All societies use stories to pass on group values. Wrapped in the sweet pill of an entertaining story, a moral goes down easily. Stories also can be useful tools that allow individuals to **chastise** or expose negative behaviors without overtly speaking the truth. The Liberian storyteller Won-Ldy Paye related how Anansi spider stories have been used to "say without saying" in front of a chief. If the chief has behaved in a greedy manner, the storyteller shows Anansi in this incorrect behavior. Everyone knows whom the storyteller is talking about. The chief hears, and he knows, too.

7   Many families draw "catch-phrases" from their favorite stories, with which they can quickly refer to a story in the course of their daily lives. A phrase, such as "It don't take long to look at a horseshoe,"[4] can bring family members back to the original story, as well as remind them of the moral of the tale.

8   Communities and families also may wrap their history in stories in order to remember details of events long past. A moment in time can be preserved by creating a story and telling it a few times. The story format bundles the facts into a neatly tied packet that is more readily stored and retrieved[5] than a number of separate details.

9   Stories also help to broaden awareness of other cultures. The folktale genre, in particular, reflects many traditions and helps to familiarize people with world cultures.

10   Stories also can be used for educational purposes. Stories can help to develop a child's literary sensibilities, and listening to tales impresses a sense of story structure into a child's mind. Stories aid in stretching vocabulary, and children who are able to tell stories often gain advanced verbal ability and an increased sense of self-worth.

---

[4] **"It don't take long to look at a horseshoe":** In an old story, a blacksmith warns a boy not to touch a hot metal horseshoe. The boy picks up the horseshoe, then quickly drops it in surprise and pain. When the blacksmith asks if the boy burned himself, the boy quickly says, "No, it just don't take me long to look at a horseshoe."

[5] **retrieve** (rĭ-trēv´): to get back or regain possession of something.

NOTICE & NOTE

trance
(trăns) *n.* When someone is in a *trance*, he or she is in a daze or daydreaming.

BIG QUESTIONS

Notice & Note: What does the author expect readers to know in paragraph 6? Mark what you're expected to know.

Analyze: Why do you think the author expects you to know this? Where could you get more information?

nurture
(nûr´chər) *v.* To *nurture* is to provide love, affection, nourishment, or something else necessary for development.

chastise
(chăs,tīz´) *v.* To *chastise* is to punish or criticize.

MAKE INFERENCES ABOUT KEY IDEAS

Annotate: Mark the ideas that are stated explicitly, or directly, in paragraph 7.

Infer: How can you use stated ideas and any other information in the paragraph to make an inference about why families use catch phrases?

NOTICE & NOTE

QUOTED WORDS

Notice & Note: What words in paragraph 11 tell you that an expert has been cited? Mark the words.

Cite Evidence: How do the expert's words or ideas support the ideas of author Josepha Sherman?

---

adversity
(ăd-vûr´sĭ-tē) *n. Adversity* is misfortune or hardship.

MAKE INFERENCES ABOUT KEY IDEAS

Annotate: Mark details in paragraphs 11–12 that describe how stories affect the imagination.

Infer: Use these details to infer the meaning of the final sentence.

11   Storytelling provides other growth opportunities, as stories help listeners to see through another's eyes and to share the protagonist's[6] feelings of anger, fear, or love—all from a safe place. The Austrian-born American writer and child psychologist Bruno Bettelheim explained that stories are important to children because battling difficulties through story can help them face real-life troubles. Stories provide role models who show us how to face demons and overcome **adversity**.

12   Perhaps best of all, stories stretch the imagination. The teller takes the listener to distant places where remarkable things happen. And once stretched, an imagination stays stretched.

---

[6] **protagonist** (prō-tăg´ĭ-nĭst): the leading character in a work of fiction, such as a novel or play.

CHECK YOUR UNDERSTANDING

Answer these questions before moving on to the **Analyze the Text** section on the following page.

1 The author included the section "Why Tell Stories?" to —

   A tell readers her favorite story about a blacksmith

   B explain the benefits and rewards of storytelling

   C persuade readers to become writers

   D tell readers about the spider Anansi

2 In paragraph 3, the author mentions that stories are told by parents and professionals and in theaters and over campfires as a way to —

   F explain that there are three kinds of storytelling

   G persuade readers to see more movies

   H provide examples of how storytelling is part of everyone's life

   J describe where stories are told

3 Which idea is not supported by information in the selection?

   A Storytelling was more popular in the past.

   B Storytelling is part of being human.

   C Storytelling is an important educational tool.

   D Anyone can be a storyteller.

RESPOND

ANALYZE THE TEXT

Support your responses with evidence from the text. **NOTEBOOK**

1. **Cite Evidence** Review paragraph 3. What key idea is presented in the paragraph? Cite evidence from the paragraph that supports the idea. How does the author organize the information in this paragraph?

2. **Predict** Reread the heading before paragraph 4. Based on the heading, what would you predict about the author's purpose for that section of the introduction? What ideas would you expect the author to discuss? Is your prediction correct?

3. **Evaluate** Review paragraphs 4–10. Identify how the author structures ideas in the text. Does the author effectively present and organize her ideas? Explain.

4. **Interpret** Use your annotations and what you've learned from the selection to determine the author's controlling idea in the introduction to *Storytelling*.

5. **Notice & Note** Review the quoted words in paragraph 6. How do the words and ideas of the expert add to the author's ideas about storytelling?

RESEARCH

RESEARCH TIP
Begin your research by exploring the website of one of the many organizations of professional storytellers. If your teacher approves, consider working in a small group to develop and send questions about storytelling to a children's storyteller. Ask your teacher or a librarian for help.

Professional storytellers know how to create and tell captivating stories. Investigate the rules or guidelines they follow for how to tell stories to children and young people. Record what you learn in the chart.

GUIDELINE	DETAILS

Extend In the first paragraph of this selection, the author includes examples of how stories begin, such as "Once upon a time." In a small group, find multiple folktales online or in the library. Make your own list that shows how these stories begin. Find at least five different examples of opening lines. Then compare them to those provided in the selection. Discuss your findings with the group.

RESPOND

CREATE AND DISCUSS

Write a Speech Summarize the selection's key ideas and use your summary to write a three-paragraph speech about the importance of storytelling.

❏ Draw upon ideas stated explicitly and implicitly in the selection. Be alert to details that will help you identify these key ideas.

❏ Paraphrase the author's key ideas by restating them in your own words. Make sure that you cite both the author and selection in your speech.

❏ Include complex sentences in your writing.

Discuss with a Small Group Work in a small group to discuss the selection's key ideas. Begin by sharing your speeches from the writing activity. Use your speeches to compile one list of key ideas.

❏ Work together to agree upon the list of ideas.

❏ Make sure the ideas are supported by evidence in the text. Refer to the selection to discuss how ideas are supported explicitly or implicitly.

❏ Make sure every group member participates fully. Listen closely and respectfully to all ideas.

Go to **Using Textual Evidence: Summarizing, Paraphrasing, and Quoting** in the **Writing Studio** for more on summarizing and paraphrasing.

 Go to **Participating in Collaborative Discussions** in the **Speaking and Listening Studio** for help with having a group discussion.

RESPOND TO THE ESSENTIAL QUESTION

? What hidden truths about people and the world are revealed in stories?

Gather Information Review your annotations and notes on the selection. Then, add relevant details to your Response Log. As you determine which information to include, think about how and why people tell stories and the importance of stories in your own life.

At the end of the unit, use your notes to write a short story or folktale.

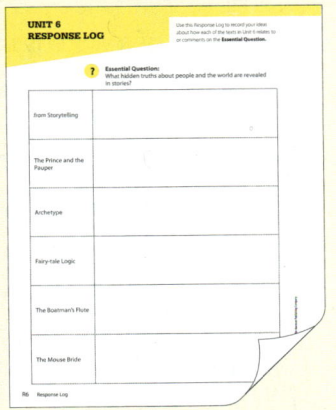

ACADEMIC VOCABULARY

As you write and discuss what you learned from the selection, be sure to use the Academic Vocabulary words. Check off each of the words that you use.

❏ emphasize
❏ occur
❏ period
❏ relevant
❏ tradition

Storytelling 431

RESPOND

WORD BANK
universal
integral
invariably
trance
nurture
chastise
adversity

CRITICAL VOCABULARY

Practice and Apply Use your understanding of the Critical Vocabulary words to answer the questions.

1. Do you think everyone **invariably** faces **adversity**? Explain.

2. Would you ever **chastise** a friend or sibling? Explain.

3. Are stories **integral** to movies? Explain.

4. How would you **nurture** a new pet?

5. If you saw a person in a **trance,** what might he or she look like?

6. Name a **universal** idea, behavior, or experience. Explain.

VOCABULARY STRATEGY: Context Clues

The **context** of a word is the words, sentences, and paragraphs that surround the word. Context can give you important clues about a word's meaning. Context clues include definitions, analogies or comparisons, and examples. Take a look at the following passage:

> **The pull of the story is <u>universal</u>. There is no known culture without some form of storytelling, and the craving to know "what comes next" has been felt by every human being, regardless of age, gender, culture, or century.**

The surrounding words "no known culture without" and "felt by every human being" provide clues to the meaning of *universal*. You can use the context clues to figure out that *universal* means "applying to every member of a group."

Practice and Apply Identify context clues that help explain the meaning of the words *trance* (paragraph 5) and *chastise* (paragraph 6). Record the context clues and explain how they hint at the meaning of each word.

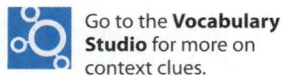

Go to the **Vocabulary Studio** for more on context clues.

432 Unit 6

LANGUAGE CONVENTIONS:
Complex Sentences

If you used only simple sentences in your writing, it would be hard for your readers to understand how your ideas connect to one another. Writers use **complex sentences** to help clarify and connect their ideas. Using complex sentences correctly will add sentence variety and improve the flow and coherence of your writing.

Writers use **subordinating conjunctions**—including *if, although, after, as, before, because, once, since, when,* and *unless*—to introduce dependent clauses. The following example from *Storytelling* shows a dependent clause beginning with the subordinating conjunction *if*:

> <u>If the chief has behaved in a greedy manner</u>, the storyteller shows Anansi in this incorrect behavior.

Writers also connect ideas within sentences by using **correlative conjunctions,** or paired conjunctions that join words or word groups. Correlative conjunctions include *both/and, either/or,* and *neither/nor*. In the following example, paired conjunctions appear in the independent clause of a complex sentence:

> <u>Neither</u> children <u>nor</u> adults will attend, if the tickets are unaffordable.

Practice and Apply Write your own complex sentences using the above examples as models. Use at least one pair of correlative conjunctions in your sentences. Write about the ideas explored in the selection or the importance of stories in your own life. When you have finished, compare your sentences with a partner's.

! Go to **Simple and Compound Sentences** in the **Grammar Studio** for more on types of sentences.

ANALYZE & APPLY

THE PRINCE AND THE PAUPER

by **Mark Twain**
dramatized by **Joellen Bland**

? ESSENTIAL QUESTION:

What hidden truths about people and the world are revealed in stories?

GET READY

QUICK START

A drama, or play, is a story performed by actors on stage, often in front of a live audience. Many dramas are also filmed. What do you think makes a drama worth reading or watching? Discuss your ideas with your group.

ANALYZE HOW PLAYWRIGHTS DEVELOP CHARACTERS

The person who writes a play, the **playwright,** uses stage directions and dialogue to develop the play's characters. **Stage directions** are instructions in the script to the actors, director, and stage crew. Stage directions might suggest scenery, lighting, sound effects, and ways for actors to move and speak. These instructions are often set in italics within parentheses in the script.

Stage directions help reveal character by:

- explaining how a character delivers, or says, his or her lines
- describing the gestures and movement of a character
- noting how characters respond to each other and to events

Dialogue is the conversation between two or more characters. Through dialogue, characters:

- express their thoughts, feelings, and motivations
- respond and react to other characters and events in the play

As you read, look for ways the playwright uses stage directions and dialogue to develop characters.

CREATE MENTAL IMAGES TO DEEPEN UNDERSTANDING

As you read a play, pause often to use stage directions and dialogue to help you visualize, or **create mental images,** of how the characters act and interact. Creating mental images can help you deepen your understanding of the text and make connections to your own experiences. Consider reading aloud, **adjusting fluency,** or how quickly you read, to suit the purposes of dialogue and stage directions.

GENRE ELEMENTS: DRAMA

- includes a script, or the text of the play
- contains a list of all the characters, called the cast of characters
- is divided into large sections called acts and smaller sections called scenes
- in a one-act play, each episode of the plot is presented as one scene
- tells a story through dialogue, the spoken words of characters
- includes stage directions that give instructions about performing the drama

ELEMENT	PURPOSE	EXAMPLE
Stage directions	describe the setting and characters' actions	*He seizes* Prince, *but* Miles *strikes him with flat of his sword.*
Dialogue	helps readers imagine what the characters think and feel	**Tom.** Oh there is no hope for me now. They will hang me for certain!

The Prince and the Pauper 435

GET READY

CRITICAL VOCABULARY

wistfully   anxiously   discreetly   rueful   jest   perplexed

To preview the Critical Vocabulary words, choose the best word to complete each sentence.

1. She _____ imagined having fun swimming in the pool.
2. I was _____ when my best friend didn't reply to my message.
3. The actors _____ with each other to make us laugh.
4. The boy was _____ after he was caught cheating.
5. The class waited _____ for the results of the final exam.
6. Not wanting to disturb the class, he whispered _____.

LANGUAGE CONVENTIONS

Prepositions and Prepositional Phrases A **preposition** shows the relationship of a noun or pronoun to another word. Commonly used prepositions include *at, by, for, from, in, of, on, to,* and *with*. A **prepositional phrase** consists of a preposition, its object, and any modifiers of the object. A prepositional phrase functions as an adverb or an adjective because it modifies, or describes, a verb or a noun. As you read the play, note the playwright's use of prepositions and prepositional phrases.

ANNOTATION MODEL

NOTICE & NOTE

As you read, note how stage directions and dialogue can help you create mental images. In the model, you can see how one student marked stage directions and made notes about mental images.

2 **Setting:** *Westminster Palace, England. Gates leading to courtyard are at right. Slightly to the left, off courtyard and inside gates, interior of palace anteroom is visible. There is a couch with a rich robe draped on it, screen at rear, bellcord, mirror, chairs, and a table with bowl of nuts, and a large golden seal on it. Piece of armor hangs on one wall. Exits are rear and downstage.*

Italics show that this is a stage direction.

The details help me picture the setting—a fancy room in a palace.

BACKGROUND

Mark Twain (1835–1910) is one of America's most beloved writers. Born Samuel Clemens, he adopted his pen name when he began his writing career. He is well known for his novels *The Adventures of Tom Sawyer* and *Adventures of Huckleberry Finn*. Twain's *The Prince and the Pauper* concerns Prince Edward, King Henry VIII's son, who became king in 1547 at the age of nine. This adaptation is by **Joellen Bland,** who has been writing scripted versions of classic stories for more than 30 years.

THE PRINCE AND THE PAUPER

by Mark Twain
dramatized by Joellen Bland

SETTING A PURPOSE

As you read, pay attention to how the stage directions and dialogue help you understand the play's characters and visualize the play's setting and action.

Notice & Note

Use the side margins to notice and note signposts in the text.

CHARACTERS

Edward, Prince of Wales
Tom Canty, the Pauper
Lord Hertford
Lord St. John
King Henry VIII
Herald
Miles Hendon
John Canty, Tom's father
Hugo, a young thief
Two Women

Justice
Constable
Jailer
Sir Hugh Hendon
Two Prisoners
Two Guards
Three Pages
Lords and Ladies
Villagers

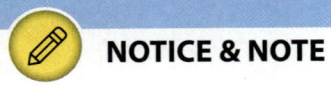# NOTICE & NOTE

LANGUAGE CONVENTIONS
The setting's description includes several prepositional phrases that add details. Mark the prepositions and prepositional phrases.

Scene 1

1 **Time:** *1547.*

2 **Setting:** *Westminster Palace, England. Gates leading to courtyard are at right. Slightly to the left, off courtyard and inside gates, interior of palace anteroom[1] is visible. There is a couch with a rich robe draped on it, screen at rear, bellcord, mirror, chairs, and a table with bowl of nuts, and a large golden seal on it. Piece of armor hangs on one wall. Exits are rear and downstage.*

3 **At Curtain Rise:** Two Guards—*one at right, one at left—stand in front of gates, and several* Villagers *hover nearby, straining to see into courtyard where* Prince *may be seen through fence, playing.* Two Women *enter right.*

4 **1st Woman.** I have walked all morning just to have a glimpse of Westminster Palace.

5 **2nd Woman.** Maybe if we can get near enough to the gates, we can have a glimpse of the young Prince. (Tom Canty, *dirty and ragged, comes out of crowd and steps close to gates.*)

6 **Tom.** I have always dreamed of seeing a real Prince! (*Excited, he presses his nose against gates.*)

7 **1st Guard.** Mind your manners, you young beggar! (*Seizes* Tom *by collar and sends him sprawling into crowd.* Villagers *laugh, as* Tom *slowly gets to his feet.*)

8 **Prince** (*rushing to gates*). How dare you treat a poor subject of the King in such a manner! Open the gates and let him in! (*As* Villagers *see* Prince, *they take off their hats and bow low.*)

9 **Villagers** (*shouting together*). Long live the Prince of Wales! (Guards *open gates and* Tom *slowly passes through, as if in a dream.*)

10 **Prince** (*to* Tom). You look tired, and you have been treated cruelly. I am Edward, Prince of Wales. What is your name?

11 **Tom** (*looking around in awe*). Tom Canty, Your Highness.

12 **Prince.** Come into the palace with me, Tom. (Prince *leads* Tom *into anteroom.* Villagers *pantomime[2] conversation, and all but a few exit.*) Where do you live, Tom?

13 **Tom.** In the city, Your Highness, in Offal Court.

14 **Prince.** Offal Court?[3] That is an odd name. Do you have parents?

ANALYZE HOW PLAYWRIGHTS DEVELOP CHARACTERS
Annotate: Mark the dialogue in paragraphs 12–18.

Analyze: What does this conversation reveal about the character of the Prince?

---

[1] **anteroom** (ăn´tē-ro͞om´): an outer room that leads to another room and is often used as a waiting room.
[2] **pantomime** (păn´tə-mīm´): to communicate by gestures and facial expressions.
[3] **Offal Court:** a place very poor people lived, named after the waste products from butchering animals.

NOTICE & NOTE

15 **Tom.** Yes, Your Highness.

16 **Prince.** How does your father treat you?

17 **Tom.** If it please you, Your Highness, when I am not able to beg a penny for our supper, he treats me to beatings.

18 **Prince** (*shocked*). What! Beatings? My father is not a calm man, but he does not beat me. (*looks at* Tom *thoughtfully*) You speak well and have an easy grace. Have you been schooled?

19 **Tom.** Very little, Your Highness. A good priest who shares our house in Offal Court has taught me from his books.

20 **Prince.** Do you have a pleasant life in Offal Court?

21 **Tom.** Pleasant enough, Your Highness, save when I am hungry. We have Punch and Judy shows,[4] and sometimes we lads have fights in the street.

22 **Prince** (*eagerly*). I should like that. Tell me more.

23 **Tom.** In summer, we run races and swim in the river, and we love to wallow in the mud.

24 **Prince** (*sighing,* **wistfully**). If I could wear your clothes and play in the mud just once, with no one to forbid me, I think I could give up the crown!

25 **Tom** (*shaking his head*). And if I could wear your fine clothes just once, Your Highness . . .

wistfully
(wĭst´fəl-ē) *adv*. When you think of something *wistfully*, you do so with sadness and longing.

[4] **Punch and Judy shows:** famous puppet show originating in 16th-century Italy, featuring Mr. Punch and his wife, Judy, who are always fighting.

NOTICE & NOTE

ANALYZE HOW PLAYWRIGHTS DEVELOP CHARACTERS

Annotate: Reread paragraphs 30–32. Mark words and phrases that help you understand the Prince's character.

Draw Conclusions: What do you learn about the Prince through his words and actions in these paragraphs?

anxiously
(ăngk´shəs-lē) *adv.* To think of something *anxiously* means that you dread it.

26 **Prince.** Would you like that? Come, then. We shall change places. You can take off your rags and put on my clothes—and I will put on yours. (*He leads* Tom *behind screen, and they return shortly, each wearing the other's clothes.*) Let's look at ourselves in this mirror. (*leads* Tom *to mirror*)

27 **Tom.** Oh, Your Highness, it is not proper for me to wear such clothes.

28 **Prince** (*excitedly, as he looks in mirror*). Heavens, do you not see it? We look like brothers! We have the same features and bearing.[5] If we went about together, dressed alike, there is no one who could say which is the Prince of Wales and which is Tom Canty!

29 **Tom** (*drawing back and rubbing his hand*). Your Highness, I am frightened. . . .

30 **Prince.** Do not worry. (*seeing* Tom *rub his hand*) Is that a bruise on your hand?

31 **Tom.** Yes, but it is a slight thing, Your Highness.

32 **Prince** (*angrily*). It was shameful and cruel of that guard to strike you. Do not stir a step until I come back. I command you! (*He picks up golden Seal of England[6] and carefully puts it into piece of armor. He then dashes out to gates.*) Open! Unbar the gates at once! (*2nd Guard opens gates, and as* Prince *runs out, in rags, 1st Guard seizes him, boxes him on the ear, and knocks him to the ground.*)

33 **1st Guard.** Take that, you little beggar, for the trouble you have made for me with the Prince. (Villagers *roar with laughter.*)

34 **Prince** (*picking himself up, turning on* Guard *furiously*). I am Prince of Wales! You shall hang for laying your hand on me!

35 **1st Guard** (*presenting arms; mockingly*). I salute Your Gracious Highness! (*Then, angrily,* 1st Guard *shoves* Prince *roughly aside.*) Be off, you mad bag of rags! (Prince *is surrounded by* Villagers, *who hustle him off.*)

36 **Villagers** (*ad lib,[7] as they exit, shouting*). Make way for His Royal Highness! Make way for the Prince of Wales! Hail to the Prince! (*etc.*)

37 **Tom** (*admiring himself in mirror*). If only the boys in Offal Court could see me! They will not believe me when I tell them about this. (*looks around* **anxiously**) But where is the Prince? (*Looks cautiously into courtyard. Two Guards immediately snap*

---

[5] **features and bearing:** parts of the face and ways of standing or walking.
[6] **Seal of England:** a device used to stamp a special design, usually a picture of the ruler, onto a document, thus indicating that it has royal approval.
[7] **ad lib:** talk together about what is going on, but without an actual script.

to attention and salute. *He quickly ducks back into anteroom as* Lords Hertford *and* St. John *enter at rear.*)

38 **Hertford** (*going toward* Tom, *then stopping and bowing low*). My Lord, you look distressed. What is wrong?

39 **Tom** (*trembling*). Oh, I beg of you, be merciful. I am no Prince, but poor Tom Canty of Offal Court. Please let me see the Prince, and he will give my rags back to me and let me go unhurt. (*kneeling*) Please, be merciful and spare me!

40 **Hertford** (*puzzled and disturbed*). Your Highness, on your knees? To me? (*bows quickly, then, aside to* St. John) The Prince has gone mad! We must inform the King. (*to* Tom) A moment, your Highness. (Hertford *and* St. John *exit rear.*)

41 **Tom.** Oh, there is no hope for me now. They will hang me for certain! (Hertford *and* St. John *re-enter, supporting* King. Tom *watches in awe as they help him to couch, where he sinks down wearily.*)

42 **King** (*beckoning* Tom *close to him*). Now, my son, Edward, my prince. What is this? Do you mean to deceive me, the King, your father, who loves you and treats you so kindly?

43 **Tom** (*dropping to his knees*). You are the King? Then I have no hope!

44 **King** (*stunned*). My child, you are not well. Do not break your father's old heart. Say you know me.

45 **Tom.** Yes, you are my lord the King, whom God preserve.

46 **King.** True, that is right. Now, you will not deny that you are Prince of Wales, as they say you did just a while ago?

47 **Tom.** I beg you, Your Grace, believe me. I am the lowest of your subjects, being born a pauper, and it is by a great mistake that I am here. I am too young to die. Oh, please, spare me, sire!

48 **King** (*amazed*). Die? Do not talk so, my child. You shall not die.

49 **Tom** (*gratefully*). God save you, my king! And now, may I go?

50 **King.** Go? Where would you go?

51 **Tom.** Back to the alley where I was born and bred to misery.

52 **King.** My poor child, rest your head here. (*He holds* Tom's *head and pats his shoulder, then turns to* Hertford *and* St. John.) Alas, I am old and ill, and my son is mad. But this shall pass. Mad or sane, he is my heir and shall rule England. Tomorrow he shall be installed and confirmed in his princely dignity! Bring the Great Seal!

NOTICE & NOTE

CREATE MENTAL IMAGES

Annotate: Reread paragraphs 39–40. Mark phrases that help you visualize the characters and the play's action.

Analyze: Why do you think Tom is "trembling"? Why is Hertford "puzzled and disturbed"?

ANALYZE HOW PLAYWRIGHTS DEVELOP CHARACTERS

Annotate: Reread paragraphs 43–47. Mark words and phrases that provide information about Tom's character.

Infer: How do you think Tom feels in the presence of the King? Why does he think he is going to die?

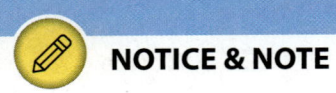

NOTICE & NOTE

53 **Hertford** (*bowing low*). Please, Your Majesty, you took the Great Seal from the Chancellor two days ago to give to His Highness the Prince.

54 **King.** So I did. (*to* Tom) My child, tell me, where is the Great Seal?

55 **Tom** (*trembling*). Indeed, my lord, I do not know.

56 **King.** Ah, your affliction[8] hangs heavily upon you. 'Tis no matter. You will remember later. Listen, carefully! (*gently, but firmly*) I command you to hide your affliction in all ways that be within your power. You shall deny to no one that you are the true prince, and if your memory should fail you upon any occasion of state, you shall be advised by your uncle, the Lord Hertford.

57 **Tom** (*resigned*). The King has spoken. The King shall be obeyed.

58 **King.** And now, my child, I go to rest. (*He stands weakly, and* Hertford *leads him off, rear.*)

59 **Tom** (*wearily, to* St. John). May it please your lordship to let me rest now?

CREATE MENTAL IMAGES
Annotate: Reread paragraphs 60–61. Mark stage directions and visualize the action.

Infer: How do the Pages' actions and Tom's reaction to them create humor in this scene?

60 **St. John.** So it please Your Highness, it is for you to command and us to obey. But it is wise that you rest, for this evening you must attend the Lord Mayor's banquet in your honor. (*He pulls bellcord, and* Three Pages *enter and kneel before* Tom.)

61 **Tom.** Banquet? (*Terrified, he sits on couch and reaches for cup of water, but* 1st Page *instantly seizes cup, drops on one knee, and serves it to him.* Tom *starts to take off his boots, but* 2nd Page *stops him and does it for him. He tries to remove his cape and gloves, and* 3rd Page *does it for him.*) I wonder that you do not try to breathe for me also! (*Lies down cautiously.* Pages *cover him with robe, then back away and exit.*)

62 **St. John** (*to* Hertford, *as he enters*). Plainly, what do you think?

63 **Hertford.** Plainly, this. The King is near death, my nephew the Prince of Wales is clearly mad and will mount the throne mad. God protect England, for she will need it!

64 **St. John.** Does it not seem strange that madness could so change his manner from what it used to be? It troubles me, his saying he is not the Prince.

ANALYZE HOW PLAYWRIGHTS DEVELOP CHARACTERS
Annotate: In paragraph 65, mark Hertford's lines in which he explains how a real impostor would act.

Analyze: Why does Hertford reason that the "Prince" cannot be an imposter? What do we know about Tom to prove that Hertford is wrong?

65 **Hertford.** Peace, my lord! If he were an impostor and called himself Prince, that would be natural. But was there ever an impostor, who being called Prince by the King and court, denied it? Never! This is the true Prince gone mad. And tonight

---
[8] **affliction** (ə-flĭk´shən): a condition that causes pain and suffering.

442 Unit 6

all London shall honor him. (Hertford *and* St. John *exit.* Tom *sits up, looks around helplessly, then gets up.*)

66 **Tom.** I should have thought to order something to eat. (*sees bowl of nuts on table*) Ah! Here are some nuts! (*looks around, sees Great Seal in armor, takes it out, looks at it curiously*) This will make a good nutcracker. (*He takes bowl of nuts, sits on couch and begins to crack nuts with Great Seal and eat them, as curtain falls.*)

Scene 2

67 **Time:** *Later that night.*

68 **Setting**: *A street in London, near Offal Court. Played before the curtain.*

69 **At Curtain Rise:** Prince *limps in, dirty and tousled. He looks around wearily. Several* Villagers *pass by, pushing against him.*

70 **Prince.** I have never seen this poor section of London. I must be near Offal Court. If I can only find it before I drop! (John Canty *steps out of crowd, seizes* Prince *roughly.*)

71 **Canty.** Out at this time of night, and I warrant you haven't brought a farthing[9] home! If that is the case and I do not break all the bones in your miserable body, then I am not John Canty!

72 **Prince** (*eagerly*). Oh, are you his father?

73 **Canty.** *His* father? I am *your* father, and—

74 **Prince.** Take me to the palace at once, and your son will be returned to you. The King, my father, will make you rich beyond your wildest dreams. Oh, save me, for I am indeed the Prince of Wales.

75 **Canty** (*staring in amazement*). Gone stark mad! But mad or not, I'll soon find where the soft places lie in your bones. Come home! (*starts to drag* Prince *off*)

76 **Prince** (*struggling*). Let me go! I am the Prince of Wales, and the King shall have your life for this!

77 **Canty** (*angrily*). I'll take no more of your madness! (*raises stick to strike, but* Prince *struggles free and runs off, and* Canty *runs after him*)

Scene 3

78 **Setting:** *Same as Scene 1, with addition of dining table, set with dishes and goblets, on raised platform. Throne-like chair is at head of table.*

---

[9] **farthing** (fär´thĭng): a former British coin worth one-fourth of a British penny.

NOTICE & NOTE

CREATE MENTAL IMAGES
Annotate: Mark information about the setting of Scene 2.

Analyze: Describe how this setting differs from the setting of Scene 1. What does the difference reveal?

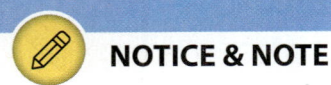

NOTICE & NOTE

79 **At Curtain Rise:** *A banquet is in progress.* Tom, *in royal robes, sits at head of table, with* Hertford *at his right and* St. John *at his left.* Lords *and* Ladies *sit around table eating and talking softly.*

80 **Tom** (*to* Hertford). What is this, my Lord? (*holds up a plate*)

81 **Hertford.** Lettuce and turnips, Your Highness.

82 **Tom.** Lettuce and turnips? I have never seen them before. Am I to eat them?

83 **Hertford** (*discreetly*). Yes, Your Highness, if you so desire. (Tom *begins to eat food with his fingers. Fanfare of trumpets is heard, and* Herald *enters, carrying scroll. All turn to look.*)

84 **Herald** (*reading from scroll*). His Majesty, King Henry VIII, is dead! The King is dead! (*All rise and turn to* Tom, *who sits, stunned.*)

85 **All** (*together*). The King is dead. Long live the King! Long live Edward, King of England! (*All bow to* Tom. Herald *bows and exits.*)

86 **Hertford** (*to* Tom). Your Majesty, we must call the council. Come, St. John. (Hertford *and* St. John *lead* Tom *off at rear.* Lords *and* Ladies *follow, talking among themselves. At gates, down right,* Villagers *enter and mill about.* Prince *enters right, pounds on gates and shouts.*)

87 **Prince.** Open the gates! I am the Prince of Wales! Open, I say! And though I am friendless with no one to help me, I will not be driven from my ground.

discreetly
(dĭ-skrēt´-lē) *adv.* To act *discreetly* means to act with self-restraint; attracting little notice.

88. **Miles Hendon** (*entering through crowd*). Though you be Prince or not, you are indeed a gallant lad and not friendless. Here I stand to prove it, and you might have a worse friend than Miles Hendon.

89. **1st Villager.** Tis another prince in disguise. Take the lad and dunk him in the pond! (*He seizes* Prince, *but* Miles *strikes him with flat of his sword. Crowd, now angry, presses forward threateningly, when fanfare of trumpets is heard offstage.* Herald, *carrying scroll, enters up left at gates.*)

90. **Herald.** Make way for the King's messenger! (*reading from scroll*) His Majesty, King Henry VIII, is dead! The King is dead! (*He exits right, repeating message, and* Villagers *stand in stunned silence.*)

91. **Prince** (*stunned*). The King is dead!

92. **1st Villager** (*shouting*). Long live Edward, King of England!

93. **Villagers** (*together*). Long live the King! (*shouting, ad lib*) Long live King Edward! Heaven protect Edward, King of England! (*etc.*)

94. **Miles** (*taking* Prince *by the arm*). Come, lad, before the crowd remembers us. I have a room at the inn, and you can stay there. (*He hurries off with stunned* Prince. Tom, *led by* Hertford, *enters courtyard up rear.* Villagers *see them.*)

95. **Villagers** (*together*). Long live the King! (*They fall to their knees as curtains close.*)

Scene 4

96. **Setting:** Miles' *room at the inn. At right is table set with dishes and bowls of food, a chair at each side. At left is bed, with table and chair next to it, and a window. Candle is on table.*

97. **At Curtain Rise:** Miles *and* Prince *approach table.*

98. **Miles.** I have had a hot supper prepared. I'll bet you're hungry, lad.

99. **Prince.** Yes, I am. It's kind of you to let me stay with you, Miles. I am truly Edward, King of England, and you shall not go unrewarded. (*sits at table*)

100. **Miles** (*to himself*). First he called himself Prince, and now he is King. Well, I will humor him. (*starts to sit*)

101. **Prince** (*angrily*). Stop! Would you sit in the presence of the King?

102. **Miles** (*surprised, standing up quickly*). I beg your pardon, Your Majesty. I was not thinking. (*Stares uncertainly at* Prince, *who sits at table, expectantly.* Miles *starts to uncover dishes of food, serves* Prince *and fills glasses.*)

NOTICE & NOTE

ANALYZE HOW PLAYWRIGHTS DEVELOP CHARACTERS

Annotate: In paragraphs 88–89, mark words and phrases that help you understand the character of Miles Hendon.

Analyze: Do you think that Miles Hendon is an important character? Why or why not?

AHA MOMENT

Notice & Note: What is Miles's opinion of the Prince? In paragraphs 100–102, mark Miles's thoughts.

Infer: Describe how Miles treats the Prince. Have his feelings changed? If so, how?

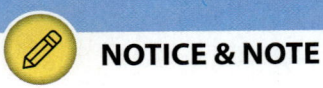

NOTICE & NOTE

ANALYZE HOW PLAYWRIGHTS DEVELOP CHARACTERS

Annotate: Reread paragraphs 104–109. Mark the Prince's response to Miles's story.

Analyze: What does the Prince's response to Miles's story reveal about him?

103 **Prince.** Miles, you have a gallant way about you. Are you nobly born?

104 **Miles.** My father is a baronet,[10] Your Majesty.

105 **Prince.** Then you must also be a baronet.

106 **Miles** (*shaking his head*). My father banished me from home seven years ago, so I fought in the wars. I was taken prisoner, and I have spent the past seven years in prison. Now I am free, and I am returning home.

107 **Prince.** You have been shamefully wronged! But I will make things right for you. You have saved me from injury and possible death. Name your reward and if it be within the compass of my royal power, it is yours.

108 **Miles** (*pausing briefly, then dropping to his knee*). Since Your Majesty is pleased to hold my simple duty worthy of reward, I ask that I and my successors[11] may hold the privilege of sitting in the presence of the King.

109 **Prince** (*taking* Miles' *sword, tapping him lightly on each shoulder*). Rise and seat yourself. (*returns sword to* Miles, *then rises and goes over to bed*)

110 **Miles** (*rising*). He should have been born a king. He plays the part to a marvel! If I had not thought of this favor, I might have had to stand for weeks. (*sits down and begins to eat*)

111 **Prince.** Sir Miles, you will stand guard while I sleep? (*lies down and instantly falls asleep*)

rueful
(rōō'fəl) *adj.* To be *rueful* is to show sorrow or regret.

112 **Miles.** Yes, Your Majesty. (*With a **rueful** look at his uneaten supper, he stands up.*) Poor little chap. I suppose his mind has been disordered with ill usage. (*covers* Prince *with his cape*) Well, I will be his friend and watch over him. (*Blows out candle, then yawns, sits on chair next to bed, and falls asleep.* John Canty *and* Hugo *appear at window, peer around room, then enter cautiously through window. They lift the sleeping* Prince, *staring nervously at* Miles.)

113 **Canty** (*in loud whisper*). I swore the day he was born he would be a thief and a beggar, and I won't lose him now. Lead the way to the camp Hugo! (Canty *and* Hugo *carry* Prince *off right, as* Miles *sleeps on and curtain falls.*)

Scene 5

114 **Time:** *Two weeks later.*

---

[10] **baronet** (băr'ə-nĭt): a rank of honor in Britain, below a baron and above a knight.
[11] **successors** (sək-sĕs'ərz): those, in sequence or line of succession, who have a right to property, to hold title or rank, or to hold the throne one after the other.

115 **Setting:** *Country village street.*

116 **Before Curtain Rise:** Villagers *walk about.* Canty, Hugo, *and* Prince *enter.*

117 **Canty.** I will go in this direction. Hugo, keep my mad son with you, and see that he doesn't escape again! (*exits*)

118 **Hugo** (*seizing* Prince *by the arm*). He won't escape! I'll see that he earns his bread today, or else!

119 **Prince** (*pulling away*). I will not beg with you, and I will not steal! I have suffered enough in this miserable company of thieves!

120 **Hugo.** You shall suffer more if you do not do as I tell you! (*raises clenched fist at* Prince) Refuse if you dare! (Woman *enters, carrying wrapped bundle in a basket on her arm.*) Wait here until I come back. (Hugo *sneaks along after* Woman, *then snatches her bundle, runs back to* Prince, *and thrusts it into his arms.*) Run after me and call, "Stop, thief!" But be sure you lead her astray! (*Runs off.* Prince *throws down bundle in disgust.*)

121 **Woman.** Help! Thief! Stop, thief! (*rushes at* Prince *and seizes him, just as several* Villagers *enter*) You little thief! What do you mean by robbing a poor woman? Somebody bring the constable! (Miles *enters and watches.*)

122 **1st Villager** (*grabbing* Prince). I'll teach him a lesson, the little villain!

123 **Prince** (*struggling*). Take your hands off me! I did not rob this woman!

124 **Miles** (*stepping out of crowd and pushing man back with the flat of his sword*). Let us proceed gently, my friends. This is a matter for the law.

125 **Prince** (*springing to* Miles' *side*). You have come just in time, Sir Miles. Carve this rabble to rags!

126 **Miles.** Speak softly. Trust in me and all shall go well.

127 **Constable** (*entering and reaching for* Prince). Come along, young rascal!

128 **Miles.** Gently, good friend. He shall go peaceably to the Justice.

129 **Prince.** I will not go before a Justice! I did not do this thing!

130 **Miles** (*taking him aside*). Sire, will you reject the laws of the realm, yet demand that your subjects respect them?

131 **Prince** (*calmer*). You are right, Sir Miles. Whatever the King requires a subject to suffer under the law, he will suffer himself while he holds the station of a subject. (Constable *leads them off right.* Villagers *follow. Curtain.*)

NOTICE & NOTE

ANALYZE HOW PLAYWRIGHTS DEVELOP CHARACTERS

Annotate: Reread paragraphs 120-131. Mark words and phrases that show the behavior of both the Prince and Miles.

Evaluate: How does their behavior fit with what you know about them?

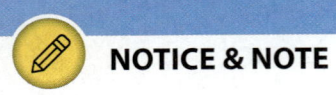
NOTICE & NOTE

ANALYZE HOW PLAYWRIGHTS DEVELOP CHARACTERS

Annotate: Reread paragraphs 134–147. Mark passages in the text that reveal the characters of the Woman and the Constable.

Analyze: Why does the Woman change the value of her pig to eight pence? Why does the Constable do what he does?

Scene 6

132 **Setting:** *Office of the Justice. A high bench is at center.*

133 **At Curtain Rise:** *Justice sits behind bench.* Constable *enters with* Miles *and* Prince, *followed by* Villagers. Woman *carries wrapped bundle.*

134 **Constable** (*to* Justice). A young thief, your worship, is accused of stealing a dressed pig from this poor woman.

135 **Justice** (*looking down at* Prince, *then* Woman). My good woman, are you absolutely certain this lad stole your pig?

136 **Woman.** It was none other than he, your worship.

137 **Justice.** Are there no witnesses to the contrary? (*All shake their heads.*) Then the lad stands convicted. (*to* Woman) What do you hold this property to be worth?

138 **Woman.** Three shillings and eight pence, your worship.

139 **Justice** (*leaning down to* Woman). Good woman, do you know that when one steals a thing above the value of thirteen pence, the law says he shall hang for it?

140 **Woman** (*upset*). Oh, what have I done? I would not hang the poor boy for the whole world! Save me from this, your worship. What can I do?

141 **Justice** (*gravely*). You may revise the value, since it is not yet written in the record.

142 **Woman.** Then call the pig eight pence, your worship.

143 **Justice.** So be it. You may take your property and go. (*Woman starts off, and is followed by* Constable. Miles *follows them cautiously down right.*)

144 **Constable** (*stopping* Woman). Good woman, I will buy your pig from you. (*takes coins from pocket*) Here is eight pence.

145 **Woman.** Eight pence! It cost me three shillings and eight pence!

146 **Constable.** Indeed! Then come back before his worship and answer for this. The lad must hang!

147 **Woman.** No! No! Say no more. Give me the eight pence and hold your peace. (Constable *hands her coins and takes pig.* Woman *exits, angrily.* Miles *returns to bench.*)

148 **Justice.** The boy is sentenced to a fortnight[12] in the common jail. Take him away, Constable! (*Justice exits.* Prince *gives* Miles *a nervous glance.*)

---

[12] **fortnight:** 14 days; two weeks.

149 **Miles** (*following* Constable). Good sir, turn your back a moment and let the poor lad escape. He is innocent.

150 **Constable** (*outraged*). What? You say this to me? Sir, I arrest you in—

151 **Miles.** Do not be so hasty! (*slyly*) The pig you have purchased for eight pence may cost you your neck, man.

152 **Constable** (*laughing nervously*). Ah, but I was merely **jesting** with the woman, sir.

153 **Miles.** Would the Justice think it a jest?

154 **Constable.** Good sir! The Justice has no more sympathy with a jest than a dead corpse! (*perplexed*) Very well, I will turn my back and see nothing! But go quickly! (*exits*)

155 **Miles** (*to* Prince). Come, my liege.[13] We are free to go. And that band of thieves shall not set hands on you again, I swear it!

156 **Prince** (*wearily*). Can you believe, Sir Miles, that in the last fortnight, I, the King of England, have escaped from thieves and begged for food on the road? I have slept in a barn with a calf! I have washed dishes in a peasant's kitchen, and narrowly escaped death. And not once in all my wanderings did I see a courier[14] searching for me! Is it no matter for commotion and distress that the head of state is gone?

157 **Miles** (*sadly, aside*). Still busy with his pathetic dream. (*to* Prince) It is strange indeed, my liege. But come, I will take you to my father's home in Kent. We are not far away. There you may rest in a house with seventy rooms! Come, I am all impatience to be home again! (*They exit,* Miles *in cheerful spirits,* Prince *looking puzzled, as curtains close.*)

Scene 7

158 **Setting:** *Village jail. Bare stage, with barred window on one wall.*

159 **At Curtain Rise:** Two Prisoners, *in chains, are onstage.* Jailer *shoves* Miles *and* Prince, *in chains, onstage. They struggle and protest.*

160 **Miles.** But I tell you, I am Miles Hendon! My brother, Sir Hugh, has stolen my bride and my estate!

161 **Jailer.** Be silent! Impostor! Sir Hugh will see that you pay well for claiming to be his dead brother and for assaulting him in his own house! (*exits*)

---

[13] **my liege** (lēj): my lord.
[14] **courier** (koor´ē-ər): messenger.

NOTICE & NOTE

ANALYZE HOW PLAYWRIGHTS DEVELOP CHARACTERS

Annotate: In paragraphs 149–157, mark how Miles gets the best of the Constable.

Infer: What does this reveal about Miles?

jest
(jĕst) *v.* To *jest* means to make playful remarks.

perplexed
(pər-plĕkst´) *adj.* When you are *perplexed,* you are puzzled.

NOTICE & NOTE

AHA MOMENT

Notice & Note: Reread paragraphs 163–165. Mark the Prince's response to the prisoners' stories.

Draw Conclusions: What lesson does the Prince learn in prison?

162 **Miles** (*sitting, with head in hands*). Oh, my dear Edith . . . now wife to my brother Hugh, against her will, and my poor father . . . dead!

163 **1st Prisoner.** At least you have your life, sir. I am sentenced to be hanged for killing a deer in the King's park.

164 **2nd Prisoner.** And I must hang for stealing a yard of cloth to dress my children.

165 **Prince** (*moved; to* Prisoners). When I mount my throne, you shall all be free. And the laws that have dishonored you shall be swept from the books. (*turning away*) Kings should go to school to learn their own laws and be merciful.

166 **1st Prisoner.** What does the lad mean? I have heard that the King is mad, but merciful.

167 **2nd Prisoner.** He is to be crowned at Westminster tomorrow.

168 **Prince** (*violently*). King? What King, good sir?

169 **1st Prisoner.** Why, we have only one, his most sacred majesty, King Edward the Sixth.

170 **2nd Prisoner.** And whether he be mad or not, his praises are on all men's lips. He has saved many innocent lives, and now he means to destroy the cruelest laws that oppress the people.

171 **Prince** (*turning away, shaking his head*). How can this be? Surely it is not that little beggar boy! (Sir Hugh *enters with* Jailer.)

172 **Sir Hugh.** Seize the impostor!

173 **Miles** (*as Jailer pulls him to his feet*). Hugh, this has gone far enough!

174 **Sir Hugh.** You will sit in the public stocks for two hours, and the boy would join you if he were not so young. See to it, jailer, and after two hours, you may release them. Meanwhile, I ride to London for the coronation![15] (*Sir Hugh exits and Miles is hustled out by Jailer.*)

175 **Prince.** Coronation! What does he mean? There can be no coronation without me! (*curtain falls*)

Scene 8

176 **Time:** *Coronation Day.*

177 **Setting:** *Outside gates of Westminster Abbey, played before curtain. Painted screen or flat at rear represents Abbey. Throne is in center. Bench is near it.*

178 **At Curtain Rise:** Lords *and* Ladies *crowd Abbey. Outside gates,* Guards *drive back cheering* Villagers, *among them* Miles.

179 **Miles** (*distraught*). I've lost him! Poor little chap! He has been swallowed up in the crowd! (*Fanfare of trumpets is heard, then silence.* Hertford, St. John, Lords *and* Ladies *enter slowly, in a procession, followed by* Pages, *one of whom carries crown on a small cushion.* Tom *follows procession, looking about nervously. Suddenly,* Prince, *in rags, steps out from crowd, his hand raised.*)

180 **Prince.** I forbid you to set the crown of England upon that head. I am the King!

181 **Hertford.** Seize the little vagabond!

182 **Tom.** I forbid it! He is the King! (*kneels before* Prince) Oh, my lord the King, let poor Tom Canty be the first to say, "Put on your crown and enter into your own right again." (Hertford *and several* Lords *look closely at both boys.*)

183 **Hertford.** This is strange indeed. (*to* Tom) By your favor, sir, I wish to ask certain questions of this lad.

184 **Prince.** I will answer truly whatever you may ask, my lord.

185 **Hertford.** But if you have been well trained, you may answer my questions as well as our lord the King. I need a definite proof. (*thinks a moment*) Ah! Where lies the Great Seal of England? It has been missing for weeks, and only the true Prince of Wales can say where it lies.

---

[15] **coronation** (kôr´ə-nā´shən): the act of crowning someone king or queen. In England, coronations usually take place at a large church in London called Westminster Abbey.

ANALYZE HOW PLAYWRIGHTS DEVELOP CHARACTERS

Annotate: Reread paragraphs 180–184. Mark key words and phrases that reveal the Prince's and Tom's behavior.

Analyze: Is their behavior consistent with how they've behaved before? Explain.

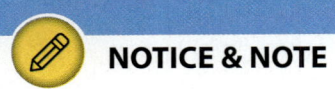

NOTICE & NOTE

AHA MOMENT

Notice & Note: What do Tom and the Prince remember about the royal seal? In paragraphs 186–189, mark their memories.

Analyze: Why is the royal seal so important here?

CREATE MENTAL IMAGES

Annotate: Reread paragraph 195. Mark the stage direction.

Evaluate: How does the stage direction help you visualize how Miles reacts to the knowledge that the "mad" boy he has been helping really is the King?

186 **Tom.** Wait! Was the seal round and thick, with letters engraved on it? (Hertford *nods.*) I know where it is, but it was not I who put it there. The rightful King shall tell you. (*to* Prince) Think, my King, it was the very last thing you did that day before you rushed out of the palace wearing my rags.

187 **Prince** (*pausing*). I recall how we exchanged clothes, but have no recollection[16] of hiding the Great Seal.

188 **Tom** (*eagerly*). Remember when you saw the bruise on my hand, you ran to the door, but first you hid this thing you call the Seal.

189 **Prince** (*suddenly*). Ah! I remember! (*to* St. John) Go, my good St. John, and you shall find the Great Seal in the armor that hangs on the wall in my chamber. (St. John *hesitates, but at a nod from* Tom, *hurries off.*)

190 **Tom** (*pleased*). Right, my King! Now the scepter[17] of England is yours again. (St. John *returns in a moment with Great Seal.*)

191 **All** (*shouting*). Long live Edward, King of England! (Tom *takes off his cape and throws it over* Prince's *rags. Trumpet fanfare is heard.* St. John *takes crown and places it on* Prince. *All kneel.*)

192 **Hertford.** Let the small impostor be flung into the Tower!

193 **Prince** (*firmly*). I will not have it so. But for him, I would not have my crown. (*to* Tom) My poor boy, how was it that you could remember where I hid the Seal, when I could not?

194 **Tom** (*embarrassed*). I did not know what it was, my King, and I used it to . . . to crack nuts. (*All laugh, and* Tom *steps back.* Miles *steps forward, staring in amazement.*)

195 **Miles.** Is he really the King? Is he indeed the sovereign of England, and not the poor and friendless Tom o' Bedlam[18] I thought he was? (*He sinks down on bench.*) I wish I had a bag to hide my head in!

196 **1st Guard** (*rushing up to him*). Stand up, you mannerless clown! How dare you sit in the presence of the King!

197 **Prince.** Do not touch him! He is my trusty servant, Miles Hendon, who saved me from shame and possible death. For his service, he owns the right to sit in my presence.

---

[16] **recollection** (rĕk´ə-lĕk´shən): a memory or recalling to mind of something that happened before.

[17] **scepter** (sĕp´tər): a staff held by a king or queen as an emblem of authority.

[18] **Tom o' Bedlam:** an insane person, such as someone hospitalized at St. Mary of Bethlehem Hospital, or Bedlam Hospital, in London.

NOTICE & NOTE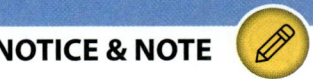

198 **Miles** (*bowing, then kneeling*). Your Majesty!

199 **Prince.** Rise, Sir Miles. I command that Sir Hugh Hendon, who sits within this hall, be seized and put under lock and key until I have need of him. (*beckons to* Tom) From what I have heard, Tom Canty, you have governed the realm with royal gentleness and mercy in my absence. Henceforth, you shall hold the honorable title of King's Ward! (Tom *kneels and kisses* Prince's *hand.*) And because I have suffered with the poorest of my subjects and felt the cruel force of unjust laws, I pledge myself to a reign of mercy for all! (*All bow low, then rise.*)

200 **All** (*shouting*). Long live the King! Long live Edward, King of England! (*curtain*)

CHECK YOUR UNDERSTANDING

Answer these questions before moving on to the **Analyze the Text** section on the following page.

1 Why don't people realize that the Prince and Tom Canty are wearing each other's clothes?

   A People think the boys are wearing costumes in a play.

   B People do realize it, but they are afraid to say anything.

   C The Prince and Tom look and move like each other.

   D The Prince often dresses in the clothes of a commoner.

2 In paragraph 32, the Prince hides the royal seal in a piece of armor. How is this significant to the plot of the play?

   F It indicates that the royal seal has no meaning.

   G The armor keeps the seal shiny.

   H The Prince is able to prove his identity because he knew where the seal was hidden.

   J He wanted to hide the seal from his father.

3 What happens to Miles and the Prince when they arrive at the home of Miles's father?

   A They are greeted with open arms.

   B They are politely turned away.

   C A huge banquet is thrown in their honor.

   D They are put in chains and thrown in jail.

RESPOND

ANALYZE THE TEXT

Support your responses with evidence from the text. 📓 **NOTEBOOK**

1. **Summarize** Review paragraphs 24–34. Summarize the events leading up to the Prince being thrown out of his own palace.

2. **Cite Evidence** Do you think Tom Canty is comfortable in his new role as the Prince? Cite evidence in the dialogue and stage directions that explains why or why not.

3. **Draw Conclusions** Review Scene 4. Based on the way Miles acts toward the Prince, what type of person do you think he is? Describe some of his character traits.

4. **Interpret** What types of information do the stage directions provide in the play? Give some examples. How do your examples help you visualize the action, guide you to adjust fluency (how quickly you read), and add to your understanding of the play?

5. **Notice & Note** How does the Prince's character change because of his experiences outside the palace? What is revealed about Tom Canty in his role as the Prince?

RESEARCH

Prince Edward became king as a young boy, after the death of his father, King Henry VIII, in 1547. Research King Edward VI and what is known about his childhood. Use the chart below to record your results.

RESEARCH TIP
The best search terms are very specific. Along with the name *King Edward VI*, you will want to include a word such as *biography* or *childhood* to make sure you get the information you need.

KING EDWARD VI: IMPORTANT CHILDHOOD EVENTS AND PEOPLE	
EVENT/PERSON	DETAILS

Connect With a small group, discuss what you learned about King Edward VI. Contrast the facts of Edward's childhood with the play's characterization of him.

RESPOND

CREATE AND PRESENT

Write a Character Study Write a brief essay in which you describe and analyze one of the major characters in *The Prince and the Pauper*. Choose Edward, Tom Canty, Miles Hendon, or John Canty.

- ❏ Think about the character's traits, and describe how the playwright develops the character throughout the play.
- ❏ Use evidence from both the dialogue and stage directions in the play to support your analysis.
- ❏ Revise and edit your draft, using prepositions and prepositional phrases correctly.

Dramatic Reading With a small group, rehearse and perform a portion of the play. Then, watch another group perform a portion of the play.

- ❏ Decide who in your group will play each character.
- ❏ As you rehearse, adjust your delivery according to the intention and purpose of the lines you are reading, taking into account stage directions and what you know about the character.
- ❏ Invite suggestions from group members and consider them carefully. Take notes about how to deliver your lines.
- ❏ When you perform, remember to make eye contact, speak clearly and loudly, and pronounce words correctly.
- ❏ When you watch others perform, contrast the performance with what you "see" and "hear" when you read the text on your own.
- ❏ Record or take a video of your dramatic readings.

Go to **Using Textual Evidence** in the **Writing Studio** for more on using textual evidence.

Go to **Giving a Presentation: Delivering Your Presentation** in the **Speaking and Listening Studio** for help delivering your lines.

RESPOND TO THE ESSENTIAL QUESTION

 What hidden truths about people and the world are revealed in stories?

Gather Information Review your annotations and notes on the play. Then, add relevant details to your Response Log. Consider what makes a person hide true feelings and how a person's behavior can reveal character.

At the end of the unit, use your notes to write a short story or folktale.

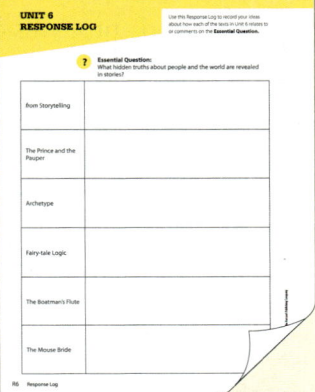

ACADEMIC VOCABULARY

As you write and discuss what you learned from the play, be sure to use the Academic Vocabulary words. Check off each of the words that you use.

- ❏ emphasize
- ❏ occur
- ❏ period
- ❏ relevant
- ❏ tradition

RESPOND

WORD BANK
wistfully
anxiously
discreetly
rueful
jest
perplexed

CRITICAL VOCABULARY

Practice and Apply Answer each question. Explain your response.

1. If you gaze **wistfully** at a picture of a sunny tropical island, does it mean you wish to be there or are you glad you are not? Why?

   _____

2. If someone looks **anxiously** at his watch, is he feeling pressed for time or relieved by the time? Why?

   _____

3. When a doctor asks to speak to you **discreetly,** is she trying to respect your privacy or to speak openly? Why?

   _____

4. If your friend is feeling **rueful,** should you congratulate or comfort your friend? Why?

   _____

5. If you and your sibling **jest** at the dinner table, are you making a joke or trying to start an argument? Why?

   _____

6. If you are **perplexed** by an algebra problem, are you finding it hard to solve or does the solution come easily to you? Why?

   _____

VOCABULARY STRATEGY: Resources

You can use a print or online dictionary and a thesaurus to identify synonyms and antonyms of vocabulary words. Using these resources to identify synonyms and antonyms of words can help you better understand the meaning and usage of unfamiliar words.

Practice and Apply Use a dictionary and a thesaurus to find a synonym and an antonym for each of these vocabulary words: *wistfully, anxiously, discreetly, rueful, jest,* and *perplexed*. For each vocabulary word, write your own sentence using the word. Then, replace the vocabulary word with a synonym to make sure that the sentence still has the same meaning. Be sure that the synonym is the same part of speech as the word it replaces.

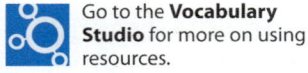 Go to the **Vocabulary Studio** for more on using resources.

LANGUAGE CONVENTIONS:
Prepositions and Prepositional Phrases

A **preposition** is a word that relates one word to another word. Prepositions include *at, by, for, from, in, of, on, to,* and *with*. A **prepositional phrase** includes a preposition and a noun—the object of the preposition. A prepositional phrase modifies or relates to another word in a sentence, telling *which one, where, why,* or *to what extent*. In writing, prepositional phrases are used to add detail and create imagery.

Here are some examples from *The Prince and the Pauper*.

> **The boy is sentenced <u>to a fortnight</u> <u>in the common jail</u>.**

The prepositional phrase "to a fortnight" describes to what extent the boy will be sentenced, and "in the common jail" describes where he will be sentenced.

Notice the importance of these prepositions and prepositional phrases in the stage directions at the opening of Scene 4.

> **Miles' room <u>at the inn</u>. <u>At right</u> is table set <u>with dishes and bowls</u> <u>of food</u>, a chair <u>at each side</u>. <u>At left</u> is bed, <u>with table and chair</u> <u>next to it</u>, and a window. Candle is <u>on table</u>.**

The prepositional phrases add details that help readers visualize the scene.

Practice and Apply Think of a scene from your everyday life; for example, walking your dog, going to school, or eating dinner with your family. Write stage directions and dialogue for your scene using prepositions and prepositional phrases. Use sentences from *The Prince and the Pauper* as a model.

RESPOND

Go to the **Grammar Studio** for more on prepositions and prepositional phrases.

COLLABORATE & COMPARE

POEM
ARCHETYPE
by **Margarita Engle**
pages 461–463

COMPARE POEMS

As you read, look for details that will help you identify themes—messages about life and the human experience. To identify themes and state them will require that you make inferences, or logical guesses based on text evidence and what you already know. After you read both poems, you will collaborate with a small group on a final project.

 ESSENTIAL QUESTION:

What hidden truths about people and the world are revealed in stories?

POEM
FAIRY-TALE LOGIC
by **A. E. Stallings**
pages 464–465

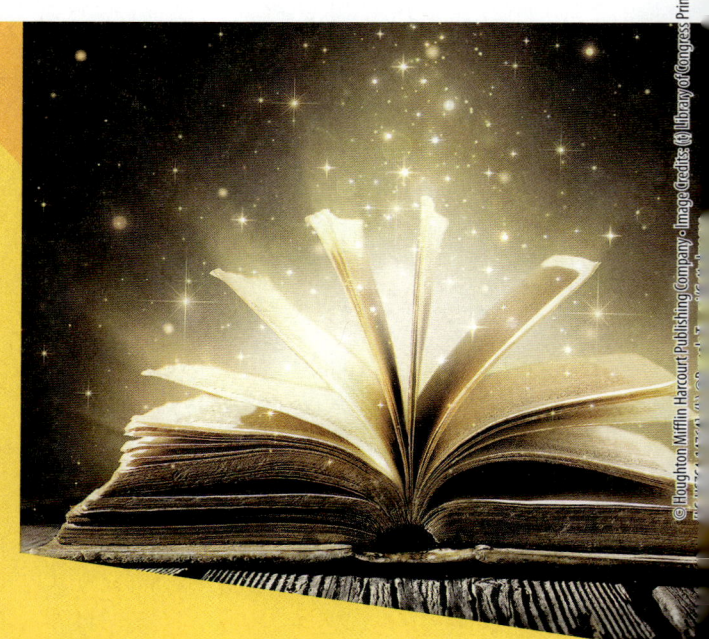

GET READY

QUICK START

Choose a favorite fairy tale, myth, or other traditional story that interests you. What message does this story have about life or the human experience? Discuss the story and its theme with your group.

ANALYZE THE EFFECTS OF METER AND STRUCTURAL ELEMENTS IN POEMS

A poem's **form,** or structure, is the way its words and lines are arranged on a page. During the writing process, poets often choose a particular form because it helps shape and express their ideas. In this way, a poem's meaning becomes closely tied to its form. Examining a poem's structure will help you discover its meaning.

"Archetype" is in **free verse,** a poetic form that has no regular patterns of line length, rhyme, or rhythm. To analyze free verse, pay attention to how line lengths and line breaks affect meaning. Note how ideas are arranged into **stanzas,** or groups of lines that form a unit.

"Fairy-tale Logic" is written in a traditional form called a **sonnet.** Sonnets generally include 14 lines with **end rhymes,** or rhyming words at the ends of lines. Sonnet structure is also established by **meter** —a pattern of stressed and unstressed syllables that create a regular rhythm.

Many poetic forms, including sonnets and free verse, use devices such as **internal rhyme** (rhymes within lines) and **alliteration** (repetition of consonant sounds at the beginnings of words) to establish rhythm and draw attention to words and ideas. Repeated sounds within words can also establish rhythm and create emphasis. As you read, pause to ask yourself, "What repeated sounds do I hear? Where are these sounds in the line?" The answers will help you identify end rhyme, internal rhyme, and alliteration. Then ask, "Why has the author created this emphasis? What does the author want me to notice or realize?"

GENRE ELEMENTS: POETRY
- may include rhyme, rhythm, and meter
- includes line breaks and white space for effects and meaning
- may use repetition and rhyme to create a melodic quality
- often includes figurative language and a variety of poetic devices

EXAMPLE	RHYME OR REPEATED SOUND AND ALLITERATION	IMPORTANCE
I never understood all the fuss/ about princesses poisoned/ or rescued from dragons. ("Archetype" lines 5–7)	• understood / fuss / princesses / rescued = repeated *s* sounds • prince*sses* / poi*s*oned / dragon*s* = repeated *z* sounds • *p*rincesses *p*oisoned = repeated initial consonant sounds	The *p* sounds make it sound as if the speaker is spitting the words out in disdain. The repeated *s* and *z* sounds hiss, sounding angry.

Archetype / Fairy-tale Logic   459

GET READY

MAKE CONNECTIONS

The poems "Fairy-tale Logic" and "Archetype" include allusions to myths, fairy tales, popular works, and biblical stories. An **allusion** is a reference to a famous person, place, event, or work of literature. Poets and authors use allusions to connect the ideas of their works to the ideas in these references. Readers can then use their own knowledge of the references to make connections to the text, creating a deeper understanding of the text's complex ideas.

Use the chart below to help you use your own understanding of allusions to make connections. One example has been done for you.

POEM	ALLUSION	TEXT CONNECTION	PERSONAL CONNECTION
"Fairy-tale Logic"	The language of snakes, perhaps, an invisible cloak....	J. K. Rowling's character, Harry Potter, can speak to snakes and has a cloak of invisibility.	I've read the books and know that Harry uses his abilities to overcome certain challenges.

ANNOTATION MODEL

NOTICE & NOTE

As you read, take notes on meter and other structural elements, text connections, and evidence that support your own ideas. This model shows one reader's notes about the beginning of "Archetype."

> 1 Is it true that nothing reveals
>   <u>more</u> about a person's secret <u>heart</u>
>   than the adult memory of a <u>favorite</u>
>   <u>childhood fairy tale</u>?

The lines are breaking in the middle of a thought, which makes me want to keep reading. The words that end each line seem important, too.
I wonder if the rest of the poem will answer this question?

BACKGROUND

Margarita Engle *(b. 1951) is an award-winning Cuban American writer. She was named the Poetry Foundation's Young People's Poet Laureate for the 2017-2019 term. She has published several children's books, novels, and young adult novels in verse. Many of her books are inspired by her Cuban American heritage and focus on history and life in Cuba. Among her many award-winning books are* The Surrender Tree: Poems of Cuba's Struggle for Freedom *(2008), and her verse memoir,* Enchanted Air.

ARCHETYPE[1]
by Margarita Engle

PREPARE TO COMPARE

As you read, pay attention to the different stories and fairy tales mentioned in the poem. Think about how the author uses these allusions, or references to famous works, to share her ideas.

1   Is it true that nothing reveals
    more about a person's secret heart
    than the adult memory of a favorite
    childhood fairy tale?

5   I never understood all the fuss
    about princesses poisoned
    or rescued from dragons.
    Hansel and Gretel seemed like a recitation[2]
    of the sorrowful evening news
10 a serial killer, the ovens, absent parents
    a famine, crumbs . . .

---

[1] **archetype** (är´kĭ-tīp´): model after which things are patterned; ideal type.
[2] **recitation** (rĕs´ĭ-tā´shən): a public presentation of memorized material.

NOTICE & NOTE

Notice & Note

Use the side margins to notice and note signposts in the text.

MAKE CONNECTIONS

Annotate: In stanza 1, mark the phrase that refers to something hidden.

Connect: What is the author asking the reader to reflect on?

NOTICE & NOTE

ANALYZE THE EFFECTS OF METER AND STRUCTURAL ELEMENTS IN POEMS

Annotate: Mark the alliteration and repeated sounds in stanza 3 (lines 12–16).

Infer: How do these elements contribute to rhythm and meaning?

MAKE CONNECTIONS

Annotate: Mark references to music and song in the poem.

Infer: What can you infer about the meaning of music and song, especially in "The Nightingale," to the poet?

Instead of magic beanstalks and man-eating giants
or wolves disguised as gentle grandmas
I chose the tale of a bird with a voice that could soothe
15   the melancholic[3] spirit of an emperor
helpless despite his wealth and power.

Of all tales, only The Nightingale[4] felt
like a story I knew before I was born
about Orpheus[5] calming wild beasts with his lyre[6]
20   King David's harp easing Saul's despair[7]
Saint Francis with his curious flocks of birds[8]
singing back and forth in a language of wishing
that even the wolf understood.

[3] **melancholic** (měl´ən-kŏl´ĭk): affected with sadness or depression.
[4] **The Nightingale:** in this fairy tale by Hans Christian Andersen, the Chinese emperor prefers a mechanical nightingale until the real nightingale saves him with her song.
[5] **Orpheus** (ôr´-fē-əs): a hero from Greek mythology who played the lyre and soothed animals and trees, causing them to sway or dance.
[6] **lyre** (līr): a stringed instrument of the harp family, used to accompany a singer or speaker of poetry, especially in Greek mythology.
[7] **King David's harp easing Saul's despair:** tale from the Bible in which David played the harp to soothe Saul from the evil spirit that bothered him.
[8] **Saint Francis with his curious flocks of birds:** Saint Francis is the patron saint of animals and nature in the Catholic Church; the allusion refers to the legend of how Francis preached to birds and other animals about divine love.

NOTICE & NOTE

CHECK YOUR UNDERSTANDING

Answer these questions about "Archetype" before moving on to the next poem.

1 The speaker in the poem questions whether —

    A a favorite story reveals something about yourself

    B fairy tales are real

    C a person can have a "secret heart"

    D fairy tales are scary or strange

2 The line <u>of the sorrowful evening news</u> does what in the poem?

    F Makes the poem into a news story

    G Connects qualities of fairy tales to the present day

    H Shows the mood of the poem is sad

    J Expresses what the poem is really about

3 What story means the most to the speaker of the poem?

    A Jack and the Beanstalk

    B Myth of Orpheus

    C The Nightingale

    D Hansel and Gretel

NOTICE & NOTE

BACKGROUND

A. E. Stallings *(b. 1968) is an award-winning poet. Her book of poetry,* Archaic Smile *(1999), won the Richard Wilbur Award. She also has won fellowships through the Guggenheim Foundation and the MacArthur Foundation for her poetry and translations. Stallings has studied Greek and Latin, and Greek mythology has influenced her poetry. She writes in sonnet form, as shown in "Fairy-tale Logic," as well as in a variety of other poetic forms. "Fairy-tale Logic" first appeared in* Poetry Magazine *in 2010.*

FAIRY-TALE LOGIC
by A. E. Stallings

Notice & Note

Use the side margins to notice and note signposts in the text.

MAKE CONNECTIONS

Annotate: This poem lists some "impossible tasks." Mark lines that comment on, rather than merely list, these tasks.

Interpret: How does the author use these comments to share ideas with the reader?

PREPARE TO COMPARE

As you read, note how the sounds, rhyme, and meter affect your reading and understanding of the poem.

Fairy tales are full of impossible tasks:
Gather the chin hairs of a man-eating goat,
Or cross a sulphuric lake[1] in a leaky boat,
Select the prince from a row of identical masks,
5 Tiptoe up to a dragon where it basks[2]
And snatch its bone; count dust specks, mote by mote,[3]
Or learn the phone directory by rote.
Always it's impossible what someone asks—

---

[1] **sulphuric lake** (sŭl-fyoor´ĭk): a lake of sulfur, which is a pale-yellow, nonmetallic element occurring widely in nature and used to make gunpowder, rubber, medicines, etc.
[2] **bask** (băsk): to expose oneself to pleasant warmth.
[3] **mote** (mōt): a very small particle; a speck.

You have to fight magic with magic. You have to believe
10 That you have something impossible up your sleeve,
The language of snakes, perhaps, an invisible cloak,
An army of ants at your beck, or a lethal[4] joke,
The will to do whatever must be done:
Marry a monster.[5] Hand over your firstborn son.[6]

---

[4] **lethal** (lē´thəl): causing or capable of causing death.
[5] **Marry a monster:** perhaps a reference to Beauty and the Beast.
[6] **Hand over your firstborn son:** in the popular fairy tale "Rumpelstiltskin," a queen promises her firstborn son in exchange for straw spun into gold.

NOTICE & NOTE

ANALYZE THE EFFECTS OF METER AND STRUCTURAL ELEMENTS IN POEMS

Annotate: Mark any alliteration or other repetition of sounds or words in lines 9–11.

Analyze: How do these elements affect your understanding of the poem?

CHECK YOUR UNDERSTANDING

Answer these questions about "Fairy-tale Logic" before moving on to the **Analyze the Texts** section on the following page.

1 In the first stanza, the speaker gives —

   A ways to overcome hard obstacles

   B remedies for the bad things that happen in fairy tales

   C lessons people can learn from stories

   D examples of tasks given in fairy tales

2 The line <u>The will to do whatever must be done</u> emphasizes what idea?

   F People should be brave when in danger.

   G People should not be scared to read fairy tales.

   H Fairy tales show characters taking big risks.

   J Fairy tales have characters that study a lot.

3 What is an important idea in the poem?

   A The impossible is actually possible.

   B It is easy to use magic.

   C Fairy tales are popular stories.

   D Fairy tales are for children.

RESPOND

ANALYZE THE TEXTS

Support your responses with evidence from the texts. 📓 NOTEBOOK

1. **Synthesize** Review stanza 1 of "Archetype." Why do you think the author began with this particular question? What does the question reveal about the poem's speaker?

2. **Interpret** Read aloud lines 12–16 of "Archetype." Notice the line breaks and line lengths. What effects do these structural elements have on how you read and understand the poem?

3. **Analyze** Read lines 1–8 of "Fairy-tale Logic" aloud quietly. Notice the words and syllables that you seem to stress naturally, as well as the end-rhyming words in each line. What is the effect of these elements? What ideas are emphasized by this structure?

4. **Connect** Reread lines 13–14 of "Fairy-tale Logic," along with the footnotes. What idea or theme do the allusions help reveal? Explain.

5. **Notice & Note** Reread stanza 2 of "Archetype." What thoughts and ideas surprise you? What do these contrasts and contradictions reveal about the poem's speaker and theme?

RESEARCH

"Archetype" and "Fairy-tale Logic" allude to, or refer to, other texts, especially to fairy tales. The Brothers Grimm and Hans Christian Andersen are among the most recognized writers of fairy tales. Complete the chart below with details about these writers and their works.

RESEARCH TIP
When you conduct online research, start by searching with key words, or in this case, the names of the writers you are researching. Often there are official sites dedicated to famous writers, which are good sites to begin your research. Once you complete background reading, extend your search using the information you learned.

QUESTION	ANSWER
Which sources did the Grimm brothers use for their first collection of fairy tales?	
Which Grimm brothers stories have you read or do you recognize?	
How did Hans Christian Andersen influence other writers?	
Which stories by Hans Christian Andersen are most familiar to you?	

Extend Read an unfamiliar story by the Brothers Grimm or Hans Christian Andersen. Discuss the story with your partner and make connections to other stories or to your personal experiences.

RESPOND

CREATE AND DISCUSS

Paraphrase Lines in a Poem Choose a set of lines in either "Archetype" or "Fairy-tale Logic" to paraphrase.

❏ Carefully reread the lines you selected, and then write your paraphrase of the lines.

❏ Be sure to capture the meaning of the lines, rephrase the meaning in your own words, and present the paraphrase in logical order.

Have a Group Discussion In a small group, discuss the meanings and messages of your favorite fairy tales or stories from childhood. The following points will help your group discussion:

❏ Discuss the possible purposes for the stories you discuss.

❏ Make connections to the stories, drawing on your own personal experience and knowledge.

❏ Make connections to other stories and their role in society.

❏ Listen attentively during the discussion, take notes, and discuss points of agreement and disagreement in a constructive and respectful way.

Go to **Using Textual Evidence: Summarizing, Paraphrasing, and Quoting** in the **Writing Studio** for more on paraphrasing.

Go to **Participating in Collaborative Discussions** in the **Speaking and Listening Studio** for more on having a group discussion.

RESPOND TO THE ESSENTIAL QUESTION

? What hidden truths about people and the world are revealed in stories?

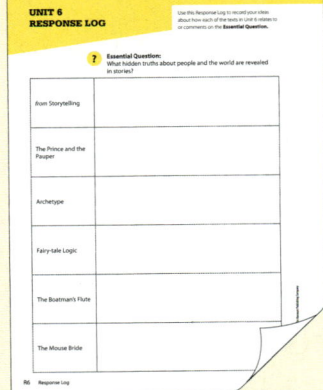

Gather Information Review your annotations and notes on "Archetype" and "Fairy-tale Logic." Then, add relevant details to your Response Log. As you determine which information to include, think about:

- what these poems reveal about stories
- what the poems reveal about society and the world
- how stories affect your own life

At the end of the unit, use your notes to write a short story or folktale.

ACADEMIC VOCABULARY

As you write and discuss what you learned from the poems, be sure to use the Academic Vocabulary words. Check off each of the words that you use.

❏ emphasize
❏ occur
❏ period
❏ relevant
❏ tradition

Archetype / Fairy-tale Logic   467

RESPOND

ARCHETYPE
Poem by Margarita Engle

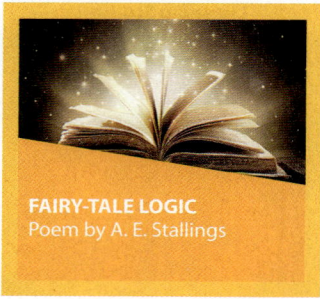

FAIRY-TALE LOGIC
Poem by A. E. Stallings

Collaborate & Compare

INFER THEMES WITHIN AND ACROSS TEXTS

Poems may have similar topics but express different themes. A **topic** is the work's subject. The work's **theme** is its message about life or human nature. Look at the following examples:

> Statement of topic: **The poem is about two friends who fight a lot.**

> Statement of theme: **Friendships can be difficult when personalities clash.**

The first example tells what the poem is about, so it states a topic, not a theme. The second example states a theme because it expresses general ideas about human nature and experience.

When you compare two texts' themes, you can draw on **explicit** (stated directly) or **implicit** (stated indirectly, or implied) information. Then you can identify similar or contrasting themes suggested in the two selections. Always use evidence from the poems to support your stated themes. Work in a small group to complete a Comparison Chart like the one that follows.

	ARCHETYPE	FAIRY-TALE LOGIC
Inferences about Theme		
Text Evidence		

ANALYZE THE TEXTS

Discuss these questions in your group.

1. **Compare** In what ways are the poems similar and different?

2. **Interpret** Both poems mention fairy tales and other stories. How does each poem use these references to reveal ideas?

3. **Connect** Which poem do you connect with more? Why?

4. **Evaluate** The poem "Archetype" names specific characters from other stories, while "Fairy-tale Logic" indirectly refers to other characters. Which use do you find more effective? Why?

COMPARE THEMES

Your group will continue to explore the themes in these poems, using evidence to support your inferences. Follow these steps:

1. **Review** In your group, review the comparison chart you created for the poems.

2. **Write Theme Statements** Use information from the chart to write a theme statement for each poem. Be sure to state each theme in a complete sentence.

Theme Statements:

"Archetype"

_____

_____

"Fairy-tale Logic"

_____

_____

3. **Compare and Contrast** Discuss similarities and differences in the themes you've identified.

4. **Connect** Share your personal opinions about these themes based on your knowledge and experience.

5. **Identify** Take notes on what others say. Do you agree or disagree? Identify points of agreement and disagreement and discuss.

6. **Share** Share your ideas with the larger group.

RESPOND

Go to the **Speaking and Listening Studio** for help with having a group discussion.

COLLABORATE & COMPARE

FOLKTALE
THE BOATMAN'S FLUTE
retold by **Sherry Garland**
pages 473–479

COMPARE THEMES

As you read, notice how the authors use plot structure and point of view to share their ideas. Pay attention to how the characters in each tale think, behave, and grow. Look for ideas and other ways that the two stories are similar to and different from each other. After you read both selections, you will work with a small group to complete a project.

 ESSENTIAL QUESTION:

What hidden truths about people and the world are revealed in stories?

FOLKTALE
THE MOUSE BRIDE
retold by **Heather Forest**
pages 487–495

470 Unit 6

The Boatman's Flute

QUICK START

Think of stories you've read that reveal a hidden truth. How did the writers reveal the truths about the world or the people involved? List a few of these stories and discuss their messages with a partner.

ANALYZE PLOT

A **plot** is a series of events in a story that center on a **conflict**—a struggle of opposing forces faced by the main character. Characters' **external** and **internal responses** to conflict, including their actions, decisions, and thoughts and feelings, help develop the plot. As you read, use the chart to identify the different stages of the plot.

PLOT STAGE	DESCRIPTION
Exposition	the first stage of plot that introduces setting and characters and provides background information
Rising Action	the events and complications that increase conflict
Climax	the point of greatest interest, where the conflict results in an important decision or action
Falling Action	the events that happen as a result of the climax
Resolution	the presentation of how the central conflict is solved

GENRE ELEMENTS: FOLKTALE
- originates in the oral tradition of a culture
- is often set in the culture of origin
- takes place in the distant past
- includes simple but powerful themes
- focuses on human strengths and weaknesses

IDENTIFY POINT OF VIEW

The **narrator** is the voice that tells the story. A writer's choice of narrator establishes **point of view.** Use the chart to help identify the point of view of the story. As you read, think about how the point of view affects your understanding of the story.

FIRST-PERSON POINT OF VIEW	THIRD-PERSON POINT OF VIEW
The narrator is a character in the story.	The narrator is not a character in the story.
The narrator uses the pronouns *I, me,* and *my*.	The narrator uses the pronouns *he, she,* and *they* to refer to the characters.
The narrator does not know what other characters are thinking and feeling.	A **third-person limited** narrator knows the thoughts and feelings of just one character, usually the main character. A **third-person omniscient** narrator knows what all of the characters think and feel.

GET READY

CRITICAL VOCABULARY

seamstress   courtyard   convince   commit   sincere   politeness

To preview the Critical Vocabulary words, replace each boldfaced vocabulary word with a word or words that have the same meaning.

1. He took the torn shirt to the (**seamstress**) _____ for repairs.

2. The museum had a (**courtyard**) _____ on the ground floor.

3. I tried to (**convince**) _____ my friend to walk with me.

4. If you (**commit**) _____ too many fouls, you will be removed from the game.

5. Her sister didn't think she was (**sincere**) _____ in her apology.

6. She thinks (**politeness**) _____ is important.

LANGUAGE CONVENTIONS

Quotation marks are used to set off a speaker's exact words. They are also used to set off the title of a story, an article, a short poem, an essay, a song, or a chapter. Punctuation marks, such as commas, question marks, and periods, appear inside the quotation marks.

ANNOTATION MODEL

NOTICE & NOTE

As you read, mark evidence that indicates plot and point of view in the folktale. You can also mark words and phrases that support your own ideas. Here are one reader's notes on the beginning of "The Boatman's Flute."

1   Once, in the <u>Land of Small Dragon</u>, a wealthy <u>mandarin</u> lived in a <u>large mansion</u> on top of a hill overlooking a peaceful river. The mandarin had only one <u>daughter</u>, and her face was as beautiful as lotus blossoms in pale moonlight that floated atop the river.

I think this is the exposition because it introduces the story, setting, and characters.

BACKGROUND

Sherry Garland *(b. 1948) is an award-winning author of more than thirty books for children, teens, and adults. She has written several books focusing on the people and country of Vietnam, where she has traveled and done research. In her home state of Texas, she has worked with Vietnamese immigrants, helping them to relocate. The selection "The Boatman's Flute" is a folktale that she retold in her book* Children of the Dragon: Selected Tales from Vietnam *(2001).*

THE BOATMAN'S FLUTE

Folktale retold by Sherry Garland

PREPARE TO COMPARE

As you read, pay attention to what the characters think they want in the beginning of the folktale. Does what they want change during the course of the story?

1   Once, in the Land of Small Dragon, a wealthy mandarin[1] lived in a large mansion on top of a hill overlooking a peaceful river. The mandarin had only one daughter, and her face was as beautiful as lotus blossoms[2] in pale moonlight that floated atop the river.

2   The mandarin loved his daughter dearly and feared for her safety so much that all her life he had never allowed her to leave the mansion. She spent her days and nights in her room, high above the river, watching the world below. Servants brought her the most delicious dishes, and talented

---

[1] **mandarin** (măn´də-rĭn): a member of an elite group, especially a person having influence or high status in intellectual or cultural circles.
[2] **lotus blossoms:** flowers of the lotus, symbolic of purity.

NOTICE & NOTE

Notice & Note

Use the side margins to notice and note signposts in the text.

ANALYZE PLOT

Annotate: In paragraph 2, mark what you learn about the mandarin's relationship with his daughter.

Predict: How do you think the mandarin's actions might influence the plot?

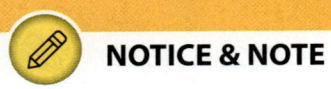

NOTICE & NOTE

seamstress
(sĕm´strĭs) *n.* A *seamstress* is a woman who sews, especially one who earns a living sewing.

courtyard
(kôrt´yärd´) *n.* A *courtyard* is an area enclosed by walls and open to the sky.

IDENTIFY POINT OF VIEW

Annotate: Review paragraphs 5–8 and mark pronouns that help you identify the folktale's point of view.

Analyze: What kind of narrator uses this point of view? How does this point of view affect your understanding? Explain.

seamstresses sewed her the finest gowns of silk. Musicians and poets sang to her the ballads of old.

3   But never had the beautiful girl walked barefoot on the dewy green grass nor plucked ripe fruit from a tree nor run along the banks of the river, flying kites and laughing like other children. The only sunlight that ever touched her fair skin was the few pale beams that peeked through the dappled shade in the walled-in **courtyard.**

4   One day the mandarin's daughter sat beside her window looking at the small boats and sampans[3] gliding over the peaceful blue waters below. Some were loaded with fresh fruit from the mountains, others with bags of rice or baskets of fish, and some ferried passengers back and forth across the river.

5   As she watched the activity below, one small *ghe*[4] caught her eye. The boatman stood up and skillfully steered the *ghe* out into deeper water with a long bamboo pole, then he sat down. He placed a bamboo flute to his lips and soon the most haunting, beautiful melody the girl had ever heard drifted up to her window. It was the sound of rippling waters and cool breezes, of tall bamboo and the night bird's song, all woven together. She watched the boatman, and as she listened to the sweet notes rise and fall, she imagined how young, strong, and handsome he must be.

6   All that day the mandarin's daughter stayed beside the window, until the sun began to set over the western mountain and the boatman steered his *ghe* away out of sight.

7   That night she dreamed of the strange melody and imagined herself stepping into the boat beside the young man, whose strong arms lifted her aboard with grace and ease. In her dream they drifted along the peaceful river by the light of a full moon. The boatman explained to her all the strange and wonderful sights that unfolded before them. She experienced things that she had only heard about from the poets — the sweet touch of the cool river waters on her hands trailing beside the boat, the gentle kiss of the night wind against her flushed cheeks, and the tingling fragrance of wild orchids hanging from trees in the nearby jungle.

8   A smile flickered across her lips, even as she slept. She dreamed of climbing out of the boat and running barefoot through the thick green grass and plucking wild berries that

---
[3] **sampans:** flatbottom Asian boats usually propelled by two oars.
[4] **ghe:** a small boat.

burst with a sour, tangy taste on her tongue. And when a green-eyed tiger roared deep in the jungle, the boatman held her tight.

9   The girl awakened to the sound of a brass gong. Without even stopping to taste the tray of delicacies laid out before her by her devoted handmaiden, the mandarin's daughter walked to the window and looked below. Her heart beat faster when she spotted the little boat and heard the haunting music floating up to the window once again.

10   All day she remained by the window, until she knew the tunes he played by heart. Whenever the boat came close to the foot of the hill, she dropped flower petals, hoping the wind would carry them to the boatman. If ever he looked in her direction, she waved her long silk scarf. She became **convinced** that he played the tunes just for her.

11   Every day the mandarin's daughter listened to the boatman's melodies, often making up her own words to sing along. Or she danced with her shadow, pretending it was the strong, young boatman. Every night she dreamed of riding down the peaceful river by his side. She knew that her father was planning for her to marry soon and prayed that somehow the boatman was really a lord in disguise who would be the one her father chose.

12   As for the boatman, he had seen a tiny figure at the window and had caught the petals floating down from above. He could only guess what the girl might look like or who she might be, but just knowing that she was listening made him pour his heart and soul into the melodies.

convince
(kən-vĭns´) v. To *convince* is to use argument or evidence to get someone to believe or be certain about something.

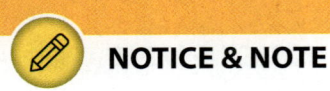

NOTICE & NOTE

LANGUAGE CONVENTIONS
Annotate: Mark the quotation marks in paragraphs 13–15.

Predict: What does the introduction of dialogue signal about the plot? What conflict does the dialogue reveal?

ANALYZE PLOT
Annotate: Mark the words that the boatman thinks to himself in paragraph 16.

Analyze: Which part of the plot is this? How does the storyteller use this view into the boatman's thoughts—his internal response to events—to develop the plot?

IDENTIFY POINT OF VIEW
Annotate: In paragraph 20, mark the sentence or sentences that focus on the handmaiden's role in this part of the story.

Analyze: How does the story's point of view affect your understanding of why the handmaiden acts as she does?

commit
(kə-mĭt´) v. To *commit* is to do or perform an action.

13   One day a gentleman he was ferrying across the river noticed the fine quality of the music. "Boatman, for whom do you play your little bamboo flute with such love and feeling? I see no maidens nearby."

14   The boatman smiled timidly and looked upward. "I do not know her name, but she comes to the window in that house high above the river every day and often drops flowers to show her approval."

15   The gentleman looked up toward the window, then laughed aloud. "You are a fool, young boatman. That is the mandarin's daughter—the most beautiful girl in all our land and one who is sought after by the most wealthy and powerful men, including myself. How could you be so foolish to think she would ever love a common, plain boatman like yourself?"

16   The boatman said nothing but sadly put away his flute and steered the boat down the river, for it was growing dark. *Better that I should leave now, while she is but a vision in my mind,* he told himself. *If ever I see her face, I will never have peace again.*

17   So it was that the boatman decided not to go to that part of the river anymore.

18   The next morning, when she went to the window, the mandarin's daughter did not see the small *ghe*. She thought of ten thousand excuses why the boatman might be late. As the day wore on, he still did not come. The girl's heart grew heavy and tears dropped from her dark, sad eyes. She refused to lie on her bed that night but instead knelt beside the window, staring at the dark river below.

19   Another day passed and the boatman did not come, and by nightfall the girl was weak from hunger and weeping. She soon fell ill. The servants placed her on her bed and summoned her father. The mandarin called in the best physicians, but they could find nothing wrong with her. As another day passed, the mandarin grew distraught.

20   Seeing the mandarin weep over his daughter, the girl's handmaiden could not hold her tongue another moment. She told the mandarin about the boatman who played tunes on his flute that seemed to make the girl very happy. The mandarin ordered his servants to search the river for a man in a small *ghe* playing a bamboo flute.

21   Soon the men returned with the boatman and his flute. He trembled before the wealthy mandarin, wondering what crime he had **committed**.

476   Unit 6

22 "Are you the young man who has been passing under my window playing tunes upon your flute for many days past?" the mandarin demanded.

23 "Yes, but I meant no harm. If I have broken a law, it was in complete ignorance. I only played the tunes to pass the long day and because it seemed to please the girl in the window. If I disturbed your household, I beg forgiveness and promise to never bother you again."

24 "It is no bother," the mandarin replied, as he studied the **sincere** young boatman. "It seems that your simple music has charmed my daughter. Now she is deathly ill, and I pray that your tunes will restore her spirit. I have been searching the lands for the finest husband for my daughter, but if fate has something else in store, who am I to question? Play your flute again, and if my daughter chooses you above all others, then so be it."

25 The boatman stood amazed. Never in his wildest dreams had he imagined that he might become the husband of this girl so rare in beauty that no man had ever been allowed to gaze upon her face. With a surge of hope in his heart, he raised the flute to his lips with trembling fingers, and he began to play his favorite melody. Soon the tender, warm notes filled the empty halls of the grand house and reached the bed where the girl lay. In a moment she opened her eyes and a smile touched her lips.

26 "He has returned," she whispered, and she begged the handmaiden to help her to her feet. With renewed energy, the girl walked through the house to the source of the music. At first her heart pounded as she saw the strong, young man from afar. But as she came nearer and saw his face, her eyes grew cold. Though his body was young and strong, the boatman's face was ugly. Out of **politeness**, she gave a slight bow.

27 "Thank you for playing the lovely music on your flute. I feel much better now. Father, please pay the boatman for his kindness and do not worry about me. I am over my illness." Quickly she returned to her room and once again looked out the window at the boats coming and going on the river below, wondering how she could have been so foolish to dream about a simple boatman.

28 But the boatman's heart was torn apart. He had gazed on a face that men see only in their dreams. He refused to take the bag of gold the mandarin offered, and left the mansion with heavy footsteps. No longer did he have the desire to play his flute, for the music reminded him of the beautiful girl. Neither

sincere
(sĭn-sîr´) *adj.* Something or someone *sincere* is genuine or heartfelt.

politeness
(pə-līt´nəs) *n. Politeness* is respectful behavior.

CONTRASTS AND CONTRADICTIONS

Notice & Note: How does the girl's attitude toward the boatman change? Mark and read aloud the dialogue spoken by the girl in paragraph 27.

Analyze: Why does the girl act this way? What does the change reveal about her?

NOTICE & NOTE

did he have the spirit to work on the peaceful river, for it, too, reminded him of the girl. Everything he saw or did caused his heart to ache with great longing for the girl that he knew could never love him. Finally, many months later, he lay down and died of a broken heart.

29   When friends and relatives prepared to send the boatman's body down the river in a farewell voyage, they saw that it was gone. But in its place, where his heart would have been, lay an exquisite piece of green jade.⁵ A relative took the jade to a carver, who shaped it into a beautiful drinking goblet.

30   Sometime later the relative sold the goblet to the mandarin, who gave it to his daughter. That night the girl's handmaiden served her cool water in the new gift. As the girl lifted the jade goblet to her lips she thought she heard a melancholy tune that she had not heard for a very long time — something that was both sad and lovely. Then, as she sipped the water, she saw in the bottom of the cup the image of a small *ghe* and the young boatman steering it down the peaceful river.

31   Suddenly the girl remembered the boatman's sweet music. She thought about all the happy hours she had spent listening to his flute and the wonderful dreams she had dreamed because of him. Since he had left, no one, not even the most handsome suitors⁶ in the land, had made her feel such warmth and happiness. Now, it seemed her days and nights were even longer and more empty than before.

32   Her heart ached with remorse, and tears filled her eyes.

33   "Dear boatman, your love was the truest I have ever known. You were good and kind, and I made a terrible mistake. Wherever you are, please forgive me," she whispered. A single teardrop slid down the girl's petal-smooth cheek into the goblet. When the tear touched the water, the goblet burst into pieces and a breeze suddenly rushed in through the window. The girl saw a thin wisp of fog rise from the shattered goblet and sail out into the night. The sound of a flute blended with the sound of the night bird's song, but this time the tune was full of joy. The boatman's soul was free at last to go in peace.

MEMORY MOMENT

Notice & Note: What triggers, or sets off, memories for the girl? In paragraphs 30–31, mark her memories.

Evaluate: How do the girl's memories at this time in the story affect its plot?

ANALYZE PLOT

Annotate: Mark the words that the girl speaks in paragraph 33.

Analyze: Which part of the plot is this? How have the story's events affected the girl?

---

⁵ **green jade:** a type of jade, a precious stone, believed to promote wisdom, balance, and peace.
⁶ **suitor** (sōō´tər): someone who tries to gain the love and attention of another person.

CHECK YOUR UNDERSTANDING

Answer these questions before moving on to the **Analyze the Text** section on the following page.

1 The mandarin's daughter dreams of riding in a boat with the boatman of the *ghe*. In her dream she —

   A traveled across a wide and stormy lake

   B experienced nature the way it had been expressed by poets

   C heard a strange bird song that was new to her

   D received a tray of delicacies to eat with the boatman

2 The boatman decides not to return to the part of river where he played to the mandarin's daughter because —

   F a gentleman he ferried across the river tells him he will report him to the mandarin

   G he learns that the mandarin's daughter is married

   H he knows if he sees her face again he'll never have peace

   J he has fruit and rice that he needs to deliver downriver

3 When the mandarin's daughter drinks from the jade cup —

   A she realizes she should have married the boatman

   B she decides to go in search of the boatman

   C she remembers the boatman's music and the dreams she had

   D she drops the goblet and it shatters

The Boatman's Flute

RESPOND

ANALYZE THE TEXT

Support your responses with evidence from the text. **NOTEBOOK**

1. **Summarize** How does the writer build the action in paragraphs 13–18? Describe how the writer uses the narrator's point of view to create conflict in this part of the rising action.

2. **Analyze** Reread paragraphs 16–17. How do the boatman's internal and external responses to conflict—his thoughts and actions—affect the development of the plot?

3. **Evaluate** Reread paragraphs 24–27. Consider the role of conflict at the climax of a story. In what ways can you identify this passage as the story's climax?

4. **Interpret** Reread from paragraph 28 to the end of the story. Describe the falling action in the story's plot. At what point does the falling action become the story's resolution?

5. **Notice & Note** Contrast the behavior of the mandarin's daughter in paragraph 18 with her behavior in paragraph 27. Why did the character act so differently in these two parts of the story?

RESEARCH

RESEARCH TIP
If you are searching for a phrase, put the words in quotation marks. For example, search "folktale structure" to bring up more targeted results.

"The Boatman's Flute" is a folktale from Vietnam. Folktales are stories from a culture's oral tradition—in other words, they were told aloud and were often passed down from one generation to another.

In a small group, research common elements of folktales. Find two or three examples of stories from different parts of the world. Use a chart like the one below to record each story's topic, structure, and tropes, or figures of speech. For example, "beautiful as lotus blossoms in pale moonlight" is a trope, or figure of speech, particular to this Vietnamese folktale.

COUNTRY OF ORIGIN	TITLE	TOPIC	STRUCTURE	TROPES

Connect With a small group, discuss how the discoveries you made in your folktale research connect to the story "The Boatman's Flute."

RESPOND

CREATE AND DISCOVER

A Different Point of View Reread the story's ending, starting at paragraph 28. Imagine you are the boatman and tell the ending from his point of view.

❑ Rewrite the last paragraphs of the story from the boatman's point of view, in the first person, beginning with "My heart was torn apart."
❑ Be sure to include dialogue.
❑ Edit your work to make sure you use quotation marks correctly.
❑ If you stall or get stuck, try reading the last paragraphs aloud, as if you are telling the story as the boatman, using "I."

Share Your Writing Gather in a small group to share your writing. When everyone has shared, discuss how the shift in point of view affects the story and its plot.

❑ Maintain eye contact as much as possible when presenting your story ending.
❑ Speak clearly, at a rate and volume that allows everyone to hear you.
❑ Speak at a pace that allows your listeners to follow you easily.
❑ Use an appropriate stance and gestures while speaking.
❑ Listen actively to each presenter and ask questions to help clarify understanding.

Go to **Writing Narratives: Point of View and Characters** in the **Writing Studio** for more on writing narrative texts, or stories.

Go to **Giving a Presentation: Delivering Your Presentation** in the **Speaking and Listening Studio** for help with presenting your writing.

RESPOND TO THE ESSENTIAL QUESTION

 What hidden truths about people and the world are revealed in stories?

Gather Information Review your annotations and notes on "The Boatman's Flute." Then, add relevant details to your Response Log. As you determine which information to include, think about:

- the plot elements
- how the internal and external responses of the characters affects the development of the plot
- whether or not you were surprised by the story's resolution

At the end of the unit, use your notes to write a short story or folktale.

ACADEMIC VOCABULARY

As you write and discuss what you learned from the selection, be sure to use the Academic Vocabulary words. Check off each of the words that you use.

❑ emphasize
❑ occur
❑ period
❑ relevant
❑ tradition

The Boatman's Flute

RESPOND

WORD BANK
- seamstress
- courtyard
- convince
- commit
- sincere
- politeness

Go to **Analyzing Word Structure** in the **Vocabulary Studio** for more on bases, roots, and affixes.

CRITICAL VOCABULARY

Practice and Apply Answer each question using a Critical Vocabulary word in a complete sentence.

1. How can you get your parents to agree to take you and your friends out for dinner?
2. If you don't know how to sew and you tear your coat, how can you repair it?
3. Where might you find a safe place to set up a basketball hoop in a busy neighborhood with lots of street traffic?
4. What characteristic is valuable in avoiding an argument?
5. What is the opposite of being deceptive?
6. Why do drivers receive traffic violations, or tickets?

VOCABULARY STRATEGY:
Word Structure

The **base** of a word is the part of the word that can stand alone. For example, the base of the word *politeness* is *polite*.

Many words in the English language have Greek or Latin **roots.** You can check a print or digital dictionary to learn about the roots of words. The entry for a word often gives details about the word's origin, or etymology. If you can identify a Greek or Latin root, such as *hydro* ("water") or *bio* ("life"), in a word you don't know, you have a clue to what the word means.

An **affix** is a letter or group of letters that changes a word's meaning. Affixes can take the form of **prefixes** added to the beginning of a root or base, or **suffixes** added to the end of a root or base. The word *convince,* for instance, comes from Latin. Its affix is the Latin prefix *con-,* which means "with." The Latin base is *vincere,* meaning "to conquer."

Use a dictionary to complete the chart.

WORD	BASE OF THE WORD	PREFIX OR SUFFIX	LATIN OR GREEK ROOT
seamstress			
commit			
sincere			

482 Unit 6

RESPOND

LANGUAGE CONVENTIONS:
Quotation Marks

Quotation marks are punctuation used to set off a speaker's exact words. Quotation marks are helpful in distinguishing narration from dialogue. For example, "The Boatman's Flute" begins with narration, and later includes dialogue between characters. The dialogue—set off with quotation marks—offers a break from the narration and brings variety and life to the writing. Use quotation marks whenever you want to express exactly what a person or character is saying.

Follow these basic rules when writing dialogue.

> Insert a question mark or exclamation mark inside the end quotes, or final quotation marks:
> **"How are you?" I asked.**
> Insert a comma before the end quotes and name the speaker after the end quotes:
> **"I'm hungry," said Henry.**
> To write a line of dialogue without naming the speaker, place the period, question mark, or exclamation point within the end quotes:
> **"Let's eat!"**
> In dialogue, begin a new paragraph each time the speaker changes.

Practice and Apply Reread the dialogue between the mandarin and the boatman in paragraphs 22–24 and study the punctuation. Then add quotations and punctuation to the following dialogue between these characters: a mother and her two daughters. The mother is unnamed, and the two daughters are Lila and Lala.

Bring the wood in for the fire and hurry up, Lila! My arms are full already, yelled Lila. Lala, help your sister unload her basket and bring the wood in before it rains! Do I have to do it now? Lila whined to her mother. Her mother yelled impatiently, Yes!

> Go to **Punctuation: Underlining, Quotation Marks, Apostrophes** in the **Grammar Studio** for more on using quotation marks.

COLLABORATE & COMPARE

FOLKTALE
THE MOUSE BRIDE
retold by **Heather Forest**
pages 487–495

COMPARE THEMES

Now that you've read "The Boatman's Flute," read "The Mouse Bride" to see how the characters and plot of this folktale from Finland compare to those in the folktale from Vietnam. Think about the stories' themes and how they are alike and different.

ESSENTIAL QUESTION:

What hidden truths about people and the world are revealed in stories?

FOLKTALE
THE BOATMAN'S FLUTE
retold by **Sherry Garland**
pages 473–479

The Mouse Bride

GET READY

QUICK START

Do you know someone who has been taunted or teased for making an unpopular choice? Would you let the possibility of being teased affect how you decide something? Discuss your thoughts with a partner.

INFER THEME

A text's **theme** is its message or big idea about life or human nature. Folktales often contain more than one theme; they may contain **multiple themes.** Some stories reveal their themes directly, but readers usually must **infer,** or make logical guesses about, a work's message based on evidence. In folktales, writers often use the thoughts, words, and actions of their characters to convey theme. To make inferences about theme in folktales, ask yourself:

- What do the characters want and how do they get what they want?
- How well do they succeed and why?
- How do the characters in the story compare to one another?

As you consider these questions, think about what the answers reveal about each character. Then, consider how the writer uses characterization to develop conflict and plot while expressing theme.

GENRE ELEMENTS: FOLKTALE
- includes universal themes
- often features the "rule of three"—characters or events happen in groups of three
- may include supernatural events
- may feature animals or superhuman beings as characters

ANALYZE PURPOSE AND TEXT STRUCTURE

Author's purpose is the main reason an author writes a text. The purpose may be to inform, entertain, persuade, or express thoughts and feelings. Often the purpose of a folktale is to teach some sort of lesson about an aspect of life. To avoid confusing purpose with theme, remember that *purpose* is why the author decided to write, while *theme* is the message the author shared. You can analyze purpose by examining what happens at key points in the plot; then, ask yourself: Why is the author telling me this?

This chart shows how to use exposition to help you analyze the author's purpose. Use a chart like this to think about what the rising action, climax, falling action, and resolution reveal about purpose.

PLOT ELEMENT	WHAT HAPPENS	HINT ABOUT PURPOSE
Exposition	I am introduced to one kind brother and two mean brothers.	The contrast between brothers may teach me something.

The Mouse Bride

GET READY

CRITICAL VOCABULARY

| amazement | enchanting | deceptive | regal | elegant |

To see how many Critical Vocabulary words you already know, use them to complete the sentences.

1. Playing the part of a king, the actor's costume was _____ .

2. The _____ gift came in a tasteful box tied with velvet ribbon.

3. The spectacular colors of the sunset fill me with _____.

4. The story was so _____ that I could not stop reading it.

5. To hide his identity, the thief responded with a _____ answer.

LANGUAGE CONVENTIONS

A **modifier** changes or modifies the meaning of another word in a sentence. **Adjectives** and **adjective phrases** or clauses modify nouns and pronouns. For example, the adjective phrase in boldface modifies *matter:*

Dark matter, **which is still unexplained,** is a subject of research.

Adverbs and **adverbial phrases** indicate time, place, manner, or cause. For example, the adverbial phrase in boldface modifies *waiting:*

I've been waiting for the bus to arrive **for 25 minutes.**

As you read, look for how the author uses modifiers to clarify ideas.

ANNOTATION MODEL

NOTICE & NOTE

As you read, mark any words and phrases that might help you infer the folktale's theme. Mark useful information about the characters and plot events. Here are one student's notes on the beginning of "The Mouse Bride."

1 Long ago, when the world was filled with wonder, there was a farmer who had three sons. The two older sons took pleasure in teasing their youngest brother, who was so kindhearted he could not even sweep a spider from the cobwebs in the corner.

Introduction = Exposition

The story seems to be using the rule of three. Details about the brothers: two are mean and one is kind.

BACKGROUND

Heather Forest (b. 1948) *is an award-winning author, storyteller, and musician. In her storytelling, she incorporates many different elements, including poetry, prose, guitar, and song. When she begins working on a story to tell, she starts by singing the story until she gets just the right rhythm and feeling she is after. She lives on a small family farm in Huntington, New York, with her husband. The selection "The Mouse Bride" is a folktale from Finland that she retold in her book* Wonder Tales from Around the World *(1995).*

THE MOUSE BRIDE

retold by Heather Forest

PREPARE TO COMPARE

As you read, pay attention to the father character in this story and consider how he compares with the father in the "The Boatman's Flute." Notice any similarities or differences between point of view in these two stories.

Notice & Note

Use the side margins to notice and note signposts in the text.

1 Long ago, when the world was filled with wonder, there was a farmer who had three sons. The two older sons took pleasure in teasing their youngest brother, who was so kindhearted he could not even sweep a spider from the cobwebs in the corner.

2 Now one day the farmer brought his sons to a field where three trees stood. "It is time for you to be wed," he said. "Each of you must cut down a sapling.[1] When it falls, walk forward in the direction it points, and you will find your sweetheart."

---

[1] **sapling:** a young tree.

NOTICE & NOTE

3   The oldest son cut the largest sapling and it fell pointing north. "What luck!" he shouted, "I know of a fine maiden who lives in a house just north of here. I will go and ask for her hand in marriage."

4   The next oldest son cut a sapling and it fell pointing south. "I too shall live in happiness," said the second son, "for there is a delightful young woman who lives in a house just south of here. I will go and ask her to be my bride!"

5   But when the youngest son cut his sapling, it pointed towards the forest where there were no houses at all.

6   "You'll find a pointy-eared sweetheart with sharp teeth in that forest," laughed his two brothers.

7   "I will trust fate and my chances," said the youngest son. He carved a beautiful walking stick from the tree and set off in the direction of the woods.

8   The young man had not gone far into the forest when he came upon a cottage made of gray logs. He knocked on the door. A pleasant voice said, "Enter, please."

9   When he walked inside, he looked everywhere but saw no one.

10   "Here I am!" said the voice, "I am so glad to have company. I have been very lonely."

11   The young man stared in **amazement**. There on the table was a dainty blue-eyed mouse with its gray fur as sleek as velvet.

12   "You can speak!" the young man said.

13   "Certainly I can speak, but I prefer to sing," she said gaily, and she began a lively tune. The young man applauded her song, amazed. Then she curtsied² and asked, "What brings you here?"

14   "I am searching for a sweetheart," he replied.

15   "Well then, how about me?" said the mouse.

16   "You are not exactly the type of sweetheart I was seeking," said the young man politely as he turned to leave.

17   "Oh," she sighed, "I am sad to hear that, for I have longed to meet someone just like you." She began such an **enchanting** love song, the young man stood motionless at the door.

18   "Please don't stop," he pleaded when she finished her song. "I want that song to go on and on ... Strange as it seems, perhaps you could be my sweetheart."

ANALYZE PURPOSE AND TEXT STRUCTURE
Annotate: Mark the statement the youngest son makes in paragraph 7.

Interpret: Describe what element of the plot this paragraph represents and what it might tell you about the author's purpose.

amazement
(ə-māz´mənt) n. *Amazement* is a state of extreme surprise or wonder.

TOUGH QUESTIONS
Notice & Note: Why might the young man have difficulty answering the mouse's question in paragraph 15?

Infer: Consider what you know about the young man and the story so far. Why might the author have the mouse pose such a question?

enchanting
(ĕn-chăn´tĭng) *adj.* Something or someone *enchanting* is charming.

---

² **curtsied:** from *curtsy*, a gesture of respect made by bending knees with one foot forward and lowering the body.

19   "Then come to visit me at this time tomorrow," she said with a smile and a twitch of her silken whiskers.

20   "I promise I will return," said the young man as he left. And all the way home, his heart quickened as he thought about the mouse and her beautiful song.

21   When he arrived at the farm that evening his two brothers were bragging to their father.

22   "The woman I met has beautiful rosy cheeks," said the oldest son.

23   "The lovely maiden I met," bragged the next oldest son, "is the fairest in the countryside. Her hair is as black as a raven's wing."[3]

24   But they teased the youngest brother before he could speak a word, saying, "Who could you find in the woods but a pointy-eared, sharp-toothed beast!"

25   "I met the most enchanting singer," said the lad hesitantly, "and I cannot stop thinking about her. She has a captivating voice, sky-blue eyes, a beautiful smile, and she dresses in the very finest gray velvet. She even invited me to return tomorrow!"

26   "A princess no doubt!" the brothers shouted sarcastically. "He is making this up! Who could love him?"

27   "Congratulations to each of you on meeting sweethearts," said their father. "But attractive looks alone do not make for a happy hearth.[4] Tomorrow, I should like to see the kind of bread your sweethearts bake."

LANGUAGE CONVENTIONS
Adverbial clauses act like adverbs to modify verbs, adjectives, or adverbs. Explain what the phrase "before he could speak a word" modifies in paragraph 24.

---

[3] **as black as a raven's wing:** a raven is a large bird with glossy black feathers.
[4] **a happy hearth:** a hearth is a fireplace, which at one time represented the center of family life.

NOTICE & NOTE

28   The next morning, the youngest son set out at dawn. When he arrived at the cottage the mouse greeted him eagerly, saying, "I am delighted that you have kept your promise to return!"

29   The lad blushed with embarrassment and said, "I told my father and brothers that ever since we met, I have not been able to stop thinking about you. But I did not tell them that you are a mouse! Now my father would like to see the kind of bread you bake! Oh," he moaned, "my cruel brothers will certainly ridicule me when I arrive home tonight empty-handed!"

30   "I cannot bear to think of them mocking you! You will not go home empty-handed!" said the mouse. "Of course I can bake bread!" She clapped her paws and one hundred gray mice appeared as she commanded, "Bring me the finest grains of wheat from the field!"

31   Fascinated, the young man stayed all day watching the marvelous effort as the little mouse directed the baking of a fine loaf of wheaten bread. She sang as she worked and enraptured the young man's ears with her music. The afternoon passed so quickly with their cheerful conversation and laughter, the young man hardly noticed that the sun was setting.

32   "I must hurry and leave," he said.

33   "Please take this loaf as a gift to your father," said the mouse, waving him goodbye. "I hope that you will come again tomorrow."

34   "Of course I'll return," assured the young man, "I would rather be here than anywhere else." He traveled back home with the loaf under his arm.

35   That night around the dinner table, the oldest brother proudly handed the farmer a loaf of rye bread made by his sweetheart and boasted, "See how hearty and well-baked it is!"

36   The second oldest brother handed the farmer some barley bread made by his sweetheart and bragged, "My sweetheart's bread is crusty and healthy to eat!"

37   But when the youngest brother handed his father the fine loaf of wheaten bread the farmer exclaimed, "Wheat bread! Only the richest among us eat wheat bread!"

38   The two older brothers bickered over who was to get the biggest piece of wheat bread and said, as they stuffed their mouths, "But there's no house in that woods for miles! What kind of sweetheart could you have found?"

39   "One whose conversation can make me forget the time of day," replied the lad.

40   "I am pleased that your sweethearts bake such fine bread!" said the farmer. "Skillful hands add comfort to a

---

AGAIN AND AGAIN

Notice & Note: Why is the youngest brother's experience of time in paragraphs 31, 39, and 45 important? Mark each reference to time.

Connect: Why might the author keep repeating this particular image of time?

NOTICE & NOTE

home. Tomorrow, I should like to see the kind of cloth they can weave."

41   The next morning the lad set out again to visit the mouse in the woods.

42   "Come in!" said the little mouse when she heard him knock. She sang him a tune and a smile spread across his face.

43   "I wish you could weave as well as you bake and sing. But how could that be possible?" said the lad with a sigh. "My father would like to see the kind of cloth you make."

44   "Love makes everything possible," said the mouse, clapping her paws. Once again, one hundred mice appeared as she said, "Fetch me strands of the finest flax."[5]

45   Each mouse quickly returned with one strand of flax. The little mouse spun the flax into thread on a tiny spinning wheel.[6] The young man stared in amazement as she wove a fine piece of linen on a miniature loom.[7] They kept company all afternoon, talking and laughing while she worked. The time sped by so quickly, the sun was setting before the young man realized it.

---

[5] **flax:** a plant whose fiber is used for making linen cloth.
[6] **spinning wheel:** a device with a foot- or hand-driven wheel and single spindle, or rod, used to make thread and yarn.
[7] **wove a fine piece of linen on a miniature loom:** fine linen fabric was woven using a loom, an apparatus for weaving strands of yarn together at right angles.

NOTICE & NOTE

46   "It's done!" she finally said, folding the small patch of delicate cloth in a walnut shell. "Take it to your father as a gift and I do hope your heart brings you here tomorrow."

47   The lad left for home with the walnut shell tucked carefully in his pocket.

48   That night around the hearth fire, each brother brought forward the cloth made by their sweethearts.

49   "Here is some coarse but sturdy cotton made by my love," boasted the first brother proudly.

50   "Here is some cotton and linen weave made by my love, and it is fancier than yours!" bragged the second brother.

51   "Here is a walnut," said the youngest brother as his older brothers howled.

52   "He has no sweetheart! He's brought a forest nut instead of some cloth!" they squealed.

53   "Appearances can be **deceptive**," said the lad. "Open the nut, Father."

54   The two older brothers stopped laughing and gawked in silence as the farmer opened the shell and held up the fine web of linen. "I have never seen such delicate work," said the farmer, admiring the cloth. "Sons, I must meet your sweethearts! Bring them home tomorrow so that I may see your brides-to-be," he said.

55   The lad's face flushed red as he imagined himself presenting the little mouse to his father and brothers as his bride. "This is ridiculous!" he thought. "I cannot marry a mouse! I must seek deeper in the forest for a proper human sweetheart."

56   But in the morning, as the young man approached the cottage he could not resist stopping for a moment. He thought, "I will tell her politely that I won't be visiting anymore. I need to find one of my own kind. But then, surely I will hurt her feelings! She is the most delightful companion I've ever met. Oh, I have never been more confused!"

57   As he nervously stood at the cottage door wondering what to do, the little mouse called out, "Welcome! Come in! I have composed a love song for you!"

58   The moment he entered the room she began to sing her beautiful song. His heart swelled with joy and every doubt he had about presenting her to his family disappeared with the first tones of her sweet voice.

59   "My Father wishes to meet you," he simply said. "Please come with me to visit him."

INFER THEME
Annotate: Mark the lad's response to his brothers in paragraph 53.

Infer: What is the meaning of this response, and how might you use the response to infer a theme?

deceptive
(dĭ-sĕp´tĭv) *adj.* Something *deceptive* is giving a false impression.

60   "Very well, I shall travel in the finest style!" replied the mouse.

61   She clapped her paws and six black mice appeared, pulling a tiny coach made of a chestnut burr with a toadstool for a canopy.⁸

62   The mouse, **regal** as a queen, climbed into the coach. With the youngest son walking alongside, they set out for his home.

63   When they arrived at the river, a hunter passed them on the bridge. He looked down at the mouse, coach, and six and exclaimed, "Ho! What is this! A pack of vile rodents! I hate rats."

64   "If you please, sir," said the lad, "these are not vile rodents. I'll not allow you to call them so!"

65   "I've killed every rodent that has crossed my path!" said the bully, looming dangerously over the lad.

66   "Open your eyes and look more carefully," said the young man bravely. "Here before you rides the most delightful creature one could chance to meet."

67   "Disgusting rats!" glowered the man and with his heavy boot he kicked the coach and six into the swift water below the bridge!

68   "Heartless cruel man!" screamed the lad as he jumped into the river to save the mouse.

69   "I've rid the world of some useless pests!" the hunter shouted and continued on his way.

70   The lad desperately tried to reach the sinking coach. But as the raging water swirled around the little mouse, she vanished in the rushing river.

71   Exhausted and almost drowned, the lad made his way to the riverbank. He climbed out of the water and wept. "Now that you are gone," he wailed, "I regret even one moment's doubt that you were indeed my true love."

72   Suddenly, with a great splash and spray of mist, out of the water came six black horses pulling a fine golden carriage. In the carriage was a beautiful woman with sparkling blue eyes, wearing a gray velvet gown.

73   "Who are you?" the lad asked, rubbing his eyes to be sure he was seeing clearly.

74   "Don't you recognize me?" she asked. Her lovely musical voice cheered his heart.

regal
(rē´gəl) *adj.* Something *regal* appears to be royal, magnificent, or splendid.

ANALYZE PURPOSE AND TEXT STRUCTURE

Annotate: Mark the character's response to events in paragraph 71 and the resulting action in paragraph 72.

Analyze: Explain what the plot element is here and how this plot element might help reveal the author's purpose.

---

⁸ **a chestnut burr with a toadstool for a canopy:** a burr is the fruit of the chestnut; a toadstool is an inedible or poisonous mushroom; and a canopy is an umbrella-like shelter.

NOTICE & NOTE

INFER THEME

Annotate: Mark the youngest son's response to the mouse in paragraph 76.

Analyze: How does this statement connect with the theme or themes you've already identified?

elegant
(ĕl´ĭ-gənt) *adj.* Someone *elegant* appears to be refined and tasteful, having a beautiful manner, form, or style.

75   She explained, "I am a royal princess. A Lapland witch,[9] jealous of my beauty, enchanted me to be a mouse until such time as a kindhearted man could truly love me for myself. You broke the spell when you risked your life and declared your love. I am your mouse bride if you will have me," she said with a shy smile.

76   "I loved you before when we were of different worlds," he said. "How could I love you less now?"

77   He climbed into the coach and together they rode to his father's house. His brothers tumbled over one another to greet the **elegant** guest at their gate. "But it's our brother!" they gawked as he stepped out of the coach holding the princess's hand.

78   After a day of celebration, the young man and the princess traveled back to the forest. Instead of finding the small cottage made of gray logs, they found a great gray stone castle filled with one hundred servants. And it was there that they dwelt in happiness for the rest of their lives.

---

[9] **Lapland witch:** witch characters and references appear in many traditional stories from Lapland, which is a region of extreme northern Europe within the Arctic circle that includes Finland (where this story originates), Norway, Sweden, and the Kola peninsula of Northwest Russia.

NOTICE & NOTE

CHECK YOUR UNDERSTANDING

Answer these questions before moving on to the **Analyze the Text** section on the following page.

1. Which of the following statements by the father helps you infer a theme of the folktale?

   A *Each of you must cut down a sapling.*

   B *Congratulations to each of you on meeting sweethearts.*

   C *Attractive looks alone do not make for a happy hearth.*

   D *I should like to see the kind of bread your sweethearts bake.*

2. When the youngest brother learns he has to bring the mouse home to meet his father and brothers, he decides that he can't marry a mouse. What stops him from telling the mouse goodbye?

   F He is curious to see what else the mouse and her 100 mouse helpers can make.

   G He thinks he might hurt her feelings.

   H He loves the wheat bread she baked.

   J He wants to learn the beautiful songs she sang to him.

3. Which passage most likely begins the plot transition from falling action to a resolution?

   A *"Here before you rides the most delightful creature one could chance to meet."*

   B *"I've rid the world of some useless pests!" the hunter shouted and continued on his way.*

   C *"Now that you are gone," he wailed, "I regret even one moment's doubt that you were indeed my true love."*

   D *"I loved you before when we were of different worlds," he said. "How could I love you less now?"*

The Mouse Bride

RESPOND

ANALYZE THE TEXT

Support your responses with evidence from the text. 📓 **NOTEBOOK**

1. **Summarize** Describe in your own words the two older brothers' attitudes toward their younger brother in paragraphs 24–26.

2. **Infer** Reread paragraph 27. What can you infer about the story's theme from the father's comments to his sons?

3. **Draw Conclusions** What ideas about human nature are expressed in paragraphs 65–70? Explain how they might reveal the author's purpose for telling this folktale.

4. **Evaluate** Reread paragraphs 70–76. How does the author use a transition in the plot to help characterize the young man? Explain how this moment in the plot contributes to the author's purpose.

5. **Notice & Note** Review paragraphs 2, 27, 40, and 54. Why do you think the father gives his sons and their sweethearts one task after another? What insights about the brothers do you gain with each task accomplished?

RESEARCH

Investigate common themes for folktales. What messages about life or human nature are common to folktales around the world? Do you notice any significant differences between countries? For example, are themes from Indian or Chinese folktales similar to or different from the Finnish folktale "The Mouse Bride"?

RESEARCH TIP
Keep track of the sources you use in your research. Copy and paste the URL for the reference into a new document. Copy the title and author if one is given. When doing research on topics such as folktales, university websites are often reliable sources of information.

FOLKTALE TITLE	COUNTRY OF ORIGIN	THEME OR THEMES

Connect How does your research connect and build upon the research you did when reading "The Boatman's Flute"?

CREATE AND DISCUSS

Write an Analytical Essay Analyze "The Mouse Bride" to identify at least one theme. Refer to your notes as you work. Then, write a three- to four-paragraph analytical essay supporting your ideas.

- ❏ Include at least one theme in your analysis. Remember that folktales and other stories sometimes have multiple themes.
- ❏ Provide text evidence to support your ideas about theme.
- ❏ Revise your work. Look for ways to enhance your writing with modifiers such as adverbs, adjectives, and modifying phrases.

Present and Discuss Present your ideas about theme to your group.

- ❏ Support your ideas with evidence.
- ❏ Ask for questions and listen carefully to what is asked.
- ❏ Respond with care, referring to the text for examples.

After each member has presented, have a small group discussion about which theme or themes seem most relevant to your own lives and why.

Go to the **Writing Studio** for more on using textual evidence.

Go to the **Speaking and Listening Studio** for help with having a group discussion.

ACTIVE PARTICIPATION
- ❏ Ask clarifying questions.
- ❏ Maintain eye contact.
- ❏ Speak at a natural rate.
- ❏ Be loud and clear.
- ❏ Gesture naturally.
- ❏ Take notes as necessary.

RESPOND TO THE ESSENTIAL QUESTION

 What hidden truths about people and the world are revealed in stories?

Gather Information Review your annotations and notes on "The Mouse Bride." Then, add relevant details to your Response Log. As you determine which information to include, think about:

- what hidden truths the story revealed
- how and why some characters changed
- how and why some characters did not change

At the end of the unit, use your notes to write a short story or folktale.

ACADEMIC VOCABULARY
As you write and discuss what you learned from the folktales, be sure to use the Academic Vocabulary words. Check off words that you use.

- ❏ emphasize
- ❏ occur
- ❏ period
- ❏ relevant
- ❏ tradition

The Mouse Bride 497

RESPOND

CRITICAL VOCABULARY

WORD BANK
amazement
enchanting
deceptive
regal
elegant

Practice and Apply With a partner, discuss and then write down an answer to each of the following questions. Then work together to write a sentence for each vocabulary word.

1. Which vocabulary word goes with *stylish*? Why?
2. Which vocabulary word goes with *wonder*? Why?
3. Which vocabulary word goes with *royal*? Why?
4. Which vocabulary word goes with *false*? Why?
5. Which vocabulary word goes with *captivating*? Why?

VOCABULARY STRATEGY:
Context Clues

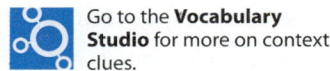 Go to the **Vocabulary Studio** for more on context clues.

Context clues are the words and phrases surrounding a word that provide hints about its meaning. The following are three types of context clues to look for when you come across an unfamiliar word.

Example clue: The writer uses words that are examples of the unknown word.

> The baker brought home three <u>loaves</u> to his children—rye, wheat, and barley—and they made French toast for breakfast.

Definition clue: The writer defines the unknown word directly in the sentence or in surrounding sentences.

> A <u>sapling</u> is a young tree.

Analogy clue: The writer pairs items that are related in some way.

> The <u>carriage</u> was like a stagecoach, only much fancier.

Practice and Apply Find the following words in the selection and identify clues to each word's meaning. Then check the definition.

WORD	CONTEXT CLUES	MEANING, ACCORDING TO CLUES	DEFINITION
amazement			
enchanting			
deceptive			
regal			
elegant			

LANGUAGE CONVENTIONS:
Adjectives and Adverbs

An **adjective** is a part of speech that modifies a noun or a pronoun. It describes *what kind, which, how many*.

An **adverb** is a part of speech that modifies or describes verbs, adjectives, or other adverbs. Adverbs provide details about *time, place, manner,* and *cause*.

A **clause** is a group of words with a subject and a predicate — the two main parts of a complete sentence. An **adjectival clause** acts like an adjective to modify a noun or pronoun in the rest of the sentence.

> **Now one day the farmer brought his sons to a field where three trees stood.**

In this sentence, *where three trees stood* modifies the noun *field*.

An **adverbial clause** acts like an adverb to modify verbs, adjectives, or adverbs. It helps convey meaning by answering the questions *when, where, why, how,* or *to what degree*. Adverbial clauses typically appear at the beginning or end of a sentence.

> **The young man had not gone far into the forest when he came upon a cottage.**

In this sentence, *when he came upon a cottage* modifies the verb *gone*.

Practice and Apply Mark and identify the adjectival and adverbial clauses in these sentences from the story, along with the words they modify. When you have finished, compare your work with a partner's and explain how you decided which clauses were adjectival and which were adverbial.

1. When he arrived at the farm that evening his two brothers were bragging to their father.

2. But they teased the youngest brother before he could speak a word. . . .

3. The second oldest brother handed the farmer some barley bread made by his sweetheart. . . .

4. The mouse, regal as a queen, climbed into the coach.

RESPOND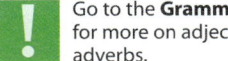

! Go to the **Grammar Studio** for more on adjectives and adverbs.

RESPOND

THE BOATMAN'S FLUTE
folktale retold by
Sherry Garland

THE MOUSE BRIDE
folktale retold by
Heather Forest

Collaborate & Compare

COMPARE THEMES

"The Boatman's Flute" from Vietnam and "The Mouse Bride" from Finland are both folktales that address the topic of love. You can infer the stories' themes by noting how each character makes decisions and responds to events, and in doing so, develops the plot. Recall that character responses may be internal (thoughts and feelings) or external (statements and actions). You can also infer themes by the lessons a folktale teaches. Making personal connections to these lessons may help you infer themes.

With your group, complete the chart by citing text evidence. As you work, remember that a folktale may have multiple themes.

	"THE BOATMAN'S FLUTE"	"THE MOUSE BRIDE"
Key statements		
Key decisions		
Lessons learned		

ANALYZE THE TEXTS

Discuss these questions in your group.

1. **Compare** Reread paragraphs 2, 20, and 24 in "The Boatman's Flute," and paragraphs 2, 27, 40, and 54 in "The Mouse Bride." What similarities do you see between the fathers in these tales?

2. **Analyze** Reread paragraphs 31–33 in "The Boatman's Flute" and paragraphs 56 and 75–76 in "The Mouse Bride." How did the mandarin's daughter and the farmer's youngest son learn important lessons, and how do these lessons differ?

3. **Infer** Both folktales feature a character who is freed. What do you infer about what actually sets the boatman and the princess free?

4. **Synthesize** What have your comparisons revealed about possible themes in each folktale?

RESPOND

COMPARE AND PRESENT

In your group, review the ideas about themes from your discussion, and determine a central theme for each story. Follow these steps:

1. **Review the lessons learned.** Thinking about lessons learned by the main characters can help you to identify a central theme.

2. **Choose a central theme for each folktale.** Discuss which of the themes in each story is most important and why. Record the themes for each story in the chart below.

3. **Record details and evidence to support each theme.** Locate specific evidence in the stories to support the themes you choose. Be sure to include specific statements made by the characters, who said it, the paragraph number, and why the statement supports the theme.

ACTIVE PARTICIPATION
- ❑ Contribute your own ideas.
- ❑ Consider the ideas of others.
- ❑ Ask clarifying questions.
- ❑ Take notes as necessary.
- ❑ Maintain eye contact.
- ❑ Speak at a natural rate.
- ❑ Be loud and clear.
- ❑ Gesture naturally.

FOLKTALE THEMES	
"The Boatman's Flute" Central Theme: Evidence:	"The Mouse Bride" Central Theme: Evidence:

4. **Present your ideas to the class.** Present the themes you've selected to the class. Explain similarities you found in the two folktales, and present any significant differences in meaning that you found. Make sure to support all of your ideas with specific evidence from the texts.

Collaborate & Compare 501

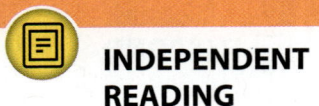
INDEPENDENT READING

Reader's Choice

? ESSENTIAL QUESTION:

What hidden truths about people and the world are revealed in stories?

Setting a Purpose Select one or more of these options from your eBook to continue your exploration of the Essential Question.

- Read the descriptions to see which text grabs your interest.
- Think about which genres you enjoy reading.

Notice & Note

In this unit, you practiced asking **Big Questions** and noticing and noting two signposts: **Word Gaps** and **Quoted Words**. As you read independently, these signposts and others will aid your understanding. Below are the anchor questions to ask when you read literature and nonfiction.

Reading Literature: Stories, Poems, and Plays		
Signpost	**Anchor Question**	**Lesson**
Contrasts and Contradictions	Why did the character act that way?	p. 3
Aha Moment	How might this change things?	p. 3
Tough Questions	What does this make me wonder about?	p. 172
Words of the Wiser	What's the lesson for the character?	p. 2
Again and Again	Why might the author keep bringing this up?	p. 92
Memory Moment	Why is this memory important?	p. 93

Reading Nonfiction: Essays, Articles, and Arguments		
Signpost	**Anchor Question(s)**	**Lesson**
Big Questions	What surprised me? What did the author think I already knew? What challenged, changed, or confirmed what I already knew?	p. 246 p. 420 p. 332
Contrasts and Contradictions	What is the difference, and why does it matter?	p. 247
Extreme or Absolute Language	Why did the author use this language?	p. 247
Numbers and Stats	Why did the author use these numbers or amounts?	p. 333
Quoted Words	Why was this person quoted or cited, and what did this add?	p. 333
Word Gaps	Do I know this word from someplace else? Does it seem like technical talk for this topic? Do clues in the sentence help me understand the word?	p. 421

INDEPENDENT READING

You can preview these texts in Unit 6 of your eBook.

Then, check off the text or texts that you select to read on your own.

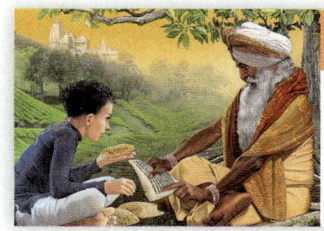

FABLE

The Golden Serpent
retold by Walter Dean Myers

A quest to find the golden serpent uncovers truths about a kingdom and the king.

MYTH

Echo and Narcissus
retold by Lancelyn Green

Goddesses prevent a beautiful nymph and her true love from ever meeting face to face.

FOLKTALE

The Fisherman and the Chamberlain
retold by Jane Yolen

A fisherman outwits a greedy bully and is royally rewarded.

INFORMATIONAL TEXT

Urban Legends, Suburban Myths
Robert T. Carroll

Beware! Which reveal truths and which spread hoaxes: urban legends or suburban myths?

Collaborate and Share With a partner, discuss what you learned from at least one of your independent readings.

- Give a brief synopsis or summary of the text.
- Describe any signposts that you noticed in the text and explain what they revealed to you.
- Describe what you most enjoyed or found most challenging about the text. Give specific examples.
- Decide if you would recommend the text to others. Why or why not?

Go to the **Reading Studio** for more resources on **Notice & Note**.

Independent Reading 503

WRITING TASK

Write a Short Story

Go to the **Writing Studio** for help writing narratives.

This unit focuses on how hidden truths are revealed through stories. For this writing task, you will write a short story or a folktale that delivers a message about life or human nature. For an example of a well-written story that you can use as a mentor text, review the folktale "The Mouse Bride."

As you write your story or folktale, you can use the notes from your Response Log, which you filled out after reading the texts in this unit.

Writing Prompt

Read the information in the box below.

This is the topic or context for your story.

> In their stories, authors often express messages or hidden truths about life and human nature.

Think carefully about the following question.

This is the essential question for the unit. How would you answer this question, based on the readings in this unit?

> What hidden truths about people and the world are revealed in stories?

Now mark the words that identify exactly what you are being asked to produce.

Write a short story or folktale that expresses a clear theme or message about life or human nature.

Be sure to—

Review these points as you write and again when you finish. Make any needed changes.

- ❏ tell a story with an exposition, rising action, a climax, falling action, and a resolution
- ❏ sequence plot events to create suspense and lead to a resolution
- ❏ invent a conflict, or a problem, that can unfold and be resolved in an interesting way
- ❏ use vivid language to make your setting and characters come alive
- ❏ use a clear point of view that suits the purpose of your story
- ❏ develop your characters through dialogue and interesting details
- ❏ clearly express your theme, or message, about life or human nature

WRITING TASK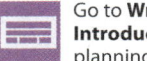

1 Plan

Before you start writing, plan your short story or folktale. Begin by thinking about what theme, or message, you would like to express in your story. Then invent a conflict, or a problem, that can unfold in an interesting way. A story usually centers on a conflict faced by the main character.

Decide who will tell your story. Are you going to create a first-person narrator or tell the story from the third-person point of view? Think about who the characters in the story are and where the story takes place. What do the characters look like? How do they act and what do they say? When and where will the story events take place? What are the sights and sounds of this place? Use the chart below to assist you in planning your draft.

Story Planning Chart	
Theme, message, or hidden truth	
Conflict or problem	
Narrator	
Characters	
Setting	
Plot events	

Background Reading Review the notes you have taken in your Response Log after reading the texts in this unit. These texts are the background reading you will use to formulate the key ideas and storytelling techniques that you will explore in your story.

Go to **Writing Narratives: Introduction** for help planning your story.

Notice & Note
From Reading to Writing

As you plan your short story, apply what you've learned about signposts to your own writing. Remember that writers use common features, called signposts, to help convey their messages to readers.

Think about how you can incorporate **Words of the Wiser** into your story.

 Go to the **Reading Studio** for more resources on **Notice & Note**.

Use the notes from your **Response Log** as you plan your story.

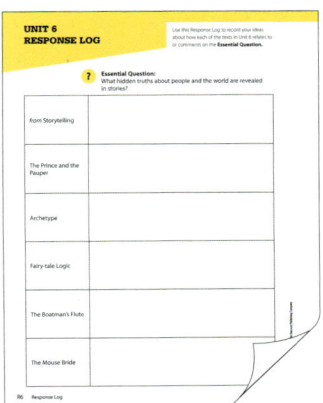

Write a Short Story   505

WRITING TASK

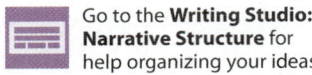 Go to the **Writing Studio: Narrative Structure** for help organizing your ideas.

Organize Your Ideas The series of events in a story is called the **plot**. The plot usually centers on a conflict faced by the main character. List the key events of your story in chronological, or time, order. When you write, you do not need to tell the events in the order in which they occurred—in fact, it helps to build suspense if you don't. However, having a "map" of the events will help you organize your story.

Place a star next to the point of highest tension—for example, the point at which a key decision determines the outcome of events. This point is called the **climax.** At this point, or shortly afterward, the problem in a story is usually resolved.

Plot Events in Chronological Order
1.
2.
3.
4.
5.

 You might prefer to draft your story online.

Develop a Draft

Once you have completed your planning activities, you will be ready to begin drafting your story. Refer to your planning charts, as well as to any notes you took as you studied the texts in the unit. Together, these will provide a kind of map for you to follow as you write.

Using a word processor or online writing application makes it easier to make changes or move sentences around later when you are ready to revise your first draft.

WRITING TASK

Use the Mentor Text

Character Development

The way a writer creates and develops characters is known as **characterization.** One method of characterization is for the writer to make direct comments about a character through the voice of the narrator. The writer may also describe the character's actions, allowing the reader to make inferences about the character. Authors use specific descriptions to develop their characters. Note the way the writer develops character in "The Mouse Bride."

The two older sons took pleasure in teasing their youngest brother, who was so kindhearted he could not even sweep a spider from the cobwebs in the corner.	*The narrator gives a specific description of the brother's kindness: he can't even kill a spider.*

Apply What You've Learned To develop your characters, show their traits through their actions. How does a brave person act? How does a timid person act?

Dialogue

Dialogue is written conversation between characters. Writers use dialogue to bring characters to life and to give readers insights into characters' qualities and traits. Note the way the writer uses dialogue to reveal insights into the mouse's character.

". . . Oh," he moaned, "my cruel brothers will certainly ridicule me when I arrive home tonight empty-handed!" **"I cannot bear to think of them mocking you! You will not go home empty-handed!" said the mouse.**	*Through dialogue the writer reveals that the mouse is confident and cares deeply about the son.*

Apply What You've Learned Reveal your characters' strengths and weaknesses through dialogue. Place hints about your characters' personalities in the statements they make and the questions they ask.

Write a Short Story 507

WRITING TASK

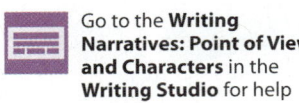

Go to the **Writing Narratives: Point of View and Characters** in the **Writing Studio** for help revising your story.

③ Revise

On Your Own Once you have written your draft, go back and look for ways to improve your story or folktale. As you reread and revise, think about whether you have achieved your purpose. The Revision Guide will help you focus on specific elements to make your writing stronger.

Revision Guide		
Ask Yourself	**Tips**	**Revision Techniques**
1. Is my theme expressed clearly?	**Mark** sections that hint at the theme.	**Add** sentences that help the reader understand the theme, or message, about life or human nature.
2. Is my narrator consistent throughout the story?	**Mark** point-of-view words such as *I*, *she*, or *them*.	**Replace** words that express an inconsistent point of view.
3. Are my plot events organized effectively?	**Mark** each event.	**Reorganize** events to build suspense and serve the plot. Use transitions to make the meaning of each plot event clear.
4. Are my characters developed with descriptive details?	**Mark** words that reveal character traits.	**Add** interesting details that help expand the reader's understanding of the characters.
5. Is the story's climax the turning point and moment of greatest tension?	**Mark** the point in the story where the climax occurs.	**Add** words, phrases, or sentences that strengthen or signal the climax.
6. Does my story have its own style reflected in word choice, sentence variety, and dialogue?	**Mark** words and phrases that reflect the style of the story.	**Add** more descriptive word choices and dialogue to develop the distinctive style and feel of the story.

ACADEMIC VOCABULARY

As you conduct your **peer review**, be sure to use these words.

☐ emphasize
☐ occur
☐ period
☐ relevant
☐ tradition

With a Partner Once you and your partner have worked through the Revision Guide on your own, exchange papers and evaluate each other's draft in a **peer review**. Focus on providing revision suggestions for at least three of the items mentioned in the chart. Explain why you think your partner's draft should be revised and what your specific suggestions are.

When receiving feedback from your partner, listen attentively and ask questions to make sure you fully understand the revision suggestions.

WRITING TASK

4 Edit

Once you have addressed the organization, development, and flow of ideas in your story, you can improve the finer points of your draft. Edit for the proper use of standard English conventions and correct any misspellings or grammatical errors.

Language Conventions: Style, Word Choice, Sentence Variety

Good writing has a particular style. A **style** is a manner of writing; it involves *how* something is said rather than *what* is said. Style is shown through elements such as the following:

- **word choice**—the author's use of powerful, vivid, and precise words, including descriptive adjectives and adverbs, to express ideas
- **sentence variety**—the author's use of a variety of sentence structures for different effects
- **dialogue**—conversation between characters, which helps to describe and reveal character traits
- **tone**—the author's attitude toward the subject, which might be serious, playful, mocking, or sympathetic

> Go to **Simple and Compound Sentences** in the **Grammar Studio** to learn more about sentence types and variety.

Notice how descriptive word choices, sentence variety, and revealing dialogue in "The Mouse Bride" capture your interest as a reader.

Style Element	Example
Descriptive Word Choice	Suddenly, with a great splash and spray of mist, out of the water came six black horses pulling a fine golden carriage.
Sentence Variety	His heart swelled with joy and every doubt he had about presenting her to his family disappeared with the first tones of her sweet voice. He climbed out of the water and wept.
Dialogue	"You'll find a pointy-eared sweetheart with sharp teeth in that forest," laughed his two brothers.

5 Publish

After you give your story its finishing touches, choose a way to share it with your audience. Consider these options:

- Present your story as a dramatization to the class.
- Post your story or folktale as a blog on a classroom or school website.

Write a Short Story

WRITING TASK

Use the scoring guide to evaluate your short story or folktale.

	Writing Task Scoring Guide: Short Story		
	Organization/Progression	**Development of Ideas**	**Use of Language and Conventions**
4	• The sequence of events is effective at building the plot and creating suspense. • The organization and pace keep the reader curious about the next plot event. • The well-designed plot begins with an intriguing conflict, builds to a climax, and the falling action leads to a satisfying resolution.	• The exposition vividly introduces the setting and main character and establishes the conflict in an engaging way. • Description and dialogue effectively develop characters and events. • The well-developed story reveals a significant theme. • The story ends satisfactorily and resolves the loose ends.	• The point of view is effective and consistent throughout. • Strong, descriptive word choices reveal the setting and characters. • Sentences vary in structure and have a rhythmic flow. • Dialogue reveals characters' personalities. • Spelling, capitalization, and punctuation are correct. • Grammar and usage are correct.
3	• The sequence of events is mostly effective at building the plot and creating suspense. • The organization is adequate, but the pace is somewhat slow or uneven. • The plot includes an interesting conflict, builds to a climax, and the falling action leads to a reasonable resolution.	• The exposition introduces the setting, a main character, and a conflict. • Description and dialogue develop characters and events. • The plot is adequately developed; the story suggests a theme. • The story resolves the conflict but needs more details to bring the plot to a satisfying resolution.	• The point of view is mostly consistent. • Setting and character need more description. • Sentence structure varies somewhat. • Dialogue is somewhat helpful in revealing personalities of the characters. • Spelling, capitalization, and punctuation mistakes occur. • Grammatical and usage errors occur.
2	• Confusion in the sequence of events weakens the plot and sense of suspense. • The organization is unclear and the pace often lags. • The story lacks thoughtful elements of plot; it does not build to a climax or include falling action ending with a resolution.	• The exposition is not engaging; it identifies a setting and a main character but only hints at a conflict. • More description and dialogue are needed to develop characters and events. • The plot development is uneven in places; a theme is only hinted at. • The story resolves some parts of the conflict.	• The point of view shifts confusingly. • Few descriptive words are used. • Sentence structures lacks variation. • Dialogue between characters is infrequent and does not provide information about the characters. • Spelling, capitalization, and punctuation are often incorrect. • Grammatical and usage errors occur often.
1	• The sequence of events and the plot are confusing; there is no sense of suspense. • The story is disorganized and the pace varies ineffectively. • The plot does not exist or does not progress to a climax and then lead to a resolution.	• Critical information about the setting and main character is missing; a conflict is not set. • Description and dialogue is missing. • The plot is barely developed and lacks a theme. • The story lacks a clear resolution.	• A clear point of view is lacking. • Unimaginative word choices and repetitive sentence structure create a dull story. • Dialogue is confusing or nonexistent. • Spelling, capitalization, and punctuation are mostly incorrect. • Grammar and usage errors occur throughout.

REFLECT

Reflect on the Unit

By completing your short story or folktale, you have created a writing product that pulls together and expresses your thoughts about the reading you have done in this unit. Now is a good time to reflect on what you have learned.

UNIT 6 SELECTIONS
- *Storytelling*
- *The Prince and the Pauper*
- "Archetype"
- "Fairy-tale Logic"
- "The Boatman's Flute"
- "The Mouse Bride"

Reflect on the Essential Question

- What hidden truths about people and the world are revealed in stories? In what ways has your understanding of how to uncover hidden truths in stories changed since you started this unit?

- What are some examples from the texts you've read of hidden truths about people and the world?

Reflect on Your Reading

- Which selection reveals a hidden truth that you'd never thought about before?

- Which selection reminds you of a fairy tale, folktale, or nursery rhyme that you enjoyed as a young child? Does the selection lead you to reconsider what that story from your childhood was really about?

Reflect on the Writing Task

- Which hidden truth were you thinking about as you wrote your story or folktale?

- How did you come up with your plot and characters?

- What strategies did you use to create a specific style for your story?

RESOURCES

Response Log	R1
Using a Glossary	R7
Pronunciation Key	R7
Glossary of Academic Vocabulary	R8
Glossary of Critical Vocabulary	R9
Index of Skills	R12
Index of Titles and Authors	R22
Acknowledgments	R23

HMH *INTO LITERATURE* STUDIOS

For more instruction and practice, visit the HMH *Into Literature* Studios.

Reading Studio

Writing Studio

Speaking & Listening Studio

Grammar Studio

Vocabulary Studio

UNIT 1 RESPONSE LOG

Use this Response Log to record your ideas about how each of the texts in Unit 1 relates to or comments on the **Essential Question.**

? Essential Question:
How do you find courage in the face of fear?

from The Breadwinner	
Life Doesn't Frighten Me	
Fears and Phobias	
Wired for Fear	
Embarrassed? Blame Your Brain	
The Ravine	

Response Log R1

UNIT 2 RESPONSE LOG

Use this Response Log to record your ideas about how each of the texts in Unit 2 relates to or comments on the **Essential Question.**

? Essential Question:
What can you learn by seeing the world through an animal's eyes?

from Pax	
Zoo	
from Animal Snoops: The Wondrous World of Wildlife Spies	
Animal Wisdom	
The Last Wolf	
Wild Animals Aren't Pets	
Let People Own Exotic Animals	

UNIT 3 RESPONSE LOG

Use this Response Log to record your ideas about how each of the texts in Unit 3 relates to or comments on the **Essential Question.**

? Essential Question:
What does it take to be a survivor?

from A Long Walk to Water	
Salva's Story	
Into the Lifeboat *from* Titanic Survivor	
from After the Hurricane	
from Ninth Ward	

Response Log R3

UNIT 4 RESPONSE LOG

Use this Response Log to record your ideas about how each of the texts in Unit 4 relates to or comments on the **Essential Question.**

? Essential Question:
What are the ways you can make yourself heard?

Text	
from Selfie: The Changing Face of Self-Portraits	
from Brown Girl Dreaming	
What's So Funny, Mr. Scieszka?	
A Voice	
Words Like Freedom	
Better Than Words: Say It with a Selfie	
OMG, Not *Another* Selfie!	

UNIT 5 RESPONSE LOG

Use this Response Log to record your ideas about how each of the texts in Unit 5 relates to or comments on the **Essential Question.**

? Essential Question:
What keeps people from giving up?

A Schoolgirl's Diary *from* I Am Malala	
The First Day of School	
Speech to the Young: Speech to the Progress-Toward	
from Into the Air	
from The Wright Brothers: How They Invented the Airplane	

Response Log R5

UNIT 6 RESPONSE LOG

Use this Response Log to record your ideas about how each of the texts in Unit 6 relates to or comments on the **Essential Question.**

? Essential Question:
What hidden truths about people and the world are revealed in stories?

from Storytelling	
The Prince and the Pauper	
Archetype	
Fairy-tale Logic	
The Boatman's Flute	
The Mouse Bride	

R6 Response Log

Using a Glossary

A glossary is an alphabetical list of vocabulary words. Use a glossary just as you would a dictionary—to determine the meanings, parts of speech, pronunciation, and syllabification of words. (Some technical, foreign, and more obscure words in this book are defined for you in the footnotes that accompany many of the selections.)

Many words in the English language have more than one meaning. This glossary gives the meanings that apply to the words as they are used in the selections in this book.

The following abbreviations are used to identify parts of speech of words:

adj. adjective   *adv.* adverb   *n.* noun   *v.* verb

Each word's pronunciation is given in parentheses. A guide to the pronunciation symbols appears in the Pronunciation Key below. The stress marks in the Pronunciation Key are used to indicate the force given to each syllable in a word. They can also help you determine where words are divided into syllables.

For more information about the words in this glossary or for information about words not listed here, consult a dictionary.

Pronunciation Key

Symbol	Examples	Symbol	Examples	Symbol	Examples
ă	pat	m	mum	ûr	urge, term, firm, word, heard
ā	pay	n	no, sudden* (sud´n)	v	valve
ä	father	ng	thing	w	with
âr	care	ŏ	pot	y	yes
b	bib	ō	toe	z	zebra, xylem
ch	church	ô	caught, paw	zh	vision, pleasure, garage
d	deed, milled	oi	noise	ə	about, item, edible, gallop, circus
ĕ	pet	ŏŏ	took	ər	butter
ē	bee	ōō	boot		
f	fife, phase, rough	ŏŏr	lure	**Sounds in Foreign Words**	
g	gag	ôr	core	KH	German ich, ach; Scottish loch
h	hat	ou	out	N	French bon (bôn)
hw	which	p	pop	œ	French feu, œuf; German schön
ĭ	pit	r	roar	ü	French tu; German über
ī	pie, by	s	sauce		
îr	pier	sh	ship, dish		
j	judge	t	tight, stopped		
k	kick, cat, pique	th	thin		
l	lid, needle* (nēd´l)	th	this		
		ŭ	cut		

*In English the consonants *l* and *n* often constitute complete syllables by themselves.

Stress Marks

The relative emphasis with which the syllables of a word or phrase are spoken, called stress, is indicated in three different ways. The strongest, or primary, stress is marked with a bold mark (´). An intermediate, or secondary, level of stress is marked with a similar but lighter mark (´). The weakest stress is unmarked. Words of one syllable show no stress mark.

GLOSSARY OF ACADEMIC VOCABULARY

achieve (ə-chēv′) *v.* to succeed in accomplishing something; to bring about by effort

appropriate (ə-prō′prē-ĭt) *adj.* suitable for a particular person, occasion, or place

authority (ə-thôr′ĭ-tē) *n.* an accepted source, such as a person or text, of expert information or advice

benefit (bĕn′ə-fĭt) *n.* something that provides help or improves something else

circumstance (sûr′kəm-stăns′) *n.* a condition, or set of conditions, that affects an event

consequence (kŏn′sĭ-kwĕns′) *n.* something that logically follows from an action or condition

constraint (kən-strānt′) *n.* something or someone that limits or restricts another's actions

distinct (dĭ-stĭngkt′) *adj.* easy to tell apart from others; not alike

element (ĕl′ə-mənt) *n.* an essential part of something

emphasize (ĕm′fə-sīz′) *v.* to give prominence or emphasis to

environment (ĕn-vī′rən-mənt) *n.* the natural world surrounding someone or something; surroundings

evident (ĕv′ĭ-dənt) *adj.* easily seen or understood; obvious

factor (făk′tər) *n.* someone or something that contributes to an accomplishment, result, or process

illustrate (ĭl′ə-strāt′) *v.* to show, or clarify, by examples or comparison

impact (ĭm′păkt′) *n.* something striking against another; also, the effect or impression of one thing on another

indicate (ĭn′dĭ-kāt′) *v.* to point out; also, to serve as a sign or symbol of something

individual (ĭn′də-vĭj′ōō-əl) *n.* a single human being apart from a society or community

injure (ĭn′jər) *v.* to hurt or cause damage

instance (ĭn′stəns) *n.* an example that is cited to prove or disprove a claim or illustrate a point

justify (jŭs′tə-fī′) *v.* to demonstrate or prove to be just, right, reasonable, or valid

occur (ə-kûr′) *v.* to take place; happen

outcome (out′kŭm′) *n.* a natural result or consequence

period (pîr′ē-əd) *n.* a particular length of time, often referring to a specific time in history or culture

principle (prĭn′sə-pəl) *n.* a rule or standard, especially of good behavior

relevant (rĕl′ə-vənt) *adj.* important to, connected to, or significant to an issue, event, or person in some way

respond (rĭ-spŏnd′) *v.* to make a reply; answer

significant (sĭg-nĭf′ĭ-kənt) *adj.* meaningful; important

similar (sĭm′ə-lər) *adj.* alike in appearance or nature, though not identical

specific (spĭ-sĭf′ĭk) *adj.* concerned with a particular thing; also, precise or exact

tradition (trə-dĭsh′ən) *n.* the passing down of various elements of culture from generation to generation; a custom

GLOSSARY OF CRITICAL VOCABULARY

accurate (ăk´yər-ĭt) *adj.* Something *accurate* is correct.

activate (ăk´tə-vāt´) *v.* To *activate* something means to cause it to start working.

adversity (ăd-vûr´sĭ-tē) *n.* *Adversity* is misfortune or hardship.

agonizing (ăg´ə-nīz´ĭng) *adj.* To be in an *agonizing* state means to feel great mental suffering and worry.

amazement (ə-māz´mənt) *n.* *Amazement* is a state of extreme surprise or wonder.

amplify (ăm´plə-fī´) *v.* To *amplify* something is to make it stronger or more intense.

angular (ăng´gyə-lər) *adj.* Something that is *angular*, such as a peaked roof, has two sides that form an angle.

anonymous (ə-nŏn´ə-məs) *adj.* Someone who is *anonymous* has an undisclosed or unknown name.

anxiety (ăng-zī´ĭ-tē) *n.* *Anxiety* is a feeling of uneasiness, fear, or worry.

anxiously (ăngk´shəs-lē) *adv.* To think of something *anxiously* means that you dread it.

apology (ə-pŏl´ə-jē) *n.* An *apology* is an expression of regret or a request for forgiveness.

apparatus (ăp´ə-răt´əs) *n.* An *apparatus* is a piece of equipment.

calculate (kăl´kyə-lāt´) *v.* To *calculate* is to figure out an answer by using math.

cascade (kăs-kād´) *v.* Something that can *cascade* will fall, pour, or rush in stages, like a waterfall over steep rocks.

celebrity (sə-lĕb´rĭ-tē) *n.* A *celebrity* is a famous person.

chastise (chăs-tīz´) *v.* To *chastise* is to punish or criticize.

collapse (kə-lăps´) *v.* When something is said to *collapse*, it falls down.

commit (kə-mĭt´) *v.* To *commit* is to do or perform an action.

constantly (kŏn´stənt-lē) *adv.* *Constantly* means something that is regularly occurring.

convince (kən-vĭns´) *v.* To *convince* is to use argument or evidence to get someone to believe or be certain about something.

courtyard (kôrt´yärd´) *n.* A *courtyard* is an area enclosed by walls and open to the sky.

debate (dĭ-bāt´) *v.* To *debate* is to discuss opposing points or ideas.

deceptive (dĭ-sĕp´tĭv) *adj.* Something *deceptive* is giving a false impression.

defeat (dĭ-fēt´) *v.* To *defeat* a person or his or her efforts is to prevent his or her success.

defy (dĭ-fī´) *v.* To *defy* someone is to oppose him or her or refuse to cooperate with that person.

demonstration (dĕm´ən-strā´shən) *n.* A *demonstration* is a presentation meant to show how something works.

dictate (dĭk´tāt´) *v.* To *dictate* something is to require it to be done or decided.

discourage (dĭ-skûr´ĭj) *v.* To *discourage* is to take away hope or confidence.

discreetly (dĭ-skrēt´lē) *adv.* To act *discreetly* means to act with self-restraint; attracting little notice.

displease (dĭs-plēz´) *v.* To *displease* someone is to cause annoyance or irritation.

eavesdrop (ēvz´drŏp´) *v.* To *eavesdrop* is to listen secretly to others' private conversations.

edict (ē´dĭkt´) *n.* An *edict* is a command or pronouncement enforced as law.

elegant (ĕl´ĭ-gənt) *adj.* Someone *elegant* appears to be refined and tasteful, having a beautiful manner, form, or style.

embrace (ĕm-brās´) *v.* To *embrace* someone is to hug or hold the person close.

enchanting (ĕn-chăn´tĭng) *adj.* Something or someone *enchanting* is charming.

GLOSSARY OF CRITICAL VOCABULARY

endure (ĕn-do͝or´) *v.* To *endure* is to carry on despite difficulty or suffering.

essential (ĭ-sĕn´shəl) *adj.* Something *essential* is so important that you can't do without it.

etch (ĕch) *v.* To *etch* is to cut or carve a drawing into a surface such as wood or metal.

eternity (ĭ-tûr´nĭ-tē) *n. Eternity* refers to infinite time, without beginning or end.

exempt (ĭg-zĕmpt´) *adj.* A person who is *exempt* is freed or excused from following a law or duty that others must obey.

exotic (ĭg-zŏt´ĭk) *adj.* Something that is *exotic* is from another part of the world.

experiment (ĭk-spĕr´ə-mənt) *n.* An *experiment* is a test to determine if an idea is true or to see if a device works.

fascinate (făs´ə-nāt´) *v.* To *fascinate* someone means to capture the interest or attention of that person.

focus (fō´kəs) *v.* When you *focus* on something, you keep attention fixed on it.

foil (foil) *v.* If you *foil* someone, you stop that person from being successful at something.

fortitude (fôr´tĭ-to͞od) *n.* To have *fortitude* is to show strength of mind and face difficulty with courage.

fume (fyo͞om) *v.* To *fume* about something is to feel or show displeasure or resentment.

generate (jĕn´ə-rāt´) *v.* To *generate* is to create and develop something.

hesitate (hĕz´ĭ-tāt´) *v.* To *hesitate* is to pause or wait in uncertainty.

history (hĭs´tə-rē) *n. History* is a chronological record of events of a person or institution.

horizon (hə-rī´zən) *n.* The *horizon* is the intersection of the earth and sky.

humiliation (hyo͞o-mĭl´ē-ā´shən) *n.* A feeling of *humiliation* is even more intense than a feeling of embarrassment.

illuminate (ĭ-lo͞o´mə-nāt´) *v.* To *illuminate* means to brighten or give light.

immaturity (ĭm´ə-tyo͝or´ĭ-tē) *n. Immaturity* is the state of not being fully developed or grown.

incorrect (ĭn´kə-rĕkt´) *adj.* Something *incorrect* is faulty or wrong.

indulgent (ĭn-dŭl´jənt) *adj. Indulgent* means excessively permissive. *Self-indulgent* is when one is overly permissive with oneself.

injury (ĭn´jə-rē) *n.* An *injury* is damage or harm done to a person or thing.

integral (ĭn´tĭ-grəl) *adj.* Something that is *integral* is necessary or essential for completeness.

intercept (ĭn´tər-sĕpt´) *v.* To *intercept* is to stop or interrupt something.

interplanetary (ĭn´tər-plăn´ĭ-tĕr´ē) *adj. Interplanetary* means existing or occurring between planets.

intimacy (ĭn´tə-mə-sē) *n. Intimacy* means close friendship and familiarity.

invariably (ĭn-vâr´ē-ə-blē) *adv.* Something that happens *invariably* occurs again and again or constantly.

jest (jĕst) *v.* To *jest* means to make playful remarks.

lament (lə-mĕnt´) *v.* If you *lament,* you are wailing or crying as a way of expressing grief.

linger (lĭng´gər) *v.* To *linger* means to leave slowly and reluctantly, not wanting to go.

microphone (mī´krə-fōn´) *n.* A *microphone* is an instrument that is often used to amplify the voice.

murky (mûr´kē) *adj.* Something *murky* is dark, obscure, and gloomy.

narcissist (när´sĭ-sĭst´) *n.* A person who is preoccupied with his or her looks is a *narcissist.*

nurture (nûr´chər) *v.* To *nurture* is to provide love, affection, nourishment, or something else necessary for development.

passion (păsh´ən) *n. Passion* means boundless enthusiasm.

pause (pôz) *v.* To *pause* is to hesitate or suspend action.

perplexed (pər-plĕkst´) *adj.* When you are *perplexed,* you are puzzled.

GLOSSARY OF CRITICAL VOCABULARY

poised (poizd) *adj.* To be *poised* means to be calm and assured, showing balanced feeling and action.

politeness (pə-līt´nəs) *n. Politeness* is respectful behavior.

portrait (pôr´trĭt) *n.* A *portrait* is a person's likeness, especially one showing the face, which may be painted, photographed, or otherwise represented.

precipice (prĕs´ə-pĭs) *n.* A *precipice* is an overhanging or extremely steep area of rock.

predator (prĕd´ə-tər) *n.* A *predator* is an animal that survives by eating other animals.

prediction (prĭ-dĭk´shən) *n.* When someone makes a *prediction*, they make a guess about something that has not yet happened.

prepare (prĭ-pâr´) *v.* To *prepare* is to get ready for an event or occasion.

preserve (prĭ-zûrv´) *v.* To *preserve* something is to keep it or save it.

pseudonym (sōōd´n-ĭm´) *n.* A *pseudonym* is a fictitious name, particularly a pen name.

reassure (rē´ə-shŏŏr´) *v.* To *reassure* someone is to give comfort or confidence to that person.

reflection (rĭ-flĕk´shən) *n.* A *reflection* is an image shown back, as from a mirror.

regal (rē´gəl) *adj.* Something *regal* appears to be royal, magnificent, or splendid.

regulate (rĕg´yə-lāt´) *v.* If you *regulate* something, you control or direct it according to a rule, principle, or law.

reluctance (rĭ-lŭk´təns) *n.* Showing *reluctance* to do something means you are unwilling.

resentment (rĭ-zĕnt´mənt) *n.* If you feel *resentment*, you feel anger or irritation.

responsibility (rĭ-spŏn´sə-bĭl´ĭ-tē) *n.* A *responsibility* is a duty, obligation, or burden.

rivulet (rĭv´yə-lĭt) *n.* A *rivulet* is a small brook or stream.

rueful (rōō´fəl) *adj.* To be *rueful* is to show sorrow or regret.

saturated (săch´ə-rāt´tĭd) *adj.* Something that is *saturated* is filled until it is unable to hold or contain more.

scurry (skûr´ē) *v.* Something that can *scurry* will run with quick, light steps.

seamstress (sēm´strĭs) *n.* A *seamstress* is a woman who sews, especially one who earns a living sewing.

sensitive (sĕn´sĭ-tĭv) *adj.* Something *sensitive* is able to perceive small differences or changes in the environment.

serene (sə-rēn´) *adj.* If you are *serene,* you are calm and unflustered.

shoulder (shōl´dər) *v.* To *shoulder* something is to carry it on one's shoulders.

sincere (sĭn-sîr´) *adj.* Something or someone *sincere* is genuine or heartfelt.

solution (sə-lōō´shən) *n.* A *solution* is a way of handling a problem.

span (spăn) *v.* To *span* is to extend over a period of time.

stake (stāk) *n.* A *stake* is something that can be gained or lost in a situation, such as money, food, or life.

stammer (stăm´ər) *v.* To *stammer* is to speak with involuntary pauses or repetitions.

stealthily (stĕl´thə-lē) *adv.* To do something *stealthily* means doing it quietly and secretly so no one notices.

terror (tĕr´ər) *n. Terror* is extreme fear of something.

trance (trăns) *n.* When someone is in a *trance,* he or she is in a daze or daydreaming.

trigger (trĭg´r) *v.* To *trigger* something means to cause it to begin.

turbulence (tûr´byə-ləns) *n.* In flying, *turbulence* is an interruption in the flow of wind that causes planes to rise, fall, or sway in a rough way.

universal (yōō´nə-vûr´səl) *adj.* Something that is *universal* affects every member of a group.

unrestrainedly (ŭn´rĭ-strā´nĭd-lē) *adv.* Doing something *unrestrainedly* means doing it without control.

veer (vîr) *v.* Something that can *veer* will swerve, or suddenly change course or direction.

wistfully (wĭst´fəl-ē) *adv.* When you think of something *wistfully,* you do so with sadness and longing.

Glossary of Critical Vocabulary R11

INDEX OF SKILLS

A

abbreviations, 6, 18, 344
absolute language. *See* Extreme or Absolute Language (Notice & Note)
Academic Vocabulary, 1, 17, 27, 39, 45, 55, 73, 84, 91, 103, 113, 127, 139, 153, 164, 171, 185, 203, 219, 229, 240, 245, 261, 275, 285, 297, 315, 326, 331, 349, 363, 373, 387, 401, 412, 419, 431, 455, 467, 481, 497, 508
acronyms, 6
active listening, 141, 219, 481
adjective clauses, 499
adjective phrases, 486
adjectives
  dictionary abbreviation for, 18
  as modifiers, 486, 499
  proper, 118, 122, 129
advantages and disadvantages pattern, 47, 391
adverb clauses, 376, 389, 499
adverbs, 18, 376, 382, 389, 413, 499
advertisements, 55
affixes. *See* prefixes; suffixes
afterwords, 375, 384
Again and Again (Notice & Note), 25, 78, 92, 98, 111, 158, 173, 180, 210, 234, 320, 406, 490, 502
Aha Moment (Notice & Note), 3, 10, 14, 70, 78, 134, 158, 173, 182, 215, 225, 234, 280, 320, 360, 406, 445, 450, 452, 502
alliteration, 207, 219, 367, 459
allusions, 460, 466
analogies, 204, 432, 498
analysis. *See also* Analyze the Text
  author's purpose and message, 202, 265, 267, 271, 285, 485, 488, 493
  author's use of language, 221, 224, 226, 277, 279–281
  character, 5, 8, 12, 59, 62–69, 175, 179
  claim in argument, 145, 152
  cultural and historical setting, 221, 223
  digital text, 42, 188
  evidence, 143, 146, 149
  figurative language, 289, 292, 294, 297
  imagery, 131, 134
  informational text, 335, 337, 343, 345, 391–394, 423, 425
  media, 44, 190
  mental image, 202, 441, 443
  multimodal text, 249, 255, 375, 378, 380, 383
  organizational patterns, 47, 51, 52
  personification, 134
  playwright character development, 435, 438–442, 445–451
  plot development, 5, 8, 11–13, 353, 356, 359–360, 471–473, 476–478
  poetic structure, 207, 209, 212–216, 367, 370, 459, 462, 465
  point of view, 95, 97, 99, 107, 110, 474, 476
  print and graphic features, 249, 252–253, 257
  refrain, 22, 24
  rhetorical device, 301, 303, 306, 309, 312
  setting, 5, 8, 12, 59, 62–69, 175, 179, 353–358
  speaker in poetry, 21, 23
  structural, 29, 31–32
  text structure, 117–119, 122, 265–267, 271, 485, 488, 493
  theme, 109
  voice, 95, 99–100
analytical essays, 363, 497
Analyze the Text, 16, 26, 38, 54, 72, 76, 102, 112, 126, 138, 140, 152, 156, 184, 202, 218, 228, 232, 260, 274, 284, 296, 298, 314, 318, 348, 362, 372, 386, 400, 404, 430, 454, 466, 468, 480, 496, 500
Anchor Questions (Notice & Note), 2–3, 78, 92–93, 158, 172–173, 234, 247, 320, 333, 406, 421, 502
anecdotes, 117
animated graphics, 188
annotate
  audience for arguments, 305, 311
  author's purpose and message, 196, 198, 267, 271, 281–282, 488, 493
  author's use of language, 224, 226, 279–281
  character, 8, 11–13, 62–69, 179
  claim in argument, 145, 148
  connections, 269, 272, 461–462, 464
  cultural and historical setting, 223
  figurative language, 200, 211, 213, 292, 294
  imagery, 134, 137
  inferences, 61, 64–67, 70, 291–294, 369, 427–428
  informational text, 337, 343, 345, 393–394, 425
  key ideas, 120–124, 379, 381, 395, 398
  mental images, 197, 200, 441–443, 452
  as monitoring strategy, 175, 181
  multimodal text, 378, 380, 383
  paraphrasing, 134, 136
  personification, 134
  playwright character development, 438, 440–442, 445–451
  plot development, 8, 11–13, 355–356, 359–360, 473, 476–478
  poetic structure, 209, 212–216, 370, 462, 465
  point of view, 97, 99, 110, 474, 476
  print and graphic features, 252–253, 257
  questions generated about text, 339, 346
  refrain, 24
  rhetorical device, 303, 306, 309, 312
  setting, 8, 12, 62–69, 179, 355, 357–358
  speaker in poetry, 23
  subheading, 49, 51, 119
  supporting evidence, 33, 35, 36
  text structure, 31–32, 119, 122, 267, 271, 488, 493
  theme, 109
  voice, 99–100
Annotation Model, 6, 22, 30, 48, 60, 96, 108, 118, 132, 144, 176, 194, 208, 222, 250, 266, 278, 290, 302, 336, 354, 368, 376, 392, 424, 436, 460, 472, 486
antecedents, 278, 282, 287, 327
antonyms, 56, 456
argumentative essays, 160–168
  develop, 162–163
  edit, 165
  introduction for, 160
  plan for, 91, 153, 161–162
  present, 167–168
  publish, 165–166
  revise, 164
  scoring guide for, 166
  thesis statements in, 161
  writing prompt for, 160
arguments. *See also* argumentative essays; multimodal arguments
  adaptation for presentation, 167
  audience for, 301, 305, 311, 325
  claims in, 143, 145, 148, 152, 161, 315
  comparison of, 142, 156, 300, 314, 318
  conclusions to, 143, 153
  counterarguments, 143, 161
  critiques of, 156, 318
  evaluation of, 318
  evidence for, 143
  gathering information for, 103, 113, 127, 139, 153
  Genre Elements, 143, 301
  logical fallacy in, 301
  present, 91
  reasoning of, 156

INDEX OF SKILLS

rhetorical devices in, 301, 303, 306, 309, 312, 325
synthesize, 318
write, 91, 153, 160–166, 315
audience
for arguments, 301, 305, 311, 325
eye contact with, 17, 27, 88, 153, 275
for informational essays, 81
for podcasts, 417
for presentations, 87, 167
author's message
analysis of, 285
explaining, 193, 198
inferences regarding, 277, 281–282
author's purpose
analysis of, 202, 265, 267, 271, 285, 485, 488, 493
of digital text, 42, 188
evaluation of, 196, 202, 496
explaining, 193, 196
inferences regarding, 277, 281–282, 368–369
in introductions, 430
of memoirs, 193, 265
in poetry, 368–369
predictions regarding, 430
repetition as method of revealing, 22
synthesizing, 372
author's use of language, 221, 224, 226, 228, 277, 279–281
autobiographies. *See* memoirs

B

background knowledge, 175, 181
background reading, 81, 161, 237, 323, 409, 505
base of words, 482
bias of sources, 77
Big Questions (Notice & Note), 78, 158, 234, 246, 257, 320, 332, 340, 384, 406, 420, 427, 502
biographical poetry, 275
biographical reports, 408–414
develop, 410–411
edit, 413
gather information for, 349, 363, 373, 387, 401
plan for, 331, 409–410
publish, 413
revise, 412
scoring guide for, 414
writing prompt for, 408
biographies, 375, 391
blogs, 241
boldfaced words, 47, 249
boxed features, 29
brainstorming, 77, 233, 319
business letters, 17, 349

C

capitalization
proper adjectives, 118, 122, 129
proper nouns, 6, 10, 19, 118, 122, 336, 344, 351
captions, 249, 375, 386, 387
catalogs, 207, 212, 219
cause-and-effect relationships
analysis of, 400
identifying, 39
in informational essays, 185
in informational texts, 394
in media, 44
as organizational pattern, 29, 391, 423
characterization, 507
characters
analysis of, 5, 8, 12, 59, 62–69, 175, 179
comparisons over time, 16
drawing conclusions regarding, 8, 13, 184
evaluation of, 16, 184, 228
external responses of, 471
inferences of, 8, 62, 68, 72
internal responses of, 471
motivations of, 59, 60, 73, 175
as narrator, 95, 107
personality of, 59, 95, 175
playwright development of, 435, 438–442, 445–451
in plot development, 5, 8, 11, 13
predictions for, 185
setting in development of, 5, 59, 175, 221, 353, 355, 357–358
traits of, 59, 60, 73, 185
character studies, 455
checklists
debate performance, 157
figurative language, 297
group work, 185, 191, 299, 349
inferences, 290
presentations, 203, 229
choral readings, 27
chronological order, 191, 238, 239, 391, 410
citation of sources, 233
Cite Evidence
annotations for, 33, 35, 36
for comparisons, 33
for connections, 35
for inferences, 59
from informational text, 38
for interpretations, 36
of key ideas, 120, 430
from memoirs, 348
for personification, 138
in plays, 454
for point of view, 102
strategies for, 29
for theme, 372
claims, in arguments, 143, 145, 148, 152, 161, 315

clarification
of event details, 45
of ideas, 73, 75, 85, 127, 168, 205
introductory elements for, 263
of sentence meaning, 250, 392
of sequence of events, 403
of time of occurrence, 108
of topic of paragraphs, 391
of understanding, 56, 335
classification patterns, 47, 391, 423
clauses. *See also* dependent clauses
adjectival, 499
adverb, 376, 389, 499
independent, 85, 96, 101, 424–425
intervening, 165
climax, 353, 362, 471, 480, 506
Collaborate & Compare, 76–77, 140–141, 156–157, 232–233, 298–299, 318–319, 404–405, 468–469, 500–501
colored type, 29, 249
commas
in complex sentences, 194, 205, 403
in compound sentences, 85, 403
introductory elements and, 48, 51, 57, 197, 205, 250–251, 263
in sentence patterns, 354, 356, 365
in transitions, 392
comma splices, 105, 205
commonly confused words, 302, 305, 310, 317
common nouns, 6, 19, 351
compare and contrast
arguments, 156
essays, 39, 73
texts, 76, 363
themes, 141, 469
comparisons. *See also* Collaborate & Compare; compare and contrast
analysis of, 112
arguments, 142, 156, 300, 314, 318
characters over time, 16
as context clues, 432
figurative language, 288
Genre Elements, 76, 206, 220, 232, 484
illustrations, 386
inferences and, 76, 291, 294
in informational texts, 33, 54
key ideas, 404, 405
main ideas, 46, 58
mental images, 202
narrator attitude, 228
poetry, 130, 140–141, 288, 298, 458
presentations, 374, 390
print and graphic features, 252
synthesizing information for, 76
themes, 46, 58, 130, 140–141, 232, 469–470, 500–501
voice and mood, 100

INDEX OF SKILLS

complex sentences
   clauses in, 85, 96, 101, 424–425
   commas in, 194, 205, 403
   common mistakes in, 105
   pattern of, 365
   subordinating conjunctions in, 60, 65, 75, 433
compound-complex sentences, 365
compound sentences, 85, 365, 403
comprehension monitoring, 132, 175, 181, 335
conclusions. *See also* drawing conclusions
   analytical essays, 363
   arguments, 143, 153
   biographical reports, 408
   informational essays, 39, 80, 82, 127
   multimodal arguments, 322
   nonfiction narratives, 236
conflict, 471, 480
conjunctions
   coordinating, 85
   correlative, 433
   subordinating, 60, 65, 75, 433
conjunctive adverbs, 389, 413
connections
   annotation of, 269, 272, 461–462, 464
   in comparison of texts, 76
   describing, 275
   in documentaries, 190
   among ideas, 127
   inferences from, 462
   in informational texts, 32, 35
   interpretation of, 464
   mental images and, 197
   as monitoring strategy, 175
   personal, 193, 266
   in poetry, 460–462, 464, 466
   rhetorical devices and, 303
   from selections of texts, 274
   setting and character, 179
   to speakers, 298, 299
consistent verb tenses, 110, 241
context clues, 74, 204, 230, 262, 316, 432, 498
contradictions. *See* Contrasts and Contradictions (Notice & Note)
Contrasts and Contradictions (Notice & Note), 3, 8, 10, 52, 78, 93, 98, 158, 196–197, 234, 247, 254, 256, 320, 406, 477, 502
controlling ideas. *See also* thesis statements
   in analytical essays, 363
   on author's purpose and message, 285
   in biographical reports, 408
   inferences regarding, 375, 387, 423
   in informational essays, 39, 80, 83, 127, 185
   interpretation of, 430

   locating, 29
   in memoirs, 335
coordinating conjunctions, 85
correlative conjunctions, 433
correspondence. *See* letters
counterarguments, 143, 161
credibility of sources, 26, 72, 77, 319, 372
Critical Vocabulary, 6, 18, 30, 40, 48, 56, 60, 74, 96, 104, 108, 114, 118, 128, 144, 154, 176, 186, 194, 204, 222, 230, 250, 262, 278, 286, 302, 316, 336, 350, 354, 364, 376, 388, 392, 402, 424, 432, 436, 456, 472, 482, 486, 498
critiques
   arguments, 156, 318
   graphics, 190, 260, 261
   informational texts, 54
   media, 44
   stereotyping, 314
cultural setting, 221, 223, 228

D

dashes, 30, 34, 41, 85
debates, 157
definition
   as context clue, 204, 262, 432, 498
   as organizational pattern, 47, 391, 423
delivering presentations, 88, 168, 319, 455
dependent clauses
   commas and, 194, 205, 263
   in complex sentences, 85, 96, 101, 424–425
   in compound sentences, 85
dialogue, 45, 435, 454, 507, 509
dictionaries, 186, 402, 456
digital sources, 233
digital texts, 42, 188
disadvantages and advantages pattern, 47, 391
discussions
   active participation in, 497, 501
   character traits, 185
   figurative language, 297
   freewriting, 349
   informational texts, 39, 55
   joke telling steps, 285
   key ideas, 405, 431
   listening in, 39, 73, 127
   main ideas, 401
   poetry, 139
   print and graphic features, 387
   research, 233, 319
   rules for, 168
   storyboards, 113
   videos, 191
   Word Networks, 1, 91, 171, 245, 331, 419
documentaries, 188–190
drafts
   argumentative essay, 162–163
   biographical report, 410–411

   edit, 85, 165, 241, 327
   folktale, 506–507
   informational essay, 82–83
   multimodal argument, 324–325
   nonfiction narrative, 238–239
   peer review of, 84, 164, 240, 326, 412, 508
   plan, 81–82, 161–162
   revise, 84, 164, 203, 326
   short story, 506–507
drama, 435, 437. *See also* plays and playwrights
dramatic readings, 455
drawing conclusions
   on audience for arguments, 305, 311
   from author's use of language, 228, 284
   on characters, 8, 13, 184
   evidence to support, 29, 202
   from figurative language, 218
   from folktales, 496
   from graphic features, 260
   from inferences, 372
   from informational texts, 38
   from key ideas, 381
   in plays, 454
   on playwright character development, 440
   on poetry, 139, 216
   from questions generated about text, 339
   from repetition, 112
   from rhetorical devices, 306
   on setting, 72, 358
   on speakers, 26
   from titles of verses, 274
drop caps, 249

E

eBooks, 78–79, 158–159, 234–235, 320–321, 406–407, 502–503
editing drafts
   argumentative essay, 165
   biographical report, 413
   folktale, 509
   informational essay, 85
   multimodal argument, 327
   nonfiction narrative, 241
   short story, 509
elegies, 21
emails, 275
emotional appeals, 143, 144, 156, 325
encyclopedias, 402
end rhyme, 459, 466
enunciation, 17, 45, 88, 319, 416
essays. *See also* informational essays
   analytical, 363, 497
   argumentative, 160–166
   character studies, 455
   compare and contrast, 39, 73
ethical use of sources, 408
etymology, 154, 482

INDEX OF SKILLS

evaluations
  arguments, 318
  author's purpose, 196, 202, 496
  captions, 386
  characters, 16, 184, 228
  conflict, 480
  debate performance, 157
  figurative language, 138, 211
  inferences and, 292
  memoirs, 348
  mental images, 452
  narrator, 284
  parallelism, 314
  playwright character development, 447
  poetry, 26, 140, 298
  point of view, 99, 112
  rhetorical devices, 309
  search results, 228
  settings, 16, 184
  text structure, 122, 430
evidence. *See also* Cite Evidence
  analysis of, 143, 146, 149
  for annotations, 33, 35, 36
  for author's purpose and message, 193, 202
  for claims in arguments, 143, 314
  for drawing conclusions, 29, 202
  explicit, 185
  fact-based, 143
  implicit, 185
  for inferences, 29, 59, 290
  main ideas supported by, 80
  personal experiences as, 143
  supporting details as, 83
examples, as context clues, 498
explicit evidence, 185
explicit statement of key ideas, 423
explicit statement of themes, 107, 468
exposition, 353, 471, 485
expository essays. *See* informational essays; writing activities
extended metaphors, 208, 219
external responses of characters, 471
Extreme or Absolute Language (Notice & Note), 78, 146, 158, 234, 247, 258, 304, 320, 406, 502
eye contact
  in dramatic readings, 455
  in group presentations, 319
  in joke telling, 285
  in multimodal presentations, 17, 103
  as nonverbal technique, 88
  in poetry presentations, 27, 219, 275
  in public service announcement presentations, 153

F

facial expressions, 27, 88, 168, 285
facts, 143
falling action, 353, 471, 480
faulty reasoning, 301
feedback from peers, 84, 164, 240, 326, 412, 508
fiction. *See also* short stories
  historical, 5, 175, 221
  novels, 7, 95, 97, 107, 177
  realistic, 5, 59, 175
  science fiction, 107, 112
  writing, 103
figurative language
  analysis of, 289, 292, 294, 297
  annotations, 200, 211, 213, 292, 294
  author's use of, 208
  comparison of, 288
  discussion of, 297
  drawing conclusions from, 218
  evaluations, 138, 211
  interpretations of, 211, 292
  metaphors, 208, 219, 289
  mood and, 221, 277
  personification, 131, 134, 138, 208, 289
  in poetry, 131, 138, 208, 211, 213, 288–289
  similes, 208, 219, 288
  summaries of, 218
films. *See* videos
first-person point of view, 21, 95, 107, 265, 471
first-person pronouns, 21, 107
flashbacks, 353
fluency of reading, 435, 454
folktales
  develop, 506–507
  draw conclusions from, 496
  edit, 509
  gather information for, 431, 455, 467, 481, 497
  Genre Elements, 471, 485
  plan for, 419, 505–506
  publish, 509
  revise, 508
  scoring guide for, 510
  themes in, 500–501
  write, 419, 504–510
fonts, 249
footage, 188, 190
footnotes, 316
formal inquiries, 17
formal language, 168
formal letters, 153, 275, 349
form of poetry, 207, 459
fragmented sentences, 105
free verse poetry, 207, 219, 275, 367, 459
freewriting, 349
friendly letters, 203

G

gathering information
  arguments, 103, 113, 127, 139, 153
  biographical reports, 349, 363, 373, 387, 401
  folktales, 431, 455, 467, 481, 497
  informational essay, 17, 27, 39, 45, 55, 73
  key idea comparisons, 405
  multimodal arguments, 261, 275, 285, 297, 315
  nonfiction narratives, 185, 191, 203, 219, 229
  research, 77, 126, 233, 319
  short stories, 431, 455, 467, 481, 497
generate questions about text, 335, 339, 346, 348
generate questions for research, 16, 77, 152, 233, 319
Genre Elements
  arguments, 143, 301
  biographies, 391
  comparison of, 76, 206, 220, 232, 484
  documentaries, 188
  drama, 435
  folktales, 471, 485
  free verse poetry, 207
  graphic biographies, 375
  historical fiction, 5, 175, 221
  humor, 277
  informational texts, 29, 47, 117
  introductions, 423
  lyric poetry, 21
  media, 42
  memoirs, 193, 265, 335
  multimodal texts, 249
  novels, 95
  poetry, 131, 289, 367, 459
  science fiction, 107, 112
  short stories, 59, 353
gestures, 168, 219, 285. *See also* natural gestures
Glossary of Academic Vocabulary, R8
Glossary of Critical Vocabulary, R9–R11
graphic biographies, 375
graphic features
  analysis of, 249, 252–253, 257
  animated, 188
  critique of, 190, 260, 261
  discussion of, 387
  draw conclusions from, 260
  predictions from, 47
  summaries of, 257, 260, 386
Greek roots, 40, 104, 114, 286, 350, 482
group work, 185, 191, 299, 349. *See also* discussions

H

headings, 29, 249
helping verbs, 115, 241
historical fiction, 5, 175, 221
historical setting, 221
humor, 117, 122, 277, 279
hyperbole, 77, 247, 301
hyphens, 30

Index of Skills R15

INDEX OF SKILLS

I

ideas. *See also* controlling ideas; key ideas; main ideas
   clarification of, 73, 75, 85, 127, 168, 205
   connections among, 127
   organization of, 82, 162, 238, 324, 410, 506
illustrations, 113, 139, 386, 387
image panels, 375
imagery. *See also* mental images
   analysis of, 131, 134
   annotations, 134, 137
   inferences regarding, 137
   interpretation of, 134
   mood and, 277
   presentation of, 139
images, 42, 45, 103
implicit evidence, 185
implicit statement of key ideas, 423
implicit statement of themes, 107, 468
indefinite pronouns, 231, 287, 327
independent clauses, 85, 96, 101, 424–425
Independent Reading, 78–79, 158–159, 234–235, 320–321, 406–407, 502–503
inferences
   annotations for, 61, 64–67, 70, 291–294, 369, 427–428
   author's purpose and message, 277, 281–282, 368–369
   author's use of language, 226, 279–281
   characters, 8, 11, 62, 68, 72
   comparisons and, 76, 291, 294
   from connections, 462
   controlling ideas, 375, 387, 423
   defined, 404, 423
   drawing conclusions from, 372
   evaluation and, 292
   evidence to support, 29, 59, 290
   imagery, 137
   key ideas, 126, 379, 423, 427–428
   meaning of words, 262
   mental images, 200, 442
   personification, 134
   playwright character development, 441, 449
   plot development, 11
   poetic structure, 462
   repetition, 218
   setting, 8, 62, 68, 72, 362
   speaker in poetry, 21, 23, 296, 298
   from speech balloons, 386
   text structure and purpose, 267
   themes, 107–109, 112, 140, 232, 368–369, 468, 485, 492–496
   thesis statements, 387
informational essays, 80–88
   compare and contrast, 39
   conclusion for, 39, 80, 82, 127
   develop, 82–83
   edit, 85
   gather information for, 17, 27, 39, 45, 55, 73
   introduction for, 80, 82–83
   plan for, 1, 81–82
   present, 87–88
   publish, 85
   revise, 84
   scoring guide for, 86
   thesis statements in, 80, 83, 127, 185
   write, 1, 39, 80–86, 127, 185, 297
informational texts
   analysis of, 335, 337, 343, 345, 391–394, 423, 425
   anecdotes in, 117
   comparisons in, 33, 54
   connections in, 32, 35
   critiques of, 54
   discussions on, 39, 55
   draw conclusions from, 38
   Genre Elements, 29, 47, 117
   interpretations of, 36, 38
   organizational patterns in, 29, 47, 51–52, 391, 423
   predictions from, 47–49, 54
   setting a purpose in, 31, 119
   structure of, 29, 31–32, 117, 119, 122, 423
information gathering. *See* gathering information
information requests, 17
initials, 6
internal responses of characters, 471
internal rhyme, 459
interpretations
   author's purpose, 488
   background information, 184
   claims in arguments, 148
   climax, 362
   connections, 464
   controlling ideas, 430
   figurative language, 211, 292
   footage, 190
   imagery, 134
   informational texts, 36, 38
   media, 44
   paraphrasing, 134, 136, 138
   plot development, 16
   poetry, 25, 140, 296, 466
   point of view, 97
   refrains, 24
   resolution, 480
   stage directions, 454
   text structure, 488
intervening phrases/clauses, 165
introductions
   argumentative essays, 160
   author's purpose in, 430
   biographical reports, 408
   Genre Elements, 423
   informational essays, 80, 82–83
   multimodal arguments, 322
   setting a purpose in, 425
introductory elements, 48, 51, 57, 197, 205, 250–251, 262

K

key ideas
   annotations, 120–124, 379, 381, 395, 398
   comparison of, 404, 405
   determining, 117, 391, 395, 398
   discussion of, 405, 431
   drawing conclusions from, 381
   evidence of, 120, 430
   implicit vs. explicit statement of, 423
   inferences regarding, 126, 379, 423, 427–428
   in multimodal texts, 375, 379, 381
   paraphrasing, 431
   summaries of, 123–124, 126, 261, 398
   synthesizing, 126

L

Language Conventions
   adjectives, 18, 118, 122, 129, 486, 499
   adverbs and adverb clauses, 18, 376, 382, 389, 413, 499
   commonly confused words, 302, 305, 310, 317
   compound sentences, 85, 365, 403
   coordinating conjunctions, 85
   correlative conjunctions, 433
   dashes, 30, 34, 41, 85
   independent clauses, 85, 96, 101, 424
   intervening phrases/clauses, 165
   modifiers, 486, 499
   prepositions and prepositional phrases, 176, 179, 187, 436, 438, 457
   quotation marks, 54, 472, 476, 480, 483
   sentence patterns, 354, 356, 365
   sentence variety, 85, 509
   simple sentences, 75, 85, 365
   spelling, 144, 146, 150, 155
   style of writing, 509
   subject-verb agreement, 165, 187
   subordinating conjunctions, 60, 65, 75, 433
   verb tenses, 108, 110, 115, 165, 241
   word choice, 95, 156, 509
Latin roots, 40, 104, 128, 350, 482
letters
   business, 17, 349
   formal, 153, 275, 349
   friendly, 203
limited point of view, 95, 471
lines and line breaks, 207, 367
listening
   active, 141, 219, 481
   to advice, 2
   in group discussions, 39, 73, 127

INDEX OF SKILLS

to peer feedback, 84, 164, 240, 326, 412, 508
to presentations, 87–88, 153, 168, 229, 416
logic, 143, 156
logical fallacy, 301
lyric poetry, 21, 22

M

magazines, 42, 102
main ideas
   comparison of, 46, 58
   discussion of, 401
   evidence for support of, 80
   summarizing, 29
maps, 335, 338
meaning of words
   context clues and, 74, 204, 230, 262, 316, 432, 498
   inferences regarding, 262
   resources for determining, 186
   roots and, 104, 114, 128, 286, 350, 482
   spelling and, 144
media. *See also* videos
   analysis of, 44, 190
   digital texts, 42, 188
   documentaries, 188–189
   Genre Elements, 42
   podcasts, 45, 373, 415–416
memoirs
   author's purpose of, 193, 265
   controlling ideas in, 335
   evaluation of, 348
   Genre Elements, 193, 265, 335
   mental images in, 193, 197, 200
   personal experiences in, 193, 266
   setting a purpose in, 195, 267, 337
   in verse, 265
Memory Moment (Notice & Note), 62, 78, 93, 100, 158, 234, 268, 270, 292, 320, 406, 478, 502
mental images. *See also* imagery
   analysis of, 202
   in letters, 203
   in memoirs, 193, 197, 200
   in narratives, 239
   in plays, 435, 441–443, 452
message of author. *See* author's message
metaphors, 208, 219, 289
meter, 207, 209, 212–214, 367, 370, 459, 462
misspelled words, 144, 146, 150
moderators, 157
modifiers, 486, 499
modulation of voice, 88, 416
monitoring comprehension, 132, 175, 181, 335
mood
   comparison of, 100
   figurative language and, 221, 277

imagery and, 277
   in nonfiction narratives, 239
   in poetry, 22, 368
   summaries of, 102
   tone and, 290
   voice and, 95
motivations of characters, 59, 60, 73, 175
multimedia presentations, 203
multimodal arguments, 322–328
   conclusion for, 322
   develop, 324–325
   edit, 327
   gather information for, 261, 275, 285, 297, 315
   introduction for, 322
   plan for, 245, 323–324
   publish, 327
   revise, 326
   scoring guide for, 328
   writing prompt for, 322
multimodal presentations, 17, 103
multimodal texts
   analysis of, 249, 255, 375, 378, 380, 383
   annotations, 378, 380, 383
   Genre Elements, 249
   key ideas in, 375, 379, 381
   rereading, 249
   setting a purpose in, 251
   synthesizing, 249
multiple themes, 107, 109, 485
myths, 459, 460

N

name-calling, 301
narrative poetry, 22, 219
narratives. *See* nonfiction narratives
narrator, 95, 107, 228, 284, 471
natural gestures, 17, 27, 88, 319
news articles, 29, 47, 117
newspapers, 42
news reports, 218
nonfiction narratives, 236–242
   conclusion for, 236
   develop, 238–239
   edit, 241
   gather information for, 185, 191, 203, 219, 229
   plan for, 171, 237–238
   publish, 241
   revise, 240
   scoring guide for, 242
   write, 45, 171
nonverbal techniques, 88
note takers, 157
Notice & Note
   Again and Again, 25, 78, 92, 98, 111, 158, 173, 180, 210, 234, 320, 406, 490, 502
   Aha Moment, 3, 10, 14, 70, 78, 134, 158, 173, 182, 215, 225, 234, 280, 320, 360, 406, 445, 450, 452, 502

   Anchor Questions, 2–3, 78, 92–93, 158, 172–173, 234, 247, 320, 333, 406, 421, 502
   Annotation Model, 6, 22, 30, 48, 60, 96, 108, 118, 132, 144, 176, 194, 208, 222, 250, 266, 278, 290, 302, 336, 354, 368, 376, 392, 424, 436, 460, 472, 486
   Big Questions, 78, 158, 234, 246, 257, 320, 332, 340, 384, 406, 420, 427, 502
   Contrasts and Contradictions, 3, 8, 10, 52, 78, 93, 98, 158, 196–197, 234, 247, 254, 256, 320, 406, 477, 502
   Extreme or Absolute Language, 78, 146, 158, 234, 247, 258, 304, 320, 406, 502
   Memory Moment, 62, 78, 93, 100, 158, 234, 268, 270, 292, 320, 406, 478, 502
   Numbers and Stats, 78, 124, 158, 234, 320, 333, 342, 396, 406, 502
   Quoted Words, 78, 81, 158, 234, 320, 333, 338, 398, 406, 421, 428, 502
   Tough Questions, 78, 158, 172, 178, 211, 234, 280, 320, 406, 488, 502
   Word Gaps, 35, 78, 158, 234, 320, 406, 421, 426, 502
   Words of the Wiser, 2, 9, 14, 78, 158, 234, 320, 370, 406, 502
nouns
   common, 6, 19, 351
   dictionary abbreviation for, 18
   proper, 6, 10, 19, 118, 122, 336, 344, 351
novels, 7, 95, 97, 107, 177
Numbers and Stats (Notice & Note), 78, 124, 158, 234, 320, 333, 342, 396, 406, 502

O

odes, 21
omniscient point of view, 95, 107, 471
online research
   of authors, 16, 274
   for children, 102
   of historical and cultural settings, 362
   key words for, 466
   sources in, 26, 44, 184, 260, 372, 386
opinions, 143, 368
organizational patterns, 29, 47, 51–52, 391, 400, 423
organizational sources, 190
organization of ideas, 82, 162, 238, 324, 410, 506
organizations, 6
outlines, 82, 410, 416
overgeneralizations, 301

P

parallelism, 301, 314, 325
paraphrasing
   annotations, 134, 136
   defined, 132
   interpretations, 134, 136, 138

INDEX OF SKILLS

key ideas, 431
poetic lines, 467
from sources, 54, 77, 233, 319
parts of speech, 18, 186. *See also specific parts of speech*
patterns. *See also* repetition
   identifying, 121
   organizational, 29, 47, 51–52, 391, 400, 423
   sentence, 354, 356, 365
peer review, 84, 164, 240, 326, 412, 508
personal attacks, 301
personal connections, 193, 266
personal experiences
   as evidence, 143
   in inferences, 368
   in memoirs, 193, 266
   thinking and responses influenced by, 185
   use in essay planning, 81
personality of characters, 59, 95, 175
personal narratives, 265
personal pronouns, 222, 224, 231, 287, 327
personification, 131, 134, 138, 208, 289
persuasion techniques, 143, 156, 163
phrases
   defined, 263
   intervening, 165
   prepositional, 176, 179, 187, 436, 438, 457
   transitional, 127, 205, 392
   verb, 115, 241
pitch of voice, 88, 168, 416
plagiarism, 233, 319, 408
planning
   argumentative essays, 91, 153, 161–162
   biographical reports, 331, 409–410
   folktales, 419, 505–506
   informational essays, 1, 81–82
   multimodal arguments, 245, 323–324
   nonfiction narratives, 171, 237–238
   podcasts, 415
   research, 72
   short stories, 419, 505–506
plays and playwrights, 435, 438, 440–442, 445–451, 454
plot development
   analysis of, 5, 8, 11–13, 353, 356, 359–360, 471–473, 476–478
   inferences, 11
   interpretations, 16
   setting and, 353, 355, 357–358
   stages of, 353, 471
   summaries of, 360
podcasts, 45, 373, 415–416
poetic elements and devices. *See also* poetry
   alliteration, 207, 219, 367, 459
   allusions, 460, 466
   end rhyme, 459, 466

figurative language, 131, 138, 208, 211, 213, 288–289
   lines and line breaks, 207, 367
   meter, 207, 209, 212–214, 367, 370, 459, 462
   mood, 22, 368
   refrain, 21, 22, 24, 26
   repetition, 21–22, 207, 209, 218–219, 367
   rhyme, 21, 207, 459, 466
   rhythm, 207, 219, 367
   stanzas, 207, 459
   themes, 368–369, 468
poetry. *See also* poetic elements and devices
   author's purpose in, 368–369
   biographical, 275
   comparisons, 130, 140–141, 288, 298, 458
   connections in, 460–462, 464, 466
   discussion of, 139
   drawing conclusions on, 139, 216
   evaluation of, 26, 140, 298
   form of, 207, 459
   free verse, 207, 219, 275, 367, 459
   Genre Elements, 131, 289, 367, 459
   interpretations of, 25, 140, 296, 466
   lyric, 21, 22
   narrative, 22, 219
   paraphrasing lines in, 467
   presentation of, 27, 275
   reading, 27, 373
   recording, 373
   setting a purpose in, 23, 369
   sonnets, 21, 459
   speaker in, 21, 23, 26, 290, 296–299
   structural elements, 207, 209, 212–216, 367, 370, 459, 462, 465
   summaries of, 274
   writing, 27, 219, 275, 373
poetry jams, 219
point of view
   analysis of, 95, 97, 99, 107, 110, 474, 476
   annotations, 97, 99, 110, 474, 476
   evaluations, 99, 112
   in fictional stories, 103
   first-person, 21, 95, 107, 265, 471
   identifying, 471, 474, 476
   interpretations, 97
   limited, 95, 471
   omniscient, 95, 107, 471
   third-person, 95, 107, 471
position, in arguments, 142, 153
posters, 229
practicing presentations, 88, 168, 319
predictions
   author's purpose, 430
   for characters, 185
   in informational texts, 47–49, 54
   plot development, 473
   from print and graphic features, 249

questions for facilitation of, 184
   from questions generated about text, 346, 348
   text structure and, 119
prefaces, 335
prefixes, 40, 350, 388, 482
prepositions and prepositional phrases, 176, 179, 187, 436, 438, 457
presentations
   argumentative essays, 167–168
   arguments, 91
   checklists for, 203, 229
   comparison of, 374, 390
   delivering, 88, 168, 319, 455
   dramatic readings, 455
   imagery, 139
   informational essays, 87–88
   listening to, 87–88, 153, 168, 229, 416
   multimedia, 203
   multimodal, 17, 103
   podcasts, 45, 373, 415–416
   poetry, 27, 275
   posters, 229
   practicing, 88, 168, 319
   public service announcements, 153
   speeches, 241, 315
   storyboards, 113
   theme statements, 141
   video, 167–168
primary sources, 188, 408, 409, 411
print features, 249, 252–253, 257, 386, 387
print sources, 233
prologues, 335
pronouns
   antecedents and, 278, 282, 287, 327
   dictionary abbreviation for, 18
   first-person, 21, 107
   indefinite, 231, 287, 327
   personal, 222, 224, 231, 287, 327
   relative, 287, 327
   third-person, 95
pronunciation, 154, 155, 186
pronunciation key, R7
proper adjectives, 118, 122, 129
proper nouns, 6, 10, 19, 118, 122, 336, 344, 351
public service announcements (PSAs), 153
publishing
   argumentative essays, 165–166
   biographical reports, 413
   folktales, 509
   informational essays, 85
   multimodal arguments, 327
   nonfiction narratives, 241
   short stories, 509
punctuation. *See specific types of punctuation*
purpose. *See* author's purpose; setting a purpose

INDEX OF SKILLS

Q

quality of characters. *See* traits of characters
questions generated about text, 335, 339, 346, 348
questions generated for research, 16, 77, 152, 233, 319
quotation marks, 54, 472, 476, 480, 483
Quoted Words (Notice & Note), 78, 81, 158, 234, 320, 333, 338, 398, 406, 421, 428, 502

R

rate of speaking, 17, 88, 103, 153, 219, 319, 416
reading. *See also* Independent Reading
  background, 81, 161, 237, 323, 409, 505
  dramatic, 455
  fluency of, 435, 454
  monitoring comprehension while, 132, 175, 181
  poetry, 27, 373
  rereading, 175, 249, 335
  skimming, 249
realistic fiction, 5, 59, 175
reasoning of arguments, 156
reference resources
  dictionaries, 186, 402, 456
  encyclopedias, 402
  footnotes, 316
  roots as, 286
  thesaurus, 364, 456
refrain, 21, 22, 24, 26
relative pronouns, 287, 327
reliability of sources, 72, 77, 184, 260, 319, 386
repetition
  drawing conclusions from, 112
  importance of, 92
  inferences regarding, 218
  as method for revealing author's purpose, 22
  in poetry, 21–22, 207, 209, 218–219, 367
  as rhetorical device, 301, 325
reputable sources, 44, 190
requests for information, 17
rereading, 175, 249, 335
research. *See also* online research; search terms; sources
  on authors, 16, 274
  biographical information for, 348
  for debates, 157
  discussion of, 233, 319
  gather information for, 77, 126, 233, 319
  generate questions for, 16, 77, 152, 233, 319
  plan for, 72
  search engine use for, 233
  on storytelling, 430
resolution, 353, 471, 480
Response Logs, R1–R6
revising drafts
  argumentative essay, 164
  biographical report, 412
  folktale, 508
  informational essay, 84
  multimodal argument, 326
  nonfiction narrative, 240
  short story, 508
rewriting stories, 481
rhetorical devices, 301, 303, 306, 309, 312, 325
rhyme, 21, 207, 459, 466
rhythm, 207, 219, 367
rising action, 353, 471, 480
roots, 40, 104, 114, 128, 286, 350, 482
rubrics. *See* scoring guides
run-on sentences, 105, 205

S

science fiction, 107, 112
science writing, 117
scoring guides
  argumentative essays, 166
  biographical reports, 414
  folktales, 510
  informational essays, 86
  multimodal arguments, 328
  nonfiction narratives, 242
  short stories, 510
script-writing techniques, 416
search engines, 233
search terms
  evaluation of, 228
  general, 296, 314
  key words as, 466
  in quotation marks, 480
  specificity of, 38, 112, 126, 152, 202, 284, 400, 454
  two-word, 54
secondary sources, 408, 409, 411
self-sustained reading. *See* Independent Reading
sensory language, 236
sentences. *See also* complex sentences
  clarification of meaning of, 250
  compound, 85, 365, 403
  compound-complex, 365
  fragmented, 105
  patterns of, 354, 356, 365
  run-on, 105, 205
  simple, 75, 85, 365
  variety in use of, 85, 509
sequence charts, 319
setting
  analysis of, 5, 8, 12, 59, 62–69, 175, 179, 353–358
  character development and, 5, 59, 175, 221, 353, 355, 357–358
  cultural and historical, 221, 223, 228
  draw conclusions on, 72, 358
  evaluation of, 16, 184
  in historical fiction, 5, 175, 221
  inferences of, 8, 62, 68, 72, 362
  for nonfiction narratives, 239
  plot development and, 353, 355, 357–358
  in realistic fiction, 59
  research on, 362
setting a purpose
  in documentaries, 189
  in drama, 437
  humor in, 279
  in informational texts, 31, 119
  in introductions, 425
  in memoirs, 195, 267, 337
  in multimodal texts, 251
  in novels, 7, 97, 177
  in poetry, 23, 369
  print and graphic features in, 249
  in short stories, 109, 355
  in videos, 43
short stories
  develop, 506–507
  edit, 509
  gather information for, 431, 455, 467, 481, 497
  Genre Elements, 59, 353
  plan for, 419, 505–506
  publish, 509
  revise, 508
  scoring guide for, 510
  setting a purpose in, 109, 355
  write, 419, 504–510
sidebars, 29
similes, 208, 219, 288
simple sentences, 75, 85, 365
skimming, 249
slang, 168
small group discussions. *See* discussions
social media posts, 229
sonnets, 21, 459
sound elements, 42, 44
sources. *See also* research
  bias of, 77
  citation of, 233
  credibility of, 26, 72, 77, 319, 372
  digital, 233
  ethical use of, 408
  keeping track of, 496
  magazines as, 102
  new reports, 218
  in online research, 26, 44, 184, 260, 372, 386
  organizational, 190
  paraphrase from, 54, 77, 233, 319
  primary, 188, 408, 409, 411
  print, 233
  reliability of, 72, 77, 184, 260, 319, 386
  reputable, 44, 190
  secondary, 408, 409, 411

Index of Skills   R19

INDEX OF SKILLS

textbooks as, 138
tracking, 319
video clips, 218
speaker
   characterizing, 297
   connections to, 298, 299
   in poetry, 21, 23, 26, 290, 296–299
   rate of, 17, 88, 103, 153, 219, 319, 416
   volume of, 17, 88, 103, 153, 219, 416
specialized dictionaries, 402
specificity of search terms, 38, 112, 126, 152, 202, 284, 400, 454
speech balloons, 375, 386, 387
speeches, 241, 315, 431
spelling, 144, 146, 150, 155
stage directions, 435, 454
stance, in arguments, 161
standard dictionaries, 402
stanzas, 207, 459
stats. *See* Numbers and Stats (Notice & Note)
stereotyping, 77, 301, 314
storyboards, 113
structure. *See also* text structure
   analysis of, 29, 31–32
   of formal letters, 17
   of memoirs in verse, 265
   of poetry, 207, 209, 212–216, 367, 370, 459, 462, 465
   of sentences, 96
   of words, 482
style of writing, 509
subheadings, 29, 47, 49, 51, 119, 249
subject-verb agreement, 165, 187
subordinate clauses. *See* dependent clauses
subordinating conjunctions, 60, 65, 75, 433
suffixes, 128, 350, 388, 482
summaries
   claims in arguments, 152
   conflict, 480
   cultural setting, 228
   figurative language, 218
   informational texts, 425
   key ideas, 123–124, 126, 261, 398
   mood, 102
   paragraphs, 72, 496
   plays, 454
   plot, 360
   poetry, 274
   print and graphic features, 257, 260, 386
   videos, 44
   voice-over narration, 190
   writing, 191, 387, 401
supporting details, 83, 391, 423
supporting evidence. *See* evidence
sweeping generalizations, 301
syllabication, 154, 186
synonyms, 56, 364, 456

synthesize
   arguments, 318
   author's purpose, 372
   in comparison of texts, 76, 404
   informational texts, 345
   key ideas, 126
   multimodal texts, 249
   refrains, 26
   setting and character, 12
   speaker in poetry, 298, 466

T

technical terms, 42
television broadcasts, 42
tense of verbs, 108, 110, 115, 165, 241
textbooks, 138
text features, 29, 30, 47, 103
text structure
   analysis of, 117–119, 122, 265–267, 271, 485, 488, 493
   annotations, 31–32, 119, 122, 267, 271
   author's purpose and, 265
   evaluation of, 122, 430
   inferences regarding, 267
   informational texts, 29, 31–32, 117, 119, 122, 423
   predictions and, 119
textual evidence. *See* evidence
themes
   analysis of, 109
   comparison of, 46, 58, 130, 140–141, 232, 469–470, 500–501
   evidence for, 372
   in folktales, 500–501
   implicit vs. explicit statement of, 107, 468
   inferences regarding, 107–109, 112, 140, 232, 368–369, 468, 485, 492–496
   multiple, 107, 109, 485
   in poetry, 368–369, 468
theme statements, 141, 469
thesaurus, 364, 456
thesis statements. *See* controlling ideas
third-person point of view, 95, 107, 471
third-person pronouns, 95
thought bubbles, 375, 387
timelines, 191
tone
   formal, 17, 153, 325
   mood and, 290
   of voice, 168, 285, 509
topics, 468
Tough Questions (Notice & Note), 78, 158, 172, 178, 211, 234, 280, 320, 406, 488, 502
traits of characters, 59, 60, 73, 185
transition words and phrases, 127, 205, 392, 416

V

Venn diagrams, 76
verbal techniques, 88, 416

verb phrases, 115, 241
verbs
   dictionary abbreviation for, 18
   helping, 115, 241
   subject-verb agreement, 165, 187
   tense of, 108, 110, 115, 165, 241
video presentations, 167–168
videos
   digital texts, 42, 188
   discussion of, 191
   documentaries, 188–189
   in multimodal presentations, 103
   in research, 218
   setting a purpose in, 43
   summaries of, 44
visual elements, 42, 44, 87, 103, 249
Vocabulary Strategy. *See also* Academic Vocabulary; Critical Vocabulary
   antonyms, 56, 456
   context clues, 74, 204, 230, 262, 316, 432, 498
   parts of speech, 18, 186
   prefixes, 40, 350, 388, 482
   reference resources, 186, 286, 402, 456
   roots, 40, 104, 114, 128, 286, 350, 482
   suffixes, 128, 350, 388, 482
   synonyms, 56, 364, 456
   thesaurus, 364, 456
   word origins, 154, 186, 482
   word structure, 482
voice. *See also* narrator; speaker
   analysis of, 95, 99–100
   comparison over time, 100
   dashes and, 41
   language in creation of, 277
   modulation of, 88, 416
   pitch of, 88, 168, 416
   tone of, 168, 285, 509
voice-over narration, 188, 190
volume of speaking, 17, 88, 103, 153, 219, 416

W

web diagrams, 266
Word Gaps (Notice & Note), 35, 78, 158, 234, 320, 406, 421, 426, 502
Word Networks, 1, 91, 171, 245, 331, 419
words. *See also* meaning of words
   base of, 482
   boldfaced, 47, 249
   choice of, 95, 156, 509
   clarification of understanding of, 56
   commonly confused, 302, 305, 310, 317
   families of, 128
   misspelled, 144, 146, 150
   origins of, 154, 186, 482
   prefixes, 40, 350, 388, 482
   pronunciation of, 154, 155, 186
   roots, 40, 104, 114, 128, 286, 350, 482
   structure of, 482

INDEX OF SKILLS

suffixes, 128, 350, 388, 482
syllabication of, 154, 186
transitional, 127, 205, 392, 416
Words of the Wiser (Notice & Note), 2, 9, 14, 78, 158, 234, 320, 370, 406, 502
writing activities
  advertisement, 55
  analytical essay, 363, 497
  argument, 91, 153, 160–166, 315
  biographical report, 331, 408–414
  character study, 455
  compare and contrast essay, 39, 73
  email, 275
  fictional story, 103
  folktale, 419, 504–510
  freewriting, 349
  informational essay, 1, 39, 80–86, 127, 185, 297
  letter, 17, 153, 203, 275, 349
  multimodal argument, 322–328
  nonfiction narrative, 45, 171, 236–242
  poetry, 27, 219, 275, 373
  rewriting stories, 481
  short story, 419, 504–510
  social media post, 229
  speech, 431
  summary, 191, 387, 401

INDEX OF TITLES AND AUTHORS

A
After the Hurricane, 209
Angelou, Maya, 23
Animal Snoops: The Wondrous World of Wildlife Spies, 119
Animal Wisdom, 133
Archetype, 461

B
Bass, Shermakaye, 308
Better Than Words: Say It with a Selfie, 303
Bland, Joellen, 437
Boatman's Flute, The, 473
Breadwinner, The, 7
Brooks, Gwendolyn, 369
Brooks, Susie, 251
Brown Girl Dreaming, 267
Burleigh, Robert, 377

C
California Science Center, The, 43
Cassill, R. V., 355
Chang, Gloria, 303
Christie, Peter, 119
Connor-Smith, Jennifer, 49

E
Ellis, Deborah, 7
Embarrassed? Blame Your Brain, 49
Engle, Margarita, 461

F
Fairy-tale Logic, 464
Fears and Phobias, 31
First Day of School, The, 355
Forest, Heather, 487
Freedman, Russell, 393

G
Garland, Sherry, 473

H
Hoch, Edward, 109
Hughes, Langston, 294

I
Into the Air, 377
Into the Lifeboat from *Titanic Survivor,* 195

J
Jessop, Violet, 195

K
kidshealth.org, 31
Kukol, Zuzana, 148

L
Last Wolf, The, 136
Let People Own Exotic Animals, 148
Life Doesn't Frighten Me, 23
Long Walk to Water, A, 177

M
McCormick, Patricia, 337
Mora, Pat, 291
Mouse Bride, The, 487

N
Ninth Ward, 223

O
OMG, Not Another Selfie!, 308

P
Park, Linda Sue, 177
Pax, 97
Pennypacker, Sara, 97
POVRoseMedia, 189
Prince and the Pauper, The, 437

R
Ravine, The, 61
Rhodes, Jewell Parker, 223

S
Salisbury, Graham, 61
Salva's Story, 189
Schoolgirl's Diary from *I Am Malala, A,* 337
Scieszka, Jon, 279
Selfie: The Changing Face of Self-Portraits, 251
Sherman, Josepha, 425
Speech to the Young: Speech to the Progress-Toward, 369
Stallings, A. E., 464
Storytelling, 425

T
TallMountain, Mary, 136
Twain, Mark, 437

U
USA Today, 145

V
Voice, A, 291

W
What's So Funny, Mr. Scieszka?, 279
Wild Animals Aren't Pets, 145
Williams-Garcia, Rita, 209
Wired for Fear, 43
Wood, Nancy, 133
Woodson, Jacqueline, 267
Words Like Freedom, 294
Wright Brothers: How They Invented the Airplane, The, 393
Wylie, Bill, 377

Y
Yousafzai, Malala, 337

Z
Zoo, 109

ACKNOWLEDGMENTS

Excerpt from "After the Hurricane" by Rita Williams-Garcia from *Free? Stories About Human Rights* by Amnesty International. Text copyright © 2009 by Rita Williams-Garcia. Reprinted by permission of Rita Williams-Garcia.

Excerpts from *The American Heritage Dictionary of The English Language, Fifth Edition*. Text copyright © 2016 by Houghton Mifflin Harcourt Publishing Company. Reprinted by permission of Houghton Mifflin Harcourt Publishing Company.

Excerpt from *Animal Snoops: The Wondrous World of Wildlife Spies*. Text copyright © 2010 by Peter Christie, published by Annick Press Ltd. Reprinted by permission of Annick Press Ltd. All rights reserved.

"Animal Wisdom" from *Sacred Fire* by Nancy Wood. Text copyright © 1998 by Nancy Wood. Reprinted by permission of the Nancy Wood Literary Trust.

"Archetype" by Margarita Engle. Text copyright © 2005 by Margarita Engle. Reprinted by permission of Margarita Engle.

"The Boatman's Flute" from *Children of the Dragon: Selected Tales from Vietnam* by Sherry Garland. Text copyright © 2001 by Sherry Garland. Reprinted by permission of Sherry Garland.

Excerpt from *The Breadwinner* by Deborah Ellis. Text copyright © 2000 by Deborah Ellis. First published in Canada by Groundwood Books Ltd. Reprinted by permission of Groundwood Books Ltd., Oxford University Press, Allen & Unwin Pty. Ltd., and Penguin Random House LLC. All rights reserved. Any third party use of this material, outside of this publication, is prohibited. Interested parties must apply directly to Penguin Random House LLC for permission.

"Embarrassed?" by Jennifer Connor-Smith from *Odyssey* March 2015 copyright © 2015 by Carus Publishing Company. Reprinted by permission of Carus Publishing Company. All Cricket Media material is copyrighted by Carus Publishing Company d/b/a Cricket Media, and/or various authors and illustrators. Any commercial use or distribution of material without permission is strictly prohibited.

"Fairy-Tale Logic" from *Olives* by A. E. Stalling. Text copyright © 2006 by A. E. Stallings. Reprinted by permission of Northwestern University Press.

"Fears and Phobias" from kidshealth.org. Text copyright © 1995-2018 by The Nemours Foundation/KidsHealth®. Reprinted by permission of The Nemours Foundation.

"The First Day of School" from *The Happy Marriage and Other Stories* by R.V. Cassill. Text copyright © 1966 by R.V. Cassill. Reprinted by permission of the Estate of R.V. Cassill.

Excerpt from *I Am Malala: How One Girl Stood Up for Education and Changed the World, Young Reader's Edition* by Malala Yousafzai with Patricia McCormick. Map by John Gilkes. Text copyright © 2014 by Salarzai Limited. Reprinted by permission of Little, Brown Books for Young Readers, New York, NY USA. All rights reserved.

Excerpt from *Into the Air* by Robert Burleigh. Illustrated by Bill Wylie. Text copyright © 2002 by Robert Burleigh. Illustration copyright © 2002 by Bill Wylie. Reprinted by permission of Rubin Pfeffer Content, LLC on behalf of Robert Burleigh and Bill Wylie.

"The Last Wolf" by Mary TallMountain. Text copyright © 1994 by the TallMountain Estate. Reprinted by permission of the TallMountain Estate. All rights reserved.

"Let People Own Exotic Animals" by Zuzana Kukol from *USA Today* October 20, 2011. Text copyright © 2011 Gannett-USA Today. Reprinted by permission of PARS International on behalf of Gannett-USA Today. All rights reserved. Protected by the Copyright Laws of the United States. The printing, copying, redistribution, or retransmission of this Content without express written permission is prohibited. www.usatoday.com

"Life Doesn't Frighten Me" from *And Still I Rise: A Book of Poems* by Maya Angelou. Text copyright © 1978 by Maya Angelou. Reprinted by permission of Random House, an imprint and division of Penguin Random House LLC, Penguin Random House Audio Publishing Group, a division of Penguin Random House LLC, and Little, Brown Book Group, Ltd. All rights reserved. Any third party use of this material, outside of this publication, is prohibited. Interested parties must apply directly to Penguin Random House LLC for permission.

Excerpt from *A Long Walk to Water* by Linda Sue Park. Text copyright © 2010 by Linda Sue Park. Reprinted by permission of Houghton Mifflin Harcourt.

"The Mouse Bride: A Folktale from Finland" from *Wonder Tales from Around the World* retold by Heather Forest. Text copyright © 1995 by Heather Forest. Reprinted by permission of Marian Reiner on behalf of the publisher August House, Inc.

Excerpt from *Ninth Ward* by Jewell Parker Rhodes. Text copyright © 2010 by Jewell Parker Rhodes. Reprinted by permission of Little Brown Books for Young Readers.

Excerpt from *Pax* by Sara Pennypacker. Text copyright © 2016 by Sara Pennypacker. Reprinted by permission of Blazer + Bray, an imprint of HarperCollins Publishers.

The Prince and the Pauper by Mark Twain, as adapted by Joellen Bland from *Plays: The Drama Magazine for Young People* and from *Stage Plays from the Classics* by Joellen Bland. Text copyright © 1987, 2012 by Joellen Bland. Reprinted by permission of the publisher Plays. This play is for reading purposes only.

"The Ravine" by Graham Salisbury from *On the Edge: Stories at the Brink* edited by Lois Duncan. Text copyright © 2000 by Graham Salisbury. Reprinted by permission of Jennifer Flannery Literary Agency.

Excerpts from *Selfie: The Changing Face of Self-Portraits* by Susie Brooks. Text copyright © 2016 by Wayland Publishers. First published in the UK by Wayland, an imprint of Hachette Children's Books, Carmelite House, 50 Victoria Embankment, London, EC4Y 0DZ. Reprinted by permission of Wayland Publishers.

"Speech to the Young, Speech to the Progress-Toward" from *Blacks* by Gwendolyn Brooks. Text copyright © 1945, 1949, 1953, 1960, 1963, 1968, 1969, 1970, 1971, 1975, 1981, 1987 by Gwendolyn Brooks. Reprinted by permission of Brooks Permissions.

ACKNOWLEDGMENTS

Excerpt from *Storytelling: An Encyclopedia of Mythology and Folklore* by Josepha Sherman. Text copyright © 2008 by M.E. Sharpe, Inc. Reprinted by permission of Taylor & Francis Group.

Excerpt from *Titanic Survivor* by Violet Jessop. Text copyright © 1997 by Sheridan House. Reprinted by permission of Rowman & Littlefield Publishers, Inc.

"A Voice" from *Communion* by Pat Mora. Text copyright © 1991 by Pat Mora. Reprinted by permission of the publisher Arte Público Press - University of Houston.

"What's So Funny, Mr. Scieszka? from *Knucklehead: Tall Tales and Almost True Stories of Growing Up Scieszka* by Jon Scieszka. Copyright © 2005, 2008 by Jon Scieszka. Illustrations, Photographs, and Text reprinted by permission of Viking Children's Books, an imprint of Penguin Young Readers Group, a division of Penguin Random House LLC. All rights reserved. Any third party use of this material, outside of this publication, is prohibited. Interested parties must apply directly to Penguin Random House LLC for permission.

"Wild Animals Aren't Pets" from *USA Today* October 23, 2011. Text copyright © 2011 Gannett-USA Today. Reprinted by permission of PARS International on behalf of Gannett-USA Today. All rights reserved. Protected by the Copyright Laws of the United States. The printing, copying, redistribution, or retransmission of this Content without express written permission is prohibited. www.usatoday.com

"writing #1," "late autumn," "the other woodson," "reading," "stevie and me," and "when i tell my family" from *Brown Girl Dreaming* by Jacqueline Woodson. Text copyright © 2014 by Jacqueline Woodson. Reprinted by permission of Nancy Paulsen Books, an imprint of Penguin Young Readers Group, a division of Penguin Random House LLC, and William Morris Endeavor Entertainment. All rights reserved. Any third party use of this material, outside of this publication, is prohibited. Interested parties must apply directly to Penguin Random House LLC for permission.

"Words Like Freedom" from *The Collected Poems of Langston Hughes* by Langston Hughes, edited by Arnold Rampersad with David Roessel, Associate Editor. Text copyright © 1994 by the Estate of Langston Hughes. Reprinted by permission of Alfred A. Knopf, an imprint of the Knopf Doubleday Publishing Group, a division of Penguin Random House LLC, and Harold Ober Associates Incorporated. All rights reserved. Any third party use of this material, outside of this publication, is prohibited. Interested parties must apply directly to Penguin Random House LLC for permission.

Excerpt from *The Wright Brothers: How They Invented the Airplane* by Russell Freedman. Text copyright © 1991 by Russell Freedman. Reprinted by permission of Holiday House, Inc.

"Zoo" by Edward D. Hoch. Text copyright © 1958 by King-Size Publications, Inc., copyright renewed © 1986 by Edward D. Hoch. Reprinted by permission of Sternig & Byrne Literary Agency.